LEGENDS OF ROCK GUITAR

The Essential Reference of Rock's Greatest Guitarists

by Pete Prown and HP Newquist

Foreword by Joe Satriani

Edited by Jon Eiche

ISBN 0-7935-4042-9

HAL•LEONARD®
CORPORATION

7777 W. BLUEMOUND RD. P.O. BOX 13819 MILWAUKEE, WI 53213

Visit Hal Leonard on the internet at http://www.halleonard.com

Table of Contents

Foreword
by Joe Satriani

My own experience as a musician is that many of us are very much a product of what we've been exposed to and the people who have gone before us. People, events, opinions, and experiences tend to be very important in how we develop our tastes in music. These things are always changing, but so is our approach to music; you will relate differently to music when you are in your thirties than you did as a teenager, because you have different sets of feelings and influences depending on what's going on in your life.

Most of the time, I think that guitar players play the types of music they like best; their styles generally have roots in the music that they've been exposed to and the music they've sought out. Someone like me, the youngest of five kids, got to hear not only what my parents were into, but what my older sisters and brother were into. It ranged from Verdi and Bach to Chuck Berry and the Supremes to the Beatles and the Stones and almost everything else you could name. Once my older siblings moved on to some other bands or types of music, I always got their hand-me-down records. Since everyone listened to different things, it was like this diverse musical library in my own house—I just had to wait a couple of years for it all to trickle down to me.

When I started playing guitar, I took a more active role in finding the music that appealed to me. I sought out music by people I liked or thought I might like, and I also spent time reading about them. I would dig up articles and interviews with great guitarists to read what they had to say about the guitar. More often than not, most of them talked about their roots and influences. I'd come across somebody like Jimmy Page talking about how he was influenced by somebody like Howlin' Wolf, so that might prompt me to check out Howlin' Wolf. I couldn't always get into some of the people that my own influences cited as their influences, but I still found it important to give them a listen

and try to understand why they were important. Because for every one that I couldn't feel any kinship with, I'd find someone else that I really did like, and that opened a huge number of doors leading in new directions for me.

While this appears to happen naturally early on, it is important for musicians to continue to search for new music and inspiration throughout their lives. It seems harder to do, though, once you've started devoting most of your time, effort, and money to your playing. For most people, it's not like you can afford to go out and buy every CD or tape around just because you think it will give you some new musical insights. And as most guitarists know, when you've got a couple of extra bucks, that means you get to buy a new set of strings. So you don't usually just go out and get the entire boxed set of *Barbecue Bob's Greatest Hits* for $45 without listening to it, because you just might find that you're incredibly disappointed by the fact that you don't like a single thing he plays.

I always found that there were two ways to get new insights into music. One, I could go hang around record stores until they played something I wanted to check out (although now most stores have some headphone stations for doing just that), or two, I could check out some books. I grew up in a house where reading was encouraged, and everyone read. It always amazed me that you could open up your brain just by taking something off the shelf and reading it. In fifteen minutes, you knew something you didn't know before.

There is a history to music that isn't always evident just by listening to records. To find some of those things—the people who started new musical movements, the people who changed what had come before and created something truly unique, the people who really made a difference—you need to begin somewhere. This book is a good place to start.

Preface

Why a book on rock guitar players? Certainly, it's been done before. Which is precisely the reason: It's been done before, but with minimal amounts of information, which, frequently, has been wrong. *Legends of Rock Guitar*, on the other hand, was intended from the outset to be as complete as possible and really cover the genre from its beginnings to the present. If nothing else, we hope this book will give you the big picture on rock 'n' roll guitar, documenting the players, the albums, and the history of this exciting rock sub-culture. To achieve this, we had to go far past the major players—Berry, Hendrix, Van Halen, Cobain—and then keep going past the notable players—Scotty Moore, Jorma Kaukonen, Rick Derringer, Vernon Reid—until we hit that special stratum of rock guitar player who has never received much praise before, but certainly helped in some way chart the course of rock guitar.

As a result, you'll meet up with Danny Cedrone, who played the blazing solo on Bill Haley's "Rock around the Clock," the guitarists of Moby Grape, arcane blues rockers like Jesse Ed Davis and Mason Ruffner, and a host of little-known studio players and sidemen, all of whom have left their mark on rock guitar history in varying degrees. After all, this is the big picture, right? And more importantly, all of the great players discussed in this book truly deserve to have their exploits written down, even if they've never had a gold record, much less a platinum one.

Where do you start? Nowhere in particular—just pick a chapter that interests you and dig in. We strongly recommend that you try to find the music of the players who catch your eye, be it a legend like Jimi Hendrix or a more obscure player like Cliff Gallup or Dave Yorko. Used record stores are a big help in this area, as are garage sales and cut-out bins at the big retail stores. In short, we hope that this book will be the beginning of a great adventure. Go for it.

Format and Foibles. As far as the current layout, we chose the chronological format because, simply, it's more fun that an A–Z encyclopedia, and it will give readers a better understanding of the rock guitar time line. Of course, one of the difficulties in organizing a chronological history like this is putting players in the correct chapters, especially when a guitarist fits into more than one genre. For example, is Allan Holdsworth a progressive guitarist or a fusion guitarist? Is Led Zeppelin a heavy metal band or not? These troubling questions were settled the hard way: We just went with our gut instincts and made a decision. Undoubtedly, some will object to certain players' placement within the text, but we stand by our decisions and hope that you

at least can understand some of the obstacles we faced in creating a work of this magnitude.

Another matter that readers should be aware of is that any guitarist's main qualification for inclusion within this book is his or her artistic contribution to the genre and not the amount of record sales they've earned. Thus, a small-name guitarist may get more text when compared to a multi-platinum rock star if they've made more of a mark on the history of rock guitar. So, for example, in the Art Rock chapter, you'll see more on Steve Hackett, who played with Genesis well before their stadium-sellout days, than on Justin Hayward of the Moody Blues, who wrote lots of hits, but contributed little to the progressive guitar *oeuvre*. This may rankle some fans a bit, but we strove here to realign the balance of previous written histories and give lesser-known, but important, players their due.

This brings us to the finished product that you hold in your hands. As with any reference book of this magnitude, we have no doubt that an error or two has crept into our text, and we invite anyone who catches one to write to us, care of the publisher, so we can get the correction into any future editions. Finally, we also have to make the shameful admission that, no matter how hard we tried, a fair amount of personal bias has seeped into this tome. Forgive us our personal weaknesses (and try to guess *who* and *what* those weaknesses are).

From time to time you'll see an arrow (◆) in the text; these are cross-references to places where you'll find more information on the artist or band in question. The index and table of contents will help you determine exact page numbers.

The special color section, entitled "Landmark Rock Guitar Albums through the Years," deserves a bit of explanation. No, this isn't a comprehensive list of all the best albums—such a list, assuming it could be assembled to everyone's satisfaction, would be many times longer than the present one. Even the discographies included throughout the text of the book (see below) only scratch the surface of great rock guitar on record. Rather, the 48 albums pictured in color can be considered points in a connect-the-dots history; they outline the twists and turns that rock guitar has taken through the years. The remainder of the book is where you'll find those points connected and the picture filled in.

Discographies. Finally, we've put quite a bit of effort into the discographies. While they're far from complete, we think that readers will enjoy many of the rare recorded delicacies we've slipped in here and there, especially in the additional "Recordings featuring..." sections. Please note that the symbol • after a record's label and date means that the work contains live concert material (example: Columbia, 1968•). The abbreviation "n/a" stands for "not available" and is album information we simply couldn't dig up. Again, if you know the correct info, please feel free to write us.

Acknowledgments

It's hard to acknowledge the people who have helped, influenced, or inspired you when you're dealing with a subject that's as important to your daily life as guitar playing. There are, however, certain guitarists I'd like to single out for their inspiration—and in some cases, their friendship—over all the years that I have slashed away at my own guitar: Jimmy Page, Steve Howe, Glen Buxton, Al Di Meola, Eddie Van Halen, Alex Lifeson, Joe Satriani, Steve Vai, Chris DeGarmo, and George Lynch.

There are certainly others who have played an essential role in my ongoing appreciation of the guitar, including Pete Prown, Rich Maloof, Jon Chappell, and Al Mowrer. Of course, I'd like to thank my compatriots at *Guitar* magazine, as well as former band members and family members who participated in my musical crimes. Thanks to my mom and dad for buying me my first guitar and amp, and for putting up with late-night loudness for years and years. Thanks to Pangborn Hall for providing electrical power and circuit breakers at 2 a.m. when I needed them, and to Trini, Madeline, and Katherine for moral support and love when I really needed that the most.

—HP Newquist

I'd like to thank the following for their help and support during the creation of this book: HP Newquist; our diligent editor Jon Eiche, as well as Brad Smith, Chris Albano, and Tom Cheney at Hal Leonard; Howard Cleff and all my colleagues at *Guitar Shop* magazine and Cherry Lane Music; historian Dan Forte for fact-checking the first eight chapters and lending us his immense knowledge on early rock players; noted guitar expert and good friend Tom Mulhern for proofreading—and greatly improving—the Art Rock chapter; Jas Obrecht and Tom Wheeler for reading an early version of the manuscript and offering helpful suggestions; guitarists Scotty Moore, Steve Morse, Allan Holdsworth, Carlos Alomar, Robby Krieger, Luther Grosvenor (Ariel Bender), Mick Abrahams, members and managers of the Outlaws, Little Feat, Kansas, Foghat, Lynyrd Skynyrd—all for offering important input on the text; not to mention my many friends and associates in the guitar industry for invaluable gear advice.

Many of the album covers in the color section of the book appear courtesy of Record Research Inc. Thanks to Kim Bloxdorf and everyone there for their generosity.

Special thanks go to my parents, Jules and Sam Prown, in addition to the Prown and Jackson families for supporting my writing activities for so long, and also my kids Max, Sophie, and Rowan for being so much fun. Finally, I'd like to dedicate this book to my wife, Shannon, for the years of love and support during the genesis of this project. I couldn't have done it without you.

—Pete Prown

INTRODUCTION

Blues and Country Masters
PreHistoric, PreElectric

It wasn't just that guitars got loud. It's a point of misinformation to think that the rise of the electric guitar came about simply because Les Paul and Leo Fender, among others, added electricity to their modified acoustic guitars. Certainly, electricity and amplification created an "electrified" guitar, an instrument that used electricity to amplify the often subtle and soft sounds found on the acoustic guitar. And, even when they decided to make their guitars out of solid wood, both Paul and Fender were still working within the framework of standard—although amplified—guitars. But electric guitar, as we know it and play it today, is not the result of advances in technology over the last five decades. Rather, it is the result of the historical fusing of several different guitar styles into one aggressive and raucous mindset.

Developed by specific individuals throughout the guitar's history, this mindset held to the belief that guitars were *not* meant to hide invisibly behind swing bands or pianists or other more "acceptable" musical instruments. Only in one Western country—Spain—did the guitar have a reputation as an instrument that could be used to convey passion, lightness, and even perhaps violence, via the sounds of classical and flamenco music. The rest of the world left this musical flexibility to more traditional instruments (pianos, violins, drums). The guitar was frequently considered too unrefined to be allowed to step forward and take center stage to display its own power and beauty. Thus, it was relegated to the role of background instrument for centuries. Its stature was equivalent, in terms of respect, to the trombone, the harmonica, and the kazoo.

While the electrification of the guitar ultimately helped change the popularly held notions of the guitar, it was the adventurousness of several individuals that allowed the playing of the electric guitar to become a musical force in its own right. They took the guitar to places it had never been before—to the front and the center—and made people notice what it could do. And while the musicians that undertook this adventure did not start out playing the electric guitar, it is because of their daring, their sheer six-string *audacity*, that the electric guitar came into its own. If not for them, electric guitars would simply be loud versions of acoustic guitars. This book, then, would be populated by guitarists like (heaven forbid) Neil Diamond and John Denver, and not masters like Chuck Berry, Jimmy Page, and

Robert Johnson

Eddie Van Halen.

Four players who helped lay the groundwork for the style that would ultimately manifest itself as rock music on the electric guitar were Robert Johnson, Merle Travis, Muddy Waters, and Chet Atkins. Two black men, two white men. Anyone who has ever used an electric guitar and an amplifier to unchain an emotion, or to test the limits of their manual dexterity, or simply to blast the clouds away, owes all four a debt of gratitude. While there are certainly other great players who deserve to be recognized for bringing the electric guitar into its own (T-Bone Walker, Lonnie Johnson, Charlie Christian, Les Paul, and B.B. King, to name just a few), these four are archetypes to be reckoned with. They, in essence, *created* electric guitar.

Robert Johnson

Born: *May 8, 1911, in Hazelhurst, Mississippi*
Died: *August 16, 1938, in Greenwood, Mississippi*
Main Guitars: *Kalamazoo archtop, Gibson L-1*

Robert Johnson was not the first blues guitarist, or the most prolific. He was not even an *electric* guitarist. He was, however, the most ferocious.

No other bluesman before him had used the guitar as the primary conduit for *all* the tortured fears and desires of his soul. Many of his predecessors may have been better technicians or more influential on their peers—players like Lonnie Johnson and Son House—but none would ultimately provide the raw materials that would allow the electric guitar to turn itself into the single most important instrument in the development of rock 'n' roll. For it was Robert Johnson that played the guitar as if his life depended on it, as if nothing else mattered. Maybe that was true. Robert, from his birth in 1911 to his mysterious death in 1938, was a wild and reckless man, rumored to have sold his soul to the devil at the crossroads. In exchange he was given a fiery talent, allowing him to play things on the guitar that others could only marvel at.

As a youth, he traveled throughout the Delta, meeting up occasionally with people like Howlin' Wolf, Memphis Slim, Son House, Johnny Shines, and Willie Moore. He would learn licks from these men at various roadhouses, or get cheap 78 recordings of other guitarists like Lonnie Johnson. An alleged master of playing anything by ear (almost everything about Johnson is "alleged," even his cause of death), Robert developed a vicious slide style, using broken bottle necks on his little finger and playing in open tunings. He also used his thumb to achieve a heavy percussive effect on the bass strings, thumping and even slapping with it while using his fingers to pluck the treble strings.

The only recordings of Johnson were made in November 1936, in the Gunter Hotel in San Antonio, Texas, and in June 1937, in a warehouse in Dallas. There he recorded his infamous "Cross Road Blues" along with other compositions including "Hell Hound on My Trail," "Me and the Devil Blues," "Traveling Riverside Blues," "Terraplane Blues," and "Sweet Home Chicago." In all, he recorded 29 tunes during these sessions, and then he went back to his life of playing for tips at levee work stations, plantation gatherings, and roadside jooks. Interestingly, while the overwhelming majority of Johnson's recorded legacy is decidedly original, a few of the lines and verses were lifted from other blues artists' tunes, a practice that future generations of rockers would use when appropriating "traditional" blues tunes for their own catalogs.

Robert's lifestyle caught up with him in 1938, when he suffered an agonizing death after a performance at a jook joint outside of Greenwood, Mississippi. He had gotten sick during the engagement and for several days was unable to leave his room. Apparently, he had been poisoned—by the husband of a girlfriend—but with no doctor in attendance and no autopsy, no one will ever be sure.

All that Johnson left to the world was an illegitimate son and his late-1930s recordings. Two photos of him were published in the mid 1980s, but prior to that, no one even knew what he looked like. In the interim, however, his records reached England, where they inspired Eric Clapton, Keith Richards, Jimmy Page, and a host of young white blues players who were looking for something to do with their newly acquired electric guitars. The fury of Johnson's playing gave them the blueprint—or indeed, the bible—for exactly how to proceed.

Johnson's life has also been the source of much written material, and a fictional movie, *Crossroads* (1986), about the search for a mythical "lost Robert Johnson song," featured hot guitar work from Ry Cooder and Steve Vai. A Broadway play by Eugene Lee and a filmed docu-drama, *Can't You Hear the Wind Howl?*, both true-to-life representations of his life and music, will further enhance the public's awareness of The King of the Delta Blues Singers.

Robert Johnson, *The Complete Recordings* (CBS, 1990).

Merle Travis

Born: *November 29, 1917, in Rosewood, Kentucky*
Died: *October 20, 1983, in Tahlequah, Oklahoma*
Main Guitar: *Custom Bigsby/Travis solidbody*

Travis grew up in Kentucky, learning from and listening to bluegrass players. Bluegrass relies to an extreme degree on banjo playing and its use of the thumb as a means to keep a melody and a chord pattern going at the same time. Travis, a guitar player, took the alternating thumb-and-finger style of bluegrass banjo players and applied it to his own guitar playing. With some modification and improvements, the result was "Travis picking," a means by which guitar players use their thumbs to pluck the low notes of a chord while using two or three fingers to play the melody. This method is so commonplace today that describing it seems to be almost too obvious—almost ridiculous, like explaining how to plug in an electric guitar. But prior to his development of the style, guitars were used almost exclusively for strumming along with other instruments. Travis' inventiveness allowed guitarists to add yet another technique to their (then) gradually growing repertoire of styles. It is not out of line to say that, as country and bluegrass marched towards rockabilly and then towards rock 'n' roll, Travis invented the means by which guitarists could become stars simply by being instrumentalists. Even guitar master Robert Johnson had relied as much on his pained vocals as he did on his guitar.

Professionally, Merle Travis appeared with the Georgia Wildcats and the Browns Ferry Four, country/bluegrass bands that were highly respected in the South. He had numerous hits in the country field, including "Sixteen Tons" (sung by

Tennessee Ernie Ford) and such intense guitar instrumentals as "Cannon Ball Stomp" and "Blue Smoke."

Merle Travis, *24 Greatest Hits* (CMH, 1989). **Various Artists,** *Legends of Guitar: Country, Vol. 1 & 2* (Rhino, 1990–91).

Muddy Waters

B o r n : *McKinley Morganfield, on April 4, 1915, in Rolling Fork, Mississippi*
D i e d : *April 30, 1983, in Westmont, Illinois*
Main Guitars: *Fender Telecaster, Gibson Les Paul goldtop*

Muddy Waters served as the transition between the frenzied acoustic blues of Robert Johnson and the British rock groups of the 1960s and beyond. He took Delta blues, cranked up the volume with electric guitars and amplifiers, and intensified the sound by putting it all into a band format. Prior to his electrification and expansion of the style, blues had remained primarily a one- or two-man show; just a couple of guys out singing and playing for enough money to buy a meal. For Muddy, as for Robert Johnson before him, playing the blues was more than a meal ticket: it was a musical assault to be unleashed on the listener.

Reveling in the same southern sexual and religious traditions as Johnson, Muddy took up guitar at about age 17. His nickname had come from his childhood habit of playing in the standing water on the plantations where his extended families lived, and it followed him as he made the acquaintance of the more experienced guitar players on the southern circuit. His personal mentor was Son House, who taught Muddy about open tunings and slide playing. And although Muddy claimed to have seen Robert Johnson a time or two, he never heard that man play live—just heard a few of those influential 78s.

After establishing a following of sorts in the South, Waters packed it up to go live in Chicago. For the most part, he wanted to escape plantation life, but there was also a growing Chicago blues scene that he thought he could tap into. Once there, though, his gritty Robert Johnsonesque style was in obvious contrast to the more refined sounds of Chicago mainstays Lonnie Johnson and Panama Red. And even though *they* were already using electric guitars, and Muddy wasn't, they were not using them to exorcise their own personal demons. Muddy, who would occasionally back these artists—using an acoustic guitar— saw that in order to be heard, he needed to play electric. When he picked one up and married it to his own snakelike blues style, he gave the guitar something it had never had before: sex appeal. The Delta "mojo" came alive in his loud and brash playing, causing a stir in the club scene from Chicago to Memphis. Muddy was loud and he was crude, and people wanted to hear both in the late 1940s and early 1950s.

With his verbal imagery and frenetic bottleneck slide soloing style, Muddy used his guitar and his voice to get people's hormones running. In addition, songs like "Hoochie Coochie Man" and "Mannish Boy" set down some of the basic chord patterns for a whole generation of rockers to come. Thus, Muddy gave them both the drive and the map, and pushed them in the right direction Among those who were aroused by the sound of Waters' guitar were Jimi Hendrix, Keith Richards (who named the Rolling Stones after a Waters tune), John Lennon, Paul McCartney, Johnny Winter, Mike Bloomfield, Buddy Guy,...the list goes on.

After a career of ups and downs, Muddy finally got the recognition he deserved in the late 1970s. He recorded some albums with Johnny Winter (◗) and played to a new generation of fans who had known him only through the Rolling Stones and their praise of his influence. Today he is widely known as the man who provided the bridge between blues and rock 'n' roll.

Muddy Waters, *The Chess Box Collection* (Chess, 1989).

Chet Atkins

B o r n : *June 20, 1924, in Luttrell, Tennessee*
Main Guitars: *Gretsch Country Gentleman and Chet Atkins 6120, Gibson Chet Atkins acoustic-electric*

Chester Atkins took Travis picking and used it to integrate country, classical, rockabilly, and pop into his own unique and accessible guitar style—one that has sustained him for the better part of the twentieth century. He grew up in a musical household—his father was a classical piano teacher—and he joined a number of Nashville country bands while still in his teens. Stints with some venerable country stars of the Grand Ole Opry soon led to a near-lifelong contract with RCA beginning in 1946. Although originally hired by RCA as a singer/guitarist, Atkins quickly came to be known as a hired gun who could play almost anything and add a spark of inventiveness to some otherwise traditional-sounding music. Musicians from Elvis Presley to Les Paul took full advantage of Atkins' abilities over the years, and he has been given such laudatory nicknames as "Mr. Nashville" and even "Mr. Guitar."

Atkins' contribution to the electric guitar was much the same as Muddy Waters': he took eclectic nontraditional guitar styles and applied them to more commercial forms of music, yet didn't miss a beat when it came time to make it all work on the electric guitar. A guitarist of many styles, Atkins was the prototype for the technically proficient multi-genre player. The people he has influenced are legion, from George Harrison to Steve Howe to Mark Knopfler. With over 100 albums to his credit, he still continues to record into the 1990s.

Chet Atkins, *The Best of Chet Atkins* (RCA, 1963), *Galloping Guitar— Retrospective* (Bear Family, 1993), *Best Selections* (RCA, 1994). **Various Artists,** *Legends of Guitar: Country, Vol. 1 & 2* (Rhino, 1990–91).

CHAPTER ONE

The Fifties
Rock 'n' Roll Begins

Who knows where rock 'n' roll began? Was it with Chicago's notorious South Side bluesmen, or R&B "jump" bands such as Louis Jordan's, or as a result of Bill Haley's Texas swing, country, and blues experiments? Or was it Elvis Presley and the boys jamming at Sun Studios in July 1954? And what did Chuck Berry sound like before his first hit in 1955? Clearly, there was no first rock 'n' roller; like any great cultural movement, rock was a large-scale trend driven by artists working towards a common goal and propelled by outside (and often unconscious) forces.

So just who were the first rockers? The first generation of rockers may have been musicians raised during the depression who didn't want to slave away at poor-paying jobs like their parents did. Instead, they wanted to create a wild, frolicking style of music based on the concept of *having fun*, sexual or otherwise. Or perhaps it was the bland but still successful pop crooners of the early fifties like Bing Crosby, Patti Page, or the Mills Brothers that spurred a horde of musicians to create a sound based on drive, energy, volume, and, above all, rhythm. There's lots of room for conjecture here, but nevertheless, the final result was that America's youth was primed and ready for a musical revolution in 1955.

Although there were earlier country/blues alchemists, such as country singer Jimmie Rodgers or acoustic bluesman Curley Weaver, in the mid fifties one began hearing on a national level the sounds of country musicians integrating blues forms into their music (à la Elvis Presley and Carl Perkins) and blues musicians using country rhythms in theirs (à la Chuck Berry), as well as various gray areas of jazz, pop, and swing in between. It was the same in the guitar department: country multi-string licks being mixed with the more soulful bends and I–IV–V chord progressions of the blues.

As became evident over the ensuing decades, rock was—and still is—a vast melting pot. The fathers of the genre—Elvis Presley, Chuck Berry, Little Richard, Jerry Lee Lewis, Buddy Holly, and others—also worked from this basic country/blues hybrid, and 40 years later, rock still regularly returns to this original formula, even with detours down other musical avenues. Finally, despite the negative connotations that most ethnic generalizations evoke in this politically correct day and age, the bare truth of the matter is that black blues and jazz, and white country, Texas swing, and pop is where rock 'n' roll came from. It's a simplistic definition, but one that works amazingly well.

Bill Haley & His Comets

Danny Cedrone
Born: *June 20, 1920, in Jamesville, New York*
Died: *June 17, 1954, in Philadelphia*
Main Guitar: *1947 Gibson ES-300*

Fran Beecher
Born: *September 29, 1921, in Norristown, Pennsylvania*
Main Guitar: *Gibson Les Paul Custom*

Coinciding with the release of the film *The Blackboard Jungle* in 1955, a song off the soundtrack—"(We're Gonna) Rock around the Clock," by Bill Haley & His Comets—took off to become what is popularly acknowledged as the first rock 'n' roll hit. Although there are earlier recorded examples of rock music, it was this song and this moment in history when rock 'n' roll became a national institution and obsession.

The song had been recorded a year earlier, on April 12, 1954, at the Pythian Temple studio in New York. Ironically, on its first release, the single flopped, and it wasn't until *The Blackboard Jungle* appeared that the tune became a hit. Of greater curiosity is the stunning guitar solo. This roaring, breakneck solo has enchanted listeners for more than 40 years, though the guitarist behind it was anonymous for decades. It was played by an obscure player from Philadelphia named Danny Cedrone (pronounced *seh-drone*), who was never actually a member of the Comets or, as they would have been known before 1953, Bill Haley & the Saddlemen. Although he had been asked to join many times by Haley (born July 6, 1925, in Highland Park, Michigan; died February 9, 1981, in Harlingen, Texas), Cedrone preferred to lead his own popular Philly duo, the Esquire Boys, with rhythm guitarist Bob Scales (*né* Scaltrito). Yet because of Cedrone's amazing soloing skills, Haley often called on him for session work, beginning with the groundbreaking "Rocket 88" of 1951, itself a very early piece of the rock 'n' roll puzzle (this was a remake of the Ike Turner tune from earlier that year; some claim *it* to be the first rock recording of all time).

As far as the solo to "Rock around the Clock" (for which the guitarist received the princely session fee of about $50), Cedrone's blast-furnace break mixes fast alternate-picking runs, string bends, and strong blues accents into one short, whirlwind solo. His powerful technique is unparalleled, too: A fluid jazz-based player from the Charlie Christian school, the guitarist is perhaps the most technically accomplished rock player of the fifties, rivaled only by Gene Vincent's guitarist Cliff Gallup. Even more intriguing is that this isn't the first time the solo appears on record. Cedrone played the same lead—nearly note for note—on a 1952 Haley B side called "Rock the Joint." His clean flatpicking chops were clearly years, perhaps *decades*, ahead of their time.

Cedrone's hot playing can also be heard on other Haley classics, like "Shake, Rattle and Roll" and "Thirteen Women," the latter employing *bluesy* string bends during the verse, which is now commonplace in rock, but at the time was rather unprecedented. Tragically, the 33-year-old guitarist died in a freak accident two months after the "Rock around the Clock" session. On June 17, 1954, the big man fell down a flight of stairs late one night at a local restaurant and broke his neck in two places. He would never know what an impact "Rock around the Clock" was to have on the music world.

After Cedrone's death, Haley hired a full-time lead guitarist named Fran Beecher to fill the void. Despite having to replace a formidable player like Cedrone, Beecher was an excellent player in his own right. Also coming from a jazz background, the new guitarist went on to cut many Comet classics, like "Choo Choo Ch' Boogie," "Razzle Dazzle," and "See You Later, Alligator," as well as be part of Bill Haley's glory days during the mid fifties.

Nevertheless, it is the Comets' early recordings that remain of the greatest historical interest, and, for guitar fans, that entails the unsung guitar work of Danny Cedrone, the bulk of whose recorded legacy currently resides on old, scratchy 78 r.p.m. records by Bill Haley or his own Esquire Boys. While his name is not known to many, Cedrone's monumental break in "Rock around the Clock" remains one of the most timeless guitar leads in rock history. Further considering the song's vast exposure via the 1973 movie *American Graffiti* and the ensuing TV sitcom "Happy Days," it is also conceivably the most widely heard rock solo of all time, far more than those in Led Zeppelin's "Stairway to Heaven" or Van Halen's "Eruption."

Bill Haley & the Saddlemen (with Danny Cedrone) [on Essex except where noted], "Rocket 88"/"Tearstains on My Heart" (Holiday, 1951), "I'm Crying" (Holiday, 1951), "Sundown Boogie" (Holiday, 1952), "Rock the Joint" (1952), "Rockin' Chair on the Moon"/"Dance with a Dolly" (1952). **Bill Haley & His Comets (with Danny Cedrone)** [on Decca except where noted], "Real Rock Drive" (Transworld, 1953), "(We're Gonna) Rock around the Clock"/"Thirteen Women" (1954), "Shake, Rattle and Roll"/"A.B.C. Boogie" (1954). **Bill Haley & His Comets (with Fran Beecher)** [on

Decca], "Razzle Dazzle" (1955), "Rock-a-Beatin' Boogie" (1955), "See You Later, Alligator" (1955), "Don't Knock the Rock" (Decca, 1956).

Chuck Berry

Born: *October 26, 1926, in St. Louis*
Main Guitars: *Gibson ES-355 and ES-350T*

To many, Chuck Berry is the greatest rock 'n' roll guitar player of all time. More than 10 years before Eric Clapton and Jimi Hendrix made the term "guitar hero" standard jargon in the musical universe, Berry was busy laying the groundwork, though the man was just as revered, if not more so, for his endlessly clever lyrics and songs. Beginning in 1955, when his song "Maybellene" became a hit on both the R&B and the pop singles charts, Chuck Berry had a string of hits throughout late fifties and early sixties that exhibited his extraordinary talents as a consummate songwriter, witty lyricist, and outrageous showman, his legendary "duck walk" always being the ultimate show stopper.

Berry's earliest musical experiences came from singing at the Baptist Sunday school he attended as a child. In the early fifties, Berry joined an R&B combo with Johnny Johnson on piano and Ebby Harding on drums and began gigging around the St. Louis area. In search of something bigger and better than local gigs offered, he left and headed towards the blues capital of Chicago, demo in hand, in search of a record deal. Eventually he landed a contract with Chess Records, the label of blues kingpins Muddy Waters, Howlin' Wolf, and Sonny Boy Williamson. During the following few years he recorded dozens of classic rock 'n' roll hits, including "Maybellene," "Rock 'n' Roll Music," "Sweet Little Sixteen," and "Carol," all of which featured his signature guitar licks, which were variations on the double stop.

While other early rock tunes occasionally featured a guitar solo (which were actually more predominant in rockabilly; saxophone was more common), Berry's songs were practically dominated by his prolific riffs. It was a Chuck Berry standard formula: He opened with a fiery barrage of double stops, and under the wry lyrics, pumped away with a I–IV–V boogie-woogie chord progression. After a repeat of the intro, he'd roar into another solo loaded with multiple bends and off-beat rhythm riffs. It was this type of reckless playing that put Chuck Berry light years ahead of most of his competition and made him among the most exciting guitarists in early rock 'n' roll.

Chuck Berry

Still, the apparent simplicity of his solos can be deceptive. In reality, they are showcases for Berry's great talent at taking a relatively simple guitar phrase and spicing it up with subtle variations in the rhythm and chord voicings to create a landmark solo. Some of this noteworthy guitar work—done using a Gibson ES-350T and, later, his trademark ES-355—can be heard in "Roll over Beethoven" and "Johnny B. Goode." "Beethoven" starts with one of his expertly crafted opening licks—of which there were many variations—and its solo is a stunning example of his rhythmic approach to lead guitar playing. During the break he jumps on the beat, using staccato string bends and his percussive, koto-like tone to create a scintillating masterpiece (it was also the blueprint for the lead in the Beach Boys' "Fun, Fun, Fun" by sessionman Tommy Tedesco). "Johnny B. Goode" follows nearly the same formula, but Berry cleverly builds the momentum of the solo by repeating the guitar intro after each chorus, before finally returning to his tale of the hot young picker named Johnny B. Goode. Here Berry proves himself a master at the use of rhythm and repetition to highlight a solo. Instead of playing a new lick in every bar, he plays off the driving drum beat and uses his guitar to accent off-beat rhythms with percussive chord riffs and repetitive double- and triple-string bends. It's an awesome sound.

Besides his masterful playing, Berry became a legendary role model for aspiring rock guitarists and, along with Jimi Hendrix, Eric Clapton, and Eddie Van Halen, is one of the most influential players in rock history. Virtually all rock guitar players, either directly or indirectly, have been influenced by Chuck Berry and his double-stop lead style, all the way from rock giants like Keith Richards to minor players like Cub Koda of the seventies boogie metal act Brownsville Station. His songs have also been covered hundreds, if not thousands, of times on record and in concert by many of the major rock groups of the past 30 years, including the Beatles, Johnny Winter, and the Grateful Dead. The Stones' Keith Richards is perhaps Berry's best-known disciple, updating the master's rhythm approach with his own chordal wizardry, and even accompanying him in the concert film and recording *Hail! Hail! Rock 'n Roll*.

But perhaps the simplest way to assess Berry's impact on the electric guitar is to say that, when rock 'n' roll began, few guitar players rocked harder—or *better*—than Chuck Berry.

Chuck Berry [on Chess except where noted], *Alan Freed's Rock 'n' Roll Dance Party, Vol. 1* (WINS Records, 1956), *After School Session* (1957), *One Dozen Berry's* (1958), *Is on Top* (1959), *Rockin' at the Hops* (1960), *New Juke Box Hits* (1961), *More Chuck Berry* (1961), *Chuck Berry on Stage* (1963•), *St. Louis to Liverpool* (1964), *Chuck Berry in London* (1965), *Fresh Berrys* (1967), *Chuck Berry's Golden Decade* (1967), *Back Home* (1970), *San Francisco Dues* (1971), *The London Chuck Berry Sessions* (1972•), *St. Louis to Frisco to Memphis* (Mercury, 1972•), *Chuck Berry's Golden Decade, Vol. 2* (1973), *Chuck Berry/Bio* (1973), *Chuck Berry* (1975), *Rockit* (Atco, 1979), *The Great Twenty-Eight* (1982), *Hail! Hail! Rock 'n Roll* [soundtrack] (MCA, 1987•), *Chuck Berry Is on Top* (MCA/Chess, 1987), *Rock 'n' Roll Rarities* (1987), *More Rock 'n' Roll Rarities* (1987). **Chuck Berry & Bo Diddley,** *Two Great Guitars* (Checker, 1964).

Bo Diddley

Born: *Elias McDaniel, on December 30, 1928, in McComb, Mississippi*
Main Guitars: *Custom rectangular Gretsch and Gretsch Duo-Jet*

Easily the most colorful and flamboyant of the early rock guitarists was a performer named Elias McDaniel, better known to the rock world as Bo Diddley. On stage Diddley has been lauded since the mid 1950s as a wild rock 'n' roll showman, raising six-string hell on his rectangular, carpet-covered guitars and playing the instrument behind his head or even with his teeth. As a songwriter he is the author of several outright rock 'n' roll classics, like "I'm a Man," "Who Do You Love," and "Bo Diddley," as well as being the creator of the legendary rock rhythm called the "Bo Diddley beat."

As a serious guitarist Bo Diddley has been no less spectacular. One of rock guitar's first technological innovators, Diddley often experimented with such effects as distortion, echo, and tremolo on his radically shaped electric guitars. He also employed other special techniques, like running a pick down the strings to create a scraping sound and turning up his amplifiers loud to get feedback effects. This doesn't even take into account his playing exclusively in open D tuning (tuned low to high: D–A–D–F♯–A–D). With his electrifying stage presence, exotic jungle rhythms, and frenzied guitar sounds, Bo Diddley became one of the most visible and outrageous performers of the fifties rock era.

Diddley began playing the violin after getting interested in music from the local Baptist church. Eventually he caught on to the electric blues that Chicago was famous for and began listening to the sounds of John Lee Hooker and Muddy Waters; not long after, he gave up the violin. After playing with various local combos in clubs and on street corners, Diddley cut a demo tape and brought it to Chess Records, who soon signed him to their adjunct label, Checker. In 1955 the single "Bo Diddley" was an immediate hit, reaching #2 on the R&B charts. From then until the early sixties he had a long string of R&B and pop hits, including "Road Runner," "Mona," "You Can't Judge a Book by Its Cover," "Cracking Up," and "Say Man." In the mid 1960s much of his music was revived due to a strong renewal of interest in the blues and early rock 'n' roll, especially by British bands. The Rolling Stones and the Yardbirds both scored hits with resurrected Bo Diddley material, helping bring Bo's music to a whole new generation of rock fans.

Among the best showcases for Bo Diddley's manic playing are his major hits "Who Do You Love," "Bo Diddley," and "Road Runner." "Who Do You Love" has a raw blues-based lead by sessionman Jody Williams and Diddley's percussive rhythm swipes over the repetitive chord vamp. The song "Bo Diddley" is noted for its heavily tremoloed power chords, as well as being a prime example of his eponymous beat. And on "Road Runner," Diddley picks a throaty bass-string riff that's highlighted with the addition of echo and distortion effects and his novel pick scraping technique.

While many rock performers use flamboyance and flash to cover up their lack of musical talent, Diddley has backed up his stage antics and eccentric guitars with fine musicianship and ever-inventive playing. Combining entertaining showmanship, good songs, infectious rhythms, and a plethora of exciting guitar parts, Bo Diddley was a formidable package of talent in those early years of rock 'n' roll. Not only that, the artist is still performing today.

Bo Diddley [on Chess/Checker], *Bo Diddley in the Spotlight* (1960), *Bo Diddley Is a Lover* (1961), *Have Guitar Will Travel* (1962), *Bo Diddley & Company* (1962), *Bo Diddley Is a Twister* (1962), *Go Bo Diddley* (1962), *Bo Diddley Is a Guitarslinger* (1963), *Beach Party* (1963), *Surfin' with Bo Diddley* (1963), *500% More Man* (1965), *I'm a Man* (1965), *Let Me Pass* (1965), *Originator* (1966), *Boss Man* (1967), *Road Runner* (1967), *Super Blues* [with Muddy Waters and Little Walter] (Chess, 1967), *Black Gladiator* (1971), *Golden Decade* (1973), *London Bo Diddley Sessions* (1973), *Greatest Hits* (1981), *Toronto Rock and Roll Revival* (Accord, 1982), *Bo Diddley* [boxed set] (Chess/MCA, 1991), *Promises* (Triple X, 1994), *A Man Amongst Men* (Atlantic, 1996). **Chuck Berry & Bo Diddley**, *Two Great Guitars* (Checker, 1964).

Recordings featuring Bo Diddley: **Various Artists,** *La Bamba* [film soundtrack] (Slash, 1987).

Buddy Holly

B o r n : *Charles H. Holley, on September 7, 1936, in Lubbock, Texas*
D i e d : *February 3, 1959, in Mason City, Iowa*
M a i n   G u i t a r : *Fender Stratocaster*

Buddy Holly helped change rhythm guitar from simple support for vocals and soloists into a major stylistic form of rock guitar during the late 1950s. Although he wasn't the first important rock rhythm player (you could list Elvis, Chuck Berry, and Bo Diddley ahead of him), Holly's innovative rhythm/lead guitar style—a subtle combination of open chord strums and near-chord melody solos—is featured on many of his biggest hits, including classics like "Peggy Sue" and "That'll Be the Day." Because of his pioneering technique and hip, tuneful songs, he eventually became a huge influence on such future greats as George Harrison and John Fogerty.

After taking up guitar at the age of 11, Holly hooked up with a guitar playing schoolmate named Bob Montgomery, and the two began playing bluegrass and country music at local dance halls as "Buddy and Bob." In 1955 Holly heard Elvis Presley for the first time, and, by all accounts, the impact was immense. Buddy dropped all of his ambitions in bluegrass and country music and became a full-fledged rock 'n'

roller. After a brief and unsuccessful stint recording for Decca Records in Nashville, Holly and his backup band, the Crickets, recorded some new material in the studio of producer Norman Petty, in Clovis, New Mexico. Recorded during the spring and summer of 1957, these legendary sessions produced such memorable Holly tunes as "Peggy Sue," "Maybe Baby," and "That'll Be the Day." When these songs were eventually released on the Coral and Brunswick labels during 1957 and 1958, they topped the U.S. pop singles charts, and, nearly overnight, Buddy Holly and the Crickets became one of the biggest acts in rock 'n' roll.

Among the many recorded examples of Buddy Holly's unique rhythm guitar style, his expert chord playing, multi-string riffs, and jangly open-chord solos are pervasive. In the classic "Not Fade Away" Holly holds down a solid chord pattern until he executes some precision sliding riffs and chord strums for the solo. Another related piece of essential listening is Holly's "Blue Days, Black Nights," which features Cricket Sonny Curtis playing a Chet Atkins-inspired lead.

Besides his inventive rhythm playing, Buddy Holly is also significant to the history of rock guitar as one of the first rock 'n' roll axemen to use a Fender Stratocaster as his primary instrument. Until then, the Stratocaster was primarily played by blues, R&B, and country-and-western players, but with Holly's widespread exposure, the Stratocaster got its start on the road to rock 'n' roll immortality, thanks to later Strat masters like Jimi Hendrix, Eric Clapton, and Stevie Ray Vaughan.

But in contrast to his immense popularity, Buddy Holly's stay in the limelight was unexpectedly short. On February 3, 1959, Holly was killed in a plane crash during a storm in Iowa, an accident that also claimed the lives of fellow rockers Ritchie Valens (a fine guitarist in his own right) and the Big Bopper.

Buddy Holly [on Coral, except where noted], *The Chirping Crickets* (Brunswick, 1957), *Buddy Holly* (1958), *That'll Be the Day* (Decca, 1958), *The Buddy Holly Story* (1959), *20 Golden Greats* (MCA, 1978), *The Complete Buddy Holly* (MCA, 1981), *Collection* (MCA 1993).

Buddy Holly

Eddie Cochran

Born: *October 3, 1938, in Albert Lea, Minnesota*
Died: *April 17, 1960, in Wiltshire, England*
Main Guitar: *Gretsch 6120*

Besides having several major rock 'n' roll hits to his credit during his brief career—including "Summertime Blues" and "C'mon Everybody"—and being an innovator in multitrack recording techniques, Eddie Cochran was also a great guitar player whose solos, acoustic guitar power chords, and rebel-cool stage presence created a blinding archetype of the early rock guitar hero. Regrettably, Cochran's brilliant career was cut short when the English taxi he was riding in (along with rockabilly star Gene Vincent) blew a tire and smashed into a lamppost. As a result of severe head injuries, Cochran, who was not yet 22 years old, died a few hours after the accident.

Cochran, who grew up in Minnesota, moved with his family to California at the age of 14. There he met Hank Cochran (no relation), with whom he formed the Cochran Brothers singing duo. They even became regulars on the "California Hayride" country music television show, but their partnership began to disintegrate when Eddie began taking strongly to the new sounds of rock 'n' roll. Soon after the duo split, the guitarist met a young songwriter named Jerry Capehart, who got him to record a single entitled "Skinny Jim." It was no hit, but it did attract the attention of several record companies. In September 1956 Cochran was signed to a recording contract with Liberty Records. In 1957 he scored his first pop hit with "Sittin' in the Balcony" and, the following year, got his biggest hit with the rock 'n' roll classic "Summertime Blues." When he scored another hit in 1959 with "C'mon Everybody," Cochran was at the height of his career, especially in England, where rock 'n' roll mania was still rampant.

A well-rounded guitarist, Eddie Cochran was equally adept at lead and rhythm playing. His guitar work on such hits as "Summertime Blues," "Twenty Flight Rock," and "Something Else" featured an aggressive bass line (Cochran was one of the first artists to highlight the electric bass extensively on his recordings) with heavy power chords played on a Martin D-18 steel-string acoustic. Cochran's stinging lead style can be heard on such tunes as "Jeanie, Jeanie, Jeanie" and "Pretty Girl," both of which show him as a skillful lead player completely at home with the double-stop licks that made Chuck Berry famous, as well as with his own melodic lines and twangy string bends. Also of special note is "Eddie's Blues," a rare slow blues (at least for a white rocker) embellished with dramatic tremolo bar bends.

Eddie Cochran, *Singin' to My Baby* (1958), *C'mon Everybody* (Sunset, 1959), *Somethin' Else* (Capehart, 1960), *Cochran* (Liberty, 1960), *Memorial Album* (Liberty, 1960), *On the Air* (EMI America, 1972), *Very Best of Eddie Cochran* (Fame/Liberty, 1975), *A Legend in Our Time* (Union Pacific, 1979), *The Eddie Cochran Singles Album* (United Artists, 1979), *Eddie Cochran: The Legend* (Charly, 1985), *Legendary Masters* (EMI America, 1987).

Bill Doggett Combo

Billy Butler

Born: *c. 1924, in Philadelphia*
Main Guitar: *Epiphone Broadway*

The roots of most early rock players aren't hard to detect: after all, before there was such a thing as "rock 'n' roll," these musicians earned their keep either playing country, blues, pop, or jazz. The first three are often noted as the key genres from which rock guitar emerged, but not much is made of the jazz school. In reality, several rock pioneers came from jazz camp, often drawing influence from either Charlie Christian or the sound of Texas swing; Danny Cedrone is one good example, as is sometime studio player Barney Kessel. But one shouldn't forget Billy Butler, the guitarist in the Bill Doggett Combo, which scored big hits in 1956 and 1961 with two versions of the track "Honky Tonk," the former version featuring a highly influential extended guitar break.

A groundbreaker in the realm of instrumental rock, the original "Honky Tonk" kicked off with Butler playing a cool blues motif before the sax took over the main riff (one would be hard-pressed to call it a melody). The guitarist's polished solo followed, expertly blending string bends, quickly strummed chords and slurs, and tasty single-note lines into one elegant break. In all, it was a very early piece of blues- and jazz-inspired playing within a rock 'n' roll context, though it could be argued that the track isn't rock at all—just an R&B song that crossed over to the pop charts and became a hit. Nevertheless, Billy Butler's lead in "Honky Tonk" gave fifties rock fans (read: aspiring young white guitarists) a fine lesson in blues and jazz phrasing, as well as an early taste of the blues-rock guitar sounds that were to pervade rock nearly a decade later via the blues revivals in America and England. His blues-jazz experiments were also a big influence on top players like Steve Miller and Danny Gatton, something you can readily hear in their own distinctive solos.

Bill Doggett, *14 Hits* (King, 1977).

CHAPTER TWO

Rockabilly
The Second Civil War

A curious hybrid emerged at the dawn of rock.

It was similar to the country music heard on radio shows (such as "The Grand Ole Opry" and "Louisiana Hayride"), but it also sounded like the blues played by blacks in the rural South. It had a bit of hillbilly bluegrass in it and a little boogie-woogie, but also a driving beat and lots of guitar. It was a powerful southern style of the rock 'n' roll revolution, and it became known as "rockabilly."

Rockabilly is essentially a fast-tempo blues with a country rhythm and accent on the offbeat. At first it was fleetingly labeled as "cat music" or "honky tonk," but eventually it was simply referred to as "rockabilly" because, as Peter Guralnick writes in *The Rolling Stone Illustrated History of Rock & Roll*, "it was not the clankety rock of Bill Haley and his Comets, nor the hillbilly sound of Roy Acuff and Ernest Tubb but a fusion of the two." From this high-powered melding, early rockers like Elvis Presley, Carl Perkins, and Buddy Holly turned rockabilly into the nonstop anthem for teenage rebellion, sexual awareness, and individual freedom that helped carve the future of rock 'n' roll.

Like the country and blues music that it was born from, rockabilly was dominated by the sound of the guitar. Rockabilly guitar borrowed the deft country fingerstyles of Merle Travis and Chet Atkins, with the soulful string-bending prowess of black bluesmen such as T-Bone Walker and B.B. King. However, some rockabilly guitarists introduced other stylistic influences to the new rock guitar sound, especially from harmonically advanced jazz guitarists like Charlie Christian, Barney Kessel, and Tal Farlow, and also from the tasty pop guitar stylings of Les Paul, who was in his heyday in the fifties. All of these diverse influences, combined with the supercharged beat of rock 'n' roll and the original techniques of such stellar pickers as Scotty Moore, James Burton, Carl Perkins, and Cliff Gallup, created the electrifying guitar sound of rockabilly, the first major school of rock guitar.

Elvis Presley

Elvis Presley
Born: *January 8, 1935, in Tupelo, Mississippi*
Died: *August 16, 1977, in Memphis*
Main Guitars: *Martin D-28 and D-18*

Scotty Moore
Born: *December 27, 1931, in Gadsden, Tennessee*
Main Guitars: *Gibson ES-295, L-5, and Super 400C*

As important as Elvis Presley was to the birth of rock 'n' roll, so too was his guitarist, Scotty Moore, important to the beginning of rock guitar. His earliest musical inspiration came from the country guitar style played by his father and older brothers. After serving in the Navy in the early fifties, Moore moved to Memphis and joined a country group called Doug Poindexter and the Starlight Wranglers. With them he recorded a single, "My Kind of Carrying On," on Sam Phillips' Sun label; it was not a big seller. The significant result of this recording was that Phillips put Moore in touch with young Elvis Presley, a fledgling country truck driver-cum-singer in whom Phillips saw some promise. Eventually, Phillips got Elvis into the studio to record a few tracks, with Moore and bassist Bill Black on instrumental backup.

As legend has it, Presley suddenly grabbed his guitar during a taping break and started belting out a wild version of Arthur Crudup's blues piece "That's All Right (Mama)." Moore and Black picked up their instruments and joined in on Elvis' raucous arrangement, and soon the staid blues tune was injected with gritty R&B vocalisms, a fast country rhythm, and Moore's peppery guitar licks.

Scotty Moore

Phillips bolted into the studio and told the three musicians to do it again—*only this time with the tape rolling.* That initial taping of "That's All Right (Mama)" on July 6, 1954, is considered by some to be the very first rock 'n' roll recording.

"That's All Right (Mama)" also marked the beginning of Elvis' Sun era (captured on RCA's excellent *Sun Sessions* album) before his eventual move to RCA and commercial stardom. During this time, Scotty Moore revealed his brilliant versatility on many of Elvis' early recordings. Among Moore's greatest guitar work during the pioneering Sun days are his Chet Atkins-inspired fingerstyle solo on "Milk Cow Blues" and the break in "Baby, Let's Play House," which features bluesy multiple string bends (this tune was also Jimmy Page's inspiration for picking up the guitar).

In addition to these significant solos, Moore cut a number of notable leads during Elvis' heyday with RCA from 1956 through '58 (before Presley's induction into the army), including his string-pushing break to "Jailhouse Rock" and the melodic single-note solo on "Hound Dog." In "Too Much" Moore even accidentally threw in a Middle Eastern-flavored lick during his solo. While most of his peers were playing straight pentatonic blues scales, Moore here landed on such notes as a flat 5th, minor 6th, and major 7th to give the break a harmonic-minor modal feel. According the guitarist, however, the track was in the unusual key of A♭, which caused him to get lost during his solo—he simply got out of key and then had to work his way back to the root note. Nevertheless, Elvis insisted that they keep the lead, mistakes and all (Moore suggests that this was done partially to tease the guitarist for hitting these odd notes). Still, the break works brilliantly and predates Ritchie Blackmore's noted use of the harmonic minor mode with Deep Purple by almost 15 years, to say nothing of the common use of similar scale tones by members of the "shred" guitar school in the eighties. Even when goofing up, Scotty Moore was making history.

Elvis Presley [on RCA except where noted], *Elvis Presley* (1956), *Elvis* (1956), *Loving You* (1957), *Elvis' Christmas Album* (1957), *Elvis' Golden Records* (1958), *King Creole* (1958), *For LP Fans Only* (1959), *A Date with Elvis* (1959), *50,000,000 Elvis Fans Can't Be Wrong—Elvis' Golden Records, Vol. 2* (1960), *G.I. Blues* (1960), *Girls, Girls, Girls!* (1962), *Elvis' Golden Records, Vol. 3* (1963), *Elvis' Golden Records, Vol. 4* (1967), *Elvis—NBC TV Special* (1968•), *The Sun Sessions* (1976), *Elvis, Scotty & Bill—The First Year* (Very Wonderful Golden Editions, 1979), *Elvis Aron Presley* (1980), *The Complete Sun Sessions* (1987), *The Top Ten Hits* (1987). **Scotty Moore,** *The Guitar that Changed the World* (Epic, 1965), *What's Left* (n/a, 1970), *706 Reunion* [with Carl Perkins] (Belle Meade, 1992), *Moore Feel Good Musichyg* (Belle Meade, 1992).

Recordings featuring Scotty Moore: **Billy Swan,** *Billy Swan* (n/a), *You're OK, I'm OK* (n/a).

Carl Perkins

Born: *April 9, 1932, in Ridgely, Tennessee*
Main Guitars: *Gibson Les Paul goldtop and ES-5 Switchmaster, Fender Telecaster*

When Elvis left Sun Records for RCA-Victor, his spot as the top recording artist for the label was filled by a talented young rockabilly performer named Carl Perkins. In addition to being a gifted singer and guitarist, Perkins was also a superb songwriter, and in early 1956 he scored a huge hit with his own tune, "Blue Suede Shoes." With its clever lyrics and driving rock 'n' roll beat, "Blue Suede Shoes" also featured a stinging Perkins guitar break, which established him as one of the foremost guitar players in the budding rockabilly genre.

Carl Perkins was first drawn to the guitar at the age of five when he heard the rural blues guitar playing of a black farmer named John Westbrook. When Perkins eventually began to play the instrument, it was Westbrook's blues licks that he first imitated on his own guitar. Later he mixed this blues with country guitar lines to help create the basic vocabulary of rockabilly guitar.

In the early fifties he and his brothers formed the Perkins Brothers Band and became regulars on a live radio show in Jackson, Tennessee. Upon hearing Elvis Presley's exciting new records from Sam Phillips' Sun Studios, the brothers Perkins took off for Memphis to audition for the label. The audition was successful enough that the band started recording for Sun in January 1955. One year later Carl Perkins, backed by his brothers, had his first and biggest hit with "Blue Suede Shoes," which topped the rock 'n' roll, country, and R&B charts simultaneously. But just as his career was taking off with "Blue Suede Shoes," Perkins was involved in a serious car accident that hospitalized him for several months. During his recuperation, most of the public's attention was diverted towards Elvis Presley. Perkins eventually recovered, but his career never really did. He had a few hits later in the decade, but he was never able to recapture those glory days when "Blue Suede Shoes" was #1. To boot, Elvis' version of the same song was an even bigger hit a few months later.

Despite this setback, there was no doubt about Carl Perkins' ability as a top-class rockabilly guitar player. In his honed leads and rhythm parts, he smoothly fused the blues styles of John Lee Hooker and Muddy Waters with the Grand Ole Opry country sounds of Ernest Tubb and the bluegrass of mandolinist Bill Monroe. As heard on such hits as "Blue Suede Shoes," "Honey Don't," and "Boppin' the Blues," his solos are veritable blueprints for rockabilly guitar, especially with their emphasis on chugging rhythms, multi-string blues bends, and a strong sense of melody. Perkins' guitar playing and songs also had a huge influence on later rock 'n' rollers like Ricky Nelson and George Harrison of the Beatles, both of whom covered several Perkins-penned tunes on their recordings (Harrison even used the stage name Carl Harrison early in his career). Later Perkins played in Johnny Cash's band, before continuing on his own as a solo artist. But he is best remembered by fans for his clever lyrics and rockabilly songs of the late 1950s, and by guitarists for his powerful blues- and country-inspired guitar solos from that era.

Carl Perkins [on Charly except where noted], *Greatest Hits* (Columbia, 1969), *On Top* (Columbia, 1969), *Boppin' the Blues* (Columbia, 1970), *Carl*

Perkins (Harvard, 1970), *Original Golden Hits* (Sun), *Blue Suede Shoes* (Sun), *The Man Behind Johnny Cash* (Columbia, c. 1970), *My Kind of Country* (Mercury), *The Rocking Guitar Man* (1975), *The Original Carl Perkins* (1976), *Sun Sound Special* (1978), *The Carl Perkins Dance Album* (1981), *The Sun Years* (Sun, 1982), *Born to Rock* (Universal, 1989), *706 Reunion* [with Scotty Moore] (Belle Meade, c. 1992). **Carl Perkins, Johnny Cash & Jerry Lee Lewis,** *Survivors* (CBS, 1982).

Recordings featuring Carl Perkins: **Paul McCartney,** *Tug of War* (Columbia, 1982).

James Burton

Born: *August 21, 1939, in Shreveport, Louisiana*
Main Guitar: *Fender Telecaster*

The funky string bend and inimitable twang of James Burton's Fender Telecaster ranks among the most easily recognizable and influential sounds in electric guitar history. As a member of teen idol Ricky Nelson's backup band, Burton was probably the most visible of the early rock guitarists, appearing weekly with Nelson on the popular television show "The Adventures of Ozzie and Harriet." (Incidentally, it was also one of the very first television shows to regularly feature live rock 'n' roll.) Besides appearing with Ricky Nelson, James Burton has also been a first-class session guitarist and sideman with many rock, pop, and country acts. Since the mid sixties he has done picking with such modern music icons as Johnny Cash, Jerry Lee Lewis, the Byrds, Frank Sinatra, Kenny Rogers, and, most importantly, Elvis Presley, with whom Burton played from 1969 until Presley's death in 1977.

A professional guitarist since his early teens, Burton was staff guitarist on the popular country radio show "Louisiana Hayride" by his sixteenth birthday. During the mid fifties he played with a variety of country and rockabilly acts and also played on Dale Hawkins' hit rockabilly single "Susie-Q," to which the young guitarman contributed the famous bass string riff and string-bending solo. Eventually Burton joined up with country singer Bob Luman's band and found himself in California, where Luman was appearing in a teen movie entitled *Carnival Rock.* It was there that Burton met Ricky Nelson, who was looking for a band to back him on his parents' television show each week. After hearing Burton's guitar licks at a local recording studio, Nelson promptly invited him to join the show. This led to Burton's recording full-time with the younger Nelson, who by 1957 was scoring huge pop hits nationwide with songs like "I'm Walkin'," "Be-Bop Baby," and "Believe What You Say" (featuring solos from the likes of jazzer Barney Kessel and country studioman Joe Maphis). From the late fifties until the late sixties, the classic rockabilly sound of James Burton's guitar was a permanent fixture on Ricky Nelson's hit records.

Burton's guitar style developed largely from his childhood exposure to country and blues music on local radio stations. On the radio he would hear the blues guitar mastery of Muddy Waters and Howlin' Wolf, as well as the country sounds of Hank Williams and Chet Atkins. He also marveled at the sliding and sustaining sounds of the pedal steel guitar, which strongly influenced the development of his innovative string bending technique. While most players used heavy strings, which discouraged string bending, Burton began to string his Telecaster with light banjo strings combined with regular A and D strings (in place of low E and A) to facilitate the string bending technique that has since become his trademark. Some classic Burton solos from his Ricky Nelson days include "It's Late," which has an ultra-rubbery Tele break, and "Believe What You Say," with its string bends and rhythmic Chuck Berry-style double stops. On Nelson's #1 hit "Travelin' Man" he picks a vibrant yet economical solo laced with tasteful melodies and blues licks, while on "Hello Mary Lou" he gives a masterful rockabilly performance that combines country-styled fingerpicking with blues runs and his patented string bending style.

Rock guitar greats such as Jimmy Page, Joe Walsh, and Dave Davies all cite Burton's rockabilly guitar style as a major influence on their own playing. His innovative blend of string bending, country fingerstyle, and blues guitar techniques have made him one of the most versatile and original guitar players of the fifties rock revolution. With his killer chops alongside credentials that include many of the biggest pop performers of the last 30 years, it is no small wonder that Burton is considered such an important player from the formative years of rock guitar.

Ricky Nelson [on Imperial], *Ricky* (1957), *Ricky Nelson* (1958), *Ricky Sings Again* (1959), *The Ricky Nelson Singles Album* (1978). **James Burton,** *Corn Pickin' & Slick Slidin'* (Capitol, 1967), *The Guitar Sounds of James Burton* (Capitol, 1971), *James Burton* (A&M, n/a). **Elvis Presley** [on RCA], *In Person at the International Hotel* (1969), *From Elvis to Memphis* (1969), *Aloha from Hawaii* (1973).

Recordings featuring James Burton: **Everly Brothers** [on Warner Bros.], *Gone Gone Gone* (n/a), *Beat & Soul* (1965). **Sandy Nelson,** *Rock 'n' Roll Revival* (Imperial, 1967). **Buffalo Springfield,** *Buffalo Springfield Again* (Atco, 1967). **Judy Collins,** *Who Knows Where the Time Goes* (Elektra, 1968). **The Byrds,** *Sweetheart of the Rodeo* (Columbia, 1968). **Mike Nesmith,** *Nevada Fighter* (RCA, c. 1972). **Gram Parsons** [on Reprise], *GP* (1972), *Grievous Angel* (1974). **Emmylou Harris,** *Pieces of the Sky* (Reprise, 1975), *Elite Hotel* (Reprise, 1976), *Luxury Liner* (Warner Bros., 1977). **Rodney Crowell,** *Ain't Living Long Like This* (Warner Bros., c. 1979). **Duane Eddy,** *Duane Eddy* (Capitol, 1987). **Roy Orbison and Friends,** *A Black and White Night Live* (Virgin, 1989).

Gene Vincent & the Blue Caps

Cliff Gallup

Born: *c. 1935, in Chesapeake, Virginia*
Died: *October 10, 1988*
Main Guitar: *Gretsch Duo-Jet*

In terms of sheer skill and technical proficiency on the electric guitar, there was probably no better guitarist in the early days of rockabilly than Cliff Gallup, lead guitarist with Gene Vincent & the Blue Caps. In terms of rock guitar history, though, there are probably few significant players whose careers were shorter or more mysterious than Gallup's. During 1956 it was Gallup who

Gene Vincent & the Blue Caps: Cliff Gallup (right)

with the Devil" that is Cliff Gallup's most lasting achievement. Coincidentally, it remains one of the few examples of blatant technical virtuosity ever recorded by a rockabilly guitarist. He starts the first solo with fast picking runs before going into a section of bluesy string bends, melodic single-note passages, and multi-string licks in the remainder of the break. In the song's second lead, Gallup sustains the momentum by modulating from E to F and using the Bigsby vibrato arm on his Gretsch Duo-Jet semihollowbody as a highlight to the solo. No question, it is an epic moment in the history of rockabilly guitar.

Since 1956 Cliff Gallup's inventive guitar playing has been a crucial influence on such famous rockers as Jimmy Page, Jeff Beck, Albert Lee, Dave Edmunds, and Brian Setzer, among others. Although Gallup gave up his public musical career after so short a time, his recordings with Gene Vincent & the Blue Caps remain testimony to his instrumental brilliance on the electric guitar. And as if to afford that notion further proof, Jeff Beck—one of rock's great improvisers—recorded the album *Crazy Legs* in 1992, featuring covers of Gene Vincent songs, right down to stylistically faithful versions of Gallup's great solos.

Gene Vincent & the Blue Caps, *Bluejean Bop* (Capitol, 1956), *Greatest!* (Capitol, c. 1970), *The Gene Vincent Box Set: Complete Capitol and Columbia Recordings 1956–1964* (EMI, 1994). **Cliff Gallup,** *Straight Down the Middle* [with The Four C's] (n/a, 1966).

The Rock 'N Roll Trio

Paul Burlison

Born: *c. 1935*
Main Guitar: *Fender Telecaster*

was responsible for the blazing guitar solos behinds such great Gene Vincent hits as "Be-Bop-A-Lula" and "Bluejean Bop." But less than a year later he quit the Blue Caps and disappeared into obscurity. To this day, the phenomenal Cliff Gallup is the most arcane hero of rockabilly guitar.

Gallup, a native of Chesapeake, Virginia, started his acoustic guitar schooling at the age of eight, switching to electric guitar at 14. By his late teens Gallup had become staff guitarist at a local radio station, and it was there that he met singer Gene Vincent in 1955. Together they cut a demo recording and sent it off to Capitol Records, which was looking for its own Elvis Presley. Out of the thousands of tapes Capitol received, they picked Vincent's demo and signed him and his band to a recording contract.

In early 1956 Gene Vincent & the Blue Caps had a Top 10 hit with "Be-Bop-A-Lula" and began extensive touring around the country to support their hit singles. Apparently, the demands of life on the road simply did not suit Gallup, and by the end of 1956 he had left the Blue Caps and returned to private life Virginia. It was a quick end to the promising public career of this rockabilly guitarist extraordinaire.

Although his career was brief by any standards, Gallup's guitar solos with Gene Vincent & the Blue Caps are timeless. His style was heavily indebted to the country fingerstyle of Chet Atkins and the melodic phrasing of Les Paul. As a result of these two powerful influences, Gallup adopted an unorthodox picking technique that involved using a regular flatpick between his thumb and forefinger coupled with the use of fingerpicks on his middle and ring fingers. One of the best examples of this versatile picking technique can be found on "Bluejean Bop," where Gallup begins one of his solos with some country-style fingerpicking and then picks a singularly tasteful blues run in the last eight bars of the solo.

In terms of recordings, it is probably his lead break on "Race

The most energetic, easily most *primal*, of all the early rockabilly pickers was Paul Burlison, lead guitarist for the Rock 'N Roll Trio. Critics and historians have called Burlison's playing style "primitive," "savage," and "raw-edged," all apt descriptions of his wild rockabilly sound. As a member of the Rock 'N Roll Trio, Burlison appeared on several classic recordings in the late fifties, including "Train Kept A-Rollin'" and "Honey Hush," both of which feature samples of his raw attack. On "Train Kept A-Rollin'," Burlison adds a percussive lead containing octave runs played entirely on the first and sixth E strings of his Fender Telecaster. Both songs also showcase Burlison's use of amplifier overdrive. Burlison discovered the distortion effect after dropping his Fender amp on his way to a gig one day. The fall loosened a tube in the back of the amp, producing the gritty feedback effect that has since become an integral part of the sound of so many contemporary guitarists. He then recreated the effect on "Train Kept A-Rollin'."

Though not as technically proficient a rockabilly player as Cliff Gallup or James Burton, Burlison was nevertheless a high-powered fifties guitarist who bridged the technical gap with gutsy improvised solos and innovative sound effects. His playing with the Rock 'N' Roll Trio was vastly influential, inspiring Foghat to cover "Honey Hush" and the Yardbirds to do "Train Kept A-Rollin'." (Aerosmith's famous version was based more on the Yardbirds version.) Eminent guitarists including Albert Lee and Jimmie Vaughan have also paid glowing tribute to Burlison's sterling work with the Rock 'N Roll Trio.

The Rock 'N Roll Trio, *The Johnny Burnette Trio, Vols. 1 and 2* (MCA, 1983).

Recordings featuring Paul Burlison: **The Sun Session Rhythm Section,** *Old Time Rock 'n' Roll* (Flying Fish, 1987).

Minor Masters

Roland Janes was a staff guitarist at Sun Studios in Memphis when many rockabilly greats recorded their most memorable tunes there. His double stop-laden solos appear on a number of legendary Sun hits, including Billy Lee Riley's "Red Hot" and "Flying Saucer Rock and Roll," as well as Warren Smith's "Ubangi Stomp." Janes also played with Jerry Lee Lewis during the late fifties and early sixties, adding his rockabilly guitar parts to such Lewis classics as "Whole Lotta Shakin' Goin' On" and "Crazy Arms." The picker is also acclaimed for his work on Bill Justis' highly influential 1957 instrumental hit "Raunchy," to which he contributed rhythm work and one solo, while much of the lead guitar on the track was handled by Justis' guitarist, Sid Manker (◗ Instrumental and Surf Rock). Another Sun player of note was Luther Perkins, who added his muted bass lines and solos to almost all of Johnny Cash's hits, from his early rockabilly days at Sun until the guitarist's death in 1968.

And one also can't forget the Collins Kids, a brother-and-sister act featuring Larry (born 1944) and Lorrie (born 1942). By the age of 13 Larry was already a hot rockabilly soloist, appearing on country package shows and national TV shows like "Town Hall Party." A fiery picker, Larry was the protégé of country studioman Joe Maphis and similarly played a Mosrite doubleneck, although his had a shorter neck tuned an octave up. In addition to the country and rockabilly records he cut with sister Lorrie, Larry also teamed up with Maphis on September 25, 1957, to cut the pile-driving instrumental "Hurricane," featuring hellacious solos from both players. Listen to it and then remember that the kid was only 13. It's pretty safe to consider him the youngest rockabilly flash ever.

CHAPTER THREE

Instrumental and Surf Rock

The Age of Innocence

Surf Beat. Instrumental Rock. Memphis Soul.

These are just a few of the explosive sounds that dominated rock guitar from the late fifties until the British Invasion of 1964. Early guitar heroes Chuck Berry, Scotty Moore, and Carl Perkins were soon joined by legions of new and somewhat different guitar innovators, all equally intent on leaving their personal mark on the sound of rock guitar. As Dan Forte wrote in *Guitar Player* magazine, "During the fifties, it seemed as though every guitarist was an innovator, a pioneer, to a certain degree. After all, the blueprint hadn't been drawn up yet; players were literally making it up as they went along."

Beginning with the instrumental prowess of Duane Eddy, the Ventures, and Britain's Hank Marvin & the Shadows, on to the surf beat of Jan and Dean, the Beach Boys, and Dick Dale & the Del-Tones, the guitar quickly became the fountainhead of pure rock 'n' roll. With the pop charts of the late fifties saturated by "doo-wop" vocal groups and crooning teen idols, these new artists filled a need for loud, danceable rock 'n' roll. They had their guitars leading the way, using crisp chord playing and solos to complement their vocals, or—in the case of instrumental bands inspired by Duane Eddy—they used the guitar alone to play the entire melody.

In the occasionally campy era between Elvis' induction into the army in 1958 and the British Invasion (highlighted by a spate of sugary pop vocalists like Pat Boone, Frankie Avalon, and Bobby Vee), rock guitar flourished in both regional instrumental groups like the Fireballs and the Wailers and in chart-topping acts like Freddie King ("Hideaway") and the Surfaris, with guitarist Jim Fuller ("Wipe Out"). During this period, Bill Justis' instrumental "Raunchy" became a hit with the help of Sid Manker's bass-string picking, while Johnny and the Hurricanes' Dave Yorko inspired guitarists with his Chuck Berry-styled guitar solos to "Reveille Rock" and "Crossfire." On the ballad side, Brooklyn brothers Santo & Johnny scored a huge #1 hit in 1959 with "Sleepwalk," later covered by guitar aces Larry Carlton and the late Danny Gatton. It was also the only #1 pop single to feature pedal steel guitar.

One also can't neglect to mention one-hit wonders like the Chantays (Bob Spickard and Brian Carman on the guitar-driven classic "Pipeline"), the Astronauts (with picker Rich Fifield), the

Pyramids, the Trashmen ("Surfin' Bird"), the Lively Ones, and many more. The Fireballs, featuring lead guitarist George Tomsco and rhythm player Dan Trammell, were another important act, influencing the Ventures. Produced early on by Norman Petty—the man behind Buddy Holly's (♪) greatest hits—the band recorded a number of instrumental classics, such as "Fireball," the Mexican-flavored "Torquay," and "Quite a Party." (Petty even employed them to cut posthumous backing tracks to a number of Buddy Holly demos.) Ironically, despite their prowess as an instrumental act, the Fireballs' greatest success came with vocal numbers, such as the #1 1963 single "Sugar Shack" (with vocalist Jimmy Gilmer) and the Top 10 1968 hit "Bottle of Wine."

Overall, these instrumental groups and guitar players are vitally important to the history of rock guitar because they laid the basic musical foundation for future rock guitarists to learn from and build upon. The guitar licks they created are inherently simple and even sometimes amusing, but therein lies the appeal.

Duane Eddy

Born: *April 26, 1938, in Corning, New York*
Main Guitar: *Gretsch 6120*

During the earliest years of rock music, the role of the guitar in any given pop song was to play backup rhythm and—on rare occasions—to take a brief solo. But when an instrumental tune called "Moovin' n' Groovin' " was released in 1958, that arrangement was changed forever. Recorded by a 19-year-old guitarist named Duane Eddy, "Moovin' n' Groovin' " featured the electric guitar playing the entire melody line. While other instrumentals had had prominent guitar parts (namely Bill Doggett's "Honky Tonk," Link Wray's "Rumble," and Bill Justis' "Raunchy"), none had ever used it as the melody instrument. There were great rock players before Eddy's arrival, but he was the first one who was recognized in the public eye as a "guitar star." No lyrics, no wild stage antics—just *guitar*.

"Moovin' n' Groovin' " also introduced the pop world to "twangy" guitar, Eddy's trademark sound. His twang was achieved by combining bass-string melodies with effects (echo and Magnatone amplifier vibrato) and gently rocking the Bigsby vibrato arm on his Gretsch model 6120 Chet Atkins guitar. This first hit was soon followed up by a long string of chart-toppers for Eddy and his group, the Rebels, including the smash hit "Rebel Rouser," "Cannonball," "Ramrod," "Some Kind-A Earthquake," and "Forty Miles of Bad Road." During his hit period from 1958 to 1963, Duane Eddy, with "twangy" guitar in hand, ranked among the most popular performers in rock. To this day he remains rock's most successful instrumentalist, scoring far more hits than modern wonders like Joe Satriani and Steve Vai.

Eddy grew up near Phoenix, Arizona, and by the time he was 15 he was already playing the guitar in a country group headed by guitarist Al Casey (who would later become a member of the Rebels). In the mid fifties Eddy signed with producer Lee Hazelwood and began looking for a new guitar style that would give his instrumental songs an extra twist. The result was their discovery of twangy guitar. This classic guitar sound was heard on nearly all of Eddy's hits, from "Moovin' n' Groovin' " all the way to "Boss Guitar," his last chart entry before the British Invasion, which brought an end to his reign on the U.S. pop charts.

Still, his rock style influenced nearly all of the top instrumental combos of the early sixties and many other great rock instrumentalists, including the Ventures and even bassist John Entwistle of the Who, who lists Eddy as his primary inspiration. Duane Eddy also won a Grammy for playing on the 1986 instrument hit "Peter Gunn" by the U.K. band the Art of Noise, thus bring his distinctive guitar sound to a whole new generation of fans. To top off this comeback was a self-titled 1987 solo album, featuring appearances from such guitar legends as George Harrison, Paul McCartney, Ry Cooder, and James Burton, all huge fans of the man who was effectively rock's first universal guitar hero.

Duane Eddy [on Jamie except where noted], *Have "Twangy" Guitar, Will Travel* (1958), *Especially for You…* (1959), *Duane Eddy Plays Songs of Our Heritage* (1959), *The "Twang's" the "Thang"* (1959), *Detour* (1960), *$1,000,000 Worth of Twang* (1960), *Girls! Girls! Girls!* (1961), *Twistin' 'n' Twangin'* (RCA, 1962), *In Person* (1962), *Twangy Guitar—Silky Strings* (RCA, 1962), *Dance with the Guitar Man* (RCA, 1962), *Twangin' up a Storm!* (RCA, 1963), *Lonely Guitar* (RCA, 1963), *Twangin' the Golden Hits* (RCA, 1965), *Duane Eddy Collection* (Pickwick 1978), *Duane Eddy* (Capitol, 1987), *Twang Thang: The Anthology* (Rhino, 1993).

Recordings featuring Duane Eddy: **Steve Douglas**, *King Cobra* (Fantasy, 1984). **The Art of Noise,** *In Visible Silence* (China/Chrysalis, 1986).

The Ventures

Bob Bogle
B o r n : *January 16, 1937, in Portland, Oregon*
M a i n   G u i t a r s : *Fender Jazzmaster, Mosrite Ventures model*

Nokie Edwards
B o r n : *May 9, 1937, in Oklahoma*
M a i n   G u i t a r : *Mosrite Ventures model*

Don Wilson
B o r n : *February 10, 1937, in Tacoma, Washington*
M a i n   G u i t a r s : *Fender Stratocaster, Mosrite Ventures model*

Gerry McGee
B o r n : *1938, in Eunice, Louisiana*
M a i n   G u i t a r : *Les Paul Deluxe goldtop*

It all started in 1960 with a slick guitar-oriented instrumental entitled "Walk, Don't Run." It was then followed with more all-guitar rockers: "Perfidia," "Ram-Bunk-Shush," and even "Walk, Don't Run '64." Soon there was a veritable avalanche of guitar hits, topping the charts all over the world and selling millions of albums. The culprits of this inspired guitar mania were not the established heroes of the day. Instead, they were a new group from Tacoma, Washington—a quartet featuring dual guitar players who called themselves the Ventures. Capitalizing on catchy melodies and slick matching suits and guitars, not to mention hot guitar playing, the Ventures (originally with Bob Bogle and Don Wilson on guitars, Nokie Edwards on bass, and Howie Johnson on drums) quickly became the top rock instrumental group of the early sixties and possibly the greatest of all time.

With Wilson—one of rock's all-time important rhythm players—handling the chordal work, early Ventures hits like "Walk, Don't Run" and "Perfidia" featured Bob Bogle on lead guitar, but around 1961 he swapped places with bassist Nokie Edwards, who was a more accomplished player. Their 1961 hit "Ram-Bunk-Shush" featured Edwards on lead, and it clearly showed his penchant for playing clean melodic solo lines à la Chet Atkins or Les Paul, as well as funky blues-style lead licks. Even better examples of his lead work can be heard on the tracks "Caravan," "Diamond Head," and "House of the Rising Sun." But "Walk, Don't Run" is the quintessential example of Ventures-style rock 'n' roll guitar. While Wilson and Edwards hold down a classic Am—G—F—E chord progression, Bogle executes a vibrato-tinged melody on his Fender Jazzmaster, clearly inspired by the master of twang, Duane Eddy.

After Nokie Edwards left the band in 1967, he was replaced by a fine guitarist named Gerry McGee, who made his mark in

Ventures history by playing on their cover of the TV theme "Hawaii Five-O," a #4 hit in 1969.

What was the secret of the Ventures' immense popularity, especially among aspiring guitarists? The most important element may have been that the melodies and arrangements of their songs were so simple and easy to learn and remember. Because of this accessibility, teenage garage bands could quickly figure out a Ventures song and, after only a few rehearsals, be playing some serious rock 'n' roll. Another reason for their vast success was that many Ventures tunes were already hit melodies. The band would often take a song that was moving up the pop charts and do their own instrumental version of it. More often than not, these would become hits, too. Because they were instrumentals, the Ventures' versions often became popular in countries where language had been a barrier to the original vocal versions—especially in Japan, where they continue to have a massive following.

The Ventures [on Dolton except where noted], *Walk, Don't Run* (1960), *The Ventures* (1961), *Another Smash!!!* (1961), *The Colorful Ventures* (1961), *Twist with the Ventures* (1962), *The Ventures Twist Party, Vol. 2* (1962), *Mashed Potatoes and Gravy* (1962), *Going to the Ventures Dance Party!* (1962), *The Ventures Play Telstar, The Lonely Bull* (1963), *"Surfing"* (1963), *Bobby Vee Meets the Ventures* (Liberty, 1963), *The Ventures Play the Country Classics* (1963), *Let's Go!* (1963), *The Ventures in Space* (1964), *The Fabulous Ventures* (1964), *Walk, Don't Run—Vol. 2* (1964), *The Ventures Knock Me Out!* (1965), *The Ventures on Stage around the World* (1965•), *Play Guitar with the Ventures* (1965), *Ventures A-Go-Go* (1965), *Where the Action Is* (1966), *The Ventures/Batman Theme* (1966), *Go! With the Ventures* (1966), *Wild Things!* (1966), *Guitar Freakout* (1967), *Super Psychedelics* (Liberty, 1967), *Golden Greats by the Ventures* (Liberty, 1967), *$1,000,000 Weekend* (1967), *Flights of Fantasy* (1968), *The Horse* (Liberty, 1968), *Underground Fire* (Liberty, 1969), *Hawaii Five-O* (Liberty, 1969), *Swamp Rock* (Liberty, 1969), *More Golden Greats* (Liberty, 1970), *The Ventures 10th Anniversary Album* (Liberty, 1970), *Theme from* Shaft (United Artists, 1972), *Joy/The Ventures Play the Classics* (United Artists, 1972), *Very Best of the Ventures* (Liberty, 1976), *Radical Guitars* (Iloki, 1987), *Walk, Don't Run: The Best of the Ventures* (EMI America, 1990).

Dick Dale *(center stage)* **& the Del-Tones**

Dick Dale & the Del-Tones

Dick Dale

Born: *Richard Monsour, c. 1938, in Boston*
Main Guitar: *Left-handed Fender Stratocaster*

Known as "The King of Surf Guitar," Dick Dale ruled the southern California rock scene in 1961 and '62 with his band, the Del-Tones. Dale drew thousands to the legendary Rendezvous Ballroom in the beach town of Balboa. He was written about in *Newsweek* and *Life* and appeared in a number of Frankie 'n' Annette surf movies. On record, the guitarist cut reverb-heavy stompers like "Let's Go Trippin'," "Miscrlou," "Surf Beat," and "Death of a Gremmie," which are now considered classics of the surf-rock genre. These songs are also excellent examples of Dale's swift left-hand picking. For gear, the guitarist played through Fender Dual Showman amps and riffed on a gold metal-flake, backwards-strung lefty Strat dubbed "The Beast" that was set up with extra-heavy strings gauged .014–.060, high to low. Like many other surf acts, however, his career was squashed by the British Invasion, despite his having a major influence on the one surf band that survived the purge, the Beach Boys.

In the mid 1990s Dale began riding a revived wave of popularity, due in part to his inclusion on several movie soundtracks, most notably the huge 1995 flick *Pulp Fiction*. He has also recorded the acclaimed comeback albums *Tribal Thunder* and *Unknown Territory* and worked with contemporary guitar shredder Gary Hoey on the soundtrack to the surf movie *Endless Summer II*.

Dick Dale, *Surfer's Choice* (Deltone, 1963), *Checkered Flag* (Capitol, 1963), *Mr. Eliminator* (Capitol, 1964), *Summer Surf* (Capitol, 1964), *Surf Family* (Dubtone, 1964), *Rock Out/Live At Ciro's* (Capitol, 1965•), *Coast to Coast* (Accent, 1967), *Greatest Hits* (GNP, 1975), *Tigers Loose* (Rhino, 1986), *King* *of Surf Guitar* (Rhino, 1989), *Tribal Thunder* (High Tone, 1993), *Unknown Territory* (High Tone, 1994), *Calling Up Spirits* (Beggar's Banquet, 1996).

Recordings featuring Dick Dale: **Various Artists,** *Legends of Guitar: Surf, Vol. 1* (Rhino, 1991). **Gary Hoey,** *Endless Summer II* (Reprise, 1994). **Various Artists,** *Pulp Fiction* (MCA, 1995).

Booker T. & the MG's

Steve Cropper

B o r n :   *October 21, 1941, in Willow Springs, Missouri*
M a i n   G u i t a r :   *Fender Telecaster*

Mixing equal doses of R&B and gospel elements, the "Memphis Sound" was one of the most exciting new rock subgenres heard in early sixties rock 'n' roll. Wilson Pickett, Carla and Rufus Thomas, and Sam and Dave, among others, created the heart of this new R&B sound, and they scored dozens of great Top 10 hits throughout the decade. Booker T. & the MG's were one of the acts spreading the Memphis gospel, and in 1962 they broke the Top Five on the singles charts with a haunting minor-key instrumental called "Green Onions." The tune featured the soulful, edgy guitar work of band member Steve Cropper, who was also staff guitarist for the prestigious Stax label and several other Memphis record companies. In this role he appeared on hit recordings by such R&B and blues greats as Eddie Floyd, Albert King, and the immortal Otis Redding. His sparse, emotive guitar playing became synonymous with the Memphis Sound, and he is one of the first white rock guitarists to whom the term "funky" can aptly be applied. Other first-rate Cropper guitar breaks include his fat multiple bends and blues licks in the MG's' 1967 hit "Hip Hug-Her" and his syncopated chord solo on their remake of the Rascals' "Groovin'."

A solid soloist, Cropper is better known as a superb rhythm guitarist whose tasty chord fills and spartan lead licks on many recordings stand out for their remarkable sense of subtlety and restraint. Cropper ultimately branched out into songwriting and production, and among his noted writing credits are Wilson Pickett's 1965 hit "In the Midnight Hour" and Otis Redding's #1 smash in 1968, "(Sittin' on) The Dock of the Bay." He also produced such top rock artists as Rod Stewart, Poco, and Jeff Beck (◗ The Jeff Beck Group), and later served in the guitar seat of the popular Blues Brothers band, fronted by comedians John Belushi and Dan Ackroyd.

Along with Bo Diddley and Buddy Holly, Cropper is one of the few early rock guitarists who emphasized the importance of rhythm in all aspects of rock 'n' roll guitar playing. His strong rhythm playing and bluesy lead style were a big influence on rock 'n' roll guitarists throughout much of the 1960s and seventies, notably inspiring Pete Townshend of the Who. If it had not been for R&B-based guitarists like Steve Cropper, there would undoubtedly be very little of that soulful "funk" in modern rock guitar.

Booker T. & the MG's [on Stax except where noted], *Green Onions* (1962), *Hip Hug-Her* (1967), *Back to Back* [with the Mar-keys] (1967), *Doin' Our Thing* (1968), *Soul Limbo* (1968), *Best of Booker T. & the MG's* (Atlantic, 1968), *Uptight* (1969), *The Booker T. Set* (1969), *McLemore Avenue* (1970), *Melting Pot* (1971), *Universal Language* (1976), *That's the Way It Should Be* (Columbia, 1994). **Steve Cropper,** *With a Little Help from My Friends* (1967), *Steve Cropper* (1981).

Recordings featuring Steve Cropper: **Wilson Pickett,** *In the Midnight Hour* (Atlantic, 1965). **Otis Redding,** *The Dock of the Bay* (Volt, 1968), *Monterey International Pop* [with Jimi Hendrix] (Reprise, 1970•). **Sam and Dave,** *The Best of Sam and Dave* (Atlantic, 1969). **Albert King/Steve Cropper/Pop Staples,** *Jammed Together* (Stax, 1969). **Roy Buchanan,** *Loading Zone* (Atlantic, 1977). **Rod Stewart** [on Warner Bros.], *Atlantic Crossing* (1975), *A Night on the Town* (1976). **Blues Brothers** [on Atlantic], *Briefcase Full of Blues* (1978•), *The Blues Brothers Soundtrack* (1980), *Made in America* (1980•). **Duane Eddy,** *Duane Eddy* (Capitol, 1987). **Dynatones,** *Shameless* (n/a, 1988). **Various Artists,** *The Bob Dylan 30th Anniversary Concert* (Columbia, 1993•).

Lonnie Mack

B o r n :   *Lonnie McIntosh, on July 17, 1941, in Harrison, Indiana*
M a i n   G u i t a r :   *1958 Gibson Flying V with Bigsby vibrato*

Lonnie Mack is something of a rock 'n' roll enigma. Outside of his two stellar 1963 hit singles "Memphis" and "Wham," Mack has spent most of his career well out of the spotlight of fame. Yet for all his obscurity, he is one of the most important and influential rock guitarists of the pre-Yardbirds 1960s. This is because he is essentially the missing guitar link between the twangy, multi-string riffing of the rockabilly guitarists and the bluesy, string-pushing players of the mid sixties—and later on, the psychedelic guitarists of San Francisco. He also made the crucial bridge between black blues and white hillbilly music via his lead work.

Hearing one of Mack's early singles makes this evident: The guitarist can be heard using the scratchy amplifier overdrive and chordal licks of the early rock guitar greats, but he infuses his breaks further with string bends, pentatonic runs, and mature blues chops, all of which became chops that eventually became trademarks of Eric Clapton, Mike Bloomfield, and Stevie Ray Vaughan. "Wham" may sound like a lost early recording from one of these famous guitarists, but it is Lonnie Mack, one of the true unsung guitar heroes of rock 'n' roll.

Mack had a musical background steeped in radio broadcasts from the Grand Ole Opry, blues, and country gospel music. His early training on guitar came from diverse sources: his mother, an uncle who played guitar using Travis-style picking, Ohio R&B player Robert Ward, and a blind gospel guitarist named Ralph Trotto, who was also well versed in jazz guitar styles. By his teen years Mack had left school and was playing music full-time with various rockabilly and country outfits around the Midwest. In 1963, while backing up a female vocal group in the studio, Mack and the Twilighters hastily recorded some instrumentals on their own, including a cover of Chuck Berry's "Memphis," which was released shortly afterwards as a single by Fraternity Records. Surprisingly, "Memphis" shot to the top of the pop charts. Lonnie, who at the time was still touring on the bar circuit, promptly shortened his name from McIntosh to Mack and quickly recorded the album *The Wham of that Memphis Man!* to back up the best-selling single.

Mack's "Memphis" is a revealing glimpse into his unparalleled guitar attack. Translating Chuck Berry's vocal line into a sliding, multi-string melody on a '58 Gibson Flying V, Mack created an exceptional version of Berry's song; his 12-bar solo is saturated with bends, blues scale maneuvers, and the warble from a Bigsby vibrato. Though "Memphis" was Mack's biggest hit, it is "Wham" with which many identify his great guitar playing. A tight chordal riff laid over a fast boogie-woogie rhythm sets the tone for the cut, which contains guitar breaks pumped up with vibrato arm highlights, echoey single-note lines, and the repetitive string-pushing licks that eventually became so prevalent in Jeff Beck's guitar style.

After the 1963 album, Fraternity continued to put his singles out, although none did as well as "Memphis." Mack eventually returned to touring and doing session work for the likes of James Brown, Freddie King, and Hank Ballard. In 1968 the guitarist's earlier hits were rediscovered, and Lonnie Mack enjoyed a small resurgence in popularity among the psychedelic rockers in San Francisco. He also played on the famous Doors rocker "Roadhouse Blues." Still, it wasn't until 1985 that he had a full-fledged "comeback" on his hands, due to the acclaimed *Strike Like Lightning* album. Produced by Stevie Ray Vaughan, the disc was highlighted by the two guitarists jamming on a smokin' remake of "Wham."

In all, it is not an exaggeration to say that Lonnie Mack was well ahead of his time when "Memphis" was released in 1963. His bluesy solos predated the pioneering blues-rock guitar work of Jeff Beck in the Yardbirds, Eric Clapton in John Mayall's Bluesbreakers, and Mike Bloomfield in the Butterfield Blues Band by nearly two years, and, considering that *they* are considered "before their time," the chronological significance of Lonnie Mack for the world of rock guitar is that much more remarkable.

Lonnie Mack, *The Wham of that Memphis Man!* (Fraternity, 1963), *Glad I'm in the Band* (Elektra, 1968), *The Hill of Indiana* (Elektra, 1971), *Home at Last* (n/a, 1977), *Strike Like Lightning* (Alligator, 1985), *Second Sight* (Alligator, 1986), *Road Houses and Dance Halls* (Epic, 1988), *Live!...Attack of the Killer V* (Alligator, 1990•). **Lonnie Mack & Pismo,** *Lonnie Mack & Pismo* (Capitol, 1977).

Recordings featuring Lonnie Mack: **The Doors,** *Morrison Hotel/Hard Rock Cafe* (Elektra, 1970). **Various Artists,** *The Alligator Records 20th Anniversary Collection* (Alligator, 1991), *Alligator 25th Anniversary Collection* (Alligator, 1996).

Link Wray

Born: *May 2, 1935, in Fort Bragg, North Carolina*
Main Guitars: *Gibson Les Paul, Danelectro Masonite "Longhorn"*

One of the earliest "heavy" rockers was Link Wray, famous for his two instrumental hits on the Cadence label, "Rumble" and "Rawhide." Wray was also one of first users of fuzztone (distortion), an effect he discovered by punching little holes in the speakers of his Premier amp. In contrast to Duane Eddy's upbeat guitar instrumentals of the same period, Wray's tunes are dense, sinister-sounding pieces that rely heavily on his flashy guitar tricks and pyrotechnic effects. "Rumble," from 1958, is the classic Link Wray showpiece: a slow, brooding blues rhythm with Wray's guitar spitting out an array of dirty fuzz riffs, power chords, and tremolo effects. On another of his early tracks, "The Black Widow," Wray plays a thick bass string motif not too dissimilar from Jeff Beck's sound with the Yardbirds, while on "Jack the Ripper" his guitar parts anticipate the heavy rock trends of the late sixties with a commanding display of power chords and fuzzy solos. He later experienced a small comeback in the late 1970s, backing rockabilly revivalist Robert Gordon.

Like another relatively obscure innovator, Paul Burlison, Link Wray was something of a guitar primitive. Not hampered by any preconceived notions of rock guitar style or method, Wray played his own brutish but inventive brand of guitar, which predated hard rock and heavy metal by nearly 10 years. He also helped introduce a myriad of sound effects to the rock guitar arena, notably distortion, feedback, reverb, tremolo, and echo. Although his name may not elicit the same public recognition as that of Duane Eddy or Dick Dale, the guitar sounds that Link Wray pioneered are virtually everywhere in rock 'n' roll today, and he's been a sizable influence on alternative and neo-surf bands everywhere.

Link Wray, *Link Wray & the Wraymen* (Edsel, 1960), *Link Wray* (Polydor, 1971), *Beans and Fatback* (Virgin, 1973), *Be What You Want To* (Polydor, 1974), *The Link Wray Rumble* (Polydor, 1975), *Stuck in Gear* (Virgin, 1976), *There's Good Rockin' Tonight* (c. 1980), *Fire and Brimstone* (n/a), *Live in '85* (Big Beat, 1986•), *Growling Guitar* (Big Beat, 1988), *Rumble! The Best of Link Wray* (Rhino, 1993). **Robert Gordon,** *Robert Gordon with Link Wray* (Private St., 1977), *Fresh Fish Special* (Private St., 1978).

The Shadows

Hank Marvin

B o r n: *October 28, 1941, in Newcastle-on-Tyne, England*
M a i n   G u i t a r: *Fender Stratocaster*

The Shadows : Jet Harris, Tony Meehan, Hank Marvin, Bruce Welch

Great Britain's equivalent to the Ventures, the Shadows began life as pop singer Cliff Richard's backing group in 1958. Originally known as the Drifters (a name change was necessary to avoid confusion with the American doo-wop group of the same name), the Shadows featured Hank Marvin on lead guitar, as well as guitarist Bruce Welch, bassist Jet Harris, and drummer Tony Meehan. This quartet backed Richard for a number of years before striking out on their own, although they continued to operate as his backup band for nearly a decade. As the Shadows, their 1960 "Apache" became a #1 hit and marked the beginning of a long number of U.K. hit singles during the early sixties, including "Kon-Tiki" (1961), "Dance On" (1962), "Man of Mystery," and "Foot Tapper" (1963). (Ironically, the Shadows' version of "Apache" never scored in America; that honor went to a one-hit Danish wonder named Jorgen Ingmann, who took the tune to #2 in 1961.)

On guitar, the image of a somewhat owlish Hank Marvin playing his trusty red Stratocaster inspired scores of British lads to take up the instrument, including everyone from art-rockers like Steve Howe and Steve Hackett to Mark Knopfler of Dire Straits, who retains a penchant for red Strats to this very day. Indeed, it might be said that Marvin was actually Britain's first guitar hero, predating Clapton's rise to prominence by half a decade.

Amidst numerous personnel changes in later years, however, the band's popularity faded. The Shadows had a small comeback when their *20 Golden Greats* album topped the charts in 1977, and then landed a Top 10 single the next year with an instrumental cover of "Don't Cry for Me Argentina," from the pop opera *Evita*. Marvin also covered Knopfler's "Local Hero" and performed it on stage with Dire Straits. Since then, the Shadows have sporadically scored singles, all of which feature the sound of Hank Marvin's timeless Stratocaster melodies.

The Shadows [on Columbia except where noted], *The Shadows* (1962), *Greatest Hits* (1963), *Dance with the Shadows* (1964), *The Sound of the Shadows* (1965), *More Hits* (1965), *Shadow Music* (1966), *Jigsaw* (1967), *Established 1958* (1968), *Something Else* (1969), *Shades of Rock* (1970), *Rockin' with Curly Leads* (EMI, 1973), *Live at Paris Olympia* (EMI, 1975•), *Rarities* (Nut, 1976), *20 Golden Greats* (EMI, 1977), *String of Hits* (EMI, 1979), *Live* (MFP, 1981•), *Life in the Jungle* (Polydor, 1982), *XXV* (Polydor), *Guardian Angel* (Polydor, 1984). **Hank Marvin,** *Hank Marvin* (Columbia, 1969), *Marvin, Welch & Farrar* (Regal Zonophone, 1971), *Words and Music* (Polydor, 1982).

Recordings featuring Hank Marvin: **Various Artists,** *Guitar Speak II* (IRS, 1990).

CHAPTER FOUR

The British Invasion

Mop Tops, Matching Suits, and Fuzztones

It was more than just pop fodder and fashion fads. The British Invasion was also pivotal to the future development of rock guitar. Until that time, the basic ingredients of rock guitar had been blues and country music influences, with small amounts of folk, jazz, and pop occasionally tossed in for good measure. But around 1963, rock 'n' roll began acquiring new sounds via the groups that were spearheading what has come to be known as the British Invasion. (The name reflects how these bands literally and swiftly took over the American pop scene.) While the Invasion may be regarded as the height of rock 'n' roll kitsch—as evidenced by the profusion of neat matching suits, scary haircuts, and embarrassing bubblegum music by acts like Freddie & the Dreamers—bands like the Beatles, the Rolling Stones, the Who, the Yardbirds, and a handful of others featured inventive guitarists who began stretching the tight stylistic boundaries that the first proponents of rock guitar had maintained until that time.

Moving beyond the standard (and even clichéd) rock 'n' roll licks, England's new generation of rockers began to include such diverse ethnic sounds as medieval Gregorian chants, American folk melodies, Indian ragas, old R&B motifs, hard U.S. blues, and Middle Eastern tonalities in their playing. These were added to the musical foundation established by early rock guitar masters such as Chuck Berry, Scotty Moore, Carl Perkins, and James Burton, thereby creating a whole new universe of playing for rock guitarists to explore. While not every band in the Invasion had a serious guitarist (indeed, some were quite amateurish), the guitarists for the Beatles, the Rolling Stones, the Kinks, and the Yardbirds became pioneers for a whole new generation of players. And looking back, it was primarily this core of mop-topped guitarists who helped set the stage for the legendary guitar explosion that was to come just a few years later.

The Beatles

George Harrison

Born: *February 25, 1943, in Liverpool*
Main Guitars: *Rickenbacker 360/12, Gretsch Country Gentleman and Tennessean, Epiphone Casino*

John Lennon

Born: *October 9, 1940, in Liverpool*
Died: *December 8, 1980, in New York City*
Main Guitars: *Rickenbacker 325, Epiphone Casino, Gibson J-160E*

Paul McCartney

Born: *June 18, 1942, in Liverpool*
Main Guitars: *Hofner bass, miscellaneous electrics and acoustics*

It was January 1964, and America was still reeling from the assassination of President John F. Kennedy the previous November. Midway through the month, a song entitled "I Want to Hold Your Hand" made its way onto the airwaves of America's pop radio stations and rapidly began ascending the singles charts. It was an upbeat rock 'n' roll song with tight vocal harmonies and an aggressive instrumental backdrop. By February 1, "I Want to Hold Your Hand" was the #1 pop single in the country. The group that performed it had once been known as the Quarrymen, Johnny and the Moondogs, and the Silver Beatles, but by the win-

The Beatles : Paul, George, Ringo, John

ter of 1964 they had long since settled on simply the Beatles.

After their performance on "The Ed Sullivan Show" on February 9, which put them on millions of television sets across the country, the Beatles had—in the span of less than one month—become America's favorite pop group. The nation's youth, who had been so devastated by the loss of their president, suddenly found some hope, and it was in the form of four Liverpudlians with an offbeat band name. Young America began to celebrate and revel in "Beatlemania," which at the time was the most frenzied period in rock 'n' roll since rock's own explosive inception barely nine years earlier.

While the Beatles' history has been amply documented, their influence on the development of rock guitar has been grossly underestimated. It is true that George Harrison, John Lennon, or even Paul McCartney (who occasionally played lead guitar on Beatles tracks) cannot be compared to any of the major guitar figures of the day, such as Duane Eddy, Keith Richards, or Eric Clapton, but they nevertheless elevated rock guitar to new and previously unparalleled levels of achievement in pop music. This was accomplished by their revolutionary use of new recording techniques, the integration of exotic ethnic music into their pop style, and, most importantly, their own uncanny creative ability, which was ultimately responsible for some of the greatest popular music of the twentieth century.

The most important aspect of the Beatles' influence on rock guitar was their expansion of the instrument's sonic horizons, done in a way that no one had, or would, until the arrival of Jimi Hendrix in England in 1966. Through the Beatles' music, the development of sixties rock guitar can be clearly traced as it moved into new realms of sound and style. The band's simple beginnings, established with early covers of Chuck Berry's "Roll over Beethoven" and Carl Perkins' "Honey Don't," later blossomed into the complex, studio-embellished backward guitar tracks of songs like "Tomorrow Never Knows." The hard-rock riffing on "Taxman" and Indian raga rhythms of "Love to You" were recorded only a few months after the folksy acoustic strumming of "Yesterday" and the experimental fuzz-bass runs of "Think for Yourself." Later on, the frenzied guitar intro to "Revolution" and Harrison's melodic solo in "Let It Be" pointed to the heavy metal and blues sounds that were beginning to take hold of rock. Overall, the diversity and substance of Harrison's, Lennon's, and McCartney's guitar work is staggering, especially considering that the Beatles were a group without a real guitar hero in the fold.

Besides these significant achievements, there is one more six-string contribution that is possibly their most important of all. At the very moment the Beatles first appeared on "The Ed Sullivan Show," thousands of young people across the country decided they wanted to—or, more accurately, *had to*—play the guitar. Teenagers and children suddenly begged their parents for a guitar. Fortunately for rock 'n' roll, many parents listened and bought their kids budget-priced electrics and acoustics. As many top rock guitarists of the last 30 years or so have testified in inter-

views, the Beatles and their appearance on the Sullivan show are often the primary reasons why these next-generation musicians to took up the guitar in the first place.

The Beatles [on Capitol except where noted], *Introducing the Beatles* (Vee-Jay, 1963), *Meet the Beatles* (1964), *The Beatles with Tony Sheridan and Their Guests* (MGM, 1964), *The Beatles' Second Album* (1964), *A Hard Day's Night* (United Artists, 1964), *Something New* (1964), *Beatles '65* (1965), *Beatles VI* (1965), *Help!* (1965), *Rubber Soul* (1965), *"Yesterday"…and Today* (1966), *Revolver* (1966), *Sgt. Pepper's Lonely Hearts Club Band* (1967), *Magical Mystery Tour* (1967), *The Beatles* ["White Album"] (Apple, 1968), *Yellow Submarine* (Apple, 1969), *Abbey Road* (Apple, 1969), *Hey Jude* (Apple, 1970), *Let It Be* (Apple, 1970), *The Beatles at the Hollywood Bowl* (1977•), *The Beatles Live! At the Star-Club in Hamburg, Germany, 1962* (Lingasong, 1977•), *Rarities* (1980), *Live at the BBC* (1994), *The Beatles Anthology, Vols. 1–3* (1995–96•).

George Harrison [on Apple except where noted], *Wonderwall Music* (1968), *Electronic Music* (Zapple, 1969), *All Things Must Pass* (1970), *The Concert for Bangla Desh* (1972•), *Living in the Material World* (1973), *Dark Horse* (1974), *Extra Texture (Read All About It)* (1975), *Thirty-Three & 1/3* (Dark Horse, 1976), *George Harrison* (Dark Horse, 1979), *Somewhere in England* (Dark Horse, 1981), *Gone Troppo* (Dark Horse, 1982), *Cloud Nine* (Dark Horse, 1987), *Best of Dark Horse, 1976–1989* (Dark Horse/Warner Bros., 1989), *Live in Japan* (Dark Horse, 1992•). **The Traveling Wilburys** [on Wilbury Records], *The Traveling Wilburys, Volume 1* (1989), *Volume 3* (1990).

Recordings featuring George Harrison: **Cream,** *Goodbye* (RSO, 1969). **Jack Bruce,** *Songs for a Tailor* (Atco, 1969). **Jackie Lomax,** *Is This What You Want* (Apple, 1969). **Billy Preston** [on A&M except where noted], *That's the Way God Planned It* (Apple, 1969), *I Wrote a Simple Song* (1972), *It's My Pleasure* (1975). **Bobby Keyes,** *Bobby Keyes* (Warner Bros., 1972). **Leon Russell,** *Leon Russell* (Shelter, 1970). **Doris Troy,** *Doris Troy* (Apple, 1970). **Derek and the Dominos,** *Layla and Other Love Songs* (Polydor, 1970). **John Lennon,** *Imagine* (Apple, 1971), *Some Time in New York City* (Apple, 1972). **Cheech & Chong,** *Los Cochinos* (Ode, 1973). **Ringo Starr,** *Ringo* (Apple, 1973). **Alvin Lee & Mylon LeFevre,** *On the Road to Freedom* (Columbia, 1974). **Ravi Shankar,** *Shankar Family & Friends* (Dark Horse, 1975). **Tom Scott,** *New York Connection* (Ode, 1975). **Hall & Oates,** *Along the Red Ledge* (RCA, 1978). **Pete Best,** *The Pete Best Story* (Savage, n/a). **Mick Fleetwood,** *The Visitor* (RCA, 1981). **Duane Eddy,** *Duane Eddy* (Capitol, 1987). **Tom Petty,** *Full Moon Fever* (MCA, 1989). **Jim Capaldi,** *Some Come Running* (Island, 1989). **Roy Orbison,** *Mystery Girl* (Virgin, 1989). **Jeff Lynne,** *Armchair Theatre* (Reprise, 1990). **Eric Clapton,** *Journeyman* (Duck/Reprise, 1990). **Gary Moore,** *Still Got the Blues* (Charisma, 1990). **Alvin Lee,** *I Hear You Rockin'* (Viceroy, 1994).

John Lennon [on Apple except where noted], *Unfinished Music No. 1: Two Virgins* (1968), *Unfinished Music No. 2: Life with the Lions* (Zapple, 1969), *Wedding Album* (1969), *The Plastic Ono Band—Live Peace in Toronto* (1969•), *John Lennon/Plastic Ono Band* (1970), *Imagine* (1971), *Some Time in New York City* (1972•), *Mind Games* (1973), *Wall and Bridges* (1974), *Rock 'n' Roll* (1975), *Shaved Fish* (1975), *Double Fantasy* (Geffen, 1980), *Milk and Honey* (Polydor, 1984), *Live in New York City* (1986•), *Menlove Avenue* (Capitol, 1986), *Imagine: John Lennon* (Capitol, 1988).

Paul McCartney [on Columbia except where noted], *McCartney* (Apple, 1970), *McCartney II* (1980), *Tug of War* (1982), *Pipes of Peace* (1983), *Give My Regards to Broad Street* (1984), *Press to Play* (Capitol, 1986), *All the Best* (Capitol, 1987), *Flowers in the Dirt* (1989), *Tripping the Live Fantastic* (1990•), *CHOBA B CCCP: The Russian Album* (Capitol, 1991•), *Unplugged* (1991•), *Paul McCartney's Liverpool Oratorio* [conducted by Carl Davis] (EMI, 1991•), *Off The Ground* (1993). **Paul & Linda McCartney,** *Ram* (Apple, 1971). **Wings** [on Capitol except where noted], *Wild Life* (Apple,

The Rolling Stones: Bill Wyman, Brian Jones, Charlie Watts, Mick Jagger, Keith Richards

their music began reflecting the feelings of teen aggression, selfishness, and insecurity that pervaded the decade. They were the musical and emotional opposite of the Beatles' sunnier pop fare. Despite the difference between the two bands, the Stones' image as the "bad boys of rock 'n' roll" garnered an equal amount of the U.K. public's attention in 1963 with the release of their single "I Wanna Be Your Man"; ironically, the song was written by Lennon and McCartney.

Early in 1963 the Stones (vocalist Mick Jagger, guitarists Keith Richards and Brian Jones, bassist Bill Wyman, and drummer Charlie Watts) landed a weekly gig as house band at the Crawdaddy Club in Richmond, a suburb of London. It was during their time at the Crawdaddy that the Stones' cover versions of black blues standards began to take on the lean, elemental rock 'n' roll characteristics that became their musical trademark. After the initial success of "I Wanna Be Your Man," the Stones (along with their extra-savvy manager, Andrew Loog Oldham) quickly garnered one of the biggest followings in England. Within two years, it would be one of the biggest followings in the world.

The nucleus of the Stones' sound during most of the sixties was the twin-guitar work of Keith Richards and Brian Jones, who was also once a member of the famed Blues Incorporated (♦ U.K. Blues Revival). While Brian Jones played slide guitar, rhythm, and some lead in the Stones' early days, Keith Richards handled the lion's share of the lead playing and was the core of the Stones guitar sound.

In the band's early recording days, it was almost a duel of Richards' and Jones' guitar influences: Chuck Berry versus slide bluesman Elmore James, respectively. Early Rolling Stones covers of "Route 66" and Berry's own "Carol" displayed Richards' obvious soloing talents with multi-string riffing, Chuck Berry style, while Jones' triplet-based slide licks à la Elmore James raced through "Little Red Rooster" and "I Wanna Be Your Man." Jones, in fact, may also be the first white rocker to play slide guitar on record (even predating the Beatles' "Drive My Car"). As a team Richards and Jones gave "Heart of Stone" its icy punch and "(I Can't Get No) Satisfaction" the hard-rock drive that made it the first Stones single to reach #1 in both England and America. "Satisfaction" (1965) also owed much of its success to Richards'

1971), *Red Rose Speedway* (Apple, 1973), *Band on the Run* (Apple, 1973), *Venus and Mars* (1975), *Wings at the Speed of Sound* (1976), *Wings over America* (1976•), *London Town* (1978), *Wings Greatest* (1978), *Back to the Egg* (Columbia, 1979).

Recordings featuring Paul McCartney: **Jackie Lomax,** *Is This What You Want* (Apple, 1969). **James Taylor,** *James Taylor* (Apple, 1969), *Walking Man* (Warner Bros., 1974). **Ringo Starr,** *Ringo* (Apple, 1973). **Denny Laine,** *Holly Days* (Capitol, 1978). **Elvis Costello,** *Spike* (Warner Bros., 1989). **Various Artists,** *Prince's 10th Anniversary Birthday Party* (A&M, 1987•). **Various Artists,** *Rock for Amnesty* (Mercury, 1987•).

The Rolling Stones (Part 1)

Keith Richards

B o r n : *December 18, 1943, in Dartford, Kent, England*
M a i n   G u i t a r s : *Gibson Les Paul and Firebird, Fender Telecaster*

Brian Jones

B o r n : *February 28, 1942, in Cheltenham, Gloucestershire, England*
D i e d : *July 3, 1969*
M a i n   G u i t a r : *Vox Mk Series "Teardrop"*

If there was any group in the British Invasion that rivaled the Beatles in popularity during the 1960s, it was the Rolling Stones. Originally a straight blues revival group, the Rolling Stones had become a tough, menacing rock outfit by 1965, when extremely novel use of a then-radical fuzzbox in the main riff, with Jones handling acoustic rhythm.

Toward the end of the decade, Brian Jones began to lose interest in guitar and began playing instruments like sitar, dulcimer, and marimba on Stones recordings, leaving the majority of the guitar playing to Richards. Keith's greased solos in "Sympathy for the Devil," the acoustic guitar power chords on "Street Fighting Man" (both from *Beggars Banquet*, 1968), and the country-style rhythm and lead on "Honky Tonk Women" (1969) all revealed that he was finally a rock player to be reckoned with; by the end of the decade he was almost universally acclaimed as one of rock's foremost rhythm guitarists. Richards was also a rock guitar pioneer in his use of open tunings in rock guitar, the use of electric five-string guitars (where the low E is left off altogether), and the use of Nashville, or "high-strung," tuning on acoustics. Nashville tuning, popular in country music, involves using the octave-higher strings from a 12-string set for the bottom three strings (E, A, D) of a six-string, along with the regular higher three strings (G, B, E), creating a glistening acoustic tone. A good example of it can be heard in the Stones' 1971 track "Wild Horses."

Eventually, the strain and stress of being a world-famous Rolling Stone proved to be too much for Brian Jones, and in June 1969 he left the group to pursue his own musical projects. A month later he drowned in his own swimming pool, ostensibly by mysterious means. As Jones had already left the band, his death did not signal the end of the Rolling Stones. In the course of their career, they would replace Jones twice, rising to even grander heights in rock 'n' roll (◗ British Invasion II).

The Rolling Stones (1964–69) [on London], *England's Newest Hitmakers/The Rolling Stones* (1964), *12 x 5* (1964), *The Rolling Stones, Now!* (1965), *Out of our Heads* (1965), *December's Children* (1965), *Big Hits: High Tides and Green Grass* (1966), *Aftermath* (1966), *Got Live if You Want It* (1966•), *Between the Buttons* (1967), *Flowers* (1967), *Their Satanic Majesties Request* (1967), *Beggars Banquet* (1968), *Through the Past Darkly: Big Hits Vol. 2* (1969).

The Kinks

Dave Davies

B o r n :   *February 3, 1947, in Muswell Hill, London*
M a i n   G u i t a r s :   *'58 Gibson Flying V and Les Paul, Guild Starfire*

Ray Davies

B o r n :   *June 21, 1944, in Muswell Hill, London*
M a i n   G u i t a r :   *Fender Telecaster*

Besides the Rolling Stones, the Kinks hold the distinction of being the only major band of the British Invasion to remain as a working rock entity well into the 1990s. At the height of the Invasion, from 1964 to 1966, the Kinks were among the most popular rock 'n' roll bands to come out of Great Britain, racking up half a dozen hits in the U.S. and nearly twice that in the U.K (although they never sold the huge number of albums the Beatles or Stones did). And of all the major groups in the Invasion, the Kinks were by far the rawest and most primitive, scoring their first few hits with a formula of raunchy R&B-influenced songs, each laden with artless guitar riffs written by singer/rhythm player Ray Davies and the feverish solos of his brother Dave.

Inspired by Chuck Berry, James Burton, and Scotty Moore, 17-year-old Dave Davies was responsible for the furious solos and barre-chord progressions in several of the Kinks' early hits, the best of which were "You Really Got Me," "I Need You," and "All Day and All of the Night," all released during 1964–65. His hot riffing also foreshadowed the sound of heavy metal with an abundance of aggressive string bends and, more importantly, his early use of amplifier feedback and distortion. Davies claims to have discovered his own distortion by slashing the back of his amp's speakers with a razor blade. He was also one of the first rockers to use the radically shaped Gibson Flying V, and his raw lead style further predated the scrappier sound of American garage bands and hard rock players by several years.

But Davies' achievements were not without controversy. For years Jimmy Page claimed to have been the lead guitarist on the Kinks' crucial early records. But the Davies brothers disputed Page's claim, although later evidence indicated that the future Led Zep guitarist did play rhythm guitar on a few of the early sessions. As further proof, Dave was also seen playing the solos live on the TV show "Shindig." Despite the years of finger pointing, Dave Davies is now deservedly appreciated for his contributions to the lexicon of heavy guitar, as is his brother Ray for writing such great rockers.

The Kinks [on Reprise except where noted], *The Kinks* (1964), *You Really Got Me* (1965), *Kinks-Size* (1965), *Kinda Kinks* (1965), *Kinks Kinkdom* (1965), *The Kinks' Greatest Hits* (1966), *Face to Face* (1967), The Live Kinks (1967•), *Something Else by the Kinks* (1968), *Arthur (or the decline and fall of the British Empire)* (1969), *Lola Versus Powerman and the Moneygoround, Part One* (1970), *Muswell Hillbillies* (RCA, 1971), *The Kink Kronikles* (1972), *Everybody's in Show Biz* (RCA, 1972•), *The Great Lost Kinks Album* (1973), *Preservation Act 1* (RCA, 1973), *Preservation Act 2* (RCA, 1974), *Soap Opera* (RCA, 1975), *Schoolboys in Disguise* (RCA, 1975), *The Kinks Greatest— Celluloid Heroes* (RCA, 1976), *Sleepwalker* (Arista, 1977), *Misfits* (Arista, 1978), *Low Budget* (Arista, 1979), *One for the Road* (Arista, 1980•), *Second Time Around* (RCA, 1980), *Give the People What They Want* (Arista, 1981), *State of Confusion* (Arista, 1983), *Word of Mouth* (Arista, 1984), *Rock & Roll Cities* (Arista, 1987), *The Road* (MCA, 1988•), *UK Jive* (MCA, 1989), *Phobia* (Columbia, 1993). **Dave Davies,** AFL1-3603 (RCA, 1980), *Glamour* (RCA, 1981).

CHAPTER FIVE

The U.K. Blues Revival

Chicago by Way of London

A second front of the British Invasion was the U.K. blues revival. This was a by-product of the "trad jazz" (i.e., Dixieland jazz) boom of the fifties. In 1960 guitarist Alexis Korner and harpist/vocalist Cyril Davies—both members of Chris Barber's popular trad-jazz band—formed Blues Incorporated, England's first white blues band. By 1962 Blues Incorporated had amassed a large following as a result of their house gig at the Marquee Club in London. More significant, however, was the group's regularly shifting personnel: at one time or another in the early sixties, the band had amongst its prestigious ranks Mick Jagger, Keith Richards, Brian Jones, Charlie Watts, Jack Bruce, and Ginger Baker, all of whom went on to impressively bigger and better things in rock 'n' roll.

Blues Incorporated's greatest achievement may have been that it brought together Jagger, Richards, Jones, and Watts, who went on to form the Rolling Stones (◊). When the Stones splintered off from Blues Incorporated, they almost immediately became the top R&B group in London, though they soon strayed from their "pure blues" roots and began mixing rock 'n' roll with their more traditional blues covers. Eventually, this unorthodox mixture of rock and blues by the Stones and other promising young groups on the British blues scene, like the Yardbirds, Savoy Brown, and Ten Years After, helped give birth to blues-rock.

Looking back, the British blues-rock boom was an extremely fertile time for rock guitar. Since many of the great American blues acts were either led by an outstanding guitarist or featured one prominently, nearly all of the U.K. blues-rock bands, in their quest to be "faithful" to the blues tradition, had to have a prominent guitarist as well. Surprisingly, they often did. The list of major blues-rock guitarists who turned up in mid-sixties Britain—Eric Clapton, Keith Richards, Jeff Beck, Jimmy Page, Peter Green, Mick Taylor, Alvin Lee of Ten Years After, and Kim Simmonds of Savoy Brown—was a staggering collection of players to be in one place at nearly the same time. It was also these guitarists (plus Americans Mike Bloomfield and Jimi Hendrix) who dominated rock guitar later in the decade.

While just a few years earlier the guitar was only an occasionally featured solo instrument in many English rock 'n' roll groups, by 1967 many of the British blues-based groups were almost completely dominated by the sounds of their guitarists, to the point where the solos seemed more important than the songs themselves. Despite the occasional overkill, the U.K. blues scene was a vitally important time for rock guitar. It marked the first time in rock music that players were really allowed to stretch out and test the limits of their improvisational abilities, and, not sur-

---

The Yardbirds: Chris Dreja, Paul Samwell-Smith, Jim McCarty, Keith Relf, Jeff Beck

prisingly, many important stylistic innovations in rock guitar playing and technology occurred as a result. It is also interesting to note that the British rock movement latched onto the electric Chicago blues style well before the American rockers, who were fixated on folk and Delta blues. It is for precisely this reason that late-sixties rock was dominated by so many great English soloists. The Yanks simply hadn't caught up yet.

The Yardbirds

Eric Clapton

Born: *March 30, 1945, in Ripley, Surrey, England*
Main Guitars: *Fender Telecaster and Jazzmaster*

Jeff Beck

Born: *June 24, 1944, in Wallington, Surrey, England*
Main Guitar: *Fender Esquire*

Jimmy Page

Born: *January 9, 1944, in Heston, England*
Main Guitar: *Fender Telecaster*

Chris Dreja

Born: *November 11, 1946, in Surbiton, Surrey, England*
Main Guitar: *Fender Telecaster, Epiphone bass*

There aren't many bands that can boast having had three of rock 'n' roll's greatest guitarists within their ranks. In fact, only one can: the Yardbirds. From their humble beginnings in 1963 to their final concert at Luton Technical College in July of 1968, the Yardbirds featured—in succession—the stunning guitarmanship of Eric "Slowhand" Clapton, Jeff Beck, and Jimmy Page, three names that in the course of five years would completely change the sound of rock guitar. Though none of these guitarists was in the group for more than two years at a stretch, each in his own brief tenure contributed more to rock guitar than most guitarists do in their entire careers. From Clapton's crucial first steps towards electric blues to Beck's pre-metal excursions to Page's ethnically influenced blues and hard rock riffs, the Yardbirds proved to be the ultimate training ground for those who would become three of rock's biggest and best.

In 1963 the newly formed Yardbirds (vocalist/harpist Keith Relf, rhythm guitarist Chris Dreja, bassist Paul Samwell-Smith, and drummer Jim McCarty) lost their lead guitarist, Anthony "Top" Topham, whose parents forbade him from quitting art school to play with the group full-time. The band recruited a little-known blues guitarist named Eric Clapton, whose only previous band experience had been in two semiprofessional groups, the Roosters and the short-lived Casey Jones & the Engineers. By the beginning of 1964 the Yardbirds landed the Rolling Stones' former house gig at the Crawdaddy Club in Richmond. Within a

short time they generated a cult following in London, and their sizzling live reputation earned them a recording contract with Epic/Columbia.

The Yardbirds' first single, "I Wish You Would," demonstrated little of Clapton's future guitar prowess, though its flip side, "A Certain Girl," had a startling solo laden with buzzy distortion. By the release of their second single, "Good Morning Little School Girl"/"I Ain't Got You," it was apparent that Clapton was a guitarist to be watched. "Good Morning Little School Girl" revealed Clapton already experimenting with blues-rock hybrids in a soulful string-bending solo, but it was on the flip side of that single that the guitarist really came alive. Halfway into "I Ain't Got You" he cut loose with a stinging 30-second break that clearly showed the developing blues phrasing and finger vibrato that eventually became so important to his soloing.

By late 1964 Yardbirds manager Giorgio Gomelsky began taking the band in a more commercial direction, picking a pop-flavored number entitled "For Your Love" for their third single. Though Clapton played on part of it—the boogie section in the middle—he was disturbed at the Yardbirds' drift away from the sanctity of the blues (even though the single's B side was a heavy Freddie King-inspired blues called "Got to Hurry"). He left the band, but this proved not to be particularly disastrous for either party. Within a few months "For Your Love" became the Yardbirds' first international hit, breaking into the Top 10 of the British and American pop charts, and Eric Clapton eventually joined John Mayall's Bluesbreakers (♦) on his way to becoming a legend.

The Yardbirds' first choice to replace Clapton was then-studio guitarist Jimmy Page, but he declined. In his stead he recommended Jeff Beck, a talented young guitarist who had been playing around London with a group called the Tridents. After joining the Yardbirds in March 1965, Beck appeared on the single "Heart Full of Soul," playing a bizarre but brilliant sitarlike riff, quickly proving he was quite capable of filling Eric Clapton's shoes. Beck's "progressive" licks also prophesied the coming of psychedelic rock.

On *For Your Love* and *Having a Rave-Up with the Yardbirds* (both 1965 and both containing earlier material with Clapton) and the hip 1966 successor *Over Under Sideways Down* (as well as on numerous singles), Jeff Beck redefined rock soloing. Many cuts on these albums and singles feature radical Beck masterpieces: "I'm Not Talkin'," a proto-metal vehicle powered by Beck's use of heavy distortion, overbent strings, and power chords; "I'm a Man," which features frenetic lick trading between Beck and harpist Keith Relf; the '66 hit "Shapes of Things," which ends in a cataclysm of feedback and fuzz chords; and his tour de force, the instrumental "Jeff's Boogie." On this signature tune, he unleashes a salvo of hammer-ons, harmonics, wry quotes from "Merrily We Roll Along," and clean, multi-tracked guitar lines reminiscent of one of Beck's own guitar heroes, Les Paul (nods to Chuck Berry and Cliff Gallup are mixed in there, too). The sheer abundance of Jeff Beck's radical guitar work with the Yardbirds is an amazing feat in and of itself and is one of the reasons why his 20-month stint with the Yardbirds marked the band's creative apex. Although the guitar hero was still a vague notion at the time, Beck—by virtue of his work with the Yardbirds—could certainly be considered rock's first true guitarslinger, as well as one of its deadliest soloists.

From March 1965 until mid 1966, Beck toured extensively with the Yardbirds, wowing audiences worldwide with his flamboyant guitar work and showmanship. But the strain of constant roadwork began to wear him down; occasionally, he missed or simply refused to play a show. Tension grew unbearable in the band, and finally, after one particularly bad gig, bassist Paul Samwell-Smith quit the Yardbirds on the spot. Once again the remaining band members asked Jimmy Page to join, this time as bass player, and he accepted. It wasn't too long, though, until Page traded places with rhythm guitarist Chris Dreja, and, for a few magical months in the second half of 1966, the Yardbirds blazed under the twin-guitar fury of Jeff Beck and Jimmy Page. While there aren't that many recorded examples of Beck's and Page's guitar work together, among the survivors are the 1966 Yardbirds hit "Happenings Ten Years Time Ago," its B side, "Psycho Daisies" (both largely dominated by Beck), and, best of all, "Stroll On," a boisterous revamping of "Train Kept A-Rollin'," which the band performed live for the 1966 pop-culture film *Blow-Up*.

Finally, Beck was fired from the Yardbirds in November of 1966. In 1967 the Yardbirds—with Jimmy Page as their sole guitarist—toured the United States, Japan, and Europe. Though they did manage to cut one album, *Little Games*, the Yardbirds as a recording entity had already been sold to U.K. hit-meister Mickie Most, who wanted the band to join his large clientele of chart-topping pop acts like Lulu and Herman's Hermits. As a result, some of *Little Games* is commercial fluff (even downright bad, as in the bubblegum numbers "Ten Little Indians" and "Ha Ha Said the Clown"). Still, Page did get some good guitar parts on vinyl, notably the instrumental "White Summer," an Indian-flavored piece performed on acoustic steel-string in DADGAD tuning (inspired by British fingerpickers like Bert Jansch and John Renbourn), and "Tinker, Tailor, Soldier, Sailor," which features Page's innovative technique of playing the guitar with a violin bow—foreshadowing Led Zeppelin's "Dazed and Confused." By the middle of 1968 pressure within the group had again become unbearable, and after a gig at Luton Technical College in July, Page and the three remaining members of the Yardbirds called it quits.

By the time the Yardbirds collapsed in 1968, Eric Clapton had already become the world's best known blues-rock guitarist as the frontman for Cream (♦), and Jeff Beck was busy anticipating heavy metal guitar with his own Jeff Beck Group (♦). Upon the Yardbirds' demise, Jimmy Page immediately set out to form what would become rock's most popular and eclectic hard rock group, Led Zeppelin (♦). These three career moves are significant because each guitarist was basically expanding upon ideas he had

pioneered in the Yardbirds: Clapton's mighty blues playing, Beck's role as rock's fiercest soloist, and Page's ethnically influenced heavy guitar sounds. Within the Yardbirds' blues and progressive rock, these players were given the opportunity to experiment and improvise on their instruments with few restraints. It is very likely that this musical freedom paved the way for many of their later historic guitar achievements.

The Yardbirds [on Epic/Columbia except where noted], *Five Live Yardbirds* (1964●), *Yardbirds with Sonny Boy Williamson* (Mercury, 1964●), *For Your Love* (1965), *Having a Rave-Up with the Yardbirds* (1965●), *Over Under Sideways Down* (1966), *Little Games* (1967), *Yardbirds Live!* (1971●), *The Yardbirds Vol. 1: Smokestack Lightning* (Sony, 1991●), *The Yardbirds Vol. 2: Blues, Backtracks & Shapes of Things* (Sony, 1991●), *Little Games Sessions & More* (EMI, 1992).

Eric Clapton

The Bluesbreakers

Eric Clapton

B o r n : *March 30, 1945, in Ripley, Surrey, England*
M a i n   G u i t a r : *Gibson Les Paul Standard*

Peter Green

B o r n : *Peter Greenbaum, on October 29, 1946, in Bethnal Green, London*
M a i n   G u i t a r : *Gibson Les Paul Standard*

Mick Taylor

Born: *January 17, 1949, in Welwyn Garden City, Hertfordshire, England*
Main Guitar: *Gibson Les Paul Standard*

Upon leaving the Yardbirds in March 1965, Eric Clapton first sought sanctuary in the home of pianist Ben Palmer, a band-mate from his days in the Roosters. During the month or so he spent at Palmer's house, Clapton became a virtual recluse, isolating himself from the rest of the world so he could just play his guitar, which he reputedly did day and night (pop gossip and fable-spinning would later extend this month-long hiatus to an entire year). Nevertheless, by the time Clapton left Palmer's house later that spring, he felt his confidence as a guitarist and a musician fully restored.

Returning to London, Clapton received a standing invitation from John Mayall (born November 29, 1933, in Macclesfield, Cheshire, England) to join his popular blues revival outfit, the Bluesbreakers. Eric accepted the offer and history was made. His position in the Bluesbreakers provided him with a rare forum, because it was the first time he was in a band that solely played the blues and allowed for extended solos. In the Bluesbreakers there were none of the rave-ups, pop tunes, or watered-down R&B covers that had inhibited his playing with the Yardbirds and earlier bands. He also started playing real Texas- and Chicago-styled blues, giving him an even greater opportunity to study the subtleties of blues guitar.

Clapton's only studio album with the band, *Bluesbreakers with Eric Clapton*, became a hit in England when released there in mid 1966. More importantly, it was a showcase for Clapton's new and improved blues-rock style. The simple blues lines he had sown during his hitch with the Yardbirds blossomed into the sophisticated sounds of a blues master during his year with the Bluesbreakers. "Key to Love" displays this growth in its lead break, composed of mature string bends and blues licks. Other powerful cuts, like "Steppin' Out" and Freddie King's "Hideaway," also demonstrate his brilliant advances on the electric guitar. Overall, it was a knockout guitar performance and one whose impact on the guitar community would be felt for years. With those mutton-chop sideburns and the (soon-to-be rock standard) combination of a Gibson Les Paul guitar and a Marshall amp, Clapton quickly became one of rock's first guitar heroes, inspiring countless teenagers to pick up the guitar in meek but determined emulation of the master. Legions of dedicated fans flocked from all over England to see the 21-year-old guitar virtuoso play with the Bluesbreakers. In London the graffiti on subway station walls righteously proclaimed, "Clapton Is God." But ironically, by the time the seminal *Bluesbreakers* album was issued in the summer of 1966, Eric Clapton had already left the group to form Cream (◗).

Fortunately, Mayall had an uncanny knack for finding the perfect guitarist to play in his band. When Clapton left the group, Mayall discovered a worthy successor in Peter Green, who had previously been with Peter B's Looners (led by Peter Bardens, later of the British art-rock band Camel), and also Shotgun Express with Rod Stewart. Green's early guitar work in the Bluesbreakers was reminiscent of Clapton's hard-edged blues sound, but before long he began to develop his own restrained, economical style (not to mention a trademark reverb tone), and soon gained a reputation as one of England's best blues guitarists. *A Hard Road*, Green's only full album with the Bluesbreakers, was praised by critics when released in 1967 and is now considered one of Mayall's finest group recordings ever. Green's masterpiece on the disc is in the instrumental "The Supernatural," a mid-tempo minor blues graced by gorgeous, ringing sustained notes (later appropriated by Carlos Santana) and his ever-tortured pentatonic licks. The guitarist's fierce, Chicago-fired blues soloing was also captured on such Mayall singles and album tracks as "Looking Back," Freddie King's upbeat "The Stumble," the slow minor blues "So Many Roads," and "Dust My Blues," an Elmore James romp featuring Green's manic lead break over Mayall's five-string slide work. Soon, however, the guitarist fancied leading his own group and left to form Fleetwood Mac (◗).

Amazingly, Mayall struck gold for a third time and chose a third extraordinary guitarist for his Bluesbreakers: 18-year-old Mick Taylor. Like Eric Clapton and Peter Green before him, Taylor quickly let it be known that he was no slouch on electric guitar. Taylor's first outing with the Bluesbreakers, the 1967 album *Crusade*, exhibited his impressive grasp of the blues-rock idiom. During his two-year stint with Mayall, he gradually gained wide recognition in England for his high-energy solos. Mayall's 1968 release *Bare Wires* contains much of Taylor's best work with the Bluesbreakers. A few of the outstanding parts include his Hendrix-like feedback intro to the solo on "I Started Walking," the R&B-flavored rhythm and lead work in "No Reply" (both notable for their early use of the wah-wah pedal), and "Killing Time," a slow blues tune in which Taylor inserts dramatic whammy bar drops that may indicate an early influence by Jimi Hendrix.

Considering his precocious talent, it is not surprising that when the Rolling Stones needed a replacement for Brian Jones in mid 1969, they asked Taylor to join the band. His heavily rock-influenced blues style and aggressive guitar method made him the perfect foil to Keith Richards' rakish rhythms—as well as a fine choice for the Stones' rowdy brand of rock 'n' roll. On June 13, 1969, Mick Taylor became the newest Rolling Stone (◗ British Invasion II).

John Mayall's Bluesbreakers [on London except where noted], *Bluesbreakers with Eric Clapton* (1966), *A Hard Road* (1967), *Crusade* (1967), *Bare Wires* (1968), *Blues from Laurel Canyon* (1969), *Looking Back* (1969•), *The Diary of a Band* (1970•), *Back to the Roots* (Polydor, 1971), *Thru the Years* (1971), *Down the Line* (1973•), *Primal Solos* (1977•). **Various Artists,** *The Great British Blues Barrelhouse and Boogie Bonanza, 1962–1968* (Decca, 1982).

Fleetwood Mac

Peter Green

Born: *Peter Greenbaum, on October 29, 1946, in Bethnal Green, London*
Main Guitar: *'59 Gibson Les Paul Standard*

Jeremy Spencer

Born: *July 4, 1948, in West Hartlepool, Durham, England*
Main Guitar: *Fender Stratocaster*

Danny Kirwan

Born: *c. 1950, in England*
Main Guitar: *Gibson Les Paul Standard*

In 1967 Peter Green decided to leave John Mayall's Bluesbreakers (♦) and form his own group. With slide guitarist Jeremy Spencer (previously with the Levi Set Blues Group) and two other members of the Bluesbreakers—bassist John McVie and drummer Mick Fleetwood—Green formed Fleetwood Mac and signed onto the blues-based Blue Horizon record label. (Bob Brunning was their bassist briefly, until McVie's arrival.) Fleetwood Mac debuted at the British National Jazz and Blues Festival on August 12, 1967, and on the strength of Green's reputation with John Mayall and the group's fine musicianship, it became one of the biggest blues bands in Great Britain. The first album was a best seller in the U.K. in early 1968, and shortly after its release, 18-year-old Danny Kirwan (from the south London band Boilerhouse) joined Fleetwood Mac as the group's *third* lead guitarist—a unique lineup at the time.

As for Peter Green's guitar work with Fleetwood Mac, his best-known playing was on "Black Magic Woman," which eventually became a U.S. hit for Santana. Opening with a shimmering harmonic, Green cuts a cool, slightly distorted solo in "Black Magic Woman," as well as contributing an electrifying jam for the rideout. Other guitar high points of Green's career in Fleetwood Mac include "Oh Well" and "The Green Manalishi with the Two-Pronged Crown" (later covered by Judas Priest), "Stop Messin' Round," and the slow blues of "Love that Burns," which had a soulful minor-key guitar break—a widely recognized Peter Green trademark. In late 1968, Fleetwood Mac began shifting away from their pure blues format and issued their first single, the bucolic "Albatross," which became a substantial hit (as well as a big influence on the Beatles' *Abbey Road* and its languid ballads "I Want You" and "Sun King"). It was followed by two more hit singles in 1969, "Man of the World" and the aforementioned "Oh Well."

Kirwan and Spencer contributed heavily to the Mac guitar sound, too. Kirwan, in particular, could solo in a style uncannily similar to Green's, albeit with a faster finger vibrato. You can hear his work on "Something inside Me" and "Coming Your Way." Spencer was the band's slide specialist and confirmed member of the Elmore James school of open-tuned bottleneck guitar.

Things seemed to be going extremely well for the band until just after the release of their fine third album, *Then Play On* (1969), when Green became a drug casualty and announced that he was leaving the group. Upon Green's departure, Fleetwood Mac's era as leaders of the British blues-rock movement was sadly ended, despite the strong performance that Kirwan and Spencer delivered on the Mac's first post-Green album, *Kiln House* (1970).

Aside from his one lackluster solo effort—*The End of the Game* (1970)—and a brief return to Fleetwood Mac in early 1971 (where he helped finish a tour disrupted by Jeremy Spencer's own sudden exit to join a religious cult), Peter Green dropped into obscurity for most of the seventies. He held menial jobs and was seen frequently wandering the streets of London in something of a daze. He was homeless for awhile and was briefly committed to a mental institution in 1977. His mental and personal decline matched that of Pink Floyd guitarist Syd Barrett almost note for note. Eventually Green did return to his music, in the late seventies, and has since recorded several well-received blues- and jazz-tinged albums, including *In the Skies* (1979) and *Little Dreamer* (1980). Despite his premature retirement, the guitarist has been highly influential, notably on rocker Gary Moore, who turned to the blues in 1990, playing Peter Green's own Les Paul, which the guitar legend had sold to him 20 years earlier. Even today there are fans who regard him as the greatest white bluesman ever, and not just as a guitarist, which further underscores the tragedy of his life and wayward musical career.

As for the rest of Fleetwood Mac history, their years as a pop sensation—first with guitarist Bob "Sentimental Lady" Welch (born July 31, 1946, in Los Angeles) and then in a far larger way with guitarist Lindsey Buckingham (♦ Pop Experimenters)—are well documented. When last heard from, the band was reinvestigating their blues roots, *sans* Peter Green, of course, with Dave Mason (♦ Traffic) and Billy Burnette on guitars.

Fleetwood Mac, *Fleetwood Mac* (Epic, 1968), *English Rose* (Epic, 1969), *Then Play On* (Reprise, 1969), *Vintage Years* (Sire, 1975), *Live in Boston* (Shanghai, 1985•), *Fleetwood Mac in Chicago 1969* (Sire, 1994•). **Peter Green,** *The End of the Game* (Reprise, 1970), *In the Skies* (PVK, 1979), *Little Dreamer* (PVK, 1980), *Whatcha Gonna Do?* (PVK, 1981), *Blue Guitar* (Creole, 1981), *White Sky* (Headline, 1982), *Kolors* (Headline, 1983), *Come on Down* (Homestead, 1986), *Case for the Blues* (Night Life, 1987), *Legend* (Creole, 1988).

Recordings featuring Peter Green: **Otis Spann (with Fleetwood Mac),** *The Biggest Thing Since Colossus* (Blue Horizon, 1969). **Various Artists,** *History of British Blues, Volume One* (Sire, 1973). **Various Artists,** *The Great British Blues Barrelhouse and Boogie Bonanza, 1962–1968* (Decca, 1982•).

Savoy Brown

Kim Simmonds

Born: *December 5, 1947, in Newbridge, Wales*
Main Guitars: *Gibson Les Paul and Flying V*

Emerging from the embers of the British blues boom, the Savoy Brown Blues Band (later shortened to just Savoy Brown) gained enough momentum in the late sixties to sustain a career throughout much of the seventies. Despite numerous personnel changes, the core of Savoy Brown has always been Kim Simmonds and his frenetic blues guitar work. Witness his soul-wrenching solos in "Mr. Downchild," a gripping minor blues from the *Getting to the Point* disc that, along with displaying the guitarist's impressive chops, revealed another player who was caught under the spell of Peter Green. Another track—"Waiting in the Bamboo Grove" (from *A Step Further*)—showed the influence of Albert Collins, which was rare for blues-rockers of the period.

Savoy Brown's 1968 album *Blue Matter* caused a stir on both sides of the Atlantic, especially in the U.S., where a following of loyal fans was building. Later albums such as *Street Corner Talkin'* and *Hellbound Train*, along with solid touring, made Savoy Brown a top blues-rock band in the early seventies, especially in America, where their intense concert boogies always went over big. But after numerous personnel shifts, their popularity began to peter out by mid decade. The band was almost completely decimated when several members left to form the boogie-rock quartet Foghat (◗). Nevertheless, with Simmonds' guitar bombastics still in the lead, Savoy Brown has continued recording into the 1990s.

Savoy Brown [on Deram except where noted], *Shake Down* (Decca, 1967), *Getting to the Point* (1968), *Blue Matter* (1969●), *A Step Further* (1969●), *Raw Sienna* (1970), *Looking In* (1970), *Street Corner Talking* (1971), *Hellbound Train* (1972), *Lion's Share* (1972), *Jack the Toad* (1973), *Boogie Brothers* (London, 1974), *Wire Fire* (London, 1975), *Skin 'n' Bone* (Polygram, 1976), *Best Of* (London, 1978), *Savage Return* (1978), *Greatest Hits Live in Concert* (Accord, 1981●), *Rock 'n' Roll Warriors* (Capitol, 1981), *Slow Train* (Relix, 1986), *Live from Central Park* (Relix, 1987●), *Make Me Sweat* (GNP Crescendo, 1988), *Kings of Boogie* (GNP Crescendo, 1989), *The Savoy Brown Collection, Featuring Kim Simmonds* (1993).

CHAPTER SIX

The U.S. Blues Revival
Electric Melting Pot

The American folk revival of the early sixties sparked renewed interest in the blues.

Acoustic musicians began digging into America's musical past and discovered the great southern bluesmen of the twenties and thirties. Among this sacred group of early country bluesmen were the legendary Robert Johnson, Son House, Skip James, Leadbelly, Blind Lemon Jefferson, and a host of others. A new group of young white folk-blues and bluegrass mavens like Danny Kalb, Jerry Garcia, and Jorma Kaukonen studied these blues masters in great depth and then began mixing the older blues guitar sounds with their own acoustic and electric rock styles. To further color their tonal palettes, some players also began exploring jazz and Indian music, adding new sounds to the growing blues-rock idiom. In short order, America had a full blown blues revival on its hands, mirroring the British revival on the other side of the Atlantic.

On the purely electric guitar side of the U.S. blues revival, there was a vast renewal of interest in the Chicago and Texas blues of electric axemen like T-Bone Walker, Muddy Waters, Howlin' Wolf, B.B. King, Buddy Guy, and Freddie King, who inspired America's best soloists of the sixties and early seventies: Mike Bloomfield, Jimi Hendrix, Johnny Winter, and Duane Allman. Thus in the course of just of few years—from roughly 1966 to 1968—the sound of *rock* guitar changed dramatically, and with the further invention of fuzz units and larger (and louder) amplifiers, the guitar took on a noticeably more significant role in bands. No longer restricted to rehashing old Chuck Berry and Carl Perkins licks, blues-based players began using the high-volume overdrive of their amps to imitate the long, sustaining sounds of a slide guitar or a saxophone and beef up the soulful string bends of their favorite blues guitarists and singers. By the end of the decade, the blues had reasserted itself as an integral part of rock 'n' roll in the United States. Blues-rock guitarists like Kalb, Bloomfield, Winter, Allman, and other lesser-known players (like Henry Vestine and Al Wilson of the highly influential Canned Heat, Harvey Mandel, and acoustic specialist John Hammond) led the growing pack of U.S. rockers who were expanding the boundaries of this powerful new rock 'n' roll subgenre. From this point in musical time until the neoclassical boom of the mid 1980s, a basic knowledge of the blues was an essential part of every rock player's vocabulary.

Mike Bloomfield

Mike Bloomfield

Born: *July 28, 1943, in Chicago*
Died: *February 15, 1981, in San Francisco*
Main Guitars: *Fender Telecaster, Gibson Les Paul*

Although fewer and fewer young players know his name, Mike Bloomfield is unquestionably a rock guitar legend. In the mid sixties, few guitarists in the U.S. could rival his dramatic blues-, jazz-, and Indian-inspired guitar excursions, which profoundly influenced the psychedelic rock guitarists of San Francisco. He also figured prominently in two of the most important concerts in rock 'n' roll history, appearing at the Newport Folk Festival in 1965 with Bob Dylan and at the Monterey International Pop Festival in 1967 with the Electric Flag. Bloomfield's pioneering blues-rock guitar playing with the Paul Butterfield Blues Band, the Electric Flag, and Al Kooper helped turn an entire generation of rock guitarists on to the blues, and to this day, many fans and critics consider Bloomfield America's first guitar hero.

In his early teens Bloomfield became infatuated with the sounds of rock 'n' roll, especially rockabilly, but eventually he discovered a whole new world of music on Chicago's South Side, which had long been famous for its great blues bands. By his late teens he was regularly heading out to the clubs where those groups played, guitar in hand, brashly asking such great bluesmen as Muddy Waters, Howlin' Wolf, B.B. King, and Otis Rush if he could sit in and play. Amazingly, many let him. He soon became a regular of the South Side blues scene, and, as his rock 'n' roll licks began to incorporate a smooth blues style, his reputation as one of Chicago's brightest young players began to grow.

In 1964 Bloomfield was signed to Columbia Records by John Hammond Sr.—the man who discovered Billie Holiday, Robert Johnson, Charlie Christian, Bob Dylan, and Bruce Springsteen, among countless others—and recorded an album in New York with an outfit simply called the Group, featuring harpist Charlie Musselwhite. (This material remained in the Columbia vaults for 30 years until the release of the excellent Bloomfield compilation *Don't Say that I Ain't Your Man, Essential Blues: 1964–69*.) By the end of '64 Bloomfield had come to the attention of Paul Butterfield, a white harmonica player whose Paul Butterfield Blues Band (♦) was the rage on the Chicago blues circuit. In early 1965 Bloomfield joined Butterfield's group, pushing the band's other guitarist, Elvin Bishop, to handle rhythm duties. Towards the end of that year the Butterfield Band's first album came out, and it was smothered with the guitarist's budding blues-rock style. On cuts like "Born in Chicago" and "Thank You, Mr. Poohbah," he picked loose, string-choking solos on his white Fender Telecaster, while on "Shake Your Moneymaker" he demonstrated his impressive skill on slide guitar. Characterized by soulful extended solos and committed bottleneck work, Bloomfield's blues guitar saturated the album. It quickly brought the young guitarist to the attention of many people and set the stage for his next musical move.

That stage happened to be the 1965 Newport Folk Festival. The Butterfield band played a powerful set there, but their electric Chicago blues caused quite a furor with many of the acoustic folk purists present at the event. Later in the concert, several members of Butterfield's band, including Bloomfield, backed up Bob Dylan during his set, in what is remembered as one of the most controversial rock performances ever. Until then, Dylan had been for the most part a purebred folk/protest singer, but on that day he appeared on stage with an electric guitar slung over his shoulder and a tight rock 'n' roll band behind him. With Bloomfield on lead guitar, he then proceeded to play a high-volume version of his new hit, "Like a Rolling Stone." Some folk purists in the audience hissed and booed throughout Dylan's set. Nonetheless, it marked a turning point in rock music—the symbolic moment when folk music met electric rock 'n' roll—and it was due in no small part to the bluesy guitar playing of Mike Bloomfield. Though still a full-time member of the Butterfield

band, the guitarist also appeared on Dylan's seminal *Highway 61 Revisited*, applying his personal touch to such classic songs as "Tombstone Blues" and "Like a Rolling Stone."

Bloomfield's next project with the Butterfield group was *East-West*, a recording that is considered both the high point of Bloomfield's career *and* the album where he laid the cornerstone for American rock guitar playing for the rest of the sixties. Cuts like "Walkin' Blues" and "Two Trains Running" featured the incisive single-note and slide playing that gained Bloomfield his initial reputation, but on the two extended pieces on the album—"The Work Song" and "East-West"—Bloomfield helped to redefine blues-based rock guitar playing. In the solos to "The Work Song" he dispenses with the bluesy pentatonic riffs that had serviced him up until that time and instead plays a new brand of rock guitar that uses off-rhythm jazz figures, angular modal lines, and a wicked wrist vibrato. Bloomfield managed to top that masterful solo on the album's spellbinding title track, "East-West." After Butterfield's harp solo reaches a hair-raising crescendo, Bloomfield lets loose a lengthy guitar solo composed of Indian-influenced modes, sitar-like open string effects, and intricate runs up and down the fingerboard of his Gibson Les Paul. The song climaxes in a guitar duel between Bloomfield and Elvin Bishop, not only foreshadowing the components of the growing West Coast rock scene, but also the twin-guitar work of the Allman Brothers Band and other groups of the southern rock movement of the seventies. Nothing like these two solos had ever been heard in rock 'n' roll. They had a dramatic influence on nearly every guitarist in San Francisco and clearly anticipated the days when long, exotic guitar solos and psychedelic jams would be commonplace in rock 'n' roll.

Towards the end of 1966 Bloomfield left Butterfield's group to find his own rock 'n' roll forum, eventually forming a sort of electrified big band known as the Electric Flag. The group debuted at the star-studded Monterey Pop Festival in June 1967 and were instantly accorded supergroup status. Though their music was solid R&B-based rock, and Bloomfield's playing was better than ever (as evidenced in his leads to "Killing Floor" and "Texas"), their first album, *A Long Time Comin'*, fizzled on the charts, and by the end of 1968 the band split up.

Bloomfield went on to do some notable work in the late sixties, releasing two popular jam-oriented records with Al Kooper: *Super Session*, also featuring future CSNY member Stephen Stills (♦ Buffalo Springfield), and *The Live Adventures of Mike Bloomfield and Al Kooper*, which features an exquisite blues solo on Albert King's "Don't Throw Your Love on Me So Strong." By the beginning of the seventies, however, Bloomfield's career had slipped; his solo album *It's Not Killing Me* (1969) was poorly received by just about everyone. Despite being hindered creatively by a long-time addiction to heroin, Bloomfield did manage to release some quality recordings towards the end of the decade, several of which showcased a talent for acoustic blues that had been hidden for most of the sixties.

Unfortunately, time was not on Mike Bloomfield's side; on

February 15, 1981, he was found dead in his car at the age of 37, apparently from an overdose of Valium. The stardom that seemed so inevitable for Bloomfield in the mid sixties had simply withered away, and despite his brilliant work with the Paul Butterfield Blues Band and others, his career was continually marred by a series of overhyped supergroups (the worst being KGB, from 1976). But it cannot be denied that Michael Bloomfield was one of the most important and prophetic rock guitarists of the 1960s, and that his playing with Butterfield dramatically influenced the shape and style of rock guitar.

Paul Butterfield Blues Band [on Elektra], *Paul Butterfield Blues Band* (1965), *East-West* (1966), *Golden Butter* (1972). **Electric Flag** [on Columbia except where noted], *The Trip* [soundtrack] (Sidewalk/Tower, 1967), *A Long Time Comin'* (1968), *The Best of the Electric Flag* (1971), *The Band Kept Playing* (1974). **Mike Bloomfield, Al Kooper & Stephen Stills,** *Super Session* (Columbia, 1968). **Mike Bloomfield and Al Kooper,** *The Live Adventures of Mike Bloomfield and Al Kooper* (Columbia, 1969•). **KGB,** *KGB* (MCA, 1976). **Michael Bloomfield,** *It's Not Killing Me* (Columbia, 1969), *Try It Before You Buy It* (Verve, 1973), *If You Love These Blues, Then Play 'em as You Please* (Guitar Player, 1977), *Analine* (Takoma, 1977), *Count Talent & the Originals* (TK, 1978), *Michael Bloomfield* (Takoma, 1978), *Between the Hard Place and the Ground* (Takoma, 1981), *Bloomfield/Harris* (Kicking Mule, 1979), *Living in the Fast Lane* (1980), *Cruisin' for a Bruisin'* (Takoma, 1981), *Bloomfield* (Columbia, 1982), *Don't Say that I Ain't Your Man, Essential Blues: 1964–69* (Columbia Legacy, 1994•). **Michael Bloomfield, John Paul Hammond & Dr. John,** *Triumvirate* (Columbia, 1973).

Recordings featuring Mike Bloomfield: **Yank Rachell's Tennessee Jug Busters,** *Mandolin Blues* (Delmark, 1963). **Sleepy John Estes,** *Broke and Hungry, Ragged and Dirty, Too* (Delmark, 1964). **Various Artists,** *The Newport Folk Festival 1965* (Vanguard, 1965•). **Bob Dylan,** *Highway 61 Revisited* (Columbia, 1965). **Peter, Paul & Mary,** *Album* (Warner Bros., 1965). **Various Artists,** *What's Shakin'* (Elektra, 1966). **John Hammond,** *So Many Roads* (Vanguard, 1965). **Eddie "Cleanhead" Vinson,** *Cherry Red* (Bluesway, 1967). **Mitch Ryder and the Detroit Wheels,** *Sock It to Me* (New Voice, 1967). **Moby Grape,** *Wow/Grape Jam* (Columbia, 1968). **Barry Goldberg,** *Two Jews Blues* (Buddah, 1969•), *Barry Goldberg and Friends* (Record Man, 1969). **Mother Earth,** *Living with the Animals* (Mercury, 1969). **Nick Gravenites,** *My Labors* (Columbia, 1969). **Janis Joplin,** *I Got Them Ol' Kozmic Blues Again, Mama!* (Columbia, 1969). **Muddy Waters and Various Artists,** *Fathers and Sons* (Chess, 1969•). **Various Artists,** *Live at Bill Graham's Fillmore West* (Columbia, 1969•). **Woody Herman,** *Brand New* (Fantasy, 1971). **Millie Foster,** *Feels the Spirit* (MGM, 1972). **Kingfish,** *Kingfish* (Round, 1976).

Johnny Winter

B o r n : *February 23, 1944, in Leland, Mississippi*
M a i n G u i t a r s : *Gibson reverse Firebird, Fender Electric XII*

An issue of *Rolling Stone* magazine from December 1968 featured an extensive article that surveyed the rock and blues scene in Texas. Among the rockers covered was a guitarist who was described as follows: "If you can imagine a hundred and thirty pound cross-eyed albino with long fleecy hair playing some of the gutsiest fluid blues guitar you have ever heard, then enter Johnny Winter." This article was all it took to motivate Steve Paul, owner of the famous Scene nightclub in New York City, to fly to

Texas and invite Johnny Winter to play in his club. Within a short time Winter was as renowned a guitarist in New York as he was in Texas, and by the end of 1968 he had headlined at the famed Fillmore East—all before he even had a recording contract. At the beginning of the next year, though, Johnny Winter signed with Columbia Records in what is reputed to be one of the biggest record deals ever made.

Raised in Beaumont, Texas, along with his similarly talented brother Edgar, Johnny Winter started learning clarinet and ukulele, but then switched to guitar and began copying solos off old blues and rock 'n' roll records note for note. By his early twenties, Winter had played on numerous blues sessions in the area around Beaumont and Houston and had already made a pilgrimage to the blues mecca of Chicago, where he met and jammed with aspiring blues guitarist Mike Bloomfield. When the aforementioned article in *Rolling Stone* came out, Winter was whisked away to New York and became a proverbial "overnight sensation" in rock 'n' roll.

With all the hoopla over his guitar playing and the subsequent rocket ride to fame, Winter's self-titled first album sounded forced, and critics were not generally charitable. Still, it contains the influential track "Leland Mississippi Blues." Another disc that suddenly appeared at the same time was *The Progressive Blues Experiment*, a record that Johnny had cut locally for the small Sonobeat label. Later sold to Imperial, it was released almost simultaneously with the first album, causing a little confusion among the record-buying public, but nevertheless bringing to light some more smokin' Winter guitar work, such as "Mean Town Blues."

By the album *Second Winter* the albino guitarman was finally ready to play guitar on his own terms. On the opening cut, a grueling blues-rocker called "Memory Pain," Winter was all over the map with distorted chord riffs and pentatonic runs. For a memorable taste of his choice bottleneck work, check out the Little Richard boogie-woogie cut "Slippin' and Slidin'," as well as his definitive slide workout in Dylan's "Highway 61."

In 1970 Winter joined forces with guitarist Rick Derringer (♦) and his group the McCoys

Johnny Winter

(famed for their 1965 hit "Hang on Sloopy") to form Johnny Winter And. With this new group, Winter began moving away from the blues-rock he'd based his reputation on and turned towards a harder brand of rock 'n' roll, noticeably closer to heavy metal. Fronted by the twin lead guitars of Winter and Derringer, Johnny Winter And gained massive popularity in the first few years of the 1970s, and both players became much-idolized guitar heroes. Some of the best examples of Winter's guitar work with the Johnny Winter And group are found on tracks like "Jumpin' Jack Flash" and "Johnny B. Goode" (from the album *Live/Johnny Winter And*), both of which are torched by the guitarist's blues-rock leads.

With the pressures of stardom mounting, along with increased drug problems, Winter eventually went into seclusion, and Derringer joined forces with Johnny's brother Edgar. When Johnny returned to active guitar duty in 1973, he released several solid albums, including the acclaimed *Still Alive and Well*. After producing Muddy Waters' (♭) last recorded efforts later in the decade, Winter returned to his blues roots with some fine records on the blues-based Alligator label, including *Guitar Slinger* (1984) and *Third Degree* (1986).

While Johnny Winter's career in the limelight dwindled substantially since the mid 1980s, his blues-inspired playing was—and still is—held in very high regard by the guitar community. He receives praise at all levels, not just for overall blues proficiency, but also for being an important part of the early hard rock scene. In 1994 Columbia/Legacy issued a collection of Winter's live and studio work, which served to reestablish him as one of America's finest white bluesmen.

Johnny Winter [on Columbia except where noted], *The Progressive Blues Experiment* (Imperial, 1969), *Johnny Winter* (1969), *The Johnny Winter Story* (GRT, 1969), *Second Winter* (1969), *Still Alive and Well* (1973), *Saints and Sinners* (1974), *John Dawson Winter III* (1974), *Captured Live* (Blue Sky, 1976●), *Nothin' but the Blues* (Blue Sky, 1977), *White, Hot & Blue* (Blue Sky, 1978), *Raisin' Cain* (Blue Sky, n/a), *Guitar Slinger* (Alligator, 1984), *Serious Business* (Alligator, 1985), *Third Degree* (Alligator, 1986), *The Winter of '88* (MCA, 1988), *Birds Can't Row Boats* (Relix, 1988), *Let Me In* (Point Blank, 1991), *Hey, Where's Your Brothers* (Point Blank, 1992), *Scorchin' Blues* (Epic, 1992), *A Rock n' Roll Collection* (1994●). **Johnny Winter And** [on Columbia], *Johnny Winter And* (1970), *Live/Johnny Winter And* (1970●). **Johnny & Edgar Winter,** *Together* (Blue Sky, 1976●).

Recordings featuring Johnny Winter: **Various Artists,** *The First Great Rock Festivals of the Seventies* (Columbia, 1971●). **Muddy Waters** [on Blue Sky], *Hard Again* (1977), *I'm Ready* (1978), *Muddy "Mississippi" Waters Live* (1979●), *King Bee* (1981). **Various Artists,** *Guitars that Destroyed the World* (Columbia, 1980). **Sonny Terry,** *Whoopin'* (Alligator, 1984). **Various Artists,** *Genuine House Rockin' Music* (Alligator, n/a). **Various Artists,** *The Alligator Records 20th Anniversary Collection* (Alligator, 1991).

The Blues Project

Danny Kalb

B o r n : *c. 1940, in New York City*
M a i n   G u i t a r : *Danelectro*

Steve Katz

B o r n : *May 9, 1945, in Brooklyn*
M a i n   G u i t a r : *Gibson ES-335*

One of the first groups on the U.S. blues-rock scene was the Blues Project, founded by lead guitarist Danny Kalb. This "underground" New York act was a direct response to the bustling American folk revival of the early sixties, and they were notably influenced by rural country blues tunes, which they transfigured into loud electric blues music. The Blues Project came out of a group Kalb had formed in 1964, the Danny Kalb Quartet, which included several future members of the Project, including rhythm guitarist Steve Katz and keyboardist Al Kooper, who had written the hit "This Diamond Ring" for Gary Lewis & the Playboys and also appeared on several classic Bob Dylan albums. Eventually, the Kalb group changed its name to the Blues Project, taken from a 1963 folk-blues compilation album on the Elektra label to which Kalb had contributed a few songs.

At the end of 1965 the Blues Project landed a steady gig at the Cafe Au Go Go in Greenwich Village, where their novel rock-influenced blues began gaining them a large following of students from nearby New York University. At the beginning of the next year, their first album, *Live at the Cafe Au Go Go*, was released on the Verve/Forecast label. Though the album was not a big seller, the popularity of the Blues Project grew vigorously via word of mouth. They embarked on several successful college tours across the country, highlighted in 1966 by three huge concerts in Central Park in New York City.

Though not the blues maestro Mike Bloomfield was, Kalb was an able soloist in his own right, putting energetic blues-inspired leads in many of the Project's recordings. Among his best are a cover of Chuck Berry's "I Want to Be Your Driver," where he fills nearly every gap with skittish blues runs and string bends, and "I Can't Keep from Crying Sometimes," which shows his rock-influenced side in a break marked by an extra-trebly tone and uncontrollable feedback. Perhaps Kalb's finest recorded solo with the Project was on "Wake Me, Shake Me," an up-tempo rave-up with a guitar break made up of quickly picked runs, over-bent strings, and finger-vibrato effects.

Internal problems soon caught up with band and in 1967 the Blues Project broke up after Al Kooper left to form Blood, Sweat & Tears (taking rhythm guitarist Katz with him). The group scattered, and Kalb completely disappeared from the music scene for several years. In 1971 the Blues Project had the first of several brief reunions, releasing several albums; Kalb and company even reunited in the early eighties for a series of well-received concerts. In all, Danny Kalb's primary historical significance remains as a blues-rock progenitor who started bridging the gap between pure blues and the oncoming hordes of blues-based rock soloists that appeared soon after.

Blues Project [on Verve except where noted], *Live at the Cafe Au Go Go* (1965●), *Projections* (1966), *Blues Project Live at Town Hall* (1967●), *Planned*

Obsolescence (1968), *Best of the Blues Project* (1969), *Lazarus* (Capitol, 1971), *Blues Project* (Capitol, 1972), *Reunion in Central Park* (MCA, 1973•), *Archetypes Blues Project* (MGM, 1974), *Best of the Blues Project* (Rhino, 1989). **Danny Kalb & Stefan Grossman,** *Crosscurrents* (Cotillion, 1971).

Recordings featuring Danny Kalb: **Phil Ochs,** *All the News that's Fit to Sing* (Elektra, 1964).

Paul Butterfield Blues Band

Elvin Bishop

B o r n : *October 21, 1942, in Tulsa*
M a i n G u i t a r : *Gibson ES-335*

Buzz Feiten

B o r n : *c. 1950*
M a i n G u i t a r : *Fender Stratocaster*

While attending the University of Chicago in the early sixties, a National Merit Scholarship student named Elvin Bishop met harpist Paul Butterfield, who shared Bishop's affinity for the electric blues that emanated from Chicago's South Side. In 1965 Bishop joined the Butterfield Blues Band as lead guitarist, and the group began tearing up South Side nightclubs with their loud, aggressive blues repertoire. By the end of that year guitar ace Mike Bloomfield (♪) had stepped in as the group's primary lead and slide player. The two classic Butterfield albums on which Bloomfield appeared, *The Paul Butterfield Blues Band* and *East-West*, show how completely Bloomfield dominated the band's guitar output. Bishop stayed in his shadow for the most part, relegated to playing rhythm and second lead guitar.

In late 1966 Bloomfield left the Butterfield Blues Band to form the Electric Flag. To commemorate Bishop's return to the lead guitar seat, the band titled their next album *The Resurrection of Pigboy Crabshaw*, referring to Bishop's self-conferred nickname. Besides the album's heavy use of horns, Bishop's incisive lead guitar work, though more simplistic and unrefined than Bloomfield's, remains one of the record's high points and gained him distinction as a highly capable blues-rocker. Choice guitar cuts include "Driftin' and Driftin'," which Bishop fills out with a long, vocal-like solo. In a funky version of Albert King's great hit "Born under a Bad Sign," Bishop pays tribute to some of his blues guitar influences, including Jimmy Reed and Otis Rush, with several tasty spot solos and an extended blues-busting lead.

Like Bloomfield before him, Bishop eventually decided to pursue his own musical vision; after one more album with the Butterfield Band—*In My Own Dream* (1968)—he bolted to San Francisco, where the huge psychedelic rock movement was already attracting interest from the blues community.

After his tenure in the Butterfield Blues Band, the guitarist formed the Elvin Bishop Band, which released several albums in the early 1970s for the Fillmore label. After a switch to Capricorn

in 1973, his popularity increased, and he scored a Top 10 single in 1975 with "Fooled around and Fell in Love" (featuring future Starship vocalist Mickey Thomas). Another highlight from the period was "Ramblin' Shoes," a juke-joint foot-stomper that mixed blues with the western swing that burst forth from his home state in the 1930s.

When Elvin Bishop left the Butterfield Blues Band for a solo career, Paul Butterfield took a chance on an unknown 19-year-old guitar player named Buzz Feiten. Feiten, who was attending the Mannes College of Music in New York City, had started playing the guitar at a young age and was heavily influenced by B.B. King and Eric Clapton. Ironically, at the time he met Butterfield he was gigging primarily as a bassist and had actually played bass during a Jimi Hendrix gig. When Feiten landed the job with the Butterfield band, he left the bass behind forever. In marked contrast to the purer blues of Mike Bloomfield and Elvin Bishop, Buzz Feiten brought a strong rock influence to the Butterfield Blues Band as well as a heavy measure of R&B and jazz guitar. On "No Amount of Loving" (from the group's 1969 album *Keep on Movin'*), Feiten displays his versatility and guitar influences, especially with rhythm work reminiscent of funk guitar pioneer Jimmy Nolen; he also delivers a distorted solo bearing a strong Clapton influence. Besides *Keep on Movin'*, Feiten also appeared with the Butterfield band at the Woodstock festival in August 1969, where he contributed an extended lead to "Everything's Gonna Be Alright" (on the *Woodstock Two* album).

After leaving the Butterfield band in 1970, Feiten moved into steady session work, appearing on albums by Stevie Wonder, Bob Dylan, and Gregg Allman, besides starting his own group, Full Moon. One of his most notable session gigs was his appearance on the Rascals' album *Island of Real* in 1972. Contained on this record is the phenomenal "Jungle Walk," an R&B gem that fully realizes Feiten's six-string ability. In it he effortlessly moves from funk to rock to jazz styles, all packed with lots of soul; in the process, he turns in one of *the* funk rhythm performances of the decade.

Paul Butterfield Blues Band [on Elektra], *Paul Butterfield Blues Band* (1965), *East-West* (1966•), *The Resurrection of Pigboy Crabshaw* (1968), *In My Own Dream* (1968), *Keep on Movin'* (1970). **Elvin Bishop** [on Capricorn except where noted], *Elvin Bishop* (Fillmore, 1969), *Feel It* (Fillmore, c. 1970), *Rock My Soul* (n/a, 1972), *Let It Flow* (1974), *Juke Joint Jump* (1975), *Struttin' My Stuff* (1976), *Hometown Boy Makes Good* (1976), *Live! Raisin' Hell* (1977•), *Big Fun* (Alligator, 1988). **Full Moon** [with Buzz Feiten], *Full Moon* (1972), *Full Moon Featuring Neil Larsen & Buzz Feiten* (Warner Bros., 1982). **Larsen/Feiten Band,** *Larsen/Feiten Band* (Warner Bros., 1980).

Recordings featuring Elvin Bishop: **Mike Bloomfield and Al Kooper,** *The Live Adventures of Mike Bloomfield and Al Kooper* (Columbia, 1969•). **Various Artists,** *Hotels, Motels, and Roadshows* (Capricorn, 1978•).

Recordings featuring Buzz Feiten: **Bob Dylan,** *New Morning* (Columbia, 1970). **Various Artists,** *Woodstock* (Cotillion, 1970•). **Various Artists,** *Woodstock Two* (Cotillion, 1971•). **The Rascals** [on Columbia], *Peaceful World* (1971), *The Island of Real* (1972). **Stevie Wonder,** *Music of My Mind* (Tamla, 1972), *Talking Book* (1972). **Gregg Allman,** *Laid Back* (Capricorn, 1973). **Love,** *Reel to Real* (Blue Thumb, 1974). **Neil Larsen,** *High Gear*

(Horizon, 1979), *Through Any Window* (1988). **Randy Crawford,** *Windsong* (Warner Bros., 1982). **Various Artists,** *Casino Lights* (Warner Bros., 1982•). **Stu Hamm** [on Relativity], *Kings of Sleep* (1989), *The Urge* (1991).

Harvey Mandel

Born: *March 11, 1945, in Detroit*
Main Guitars: *Gibson Les Paul and ES-335, Fender Stratocaster*

Given Harvey Mandel's impressive credentials in rock 'n' roll, it is a mystery why he is not one of its best-known guitar heroes. He was an active part of both the mid-sixties blues revival in Chicago and the San Francisco psychedelic movement, played with rock 'n' blues icons John Mayall and the Rolling Stones, and helped pioneer rock guitar techniques including feedback, distortion, and two-handed tapping. Still, Mandel is known only to a relatively small cult of rock guitar fans.

In the mid sixties Mandel was in Chicago during the genesis of the U.S. blues-rock scene. There he played with a plethora of blues heavyweights, from Otis Rush to Muddy Waters to Buddy Guy, in addition to white bluesman Barry Goldberg and blues harpist/vocalist Charlie Musselwhite. By 1966 he had joined Musselwhite's band and quickly became one of Chicago's guitar wonders. His guitar work on the legendary *Stand Back! Here Comes Charlie Musselwhite's South Side Band* (1966) rivaled the playing of both Mike Bloomfield and Eric Clapton and brought blues and rock 'n' roll another step closer to one another with his relentless fuzztone, feedback-edged solos, and unusual syncopated phrasing.

Around the time the Musselwhite band relocated to San Francisco, Mandel began his solo career with the impressive blues and jazz-based recordings *Cristo Redentor* and *Righteous*. In 1969 he replaced Henry Vestine as guitarist for Canned Heat, a band that was riding high on the single "Going up the Country." That August Mandel and the Heat—known as the primary advocates of the rock 'n' roll boogie—electrified fans at the Woodstock festival with an energetic performance that would later appear on both Woodstock albums. Mandel also recorded with the band and appeared on its 1970 *Future Blues* set, contributing the fiery leads to "My Time Ain't Long" and "4 P.M.," the latter noted for the guitarist's choppy stutters during his solo. Later in 1970 Mandel joined up with John Mayall for his *U.S.A. Union* album, a soft blues disc that featured such instrumentation as electric guitar and bass, violin, but curiously, no drummer. Mandel then formed the Pure Food and Drug Act with violinist Don "Sugarcane" Harris (who had also played on the Mayall disc) and recorded the *Choice Cuts* record. Another interesting recording he played on was the Ventures' 1971 *Rock and Roll Forever*, which revealed Mandel's strong influence from instrumental rock.

Mandel continued releasing solo albums, among them such standouts as *Baby Batter*, *The Snake*, and *Shangrenade*. All three of these records show Mandel moving away from his blues base and experimenting with a variety of styles, notably jazz, funk, and fusion. By the time of *Feel the Sound of Harvey Mandel* (1974), he was incorporating a new technique into his funk-fusion rock that was well ahead of its time in rock circles: two-hand tapping. Though ZZ Top's Billy Gibbons and sessionman Larry Carlton had used one-note taps before, Mandel—along with Steve Hackett of Genesis—was one of the first guitarists to fully develop repeating arpeggios via the two-hand method. Most rock fans became aware of this style only after Eddie Van Halen's thunderous debut in 1978.

In 1975 Mandel was offered a chance to play with and possibly join the Rolling Stones. Mick Taylor had quit the Stones in 1974 and Mandel's name was high on a list of potential replacements (including Ron Wood, Wayne Perkins, and Jeff Beck). The guitarist was flown to Munich, Germany, to audition and do some recording with the band. From these sessions came tracks such as "Memory Motel" and "Hot Stuff," which eventually surfaced on the Stones' *Black and Blue* set. "Hot Stuff," which garnered ample radio airplay in 1976, contained a scorching Mandel lead steeped in funk and fusion textures. The full-time Stones gig, however, went to British guitarist Ron Wood (♦ The Rolling Stones [Part 2]). Not coincidentally, that is where the saga of Harvey Mandel trails off, though he did cut the well-received *Twist City* platter in 1994.

Considering his achievements, Mandel seemed at one time poised to become a rock guitar celebrity. But the guitarist never achieved the popularity and acclaim accorded to Eric Clapton, Jimi Hendrix, and Jeff Beck because he never embraced hard rock or heavy metal in a manner that would have made him more accessible to commercial audiences. Instead, he pursued his own particular guitar visions, which included a firm commitment to instrumental rock, a musical form that rarely wins widespread commercial support.

Charlie Musselwhite, *Stand Back! Here Comes Charlie Musselwhite's South Side Band* (Vanguard, 1966). **Harvey Mandel** [on Janus except where noted], *Cristo Redentor* (Philips, 1969), *Righteous* (Philips, 1969), *Games Guitars Play* (Phillips, c. 1971), *Baby Batter* (c. 1971–72), *The Snake* (1972), *Shangrenade* (c. 1973), *Feel the Sound of Harvey Mandel* (1974), *The Best of Harvey Mandel* (1975), *Live Boot: Harvey Mandel Live In California* (Fresh Squeezed, 1990•), *Twist City* (Western Front, 1994). **Canned Heat,** *Future Blues* (Liberty, 1970), *Canned Heat Concert* (United Artists, 1971•). **John Mayall** [on Polydor], *U.S.A. Union* (1970), *Back to the Roots* (1971).

Recordings featuring Harvey Mandel: **Barry Goldberg,** *Blowing My Mind* (Epic, 1966), *There's No Hole in My Soul* (Buddah, c. 1968), *Two Jews Blues* (Buddah, c. 1969•), *Barry Goldberg and Friends* (Record Man, c. 1970), *Blasts from the Past* (Buddah, 1971). **The Ventures,** *Rock and Roll Forever* (United Artists, 1971). **Various Artists,** *Woodstock* (Cotillion, 1970•), *Woodstock Two* (Cotillion, 1971•). **Pure Food and Drug Act,** *Choice Cuts* (Epic, c. 1971). **Don "Sugarcane" Harris** [on MPS/BASF], *Fiddler on the Rock* (1972), *Cup Full of Dreams* (c. 1973). **Love,** *Reel to Real* (Blue Thumb, 1974). **The Rolling Stones,** *Black and Blue* (Rolling Stones, 1976). **Various Artists,** *Guitar Speak II* (IRS, 1990).

CHAPTER SEVEN

Folk Rock
Electric Meets Acoustic

In the early sixties the U.S. saw a surge in the popularity of folk music. Leading the way were artists like Bob Dylan, Peter, Paul & Mary, Joan Baez, the Rooftop Singers, Ramblin' Jack Elliott, the Kingston Trio, the Limelighters, Trini Lopez, Phil Ochs, and Judy Collins. These young musicians updated and, in some cases, simply revisited the form and content of American folk music as it had existed for the three previous decades. In the process, they reacquainted American listeners with the rich music of folk and country legends such as Woody Guthrie, the Weavers (with the great Pete Seeger), and Hank Williams, as well as bluegrass innovators like Bill Monroe and the newly discovered guitar master Doc Watson. While singers like Dylan and Baez were leading the U.S. folk revival—and would give folk *rock* much of its gentle poetic influence—there were two events that really provided the movement with its push towards electric rock music. The first event was the meteoric rise of the Beatles, and the second (and more important) was Bob Dylan's dramatic conversion to electric rock 'n' roll. When Dylan and the Byrds crashed the pure folk music of Woody Guthrie and Pete Seeger into the Beatles' wall of vocals and electric guitars, folk rock emerged.

Since the guitar figured so heavily in American folk musics (i.e., blues, country, folk, bluegrass), it also came to be of vital importance in folk rock. The delicate strumming and fingerpicking of folk and bluegrass styles meshed surprisingly well with the roar of an amplified electric guitar. By 1965 many hit recordings by top folk rock groups like the Byrds, Lovin' Spoonful (with influential guitarist Zal Yanovsky), the Turtles, the Mamas & the Papas, Simon & Garfunkel, and Buffalo Springfield featured electric guitars. This uncanny synthesis of folk and rock music, acoustic and electric guitar styles, and old and new musical traditions, had a direct impact on rock musicians of the late sixties and seventies. The folk rock sound proved highly influential on the guitarists of such groups as the Eagles, Poco, the Flying Burrito Brothers, Pure Prairie League, and even Led Zeppelin.

Bob Dylan

Born: *Robert Zimmerman, May 24, 1941, in Duluth, Minnesota*
Main Guitars: *Gibson and Martin acoustics, Fender Telecaster and Stratocaster*

Without question, Bob Dylan was *the* pivotal force in folk rock and extremely influential on sixties rock as a whole. Almost everybody—including various members of the Beatles—wanted to sound, look, and write songs like Dylan. Despite his universal fame as a songwriter, Dylan to this day is not a famous guitarist. Perhaps he ought to be, given that most of his best music is guitar-driven, and he has always appeared on stage with guitar in hand, from flat-top acoustics to Fender solidbodies. Further investigation of his early acoustic records, which feature minimal standup bass accompaniment, reveal an accomplished fingerpicker ("It's Alright Ma, I'm Only Bleeding," "Girl from the North Country," "Don't Think Twice, It's All Right"), while his later electric work shows an aggressive rock rhythm player ("Like a Rolling Stone," "Positively 4th Street"). In recent years, the 50-something rocker has even taken to playing fiery guitar

Bob Dylan

solos in concert.

Overall, however, Dylan's importance to electric guitar is more as a visual icon than as a masterful player. Like Elvis Presley, John Lennon, or Kurt Cobain of Nirvana, he is an influential rhythm player who simply uses the guitar as a tool to deliver his songs, not as an improvisational instrument. So while Mr. Dylan may not rival Jimi Hendrix as a guitar god, few would argue about his impact on the guitar universe of the 1960s and beyond.

Bob Dylan [on Columbia], *Bob Dylan* (1962), *The Freewheelin' Bob Dylan* (1963), *The Times They Are A-Changin'* (1964), *Another Side of Bob Dylan* (1964), *Bringing It All Back Home* (1965), *Highway 61 Revisited* (1965), *Blonde on Blonde* (1966), *John Wesley Harding* (1967), *Nashville Skyline* (1969), *Self-Portrait* (1970), *New Morning* (1970), *Pat Garrett & Billy the Kid* [soundtrack] (1973), *Dylan* (1973), *Planet Waves* (1974), *Before the Flood* (1974•), *Blood on the Tracks* (1975), *The Basement Tapes* [with the Band] (1975), *Desire* (1976), *Hard Rain* (1976•), *Street-Legal* (1978), *Bob Dylan at Budokan* (1979•), *Slow Train Coming* (1979), *Saved* (1980), *Shot of Love* (1981), *Infidels* (1983), *Real Live* (1985•), *Empire Burlesque* (1985), *Biograph* (1985•), *Knocked out Loaded* (1986), *Down in the Groove* (1988), *Dylan & the Dead* (1989•), *Oh Mercy* (1989), *Under the Red Sky* (1990), *The Bootleg Series—Vols. 1–3* (1991•), *Good as I Been to You* (1992), *World Gone Wrong* (1993), *Unplugged* (1995•). **Various Artists,** *Bob Dylan: The 30th Anniversary Concert Celebration* (1993•).

The Byrds

Jim "Roger" McGuinn

Born: *July 13, 1942, in Chicago*
Main Guitars: *Rickenbacker 370/12 and 360/12*

David Crosby

Born: *August 14, 1941, in Los Angeles*
Main Guitar: *Gretsch Tennessean*

If folk rock was the marriage of folk music with the Beatles, then its first child was the Byrds. Rich vocal harmonies, electrified Dylan tunes, and electric 12-string guitars made up the band's special sound. In 1965 it catapulted them to the top of the pop charts, and for the next three years the Byrds led the folkies-turned-rockers with a handful of timely hits and albums that ranged from Beatlesque folk-pop ("Mr. Tambourine Man," "Turn, Turn, Turn," "I'll Feel a Whole Lot Better") to spacy pre-psychedelia ("Eight Miles High," "Mr. Spaceman"). At the core of their sound was the electric Rickenbacker 12-string of Roger McGuinn. That element, combined with the band's harmonies and catchy pop tunes, helped cement the Byrds' reputation as America's rock 'n' roll answer to the Beatles (though Crosby and McGuinn often try to play down that flattering comparison).

McGuinn had worked as a folksinger in Greenwich Village and as a backup musician for Bobby Darin and Judy Collins. He went to Los Angeles in 1964, where he put together the Byrds with David Crosby on rhythm guitar, bluegrass veteran Chris Hillman on bass, Gene Clark on vocals, and Mike Clarke on drums. At the beginning of 1965 this band recorded a version of Bob Dylan's "Mr. Tambourine Man." Dylan's original version had featured only folksy acoustic strumming and harmonica under his coarse singing, but the Byrds supercharged it with choirlike vocalizing, a pungent bass line, and McGuinn's ubiquitous Ricky 12-string. Released in March 1965, the song became an immediate sensation, and the Byrds turned out another folk-rock epic just a few months later with "Turn, Turn, Turn," a song derived from a biblical passage revamped by folksinger Pete Seeger.

Riding the crest of popularity, the Byrds broke new ground in mid 1966 with the release of the proto-psychedelic single "Eight Miles High" (from their third album, *Fifth Dimension*), marking the peak of their "space cowboy" period. Leading off with Hillman's ominous bass riff, "Eight Miles High" brims with ethereal vocals and McGuinn's jagged, menacing electronic guitar riffs, which occasionally border on total chaos. Inspired by jazz saxophonist John Coltrane, it was Roger McGuinn's finest moment with the Byrds.

Internal friction, however, began to grow within the band. During 1966 Gene Clark left the group—the first of many personnel changes. After another successful album, *Younger than Yesterday*, David Crosby also departed from the Byrds, and went on to form Crosby, Stills & Nash (♦). He was soon followed out the door by drummer Mike Clarke. With McGuinn at the helm, session musicians were brought in to round out the Byrds' next few efforts, including *Sweetheart of the Rodeo* (1968), which may have single-handedly triggered the country-rock movement of the seventies. The record prominently featured the talents of L.A. rock guru Gram Parsons and bluegrass superpicker Clarence White, who had also made an uncredited session performance on *Younger than Yesterday*. (White was also the inventor of the Parsons/White string-bender device, later favored by Jimmy Page and other rock giants.) Soon after the release of *Sweetheart*, Chris Hillman decided to call it a day, and Roger McGuinn was the only remaining Byrd in the nest. Though he managed to keep the name going for a couple more albums (including *Untitled*, which contained the beautiful "Chestnut Mare"), the golden era of the Byrds was behind him.

Though the original Byrds splintered after only three years in the limelight, they left a considerable mark on the future sound of rock 'n' roll. The sound of McGuinn's electric 12-string guitar became immensely influential, having a significant impact on rockers like Tom Petty, Marshall Crenshaw, and the Gin Blossoms, all of whom regularly duplicated it, as did many other guitarists and bands of the post-punk era. The Byrds also had a lasting effect on many of the L.A. folk and country-rock acts that followed them, including Poco, the Eagles, the Grateful Dead, Pure Prairie League, and Stephen Stills' Manassas, which, ironically, included Chris Hillman. The Beatles also soaked up much of the Byrds' early sounds, as is evidenced by their strongly folk-influenced *Rubber Soul* LP, which came out a scant nine months after the appearance of "Mr. Tambourine Man." George

Harrison even admitted copping a Byrds lick for his guitar part to "If I Needed Someone."

The Byrds [on Columbia except where noted], *Mr. Tambourine Man* (1965), *Turn, Turn, Turn* (1965), *Fifth Dimension* (1966), *Younger than Yesterday* (1967), *Greatest Hits* (1967), *The Notorious Byrd Brothers* (1968), *Sweetheart of the Rodeo* (1968), *Dr. Byrds & Mr. Hyde* (1969), *Preflyte* (Together, 1969), *Ballad of Easy Rider* (1969), *The Byrds* [Untitled] (1970•), *Byrdmaniax* (1971), *Farther Along* (1971), *Greatest Hits Volume II* (1972), *Byrds* (Asylum, 1973), *Never Before* (Murray Hill, 1988), *In the Beginning* (Rhino, 1988), *Preflyte, The Byrds* [boxed set] (1990•). **Roger McGuinn** [on Columbia except where noted], *Roger McGuinn* (1973), *Peace on You* (1974), *Roger McGuinn & Band* (1975), *Cardiff Rose* (1976), *McGuinn, Clarke & Hillman* (Capitol, 1979), *Back from Rio* (Arista, 1991).

Recordings featuring Roger McGuinn: **Chad Mitchell Trio** [on Kapp], *Mighty Day on Campus* (1962), *The Chad Mitchell Trio at the Bitter End* (1962). **Various Artists,** *Bob Dylan: The 30th Anniversary Concert Celebration* (1993•).

Buffalo Springfield

Stephen Stills

Born: *January 3, 1945, in Dallas*
Main Guitars: *Fender Telecaster, Gibson Byrdland*

Neil Young

Born: *November 12, 1945, in Toronto*
Main Guitars: *Gretsch White Falcon and Chet Atkins*

Richie Furay

Born: *May 9, 1944, in Yellow Springs, Ohio*
Main Guitar: *Gibson ES-335 12-string*

The stereotypical image of the sixties folk rock guitarist has often been of a pre-hippie softly strumming chords and arpeggios behind layered vocal harmonies and softly electrified folk tunes. In many cases this bland generalization holds true, but when considering folk rock guitarists Stephen Stills and Neil Young, nothing could be further from the truth. Their playing in Buffalo Springfield was fully electrified and added a whole new dimension to what a folk rock guitarist could be.

After a lengthy stint in New York City with a vocal-oriented folk group called the Au Go Go Singers, Stephen Stills went to Los Angeles in the mid sixties, where new folk sounds were being generated by the Byrds. It was there that he auditioned for the Monkees (supposedly being turned down because of crooked teeth) and eventually hooked up with Richie Furay (who had also played in the Au Go Go Singers) and Neil Young, a Canadian folksinger Stills had met a few years earlier. Together with drummer Dewey Martin and bassist Bruce Palmer, they formed Buffalo Springfield (named for a fire engine manufacturer) in the beginning of 1966. With the release of their first album the following year, Buffalo Springfield scored a hit single with a composition by Stills, "For What It's Worth," based on the infamous Sunset Strip riot of 1966.

Much of Buffalo Springfield's reputation was based on their blend of delicate folk influences with the electric attack of Stills and Young. "For What It's Worth" demonstrated this formula with Stills and Furay playing acoustic rhythm while Young handled the twangy electric lead parts, heavy with reverb and cheesy amplifier tremolo. "Rock 'n' Roll Woman" (from *Buffalo Springfield Again*) was another example, with Stills playing the thickly distorted blues solos over the bridge and rideout. Also of importance is the original version of "Bluebird," which showcased solos alternating between Young's distorted electric licks and Stills' acoustic fingerpicking.

Personality problems grew within the band (reputedly between Stills and Young), and, after only three albums, Buffalo Springfield disbanded in the spring of 1968. Neil Young (♦) went off to do solo work, while Stills almost immediately appeared on a hit album called *Super Session*. Masterminded by Al Kooper (formerly of the Blues Project [♦] and Blood, Sweat & Tears), *Super Session* was a series of impromptu jam sessions; one side of the album featuring Mike Bloomfield (♦), and the other featuring Stills. His wah-wah breaks in "Season of the Witch" and phase-shifted solo on "You Don't Love Me" revealed his movement towards a heavier, more electronic guitar sound than his work in Buffalo Springfield, quite likely the influence of his frequent jamming partner, Jimi Hendrix.

Buffalo Springfield [on Atco], *Buffalo Springfield* (1967), *Buffalo Springfield Again* (1967), *Last Time Around* (1968), *Retrospective* (1969). **Mike Bloomfield, Al Kooper & Stephen Stills,** *Super Session* (Columbia, 1969).

Crosby, Stills, Nash & Young

David Crosby

Born: *August 14, 1941, in Los Angeles*
Main Guitars: *Gretsch hollowbodies*

Stephen Stills

Born: *January 3, 1945, in Dallas*
Main Guitars: *Gretsch hollowbodies, Fender Telecaster*

Graham Nash

Born: *February 2, 1942, in Blackpool, England*
Main Guitars: *Gretsch hollowbodies*

Neil Young

Born: *November 12, 1945, in Toronto*
Main Guitars: *Gretsch hollowbodies, Gibson Les Paul*

At the end of 1968 Stephen Stills formed a new group with ex-Byrd David Crosby and Graham Nash from the Hollies. Calling themselves simply Crosby, Stills & Nash, their self-titled first album gained immediate acclaim for beautiful original compositions by all three members. Opening the album was Stills' opus "Suite: Judy Blue Eyes" (written for folk singer Judy Collins), which provided a good look at Stills' impressive multi-instrumental

Neil Young, David Crosby, Graham Nash, Stephen Stills

career went into a period of decline. In 1977 he again joined forces with David Crosby and Graham Nash, who had been performing and recording as a duo, and recorded the extremely well-received reunion album *CSN*, featuring good acoustic work on "Dark Star" and fierce electric breaks in "I Give You Give Blind." As for Neil Young (♪), after CSNY's golden era he went on to become one of the most celebrated singer-songwriters of the seventies with his band, Crazy Horse,

capabilities, as he played electric and acoustic guitars, bass, and organ on the track. "Wooden Ships" was the album's guitar high point, featuring several extended Stills solos that alternate between funky chordal licks on a Telecaster (with extensive string pops) and muted melodic phrases, which he achieved by rolling off the tone knob.

As if Stills' guitar talents weren't enough on their own, it was announced in mid 1969 (right before their debut gig at Woodstock) that Neil Young would be joining the trio on second lead guitar and vocals to create a quartet, CSNY. On the newly expanded band's popular 1970 album, *Deja Vu*, Stills' and Young's electric trade-offs were so fervent that they almost overshadowed the subtler acoustic moments of the set (though the players still relied heavily on the mixture of acoustic and electric they frequently used in Buffalo Springfield). "Carry On," the album opener, belongs mostly to Stills, with his typically rough acoustic strumming, gritty electric leads, and wah-wah'd Telecaster breaks. Young dominates the rocker "I Almost Cut My Hair," cutting blistering distortion- and echo-laced leads on stereo tracks.

Like Buffalo Springfield, the original Crosby, Stills, Nash & Young had only a brief life span. After *Deja Vu* and a tour—captured on the album *4 Way Street*—the four splintered off into various solo projects. Stephen Stills cut an excellent debut album in 1970 with guests Jimi Hendrix and Eric Clapton that yielded the hit single "Love the One You're With." In 1972 he formed a country-rock congregation with ex-Byrds bassist Chris Hillman called Manassas, but after two albums, that act broke up, and Stills'

and as a solo artist. The four have only reunited for a 1974 tour and the largely forgettable *American Dream* album of 1988.

Crosby, Stills & Nash [on Atlantic], *Crosby, Stills & Nash* (1969), *CSN* (1977), *Daylight Again* (1982), *Allies* (1983●), *Live It Up* (1990), *CSN* [boxed set] (1991●), *After the Storm* (1994). **Crosby, Stills, Nash & Young** [on Atlantic], *Deja Vu* (1970), *4 Way Street* (1971●), *So Far* (1974), *American Dream* (1988). **Stephen Stills** [on Atlantic except where noted], *Stephen Stills* (1970), *Stephen Stills 2* (1971), *Stills* (Columbia, 1975), *Stephen Stills Live* (1975●), *Illegal Stills* (Columbia, 1976), *The Best of Stephen Stills* (1976), *Thoroughfare Gap* (Columbia, 1978), *Right by You* (1984). **Manassas** [on Atlantic], *Manassas* (1972), *Down the Road* (1973). **Stills-Young Band,** *Long May You Run* (Reprise, 1976).

Recordings featuring Stephen Stills: **Various Artists,** *Woodstock* (Cotillion, 1970●). **Eric Clapton,** *Eric Clapton* (Atco/Polydor, 1970), *Crossroads* (Polydor, 1988●). **Doris Troy,** *Doris Troy* (Apple, 1970). **Mickey Hart,** *Rolling Thunder* (Warner Bros., 1972). **Various Artists,** *Havana Jam* (Columbia, 1979●).

The Band

Robbie Robertson

B o r n : *Jaime Robertson, on July 5, 1944, in Toronto*
M a i n G u i t a r s : *Fender Telecaster and Stratocaster, Gibson "O" Style archtop*

When the Band's first record, *Music from Big Pink*, was released in the summer of 1968, it was hailed by the rock press as one of the most distinctive and original rock albums of the year. Combining rustic folk ballads, New Orleans ragtime and jazz, rock 'n' roll, and a slew of other diverse influences (including lyrics about life in nineteenth century America), the Band established themselves as pioneers in the emergence of folk rock, due mostly to the unquestionable genius of Robbie Robertson. In addition to composing much of the Band's music, Robertson was also the group's lead guitarist, lending his inventive rock-, country-, and blues-based guitar solos to many of the great Band songs, from *Music from Big Pink* until their final release, *The Last Waltz*, in 1978.

Though *Big Pink* was the Band's first official album, they were actually rock 'n' roll veterans. The members of the Band—Robertson, drummer Levon Helm, bassist Rick Danko, and keyboardists Richard Manuel and Garth Hudson—had formed in the late 1950s as the Hawks, a backup band for rockabilly singer Ronnie Hawkins. With Hawkins they recorded the 1963 hit "Who Do You Love," which contains an early and very intense Robertson solo. Around 1964 Robertson and the Hawks left Hawkins and began touring the East Coast on their own. Credited as "Jaime Robertson," Robbie can be heard on John Hammond's 1965 urban-blues disc *So Many Roads*, where his blues ideas and string bends were well ahead of their time for a white rocker.

Later in 1965 the Hawks made contact with Bob Dylan, who hired them as his backup band for the controversial 1965–1966 world tour, which marked Dylan's legendary conversion to electric rock 'n' roll. Due in large part to Robertson's electrifying guitar work and the Hawks' energetic backup playing, this riotous tour is almost universally regarded by both rock fans and critics as one of the outstanding periods of Bob Dylan's career. (A bootleg recording of their famous concert at Royal Albert Hall in London remains a popular underground seller to this day.) After the tour, Dylan was involved a serious motorcycle accident and went into seclusion in the rural village of Woodstock, New York, to recuperate. The Hawks followed him there and began informally recording some new material with him as well as cutting some tracks by themselves. The recordings with Dylan came out in 1975 as *The Basement Tapes*, but the other material was earmarked for *Big Pink*. By the time these recordings were finished, the Hawks had already changed their name to simply the Band.

Despite the widespread success the Band achieved after the release of *Big Pink*, they toured and recorded only sporadically. The quintet issued several brilliant albums, including *The Band* (1969), the live *Rock of Ages* (1972), and *Northern Lights—Southern Cross* (1975); other efforts, notably *Cahoots* and *Islands*, were unpopular with both the press and the public. But in all of their recordings and stage work, the powerful guitar playing of Robbie Robertson is omnipresent. On their second and most popular album, *The Band*, his guitar playing shines on "Jemima Surrender" with tough rhythm progressions and a tart, Claptonesque solo, while on "Jawbone" he plays a funky multistring break across the fretboard of a Fender Telecaster. On *Rock of Ages* he adds a reeling Telecaster solo to "Don't Do It," and in

"This Wheel's on Fire" his break roams from tasty chordal licks to twangy single-note blues lines. On the 1974 live set with Bob Dylan, *Before the Flood*, Robertson lends his guitar to "All along the Watchtower" and "Highway 61 Revisited" with some more characteristically aggressive leads. The Band's tour-de-force finale, *The Last Waltz*, includes Robertson trading licks with Eric Clapton (who had been hugely influenced by the Band's first album), plus featuring Joni Mitchell, Muddy Waters, Ron Wood, and Neil Young, among others.

After leaving the Band, Robertson did film scores for Martin Scorsese (*Raging Bull*, *The Color of Money*, *The King of Comedy*) and dabbled in acting (*Carny*, *Crossing Guards*). He released three solo albums, beginning with his well-received debut album of 1987. In 1994 he released his third album, which was the soundtrack to a documentary for Turner Broadcasting, "The Native Americans." He continues to work with other artists, such as Eric Clapton and Bruce Hornsby; Clapton inducted all the members of the Band into the Rock and Roll Hall of Fame in January 1994.

The Band [on Capitol except where noted], *Music from Big Pink* (1968), *The Band* (1969), *Stagefright* (1970), *Cahoots* (1971), *Rock of Ages* (1972●), *Moondog Matinee* (1973), *Northern Lights—Southern Cross* (1975), *Islands* (1977), *The Last Waltz* (Warner Bros., 1978●), *To Kingdom Come* (1989●), *Across the Great Divide* (1995●). **Bob Dylan and the Band**, *Planet Waves* (Asylum, 1973), *Before the Flood* (1974●), *The Basement Tapes* (Columbia, 1975). **Robbie Robertson**, *Robbie Robertson* (Geffen, 1987), *Storyville* (Geffen, 1991), *Music for "The Native Americans"* [with the Red River Ensemble] (Capitol, 1994).

Recordings featuring Robbie Robertson: **John Hammond**, *So Many Roads* (Vanguard, 1965). **Ronnie Hawkins**, *The Best of Ronnie Hawkins Featuring His Band* (Roulette, c. 1970). **Joni Mitchell**, *Court and Spark* (Asylum, 1974). **Eric Clapton**, *No Reason to Cry* (RSO, 1976), *Crossroads* (Polydor, 1988●). **Neil Diamond**, *Beautiful Noise* (Columbia, 1976), *Love at the Greek* (Columbia, 1977●). **Bob Dylan**, *Biograph* (Columbia, 1985●). **Various Artists**, *The Color of Money* [soundtrack] (MCA, 1987).

CHAPTER EIGHT

Psychedelia
Rockin' the Aquarian Age

Acid rock. Haight-Ashbury. The Fillmore. Though these terms don't mean much to the current generation of rock 'n' rollers, they meant almost everything to rock fans in San Francisco in 1967. During that year a new style of music called acid rock (also known as psychedelic rock) took hold in free "dance concerts" and dance halls (like the groundbreaking Fillmore Auditorium and the Avalon Ballroom) around the Bay Area. The terms reflected the trippiness of the music as it related to the drugs of choice in San Francisco, which—with its now-infamous Haight-Ashbury district—was a national magnet for the minions of the growing sixties counterculture.

It didn't take long for this form of rock 'n' roll to filter out to the rest of country. This was due in no small part to the Monterey Pop Festival of June 1967. The festival was the ultimate showplace for many of the great psychedelic groups of the late sixties, including Big Brother & the Holding Company (with Janis Joplin on vocals), the Steve Miller Band, and Quicksilver Messenger Service. More importantly, Monterey focused national attention on these and other bands, instantly adding psychedelic rock to the American musical lexicon.

Groups like the Grateful Dead, the Great Society, the Jefferson Airplane, and the Charlatans were just a few of the psychedelic groups that rose up from the bohemian Haight-Ashbury district, bringing with them a musical message of love, drugs, peace, and togetherness, as well as a whole new grab bag of rock 'n' roll sounds. Yet, contrary to this philosophy, psychedelic rock was loud, aggressive, and rather long-winded. It found its most comfortable ground by fusing the folk-rock earthiness of musicians like Bob Dylan and the Byrds with the aggressive rock 'n' blues of the Rolling Stones and the Paul Butterfield Blues Band. In particular, the long, improvisational jam sessions of Butterfield and his guitarist Mike Bloomfield were highly influential on the whole psychedelic movement.

With such diverse musical influences, psychedelic rock quickly became a new forum for rock guitarists, who were freshly inspired by the innovative guitar sounds of contemporaries Mike Bloomfield, Keith Richards, Jeff Beck, Roger McGuinn, Jerry Garcia, Eric Clapton, and, of course, psychedelia's own favorite son, Jimi Hendrix. The psychedelic guitarists, many of whom were ex-acoustic folk strummers, took advantage of the long jams that were ubiquitous in the genre and began craftily experimenting with electronic sound effects like fuzzboxes, wah-wah pedals, and feedback. They also made great use of the emotive pentatonic blues solos that were part and parcel of blues-rock guitar.

Psychedelic rock and the sound of San Francisco had a brief life span, however, and by 1970 the musical form as a commercial entity was dead. Major contributors to its downfall were, among others, the inevitable arrival of too many musicians trying to get in on the action, in addition to extensive media hype. Nevertheless, during its peak years from 1966 to 1969, psychedelia was a hotbed for some of the most interesting rock guitarists of the time. By today's standards these players sound rather primitive, with their squawking fuzzboxes, tremolo amplifier effects, and slowly developing finger vibrato, but at the time, they represented the triumphant sound of change in rock guitar. They freely plundered the guitar licks of Hendrix, Clapton, Bloomfield, and many other guitar masters and, in the process, pushed the stylistic, technical, and electronic limits of the instrument and the genre. A good example of the typical acid rocker is Barry Melton. As part of the popular group Country Joe & the Fish, Melton was one of the most far-out pickers in San Francisco. For a quick sampler of his heavy guitar tripping, "Superbird" or "Flying High" (from the

Jimi Hendrix

Fish's 1967 album *Electric Music for the Mind and Body*) are emblematic of the guitarist's fast, string-pushing breaks. Even better is "Happiness Is a Porpoise Mouth," which is enhanced with harpsichord-like guitar lines and fuzzy string drones from Melton's electric guitar. Surely, this is rock guitar at its trippiest.

So while there were few truly great guitarists in psychedelic rock outside of Hendrix, through the collective effort of all the players of that period, the sound of psychedelia became an instantly recognizable style of rock 'n' roll. Despite its negative connotations, it's also one of the more colorful periods in rock history.

Jimi Hendrix

Born: *Johnny Allen Hendrix, on November 27, 1942, in Seattle*
Died: *September 18, 1970, in London*
Main Guitar: *Fender Stratocaster*

At the moment Jimi Hendrix struck his first power chord on Sunday, June 18, 1967, at the Monterey Pop Festival, the sound of rock guitar was changed forever. It was the last concert of the three-day festival, and the Jimi Hendrix Experience was among the final acts to appear. After the Who's bombastic finale of smoke bombs and smashed guitars, Brian Jones, guitarist for the Rolling Stones, came on stage and calmly announced the next group. The Experience hit the stage with a blitzkrieg version of Howlin' Wolf's "Killing Floor" that was loaded with Hendrix's feedback-ridden lead licks and funky chordings.

Assisted by the electrifying rhythm section of drummer Mitch Mitchell and bassist Noel Redding, Hendrix followed "Killing Floor" with a dazzling set that included "Hey Joe," "Like a Rolling Stone," and "Can You See Me." The audience was mesmerized throughout the entire set.

For the finale, Hendrix announced to the crowd of thousands, "I'm gonna sacrifice something that I really love...." As he strummed the familiar power chords, the audience roared in recognition of the Troggs' 1966 hit "Wild Thing." Hendrix pulled out all the stops and made his guitar scream with feedback, tremolo bar drops, wide string bends, trills, distorted blues lines, and much more. As the band was screaming to the end of its sonic melee, Hendrix whipped off his Fender Stratocaster, doused it with lighter fluid, and set it on fire. In front of the thousands of stunned concert-goers, Hendrix bowed to his burning axe, humped it, smashed it, threw the smoldering Strat shards to the audience, and then calmly left the stage. In the course of just a few minutes, Jimi Hendrix had gone from being an unknown rocker to a virtual superstar, simultaneously stealing the show and forever changing the future of rock guitar.

In his brief career, Jimi Hendrix brought rock guitar out of its comparative dark ages and into the modern era. He changed the instrument from just being six amplified strings to a limitless electronic instrument, using sonic experimentation, sound effects, volume, novel techniques, and plain audacity. His onstage guitar theatrics and offstage mystique only made his reputation larger and his fans more ardent.

Early Years. Hendrix was born in Seattle, Washington, as Johnny Allen Hendrix. Later his parents separated and his father changed the youngster's name to James Marshall Hendrix. The boy had a normal but musical childhood: he started to play the guitar at about 12—regularly delving into his father's large R&B record collection for inspiration—and in his teens he played with many groups in clubs around Seattle and nearby Vancouver. After a two-year stint in the army, he jumped on the southern bar, or "chitlin'," circuit, where he played guitar with R&B and soul acts like Little Richard, Wilson Pickett, Ike and Tina Turner, and the Isley Brothers. In late 1965 he made his way to New York, where he formed his own group, Jimmy James and the Blue Flames (Hendrix was Jimmy James). The Blue Flames gigged around Greenwich Village, and for a while in 1966 Hendrix joined blues revivalist John Hammond's band as lead guitarist. It was during this time that Hendrix was first heard by Chas Chandler, then bassist for the Animals. Chandler was greatly impressed by Hendrix's astounding guitar playing and invited him to England, where he promised to make him a superstar (and offered him the opportunity to meet Eric Clapton, who was just beginning to make waves with Cream).

Recordings. Once Hendrix arrived in England, Chandler hooked him up with drummer Mitch Mitchell and bassist Noel Redding, and the Jimi Hendrix Experience was born. With Chandler managing them, the Experience quickly released a single, "Hey Joe," and began playing in London and on the continent. They signed a record contract with Track Records (the Who's label) and were regularly blowing away audiences at club gigs throughout Britain. In the space of a few months during 1967, the Jimi Hendrix Experience became the rage of Europe. Returning to the U.S. in June, Hendrix and band destroyed the audience at Monterey and—with the release of their first album, *Are You Experienced?*, later that summer—set out to conquer the rest of the country. Their first tour, though, began as a disaster. Unbelievably, they opened for the Monkees, the made-for-TV mop-tops who were the rage of teenybopper America. Naturally, the Monkees' fans didn't connect with Hendrix's music or his suggestive stage moves. After a few dates Hendrix and the group got off the tour and played out the summer of 1967 touring on their own.

Meanwhile, the single "Purple Haze" became a new anthem for rock guitarists everywhere. Nothing like "Purple Haze" had ever been heard before. Opening with the classic flatted-fifth fuzz riff, the song employed lavish sound effects and brazen guitar playing throughout. Hendrix also gave it one of the most memorable rock guitar solos of all time. Of course, the rest of the guitar work on the album was just as apocalyptic. The material ranged from studio-enhanced psychedelia like "Third Stone from the Sun" and "Are You Experienced?" to the softer, balladlike numbers "May This Be Love" and "The Wind Cries Mary" (a rhythm guitar tour de force influenced by Curtis Mayfield and Bobby Womack) to heavy tracks like "Fire" and "Foxey Lady." Throughout *Are You Experienced?*, Hendrix's guitar playing was nothing short of revolutionary.

Released at the beginning of 1968, their second album, *Axis: Bold as Love*, was another instant hit for Hendrix and the Experience. The new album was musically lighter than the previous one, featuring more spacey, psychedelic tunes and an increased use of studio gimmickry. Hendrix's songwriting talents had improved noticeably, most obviously on the beautiful ballad "Little Wing." Among his heavy guitar standouts were the solos on "If 6 Was 9." On that particular song he began to exercise the freedom offered by the technology of the studio. The guitar solo travels throughout the stereo spectrum, panning left to right and back again, complemented by slap echo, fuzzbox distortion, reverb, and other effects. Like its predecessor, *Axis: Bold as Love* lodged itself in the pop album charts for a lengthy stay.

By the beginning of 1968 Hendrix was working on his most ambitious album in studios in London and New York. Reflecting his interest in playing with different musicians (as evidenced by many after-hours jams with fellow guitar flashes like John McLaughlin, Larry Coryell, Stephen Stills, and Johnny Winter), Hendrix's new recordings featured various members of Traffic and Jefferson Airplane as well as the Experience. The album, *Electric Ladyland*, was released in the fall of 1968 and quickly moved to the top of the charts. Hendrix offered up bluesy layered breaks in "Gypsy Eyes," wah-wah effects in "Still Raining, Still Dreaming," and phase-shifted solos on "House Burning Down."

Two tracks in particular cemented Jimi Hendrix's rock guitar immortality. He took Bob Dylan's "All along the Watchtower" and gave it a completely new feel and arrangement. In the space of just a few minutes, Hendrix runs through the gamut of guitar techniques and effects—octave lines à la Wes Montgomery, pentatonic runs, chord melody work, string bends, and slide guitar— all fed through echo, reverb, and wah-wah effects. Topping even this brilliant achievement, Hendrix closed the album with the track "Voodoo Child (Slight Return)," his own perfect blues. The prowling rhythm sets the tone for this Hendrix masterwork: a harmonious blend of psychedelic imagery, mournful blues vocals, and high-tech electronic guitar. His solos on the song are among the most aggressive and vital he ever cut on tape. It is arguably his finest moment in the recording studio.

Despite the success of his records and numerous tours, Hendrix's personal life was fragile, to say the least. He was constantly surrounded by hangers-on who wanted a piece of his success, draining him both mentally and physically. This, combined with an arrest for heroin possession and another legal battle over an old recording contract, merely added to his problems. In mid 1969 Hendrix dissolved the Experience and moved to the rural community of Woodstock, New York, with a new group of musicians that featured a strong African influence. With this new aggregation, dubbed the "electric sky church" (or the Band of Gypsys, Suns, Moons, and Rainbows), Hendrix appeared that

summer at the Woodstock festival, where he performed his legendary version of "The Star-Spangled Banner," complete with overloaded feedback, distortion, and his trademark whammy bar dives.

Eventually Hendrix went back to his trio format; he played at the Fillmore East in New York on New Year's Eve 1969 with Buddy Miles (from the Electric Flag) on drums and an Army buddy, Billy Cox, on bass. The trio was billed as the Band of Gypsys. The highlight of the concert was "Machine Gun," a song about Vietnam that contained one of Hendrix's most dramatic solos. This dark, brooding concert was recorded and eventually released as an album on Capitol (helping settle the recording suit), though the group never toured.

Later in the year, Hendrix toured with Cox, bringing Mitch Mitchell back on drums. By the end of the summer of 1970, the Experience was rumored to be reforming. Hendrix had also been busy with the construction of his own studio in New York City, called Electric Lady Studios, where he would be able to record and jam whenever he wanted. After many delays, the studio was finally opened for business in August 1970. Immediately after, Hendrix left for England to play the huge Isle of Wight festival and tour Europe. He would never return to America or his Electric Lady Studios. On September 18, 1970, Jimi Hendrix died in the apartment of a girlfriend in London, suffocating on his own vomit after taking an accidental overdose of barbiturates.

When he died, Hendrix was in the midst of recording a double studio album, which had tentatively been titled *First Rays of the New Rising Sun*. He also had plans to do some recordings with progressive jazz bandleader Gil Evans, which undoubtedly would have yielded some interesting results. After Hendrix's death, unfinished recordings he had made over the course of his life were issued as albums through the seventies, though none was of the quality of his first three records with the Jimi Hendrix Experience. What remained of *First Rays of the New Rising Sun* turned up on the first two posthumous Hendrix releases, *Cry of Love* and *Rainbow Bridge*. While few of the countless albums released after his death merit any serious discussion, Hendrix's *Live at Winterland* concert was issued on compact disc in 1987 and was acclaimed as one of his finest live documents ever.

Gear and Technique. In his short career Hendrix revolutionized nearly every aspect of rock guitar playing. In his quest to broaden the electronic boundaries of the guitar and express his unique sonic vision, he employed nearly every available effect and guitar gadget of the late 1960s. Among his regular effects were a Dallas-Arbiter Fuzz Face, a Mayer Octavia (produces octaves above and below the note played), a Vox wah-wah pedal, a Leslie rotating speaker, and a Univox Univibe (which simulated a rotating speaker), not to mention the vast array of studio effects he used, like echo and phasing. His universally recognized signature guitar was a right-handed Fender Stratocaster flipped over and restrung for his lefty technique, though he could occasionally be found wailing away on a Gibson Les Paul or Flying V. His amps were almost always Marshall 100-watt stacks, though his rig did include Sunn and Sound City gear from time to time.

Another of his guitar revolutions was in the many techniques he used to conjure different sounds out of his guitars. The "whammy" (tremolo) bar was nothing new to rock 'n' roll when Hendrix came out in 1967, but the way he used it definitely was. Previously used as a subtle vibrato highlight to a note or chord, in his hands it was coupled with extreme feedback to achieve extreme pitch drops on certain notes and chords, and also to imitate the sound of bombs dropping and exploding. Among his other techniques were sliding his pick or fingers down the strings to make grinding noises and thumping the body of the guitar to create even more feedback effects.

One of his most novel uses for the guitar was as a prop in his live stage show. Taking many of his moves from old black R&B and showboat performers, Hendrix would play his guitar behind his head and back for flash, and would play leads with his teeth and tongue for even more camp. Though Hendrix used his stage antics to get people's attention, he eventually found it a burden to his image, as the title of a 1969 *Rolling Stone* article on Hendrix attested. Called "I Don't Want to Be a Clown Any More...," it clearly showed Hendrix's deep desire to be taken more seriously as a musician—and not as a freak-show performer.

Legacy. Despite the bad press he regularly received, and frequent drug and legal problems, Hendrix's popularity was immense, due in equal parts to his outrageous showmanship, rock star reputation, and inspired music. He was the ultimate symbol of the late sixties: his dress defined the "hippie" look, his aggressive blues-based music connoted the sad realities of the time, his skin color and popularity among whites (more so than blacks) was a sign of social change, and his playing was the ultimate sound of sixties rock guitar. Now, nearly three decades since his death, Jimi Hendrix is more popular—or better, revered—than ever.

The impact Jimi Hendrix has had on other guitarists has also been enormous. Even the most respected rock players, from Eric Clapton to Jeff Beck, on to Steve Vai and Stevie Ray Vaughan, admit to having been influenced by Hendrix. Like Chuck Berry before him, Hendrix has proven influential in every aspect of guitar playing—sound, technique, and showmanship. His sound or the spirit of his music has somehow found its way into the playing style of nearly every rock player since the end of the sixties.

To project what Hendrix might have achieved had he lived on is mind-boggling, but effectively fruitless. What remain to be most appreciated about Jimi Hendrix's playing are the recordings released before his death (unfortunately, there were so many sub-standard releases after his death), especially the three albums with the Experience and one with the Band of Gypsys. Those recordings are treasure troves of Hendrix's great guitar style and sound, gems of another era of rock 'n' roll. Thousands of rock guitarists have come and gone since Hendrix's untimely death in 1970, and thousands more are on the way, but over time it has become painfully clear that there will never again be another rock guitar hero like Jimi Hendrix.

Jimi Hendrix Experience [on Reprise except where noted], *Are You Experienced?* (1967; reissued on MCA, 1993), *Axis: Bold as Love* (1968; reissued on MCA, 1993), *Smash Hits* (1968), *Electric Ladyland* (1968; reissued on MCA, 1993), *Monterey International Pop Festival* [one side only] (1970•), *Live at Winterland* (Ryko, 1987•). **Band of Gypsys,** *Band of Gypsys* (Capitol, 1970•; reissued on MCA, 1995), *Band of Gypsies 2* (Capitol, 1986). **Jimi Hendrix** [on Reprise except where noted], *The Cry of Love* (1971), *Rainbow Bridge* (1971), *Isle of Wight* (Polydor, 1971•), *In the West* (1972•), *Crash Landing* (1975), *Midnight Lightning* (1975), *Loose Ends* (Polydor, 1973), *The Essential Jimi Hendrix, Vol. 1* (1978), *The Essential Jimi Hendrix, Vol. 2* (1978), *9 to the Universe* (1980), *The Jimi Hendrix Concerts* (1982), *Early Hendrix* (Baron, n/a), *Kiss the Sky* (1984), *Jimi Plays Monterey* (1986•), *Johnny B. Goode: Original Video Soundtrack* (Capitol, 1986•), *Fuzz, Feedback, and Wah-Wah* (Hal Leonard, 1989), *Whammy Bar and Finger Grease* (Hal Leonard, 1989), *Octavia and Univibe* (Hal Leonard, 1989), *Rhythm* (Hal Leonard, 1989), *Variations on a Theme: Red House* (Hal Leonard, 1989), *Lifelines: The Jimi Hendrix Story* (1991•), *Stages* (1991•), *The Ultimate Experience* (MCA, 1993), *Blues* (MCA, 1994•), *Voodoo Soup* (MCA, 1995). **Jimi Hendrix and Lonnie Youngblood,** *Two Great Experiences Together* (Maple, 1971), *Rare Hendrix* (Trip, 1972).

Other recordings featuring Jimi Hendrix: **Curtis Knight with Jimi Hendrix,** *Get that Feeling* (Capitol, 1967). **Stephen Stills,** *Stephen Stills* (Atlantic, 1970). **Various Artists,** *Woodstock* (Cotillion, 1970•). **Love,** *False Start* (Blue Thumb, 1970). **Various Artists,** *Woodstock Two* (Cotillion, 1971•). **Various Artists,** *The First Great Rock Festivals of the Seventies* (Columbia, 1971•).

Grateful Dead

Jerry Garcia

B o r n : *August 1, 1942, in San Francisco*
D i e d : *August 9, 1995, in Marin County, California*
M a i n   G u i t a r s : *Custom Doug Irwin solidbody, Gibson Les Paul and SG, miscellaneous solidbodies*

Bob Weir

B o r n : *October 16, 1947, in San Francisco*
M a i n   G u i t a r s : *Travis Bean and Ibanez solidbodies*

For some of the best rock 'n' roll of 1967, the place to be was San Francisco, the music to hear was acid rock, and the band to see was the Grateful Dead. Arguably the defining act of the whole Bay Area experience, the Dead personified the exciting new music coming out of the city with their so-called hippie looks, extended jam sessions, and well-publicized drug busts. The band quickly acquired a sizable following, which has since evolved into a vast cult of loyal fans known as Deadheads. Furthermore, their eclectic blend of rock, blues, country, jazz, folk, bluegrass, and jug band music was applauded by fans and critics alike in the late sixties, and their live reputation was widely renowned and praised.

Heading the band for 30 years was lead guitarist Jerry Garcia, whose melodic, bluegrass-rooted solos earned him a reputation as one of rock's most inventive guitarists. Garcia, however, wasn't the only guitarist of note in the band. Bob Weir provided the Grateful Dead's tight rhythm guitar underpinning, while bassist Phil Lesh held down their sound with prominent bass lines reminiscent of Paul McCartney and John Entwistle. Eschewing the three-minute pop song format, Garcia and the Grateful Dead frequently delved into long, improvisational jam sessions, similar to those the Paul Butterfield Blues Band pioneered on its landmark 1965 album *East-West*, though the Dead concentrated more on intricate ensemble playing than individual solo virtuosity.

Garcia, a self-taught guitar player, started to play rock and blues guitar in his mid teens. After a brief stint in the army, he played in various bluegrass bands around the San Francisco area, including the Hart Valley Drifters (winners at the 1963 Monterey Folk Festival). His next group was another acoustic outfit, Mother McCree's Uptown Jug Band, which had in its ranks future Dead members Bob Weir and Ron "Pigpen" McKernan. A lack of gigs forced the group to rethink their musical direction. In early 1965 they transformed themselves into a rock 'n' roll band and changed their name to the Warlocks. Now an electric group, they added Bill Kreutzmann on drums and Lesh on bass to get more of a rock 'n' roll feel. For a while the Warlocks played the local bar circuit (five sets a night, seven days a week), but it wasn't long until they met up with writer Ken Kesey and his Merry Pranksters, and became the official house band for the infamous Acid Tests of 1965. These multimedia drug fests featured the Warlocks in a series of impromptu performances in front of exotic light shows and thousands of stoned spectators who were experimenting with LSD. It was here that the seeds of psychedelia were being sown.

The Grateful Dead's live reputation and extensive local following earned them a recording contract with Warner Brothers in 1967; soon after, their self-titled first album was released. Opening with a rocker called "The Golden Road (To Unlimited Devotion)," the Grateful Dead began defining the sound of the San Francisco psychedelic era and displayed the unique, though still developing, guitar work of Garcia via a fuzzy, string-bending solo. The rendition of "Sittin' on Top of the World" is also a vintage piece of early Dead, especially with Garcia's fast, bluegrass-styled solo. The album hits closest to the true psychedelic jam in "Viola Lee Blues," a 10-minute blues groove that features a long, melodic solo by Garcia (showing his strong blues influences) and an uptempo rave-up at the conclusion.

In 1970 the Dead hit their stride with two near-classic albums, *Workingman's Dead* and *American Beauty*. Garcia also began to demonstrate his proficiency on pedal steel guitar, which he used on "Sugar Magnolia," from *American Beauty* (as well as on "Teach Your Children," from Crosby, Stills, Nash & Young's *Deja Vu*).

Another side of Garcia and the Grateful Dead has been that of an acoustic band, occasionally taking the stage without any electric instruments besides Lesh's bass. Some good recorded examples of the acoustic Dead are "Uncle John's Band," which has a beautiful acoustic guitar solo by Garcia, and "Friend of the Devil," noted as much for Lesh's up-front bass work and Weir's

rhythm excursions as for Garcia's accomplished leads. At the other end of the technological spectrum, the band delved into guitar synthesizers and the use of MIDI onstage during the 1980s and the first half of the nineties.

In 1987 the band scored their biggest hit with the single "Touch of Grey," bringing an even larger swarm of young fans into the already huge Deadhead camp. The following eight years were marked by sellout concerts and a broadening of their popularity, from young children to more than one U.S. Senator. The former beacons of the hippie counterculture had at last become respectable, their shows becoming less known as drug parties (although illegal substances still had a firm place in Dead life and lore) and more as a pleasant night out for the whole family. Not surprisingly, this global Dead community was shattered by news of Garcia's sudden death from a heart attack in 1995 (he was at a drug rehab center trying to overcome a lingering heroin addiction). Beyond being the band's signature voice and guitarist, he was the focal point of the entire Dead experience.

In hindsight, Garcia was a truly unique soloist, while the Grateful Dead was the only psychedelic band to survive past the fall of the San Francisco scene in the late sixties and successfully carry on the improvisational acid-rock format for another 25 years. That alone is a mighty impressive achievement.

Grateful Dead [on Warner Bros. except where noted], *The Grateful Dead* (1967), *Anthem for the Sun* (1968), *Aoxomoxoa* (1969), *Live Dead* (1970•), *Workingman's Dead* (1970), *Vintage Dead* (Sunflower, 1970•), *American Beauty* (1970), *Historic Dead* (Sunflower, 1971•), *The Grateful Dead* (1971•), *Europe '72* (1972•), *History of the Grateful Dead, Vol. 1, Bear's Choice* (1973•), *Wake of the Flood* (Grateful Dead, 1973), *The Best Of/Skeletons from the Closet* (1974), *Grateful Dead from the Mars Hotel* (Grateful Dead, 1974), *Blues for Allah* (Grateful Dead, 1975), *Steal Your Face* (Grateful Dead, 1976•), *Terrapin Station* (Arista, 1977), *What a Long Strange Trip It's Been* (1977), *Shakedown Street* (Arista, 1978), *Go to Heaven* (Arista, 1980), *Reckoning* (Arista, 1981•), *Dead Set* (Arista, 1981•), *In the Dark* (Arista, 1987), *Dylan and the Dead* (Columbia, 1989•), *Built to Last* (Arista, 1989), *Without a Net* (1990•), *One from the Vault* (Grateful Dead, 1991•), *Two from the Vault* (Grateful Dead, 1992•). **Jerry Garcia**, *Garcia* (Warner Bros., 1972), *Reflections* (Round, 1976), *Cats under the Stars* (Arista, 1978), *Run for the Roses* (Arista, 1982). **Howard Wales and Jerry Garcia**, *Hooteroll?* (Douglas, 1971). **Jerry Garcia Band**, *Jerry Garcia Band* (Arista, 1991•). **Bob Weir**, *Ace* (Warner Bros., 1972), *Heaven Help the Fool* (Arista, 1978). **Bobby & the Midnites**, *Bobby & The Midnites* (Arista, 1981), *Where the Beat Meets the Street* (Columbia, 1984). **Kingfish**, *Kingfish* (Round, 1976), *Live 'n' Kickin'* (Jet, 1977•), *Live in '85* (Relix, 1985•). **Seastones**, *Seastones* (Round, c. 1975).

Recordings featuring Jerry Garcia: **Jefferson Airplane**, *Surrealistic Pillow* (RCA, 1967). **Crosby, Stills, Nash & Young**, *Deja Vu* (Atlantic, 1970). **Jefferson Starship**, *Blows against the Empire* (RCA, 1970). **Paul Kantner & Grace Slick**, *Sunfighter* (Grunt, 1971). **Mickey Hart**, *Rolling Thunder* (Warner Bros., 1972). **Paul Kantner, Grace Slick, and David Freiberg**, *Baron Von Tollbooth & the Chrome Nun* (Grunt, 1973). **Merl Saunders** [on Fantasy], *Live at Keystone* (1972•), *Fire Up* (1973). **Old and in the Way**, *Old and in the Way* (Round, 1975•). **Robert Hunter**, *Liberty* (Relix, n/a), *Promontory Rider* (Relix, 1982). **Matt Kelly**, *A Wing and a Prayer* (Relix, n/a). **New Riders of the Purple Sage**, *New Riders of the Purple Sage* (Columbia, 1971), *Before Time Began* (Relix, 1976).

Cream

Eric Clapton

Born: *March 30, 1945, in Ripley, Surrey, England*
Main Guitars: *'61 Gibson Les Paul/SG (painted by The Fool), ES-335, '59 Les Paul*

During Eric Clapton's last few months in the Bluesbreakers (♦), John Mayall had at one point temporarily replaced his regular bassist (John McVie, of Fleetwood Mac fame) with Jack Bruce, who had just left the Graham Bond Organization. Clapton and Bruce played together in the Bluesbreakers for several months, but eventually Bruce went off to play bass for Manfred Mann, who had scored a huge hit in 1964 with "Do Wah Diddy Diddy." Soon after, Clapton was approached by Ginger Baker, the Graham Bond Organization's powerhouse drummer, who asked him to form a band. Clapton agreed, but only on the condition that Bruce—who had so impressed him in the Bluesbreakers—would play bass. When the three got together for a jam at Baker's house, they were so inspired by the musical chemistry between them that the decision to form a group was made right on the spot.

Within a short time they had dubbed themselves Cream; since Clapton, Bruce, and Baker were regarded as the best musicians in England, their name referred to the notion that they were the "cream of the crop," so to speak (Clapton often refers to the band as *The* Cream"). By the end of 1966 they had already released several singles, including "I Feel Free," and their debut album, *Fresh Cream*. Amidst the churning blues and jazz-influenced rhythms of Jack Bruce and Ginger Baker, Clapton's huge, Marshall amp-powered sound on *Fresh Cream* was a revelation to guitar fans in England and in the U.S. when it was released stateside in the spring of 1967. On tracks like "I'm So Glad" and "Rollin' and Tumblin'," Clapton played blues-rock guitar with a forcefulness and freedom never before heard in rock 'n' roll.

One element behind Clapton's adventurous new style was the intense energy of the Bruce-Baker rhythm section. With their combined fury behind him, Clapton improvised freely over the changes, applying the blues guitar style he'd mastered in the Bluesbreakers in this newfound outlet for rock 'n' roll jamming. Without the restrictions of the 12-bar blues, Clapton's playing was faster, louder, and more daring than almost anything his peers were doing at the time. His popularity grew at an alarming rate, and Eric Clapton quickly became an international rock superstar.

By Cream's second album, *Disraeli Gears*, the guitarist's lead work had moved even further towards psychedelia, though as always, his solos remained rooted in the blues. As a replacement for his stolen '59 Les Paul, he began using his famous Gibson Les Paul/SG (painted by two artists known collectively as The Fool and later owned by pop wizard Todd Rundgren). Clapton's playing was also becoming flashier, with extensive use of echo, heavy fuzz, and the newly introduced wah wah pedal. Much of the moti-

vation behind Clapton's newly developed guitar sound was the arrival of Jimi Hendrix between the recording of *Fresh Cream* and *Disraeli Gears*. Besides influencing thousands of players around the world, Hendrix's wild, effects-ridden blues guitar had a huge impact on Clapton's style. Another influence was the late-sixties work of blues picker Albert King on the Stax label (notably his album *Born under a Bad Sign*). *Gears* also produced Cream's first stateside hit single, "Sunshine of Your Love," featuring a killer low-register guitar break (inspired by Hendrix and beginning with a quote from the standard "Blue Moon"), as well as Clapton's sharing of vocal duties with Jack Bruce, revealing his increasing talent as a singer and frontman. Another change for Clapton came in the fashion department, where he updated his prim British look with a Dylanesque mop of curly hair and the *de rigueur* "Summer of Love" outfit of brilliantly colored fabrics and ceramic love beads. With the radical new sound and image he presented on *Disraeli Gears*, Clapton became the most popular rock guitarist of his day, rivaled only by his friend Jimi Hendrix.

There was yet another side to Clapton and Cream. In the studio Cream may have played concise, well-arranged pop tunes, but onstage they were almost an entirely different band. When Cream hit U.S. clubs and concert halls in late summer 1967, they showed the Americans that the psychedelic rockers in San Francisco were mere neophytes when it came to jamming, though Cream reportedly arrived at this by default: when they ran out of tunes, audiences would inevitably shout out "Just play!," forcing them to jam over their material. As a result, Clapton, Bruce, and Baker would often take one of their album tunes and expand it to over 20 minutes long, with all three members improvising simultaneously. They even crossed that tenuous bridge between rock 'n' roll and free-form jazz. Many listeners were baffled by this new sound, but many more went to see the action for themselves. The fans and critics raved, and it wasn't long until Cream was recognized as one of the best live bands in the world.

To prove this to everyone who had missed them on tour, Cream's next effort was a half live/half studio album in 1968, called *Wheels of Fire*. Besides the great studio tracks—including the hit "White Room" and "Sitting on Top of the World" (also recorded the previous year on the Grateful Dead's debut set)—the live cut "Crossroads" became a Clapton milestone. Written by Delta blues legend Robert Johnson as "Crossroads Blues," this electrified version of "Crossroads" contains two magnificent Clapton breaks, which helped establish the formula of high volume plus blues scales as the soloing format of the future and solidified Clapton's position at the forefront of rock guitar. In fact, Clapton's berserk second lead to "Crossroads" is widely considered to be his finest solo with Cream.

Besides the mass adulation they received, Cream also had to deal with grueling concert tours and recording sessions, as well as a steady dose of inflated egos, hyped media coverage, drug use, and internal quarrels (stemming largely from Baker's and Bruce's well-publicized disputes). At this frantic pace it was inevitable that the band would eventually burn out. The final straw came in May

1968, when an editorial in *Rolling Stone* magazine incisively criticized the band's lack of depth and musical development. Personally disillusioned by this heated criticism and other pressures of rock stardom, Clapton announced that Cream would break up that fall. A farewell tour and final album ensued (*Goodbye*), and Cream played their final concert on November 26, 1968, at the Royal Albert Hall in London. It was the end of rock 'n' roll's first—and arguably best—"supergroup," as well as the beginning of a whole new career for Eric Clapton (◗).

Cream [on Atco except where noted], *Fresh Cream* (1967, 1966 in U.K.), *Disraeli Gears* (1967), *Wheels of Fire* (1968•), *Goodbye* (1969), *Live Cream* (1970•), *Live Cream, Vol. 2* (1972•), *The Very Best of Cream* (Polydor, 1983). **Eric Clapton,** *The Cream of Eric Clapton* (A&M, 1995).

Jefferson Airplane

Jorma Kaukonen

B o r n : *December 23, 1940, in Washington, D.C.*
M a i n   G u i t a r : *Gibson reverse Firebird*

Paul Kantner

B o r n : *March 12, 1942, in San Francisco*

Among the crucial psychedelic bands to come out of the blossoming San Francisco rock 'n' roll scene during the late sixties was the Jefferson Airplane. Whereas the Grateful Dead played a somewhat softer style of psychedelic rock and stressed the laid-back motto "Whatever turns you on," the Airplane's peak-era music was closer to heavy rock, with a blend of socially conscious protest themes and aggressive riffing. Behind the lyrics of drugs, free love, and political activism, ex-folk guitarist Jorma

(pronounced *Yorma*) Kaukonen added screechy solos and fuzz chords on nearly all of the Airplane's early recordings and concert appearances.

Born and raised in Washington, D.C., Kaukonen was first drawn to bluegrass, which he began playing in clubs around the capital. He had been greatly inspired by country blues guitarists such as the Reverend Gary Davis and Blind Lemon Jefferson, as well as by the seminal rock playing of Mike Bloomfield, Eric Clapton, and Pete Townshend. In his late teens he even formed a band with future Airplane bassist Jack Casady, who played lead guitar at the time, while Kaukonen himself handled acoustic rhythm. After a couple of years at college, Kaukonen wound up in San Francisco, jamming with various members of the folk community there, including rhythm guitarist Paul Kantner. When Kantner eventually decided to put together a folk rock group with singer Marty Balin and a few others, he asked Kaukonen to join as lead guitarist. Kaukonen in turn knew Jack Casady (who was by then playing bass), and in a short time the Jefferson Airplane was born.

By the beginning of 1966 the Airplane had signed with RCA (one of the first San Francisco groups to sign with a major label), and within a few months their folky first album, The *Jefferson Airplane Takes Off*, was released. By their harder-edged second set, *Surrealistic Pillow*, the group had replaced singer Signe Anderson with the great Grace Slick, and then the Jefferson Airplane really did take off. It was mid 1967, and both the fabled "Summer of Love" and psychedelic San Francisco were at their absolute zenith. The Airplane's first single from the album was a hard-edged love anthem called "Somebody to Love," and it soon became a major hit across the nation, incisively capturing the spirit of the times. "Somebody to Love" also shows off Kaukonen's developing electric style, stiff string bends, and heavy use of reverb and distortion effects. At the time, this was cutting-edge rock guitar. Another important track on the album is the acoustic instrumental "Embryonic Journey," the first song Kaukonen ever wrote and one of the earliest examples of a rock player using dropped-D

Jefferson Airplane: Marty Balin, Jack Casady, Grace Slick, Jorma Kaukonen, Paul Kantner, Spencer Dryden

tuning. Inspired by British folk players like Bert Jansch and John Renbourn, this song also prophesies Kaukonen's later acoustic work with Hot Tuna.

On the band's critically acclaimed *Crown of Creation* (1968), Kaukonen further revealed his heavier inclinations—for example, in the Hendrix-like wah-wah breaks of "If You Feel." In the Airplane's version of the Crosby, Stills & Nash song "Wooden Ships" (from the Airplane's 1969 LP *Volunteers*), Kaukonen cleverly uses his guitar as a dramatic melodic counterpoint to the vocal harmonies of Kantner, Balin, and Slick, weaving in and out of their singing with linear phrases and impassioned solos.

In 1970 Kaukonen and Casady formed Hot Tuna, a group that was designed to fill in the gaps when the Airplane wasn't in the studio or on tour. Starting out as just an acoustic duo, Hot Tuna expanded into a heavy blues-rock outfit with the addition of a drummer and, for a while, electric violinist Papa John Creach. While specializing in hard rock 'n' roll that featured Kaukonen's blazing guitar solos, Hot Tuna also played a large number of tunes showcasing the guitarist's extraordinary acoustic finger-style talents. The best of these include "Hesitation Blues," "Keep on Truckin'," and the daring instrumental "Water Song," which interestingly contrasts acoustic fingerpicking with Casady's thunderous fuzz-bass lines. (In a similar vein is the beautiful acoustic guitar ballad "Genesis," from Kaukonen's 1973 solo album *Quah*.) Best of all, the band is still going strong today.

Though Hot Tuna may be where the bulk of Jorma Kaukonen's most proficient guitar playing lies, it is with the Jefferson Airplane that he made his most lasting contribution to rock guitar. In psychedelic San Francisco, and indeed, everywhere else the Jefferson Airplane played in the sixties (which included both Woodstock and the Rolling Stones' ill-fated Altamont concert), Kaukonen's brash fuzztone and wah-wah-inflected guitar work gave the Airplane much of its rock energy and made him one of the electric guitar standouts of the entire psychedelic era. Along with Jerry Garcia of the Dead, Jorma Kaukonen was central to the development of the psychedelic guitar sound and was also among the most impressive Bay Area guitarists of the time.

Jefferson Airplane [on RCA except where noted], *Jefferson Airplane Takes Off* (1966), *Surrealistic Pillow* (1967), *After Bathing at Baxter's* (1967), *Crown of Creation* (1968), *Bless Its Pointed Little Head* (1969•), *Volunteers* (1969), *The Worst of the Jefferson Airplane* (1970), *Bark* (Grunt, 1971), *Long John Silver* (Grunt, 1972), *Thirty Seconds Over Winterland* (Grunt, 1973•), *Early Flight* (Grunt/RCA, 1974), *Flight Log 1966–1976* (Grunt, 1977), *2400 Fulton Street* (1987), *Jefferson Airplane* (Epic, 1989). **Hot Tuna,** *Hot Tuna* (RCA, 1970•), *First Pull up Then Pull Down* (RCA, 1971•), *Burgers* (Grunt, 1972), *The Phosphorescent Rat* (Grunt, 1974), *America's Choice* (Grunt, 1975), *Yellow Fever* (Grunt, 1975), *Hoppkorv* (Grunt, 1976), *Double Dose* (Grunt, 1978•), *Finyl Vinyl* (Grunt, c. 1979), *Pair a Dice Found* (Epic, 1991). **Jorma Kaukonen,** *Quah* (Grunt, 1973), *Jorma* (RCA, 1978), *Barbeque King* (RCA, 1980), *Too Hot to Handle* (Relix, 1985), *Magic* (Relix, 1985•).

Recordings featuring Jorma Kaukonen: **Various Artists,** *Woodstock* (Cotillion, 1970•). **Various Artists,** *Woodstock Two* (Cotillion, 1971•). **David Crosby,** *If Only I Could Remember My Name* (Atlantic, 1971). **Paul Kantner & Grace Slick,** *Sunfighter* (Grunt, 1971). **Paul Kantner, Grace Slick, and David Freiberg,** *Baron Von Tollbooth & the Chrome Nun* (Grunt, 1973). **Papa John Creach,** *Papa John Creach* (Grunt, 1971), *Filthy* (Grunt, c. 1972). **Robert Hunter,** *Amagamalin St.* (Relix, c. 1987).

Moby Grape

Jerry Miller
B o r n : *Tacoma, Washington*
M a i n   G u i t a r : *Gibson L-5*

Skip Spence
B o r n : *Windsor, Ontario*
M a i n   G u i t a r s : *Gibson ES-355, Martin electric*

Peter Lewis
B o r n : *Los Angeles*

After playing drums with the Jefferson Airplane for one album, guitarist Skip Spence left the band to form Moby Grape towards the end of 1966. Besides their unusual name, Moby Grape had another unique attribute—*three* guitarists: rhythm players Spence and Peter Lewis, and leadman Jerry Miller, formerly of a Seattle garage-rock band called the Frantics. Bypassing the rambling jam sessions common to most psychedelic rock groups, the Grape instead played tight, power-packed songs that rivaled even the Steve Miller Band's pointed sense of efficient energy and timing. With well-honed vocal harmonies, intelligent songwriting, and the triple guitar threat of Spence, Lewis, and Miller, Moby Grape was an instant hit with both fans and critics.

Through a series of appearances at the Fillmore, the Avalon, and other Bay Area dance halls, Moby Grape acquired a sizable cult following and, in 1967, signed a record deal with Columbia. Their first album, *Moby Grape* (1967), was released during the height of the "Summer of Love" and contained plenty of top-form guitar playing from Spence, Lewis, and Miller. On the popular "Changes," Spence and Lewis laid down the churning rhythm for Miller, who took off with biting blues solos and spot licks around the vocals. "Hey Grandma" and "Indifference" are more examples of the Grape's triple guitar formula, demonstrating Miller's strength as a high-powered blues soloist. Unfortunately, someone at Columbia with no marketing sense decided to capitalize on the Grape's local popularity and released 10 singles off the album—all at once. Each of them flopped, and the album stalled at #24 on the charts.

After that fiasco Moby Grape's days in the limelight were numbered. Following a second album in 1968, *Wow/Grape Jam* (which had more punchy guitar parts on tunes like "Can't Be So Bad" and "Miller's Blues" and had a guest appearance by Mike Bloomfield), the quality of the band's albums dropped about as quickly as their record sales. The night of the big coming-out party for *Wow/Grape Jam* at the Avalon, two members of the band were caught *in flagrante delicto* with a pair of minors in the Marin County hills, eventually marking the band as untouchable by still-highly-conservative AM radio programmers. Several breakups and re-formations quickly followed, each one more watered down than the last, and by the early seventies, Moby Grape was all but a psychedelic flashback (sadly, Spence became a drug casualty and, at last report, was homeless). Despite their rapid descent into obscurity, Moby Grape was still one of the most exciting bands of the Summer of Love, and Jerry Miller was among the best rock soloists psychedelia had to offer.

Moby Grape [on Columbia except where noted], *Moby Grape* (1967), *Wow/Grape Jam* (1968), *Moby Grape '69* (1969), *Truly Fine Citizen* (1969), *20 Granite Creek* (Reprise, 1971), *Moby Grape* [set of six 12-inch singles] (San Francisco Sound, 1984), *The Legendary Grape* (Herman, 1990).

Quicksilver Messenger Service

John Cipollina

Born: *August 24, 1943, in Berkeley, California*
Died: *May 29, 1989*
Main Guitar: *Gibson SG*

Gary Duncan

Born: *September 4, 1946, in San Francisco*

Another leading group from the Bay Area was Quicksilver Messenger Service. Featuring lead guitarist John Cipollina, Quicksilver played letter-perfect acid rock, with long improvisational songs, mystical lyrics, and Cipollina's extended, raving solos in nearly every song. Originally a classical guitarist, Cipollina got turned on to rock 'n' roll, blues, and folk music in his mid teens and began listening to the guitar sounds of Link Wray, Mickey Baker, Leadbelly, Chet Atkins, and various classical artists. Soon he was gigging around San Francisco as a solo folksinger and eventually met up with Dino Valenti (who spent much of the band's heyday in jail over a drug bust) and several other folk musicians who later formed the Quicksilver Messenger Service.

Though Quicksilver's roots go back to 1965, it didn't land a major record contract until 1968, when it finally signed with Capitol. The band released its debut, *Quicksilver Messenger Service*, and followed it up a few months later with *Happy Trails* (1969). These two albums are widely considered Quicksilver's best efforts, and they contain many examples of Cipollina's dizzy acid-guitar playing, usually on a Gibson SG. Technically, Cipollina is perhaps the archetypal psychedelic player, largely because—like many of the other Bay Area pickers—he was an acoustic folkie who had switched to electric in the wake of the British Invasion and folk rock revolution. Not surprisingly, his playing was not as polished as contemporary British players who'd been playing electric blues for a while, namely Eric Clapton, Jeff Beck, and Peter Green.

Although Quicksilver's *Happy Trails* is hopelessly dated today, it does contain the best representation of Cipollina's flower-powered guitar approach. On the atmospheric "Calvary," it sounds as if Cipollina is at work writing the textbook of psychedelic guitar, as he pulls out murky harmonic minor runs, distorted blues licks, and feedback effects, all supported by second guitarist Gary Duncan's heavy wah-wah strums and power chording. In a numbing 25-minute version of Bo Diddley's "Who Do You Love," the guitarist whips out nearly every technique and effect known to rock guitarists at the time, including heavy distortion, feedback, tremolo, echo, and slide effects, as well as his novel jazz influences, whammy vibrato, and string-bending techniques.

After *Happy Trails*, Quicksilver released several more albums, but none matched the intensity of its first two efforts. In October 1970 Cipollina left the group to do session work and later formed a hard rock group called Copperhead. Quicksilver Messenger Service, meanwhile, floundered about for a few more years and eventually folded in mid 1972. After Copperhead's demise, Cipollina stayed out of the spotlight for many years until latching onto a local San Francisco act called the Dinosaurs (with Barry Melton of Country Joe & the Fish and Big Brother's Peter Albin) in the late eighties. Sadly, the guitarist passed away from a chronic illness before regaining any momentum with his career.

Quicksilver Messenger Service [on Capitol except where noted], *Quicksilver Messenger Service* (1968), *Happy Trails* (1969), *Shady Grove* (1969), *Just for Love* (1970), *What about Me* (1970), *Anthology* (1973), *Solid Silver* (1975), *Peace by Piece* (1986), *Sons of Mercury 1968–75* (Rhino, 1991•), *Shape Shifter* (Pymander, 1996). **Dinosaurs,** *Dinosaurs* (Relix, 1988).

Recordings featuring John Cipollina: **Robert Hunter,** *Amagamalin St.* (Relix, c. 1987). **Zero,** *Here Goes Nothing* (Relix, 1988).

The Doors

Robby Krieger

Born: *January 8, 1946, in Los Angeles*
Main Guitar: *Gibson SG*

About the time psychedelic acts like the Grateful Dead and the Jefferson Airplane were getting off the ground in San Francisco, another important rock band was in its formative stages several hundred miles to the south, in Los Angeles. Dubbing themselves the Doors, this group began playing the bar circuit around L.A., most frequently at the Whiskey-A-Go-Go. They were soon signed by a small folk label called Elektra, and in early 1967 their self-titled debut album was released. The record was immensely popular, and the single "Light My Fire" went to the top of the pop charts. The group's most obvious asset was frontman Jim Morrison, who ignited the Doors' music with his charismatic vocals and compelling lyrics. Instrumentally, the band packed just as much of a punch, especially with organist Ray Manzarek and inventive guitarist Robby Kreiger.

When the Doors broke big in 1967, Krieger was just 19 and had only been playing the guitar for three years. He had first picked up the instrument in high school and had been drawn to the sounds of flamenco guitar. His interest moved towards rock 'n' roll after he attended a Chuck Berry concert, and he purchased his first electric guitar, a Gibson SG. He joined a group called the Psychedelic Rangers, which included future Doors drummer John Densmore. Krieger then met keyboardist Ray Manzarek at a meditation class. Manzarek, in turn, had a great lead singer in his band: Jim Morrison. A few weeks later, the Doors were born.

Robby Krieger was not your typical rock guitarist, especially for the mid sixties. Instead of the usual pentatonic-based solos that almost all rock guitarists of the time were using, Krieger delved more into the melodic side of rock guitar, often playing in a style that bordered on jazz. The Doors' first hit, "Light My Fire" (written by Krieger), shows the guitarist's impressive flamenco-inspired fingerstyle chordings as well as his strong melodic sensibility in the legato-filled solo. Other noteworthy Doors tunes that feature Krieger's melodic lead style are "Summer's Almost Gone" (from *Waiting for the Sun*) and "Ship of Fools" (from *Morrison Hotel*). Another interesting track is "Spanish Caravan," which has a strong bass-string break after the flamenco guitar intro.

The Doors' promising career was cut short in 1971 when Morrison died in Paris under mysterious circumstances. During the rest of the 1970s Robby Krieger cut a few more albums with the remaining members of the group before striking out on his own with the Butts Band, which recorded two albums between 1973 and 1975. He has also released several solo albums and played small clubs on the West Coast. Although more than two decades have passed since Morrison's death, the Doors remain as popular today as they ever were (if not more so, thanks to Oliver Stone's big-budget film on the band), and Robby Krieger's creative guitar work is still reaching the ears of countless guitarists.

The Doors [on Elektra], *The Doors* (1967), *Strange Days* (1967), *Waiting for the Sun* (1968), *The Soft Parade* (1969), *Morrison Hotel* (1970), *Absolutely Live* (1970•), *13* (1971), *L.A. Woman* (1971), *Other Voices* (1971), *Weird Scenes inside the Gold Mine* (1972), *Full Circle* (1972), *An American Prayer* (1978), *The Doors' Greatest Hits* (1980), *Alive, She Cried* (1983•). **The Butts Band** [on Blue Thumb], *The Butts Band* (1974), *Hear and Now* (1975). **Robby Krieger,** *Robby Krieger and Friends* (Blue Note, 1977), *Versions* (Passport, 1982), *No Habla* (IRS, 1989).

Recordings featuring Robby Krieger: **Blue Öyster Cult,** *Extraterrestrial Live* (Columbia, 1982•). **Various Artists,** *Guitar Speak* (IRS, 1989), *Night of the Guitar Live!* (IRS, 1989•).

Steve Miller

Born: *October 5, 1943, in Milwaukee, Wisconsin*
Main Guitars: *Fender Stratocaster (lefty model played right-handed), Gibson Barney Kessel Custom, Ibanez Iceman and Artist*

One of the most unusual guitarists of the psychedelic era was Steve Miller, leader of the Steve Miller Band. Unlike most of his peers—who were defining late-sixties guitar with long, fuzztone-riddled guitar improvisations—Miller gained a reputation for playing short solos and sometimes even no solos at all. Instead, he filled in the gaps with plenty of crisp rhythm guitar work. As a group, the Steve Miller Band was not the usual psychedelic outfit, either. Rather than the stock 30-minute-plus jam sessions that were so prevalent in acid rock, the Miller band's music often consisted of catchy, well-planned pop songs that stand out for their compact ensemble playing and fine studio techniques as well as for Miller's smart guitarmanship.

Steve Miller started to play the guitar at the age of four with a six-string training few can boast of. Miller's father, an avid music enthusiast, was friends with several legends of the guitar, among them pop guitar duo Les Paul and Mary Ford, Texas blues great T-Bone Walker, and jazzman Tal Farlow. Mary Ford showed Miller his first chords, and other guitarists, especially T-Bone Walker, were to have a lasting impression on the youngster's developing guitar style. After playing guitar professionally in his teenage and college years (occasionally with school chum Boz Scaggs), Miller headed for Chicago, where he formed the Goldberg/Miller Blues Band with keyboardist Barry Goldberg, later of the Electric Flag. But it wasn't long until he was lured to the thriving rock scene in San Francisco. Upon arriving in the City by the Bay, he assembled the Steve Miller Band and gained a substantial following with appearances at the Fillmore and Avalon dance halls (the Miller band even backed up Chuck Berry for a gig at the Fillmore, which later appeared as a Berry live album).

After signing with Capitol, the Steve Miller Band (with Boz Scaggs on rhythm guitar) finally hit the studio and produced a series of albums that remain among the best of psychedelic rock: *Children of the Future, Sailor, Brave New World*, and several others. More than just containing some clever psychedelic pop, these albums also made room for Miller's restrained but effective guitar playing. On "Going to Mexico" he reveals his blues influences during a distorted string-bending solo. In "Space Cowboy" he plays a lead break drenched with distortion, power chords, and a memorable bass-string riff, all reminiscent of Eric Clapton's guitar playing with Cream circa *Disraeli Gears*.

Though Miller was an important part of the psychedelic movement, he didn't achieve superstar status until his album *The Joker* topped the pop charts in 1973. Three years later he did it again with the hit album *Fly Like an Eagle*, followed in 1977 with another platinum-seller, *Book of Dreams*, and in 1983 with the hit *Abracadabra*. From his roots in the psychedelic sixties, Miller became one of the premier arena rock guitarists of the 1970s and is still recording successfully today.

Steve Miller Band [on Capitol except where noted] *Children of the Future* (1968), *Sailor* (1968), *Brave New World* (1969), *Your Saving Grace* (1969), *Number 5* (1970), *Rock Love* (1971), *Recall the Beginning...A Journey from Eden* (1972), *Anthology* (1973), *The Joker* (1973), *Fly Like an Eagle* (1976), *Book of Dreams* (1977), *Greatest Hits 1974–1978* (1978), *Circle of Love* (1981),

Abracadabra (1982), *Steve Miller Band—Live!* (1983•), *Italian X-Rays* (1984), *Living in the 20th Century* (1986), *Born 2 B Blue* (1988), *Wide River* (Polydor, 1993).

Recordings featuring Steve Miller: **Chuck Berry,** *St. Louie to Frisco to Memphis* (Mercury, 1972•).

Creedence Clearwater Revival

John Fogerty

B o r n : *May 28, 1945, in Berkeley, California*
M a i n   G u i t a r s : *Rickenbacker 325 with Bigsby vibrato, Gibson Les Paul*

Tom Fogerty

B o r n : *November 9, 1941, in Berkeley, California*
D i e d : *September 6, 1990, in Scottsdale, Arizona*
M a i n   G u i t a r : *Rickenbacker hollowbody*

Although Creedence Clearwater Revival emerged from the same San Francisco rock scene that spawned the Grateful Dead and the Jefferson Airplane, they actually had little to do with psychedelic rock. While bands like the Dead and Quicksilver Messenger Service were jamming away with kaleidoscopic light shows, half-hour guitar solos, and mystical lyrics, Creedence played radio-friendly three-minute pop songs with catchy hooks and a clean rock 'n' roll beat. No dense jams, no wild outfits—just hip, no-frills rock 'n' roll that paid reverent tribute to rockabilly, the Memphis sound, country, R&B, and early rock 'n' roll. Led by the genius of John Fogerty, the group's lead guitarist, vocalist, and songwriter, Creedence took America by storm beginning in 1969. From then until 1972 they dominated the AM airwaves with a succession of singles that hit gold virtually every time and, along the way, created a lasting legacy of great rock 'n' roll.

The core of Creedence's "swamp rock" sound was John Fogerty's powerful voice, backed up by the compelling guitars of Fogerty and his brother Tom, who played rhythm. While Creedence isn't particularly known as a "guitar band," the quality of John and Tom Fogerty's guitar playing shouldn't be undervalued by any means. John Fogerty's expressive lead guitar drew heavily on rockabilly players like Scotty Moore and James Burton, as well as other early rock 'n' roll influences. The album *Bayou Country* is a superb primer on John Fogerty's lead playing, especially for his Steve Cropper-like chordal solo on "Proud Mary" and contrasting fuzztoned lead in "Keep on Chooglin'." Tracks like these make John Fogerty's versatility as lead guitarist readily apparent.

Tom Fogerty left the band in 1970, and the group continued on as a threesome. Creedence broke up for good in 1972 due to internal friction and management problems. John Fogerty released a solo album the following year under the name *Blue Ridge Rangers* and another one in 1975 called simply *John Fogerty*; neither was a big seller. However, after a 10-year hiatus,

Fogerty returned to rock 'n' roll in 1985 with a fine album called *Centerfield* that showed his voice, songwriting, and guitar playing were just as good as ever (he also played all the instruments). Like all talented shooting-star bands (such as the original Byrds, Cream, the Electric Flag, Blind Faith), it's not surprising that Creedence Clearwater Revival burned out after only a few years on top. What remains from those days is a collection of music that is as memorable for its restraint, simplicity, and reverence as for its lively rock 'n' roll energy.

Creedence Clearwater Revival [on Fantasy], *Creedence Clearwater Revival* (1968), *Bayou Country* (1969), *Green River* (1969), *Willie and the Poor Boys* (1969), *Cosmo's Factory* (1970), *Mardi Gras* (1971), *Creedence Gold* (1972), *More Creedence Gold* (1973), *Live in Europe* (1973•), *The Concert* (1980•). **John Fogerty,** *Blue Ridge Rangers* (Fantasy, 1973), *John Fogerty* (Asylum, 1975), *Centerfield* (Warner Bros., 1985), *Eye of the Zombie* (Warner Bros., 1986). **Tom Fogerty,** *Tom Fogerty* (Fantasy, 1972).

Recordings featuring John Fogerty: **Duane Eddy,** *Duane Eddy* (Capitol, 1987).

Big Brother & the Holding Company

Sam Andrew

B o r n : *December 18, 1941, in Taft, California*
M a i n   G u i t a r s : *Gibson SG and Les Paul Junior*

James Gurley

B o r n : *c. 1941, in Detroit*
M a i n   G u i t a r : *Gibson SG*

Behind Janis Joplin's passionate, leonine vocals, the lead guitars of Sam Andrew and James Gurley personified the sound of electric psychedelia in Big Brother & the Holding Company. On the album *Cheap Thrills*, Andrew took lead duties for the hit "Piece of My Heart" with a wrenching distortion- and feedback-laden break, while on the band's rendition of Big Mama Thornton's "Ball and Chain," Gurley's solos are fully immersed in heavy fuzztone and uncontrollable amplifier feedback—true trademarks of that era. Though Joplin eventually left the group for a solo career backed by more polished ensembles, none of those groups matched the original psychedelic spirit and energy produced by Big Brother & the Holding Company or their guitarists. This is Aquarian guitar rock at its prime.

Big Brother & the Holding Company [on Columbia except where noted], *Big Brother & the Holding Company* (Mainstream, 1967), *Cheap Thrills* (1968•), *Be a Brother* (1970), *How Hard It Is* (1971). **Janis Joplin** [on Columbia], *I Got Them Ol' Kozmic Blues Again Mama!* (1969), *Joplin in Concert* (1972•), *Janis Joplin's Greatest Hits* (1973), *Janis* (1975), *Farewell Song* (1982).

CHAPTER NINE

Hard Rock and Heavy Metal

Birth of a Behemoth

It began with Led Zeppelin's first album in January 1969. There had been great "heavy" bands before—Cream, the Jimi Hendrix Experience, the Jeff Beck Group—but Zeppelin violently stirred a concoction of pounding drums, shrill vocals, and sledgehammer guitar riffs into what is now called heavy metal. Aside from stirring the white suburban masses into hysteria, metal also codified the notion of the guitar hero, which had been developed earlier by Clapton, Beck, and Hendrix. And after Jimmy Page and Led Zep pounced on the pavement, guitarists ruled the rock landscape like a pack of hungry Tyrannosauruses—that is, until an obscure Seattle trio called Nirvana unceremoniously beheaded the glittering guitar god with their 1991 manifesto "Smells Like Teen Spirit." Still, for the roughly 22-year span in between, the guitar hero was undeniably king of the realm.

Among the first guitar heroes were such British pickers as Eric Clapton, Jeff Beck, and Jimmy Page, each of whom specialized in the kind of long, fuzztone-ridden solos that drove their mostly teenage-white-male fans into fist-pumping frenzies. In America, many fans were also hip to the blues-rock improvisations of Mike Bloomfield and, of course, the king of sixties rock guitar, Jimi Hendrix. By the beginning of the seventies, metal fans were pouring out of the woodwork to hear near-hard rockers like Vanilla Fudge, Mountain, Grand Funk, Deep Purple, Steppenwolf, Black Pearl, Cactus, Uriah Heep, the Frost, Black Sabbath, Status Quo, Humble Pie, and a slew of others. For better or worse, the age of metal had arrived.

Despite the sudden appearance and success of heavy metal, its roots actually go back to the early years of rock 'n' roll. There is a definite chain of guitarists that led to the metal explosion c. 1968–69. Among the first "heavy" rock guitarists were Link Wray, whose distorted guitar appeared on a few instrumental hits in the late fifties, and Paul Burlison, the rock 'n' roll wild man whose octave-styled rockabilly solos fired up recordings by Johnny Burnette and the Rock 'N Roll Trio. By 1964, two more guitarists upped the ante of "heavy rock guitar." Lonnie Mack put out the hits "Memphis" and "Wham" in 1963, becoming the first rock guitarist to combine mature blues guitar technique and phrasing with the rhythmic focus of fifties rock playing. The following year, lead guitarist Dave Davies was riding high on the pop charts with the Kinks and their hits "You Really Got Me" and "All Day and All of the Night," both of which had proto-metal leads.

In 1965 the Who's single "My Generation" came out, and guitarist Pete Townshend set new standards for rock guitar with his innovative power chording and intentional use of volume-induced amplifier feedback (not to mention John Entwistle's heavy leads...on *bass*). In the same year, the Rolling Stones recorded "Satisfaction," one of the first hit singles to utilize the sound of a distorted guitar—with Keith Richards' memorable fuzztone hook. The Beatles also hinted at heavier things to come with guitar-based rockers like "Paperback Writer" and "Taxman."

Some of the greatest heavy rock guitar innovation of the mid sixties took place in the Yardbirds, first with Eric Clapton's rapid ascension, and then with the fuzztone and feedback mannerisms of Jeff Beck and Jimmy Page. Clapton also took blues-rock guitar to new heights in his seminal work with John Mayall's Bluesbreakers during 1965–66.

In 1966 Cream was born, and within two years Eric Clapton's famed blues-fueled solos with the power trio had convinced the world that *he* was the sound of rock guitar future. The march towards metal took another huge step forward the following year when Jimi Hendrix blew all of his competition off the stage at the Monterey Pop Festival. At the same time, he redefined rock

Jimmy Page

guitar with massive amounts of distortion and volume, radical technique, and a voracious use of studio effects. In 1968 the legendary Jeff Beck Group released *Truth*, an album that contained the final blueprints for heavy metal guitar. Ex-Yardbird Jimmy Page was close behind, and when the first Led Zeppelin album came out in January 1969, heavy metal was born at last.

The common thread for these and, in fact, all heavy metal guitarists past and present is *distortion*, i.e., the sound of an electric guitar being sonically contorted into a fuzzy, high-volume crunch (electronics enthusiasts can also wax philosophic on how distortion takes a guitar's round-wave "clean" tone and shapes it into a square-wave "distorted" tone). With this sound, metal guitarists are able to produce sustained string bends, piercing harmonics, huge power chords, and many other effects—a far cry from the clean "twang" of earlier rock players.

In the early days of metal, guitarists didn't have to be good—just loud 'n' heavy. Many pre-metal guitarists in 1968 fit that bill perfectly, like Leigh Stephens of Blue Cheer, a power trio that briefly hit it big in 1968 with a molten version of Eddie Cochran's "Summertime Blues" (from *Vinebus Eruptum*), or Erik Brann of Iron Butterfly, a band that scored with the 17-minute dirge "In-A-Gadda-Da-Vida." But with the simultaneous and far more proficient guitar exploits of Hendrix, Clapton, Beck, and Page, quality soon became as important as quantity. Before long, polished technique and original style became decisive factors in the grading and popularity of metal guitar heroes. The formula of *flash*, *fire*, and *fast chops* soon became the norm for heavy metal guitarists everywhere. And while metal guitar has often been criticized (rightfully at times) for the inflated egos, ear-splitting solos, and theoretical ignorance of its players, it has still produced some of the greatest guitarists known to rock 'n' roll, as well as some of its absolutely most exhilarating music.

Led Zeppelin

Jimmy Page

Born: *January 9, 1944, in Heston, England*
Main Guitars: *Gibson Les Paul Standard and ES-1275 doubleneck, Fender Telecaster*

To many rock fans, Led Zeppelin represents the ultimate in heavy metal, while others argue that they weren't a metal band at all, owing to their fondness for acoustic and Third World textures. No matter which way the argument falls, Led Zep still put the *heavy* in heavy rock 'n' roll.

Formed in 1968 by ex-Yardbirds (♪) guitarist Jimmy Page, Led Zeppelin learned and assimilated the heavy rock lessons of the Yardbirds, John Mayall's Bluesbreakers, Cream, Jimi Hendrix, and the Jeff Beck Group with unerring precision. The band went on to become one of the most popular rock acts of all time. Zeppelin's primary formula for hard rock was simple but devas-

tatingly effective: in the rhythm section, a massive low end was alchemized by bassist/keyboardist John Paul Jones and drummer John Bonham, whose kit was so loud on record that it often sounded like he used baseball bats instead of drumsticks. Page controlled the sonic midsection with towering structures of multitracked guitars and torrid solos, and on top of it all, vocalist Robert Plant pierced through the heavy mix with a treble scream that few could ever forget. Like all great bands, the members of Zeppelin had a magic chemistry that made the music work on every level.

Background. Page had played guitar since being given an acoustic when he was about 15. Directly inspired by Elvis' "Baby, Let's Play House," he soon began playing blues tunes in bands and pickup groups throughout England with other interested teenagers, including Jeff Beck. Ultimately, his poor health (continual bouts of fatigue and mononucleosis) led him into the safe confines of the studio and away from the rigors of the road and stage. By 1964 he had broken into the London studio scene and quickly became a top session guitarist, playing on records by the Who, Donovan, the Rolling Stones, and other popular British artists. When Clapton left the Yardbirds, Page was approached to replace him, but was reluctant to give up his lucrative studio career. Instead, he recommended Jeff Beck for the slot, and the Yardbirds carried on.

Page reconsidered the offer when the Yardbirds asked him yet again to join the band, this time to replace bass player Paul Samwell-Smith. Tiring of studio life, he joined the Yardbirds in June 1966 as their bassist. Later he shared guitar duties with Beck, until Beck left the band at the end of that year. Page remained with the Yardbirds until July 1968, when they finally broke up for good. Shortly thereafter, Page showed up on Joe Cocker's seminal album *With a Little Help from My Friends* and then set about to form another group, tentatively to be called the New Yardbirds (the name was chosen to fulfill contractual obligations). After snatching up John Paul Jones from the session scene, he enlisted Robert Plant (then singing for a Birmingham-based group called Hobbstweedle) and Plant's drummer friend John Bonham. By the end of the summer the new lineup was complete. In September 1968 Page, Plant, Jones, and Bonham toured Scandinavia as the New Yardbirds, but by the time they returned to London they were calling themselves Led Zeppelin (taken from a name coined by Who drummer Keith Moon, who during the "Beck's Bolero" session mocked that a supergroup featuring Beck, Page, Jones, and Moon would probably go over with the public like a "lead zeppelin").

Recordings. When their debut album, *Led Zeppelin*, was released in January 1969 (the result of a reportedly huge record deal with Atlantic Records), guitar fans got a whopping dose of Page's metallish playing firsthand. From the fast blues-scale runs of "Communication Breakdown" to the echo-enhanced slide work on their oft-criticized version of "You Shook Me" (it was covered just a few months before by the Jeff Beck Group on *Truth*), on to their soon-to-be concert classic "Dazed and

Confused"—which featured a Hendrix-like use of studio techniques and Page's famed violin-bowed guitar break—this record proved to be a critical influence on the coming hordes of young metal guitarists. Ironically, although Page would soon help standardize the setup of Gibson Les Paul with Marshall amp among rising players, he cut this album on a Fender Telecaster and a Vox AC30 amp, with a Sola-Sound fuzzbox. To boot, the record was cut in a mere 30 hours of studio time.

By the time *Led Zeppelin II* came out in October 1969, Page had moved up to using Marshall 100-watt stacks and his trademark 1958 Gibson Les Paul Standard. With this record Page also secured his place along with Clapton, Beck, and Hendrix as one of the best heavy rock players of the time. Though the entire record is brimming with Page's ingenious guitar forays, just two cuts alone, "Whole Lotta Love" (Zeppelin's first hit single) and "Heartbreaker," would have qualified him as a virtuoso. With its impossibly distorted intro, "Whole Lotta Love" became famous for its spacey midsection of studio tape experiments, string grinding effects, and the eerie howl of a theremin. The crack of Bonham's snare then signals the climax: a brutal burst of short, string-pushing guitar breaks from Page's Les Paul. "Heartbreaker" also features a bone-crunching intro riff, but it is Page's dramatic solo of fast hammer-ons and string bends that upstages everything, nearly including the song itself. Until Van Halen's "Eruption" of 1978, the "Heartbreaker" solo was the premier unaccompanied electric solo on the planet.

Despite Led Zeppelin's reputation for loud and heavy rock, the band's third record, aptly titled *Led Zeppelin III*, took a decisive turn away from straight-ahead heavy metal and into the distinctly lighter realm of folk music. On this 1970 recording, Page professed his strong penchant for the Celtic music of the British Isles, as well as for the smooth rock sounds emanating from America's West Coast, especially those of the Byrds, Joni Mitchell, and Crosby, Stills, Nash & Young. On *Zeppelin III* he also further displayed his considerable talent on acoustic guitar, which was only hinted at before on cuts like "Black Mountain Side" and "Babe, I'm Gonna Leave You" (both from the first album). Inspired by British folk guitarist Bert Jansch and other acoustic fingerstylists, he wove many ethnically derived guitar patterns into album tracks like "Friends" and "That's the Way," relying primarily on open tunings, like open C (low to high: C–G–C–G–C–E) for the record's exotic acoustic timbres. Another peak was "Since I've Been Loving You," an almost Wagnerian minor blues track highlighted by Page's mournful solos. Muddy Waters it wasn't.

Late in 1971 the band released its untitled fourth album, commonly referred to as *Led Zeppelin IV*, or *Zo-So* (in reference to Page's personal icon, displayed on the album's inner sleeve). Combining the metal thunder of the first two records with the folk excursions of the third, Led Zeppelin found their perfect rock 'n' roll niche on the fourth album. The disc opens with two rockers: "Black Dog," featuring a berserk multitracked riff, and "Rock and Roll," a boogie tribute to the rock 'n' roll sounds of

the fifties, not to mention to Page's rockabilly guitar heroes like Scotty Moore, James Burton, and Cliff Gallup.

The record's centerpiece, undeniably, is the rock opus "Stairway to Heaven." The song begins in ballad form with gentle acoustic guitar and harmonized recorder filling the background behind Robert Plant's mystical lyrics. Like Ravel's "Bolero," the song is structured to rise slowly in dramatic tension with subtle increases in instrumentation and volume, with the addition of drums, Mellotron, bass, and Page's ringing electric 12-string guitar. Finally, a shimmering open D chord breaks through the melody, ushering in Page's guitar solo. Cut in one take on a Fender Telecaster plugged into a Supro amp, it finds Page ripping out a succession of blues runs and melodic phrases, with sighing slide overdubs, in a performance rarely matched for sheer emotion, melody, and raw energy. A final melee of power chords and unison string bends quickly ensues, leading to Plant's graceful vocal finale. It is a great moment in rock 'n' roll.

With the success of "Stairway to Heaven" under their belt, Zeppelin again toured the States in 1972 and 1973, this time with Page introducing his other signature guitar, the Gibson ES-1275 doubleneck. Throughout the rest of the seventies Led Zeppelin put out several more huge albums, including *Houses of the Holy* in 1973, a diverse collection of rockers, ballads, reggae, funk, and fifties-style rock 'n' roll, and the even more ambitious 1975 set *Physical Graffiti*, which contained several epic-length pieces: "Ten Years Gone," "In My Time of Dying," and the Arabic-flavored "Kashmir," a groundbreaking epic on which Page and Plant further reveal their passion for global music, especially that of Morocco. Another major U.S. tour came in 1975, showing Zeppelin at the height of their fame and Page wowing audiences everywhere with his patented guitar flash and infamous stage outfits with their embroidered symbols of the occult.

The excellent *Presence* followed in 1976 (with the extensively multitracked guitar masterpiece "Achilles Last Stand"), as did the live soundtrack to their critically panned concert movie *The Song Remains the Same*. Zeppelin toured America in 1977, but the tour was cut short due to the sudden death of Plant's son. They finally reemerged in August 1979 with the softer, more commercial *In through the Out Door*—their only non-hard rock album—and played their first concert dates in several years. Tragedy struck again before the band could mount a full-scale tour: In September 1980, drummer John Bonham died of an alcohol overdose at Page's home in Windsor. In the first week of December that year, the remaining members of the band issued a statement to the press proclaiming that Led Zeppelin would break up as a result of Bonham's death.

Post-Zep. Aside from creating the soundtrack to the film *Death Wish II* in 1982 and appearing in the brief ARMS (Action Research into Multiple Sclerosis) tour in late 1983 (with fellow British guitar heroes Eric Clapton and Jeff Beck), Jimmy Page was barely heard from in the first few years of the eighties. He finally saw the light of day at the beginning of 1985 with a new band and album under the name of the Firm, an outfit led by Page and former Bad Company vocalist Paul Rodgers. Unfortunately, the Firm's music paled in comparison to its leaders' previous achievements, and Page's playing was markedly half-hearted, despite stellar cuts like "Cadillac" and "Live in Peace." Brief Led Zeppelin reunions occurred too, including uninspired appearances at the Live Aid concert in Philadelphia in 1985 and at the Atlantic Records 40th Anniversary concert in 1988. On a more positive note, Jimmy Page and Robert Plant reunited for an acclaimed "Unplugged" show on MTV in 1994 and released the album *No Quarter–Unledded*. In early 1995 Led Zeppelin was inducted into the Rock and Roll Hall of Fame.

Style and Impact. Over the past 25 years Jimmy Page's guitar style has changed from a brash blues-rock attack to the cutting edge of metal guitar to a progressive style that owed as much to his studio wizardry and songwriting as to the overall aggressiveness of his playing. One constant throughout Zeppelin recordings is the huge scope of Page's sonic range. On high-volume rockers like "The Song Remains the Same" or "The Wanton Song," he would employ several tracks of processed guitars to enhance the song, adding different tonal colors and textures like echo, phasing, and Leslie effects to each guitar track. He would later call this fondness for multitracking (perhaps itself an influence of Page's mentor, recording pioneer Les Paul) his "guitar army." Like the grand scale of most Zep songs, Page's *modus operandi* seemed to be, "Why use one guitar when you can use five?"

Another of Page's notable feats on Zeppelin sessions was that no matter how dense a recording got with multitracked guitar lines, he never sacrificed his big, muscular guitar sound for the complexities of studio gadgetry. A good example is "Ten Years Gone," from *Physical Graffiti*. At times there are upwards of three or four guitar riffs playing simultaneously, yet each one of his guitars sounds like a single Les Paul roaring through Marshall at a live concert, with nothing lost in sound quality or emotional intensity. Clearly, the man knows his way around a mixing console. And while Eric Clapton and Jeff Beck may be more dazzling improvisationalists, there is no doubt of Page's command of rock guitar in the studio. As the increasingly popular recordings of Led Zeppelin prove, he has the singular talent of writing straightforward guitar tracks and turning them into something much larger than life.

Led Zeppelin [on Atlantic except where noted], *Led Zeppelin* (1968), *Led Zeppelin II* (1969), *Led Zeppelin III* (1970), *Led Zeppelin IV* (1971), *Houses of the Holy* (1973), *Physical Graffiti* (Swan Song, 1975), *Presence* (Swan Song, 1976), *The Song Remains the Same* (Swan Song, 1976•), *In through the Out Door* (Swan Song, 1979), *Coda* (Swan Song, 1982), *Led Zeppelin* [boxed set] (1990). **Jimmy Page,** *James Patrick Page: Session Man, Vols. I & II* (Hoff/Slipped Disc, 1979), *Death Wish II* (Swan Song, 1982), *Outrider* (Geffen, 1988). **The Firm** [on Atlantic], *The Firm* (1984), *Mean Business* (1986). **Jimmy Page & Robert Plant,** *No Quarter—Unledded* (Atlantic, 1994•).

Recordings featuring Jimmy Page: **Them,** *Them* (Parrot, 1965). **Herbie Hancock** [Yardbirds on one song], *Blow Up* (MGM, 1966). **Donovan,** *The Hurdy Gurdy Man* (Epic, 1968). **Joe Cocker,** *With a Little Help from My Friends* (A&M, 1968). **Jeff Beck Group,** *Truth* (Epic, 1968). **Screaming**

Lord Sutch, *Lord Sutch and Heavy Friends* (Cotillion/Atlantic, 1970). **Maggie Bell,** *Suicide Sal* (Swan Song, 1975). **Various Artists,** *White Boy Blues: Classic Guitars of Clapton, Beck, and Page* (Compleat, 1984). **The Honeydrippers,** *The Honeydrippers, Vol. 1* (Es Paranza, 1984). **Stephen Stills,** *Right by You* (Atlantic, 1984). **John Paul Jones,** *Music from the Film: Scream for Help* (Atlantic, 1985). **Box of Frogs,** *Strange Land* (Epic, 1986). **Robert Plant,** *Now and Zen* (Es Paranza, 1988).

The Jeff Beck Group

Jeff Beck

B o r n : *June 24, 1944, in Wallington, Surrey, England*
Main Guitars: *Fender Stratocaster, Gibson Les Paul Standard*

Soon after Jeff Beck left the Yardbirds (♦) in November 1966, he began putting together his own rock 'n' roll act, the Jeff Beck Group. But before Beck could get it off the ground, he had to fulfill some contractual recording obligations to bugglegum-pop producer Mickie Most. The results of the Beck/Most recordings, circa 1967, were a number of chart-topping singles for Beck, including "Love Is Blue," "Beck's Bolero," and the extra-hokey but still successful bubblegum hit "Hi-Ho Silver Lining." Fortunately, Beck found his way clear of Most's syrupy productions to assemble the first Jeff Beck Group, which by late 1967 included Rod Stewart on vocals, Ron Wood (♦) on bass, and Mick Waller on drums.

Drawing on Beck's thunderous guitar work and Stewart's raspy vocals, the Jeff Beck Group was nothing short of a revelation to heavy rock 'n' roll, as was quickly proved on their seminal debut album, *Truth*, released in mid 1968. Although some have claimed that this disc was the first metal album, the sound actually leaned more towards a heavy brand of blues rock. The group took the old blues standards and song stylings from the blues boom earlier in the decade and beefed them up with Beck's Gibson Les Paul guitar and Vox AC30 amplifier, Stewart's powerful voice, and the muscular rhythm section of Wood and Waller (this in contrast to Led Zeppelin, who, with Robert Plant's piercing voice and Jimmy Page's over-the-top guitar riffs, would truly usher in metal with their earth-shaking first album a few months later).

Aside from containing the band's charged-up revamping of the Yardbirds' hit "Shapes of Things" and the bluesy "You Shook Me," *Truth* also included the heavy instrumental "Beck's Bolero," a late-1966 or early-'67 recording from Beck's stint with Mickie Most. Playing on that particular session was a proposed "super-group" that included Beck on lead guitar, Jimmy Page (then still with the Yardbirds) on 12-string rhythm, Keith Moon of the Who on drums, and future Led Zeppelin member John Paul Jones, who was a session musician in London at the time, playing bass. The band never happened, but "Beck's Bolero" still remains a great memento of their once-in-a-lifetime "supersession." The two guitarists also continue to squabble in the press about who actually came up with and played the tune's main riff, although it is technically credited to Page.

On the strength of the chart success garnered by *Truth*, the Beck Group toured the United States extensively and eventually got around to recording their second album in about four days at Chicago's famed Chess studios. Despite its quick creation, *Beck-Ola* was instantly acclaimed as another "heavy" masterpiece upon its release in the summer of 1969. With *Beck-Ola*, Beck took the beefy blues of *Truth* and made it even heavier on tracks like "Jailhouse Rock," "Plynth (Water down the Drain)," "Hangman's Knee," and, notably, the extended instrumental metal jam "Rice Pudding," which contains the kind of power chord riff that would later be a staple of Deep Purple and other metal stalwarts of the seventies and eighties. By this time Beck had also traded in his Gibson and Vox amp for a Fender Stratocaster and several Marshall 100-watt stacks, a setup presumably inspired by one of his major influences, Jimi Hendrix. Still, the tolls of finances, long tours, and interpersonal problems began mounting within the band, and—just before an invitation to play at Woodstock came in mid 1969—Beck broke up the group.

At that point he was set to form a new group with Tim Bogert and Carmine Appice of Vanilla Fudge, but was involved in a near-fatal car accident in the fall of 1969. During his extended recovery, Bogert and Appice formed the early hard-rock group Cactus, and plans for a Beck/Fudge band promptly fell apart. Beck finally got his act together in 1971 when he formed the second Jeff Beck Group, this time with Max Middleton on keys, Bobby Tench on vocals, and a rhythm section consisting of bassist Clive Chaman and drummer Cozy Powell. The guitar hero had grown weary of the loud *blooze* he'd been playing for the previous six years with the Yardbirds and the original Jeff Beck Group, so with this new group he tried to create a new musical style that combined heavy rock, funk, jazz, and the Motown/Atlantic soul sounds of his favorite R&B performers, like Otis Redding, Tina Turner, and Stevie Wonder. The idea sounded good on paper, but as the second Jeff Beck Group proved on their two albums, *Rough and Ready* (1971) and *Jeff Beck Group* (1972), it was not a complete musical success, especially when they tried to marry soulful R&B with Powell's ham-fisted rock drumming. Still, there are several six-string high points on these discs, such as the soulful ballads "Definitely" and "I Can't Give Back the Love I Feel for You" and the rocker "Going Down," which contains a hellacious Strat break drenched in feedback and distortion. Incidentally, this track was produced by another guitar great, Steve Cropper (♦).

In late 1972 Beck scrubbed this band and finally made the musical union with Tim Bogert and Carmine Appice, who had left Cactus. Calling themselves Beck, Bogert & Appice, this Cream-styled power trio was awarded "supergroup" status by the press, yet Jeff Beck's career slump seemed to worsen. The members of BBA were renowned individually for their musical expertise, but it soon became apparent that the band suffered from weak songwriting and often embarrassing vocals. After one befuddled album and an overdose of media hype, Beck disbanded the trio in 1973, though a Japanese live album that was more representative of their musical prowess appeared in 1978. Better still, the BBA fiasco would not deter the guitarist's career for long (♦ Jeff Beck).

The Jeff Beck Group [on Epic except where noted], *Truth* (1968), *Beck-Ola* (1969), *Rough and Ready* (1971), *Jeff Beck Group* (1972), *The Best of Jeff Beck, 1967–1969* (Fame, 1985). **Beck, Bogert & Appice,** *Beck, Bogert & Appice* (Epic, 1973), *Live* (Epic Japan, 1978•) **Jeff Beck,** *Beckology* [boxed set] (Epic, 1991•).

Recordings featuring Jeff Beck (1969–74): **Donovan,** *Barabajagal* (Epic, 1969). **Screaming Lord Sutch,** *Lord Sutch and Heavy Friends* (Cotillion/Atlantic, 1970). **Stevie Wonder,** *Talking Book* (Tamla, 1972). **Eddie Harris,** *E.H. in the U.K.* (Atlantic, 1974).

Black Sabbath

Tony Iommi

B o r n : *February 19, 1948, in Birmingham, England*

Main Guitar: *Gibson SG, John Birch Custom "SG"*

Doom, gloom, and the heaviest of heavy metal has been how Black Sabbath and their music have been critiqued and, more often than not, reviled by the rock press since their rise to fame in 1970. Like their American peers in Grand Funk Railroad, it seemed the more critics despised Black Sabbath, the more the fans loved them, making way for countless hit albums and sellout tours by the band. Vintage Sabbath is best known for front man Ozzy Osbourne's vocal whine and Geezer Butler's murky lyrics about Satan, war, paranoia, and sorcery. Still, the band boasted solid instrumental backup to Ozzy's pessimistic rantings, especially from lead guitarist Tony Iommi. One of the earliest metal heroes,

Tony Iommi

Iommi cut a mysterious figure on concert stages with his all-black outfits, gleaming crucifix around his neck, and fast guitar solos issuing forth from the huge wall of Laney amps behind him. Like Sabbath's best songs, Iommi is unquestionably *spooky*.

One of the most unusual aspects of Iommi's guitar style was directly related to a welding accident he had while a teenager, in which he lost the fingertips of his fretting hand (his right hand; Iommi is left-handed). He had already been playing for a few years and, following the accident, was prepared to give it up altogether had it not been for a recording he heard by Django Reinhardt, the legendary gypsy guitarist of jazz. Reinhardt had crippled his fretting hand in a caravan fire, but had overcome the handicap by developing a revolutionary two-finger technique. Inspired by the story of Django's amazing recovery, Iommi fitted his damaged fingers with plastic tips covered with leather and proceeded to relearn the guitar. Within a few years he was playing better than ever with the aid of these artificial fingertips.

In January 1969 Iommi formed Earth, a jazz and blues group, with Ozzy Osbourne, bassist/lyricist Geezer Butler, and drummer Bill Ward. After playing with them for a few months, Iommi left to join Jethro Tull (♦) and played with them in the Rolling Stones' never-released television special, "The Rolling Stones' Rock and Roll Circus." But Iommi was ill at ease in Jethro Tull and soon returned to Earth. Towards the end of that year they changed their name to Black Sabbath, and in 1970 they issued their eponymous debut. The album quickly became an underground hit in the U.S. and Europe, and with the appearance of their popular second set, *Paranoid* (1971), Black Sabbath were well on their way to heavy metal immortality.

Throughout all of Sabbath's releases in the 1970s, Iommi maintained a rigid method of soloing, rarely varying styles or ideas. He consistently blazed through Sabbath standards with power chords and fast blues chops on his trademark black SG-style guitar with crucifix inlays. He used this signature sound on such Sab tracks as "Paranoid," "War Pigs," "N.I.B.," and the ever-popular concert favorite "Iron Man." Even after Ozzy left in 1979, Iommi continued his lead guitar fury, especially on pummeling albums like *Heaven and Hell* (1980, with vocalist Ronnie James Dio) and *Dehumanizer* (1992).

While many rock critics are still baffled by Sabbath's ceaseless existence, a likely reason for their popularity in the seventies was a combination of a powerful rhythm section, Iommi's cro-metal guitar work, and the spiritual rapport between Sabbath's cynical lyrics and a generation of teenagers disillusioned by the Vietnam war, political corruption, and other downers from the "Have a Nice Day" decade. Despite frequent attacks from the rock press over the years, Black Sabbath remains an immovable icon of heavy metal, and Iommi remains a metal guitar hero of notable distinction. His dirge-like tone and trademark spartan riffs are arguably among the most influential in all of heavy rock, adapted in near-carbon copy form during the late 1980s and 1990s by bands like Metallica, Megadeth, Pantera, Helmet, and much of the industrial and British grindcore movement. Tony

Iommi may not be a household name, but his riffs are forever chiseled into the cliffs of heavy metal.

Black Sabbath [on Warner Bros. except where noted], *Black Sabbath* (1970), *Paranoid* (1970), *Master of Reality* (1971), *Black Sabbath, Vol. 4* (1972), *Sabbath Bloody Sabbath* (1973), *Sabotage* (1975), *We Sold Our Soul for Rock 'n' Roll* (1976), *Technical Ecstasy* (1976), *Greatest Hits* (1977), *Never Say Die* (1978), *Heaven and Hell* (1980), *Mob Rules* (1981), *Live Evil* (1983•), *Born Again* (1983), *Seventh Star* (1986), *Eternal Idol* (1988), *Headless Cross* (IRS, 1990), *TYR* (IRS, 1991), *Dehumanizer* (Reprise, 1992), *Forbidden* (IRS, 1995).

Recordings featuring Tony Iommi: **Various Artists,** *Guitar Speak II* (IRS, 1990). **Cathedral,** *The Carnival Bizarre* (n/a, 1995).

Deep Purple

Ritchie Blackmore

B o r n : *April 14, 1945, in Weston-super-Mare, England*
M a i n   G u i t a r : *Fender Stratocaster*

Deep Purple first entered America's rock consciousness in 1968 with a hit version of Joe South's "Hush," but it wasn't until the release of *In Rock* in 1970 that they began to get wider recognition for their abilities, especially in England. Besides the bombastic instrumental work of organist Jon Lord, drummer Ian Paice, and bassist Roger Glover (not to mention the lead vocals of Ian Gillan), Purple introduced an exciting guitar innovator to the rising world of heavy metal: Ritchie Blackmore.

Blackmore was no newcomer to rock 'n' roll. After learning guitar in the mid fifties and playing in local pop groups like Neil Christian and the Crusaders, Mandrake Root, and Roundabout, Blackmore had become much sought after as a session guitarist in the sixties—often sharing studio dates with Jimmy Page and Big Jim Sullivan—and also going through several stints with Screaming Lord Sutch's highly theatrical rock group. Eventually, he grew weary of session work and moved to Hamburg, to look for new musical horizons. Besides playing regularly at the fabled Star Club (one of the Beatles' early haunts), Blackmore gigged with several bands, in the process meeting future Deep Purple bandmates Jon Lord and Ian Paice. Together with singer Rod Evans and bassist Nick Simper, they formed Deep Purple in 1968.

Deep Purple's first album came out that fall and contained the U.S. hit "Hush." About a year later, Evans and Simper were replaced by Gillan and Glover, at which point the metal guitar vocabulary of Blackmore (then playing a Gibson ES-335 hollow-body) really began to take shape. The band's critically praised but musically shaky album *Concerto for Group and Orchestra* (with the Royal Philharmonic Orchestra) followed, after which the group got to work on *In Rock*. Containing such fine rockers as "Speed King" and "Child in Time," this album finally pushed Blackmore's flashy guitarmanship to the fore. The equally impressive *Fireball* followed in 1971, but it wasn't until *Machine Head* in 1972 that Deep Purple finally struck gold in international circles, via the definitive hard rock anthem "Smoke on the

Water," which has one of the best—*and easiest to learn*—guitar riffs in rock history. Blackmore's soulful Strat solo on "Smoke" further slammed the point home that he was a guitar ace to be reckoned with in the early seventies.

Other vintage Deep Purple tracks like "Highway Star," "Strange Kind of Woman," "Mistreated," "Woman from Tokyo," and "Burn" all display Blackmore's patented solo trademarks: fast hammer-ons, violent tremolo bar jerks, and, generally, a more sophisticated harmonic vocabulary than most other metal players of the day. A few solos reveal his groundbreaking use of the harmonic minor scale, once commonly known as the "snake charmer" scale. One of the best examples of this is in "Mistreated," while in "Highway Star" (from *Machine Head*), Blackmore constructs a stunning break composed of rapidly picked arpeggios based on a passage by baroque composer J.S. Bach, mirroring the rise of classical rock around the same time.

Several successful albums came after *Machine Head*: *Who Do We Think We Are!*, *Made in Japan* (both from 1973), and *Burn* (1974), but before long, Deep Purple began to burn out from the pressures of fame and heavy touring. Gillan and Glover dropped out of the band in 1973 (replaced by future Whitesnake vocalist David Coverdale and bassist Glenn Hughes), and in 1975 Blackmore followed suit after the release of the inferior *Stormbringer*. He was later replaced by ex-James Gang guitarist Tommy Bolin (♪). Not wasting any time, Blackmore hired a New York-based band called Elf, led by singer Ronnie James Dio, and turned them into Ritchie Blackmore's Rainbow. For the rest of the seventies Rainbow was a fairly successful act in the U.K., renowned as much for their frequent personnel changes as for their leader's cranked guitar solos (peak single: "I Surrender" hit #3 in England in 1981.)

Blackmore finally broke up Rainbow in 1983 to join Lord, Paice, Glover, and Gillan in a reunion of Deep Purple. They produced a major comeback album (*Perfect Strangers*) and tour in 1984, which successfully resurrected the classic metal sound of their earlier days (replete with several fine Blackmore solos) and made it fit right into the musical mood of the 1980s. Deep Purple followed it up in 1987 with an equally strong outing called *The House of Blue Light*. Various and sundry lineups of the band followed from this point onward, with Gillan dropping out occasionally to be replaced by Joe Lynn Turner. In 1993 Gillan and Blackmore got together for *The Battle Rages On*, but Blackmore left before a Japanese tour and was temporarily replaced by American flash Joe Satriani (♪), before the great Steve Morse (♪) joined Deep Purple full-time.

In all, Blackmore's greatest contribution to heavy metal came during the prime 1970–74 epoch of Purple history. During that time he greatly popularized the metal style for rock guitarists all over the world and deeply influenced many of the greats of the late seventies and eighties, most importantly Eddie Van Halen and Yngwie Malmsteen. His use of classically derived themes was the precursor to the "Bach and roll" guitar shredders that dominated the instrument in the mid 1980s. He has also been one of

the few guitarists who dared carry on the unique Stratocaster/Marshall sound pioneered by Jimi Hendrix. In truth, when many metal guitarists were just getting to their feet in the early seventies, Ritchie Blackmore was already miles ahead of the pack.

Deep Purple [on Warner Bros. except where noted], *Shades of Deep Purple* (Tetragram, 1968), *Book of Taliesyn* (Tetragram, 1969), *In Concert* (Tetragram, 1969•), *Concerto for Group and Orchestra* (1970•), *In Rock* (1970), *Fireball* (1971), *Machine Head* (1972), *Made in Japan* (1973•), *Who Do We Think We Are* (1973), *Burn* (1974), *Stormbringer* (1974), *Made in Europe* (1976•), *Perfect Strangers* (Mercury, 1984), *House of Blue Light* (Mercury, 1987), *Nobody's Perfect* (Mercury, 1988•), *Slaves and Masters* (RCA, 1990), *The Battle Rages On* (Giant, 1993), *Live at California Jam* (Mausoleum, 1996•). **Rainbow,** *Ritchie Blackmore's Rainbow* (Oyster, 1975), *Rainbow Rising* (Oyster, 1976), *On Stage* (Oyster, 1977•), *Long Live Rock 'n' Roll* (Polydor, 1978), *Down to Earth* (Polydor, 1979), *Difficult to Cure* (Polydor, 1981), *Jealous Lover* [EP] (Polydor, 1981), *Straight between the Eyes* (Mercury, 1982), *Bent out of Shape* (Mercury, 1983), *Finyl Vinyl* (Mercury, 1986•), *Live in Europe* (Mausoleum, 1996•), *Stranger in Us All* (Fuel, 1996). **Ritchie Blackmore,** *Take It!—Sessions 63/68* (RPM, 1995).

Recordings featuring Ritchie Blackmore: **Screaming Lord Sutch,** *Hands of Jack the Ripper* (Cotillion/Atlantic, c. 1970). **Green Bullfrog,** *Green Bullfrog* (Decca, 1971).

Mountain

Leslie West

Born: *October 22, 1945, in Queens, New York*
Main Guitar: *Gibson Les Paul Junior "TV"*

After only a few gigs together, Mountain—a power trio led by guitarist Leslie West and bassist Felix Pappalardi—made their national debut at the Woodstock festival in August 1969. Before an audience of 300,000 people, they cranked out epic tunes like "Blood of the Sun" and "Theme from an Imaginary Western," announcing the arrival of the then-new sound of heavy metal. The performance was a high point of the festival, and for the next few years Mountain was at the summit of heavy rock 'n' roll, rivaling Led Zeppelin, Black Sabbath, and Grand Funk Railroad.

Mountain developed from a group called the Vagrants, which featured the impressive playing of West, a player whose size made him something of a landmark in his own right—an anomaly in the "rock star" universe. The Vagrants signed to Atlantic's Atco label and were assigned Felix Pappalardi as producer; Pappalardi had previously produced such rock acts as Cream, Jack Bruce, the Lovin' Spoonful, and Richie Havens. The Vagrants cut two singles for Atco, both of which bombed, and the band eventually broke up. Soon after, Pappalardi produced and played bass on West's first solo album, *Mountain*, in 1969. The album was so successful musically that West proposed forming a group to Pappalardi, and the producer agreed to give it a try. Mountain finally came together in early summer 1969 as a conspicuously Cream-styled trio, consisting of West, Pappalardi, and drummer Norman Smart.

Mountain debuted to overwhelming acclaim at the Fillmore West, in San Francisco, and played a few other warm-up gigs before burning up the stage at Woodstock later that summer. By the beginning of 1970 their first record, *Mountain Climbing*, was released to the approval of metal fans and critics alike. *Mountain Climbing* contained the band's first and most enduring hit, "Mississippi Queen," one of the first heavy guitar songs to garner regular radio airplay. They followed it up with another gold record, *Nantucket Sleighride* (1971), featuring new drummer Corky Laing and the single "For Yasgur's Farm" (a tribute to farmer Max Yasgur, on whose land the Woodstock festival was held).

Leslie West's best guitar moment with Mountain was "Mississippi Queen." He launches the tune with a fuzz-heavy riff on his trademark Gibson Les Paul Junior before picking the familiar power chords and fat lead lines reminiscent of his hero, Eric Clapton. Another great West solo is in the Jack Bruce-penned song "Theme from an Imaginary Western." In this moving power ballad (probably the first metal track to warrant this distinction) the guitarist plays two soulful solos, each rich in tasteful string bends, distortion effects, and his melodic use of the pentatonic blues scale. This version and the one included on the *Woodstock Two* record are both excellent examples of Leslie West's control, emotion, and overpowering aggressiveness on the electric guitar. Another gem is "Travelin' in the Dark," which blends power chords and crisp Hammond organ to create one of the first traces of "art metal," a sound later capitalized on by Jethro Tull, Kansas, and Rush.

After *Nantucket Sleighride*, Mountain put out two more albums before disbanding due to a rift between West and Pappalardi. In 1972 West and Laing were joined by bassist Jack Bruce in yet another Cream-like supergroup: West, Bruce, and Laing. Bent on rehashing old Cream and Mountain riffs, the group churned out an unappetizing mishmash of metal clichés, and after two mediocre albums, the band folded in 1973 (their third album—a truly dismal live set—came out in 1974). Later touring briefly as Leslie West's Wild West Show, West and Laing decided to give Mountain another try with Pappalardi back in the group. Two more poorly received records were released, and then Mountain gave up again. West still tours and records—and is considerably slimmed down—under the Mountain name. (Tragically, Pappalardi was murdered in 1983.)

Besides his tone and aggression, Leslie West's individuality as a metal guitarist came from his not being a fast player. He almost never sacrificed melody and taste for the cheap metal thrills of speed and flash, preferring instead to construct a soulful but heavy break using his admittedly "two-fingered" technique (he only used the first and third fingers on his fretting hand). Despite this technical limitation, few would dispute the power and influence of West's vintage guitar work with Mountain. Furthermore, his clear, ringing lead style was also highly influential, inspiring, among others, Michael Schenker of UFO.

Leslie West, *Mountain* (Windfall, 1969), *The Great Fatsby* (Phantom, 1975), *The Leslie West Band* (Phantom, 1976), *Theme* (Passport, 1988), *Live* (BBI, 1993•), *Dodgin' the Dirt* (BBI, 1994). **Mountain** [on Windfall except where noted], *Mountain Climbing* (1970), *Nantucket Sleighride* (1971), *Flowers of Evil* (1971), *Mountain Live: The Road Goes on Forever* (1972•), *The Best of Mountain* (Columbia, 1973), *Twin Peaks* (Columbia, 1974•), *Avalanche* (Columbia, 1974), *Go for Your Life* (Scotti Bros., 1985), *Over the Top* (Columbia Legacy, 1995•). **West, Bruce, and Laing** [on Windfall], *Why Doncha'* (1972), *Whatever Turns You On* (1973), *Live 'n' Kickin'* (1974•). **The Vagrants,** *The Great Lost Album* (Arista, 1987).

Recordings featuring Leslie West: **Various Artists,** *Woodstock Two* (Cotillion, 1971•), *The First Great Rock Festivals of the Seventies* (Columbia, 1971•), *Guitar Speak* (IRS, 1989), *Night of the Guitar Live!* (IRS, 1989•), *Guitar's Practicing Musicians* (Guitar Recordings, 1989). **Bobby Keyes,** *Bobby Keyes* (Warner Bros., 1972). **Dana Valery,** *Dana Valery* (Phantom, 1975). **Billy Joel,** *River of Dreams* (Columbia, 1993).

Grand Funk

Mark Farner

Born: *September 29, 1948, in Flint, Michigan*
Main Guitars: *Micro-Frets and Messenger electrics*

Rock 'n' roll bands that are roundly hated by the critics and receive little radio airplay often end up nowhere fast. But Grand Funk Railroad, a power trio from Flint, Michigan, received this treatment and still went on to become one of America's most popular hard rock groups of the early seventies. Musically, early Grand Funk offered the usual barrage of high-volume riffing, but they nevertheless found a huge audience who bought their albums in droves. It seemed that the more critics hated Grand Funk Railroad, the more their fans loved them.

Grand Funk grew out of a group from Flint called the Pack, which featured singer Terry Knight and drummer Don Brewer. When the group folded around 1968, Knight left to find fame in New York, while Brewer brought in guitarist Mark Farner and bassist Mel Schacher to round out the bill. The trio eventually contacted Knight to be their manager. He agreed and swiftly showed off his business savvy by booking the band, now called Grand Funk Railroad, to play for free at the Atlanta Pop Festival in July 1969. The concert was a huge success for Grand Funk, and after a few initial rejections they were signed to Capitol Records.

Grand Funk Railroad's first album, *On Time* (1969), is a case study in early metal style. Throughout each song, Brewer and Schacher hold down the plodding rhythm section while Farner fills up the rest of sonic spectrum with high-pitched vocals and distorted guitar riffs. From *On Time* they placed "Time Machine" on the singles charts and scored their first gold album. *Grand Funk* followed in 1970 with another single, "Mr. Limousine Driver," and another gold album. Grand Funk's popularity soared, and in addition to having a long string of hit albums, they played sellout concerts across the country (due in part to the massive popularity of their hit "I'm Your Captain"), even managing a sellout gig at Shea Stadium.

The musical fuel for Grand Funk Railroad was Farner's guitar. While not as a technically skilled or imaginative a guitarist as early metal men like Leslie West and Ritchie Blackmore, Farner still possessed an ample vocabulary of heavy licks including fast, repeating hammer-ons, string bends, power chords, and of course, omnipresent heavy distortion effects. A few samples of Farner's aggressive solos with the Funk are in tracks like their perennial concert opener, "Are You Ready," as well as "Time Machine" and "Mr. Limousine Driver."

Eventually, Grand Funk began to change from their early metal sounds to a more commercial hard rock style. In 1973 they dropped the "Railroad" from their name and issued *We're an American Band*—produced by guitarist Todd Rundgren—scoring a hit with the title track, which also had a killer wah-wah/fuzz solo. Several more Top 10 hits followed for the band in 1974: "The Locomotion" (with a wild, phase-shifted Farner solo), "Some Kind of Wonderful," and "Bad Time." Grand Funk finally broke up in 1976, with a short reunion in 1981. Later, Mark Farner was recording albums of contemporary Christian music—a long way from his days at the head of America's most notorious hard rock band.

Grand Funk Railroad [on Capitol], *On Time* (1969), *Grand Funk* (1970), *Closer to Home* (1970), *Live Album* (1970•), *Survival* (1971), *E Pluribus Funk* (1972), *Mark, Don, and Mel 1969–1971* (1972), *Phoenix* (1973). **Grand Funk** [on Capitol except where noted], *We're an American Band* (1973), *Shinin' On* (1974), *All the Girls in the World Beware!!!* (1974), *Caught in the Act* (1975•), *Born to Die* (1975), *Good Singin' Good Playin'* (MCA, 1976), *Grand Funk Hits* (1977), *Grand Funk Lives* (Full Moon, 1981). **Mark Farner,** *Just Another Injustice* (Frontline, 1988).

Rick Derringer

B o r n : *Richard Zehringer, on August 5, 1947, in Celina, Ohio*
M a i n   G u i t a r s : *Gibson Explorer, B.C. Rich Rick Derringer Stealth*

Rick Derringer might well be described as the everyman of 1970s hard rock. His guitar style has always been simple, no-frills rock, and his frequent use of ideas derived from Clapton, Beck, and Hendrix seems to have been in fond appreciation of and respect for their guitar heroics more than in cheap imitation. In his musical associations with Johnny and Edgar Winter, and in various solo projects, Derringer successfully updated the sixties guitar sounds into his own hard-rocking style, and he's also gained recognition for his appearances as a record producer and songwriter, penning such outright rock classics as "Hang on Sloopy" and "Rock and Roll Hoochie Koo."

After starting guitar at about the age of nine, Derringer quickly progressed to playing in local bands and, at 15, formed a group called the McCoys. In 1965 the McCoys released the single "Hang on Sloopy," which promptly became a hit. As the overnight success began to wear off, the McCoys found themselves in Greenwich Village as house band for Steve Paul's famous Scene club. There they became the backup group for Paul's new protégé, Texas guitarist Johnny Winter (◗), during 1969–70. With both Winter and Derringer on lead guitars, Johnny Winter And (as they now began to call themselves) became a popular attraction and tore up concert stages all over the country. The group's '71 live album, *Johnny Winter And Live!*, is particularly memorable, especially for their explosive version of "Johnny B. Goode."

After two well-received albums with the group, Derringer parted company with the Winter/McCoys conglomeration in 1971 and started working with Edgar Winter's R&B-influenced group White Trash. The guitarist produced two albums for Winter before finally joining the Edgar Winter Group for the 1974 recording *Shock Treatment* (he had guested with then-guitarist Ronnie Montrose on *They Only Come out at Night*). At the time, Derringer had just released his first solo album, *All American Boy* (1973), containing his own fiery rendition of "Rock and Roll Hoochie Koo" (originally a hit for Johnny Winter several years earlier). On this tune he combines power chording and single-note riffs in the rhythm tracks before setting up a solo that fuses Beck- and Hendrix-inspired bends, blues scale runs, and rhythmic chordal riffing. But Derringer wasn't a one-dimensional player: on the ballad "Jump, Jump, Jump," he performs a long, echo-enhanced lead that scores high marks for emotion and melodic content.

Since his heyday in the seventies, the guitarist has recorded with various artists and groups, including his own metal quartet Derringer, pop diva Cyndi Lauper, and Weird Al Yankovic (he mimics the Eddie Van Halen solo in "Eat It"), as well as cutting a critically praised solo disc in 1993 called *Back to the Blues* and an instructional guitar video called *Secrets* (Warner Bros.).

The McCoys, *Hang on Sloopy* (Bang, 1965), *Human Ball* (Mercury, 1968), *Infinite McCoys* (1969). **Johnny Winter And** [on Columbia], *Johnny Winter And* (1970), *Live/Johnny Winter And* (1971). **Edgar Winter** [on Epic], *Edgar Winter's White Trash* (1971), *Roadwork* (1972), *They Only Come out at Night* (1972), *Shock Treatment* (1974), *The Edgar Winter Group with Rick Derringer* (1975). **Rick Derringer** [on Blue Sky except where noted], *All American Boy* (1973), *Spring Fever* (1975), *If I Weren't So Romantic, I'd Shoot You* (1978), *Guitars and Women* (1979), *Face to Face* (1980), *Rick Derringer* (n/a, 1981), *Good Dirty Fun* (Passport, 1983), *Back to the Blues* (BBI, 1993), *Elektra Blues* (BBI, 1994). **Derringer** [on Blue Sky], *Derringer* (1976), *Sweet Evil* (1977), *Live* (1977•). **DNA,** *Party Tested* (Boardwalk, 1983).

Recordings featuring Rick Derringer: **Todd Rundgren,** *Something/Anything* (Bearsville, 1972). **Steely Dan,** *Countdown to Ecstasy* (ABC, 1973), *Katy Lied* (ABC, 1975), *Gaucho* (MCA, 1980). **Eye to Eye,** *Eye to Eye* (Warner Bros., 1982). **Donald Fagen,** *The Nightfly* (Warner Bros., 1982). **Cyndi Lauper,** *True Colors* (1986). **Mason Ruffner,** *Mason Ruffner* (CBS/Associated, 1985).

CHAPTER TEN

British Invasion II
The Second Wave

In the late sixties, a second British Invasion commenced. This despite the shift in focus towards American rock 'n' roll bands—thanks to psychedelia and the L.A. folk-rock scene. In addition to perennial mega-acts like the Rolling Stones and the Who (both of whom were fast approaching the apex of their careers), there were fresh, talented performers emerging on the U.K. pop scene, including bands such as Traffic, the Move, Rod Stewart and the Faces, Free, and Procol Harum.

By the time of this Second Invasion, the effects of the U.K. blues revival had permanently infiltrated mainstream pop and rock, providing the new wave with a strong basis in both the blues and gospel music. And while much of the music in the second British wave was shrouded in psychedelic imagery, flowery lyrics, and heavily ornamented arrangements, electric Chicago blues was still very much at the heart of the music and its attendant guitar styles.

Eric Clapton

Born: *March 30, 1945, in Ripley, Surrey, England*
Main Guitars: *Fender Stratocaster, Gibson ES-335*

Transformation. By the summer of 1969, several months after the dissolution of Cream (◗), Clapton had formed a new band, Blind Faith. Composed of Clapton, Ginger Baker, bassist Rick Grech (from Family), and Stevie Winwood (of the Spencer Davis Group and Traffic) on vocals, keyboards, and guitar, Blind Faith was radically different from Cream. In contrast to Cream's long jam sessions and psychedelic fashion statements, Blind Faith played shorter, catchier tunes and featured considerably toned-down guitar work from Clapton. During this phase, Clapton also began developing his singing and songwriting skills, which had largely been overshadowed in Cream by Jack Bruce's prolif-ic abilities as head tunesmith and vocalist.

Despite the multi-talented lineup, Blind Faith was plagued by problems from the beginning. They were tagged by the press as a "supergroup" and touted as the next Cream, which put extreme pressures on the band members. On their debut tour they were booked into massive venues like Madison Square Garden, instead of easing into the music scene with a series of small theater or club appearances. With all the external expectations laid on the group, Blind Faith collapsed under the weight of egos and marketing hype before it had a chance to start. Yet their eponymous studio album—with controversial artwork of a pre-pubescent nude—yielded several solid songs (notably Winwood's mesmerizing "Can't Find My Way Home" and Clapton's "Presence of the Lord," which dealt with his conversion to Christianity). Unfortunately, Clapton's guitar playing was meek in comparison to his work with Cream.

During Blind Faith's one and only tour, Clapton became friendly with the opening act, an American gospel-rock duo named Delaney and Bonnie, fronted by the husband-and-wife team of Delaney and Bonnie Bramlett. When Blind Faith disintegrated, Clapton hooked up with the Bramletts and joined them on a late-1969/early-1970 tour of the U.K. and Europe (which also included Traffic guitarist Dave Mason), which resulted in an unremarkable live album called, artfully enough, *Delaney & Bonnie and Friends on Tour with Eric Clapton*. Around the same time, Clapton appeared with John Lennon's Plastic Ono Band at the Toronto Rock and Roll Festival for an odd set of oldies and avant-garde rock (an embarrassing concert disc resulted, *Live Peace in Toronto*). The guitarist also showed up on the Beatles' 1968 "White Album," where he played the sultry solo on George Harrison's "While My Guitar Gently Weeps," using one of Harrison's own Les Pauls.

After this series of sideman gigs, Clapton set about recording his first solo album, with Delaney Bramlett in the producer's chair.

Eric Clapton

Released in the summer of 1970, the album—titled simply *Eric Clapton*—was a sizable seller and had a U.S. hit with J.J. Cale's "After Midnight." Like the Blind Faith album, *Eric Clapton* was a mixed bag of filler songs and a few gems, like the terrific "Let It Rain," "Easy Now," and "Blues Power." On this album Clapton abandoned the high-volume guitar work of his Cream days in favor of a lightly overdriven electric guitar sound that showed a more melodic side of his soloing talents. He had also switched from the humbucker-powered Gibsons of Cream and Blind Faith to the less powerful, but just as distinctive, Fender Stratocaster, with three single-coil pickups. It would ultimately become his signature guitar.

Eric's Masterpiece. After the release of the solo album, Clapton exited the Delaney and Bonnie camp, taking with him the rhythm section of Bobby Whitlock (keyboards and vocals), Jim Gordon (drums), and Carl Radle (bass). They formed Derek & the Dominos, with Eric in the lead role of "Derek." This new ensemble undertook a low-key British club tour that proved highly successful, and by the fall of 1970, the quartet was in Miami working on their first record, *Layla and Other Assorted Love Songs*. The album's theme was of lost love, based largely on Clapton's love affair with Patti Boyd Harrison (at that time the wife of George Harrison; she later left Harrison to marry Clapton). Compounding his personal torment was Clapton's increasing use of heroin, to which he had become addicted. The expression of this turmoil was the *Layla* album, a two-record set that contained intensely introspective and revealing songs, in addition to what is arguably the best recorded guitar playing of his career.

During the recording of *Layla*, Clapton invited Duane Allman, slide and lead guitarist for the Allman Brothers (♪) to play on several songs. After cutting a few tracks, Allman became the fifth Domino and played on the rest of the album. Though the record didn't create an immediate sensation upon its release in November 1970, it was readily apparent that the guitar team of Clapton and Allman was something special. From potent blues cuts like "Key to the Highway" and "Have You Ever Loved a Woman" to the rockers "Anyday" and "Why Does Love Have to Be So Sad" to their bombastic version of Jimi Hendrix's "Little Wing," the two players formed one of the greatest guitar teams rock has ever known.

Addiction. Unfortunately, it was to be short-lived. Derek & the Dominos completed a large stateside tour in early 1971 and were in the process of recording their second album that May when the band broke down completely. Most of the members were using large amounts of drugs, and tensions were mounting between them, so they decided to call it quits. Clapton did George Harrison's "Concert for Bangla Desh" in New York on August 1, 1971, but then went into seclusion. For the next year and a half he remained reclusive, avoiding outside contact or gigs. At one low point, the "guitar hero" even resorted to selling his guitars to raise money for drugs. For recreation, meanwhile, he spent a lot of time listening to short-wave radio and building model cars and airplanes; he even worked as a farmhand in

Wales.

Several friends, including Pete Townshend, prodded Clapton into the spotlight in an attempt to bring him back to music. They arranged a comeback show for him at the Rainbow Theatre in London during January 1973, which eventually resulted in a restrained live album (a live set from his days with Derek & the Dominos was released that year as well).

Solo Career. By 1974 Clapton partially got his act together, swearing off drugs (though not alcohol, which would plague him for another decade) and recording his first studio album in three and a half years. Titled *461 Ocean Boulevard*, the album made it to #1 and yielded a hit single, "I Shot the Sheriff." Despite the solid collection of songs on *461*, Clapton's guitar playing lacked the authority it had possessed in the days of the Bluesbreakers, Cream, and Derek & the Dominos. Vocally, too, Clapton seemed a milder frontman, at times mumbling and whispering his lyrics on the album.

For the rest of the seventies he continued on in this manner, making lightweight studio albums of soft country-style pop and blues. He did create a considerable name for himself as a pop performer, garnering several Top 40 singles during the next decade. His live albums, *E.C. Was Here* and *Just One Night*, showed the guitarist in better form, soloing with some of his renowned fire, but Eric Clapton the guitar hero seemed a hazy rock 'n' roll memory. As many of his fans came to realize, Clapton was not God.

A glimmer of hope came in 1985 when he released the single "Forever Man" (from the album *Behind the Sun*), which featured a blazing Clapton solo in the style of old and his most impassioned singing in years; he had also finally kicked his alcoholism. In 1986 Clapton came back with *August*, a guitar dominated pop album (produced by Genesis drummer and solo artist Phil Collins) that was replete with some of the guitarist's most explosive guitar solos since the Derek & the Dominos period—his break on "Miss You" was a true return to form. Clapton toured behind the album with Collins and several top L.A. session players. The tour included a very popular appearance at the Live Aid concert in 1985, which regained him a large audience among the rock youth of the world. After both *August* and the tour, Clapton seemed finally to be at ease with the responsibility of being one of rock's greatest guitar heroes, a designation that had haunted him since the mid sixties.

More recently, he has returned to his earliest blues influences and a stripped-down style, which resulted in his most successful album ever, *Unplugged* (1992). The acoustic album, taken from an appearance on MTV, featured a moving tribute to his deceased son, "Tears in Heaven," and the entire collection swept the Grammys that year. In 1994, the all-blues disc *From the Cradle* featured the guitarist roaring through a collection of Chicago blues tunes. It debuted at #1.

Legacy. While his career is booming these days, Clapton's music from 1965 through 1970 stands out as the showcase for his mastery of the guitar. His blues-rock style was not as sonically adventurous as Jimi Hendrix's, but Eric Clapton's synthesis of blues guitar techniques and rock sounds was more accessible than Hendrix's wild aural assault. Because of this, Clapton helped formulate the basic vocabulary for a generation of rock guitar players, and echoes of his instrumental voice can be found in the styles of most rock guitarists, especially those who emerged in the pre-Van Halen period from 1966 to 1978. Thus, while new guitar heroes will come and go, it is doubtful that the timeless sound of Clapton's electric guitar will ever cease to be important to the world of rock 'n' roll.

Blind Faith, *Blind Faith* (Atlantic, 1969). **Derek & the Dominos,** *Layla and Other Assorted Love Songs* (Atco, 1970), *In Concert* (Polydor, 1973•), *The Layla Sessions* (Polygram, 1991). **Eric Clapton** [on RSO except where noted], *Eric Clapton* (Atco,1970), *History of Eric Clapton* (Atco, 1972), *Eric Clapton at His Best* (Polydor, 1972), *Eric Clapton's Rainbow Concert* (1973•), *461 Ocean Boulevard* (1974), *There's One in Every Crowd* (1975), *E.C. Was Here* (1975•), *No Reason to Cry* (1976), *Slowhand* (1977), *Backless* (1978), *Just One Night* (1980•), *Another Ticket* (1981), *Timepieces/Best of Eric Clapton* (1982), *Money and Cigarettes* (Duck/Warner Bros., 1983), *Behind the Sun* (Duck/Warner Bros., 1985), *August* (Duck/Warner Bros., 1986), *Crossroads* (Polydor, 1988•), *Journeyman* (Duck/Reprise, 1990), *24 Nights* (Reprise, 1991•), *Rush* [soundtrack] (1992), *Unplugged* (1992•), *From the Cradle* (1994), *The Cream of Eric Clapton* (1995).

Recordings featuring Eric Clapton: **Various Artists,** *What's Shakin'* (Elektra, 1966). **Various Artists** [on Immediate], *Blues Anytime Vol. 1* (1968), *Blues Anytime Vol. 2* (1968), *Blues Anytime Vol. 3* (1968). **George Harrison,** *Wonderwall Music* (Apple, 1968), *All Things Must Pass* (Apple, 1970), *Dark Horse* (Apple, 1974), *George Harrison* (Dark Horse, 1979), *Cloud Nine* (Dark Horse, 1987). **The Beatles,** *The Beatles* ["White Album"] (Apple, 1968). **Aretha Franklin,** *Lady Soul* (Atlantic, 1968). **Champion Jack Dupree,** *From New Orleans to Chicago* (London, 1969). **Jackie Lomax,** *Is This What You Want?* (Apple, 1969). **John Lennon/Plastic Ono Band** [on Apple], *Live Peace in Toronto* (1969•), *Plastic Ono Band* (1970), *Some Time in New York City* (1972•). **Billy Preston** [on Apple], *That's the Way God Planned It* (1969), *Encouraging Words* (1970). **King Curtis,** *Get Ready* (Atlantic, 1970). **Leon Russell** [on Shelter], *Leon Russell* (1970), *Leon Russell & The Shelter People* (1971). **Delaney and Bonnie & Friends,** *On Tour* (Atco, 1970•). **Shawn Phillips,** *Contribution* (n/a, 1970). **Ashton, Gardner & Dyke,** *Ashton, Gardner, and Dyke* (Capitol, 1970). **Jesse Ed Davis,** *¡Jesse Davis!* (Atlantic, 1970). **Doris Troy,** *Doris Troy* (Apple, 1970). **Stephen Stills** [on Atlantic], *Stephen Stills* (1970), *Stephen Stills 2* (1971). **Buddy Guy & Junior Wells,** *Play the Blues* (Atlantic, 1971). **Yoko Ono,** *Fly* (Apple, 1971). **Howlin' Wolf,** *The London Howlin' Wolf Sessions* (Chess, 1971). **Various Artists,** *The Concert for Bangla Desh* (Apple, 1971•). **The Crickets,** *Rockin' 50's Rock 'n' Roll* (Barnaby, 1971). **Dr. John,** *The Sun, Moon, and Herbs* (Atco, 1971), *Hollywood Be Thy Name* (United Artists, 1975). **Bobby Keyes,** *Bobby Keyes* (Warner Bros., 1972). **Bobby Whitlock,** *Raw Velvet* (ABC, 1972). **Duane Allman,** *An Anthology* (Capricorn, 1972). **Various Artists,** *History of British Rock, Vol. 2* (Sire, 1974). **The Who & Various Artists,** *Tommy* (Polydor, 1975) **Joe Cocker,** *Stingray* (A&M, 1976). **Ringo Starr,** *Ringo's Rotogravure* (Atlantic, 1976). **Kinky Friedman,** *Lasso from El Paso* (Columbia, 1976). **Stephen Bishop** [on ABC], *Careless* (1976), *Red Cab to Manhattan* (1980). **Roger Daltrey,** *One of the Boys* (MCA, 1977). **Rick Danko,** *Rick Danko* (Arista, 1977). **Pete Townshend & Ronnie Lane,** *Rough Mix* (MCA, 1977). **Various Artists,** *White Mansions* (A&M, 1978). **Marc Benno,** *Lost in Austin* (A&M, 1979). **Danny Douma,** *Night Eyes* (Night Eyes, 1979). **Phil Collins** [on Atlantic], *Face Value* (1981), *…But Seriously* (1990). **John Martyn,** *Glorious Fool* (Warner Bros., 1981). **Various Artists,** *The Secret Policeman's Other Ball, The Music* (Island, 1982•). **Various Artists,** *The Great British Blues Barrelhouse and Boogie Bonanza, 1962–1968* (Decca, 1982). **Gary Brooker** [on Polygram], *Lead Me to Water* (1982), *Echoes in the Night* (1985). **Corey Hart,** *First Offense* (EMI America, 1983). **Roger Waters,** *The Pros and Cons of Hitchhiking* (Columbia, 1984). **Various Artists,** *White Boy Blues, Classic Guitars of Clapton, Beck, and Page* (Compleat, 1984). **Christine McVie,** *Christine McVie* (Warner Bros., 1984). **Liona Boyd,** *Persona* (CBS, 1986). **Lionel Richie,** *Dancing on the Ceiling* (Motown, 1986). **Bob Geldof,** *Deep in the Heart of Nowhere* (Atlantic, 1986). **Various Artists** [on Warner Bros.], *Lethal Weapon* [soundtrack] (1987), *Lethal Weapon 2* [soundtrack] (1989). **Various Artists,** *The Color of Money* [soundtrack] (MCA, 1987). **Sting,** *…Nothing Like the Sun* (A&M, 1987). **Bob Dylan,** *Down in the Groove* (Columbia, 1988). **Jim Capaldi,** *Some Come Running* (Island, 1989). **Jack Bruce,** *Willpower—A Twenty Year Retrospective* (Polydor, 1989). **Richie Sambora,** *Stranger in this Town* (Mercury, 1991). **Various Artists,** *Two Rooms* (Polydor, 1991). **Various Artists,** *A Tribute to Stevie Ray Vaughan* (Epic, 1996).

The Rolling Stones (Part 2)

Keith Richards
Born: *December 18, 1943, in Dartford, Kent, England*
Main Guitars: *Gibson Les Paul, Fender Telecaster*

Mick Taylor
Born: *January 17, 1949, in Welwyn Garden City, Hertfordshire, England*
Main Guitar: *Gibson Les Paul Standard*

Ron Wood
Born: *June 1, 1947, in Hillingdon, Middlesex, England*
Main Guitars: *ESP, Zemaitis, and Ernie Ball/Music Man solidbodies*

On July 5, 1969, ex-Bluesbreaker (♦) guitarist Mick Taylor made his debut with the Rolling Stones at Hyde Park in London in front of an audience of 250,000. Originally planned as a comeback show, it became a tribute performance to Brian Jones, who had died just a few days earlier (♦ The Rolling Stones [Part 1]). With Taylor in the lineup, the Rolling Stones made it clear that they were back in action, planning both a new album and a tour. Soon after the successful Hyde Park concert, the single "Honky Tonk Women"—a Keith Richards masterpiece of rhythm guitar—was released to universal popular and critical acclaim. Taylor's deft soloing abilities, honed during his stint with Mayall, contrasted superbly with Richards' visceral rhythm style. With the late-1969 release of *Let It Bleed*, the Stones first album with Taylor, it was evident that the Richards-Taylor guitar combination was indeed going to be the beginning of an entirely new chapter of Rolling Stones rock 'n' roll.

At the end of 1969 the Stones launched their first U.S. tour in several years and swiftly reconquered the States. In November they recorded their concert at Madison Square Garden and released it as the seminal 1970 live set *Get Yer Ya Ya's Out*, which contained a couple of great Chuck Berry covers, "Carol" (with Taylor taking the solos) and "Little Queenie" (Richards handling lead duties). In 1971 they released the brilliant *Sticky Fingers*. Whereas the guitar pairing of Keith Richards and Brian Jones was essentially that of two guitars completely intermeshed with one another, the Richards and Taylor combination was more of a straight-ahead lead/rhythm setup, with Taylor handing most of the leads and Richards cranking out his in-the-pocket rhythm grooves. Some guitar peaks on *Sticky Fingers* include Taylor's heavy blues solo on "Sway" (ironically, with Mick Jagger on rhythm guitar instead of Richards), Richards' updated Chuck Berry-style break on the bruising rocker "Bitch," and "Can't You Hear Me Knocking," which is a Richards master class on rock rhythm guitar with Taylor checking in on lead.

In mid 1972 the critically lauded *Exile on Main St.* was released, featuring more electrifying guitar workouts by Richards and Taylor (notably on "Rocks Off" and "Happy," the latter featuring Richards on lead vocals), as well as the single, "Tumbling Dice." *Goats Head Soup* followed in 1973 with the single "Doo Doo Doo Doo Doo (Heartbreaker)"—notable for Taylor's melodic phase shifted break—and 1974 brought *It's Only Rock 'n' Roll*. In addition to the classic title track, Taylor delivers a stunning extended and soulful solo on "Time Waits for No One." *It's Only Rock 'n' Roll* proved to be Mick Taylor's last album with the Stones. After five and a half years of lead guitar with "the World's Greatest Rock 'n' Roll Band," Taylor left the Stones because, as he stated at the time, he wanted to evolve as a musician and play with some different artists, especially ex-Cream bassist Jack Bruce. Like Clapton before him, he wanted more than just the spotlight of fame.

In 1975 the Stones replaced Taylor with Ron Wood, who had served as bassist for Jeff Beck and then as guitarist and foil for Rod Stewart. With Wood the Stones continued creating their patented brand of rock 'n' roll,

Keith Richards

arguably with less panache than during the Taylor years. Wood brought the Rolling Stones' guitar sound full circle back to the days when Brian Jones and Keith Richards were at the guitar helm. Unlike Mick Taylor, neither Richards nor Wood was—or is—strictly a "lead" or a "rhythm" guitarist; both simply played to enhance the song, just as Richards and Jones did in the sixties. On Stones albums since 1976, including *Some Girls*, *Tattoo You*, *Voodoo Lounge*, and the live set *Still Life*, the combined guitar playing of Ron Wood and Keith Richards almost amounts to the sound of one big guitar, since their playing is so fully integrated.

Of course, the heart of the entire Rolling Stones guitar sound is unquestionably Richards' rhythm playing, which leans heavily on simple fourths and open tunings. As his solo recordings have proved, he is the one singularly responsible for defining the overall Stones sound. Co-guitarists may come and go, but Keith Richards is surely the electric heart and soul of the Rolling Stones.

Rolling Stones (1969–94) [on Rolling Stones Records, except where noted], *Let It Bleed* (London, 1969), *Get Yer Ya Ya's Out* (London, 1970•), *Sticky Fingers* (1971), *Hot Rocks: 1964–1971* (1972), *Exile on Main St.* (1972), *More Hot Rocks* (1972), *Goats Head Soup* (1973), *It's Only Rock 'n' Roll* (1975), *Made in the Shade* (1975), *Metamorphosis* (Abkco, 1975), *Black and Blue* (1976) *Love You Live* (1977•), *Some Girls* (1978), *Emotional Rescue* (1980), *Sucking in the Seventies* (1981), *Tattoo You* (1981), *Still Life* (1982•), *Undercover* (1983), *Rewind* [1971–1984] (1984), *Dirty Work* (1986), *Steel Wheels* (1989), *Flashpoint* (1991•), *Voodoo Lounge* (1994), *Stripped* (1995•). **Keith Richards**, *Talk Is Cheap* (Virgin, 1988), *The X-Pensive Winos Live at the Hollywood Palladium* (Virgin, 1991•), *Main Offender* (1992). **Mick Taylor**, *Mick Taylor* (Columbia, 1979). [♦ The Faces for Ron Wood discography]

Recordings featuring Keith Richards: **Ron Wood**, *I've Got My Own Album to Do* (Warner Bros., 1974), *Now Look* (Warner Bros., 1975), *Gimme Some Neck* (Columbia, 1979). **Chuck Berry**, *Rockit* (Atco, 1979), *Hail! Hail! Rock 'n Roll* [soundtrack] (MCA, 1987•). **Aretha Franklin**, *Aretha* (Arista, 1986).

Recordings featuring Mick Taylor: **John Mayall** [on London/Decca], *Crusade* (1967), *Bare Wires* (1968), *Blues from Laurel Canyon* (1969), *Looking Back* (1969), *The Diary of a Band* (1970•), *Primal Solos* (1977•). **Various Artists**, *The Great British Blues Barrelhouse and Boogie Bonanza, 1962–1968* (Decca, 1982). **Bob Dylan**, *Real Live* (1984•). **Various Artists**, *Guitar Speak III* (IRS, 1991).

The Who

Pete Townshend

Born: *May 19, 1945, in Chiswick, England*
Main Guitars: *Rickenbacker hollowbodies, Gibson Les Paul Deluxe, Fender Stratocaster*

Howling feedback. Crashing power chords. Manic spot solos. These are all attributes of rock 'n' roll's most physical guitar player, Pete Townshend of the Who. Townshend—acclaimed as one of rock's greatest songwriters and spokesmen—revolutionized rock guitar in the sixties with his brutal guitar playing and onstage acrobatics. During Who numbers such as "I Can't Explain," "Anyway,'Anyhow, Anywhere," 'Pinball Wizard," and "Baba O'Riley," Townshend characteristically played frenzied barre-chord progressions with barbaric delight, complemented equally by the primal lead vocals of Roger Daltrey and the Who's ominously thundering rhythm section, bassist John Entwistle and drummer Keith Moon.

Onstage, the Who had few rivals in the sixties and seventies. Centerstage, Roger Daltrey would swing his mike by the cable ten feet over his head while Keith Moon alternated between playing brilliant drum fills and trashing his entire kit. Stage right, Entwistle would stand off to the side, looking bored, but playing lightning-quick runs on bass. Finally, Townshend would top them all by flailing his arm around like a windmill, leaping all over the stage. As a finale, he would smash his Rickenbacker or Gibson guitar to pieces or ram it through one of his speaker cabinets. With their tough, bombastic recordings and blitzkrieg stage act, it is easy to understand how the Who became one of the most popular and exciting groups in rock 'n' roll.

Early Years. In London in 1965, the Who (formed the previous year) were at the forefront of a pop fashion movement sweeping the country called "mod." Mods, as its adherents were known, were amphetamine-popping teenagers whose credo insisted on their dressing better than anybody else (including each other), driving motor scooters, snubbing adults, and fighting their punkish rivals, the "rockers." Before long, the Who became the mods' favorite band, mostly because of their aggressive music, wild stage act, and Townshend's and Moon's tendency to destroy their instruments at the end of each performance. With the help of ambitious managers Kit Lambert and Chris Stamp, the group began building a large following in England through numerous club appearances and hit singles like "I Can't Explain" and "My Generation."

In 1967 the Who tried to crack America with a series of grueling concert tours and television appearances. During that year the band charted in the Top 10 on both sides of the Atlantic with the quasi-psychedelic single "I Can See for Miles." By the time they hit the stage at the Monterey Pop Festival in that California summer of 1967 (where they were topped only by Jimi Hendrix), they were one of the hottest acts to come out of England.

After the success of "I Can See for Miles," Townshend and the Who began work on a more ambitious piece of rock music. When it was released in 1969, the album, called *Tommy*, immediately set the rock world on its ear. The tale of a deaf, dumb, and

Pete Townshend

blind boy-turned-messiah, *Tommy* was a radical new idea in rock music: the rock opera. Although the Who weren't the inventors of the rock opera, they were undoubtedly the most successful with it, and within a few months of the album's release, the Who were virtual superstars around the globe.

Kerr-chang! The definitive Who guitar sound was that of Pete Townshend's power chords. Usually it was the sound of a single guitar chord (often a triad or simple configuration of root and fifth) being strummed hard with excessive amplifier feedback and sustain for added punch. Townshend's trademark power chordings run rampant through nearly all of the Who's early hits: "I'm a Boy," "I Can't Explain," "The Kids Are Alright," and especially "I Can See for Miles," with its multi-tracked guitars, brief single-note solos, and distorted chords. But the best of Townshend's early work by far is "My Generation," from 1965, one of the great rock singles of all time. Behind the stuttering vocals of Roger Daltrey, Townshend's rhythm guitar work slashes about the song recklessly, while Entwistle takes a twangy Duane Eddy-influenced solo on his dual-horned Danelectro bass. "My Generation" concluded in an instrumental tour de force as Townshend, straining the limits of his guitar, strums long, hellish power chords with feedback and total distortion.

Within the *Tommy* set are more displays of Townshend's great guitar playing. Among the best are "Sparks," an instrumental that features Townshend's pedal-based chordings on acoustic guitar, and "Pinball Wizard" with its frenetically strummed acoustic intro and echo-panned electric work. The strong acoustic rhythm guitar parts on "Pinball Wizard" also proved that, above all else, the acoustic guitar could hold its own with an electric guitar in a heavy rock setting.

Later Recordings. The Who's reputation as a great stage act spread quickly, and after a stunning live performance at Woodstock, the band released *Live at Leeds* in mid 1970. While Townshend had established the acoustic guitar as a great rock instrument on *Tommy*, Leeds was his tribute to the electric guitar. Of note are the Hendrix-influenced guitar parts to "Young Man Blues" and Eddie Cochran's "Summertime Blues." In fact, the whole of *Live at Leeds* is a pyrotechnical monument to the heavy side of Townshend's guitar playing with the Who.

In 1971 the Who released what's considered their finest recorded work, *Who's Next*. Composed of tracks from an aborted concept album called *Lifehouse*, *Who's Next* was a revolutionary album in rock 'n' roll, not only for Townshend's powerful songwriting and guitar playing, but also for establishing the synthesizer as a serious rock instrument (especially on the power chord-filled "Baba O'Riley"). Throughout the recording Townshend deftly combines the acoustic guitar lyricism of *Tommy* with the molten electric assaults of *Live at Leeds* to create some of his best six-string work ever. On "Bargain" he gives a stunning electric/acoustic performance, while on "Behind Blue Eyes," he plays a quiet, fingerpicked intro before launching into an electric hard rock section. The summit of *Who's Next* is "Won't Get Fooled Again," one of the finest exhibitions of rock guitar power chording ever captured on vinyl. Townshend's and Daltrey's fuzz-chord-and-scream finale is still an unrivaled moment in rock 'n' roll.

Quadrophenia (1973), another large-scale rock opera from the band, moved towards more orchestrated and keyboard-inspired tracks. The hard edge of *Who's Next* was found only on tracks like "The Punk Meets the Godfather" and "Dr. Jimmy." Many lamented the subdued dose of guitar bombast on the disc, a feature that Townshend dispensed with until the muscular *Who Are You* of 1978. Unfortunately, this was to be the last album with Keith Moon, who died from an overdose shortly after its release. Attempts to keep the band going with ex-Faces drummer Kenny Jones proved futile, as his restrained style did little to revive the guitar mayhem of Townshend's earlier days.

Townshend recorded a number of hit-and-miss solo albums (the best of which are *Empty Glass* and *All the Best Cowboys Have Chinese Eyes*) and battled drugs throughout the 1980s. He also revealed that he had a severe case of tinnitus–ringing in the ears–making him one of the first electric guitarists to admit to the dangerous effects of deafening amplification. The Who itself has existed in a fractured form since the early 1980s, getting together occasionally for high-profile concerts. For all his social concerns as a young adult ("Hope I die before I get old"), Townshend now has become something of a rock hypocrite, shamelessly reuniting the band for cash and glitzing up *Tommy* for the Broadway stage. His status as rock's angriest young man has given way to a reputation as one of rock's oldest sellouts.

Legacy. Though he is not the technically proficient lead guitarist some of his peers are, Townshend has still earned equal billing with them in the history of rock guitar–not just as a guitar smasher, but as a great stylist in his own right. For his incandescent use of amplifier distortion and feedback, he is undoubtedly one of the great sonic innovators of rock guitar, and he stands among the best as a rhythm guitarist. Who else could strum his guitar like a windmill and turn it into a respected playing technique?

The Who [on Decca except where noted], *The Who Sings My Generation* (1966), *Happy Jack* [U.S. title of *A Quick One*] (1967), *The Who Sell Out* (1967), *Magic Bus—The Who on Tour* (1968), *Tommy* (1969), *Live at Leeds* (1970•), *Who's Next* (1971), *Meaty, Beaty, Big, and Bouncy* (1971), *Quadrophenia* (MCA, 1973), *Odds and Sods* (MCA, 1974), *The Who by Numbers* (MCA, 1975), *Who Are You* (1978), *The Kids Are Alright* (1979•), *Quadrophenia* [soundtrack] (Polydor, 1979), *Face Dances* (Warner Bros., 1981), *It's Hard* (Warner Bros., 1982), *Hooligans* (MCA, 1982), *Who's Last* (MCA, 1984•), *Who's Missing* (MCA, 1986), *Two's Missing* (MCA, 1987), *Join Together* (MCA, 1990•), *30 Years of Maximum Rock & Roll* (1994•), *Live at Leeds* [reissue with bonus tracks] (MCA, 1995•). **Pete Townshend** [on Atco except where noted], *Who Came First* (MCA, 1972), *Empty Glass* (1980), *All the Best Cowboys Have Chinese Eyes* (1982), *Scoop* (1983), *White City* (1985), *Deep End Live* (1986•), *Another Scoop* (1987), *The Iron Man* (1989), *Psychoderelict* (1993), *The Best of Pete Townshend—coolwalkingsmoothtalking...* (Atlantic, 1996). **Pete Townshend & Ronnie Lane,** *Rough Mix* (MCA, 1977).

Recordings featuring Pete Townshend: **Various Artists,** *Woodstock* (Cotillion, 1970•). **Eric Clapton,** *Rainbow Concert* (RSO, 1973•). **Various Artists,** *History of British Rock, Vol. 2* (Sire, 1974). **The Who & Various Artists,** *Tommy* [soundtrack] (Polydor, 1975). **Various Artists,** *The Secret Policeman's Ball* (Island, 1979•). **Paul McCartney,** *Press to Play* (Capitol, 1986). **Various Artists,** *Two Rooms* (Polydor, 1991).

Ten Years After

Alvin Lee

Born: *December 19, 1944, in Nottingham, England*
Main Guitar: *Gibson ES-335*

On August 17, 1969, Alvin Lee cranked out the loud guitar riff of "I'm Going Home" in front of a quarter of a million people at Woodstock and achieved instant rock guitar stardom. Wailing away on a red Gibson ES-335 emblazoned with its signature "peace" decal, Lee turned this historic nine-minute-plus boogie into what many remember as one of the highlights of the entire Woodstock festival. On the strength of that performance and its inclusion in the accompanying concert film, Lee–a.k.a. "the Fastest Guitar in the West" and leader of the British blues-rock outfit Ten Years After–became one of the most popular blues-rock imports from Britain.

Instead of imitating American blues guitar masters, as many of his blues-rock peers did, Lee drew from the jazz guitar mastery of Charlie Christian and Tal Farlow, whose fast right-hand picking he smoothly incorporated into his own fleet-fingered style. Some of Lee's best guitar frenzies with Ten Years After are on tracks like "Spoonful" (from their eponymous 1967 debut album) and their pyrotechnical cover of Woody Herman's big-band classic "Woodchopper's Ball," both of which have guitar solos taken at lightning-fast tempos. Another guitar peak of Lee's recording career with TYA is "I'd Love to Change the World" (from the 1971 album *A Space in Time*), where he cuts a fine pentatonic solo with just the right amounts of distortion and echo. It's one of his most memorable leads with the band.

The endless high-speed boogies of Ten Years After lost steam by the mid seventies, and U.S. fans found new artists to rock to; the band broke up not long after. Still, Alvin Lee is recording today and, along with Jimi Hendrix and Carlos Santana, remains one of the quintessential guitar heroes of the Woodstock experience. His penchant for speed also prophesied the coming shredders of the 1980s, who, like him, used technique as an art unto itself and similarly blew more than a few minds.

Ten Years After [on Deram except where noted], *Ten Years After* (1967), *Undead* (1968), *Stonehenge* (1969), *Ssssssh* (1969), *Cricklewood Green* (1970), *Watt* (1970), *A Space in Time* (Columbia, 1971), *Recorded Live* (Columbia, 1973•), *Goin' Home, Their Greatest Hits* (Columbia, 1975). **Ten Years Later, Rocket Fuel** (RSO, 1978), *Ride On* (RSO, 1979), *Essential* (EMI, 1991). **Alvin Lee** [on Columbia except where noted], *On the Road to Freedom* [with Mylon LeFevre] (1974), *In Flight* (1975), *Pump Iron* (1975), *Free Fall* (Atlantic, 1980), *RX5* (Atlantic, 1981), *Detroit Diesel* (21/Atco, 1986), *I Hear You Rockin'* (Victory, 1994).

Recordings featuring Alvin Lee: **Various Artists,** *Woodstock* (Cotillion, 1970•). **Various Artists,** *The First Great Rock Festivals of the Seventies* (Columbia, 1971•). **Jerry Lee Lewis,** *The Session* (Mercury, 1973). **George Harrison,** *Dark Horse* (Apple, 1974). **Various Artists,** *The Great British Blues Barrelhouse and Boogie Bonanza, 1962–1968* (Decca, 1982•).

Traffic

Dave Mason

B o r n : *May 10, 1946, in Worcester, England*
M a i n   G u i t a r : *Fender Stratocaster*

Steve Winwood

B o r n : *May 12, 1948, in Birmingham, England*
M a i n   G u i t a r : *Fender Stratocaster*

One British guitarist whose name was heard frequently in the late sixties and early seventies was Dave Mason. Aside from his acclaimed solo career, Mason was best known for his work with Traffic, the English supergroup he co-founded with singer and multi-instrumentalist Steve Winwood. Mason was also a top-notch sideman, appearing at times with such legendary performers as the Rolling Stones, Derek & the Dominos, George Harrison, and even Jimi Hendrix. Through his associations with Traffic and other groups, Mason gained a sizable reputation as an ace guitarslinger, renowned as much for his controlled and melodic lead style as for his solid rhythm playing, which was featured on Jimi Hendrix's classic version of "All along the Watchtower".

After playing as a teenager in local groups the Jaguars, the Hellions, and Deep Feeling, Mason hooked up with the Spencer Davis Group as a roadie in the mid sixties. There he met the group's much-praised vocalist, Steve Winwood, whose powerful R&B singing had given the group their 1967 hit "Gimme Some Lovin'." Mason appeared on the band's last single, "I'm a Man" (reportedly playing tambourine), as did horn player Chris Wood.

After the release of the recording in 1967, Winwood, Mason, and Wood left Spencer Davis to form Traffic with drummer Jim Capaldi. Within a few months they released their debut album, *Mr. Fantasy*. It was an immediate hit in the U.K., as were the first singles, "Paper Sun" and the Mason-penned number "Hole in My Shoe."

In late 1967 Mason left the group, citing musical conflicts, but he was back within a few months to play on the second album, *Traffic*. The album was even more successful than the first (due in part to Mason's composition "Feelin' Alright") and quickly broke into the upper reaches of the U.S. album charts. Mason left the band again in October 1968, and soon after, Traffic folded. Among his finest recorded moments with the band are songs like "Pearly Queen," on which he plays some Hendrix-like solos and R&B-styled rhythm riffs, and "Dear Mr. Fantasy," which is notable for a bluesy, Claptonesque guitar break.

With above-average singing and songwriting talents, Mason was determined to make it as a solo act. His first record, *Alone Together* (1970), proved he had the potential to be a major rock performer. The album was a hit in both the U.S. and the U.K. and showcased Mason's guitar acrobatics, gaining him wider recognition as a guitarist of sizable talent. Standout cuts included "Shouldn't Have Took More than You Gave," which features a long wah-wah solo, and "Look at You Look at Me," with a solo composed of echoey bends, repeated licks, and melodic phrasing.

After *Alone Together*, however, Mason's solo career was plagued with poorly received albums and numerous conflicts with his record company. He did briefly pull out of the slump in 1977 with the album *Let It Flow*, which yielded the light pop hit "We Just Disagree." As of 1995 he was lead guitarist in the latest incarnation of Fleetwood Mac (♦), while Traffic, which had broken up in 1975, was resurrected by Jim Capaldi and Steve Winwood, the latter serving as the band's lead guitarist.

Traffic [on UA except where noted], *Mr. Fantasy* (1968), *Traffic* (1968), *Best of Traffic* (1970), *Welcome to the Canteen* (1971•), *Far from Home* (Virgin, 1994). **Dave Mason** [on Blue Thumb except where noted], *Alone Together* (1970), *Dave Mason and Cass Elliot* (1971), *Headkeeper* (1972•), *Dave Mason Is Alive* (1973•), *It's Like You Never Left* (Columbia, 1973), *The Best of Dave Mason* (1974), *Dave Mason* (Columbia, 1974), *Split Coconut* (Columbia, 1975), *Certified Live* (Columbia, 1976•), *Let It Flow* (Columbia, 1977), *Mariposa de Oro* (Columbia, 1978), *Very Best of Dave Mason* (1978), *Old Crest on a New Wave* (Columbia, 1980). **Fleetwood Mac,** *Time* (Warner Bros., 1995).

Recordings featuring Dave Mason: **The Rolling Stones,** *Beggars Banquet* (London, 1968). **Jimi Hendrix,** *Electric Ladyland* (Reprise, 1968). **Delaney and Bonnie,** *Delaney and Bonnie & Friends on Tour with Eric Clapton* (Atco, 1970•). **George Harrison,** *All Things Must Pass* (Apple, 1970). **Bobby Keyes,** *Bobby Keyes* (Warner Bros., 1972). **Eric Clapton,** *Crossroads* (Polydor, 1988•).

The Faces

Ron Wood

Born: *June 1, 1947, in Hillingdon, Middlesex, England*
Main Guitars: *Zemaitis custom, Fender Stratocaster, ESP Ron Wood model*

There are not many guitarists who can claim to have played with such stellar rock acts as the Jeff Beck Group, the Faces, Rod Stewart, and the Rolling Stones. Ron Wood, however, can. While playing in a London band called the Birds in the mid sixties (not to be confused with the Byrds of folk-rock fame), he became acquainted with Jeff Beck (♦), who at the time was with the Yardbirds (♦). When Beck left that group in late 1966, Wood promptly got in touch with him about forming a new band. Beck agreed, and the lineup of the first Jeff Beck Group was set with both Beck and Wood on guitar and Rod Stewart (formerly of Shotgun Express) on vocals. Their original bass player didn't work out, so Wood volunteered for the part. On their seminal albums *Truth* (1968) and *Beck-Ola* (1969), the Jeff Beck Group—with Wood on bass—blazed new trails in hard rock and were instrumental in the creation of what came to be called heavy metal.

The Jeff Beck Group fell apart just before Woodstock in mid 1969, and Ron Wood was again in search of a band. At about the same time, the Small Faces (known for such hits as "Itchycoo Park" and "Tin Soldier") lost their lead vocalist and guitarist Steve Marriott, who had left to form Humble Pie (♦). Taking advantage of the circumstances, Wood and Stewart joined up with the remaining Small Faces (bassist Ronnie Lane, keyboardist Ian McLagan, and drummer Kenny Jones), and the new group renamed itself Faces. With their wild antics and drunken-sailors image, the Faces established themselves as a booze-swigging party band. Their albums were often lacking in focus and sales, but nevertheless, the Faces were regarded as a powerhouse live act and became a very popular concert band in the first half of the seventies.

Contrasting with the up-and-down career of the Faces was Rod Stewart's meteoric rise as a solo artist during the same time. On the brilliant solo albums *Every Picture Tells a Story* and *Never a Dull Moment*, Stewart's gutsy vocal lines were complemented by Ron Wood's charac-

teristically raw guitar excursions. From his neo-rockabilly break on "That's All Right, Mama" to his melodic solo on Stewart's big hit "Maggie May" to the greasy slide guitar on "Twistin' the Night Away" (with Mick Waller's memorable drum intro), Wood's guitar playing became an integral part of the early Rod Stewart sound and contributed much to the singer's success.

By mid decade the relationship between Rod Stewart and the Faces frayed as Stewart's solo career skyrocketed. Adding to the rift was the release of Wood's first solo album, *I've Got My Own Album to Do* (1974), and also his widely publicized appearance with the Rolling Stones on their 1975 U.S. tour as a fill-in for Mick Taylor. When Taylor left the Stones in December 1974, the band was beginning to record a new studio album, so a replacement was needed posthaste. After considering everyone from Jeff Beck to Rory Gallagher to Harvey Mandel, the Stones finally asked Wood to join in late 1975. At the same time, Rod Stewart announced he was quitting the Faces, effectively putting that band out to pasture and leaving Wood with his options completely open. Since the Faces were now defunct, he agreed to become the Rolling Stones' newest guitar player.

As a rock guitarist of note, Ron Wood's main asset on the instrument has been his ability to complement the song, rather than attempting to seek his own solo spot. Whether he's backing Rod Stewart or Mick Jagger or even himself, Wood generally lays low on the guitar, tastefully adding to the vocal melody with a sly bottleneck run, a Chuck Berry-styled lick, or fat power chords. And though he may never be regarded as highly as Eric Clapton, Jimi Hendrix, or Jimmy Page, Ron Wood is surely a significant journeyman of British rock guitar.

Jeff Beck Group [on Epic], *Truth* (1968), *Beck-Ola* (1969), *Beckology* (1991•). **The Faces** [on Warner Bros. except where noted] *First Step* (1970), *Long Player* (1971), *A Nod Is as Good as a Wink...to a Blind Horse* (1971), *Ooh La La* (1973), *Overtures and Beginners* (Mercury, 1973•), *Snakes and Ladders: The Best of the Faces* (1977). **Rod Stewart** [on Mercury], *Gasoline Alley* (1970), *Every Picture Tells a Story* (1971), *Never a Dull Moment* (1972), *Sing It Again Rod* (1973), *Smiler* (1974), *Storyteller—The Complete Anthology, 1964–1990* (Warner Bros., 1990). **Ron Wood,** *I've Got My Own Album to Do* (Warner Bros., 1974), *Now Look* (Warner Bros., 1975), *Mahoney's Last Stand* (Warner Bros., 1976), *Gimme Some Neck* (Columbia, 1979), *1234* (Columbia, 1981), *Slide on This* (Continuum, 1992). **Rolling Stones** [on Rolling Stones], *Black and Blue* (1976), *Love You Live* (1977•), *Some Girls* (1978), *Emotional Rescue* (1980), *Sucking in the Seventies* (1981), *Tattoo You* (1981), *Still Life* (1982•), *Undercover* (1983), *Rewind* (1984), *Dirty Work* (1986), *Steel Wheels* (1989), *Flashpoint* (1991•), *Voodoo Lounge* (1994), *Stripped* (1995•).

Ron Wood

Recordings featuring Ron Wood: **Eric Clapton,** *Eric Clapton's Rainbow Concert* (RSO, 1973•), *No Reason to Cry* (Polydor,

1976), *Crossroads* (Polydor, 1988•). **Alvin Lee & Mylon LeFevre,** *On the Road to Freedom* (Columbia, 1974). **The Band & Various Artists,** *The Last Waltz* (Warner Bros., 1978•). **Various Artists,** *White Boy Blues, Classic Guitars of Clapton, Beck, and Page* (Compleat, 1984). **Don Johnson,** *Heartbeat* (Epic, 1986).

Robin Trower

B o r n : *March 9, 1945, in Catford, London*
M a i n   G u i t a r : *Fender Stratocaster*

An important figure on the hard rock scene in the seventies was British guitarslinger Robin Trower. Trower's trademark sound was a supple tone that emanated from a Fender Stratocaster and a horde of effects. Because of his phased-shifted sound and spacey R&B-flavored compositions, Trower was regularly likened to Jimi Hendrix, a comparison that both helped and hindered his career. Despite the sonic similarities, Trower carved out a unique niche for himself in heavy rock, and by the middle of the 1970s was elevated to guitar hero status, propelled in large part by his 1974 album *Bridge of Sighs*.

Trower first gained recognition in Procol Harum, the British art-rock outfit whose hits included "A Whiter Shade of Pale" and "Conquistador." Before joining Procol Harum in 1967, Trower had a lengthy stint in the Paramounts, an R&B band that had several singles in the U.K. during the mid sixties. During his time in the Paramounts, Trower discovered the blues, and by the time he hooked up with Procol Harum, he'd already begun to shift his guitar style in a more bluesy direction. The coming of Hendrix in 1967 spurred Trower's blues development even more, and by the time of his last album with Procol Harum, *Broken Barricades* (1971), he was a formidable soloist in the blues/Hendrix vein (as evidenced in his tribute to Jimi on that recording, "Song for a Dreamer").

The following year Trower formed Jude, a hard rock outfit fronted by vocalist James Dewar, but the band folded within a few months. The guitarist then assembled his own trio with Dewar on bass and vocals and Reg Isadore on drums. Nineteen seventy-three saw the release of their first album, *Twice Removed from Yesterday*, and the next year brought forth Trower's chart-busting *Bridge of Sighs*. For much of the seventies, Trower was a highly esteemed guitarist and issued several fine albums, like *For Earth Below* (1975) and *Long Misty Days* (1976), as well as mounting several stateside tours.

Many of the best examples of Trower's "post-Hendrix"-styled guitar playing come from *Bridge of Sighs*. The opener, "Day of the Eagle," is a metallish rocker filled with the guitarist's funky chording, melodic lead work, and a menagerie of electronic sound effects (distortion, echo, and the swishing, Leslie-like sound of a Univox Univibe). Trower sets a moody tone for the title ballad with a cool, ethereal rhythm guitar track and a hyp-

notic single-note figure in the fadeout. Another key Trower song is the title cut of *Long Misty Days*, which has a huge, cathedral-like rhythm guitar tone and lead lines highlighted by his impressive wrist vibrato, string-bends, and melodic pentatonic lines.

In the early eighties Trower teamed up with ex-Cream bassist Jack Bruce and drummer Bill Lordan for a well-received album under the moniker B.L.T. He continues to release solo albums, though his fame relies solely on his guitar work from the 1970s.

Procol Harum [on A&M except where noted], *Procol Harum* (Deram, 1967), *Shine on Brightly* (1968), *A Salty Dog* (1969), *Home* (1970), *Broken Barricades* (1971), *The Prodigal Stranger* (RCA, 1991). **Robin Trower** [on Chrysalis except where noted], *Twice Removed from Yesterday* (1973), *Bridge of Sighs* (1974), *For Earth Below* (1975), *Robin Trower Live!* (1976•), *Long Misty Days* (1976), *In City Dreams* (1977), *Caravan to Midnight* (1978), *Victims of the Fury* (1980), *Back It Up* (1983), *Beyond the Mist* (Passport, 1986), *Passion* (GNP/Crescendo, 1987), *Take What You Need* (Atlantic, 1987•), *In the Line of Fire* (Atlantic, 1990), *Essential Robin Trower* (1991), *20th Century Blues* (Vtwelve, 1994), *Anthology* (Import, 1994). **Bruce, Lordan & Trower** [on Chrysalis], *B.L.T.* (1981), *Truce* (1982), *No Stopping Anytime* (1989).

Recordings featuring Robin Trower: **Various Artists,** *Guitar Speak II* (IRS, 1990).

Free

Paul Kossoff

B o r n : *September 14, 1950, in Hampstead, London*
D i e d : *March 19, 1976*
M a i n   G u i t a r : *Gibson Les Paul*

One of the biggest hits of 1970 was "All Right Now," by an up-and-coming British blues-rock outfit named Free. "All Right Now" showcased one of Free's most appealing assets: the deep, R&B-styled vocals of singer Paul Rodgers. But the band also had a singular force in Paul Kossoff, a guitarist whose taut, bluesy lines were the essence of many Free compositions. What differentiated Kossoff from many of his peers of the time was a highly developed wrist vibrato technique. Whereas many rock players have a weak and off-key vibrato, Kossoff's strong left-hand approach could gracefully flutter a note indefinitely, right on pitch. He was also a top-notch soloist, lauded as much for the sheer simplicity and restraint of his lines as for his aggressive blues-rock style.

In 1967 Kossoff was playing in a band called Black Cat Bones with drummer Simon Kirke. After discovering Paul Rodgers in the group Brown Sugar, Kossoff and Kirke decided to put together a new group with him and bassist/songwriter Andy Fraser, late of John Mayall's Bluesbreakers. Dubbing themselves Free (a name given to them by Alexis Korner, the godfather of British blues), they played their debut gig in the spring of 1968. They signed with Island Records and released their first album, *Tons of Sobs*, in 1969, to immense acclaim in the U.K. Another album followed, but it was their third, *Fire and Water* (1970), that made the band's fame in America, riding on the back of the single "All Right Now."

The song marked the peak of Free's popularity in America and is an exceptional example of Kossoff's guitar style. Opening with stereo power chordings, Kossoff churns through the number until the instrumental midsection, where he takes a break of lightly distorted melody phrases, fast, repeated hammer-ons, and wrist vibrato effects. Other significant guitar moments with Free include "I'll Be Creepin'," replete with string bends, fast vibrato, and quirky blues runs, and "Mr. Big," from *Free Live* (1971).

In early 1971 Free broke up, and Kossoff formed a band called Kossoff Kirke Tetsu Rabbit with bassist Tetsu Yamauchi (later of the Faces) and keyboardist John "Rabbit" Bundrick. Free eventually regrouped in 1972 and cut *Free at Last*, which was released to mixed reviews. Bassist Fraser left at the end of the year, and during the recording of *Heartbreaker* in 1973 Kossoff also decided it was time to move on. He recorded his first solo album that year, *Back Street Crawler*, but was out of action until 1975 due to drug and health problems. When he returned to playing, he formed a band called Back Street Crawler and recorded *The Band Plays On*. A tour was planned, but was shelved when Kossoff suffered a major heart attack. Arrangements were then made for a spring tour of the U.K., but on March 19, 1976, Kossoff died in his sleep on a flight to New York en route to a meeting with record executives.

Free [on A&M except where noted], *Tons of Sobs* (1969), *Free* (1969), *Fire and Water* (1970), *Highway* (1971), *Live* (1971•), *Free at Last* (1972), *Heartbreaker* (Island, 1973), *The Free Story* (1973), *Best of Free* (1975). **Kossoff Kirke Tetsu Rabbit,** *Kossoff Kirke Tetsu Rabbit* (Island, 1971). **Paul Kossoff,** *Back Street Crawler* (Island, 1973), *Koss* (DJM, c. 1978). **Back Street Crawler** [on Atco], *The Band Plays On* (1975), *2nd Street* (1976).

Recordings featuring Paul Kossoff: **Jim Capaldi,** *Oh How We Danced* (Island, 1972).

CHAPTER ELEVEN

Art Rock
Progressive Pomp

By 1970 a new sub-genre of psychedelia arose: art rock. Instead of plundering the blues, as so many sixties rock bands had, British art rock groups such as the Nice, Yes, Genesis, ELP, King Crimson, the Moody Blues, and Procol Harum drew from the grand symphonic sounds of classical music for their primary inspiration, as well as the dreamy, fantasy mindset of psychedelic rock. They were also influenced by "progressive" pop groups like the Beatles and the Yardbirds, both of which were successful in combining rock 'n' roll with various other musical styles, including Indian ragas, oriental melodies, and Gregorian chants. With this combination of classical grandeur and sixties pop experimentalism, the era of art rock—also called *progressive rock*, or simply *prog rock*—was ushered in during the seventies.

Art rock was also voraciously eclectic. Where Hawkwind and Tangerine Dream were spacey, Yes and U.K. (♦ Allan Holdsworth) rocked out. Where ELP and the Moody Blues shot for orchestral orgasms, Renaissance and Gentle Giant toyed with madrigals and medievalism. Where Kansas and Jethro Tull mixed metal and the classics, Soft Machine and Gong fused jazz and psychedelia. Even groups not considered part of the genre strayed into an arty mode every once in a while: witness Deep Purple's "Child in Time," Love Sculpture's "Sabre Dance" (♦ Dave Edmunds), the Edgar Winter Group's '72 hit "Frankenstein" (♦ Montrose), or UFO's Elizabethan-tinged "Arbory Hill" or their symphonic ballad "Love to Love," both featuring solos by *metal* guitarist Michael Schenker (♦). And what are we to make of Walter Murphy's 1976 prog-disco hit, "A Fifth of Beethoven," or the Yes clones in Starcastle—where do they fit in? (In the cut-out bin, one hopes.) Scriously, progressive rock is perhaps the most diverse style in all of rock 'n' roll. There are no rules and no sonic standards—just a vast canvas on which any bold artist can experiment freely.

Then there is the subject of art rock's inherent "British-ness," since, of course, 90 percent of all great prog bands came from Great Britain. One might speculate that when American acid rock à la Janis Joplin and the Grateful Dead collided with Anglican church music, the Beatles, and an English art-school education, the resulting progeny was progressive rock. But that's far too simple a description for such a complex genre.

Despite their differences, a prominent feature of many of these new art rock groups was the emergence of instrumental virtuosos from within their ranks—musicians who in many cases were trained in prestigious classical academies and well-considered musical institutions. Among the top progressive instrumentalists were keyboardists Rick Wakeman of Yes and Keith Emerson of Emerson, Lake & Palmer. The skill of art rock guitarists was not to be overlooked, however, and players like Steve Howe of Yes and Robert Fripp of King Crimson became instrumental stars in their own right. They effectively dazzled fans with their clean technique, clever soloing ideas, and radical sonic experiments, heralding the arrival of a new type of rock hero: the guitar virtuoso.

Superficially, art rock guitar combined the raw-edged heavy rock of Jimi Hendrix, Jeff Beck, and Jimmy Page with the sublime majesty of solo classical guitar. But the average art rock guitarist's influences didn't stop there: jazz also figured heavily in this category, with guitarists sometimes copping licks from Charlie Christian, Tal Farlow, and Wes Montgomery for their intricate solos. And, from time to time, snippets of country, Indian, and atonal "avant garde" styled riffs would also show up in their work. In art rock guitar, the more diverse a player's influences, the better he was.

Though the entire category of art rock has been denigrated for its bombast and heavy-handedness, little of that same criticism can be leveled at its guitar players. Despite the occasional bout of self-seriousness, they represented the first school of rock guitar that consciously attempted to raise the standard of guitar playing to new heights of technical and instrumental expertise—without sacrificing either emotion or melodic content. Names like Steve Howe, Robert Fripp, and, later, Alex Lifeson of Rush (♦) all stand out as being among the most important innovators of rock guitar, and they continue to shape the current guitar sounds of rock 'n' roll.

Interestingly, the genre seemed to experience a bit of a revival in the nineties, notably through the popular work of bands like Queensrÿche (♦), King's X, Dream Theater, and British space-rockers Ozric Tentacles. For a rock idiom that garnered so much criticism over the years, art rock actually produced more than its fair share of important rock guitarists.

Yes

Steve Howe

Born: *April 8, 1947, in London*
Main Guitars: *'64 Gibson ES-175, ES-5 Switchmaster, and ES-345; Fender Stratocaster, Telecaster, and steel guitar*

Peter Banks

Born: *July 7, 1947, in Hertfordshire, England*
Main Guitar: *Rickenbacker Model 1997*

Besides being among the finest guitarists of the art rock movement, Steve Howe was also one of the first seriously eclectic rock players. In his stint with Yes, Howe combined classical, jazz, ragtime, rockabilly, country, blues, and various other guitar styles into his own individual brew of guitar playing. For a good part of the 1970s he was considered by many to be rock's most skilled guitarist and was a frequent winner of various guitar polls.

Early Years. Howe took up the guitar up around the age of 12. His first influences included early rock 'n' rollers like Danny Cedrone and Fran Beecher of Bill Haley's Comets, Buddy Holly, and Hank Marvin of the Shadows, as well as pop guitar superstars Les Paul and Mary Ford. But when his brother bought him an album by jazz master Barney Kessel, it opened young Steve's ears to other forms of guitar music. Soon he was soaking up material by guitarists such as Django Reinhardt, Charlie Christian, and Tal Farlow, flamenco legend Carlos Montoya, Julian Bream of classical guitar and lute fame, and country instrumentalists such as Jimmy Bryant and pedal steel player Speedy West. Howe began developing his own unique voice on the guitar by culling technical and stylistic elements from all these different players.

By his teens Howe was playing in professional rock groups like the Syndicats, the In Crowd, and Tomorrow. He got his first taste of success with the psychedelic outfit Tomorrow, when they scored a hit in 1968 with "My White Bicycle." The band broke up soon after, and Howe h o o k e d up with Bodast, a group that last-

Steve Howe

ed about a year and a half and recorded one album that was never released. (Bodast drew its name from the first two letters of each member's first name: Bob, Dave, and Steve.)

Breakthrough. In March 1970 Howe was asked to join Yes, a vocal-oriented progressive group that already had released two albums on the Atlantic label. Yes' previous guitarist, Peter Banks, had departed to form his own band, Flash, despite having played for years with Yes co-founders Jon Anderson and Chris Squire. Banks had also been instrumental in developing Yes' arty sound, though his guitaristic efforts were soon to be dwarfed by Howe's. When Banks left, Howe joined Anderson (vocals), Squire (bass), Bill Bruford (drums), and Tony Kaye (keyboards) in time to start work on the band's third album that fall.

When released in early 1971, Howe's first Yes album, entitled *The Yes Album*, set a precedent in rock 'n' roll. In addition to containing future band classics like "Perpetual Change" and "All Good People/Your Move," *The Yes Album* also provided an open forum for Howe's expansive guitar work. On "Yours Is No Disgrace," a nearly 10-minute-long suite with several interlocking sections, the guitarist takes off on his Gibson ES-175 with uncharacteristically—at least for seventies rock music—clean-toned riffs and fast scalar runs. Other examples of his guitar wizardry include "Clap," a bouncy fingerstyle ragtime piece performed on acoustic steel string (and inadvertently misprinted on the record label as "*The* Clap"), and "Würm," the Howe-penned closing section of the "Starship Trooper" suite, which features a mesmerizing three-chord motif and stereo solo (adapted from a Bodast track called "Nether Street").

Later in 1971, Yes' fourth album, *Fragile*, was released. It introduced keyboard virtuoso Rick Wakeman as Tony Kaye's replacement and contains the single "Roundabout," the band's first major U.S. hit. With "Roundabout," Yes became a heavyweight art rock group around the world. One of the most captivating aspects of this track—at least for many guitar fans—is Howe's simple but memorable intro: a charming blend of twelfth-fret harmonics and hammer-on phrases performed on a nylon-string guitar. The riff soon became a staple in the vocabulary of beginning guitarists and dramatically increased Howe's visibility among fans of rock guitar. For the record the guitarist also switched to a fat-body Gibson Switchmaster, except for the classic "Heart of the Sunrise," where he plugged in his old ES-175.

In addition to his usual array of facile fretboard moves and intricately picked melodies, Howe also recorded his "Mood for a Day" for *Fragile*. A baroque-styled solo for nylon-string guitar, this light melodic piece opened up a whole new world of music for rock guitarists.

Because of this instrumental, many rock guitarists realized that classical guitar was not the dull, stuffy music of an older generation of players, but rather a vital form of music that was relevant to modern guitar playing. Such top rock guitarists as Alex Lifeson of Rush and Rik Emmett of Triumph would later cite this particular piece of Howe's as a major influence on their own developments of classical-style guitar.

Several successful Yes albums followed *Fragile*: *Close to the Edge* (which showcases Howe's 12-string acoustic skills on "And You and I" and more electric chops via a Gibson ES-345 Stereo on "Siberian Khatru"), the 1973 triple live *Yessongs*, and *Tales from Topographic Oceans*, a wildly (and perhaps overly) adventurous double album based on a single composition by Howe and Anderson. With each new album, Yes' music became increasingly dense and complex as the band reached for increasingly lofty levels of expression. Not surprisingly, they alienated more and more of their audience with each successive release. In 1974 the band put out *Relayer*, an album that marked Yes at their most extreme. Alongside the cacophonous synth playing of Patrick Moraz and drumming of Alan White, the album included beautiful work by Howe, notably the stunning pedal steel solo during the balladic conclusion to the "Gates of Delirium" suite.

After *Relayer*, Yes went on an extended hiatus, and each member began work on a solo album. Howe recorded the excellent *Beginnings* in 1975, while bassist Chris Squire cut his own solo masterpiece, the highly recommended *Fish out of Water*. In 1977 Yes reunited for the superb comeback album *Going for the One*, which accented Howe's better-than-ever guitar chops in the fast-picked solos to "Parallels" and eclectic guitar stylings on "Awaken." After a less-than-stellar Yes followup in 1978 (*Tormato*), and the release of *The Steve Howe Album* in 1979, Yes underwent series of dramatic personnel changes that saw singer Jon Anderson and keyboardist Rick Wakeman leave. In late 1980 a final lineup of Yes broke up after issuing the New Wave-inspired album *Drama*.

Beyond Yes. Following *Drama*, Howe joined up with bassist and vocalist John Wetton (previously with King Crimson, Roxy Music, Uriah Heep, and U.K.), keyboardist Geoff Downes, and drummer Carl Palmer (formerly one third of Emerson, Lake & Palmer) to form an art rock supergroup, Asia. Their first album became one of the best sellers of 1982 and established Asia as a commercially viable act, especially since its bombastic progressive roots had been carefully pruned for an eighties post-punk audience. Howe's tenure with Asia was short, however; after the second album, *Alpha*, a critical and commercial loser, he promptly left the band. He reemerged in 1986 with a guitar synthesizer-oriented band called GTR, featuring ex-Genesis guitarist Steve Hackett. On the strength of the pop-flavored but somewhat bland single "When the Heart Rules the Mind," GTR's debut set became a solid MTV and chart hit in America. But Hackett bowed out before work could commence on a second album.

During Howe's stint with GTR, Chris Squire and Alan White had formed a band called Cinema, featuring Trevor Rabin on guitar. (White and Squire had briefly rehearsed with Jimmy Page under the moniker XYZ.) When Jon Anderson and Tony Kaye joined this lineup, they decided to bill themselves as the reformed Yes. Former Yes-men who were not part of the new lineup, including Howe, joined together to create Anderson, Bruford, Wakeman & Howe, which competed for concert goers and album buyers with the Rabin-led Yes. The two bands merged for a half-baked album in 1991 called *Union* and embarked on a worldwide tour with eight past and present Yes-men appearing simultaneously on stage. While the union was at times acrimonious, the concerts were quite successful. Still, the band broke up into its disparate parts upon the completion of the tour.

The Rabin lineup released one last album in 1994, entitled *Talk*. The album was poorly received even by diehard fans, and this incarnation of Yes crumbled in 1995. Rabin was subsequently lured into the session and production world (⧫ Pop Experimenters).

Howe recorded three fine solo albums in the aftermath of *Union*, with varying degrees of commercial success. In 1994 he released an album of rarities from his pre-Yes days, as well as putting together a live symphonic version of Yes, an instructional guitar video, and a book showcasing his impressive guitar collection. He also worked with guitarist Martin Taylor and ex-Renaissance vocalist Annie Haslam on two separate recording projects in 1995 and 1996. And he said "Yes" once more in 1996, recording *Keys to Ascension* with Anderson, Wakeman, Squire, and White—the classic "Topographic" lineup. The band recorded the live album, which included two new tracks, in California, and further plans called for a second live album and new material in 1997. According to Howe, he might even be around to see this version of Yes into the year 2000.

Legacy. While he continues to record and stage small tours, Howe's most innovative and important contributions to rock guitar have been his early-seventies work with Yes. With his unparalleled guitar style—a mixture of jazz, classical, neo-rockabilly, country, and ethnic elements—he pushed the borders of rock guitar further in just a few years than most top rock guitarists do in several decades. In addition to his relentless eclecticism, Howe is also important for his avoidance of using rock guitar clichés. Rarely has he relied on old blues licks or pentatonic scale patterns for his lead or rhythm playing. Instead, he has used his fast right-hand picking technique and a thorough knowledge of scales and arpeggios to make his solos and rhythm playing stand above that of mainstream rock guitarists. In hindsight, he stands among that small handful of truly masterful musicians that rock 'n' roll has produced.

Tomorrow, *Tomorrow* (Sire, 1968). **Yes** [on Atlantic except where noted], *The Yes Album* (1971), *Fragile* (1971), *Close to the Edge* (1972), *Yessongs* (1973•), *Tales from Topographic Oceans* (1973), *Relayer* (1974), *Yesterdays* (1975), *Going for the One* (1977), *Tormato* (1978), *Drama* (1980), *Yesshows* (1980•), *Classic Yes* (1982), *Union* (Arista, 1991), *Yes Years* (1991•), *Keys to Ascension* (CMC/BMG, 1996•). **Steve Howe** [on Atlantic except where noted], *Beginnings* (1975), *The Steve Howe Album* (1980), *The Bodast Tapes*

Featuring Steve Howe (n/a, 1981), *Turbulence* (Relativity, 1991), *The Grand Scheme of Things* (Relativity, 1993), *Mothballs* (RPM, 1994), *Not Necessarily Acoustic* (Herald, 1995●), *Homebrew* (Caroline, 1996). **Asia** [on Geffen], *Asia* (1982), *Alpha* (1983), *Then and Now* (1990), *Aqua* (1992). **GTR,** *GTR* (Arista, 1986). **Anderson, Bruford, Wakeman & Howe,** *Anderson, Bruford, Wakeman & Howe* (Arista, 1989), *An Evening of Yes Music Plus* (Herald, 1993●). **Steve Howe & Paul Sutin** [on CMC], *Voyagers* (1995), *Seraphim* (1995).

Recordings featuring Steve Howe: **Lou Reed,** *Lou Reed* (RCA, 1972). **Rick Wakeman,** *The Six Wives of Henry the Eighth* (A&M, 1973). **The Dregs,** *Industry Standard* (Arista, 1982). **Frankie Goes to Hollywood,** *Pleasure Dome* (Island, 1984), *Liverpool* (Island, 1986). **Propaganda,** *Secret Wish* (c. 1985). **Andy Leek,** *Say Something* (c. 1988). **Bill Currie,** *Transportation* (c. 1988). **Animal Logic,** *Animal Logic* (IRS, 1989). **Various Artists,** *Guitar Speak* (IRS, 1989), *Night of the Guitar Live!* (IRS, 1989●). **Queen,** *Innuendo* (Hollywood, 1991). **Bee Gees,** *Size Isn't Everything* (Polydor, 1993). **Various Artists,** *Tales from Yesterday* (Magna Carta, 1995).

King Crimson

Robert Fripp

Born: *May 16, 1946, in Wimbourne, Dorset, England*
Main Guitars: *Gibson Les Paul Custom, Roland guitar synthesizer*

Adrian Belew

Born: *1949, in Covington, Kentucky*
Main Guitars: *Fender Stratocaster and Jaguar, Roland guitar synthesizer*

Among his numerous other achievements, Robert Fripp was *the* first major art rock guitarist. With King Crimson—the acclaimed band he has led on and off for over 25 years—Fripp burst onto the guitar scene in late 1969. The band's first album, *In the Court of the Crimson King*, was instantly hailed as a rock masterpiece, featuring the work of bassist and vocalist Greg Lake (later of ELP), lyricist Pete Sinfield, keyboardist Ian MacDonald (later of Foreigner), drummer Michael Giles, and Fripp. It was a clever blend of modern classical and rock influences, further enhanced by layers of string-like Mellotron parts and Fripp's ferocious guitar assaults, played on his ubiquitous Gibson Les Paul Custom. His approach combined fine technique with an inventive use of unusual scales (at least for rock) and odd-meter rhythmic patterns. Though most of the songs on *Crimson King* are pri-

Robert Fripp

marily gentle ballads revolving around Mellotron and acoustic guitar, they are offset by "21st Century Schizoid Man," an jarring tune highlighted by Fripp's abrasive power chords and solos.

Beginnings. Having taken up guitar with a studious fervor at a young age, the rather owlish Fripp was the prize pupil of the local music teacher, whose other students included Greg Lake and Al Stewart. Fripp formed a small band called Giles, Giles & Fripp, which ultimately turned into King Crimson. After their debut at the Speakeasy Club in London in April 1969, the newly founded Crimson acquired a substantial word-of-mouth reputation as a radical rock band. The group landed a spot at the Rolling Stones' concert in Hyde Park on July 5 (Mick Taylor's debut gig) and quickly won the audience over with their inventive amalgam of rock and classical music. While recording their second album (*In the Wake of Poseidon*) a few months later, the group lost Greg Lake, who was lured away to join Keith Emerson in the art rock super trio Emerson, Lake & Palmer. A series of poor-selling albums followed, including *Lizard* (1971), *Islands* (1971), and the live *Earthbound* (1972), each featuring several personnel changes except for the omnipresent Fripp.

Next Generation. In 1973 Fripp reemerged with an entirely new King Crimson band, consisting of ex-Yes drummer Bill Bruford, bassist and vocalist John Wetton, violinist and keyboardist David Cross, and percussionist Jamie Muir. That spring they released the stunning *Larks' Tongues in Aspic*. Easily among King Crimson's best recordings, *Larks' Tongues* showed the band delving even further into the experimental rock that Fripp had initiated in "21st Century Schizoid Man." The album's centerpiece was the two-part "Larks' Tongues in Aspic" suite, "Part One" of which had Fripp serving up fuzz chords, fast atonal scale runs, and distorted string bends. It is perhaps not out of line to claim that Fripp pioneered the sound of "industrial rock" long before it ever had a name.

After a solid follow-up with both *Starless and Bible Black* and *Red* (1974), Fripp broke up the band yet again, even though he felt that the latter was a definitive Crimson endeavor. For the rest of the seventies Fripp kept a low profile, occasionally recording solo albums, playing on other artists' albums (such as David Bowie's *Heroes*, Peter Gabriel's solo debut, and Blondie's *Parallel Lines*), or producing artists like the Roches or Daryl Hall of Hall and Oates. During that time he also unveiled "Frippertronics," a performance method he invented that used two reel-to-reel tape decks to provide instrumental backup to his solo improvisations, thereby allowing him to successfully play solo concerts.

Reinvention. Returning once again to Crimson (he claims to only form the band when Crimson music—as an ethereal entity—requires a mouthpiece), Fripp hired Bill Bruford, Zappa alumnus Adrian Belew (♪) on guitar and vocals, and New York session bassist Tony Levin, who doubled on Stick. Based in part on the complex rhythms of Balinese gamelan orchestras, this King Crimson's debut album, *Discipline* (1981), was unanimously lauded and had more close ensemble playing than any previous Crimson incarnation. Two more superb albums followed, *Beat* (1982) and *Three of a Perfect Pair* (1984), as well as several popular U.S. club tours. With this Crimson group Fripp also began using the guitar synthesizer extensively in conjunction with his usual electric guitar playing.

During this time Fripp also paired up with Andy Summers, of the Police (♪), for a pair of albums dominated by guitar synthesizer, *I Advanced Masked* (1982) and *Bewitched* (1984). In 1984 Fripp yet again dissolved King Crimson and quietly moved into the educational sector. He founded the League of Crafty Guitarists, an ensemble designed to immerse interested guitarists in the philosophy of eating, drinking, and breathing the guitar. Fripp also developed a guitar tuning (C–G–D–A–E–G, low to high) that he hoped would ultimately replace the standard E–A–D–G–B–E tuning.

Through the late eighties and early nineties, Fripp spent much of his time in bitter litigation with EG, the company that had managed and promoted Crimson since its formation. Upon the completion of those legal wranglings, Fripp re-formed King Crimson in 1994 as a double trio, featuring Fripp and Belew on guitar, Levin and Trey Gunn on bass and Stick, and Bill Bruford and Pat Mastelotto on percussion. The group released *Thrak* in early 1995, allowing King Crimson to once again terrorize the music world with the sound of rock 'n' roll chaos.

Giles, Giles & Fripp, *The Cheerful Insanity of Giles, Giles & Fripp* (Deram, 1968). **King Crimson** [on Atlantic except where noted], *In the Court of the Crimson King* (1969), *In the Wake of Poseidon* (1970), *Lizard* (1971), *Islands* (1971), *Earthbound* (1972•), *Larks' Tongues in Aspic* (1973), *Starless and Bible Black* (1974), *Red* (1974), *USA* (1975•), *A Young Person's Guide to King Crimson* (1976), *Discipline* (Warner Bros., 1981), *Beat* (Warner Bros., 1982), *Three of a Perfect Pair* (Warner Bros., 1984), *Vroom* [EP] (Discipline, 1994), *Thrak* (Virgin, 1995), *B'Boom* (Discipline, 1995•), *Thrakattak* (Discipline, 1996•). **Robert Fripp & Eno** [on Antilles], *No Pussyfooting* (1973), *Evening Star* (1975). **Robert Fripp,** *Exposure* (Editions EG, 1979), *God Save the Queen/Under Heavy Manners* (Polydor, 1980), *Let the Power Fall* (Editions EG, 1981), *Network* (EG, 1985), *Robert Fripp & the League of Crafty Guitarists Live!* (EG, 1986•), *Intergalactic Boogie Express* (Discipline,

1995•). **The League of Gentlemen,** *The League of Gentlemen* (Polydor, 1981), *Thrang Thrang Gozinbulx* (Discipline, 1996•). **Robert Fripp & Andy Summers** [on A&M], *I Advanced Masked* (1982), *Bewitched* (1984). **Sunday All over the World,** *Kneeling at the Shrine* (n/a, 1991).

Recordings featuring Robert Fripp: **Van Der Graaf Generator** [on Blue Plate], *H to He, Who Am the Only One* (1970), *Pawn Hearts* (1971). **Brian Eno** [on Island except where noted], *Here Come the Warm Jets* (1974), *Another Green World* (1975), *Before and after Science* (1977), *Music for Films* (Polydor, 1977). **David Bowie,** *Heroes* (RCA, 1977), *Scary Monsters* (RCA, 1980), *Sound + Vision* (Rykodisc, 1989). **Peter Gabriel,** *Peter Gabriel* (Atco, 1977), *Peter Gabriel* (Atlantic, 1978), *Peter Gabriel* (Mercury, 1980). **Blondie,** *Parallel Lines* (Chrysalis, 1978). **The Roches,** *The Roches* (Warner Bros., 1979). **Talking Heads,** *Fear of Music* (Sire, 1979). **Daryl Hall,** *Sacred Songs* (RCA, 1980). **Various Artists,** *Guitar Speak III* (IRS, 1991).

Pink Floyd

David Gilmour

B o r n : *March 6, 1947, in Cambridge, England*
M a i n   G u i t a r : *Fender Stratocaster*

Syd Barrett

B o r n : *January 6, 1946, in Cambridge, England*
M a i n   G u i t a r s : *Danelectro, Fender Stratocaster*

During the seventies Pink Floyd ranked among the premier rock acts in the world, their albums selling well into the *gazillions* and then some. Though little was done to promote the individuality of the band members, guitarist David Gilmour's melodic, bluesy electric guitar solos became a Pink Floyd hallmark, highlighting many of their multi-platinum albums, including *Wish You Were Here*, *The Wall*, and the phenomenally successful *Dark Side of the Moon*.

Background. Gilmour started his guitar training at 14 and played guitar in several rock and folk groups throughout his teen years. In high school he met future Floyd members Roger Waters and Syd Barrett (for a while he even played with Barrett in a folk duo). Bassist/vocalist Waters and guitarist/songwriter Barrett put together Pink Floyd in 1966 with keyboardist Richard Wright and drummer Nick Mason. Within a short time Pink Floyd was gar-

David Gilmour

nering a great deal of attention in London's underground psychedelic scene, primarily for their wild light shows and for Barrett's brilliance as a composer and rock visionary. In early 1967 the group put out their first album, *Piper at the Gates of Dawn*, and toured America. At the same time, Barrett became increasingly dependent on drugs, and would often simply stop playing–or play something different–during live shows. By the beginning of 1968 his position in Pink Floyd was on questionable ground.

In February 1968 the members of the band decided to bring their old schoolmate David Gilmour into the fold to support Barrett's sporadic guitar playing. Within two months, however, Barrett's mental state was such that he wandered away from the group. He was never formally fired and never formally quit–he just stopped showing up. Gilmour, who had been earning a living as a male model, then became Pink Floyd's sole guitarist, although Barrett was expected to return at any time. Several fine albums ensued with Gilmour in the guitar seat–*A Saucerful of Secrets* (1968), *Ummagumma* (1969), *Atom Heart Mother* (1970), and *Meddle* (1971)–as well as several movie soundtracks, each one progressively more electronic and ethereal than its predecessor.

Landslide. Floyd took most of 1972 off to work on a new studio album. When released in early 1973, *Dark Side of the Moon* shot up album charts all over the world and established Pink Floyd as a world-class rock act. They followed it up with *Wish You Were Here* in 1975, *Animals* in 1977, and *The Wall* in 1979, each one selling millions of copies and cementing the band's massive international popularity. Pink Floyd clearly had a sound that appealed to the album-buying masses: a soft, flowing rock style with extensive synthesizer layerings and cloudy, message-riddled lyrics. Another major selling point was the accompanying stage extravaganzas, which at times involved laser light shows, massive floating dirigibles in the shapes of farm animals, and, on the *Wall* tour of 1980, a huge wall that eventually crumbled around the band as they played. Snowy White, later of Thin Lizzy (♦), was the band's second guitarist on these mega-tours.

Gilmour recorded several solo albums, and after an internal blow-out, Pink Floyd broke up in the mid eighties. The band reformed in 1987 without Roger Waters, who sued over the use of the Pink Floyd name. He lost, and fans didn't seem to care, as the success of *A Momentary Lapse of Reason* proved. A Waters-less live set followed, and then the mega-selling *Division Bell* (1994).

Legacy. While Pink Floyd's albums still sell into the millions, and the tours are sell-outs, their once-daring inflatable pig now seems more of a bloated cash cow. Gilmour's heyday as a guitarist of note is also behind him, yet he remains one of the most soulful players to emerge in rock, progressive or otherwise. His haunting blues-based guitar solos helped to define the Floyd sound as much as the strange lyrics and synth experimentation did. Fine examples can be heard on "Time" (from *Dark Side of the Moon*), where Gilmour cuts an echo- and distortion-fueled break with sustaining bends and an effective use of chord tensions and blues

scales. "Shine on You Crazy Diamond, Parts I–V" (a tribute to Barrett, who had lost most of his mental faculties), from *Wish You Were Here*, shows more of the distinctive Gilmour guitar sound in a series of emotive solos over a minor blues variation, all featuring the guitarist's keen sense of melody and blues feel. Most famous of all is his orgasmic string bending in the power ballad from *The Wall*, "Comfortably Numb," which is quite possibly one of the finest rock solos ever recorded.

Pink Floyd [on Harvest except where noted] *Piper at the Gates of Dawn* (1967), *A Saucerful of Secrets* (1968), *More* (1969), *Ummagumma* (1969●), *Atom Heart Mother* (1970), *Relics* (1971), *Meddle* (1971), *Obscured by Clouds* (1972), *Dark Side of the Moon* (1973), *Wish You Were Here* (Columbia, 1975), *Animals* (Columbia, 1977), *The Wall* (Columbia, 1979), *A Collection of Great Dance Songs* (Columbia, 1981), *The Final Cut* (Columbia, 1983), *A Momentary Lapse of Reason* (Columbia, 1987), *The Delicate Sound of Thunder* (1989●), *The Division Bell* (Columbia, 1994). **Syd Barrett** [on Capitol except where noted], *The Madcap Laughs* (1969), *Barrett* (1970), *Opel* (1988), *Octopus: The Best of Syd Barrett* (Cleopatra, 1992), *Crazy Diamond* (1993). **David Gilmour** [on Columbia] *David Gilmour* (1978), *About Face* (1984).

Recordings featuring David Gilmour: **Paul McCartney,** *Give My Regards to Broad Street* (Columbia, 1984). **Pete Townshend,** *White City: A Novel* (Atco, 1985). **Liona Boyd,** *Persona* (CBS, 1986).

Frank Zappa

Born: *December 21, 1940, in Baltimore*
Died: *December 4, 1993*
Main Guitars: *Fender Stratocaster, Gibson SG*

One of the most original–and downright bizarre–figures in art rock was guitarist Frank Zappa. From the mid sixties until his death from cancer in 1993, Zappa provided rock listeners with a strange, enjoyable blend of arty rock 'n' roll, pubescent bathroom humor, and futuristic orchestral music. Outside of his outrageous compositions, he was a killer lead guitarist who tore through many of his pieces with high-speed solos laced with thick distortion and wah-wah effects.

Starting out as a drummer at age 12, Zappa switched to the guitar when he was 18. He then played professionally for several years in groups like the Soul Giants, and Joe Perrino and the Mellow Tones. By 1965 he had formed the outrageous Mothers of Invention. That band's first album, *Freak Out*, was released in 1966 and immediately earned the distinction of being the first rock 'n' roll concept album. Zappa and the Mothers followed it up with a lengthy succession of albums like *We're Only in It for the Money* (1968), *Weasels Ripped My Flesh* (1970), and *Overnite Sensation* (1973), many of which gained public attention due to Zappa's quirky humor, jazzy excursions, and impressively raw guitar solos.

Zappa recorded prodigiously, replacing members at a dizzying pace for each album. Both demanding and abrasive, Zappa had a knack for finding talented guitar players to help him realize his complex and complicated musical visions. Yet he was also an astounding player himself, one who experimented with pickup placement and guitar electronics. One of Zappa's best guitar performances was *Apostrophe* (1974). He bursts forth on nearly every cut with one of his typically fuzz- and wah-saturated solos from his Gibson SG or Fender Stratocaster (he even owned and used a burned Hendrix Strat that he repaired and modified). Strong tracks include "Nanook Rubs It," "Cosmik Debris," and "Excentrifugal Forz," each of which showcases the speedy, off-rhythm runs that Zappa achieved using extensive hammer-ons and fast picking.

Zappa's most famous, and arguably his best, solo is on "Muffin Man," from the live album *Bongo Fury* (1975). Using a muffled Hendrix-like tone, Zappa comes close to a full six-string meltdown during two stunning breaks, with lighting-quick fretboard climbs, spastic phrasing, and, of course, the polyrhythmic lines that mark every great Zappa solo. Other major guitar releases from Zappa include his multi-record anthology *Shut up 'n Play Yer Guitar* and the 1988 CD set *Guitar*.

Like Miles Davis or David Bowie, Frank Zappa was also important for introducing many fine musicians to the record-buying public. Among his many associates were such stellar names as Aynsley Dunbar, George Duke, and Jean-Luc Ponty, not to mention noted guitarists like Adrian Belew (♪), son Dweezil Zappa, Warren Cuccurullo of Missing Persons and Duran Duran fame, Mike Keneally, Lowell George of Little Feat (♪), and especially Steve Vai (♪), who was immortalized in the Zappa tune "Stevie's Spanking." Only time will tell if Frank Zappa is to be remembered as a bizarre musical comic or a brilliant rock visionary and composer, but it is certain that his guitar playing will be held in the high regard it has been for nearly three decades.

Mothers of Invention [on Bizarre except where noted], *Freak Out* (Verve, 1966), *Absolutely Free* (Verve, 1967), *We're Only in It for the Money* (Verve, 1968), *Cruising with Ruben & the Jets* (Verve, 1968), *Mothermania/Best of the Mothers* (Verve, 1969), *Uncle Meat* (1969), *Burnt Weeny Sandwich* (1970), *Weasels Ripped My Flesh* (1970), *The Mothers/Fillmore East—June 1971* (1971•), *200 Motels* (United Artists, 1971), *Just Another Band from L.A.* (1972), *Grand Wazoo* (1972), *Over-nite Sensation* (Discreet, 1973), *Roxy & Elsewhere* (Discreet, 1974•), *One Size Fits All* (Discreet, 1975). **Frank Zappa** [on Barking Pumpkin except where noted], *Lumpy Gravy* (Verve, 1968), *Hot Rats* (Bizarre, 1969), *Chunga's Revenge* (Bizarre, 1970), *Waka/Jawaka* (Bizarre, 1972), *Apostrophe* (Discreet, 1974), *Bongo Fury* [with Captain Beefheart and the Mothers] (Discreet, 1975•), *Zoot Allures* (Warner Bros., 1976), *Zappa in New York* (Discreet, 1978•), *Studio Tan* (Discreet, 1978), *Sleep Dirt* (Discreet, 1979), *Sheik Yerbouti* (Zappa, 1979), *Orchestral Favorites* (Discreet, 1979), *Joe's Garage, Act I* (Zappa, 1979), *Joe's Garage, Acts II & III* (Zappa, 1979), *Tinsel Town Rebellion* (1981), *You Are What You Is* (1981), *Ship Arriving too Late to Save a Drowning Witch* (1982), *Shut up 'n Play Yer Guitar* (1981), *Shut up 'n Play Yer Guitar Some More* (1981), *Return of the Son of Shut up 'n Play Yer Guitar* (1981), *Man from Utopia* (1983), *Zappa, Vol. 1* [with the London Symphony Orchestra] (1983), *Thing-Fish* (1984), *Them or Us* (1984), *Frank Zappa Meets the Mothers of Prevention* (1986), *Jazz from Hell* (1987), *You Can't Do that on Stage Anymore* (Rykodisc, 1988•), *Guitar* (Rykodisc, 1988•), *Fillmore East 1971* (Rykodisc, 1990•), *Beat the Boots! Box* (Rykodisc, 1991•).

Genesis

Steve Hackett

B o r n : *February 12, 1950, in London*
M a i n   G u i t a r : *Gibson Les Paul goldtop*

Mike Rutherford

B o r n : *October 2, 1950, in Guildford, England*
M a i n   G u i t a r s : *Rickenbacker and Shergold doublenecks, Steinberger GM*

In contrast to the incessant soloing and technical displays of many art rock guitarists of the seventies, Steve Hackett's playing was dedicated to embellishing the entire song rather than stealing the guitar limelight. In his six and a half years with Genesis, Hackett developed his guitar into a something of a symphonic instrument, complementing songs with lilting guitar melodies in the background, a creative use of special effects, and on rare occasion, fiery solos that sounded more like an integral part of the song structure than an off-the-cuff lead break. He also helped pioneer the "two-handed" tapping technique that Eddie Van Halen brought to fame later in the decade, and claims that Van Halen picked up the idea after seeing a Genesis concert in the mid seventies.

Whether he was playing a solo acoustic interlude or a Wagnerian rocker with the band, Hackett was always a team player within the group. Some of his finest work with Genesis was on tracks such as "Watcher of the Skies" (from *Foxtrot*), where he contributes melodic background phrases, volume pedal swells, and a harsh fuzztone solo, and "Firth of Fifth," from *Selling England by the Pound* (1973) and the 1977 live set *Seconds Out*, which contains a long, haunting solo filled with volume swells, hammer-on trills, and linear phrases, all bathed in thick distortion and echo. He shows off his acoustic talents on "Horizons," a beautiful steel-string solo that serves as a prelude to the acclaimed centerpiece on *Foxtrot*, "Supper's Ready," and also in the nylon string intro to "Blood on the Rooftops," from *Wind and Wuthering* (1976). Hackett left Genesis to pursue a solo career after that album, after which the band carried on as a trio (hence the name of their first disc following his departure, *...And Then There Were Three*).

Besides his work with Genesis, Hackett has had an intriguing solo career, marked by several fine albums, including *Please Don't Touch* (1978), *Spectral Mornings* (1979), *Cured* (1981), and *Guitar Noir* (1993). In 1986 he joined Steve Howe in GTR, which saw a fair amount commercial success, despite the fact that GTR's one album is largely forgettable. And while Hackett's visibility in the early seventies was limited by Genesis' painfully slow journey to international success, he is still a vital part of the art-rock guitar school, especially for his near-symphonic approach to the electric guitar and also for his use of special effects and classical guitar in a rock setting. Of those in the art rock camp,

Hackett is one player who deserves more acclaim than history has given him.

Genesis bassist Mike Rutherford assumed guitar duties after Hackett left the band. He had backed Hackett up during Genesis' early days by providing acoustic 12-string arpeggio patterns on various tunes. His debut as the group's sole guitarist was on ...*And Then There Were Three*, which showed he was capable of picking up where Hackett left off, with solid single-line riffs on "The Ballad of Big," "Down and Out," "Scenes from a Night's Dream," and the single "Follow You, Follow Me" (in concert, the loss of Hackett was offset by Daryl Stuermer, an excellent guitarist who had played fusion in violinist Jean-Luc Ponty's band).

As Genesis moved from art rock to power pop during the 1980s and 1990s, it was Rutherford who became the band's most visible guitarist. Though not as flashy or singularly unique a guitarist as his predecessor, Rutherford has nonetheless proven to be an imaginative player. His work on ...*And Then There Were Three*, *Duke*, *Abacab*, and *Genesis* is worth noting for his odd time signatures and heavy chording, although recent Genesis recordings contain little guitar material of interest. Rutherford has also had pop success with his side project Mike + the Mechanics.

Genesis [on Charisma except where noted], *Trespass* (1970), *Nursery Crime* (1971), *Foxtrot* (1972), *Genesis Live* (1973•), *Selling England by the Pound* (1974), *In the Beginning* (London, 1974), *The Lamb Lies Down on Broadway* (Atco, 1974), *A Trick of the Tail* (Atco, 1976), *Wind and Wuthering* (Atco, 1976), *Seconds Out* (Atlantic, 1977•), *And Then There Were Three* (Atlantic, 1978), *Duke* (Atlantic, 1980), *Abacab* (Atlantic, 1981), *Three Sides Live* [U.K. version] (Atlantic, 1982•), *Genesis* (Atlantic, 1983), *Invisible Touch* (Atlantic, 1986), *We Can't Dance* (Atlantic, 1991), *Live/The Way We Walk: The Shorts & the Longs* (Atlantic, 1992•). **Steve Hackett** [on Chrysalis except where noted], *Voyage of the Acolyte* (1976), *Please Don't Touch* (1978), *Spectral Mornings* (1979), *Defector* (1980), *Cured* (Epic, 1981), *Highly Strung* (Epic, 1983), *Bay of Kings* (1983), *Till We Have Faces* (1983), *Momentum* (Herald, 1988), *Time Lapse* (Caroline, 1992•), *Guitar Noir* (Viceroy, 1993), *Blues with a Feeling* (Herald, 1995). **GTR**, *GTR* (Arista, 1986). **Mike Rutherford,** *Smallcreep's Day* (Passport, 1980), *Acting Very Strange* (Atlantic, 1982). **Mike + the Mechanics** [on Atlantic], *Mike + the Mechanics* (1985), *Living Years* (1988), *Word of Mouth* (1991), *Beggar on a Beach of Gold* (1995).

Recordings featuring Steve Hackett: **Peter Banks,** *Two Sides of Peter Banks* (Sovereign, 1973). **Box of Frogs,** *Strange Land* (Epic, 1986). **Various Artists,** *Guitar Speak III* (IRS, 1991).

Jethro Tull

Martin Barre
B o r n : *November 17, 1946, in Birmingham, England*
M a i n G u i t a r s : *Gibson Les Paul, Hamer archtop custom*

Ian Anderson
B o r n : *August 10, 1946, in Edinburgh*
M a i n G u i t a r s : *miscellaneous acoustics*

Mick Abrahams
B o r n : *April 7, 1943, in Luton, Bedfordshire, England*
M a i n G u i t a r : *Gibson SG Standard*

On the periphery of the art-rock movement of the 1970s was Jethro Tull, a group whose baroque and Celtic folk-inspired hard rock earned them a large following in both the U.S. and Europe. Though Tull has always been dominated by their multi-faceted leader, Ian Anderson (who provides the group's music, vocals, flute, and acoustic guitar), electric guitarist Martin Barre has instilled a strong electric six-string presence into Jethro Tull's unique rock sound.

Tull was formed in late 1967 by Anderson, and initially featured guitarist Mick Abrahams. Abrahams' bluesy playing style was evident on the band's 1968 debut album, *This Was*. Abrahams left that year to form the more primitively driven Blodwyn Pig, and was replaced temporarily by Tony Iommi, later of Black Sabbath (♦). Iommi appeared with the group long enough to play on the Rolling Stones' ill-fated "Rock and Roll Circus" TV special, and then departed when he realized he wasn't the right person to be working for Ian Anderson.

Martin Barre joined Tull in time for *Stand Up* (1969) and has been the band's electric guitar mainstay ever since. His best-known guitar work with Jethro Tull is on early seventies hits like "Cross-Eyed Mary," "Locomotive Breath," and the ever-popular "Aqualung." His exceptionally fluid and melodic hard rock solo on "Aqualung" is one of the finest extended solos by any guitarist of the period, especially since it avoids all of the blues jam clichés so prevalent in rock at the time. In contrast to most of his heavy rock peers—who were concentrating on the approach to extended improvisation laid down by Eric Clapton and Jeff Beck—Barre stood out for his precision and attention to melody.

Through more than two decades with Tull, Barre has held fairly close to the combination of heavy chords and deft solos he displayed on "Aqualung." At times he has been a little harder, as on *Minstrel in the Gallery*, and at times lighter, as on *Heavy Horses*. Despite a certain sameness to his playing in recent years, he is nonetheless always enjoyable to listen to, and is a perfect example of the kind of guitar playing that exists beyond standard blues-rock.

Jethro Tull [on Chrysalis except where noted], *This Was* (1968), *Stand Up* (Reprise, 1969), *Benefit* (Reprise, 1970), *Aqualung* (Reprise, 1971), *Thick as a Brick* (Reprise, 1972), *Living in the Past* (1972•), *A Passion Play* (1973), *War Child* (1974), *Minstrel in the Gallery* (1975), *M.U. The Best of Jethro Tull* (1975), *Too Old to Rock 'n' Rock, Too Young to Die!* (1976), *Songs from the Wood* (1977), *Repeat: The Best of Jethro Tull, Vol. 2* (1977), *Heavy Horses* (1978), *Bursting Out* (1978•), *Stormwatch* (1979), *"A"* (1980), *The Broadsword and the Beast* (1982), *Under Wraps* (1984), *Original Masters* (1985) , *Crest of a Knave* (1987), *20 Years of Jethro Tull* [boxed set] (1988•), *Rock Island* (1989), *Catfish Rising* (1991), *A Little Light Music* (1992•), *Nightcap* (Import, 1994). **Mick Abrahams (& Blodwyn Pig)** [on A&M except where noted], *Ahead Rings Out* (1969), *Getting to This* (1970), *Musical Evening with Mick Abrahams* (n/a, 1971), *At Last* (n/a, 1972), *Having Fun Learning the Guitar* (SRT, 1974), *All Said and Done* (Elite/Pickwick, 1991), *Lies* (Viceroy, 1993).

Emerson, Lake & Palmer

Greg Lake

B o r n : *November 10, 1948, in Bournemouth, England*
M a i n   G u i t a r s : *Alembic basses, Fender Stratocaster, Zemaitis electrics and acoustics, Gibson J-200*

While best known as the bassist and vocalist for Emerson, Lake & Palmer and King Crimson, Greg Lake has also received accolades as a skilled acoustic fingerstyle player, and deservedly so. His vaguely classical-styled songs with ELP, including "The Sage" (from *Pictures at an Exhibition*), "From the Beginning" (*Trilogy*), "Still...You Turn Me On" (*Brain Salad Surgery*), "C'est la Vie" (*Works, Vol. 1*), and "Father Christmas" (*Works, Vol. II*), fostered a new level of appreciation of the acoustic guitar within rock guitar circles in the 1970s.

Lake grew up in the same town that produced Robert Fripp and Andy Summers, all of whom played guitar in local groups. Although considered a decent guitarist, Lake found himself playing bass in various bands with more esteemed players, including the Gods (which featured Mick Taylor, of Rolling Stones fame) and King Crimson (which featured Fripp). Upon teaming up with Keith Emerson, formerly of The Nice, and Carl Palmer, of Atomic Rooster, Lake became ELP's vocalist, bass player, and guitarist. There was talk within the band of bringing in a full-time guitarist, but the only candidate considered enough of a virtuoso by any of the three was Jimi Hendrix, which would have allowed them to use the acronym HELP. Instead, Lake handled all the guitar parts from day one, and did so admirably.

On ELP's first album he relied almost exclusively on his bass talents, and many tracks, like "The Barbarian," feature a distorted fuzz bass that sounds like a guitar. On "Lucky Man," though, his affinity for writing and playing shimmering acoustic pieces is quite evident. This track also shows that it would be Emerson's strange synth sounds, and not the tortured wails of an electric guitar, that would be used for solos and leads in ELP. With only occasional exceptions, Lake would employ acoustic guitar for the vast majority of his six-string contributions to the band.

His most extensive electric work occurred on *Tarkus* (1971).

Songs like "Mass" and "Battlefield" include tastefully restrained electric guitar solos and fills by Lake, who demonstrates a sharp but spacey tone in the vein of Pink Floyd's David Gilmour, as well as a penchant for multitracked guitar parts. Still, Lake's electric bass playing was his primary contribution to most Emerson, Lake & Palmer projects, although it was often overshadowed by the more accomplished stylings of other art rock bassists, like Chris Squire of Yes and Mike Rutherford of Genesis. His work on pieces like "Tank" and "Pirates," however, are *tours de force* of bass playing, especially within the complex realm of prog rock.

ELP, like most art rock bands, went through highly publicized personnel skirmishes, and the band has broken up and reformed innumerable times. In the time between the various ELP incarnations, Lake released a solo album and toured as John Wetton's replacement in Asia, which at that time still had Steve Howe in its lineup.

ELP lost much of its popularity in the U.S. during the eighties and nineties, but the band remains a huge international concert draw. Time has not diminished Lake's playing, as attested to by his moving acoustic piece "Daddy," from the 1994 ELP set *In the Hot Seat*. Moreover, his acoustic legacy should not be underestimated; in terms of groundbreaking guitar work, songs like "The Sage" and "Still...You Turn Me On" rank with Steve Howe's "Mood for a Day" and Jimmy Page's "Bron-Yr-Aur" as great acoustic classics of the 1970s.

King Crimson [on Atlantic], *In the Court of the Crimson King* (1969), *In the Wake of Poseidon* (1970). **Emerson, Lake & Palmer** [on Cotillion except where noted], *Emerson, Lake, and Palmer* (1970), *Tarkus* (1971), *Pictures at an Exhibition* (1971•), *Trilogy* (1972), *Brain Salad Surgery* (Manticore, 1973), *Welcome Back, My Friends, to the Show that Never Ends…* (Manticore, 1974•), *Works, Vol. 1* (1977), *Works, Vol. 2* (1978), *Love Beach* (1978), *In Concert* (1979•), *Black Moon* (Victory, 1992), *Live at the Royal Albert Hall* (Victory, 1993•), *In the Hot Seat* (Victory, 1994), *I Believe in Father Christmas* [EP] (Rhino, 1995•). **Greg Lake** [on Chrysalis], *Greg Lake* (1981), *Manoeuvres* (1983). **Emerson, Lake & Powell,** *Emerson, Lake, and Powell* (Polydor, 1986).

Recordings featuring ELP: **Various Artists,** *Mar y Sol* (Atco, 1973•).

Be Bop Deluxe

Bill Nelson

B o r n : *December 18, 1948, in Wakefield, Yorkshire, England*
M a i n   G u i t a r s : *Gibson ES-345, Yamaha SG2000, Hagstrom Patchmate 2000 guitar synthesizer*

One of *the* most underrated guitarists of the seventies art rock movement, Bill Nelson of Be Bop Deluxe not only played excellent guitar, but was this seminal band's chief songwriter and vocalist. Initially under the influence of the London glam-rock scene, the first Be Bop Deluxe album, *Axe Victim*, was released in 1974, but it was not until *Live! In the Air Age* (1977) that the group attracted major attention on both sides of the Atlantic. Besides running through Be Bop Deluxe's greatest hits, this live album provided a stellar showcase for Nelson's dazzling, often ingenious solos. On this stellar set, the guitarist's parts range from to funk chordings in "Shine" to the hard rock 'n' roll riffs of "Ships in the Night" and "Blazing Apostles."

More important is the first solo to "Adventures on a Yorkshire Landscape," where Nelson uses fluid legato hammer-ons in a way that didn't become standard in rock for another decade. And considering the date of recording (1976), the only precedents for this style of playing came from Allan Holdsworth and Spirit's Randy California, both of whom were relatively obscure at the time; a few years later, Eddie Van Halen would popularize the technique on a far wider scale. In any case, it's clear that the man was playing licks on a level far higher than your average seventies rocker.

Sadly, this release marked Be Bop Deluxe's high point. Without a glittery frontman like David Bowie or Roxy Music's Brian Ferry, the band's glam-rock never caught on successfully in either America or the U.K., and the group folded in 1978 after a series of poor-selling albums. Bill Nelson has since continued on as a cult favorite, releasing a number of moderately well-received solo albums since Be Bop's demise, although few featuring the high-powered guitar work of his earlier years. He has most recently appeared with the ambient ensemble Light Channel Vessel and released the all-instrumental guitar album *Practically Wired* to very positive reviews.

Be Bop Deluxe [on Harvest], *Axe Victim* (1974), *Futurama* (1975), *Sunburst Finish* (1976), *Modern Music* (1976), *Live! In the Air Age* (1977•), *Drastic Plastic* (1978). **Bill Nelson's Red Noise,** *Sound-on-Sound* (Harvest, 1979). **Bill Nelson** [on Cocteau except where noted], *Quit Dreaming and Get on the Beam* (1981), *Sounding the Ritual Echo* (1981), *Das Kabinett* (1981), *The Love that Whirls* (1982), *On a Blue Wing* (1986), *Trial by Intimacy* (1984), *Map of Dreams* (1987), *Simplex* [soundtrack] (1989), *Blue Moons and Laughing Guitars* (1992), *Practically Wired* (Gyroscope, 1995), *After the Satellite Sings* (Gyroscope, 1996). **Light Channel Vessel,** *Automatic* (Gyroscope, 1994).

Recordings featuring Bill Nelson: **Cabaret Voltaire,** *Code* (EMI/Manhattan, 1987). **David Sylvian,** *Gone to Earth* (Virgin, 1986).

Kansas

Kerry Livgren
Born: *September 1949*
Main Guitar: *Gibson Les Paul*

Rich Williams
Born: *February 1950*
Main Guitar: *Gibson Les Paul*

Steve Morse
Born: *July 28, 1954, in Hamilton, Ohio*
Main Guitar: *Ernie Ball/Music Man Steve Morse model*

Kansas was one of the few American art-rock bands to achieve any sort of major success. Showcasing the twin guitars of Kerry Livgren on lead and Rich Williams on rhythm, the band actually was very riff-heavy at its core (as was much of the midwestern rock of the time—notably Ted Nugent and REO Speedwagon). However, Kansas achieved a progressive sound largely due to its utilization of both a keyboardist (Steve Walsh) and a violinist (Robby Steinhardt) to round out its hard-edged sound. Dividing its longer pieces into suites and using mystical and religious imagery also encouraged the art rock tag.

After touring regionally in the American Midwest during the early 1970s, the band from Topeka signed a record deal with rock impresario Don Kirshner—the man behind the Monkees. Kansas impressed him with a sold-out show; Kirshner was not aware that free beer was offered to all attendees. Nonetheless, his label released Kansas' eponymous debut in 1974. It was followed up with a pair of stunners, *Song for America* and *Masque*, both of which veered from hard blues rock ("Lonely Street") to intricately constructed tempo changes ("Child of Innocence"). Despite incessant touring, the band did not reach a wide audience until the release of *Leftoverture* in 1976. The record featured the FM smash "Carry on Wayward Son," a track that combined Led Zeppelin's heavy guitar bombast with the prog-rock leanings of Yes, King Crimson, and Genesis. The success of *Leftoverture*, coupled with a reputation as an amazing live act, turned Kansas into arena rock stars by the year's end.

The two Kansas guitarists showed off their acoustic abilities on the 1977 single "Dust in the Wind," from *Point of Know Return*. This release marked the band's peak; subsequent albums didn't fare as well in the marketplace and showed an increasing lack of original ideas from bandleader Livgren. In the early eighties Livgren left the band to pursue a career in Christian music (which resulted in a fine solo album featuring Ronnie James Dio on lead vocals). Kansas carried on and in 1986 added ex-Dixie Dregs leader Steve Morse (•) on guitar for a pop-metal release entitled *Power*. Morse played on one more studio album and then went back to his own solo projects and Dregs reunions. Currently, Kansas tours with much of its original lineup, *sans* violinist Steinhardt and Livgren, leaving Rich Williams to handle all the guitar parts on his own.

Kansas [on Kirshner except where noted], *Kansas* (1974), *Song for America* (1975), *Masque* (1975), *Leftoverture* (1976), *Point of Know Return* (1977), *Two for the Show* (1978•), *Monolith* (1979), *Audio-Visions* (1980), *Vinyl Confessions* (1982), *Drastic Measures* (CBS Associated, 1983), *The Best of Kansas* (CBS Associated, 1984), *Power* (MCA, 1986), *In the Spirit of Things* (MCA, 1988), *Kansas* [boxed set] (Sony, 1994•).

Focus

Jan Akkerman

B o r n : *December 24, 1946, in Amsterdam*
M a i n G u i t a r : *Framus Jan Akkerman model*

A fine example of the ever-eclectic art rocker is Jan Akkerman, guitarist with Focus, a minor Dutch band that produced one of the biggest U.S. singles of 1973, "Hocus Pocus." Alternating between sections of distorted chords and the multi-octave vocals of keyboardist and flutist Thijs van Leer, the song was laced with Akkerman's spellbinding and fleet-fingered solos. Simultaneously bridging the gaps between art rock, fusion, and heavy metal, he added energetic string bending and modal flurries to "Hocus Pocus," making it among the wildest and most technically accomplished lead guitar tracks ever heard in a Top 40 single.

Akkerman and Focus recorded their eclectic progressive rock during the mid seventies, earning two gold albums in 1973 for *Moving Pictures* (originally released in 1971) and *Focus 3*. Yet the band's popularity died in the U.S. with the final strains of "Hocus Pocus." Akkerman went on to record a number of acclaimed solo albums, several of which reflected his interest in instrumental guitar music and fusion. Of special note is his 1989 effort *The Noise of Art*, which features his unique heavy rock/bebop soloing abilities.

Focus [on Sire except where noted], *In and out of Focus* (1971), *Moving Waves* (1971), *Focus 3* (1973), *Focus at the Rainbow* (1973•), *Hamburger Concerto* (Atco, 1974), *Dutch Masters, 1969–1973* (1975), *Mother Focus* (Atco, 1975). **Jan Akkerman** [on Atlantic except where noted], *Profile* (Sire, 1973), *Guitar for Sale* (Bovema, 1973), *Tabernakel* (Atco, 1974), *Eli* (1977), *Aranjuez* (CBS, 1978), *Live* (1979•), *Jan Akkerman 3* (1980), *The Noise of Art* (No Speak, 1989). **Jan Akkerman & Thijs Van Leer,** *Focus* (Mercury, 1986).

Wishbone Ash

Andy Powell

B o r n : *February 8, 1950, in England*
M a i n G u i t a r : *Gibson Flying V*

Ted Turner

B o r n : *August 2, 1950, in Birmingham, England*
M a i n G u i t a r : *Gibson Les Paul*

Laurie Wisefield

B o r n : *1953, in England*
M a i n G u i t a r : *Fender Stratocaster*

W ishbone Ash was one of Britain's most unusual rock exports circa the mid seventies, creating a sound based on guitar harmonies and dazzling instrumental ensemble playing.

Featuring guitarists Andy Powell (known for his trademark Gibson Flying V) and Ted Turner, as well as bassist Martin Turner (no relation) and drummer Steve Upton, Wishbone Ash emphasized the guitar players' instrumental prowess in long compositions that included odd meters and near-orchestral guitar parts.

Their 1970 debut, *Wishbone Ash*, and its follow-up, *Pilgrimage*, gained the group a solid core of fans in the U.K., especially among college listeners. This paved the way for the 1972 album *Argus*, which many felt was the group's best work.

Ted Turner left the band when he found religion in 1974 and was replaced by guitarist Laurie Wisefield, formerly of Home. When the band moved to the U.S. to escape the heavy British taxes, its popularity began to wane. Turner returned in 1987, and the band recorded *Nouveau Calls* in addition to reclaiming a large concert audience in Japan. Despite its lack of mainstream commercial success, Wishbone Ash was influential on other musicians: Phil Lynott cited it as a central reason for turning his Thin Lizzy trio into a harmony-driven, two-guitar quartet, like Ash's guitar team of Powell and Turner. In the long run, Powell and Turner should be considered England's version of Duane Allman and Dickey Betts.

Wishbone Ash [on MCA except where noted], *Wishbone Ash* (1970), *Pilgrimage* (1971•), *Argus* (1972), *Wishbone 4* (1973), *Live Dates* (1974•), *There's the Rub* (1974), *New England* (1976), *Locked* (Atlantic, 1976), *Front Page News* (Atlantic, 1977), *Classic Ash* (1977), *No Smoke without Fire* (1978), *Just Testing* (1979), *Live Dates II* (1980•), *Number the Brave* (1981), *Both Barrels Burning* (AVM, 1982), *Best of Wishbone Ash* (1982), *Nouveau Calls* (No Speak, 1988).

Recordings featuring Andy Powell: **Blue Law,** *Blue Law* (Griffin, 1995).

Sky

John Williams

B o r n : *April 24, 1941, in Melbourne*
M a i n G u i t a r s : *Ovation nylon-string,* *Gibson RD Artist*

Kevin Peek

M a i n G u i t a r : *Gibson L-5S*

H ere's an art rocker of a different color: John Williams, the internationally renowned classical guitarist, occasionally dabbled in the rock field when not recording and performing traditional Spanish and baroque guitar pieces. Among his better forays into rock was with the British group Sky. This quintet was formed in 1978 with a lineup that included Williams, guitarist Kevin Peek, and noted U.K. session bassist Herbie Flowers. With Peek handling most of the electric guitar parts, Williams' contribution to Sky was on an Ovation nylon-string guitar plugged—surprisingly—into a Marshall amp. Sky's souped-up metal version of J.S. Bach's "Toccata in D Minor" and rip-roaring "Vivaldi" (from their 1980 album *Sky*) were entirely successful. While receiving little notoriety in the U.S., Sky became popular in Britain, with "Toccata" going to #5 on the singles charts. The band's next several releases placed extremely high in the album charts as well. All in all, a daring and original art-rock band.

Sky [on Arista], *Sky* (1979), *Sky 2* (1980), *Sky 3* (1981), *Forthcoming* (1983), *Sky Five Live* (1983).

Recordings featuring John Williams: **Various Artists,** *The Secret Policeman's Ball* (Island, 1979). **Kate Bush,** *Hounds of Love* (EMI America, 1985).

Minor Masters

In the late sixties there was a handful of daring European bands who wound up taking psychedelic rock on a more progressive path than their acid popping San Francisco brethren. Among the earliest progressive bands were Soft Machine and Gong, both of which had endlessly revolving lineups. The Softs' noted psyche-delic-jazz formula was co-hatched by Australian guitarist Daevid Allen, but he was forced to quit after being denied a visa to enter England in 1967. Later, Allen turned up in Gong, working on their hip avant-rock releases like *The Flying Teapot* and *Angel's Egg* (both 1973). These albums also featured the guitar talents of Steve Hillage, who cut a well-received solo album in 1975 called *Fish Rising*. With its success the axeman went solo full-time, recording *L* the following year with the aid of producer and sometime prog-rocker Todd Rundgren; currently, Hillage plays with the ambient synth-dance act 777. Back in the Soft Machine camp, guitar duties were briefly taken over by the great Allan Holdsworth (♦) for *Bundles*; he was later replaced noted jazz picker John Etheridge. Given the incredible turnover in these prog acts, it shouldn't be surprising to learn that Holdsworth later joined Gong for a pair of fine albums, *Expresso* and *Expresso II*.

Other unsung prog players include Gary Green of Gentle Giant and Phil Manzanera of Roxy Music. Gentle Giant never did well at home in the U.K., but in the U.S. the band generated a cult following from discs like *Octopus* (1973), *The Power and the Glory* (1974), and *Freehand* (1975). Gary Green was an eclectic player, as he proved on tracks like "A Cry for Everyone" (odd meters, fast picking), "Dog's Life" (tasteful Elizabethan acoustic fingerstyle), and "River" (distorted blues-rock soloing)—all from *Octopus*. More towards the "glam" side of art rock was Roxy Music, fronted by chic vocalist Brian Ferry. Guitarist Phil Manzanera, however, was a powerhouse player whose stinging solos ranged from Fripp-like sustain to jagged blues licks. A great sampling of his wild, aggressive playing can be heard on Roxy's live albums *Viva! Roxy Music* (1976) and *Musique/The High Road* (1983), the latter including a cool, guitar-drenched cover of Neil Young's "Like a Hurricane." He also appears on the band's one bona fide masterpiece, the R&B-inspired epic *Avalon*.

Also of note is Andy Latimer of Camel, another fine, melodic player, important for his instrumental workouts on such cult favorites as *The Snow Goose* (1975), *Moonmadness* (1976), and *Rain Dances* (1977). And not to be forgotten is Brand X, which is generally remembered as one of drummer Phil Collins' side projects. But fans of the group will rave endlessly about their fusion guitar monster, John Goodsall, who torched albums like *Unorthodox Behavior* (1976), *Moroccan Roll* (1977), and *Product* (1979), as well as their concert set, *Livestock*.

Of course, there are zillions of other hip English acts that were an essential part of the art rock revolution, among them, Keith Emerson's The Nice (which briefly sported guitarist David O'List), National Health, Van Der Graaf Generator, Curved Air, Henry Cow, Nektar, Greenslade, Spooky Tooth, and Marillion. And there's more to prog rock than just the British bands. Global prog-rockers include PFM from Italy, Magma from France, Tasavallen Presidenti from Iceland, Rush and Saga from Canada, Guru-Guru from Germany, and, from America, Kansas, Todd Rundgren's original Utopia, King's X, and the aforementioned but best forgotten Starcastle. In all, art rock was a worldwide phenomenon of the first order. Happily, this fact remains a thorn in the side of those mainstream rock critics who have lambasted the genre for decades.

CHAPTER TWELVE

Roots Rock

In Search of Soul

The early seventies in rock were a fertile time for the blues. Only a handful of rockers were stretching the harmonic limits of guitar via fusion and art rock, while the rest were content to rehash blues-scale solos à la Eric Clapton, Peter Green, and Jimi Hendrix, especially in the hard rock camp. But a few strove to go beyond, to get in touch with the blues, and make it a part of their rock sound.

Preeminent blues-rockers of the era include Johnny Winter, Roy Buchanan, and Billy Gibbons of ZZ Top, but there were minor blues-based players who made their mark. One good example was Jesse Ed Davis (born c. 1947 in Oklahoma City). Of Native American heritage, Davis turned in strong lead and slide work on several solo albums for the Atco label, the first of which, *¡Jesse Davis!* (1970), included a guest appearance by Eric Clapton. Besides the Clapton connection, Davis had other famous friends, especially in the British rock scene. For example, his fine Strat playing appeared on recordings by Joe Cocker and ex-Beatles George Harrison (*Concert for Bangla Desh*, *Extra Texture*) and John Lennon (*Walls and Bridges*, *Rock 'n' Roll*), as well as such American performers as Jackson Browne and Leon Russell. Reportedly, after witnessing Davis' hot slide work at a concert in the late sixties, Duane Allman took up the style for himself, with legendary results. But after 1975 little was heard from Davis aside from the odd solo album, and the guitarist died in obscurity in 1988.

Les Dudek (born c. 1950 in Auburndale, Florida) achieved recognition in the middle seventies for his work with the Allman Brothers (adding harmonies to their 1973 hit "Ramblin' Man"), in addition to touring with Boz Scaggs and playing on his hit album *Silk Degrees*. Some of Dudek's best playing, however, could be found on his solo albums of the seventies. On tracks like "City Magic" (from *Les Dudek* [1976]) and "Old Judge Jones" and "Zorro Rides Again" (both from *Say No More* [1977]), Dudek carried on the versatility of Duane Allman with a lead guitar style that blended blues, rock, and jazz idioms, while retaining a strong sense of melody and emotion. And, like Allman, Dudek was praised for his accomplished slide playing. Despite his many strengths as a player, however, the guitarist was not able to sustain a solo career into the eighties, opting to perform with then-girlfriend Cher in the ill-fated band Black Rose and re-emerging on his own in 1995 with a solo album entitled *Deeper Shade of Blues* (on Geosynchronous Records).

Of course, one can't forget George Thorogood, the Delaware-based party rocker who burst into prominence late in the seventies with his electric tributes to Chuck Berry and bluesmen Elmore James and John Lee Hooker. While doing covers of rock 'n' blues classics like Bo Diddley's "Who Do You Love," Elmore James' "Madison Blues," and others, Thorogood effectively showed off double-stop injected solos à la Berry and tough slide work through his cheapo Gibson ES-125/Fender amp combination. Further, his overall rawness as a player simply added to his appeal as a blue-collar bluesman. Among Thorogood's many enjoyable, but similar sounding, albums are *Move It on Over* (1978), *Bad to the Bone* (1982), and *Boogie People* (1991). No question, the guy rocks, as his 1995 live collection, *Let's Work Together Live*, proves beyond a doubt.

Billy Gibbons

ZZ Top

Billy Gibbons

Born: *December 12, 1949, in Houston*
Main Guitars: *'59 Gibson Les Paul, various custom solidbodies*

At the beginning of the 1980s few would have predicted that ZZ Top, that little old blues-boogie trio from Texas, was to be among the biggest and most popular rock groups of the decade. Nothing in its 1960s blues roots gave any indication of the phenomenal success the band would enjoy until the early 1990s. But numerous platinum albums and hit videos later, the band is virtually a rock institution.

Back in the 1960s, Billy Gibbons had moved through a succession of bands before winding up in the psychedelic band the Moving Sidewalks late in the decade. During his stint with the Sidewalks, Gibbons got his first taste of success when the band scored a hit in 1968 with the single "99th Floor." The band then landed the opening spot on a tour with the Jimi Hendrix Experience. Gibbons and Hendrix became friends during this time, and Hendrix's playing was to have a lasting influence on the young Texan's guitar style.

By 1970 Gibbons had left the Moving Sidewalks and began assembling a new group with drummer Frank Beard and bassist/vocalist Dusty Hill. They dubbed themselves ZZ Top (possibly as a tribute to bluesman ZZ Hill; Gibbons won't 'fess up) and released *First Album*. They followed in 1972 with *Rio Grande Mud*, which yielded the minor uptempo rock hit "Francine." In 1973 they released *Tres Hombres*, with Gibbons' six-string barn-burner "Waiting for the Bus/Jesus Just Left Chicago" and the ultimate Texas blues rocker, "La Grange." The following year, that "li'l ol' band from Texas" (as they are affectionately known by fans) established themselves as a major concert draw by headlining in front of a gathering of 80,000 at the Texas Memorial Stadium in Austin.

Nineteen seventy-five was another banner year for the group. First they hit big with the single "Tush," which encapsulated several energized bottleneck solos into a compact, two-minute arrangement. Then *Fandango*, the album that featured "Tush," went platinum. Another good cut on the record was the minor blues "Blues Jean Blues," with its tasty, Peter Green-styled guitar solos. Several popular albums followed on the heels of *Fandango*: *Tejas* (1976), *Deguello* (1978), and *El Loco* (1981), each full of Gibbons' blues breaks and the band's relentless Texas boogie sound.

Thus, for most its first 10 years (c. 1970–1980), ZZ Top produced a handful of albums that successfully mixed the hard rock appeal of Led Zeppelin and Cream with the deep blues of Muddy Waters and Howlin' Wolf. But at the beginning of the eighties, mainstream rock took a decisive turn away from blues-based rock and plunged headfirst into the world of synthesizers and "techno-rock." This seemingly spelled trouble for a band of bluesy roots rockers like ZZ Top. For many roots rock bands, this fad meant the end of the road, but in 1983 ZZ Top pulled off a major coup by releasing *Eliminator*. On this record the band presented an updated ZZ Top sound, replete with synths and drum machines. Despite the technology, they remained faithful to their blues-rock roots, as demonstrated in raunchy hit rockers like "Legs" and "Sharp-Dressed Man." The trio's lighthearted videos and outrageous visual appeal (e.g., waist-length beards and fur-covered Dean guitars) only served to increase their mainstream popularity. By the middle of the decade, ZZ Top mania was in full swing across America.

While some older fans may have been alienated by the new ZZ Top sound and image, millions of new ones picked up on it and turned the band into one of the biggest sensations of rock music in the eighties. In late 1985 the trio followed *Eliminator* with the chart-busting *Afterburner*, which produced another bumper crop of guitar- and synthesizer-filled rockers ("Can't Stop Rockin'," "Sleeping Bag," and the guitar ballad "Rough Boy"). Staying close to these roots, the band unveiled *Recycler* in 1990, which featured "Doubleback," the main cut from the movie *Back to the Future, Part III* (the band had a cameo role in the otherwise silly film).

After a huge bidding war in the early 1990s that ranked up there with contract negotiations for the Rolling Stones and Aerosmith, ZZ Top left their longtime record company Warner Brothers for RCA. The boys delivered *Antenna* in 1994, but it didn't chart as well as its slick predecessors, despite a long-awaited return to some bluesier sounds from Gibbons. Capitalizing on the departure of the band, Warner issued *One Foot in the Blues* in late 1994, a fine compilation of pre-*Eliminator* blues cuts and outtakes.

Ever since their inception, ZZ Top's greatest asset has been the throaty electric tones of Billy Gibbons' guitar. While many rock guitarists of the seventies chose to follow in the high-powered footsteps of Jimmy Page and Jeff Beck, Gibbons absorbed these influences, but included a heady amount of pure blues guitar in his playing, largely inspired by blues kings like Howlin' Wolf, T-Bone Walker, and Jimmy Reed. Much of his meaty sound comes from his use of a quarter for a plectrum, instead of a regular plastic pick. This he applies with nimbleness to his trademark 1959 Gibson Les Paul Standard flametop, known as "Pearly Gates."

One of Gibbons' finest attributes is that, during the eighties era of fast-picking soloists and tremolo-bar acrobats, he found a comfortable niche for the classic sound of blues-rock guitar. At the same time, he made it sound as contemporary as any other current style. His harmonic squeals (also called pinch harmonics) and distortion tones have become veritable trademarks and make up a huge part of the ZZ Top sound (Mark Knopfler reportedly tried to cop Gibbons' tone precisely for the intro to the 1985 Dire Straits hit "Money for Nothing"). In all, Billy Gibbons' world-class tone and deep blues influences have set him a world apart from the average rock player.

ZZ Top [on Warner Bros. except where noted], *First Album* (1970), *Rio Grande Mud* (1972), *Tres Hombres* (1973), *Fandango* (1975•), *The Best of ZZ Top* (1977), *Deguello* (1979), *El Loco* (1981), *Eliminator* (1983), *Afterburner* (1985), *The ZZ Top Sixpack* (1988), *Recycler* (1991), *Greatest Hits* (1992), *Antenna* (RCA, 1994), *One Foot in the Blues* (1994), *Rhythmeen* (RCA, 1996). **Various Artists,** *Back to the Future III* [soundtrack] (Varese Sarabande, 1990).

Roy Buchanan

Born: *September 23, 1939, in Ozark, Tennessee*
Died: *August 14, 1988, in Fairfax, Virginia*
Main Guitar: *Fender Telecaster*

The late Roy Buchanan was one of those great guitarists who rightfully laid claim to being a reluctant guitar hero. Fame and Roy Buchanan seemingly butted heads at every opportunity, and Roy rarely seemed the better off for it.

At the beginning of the sixties Buchanan hooked up with rockabilly singer Dale Hawkins for a three-year stint of tours, club gigs, and recording sessions (he appeared on Hawkins' hit "My Babe"). After that, Buchanan played with Canadian rockabilly singer Ronnie Hawkins' outfit for several years, as well as with singer Freddie Cannon. For the rest of the decade, Buchanan mostly laid low, playing sessions on the East Coast or playing gigs with countless rock 'n' roll bar bands. Yet his reputation—and his reluctance—was such that the Rolling Stones offered him their rhythm guitar slot after Brian Jones' death in 1969. Shunning the guaranteed fame and fortune, he turned them down.

In 1970 Buchanan was discovered at a bar outside of Washington, D.C., playing the raw, incandescent blues that had already earned him a massive reputation as a blues-rock guitar master. National Educational Television got wind of this fiery guitarist and decided to do a show on him. In 1971 "The Best Unknown Guitarist in the World" aired on public TV, and, in a very short time, his Fender Telecaster sound was known throughout the guitar world. After this TV discovery, he finally started getting material together for his first solo album. In 1972 *Roy Buchanan* was released, to applause from critics and fans alike, and within his own showcase Buchanan showed the rest of the world what all the fuss was about. On "Pete's Blues," for example, he takes a standard slow blues groove and inflects it with powerful string pushes, chordal licks, and glissandos. In the classic "The Messiah Will Come Again," the guitarist gives a blues master class as he runs through melodic phrases and bends. He also incorporates volume knob swells, "seagull" harmonics, and his patented, speed-picked Telecaster runs throughout. It's a brilliant performance.

Throughout the rest of the seventies, Buchanan continued to put out albums brimming with his blues/country/rock 'n' roll-based guitar music: *Second Album* (1973), *That's What I'm Here For* (1974), and *A Street Called Straight* (1976). In 1977 he recorded one of his finest efforts, *Loading Zone*, produced by fusion bass master Stanley Clarke. On this disc the scope of the material ranges from heavy fusion ("The Heat of the Battle") to cornball country (his duet with Clarke on "Adventures of Brer Rabbit and Tar Baby") to the heavy blues workouts ("Ramon's Blues" and "Green Onions," both of which feature him trading solos with R&B legend Steve Cropper [♦], who wrote "Green Onions").

A creative lull followed *Loading Zone*, during which Buchanan released several poorly received albums and battled his own addictions. But in 1985 he resurrected his career with *When a Guitar Plays the Blues*, released on the independent Alligator label. With this record he finally committed himself wholeheartedly to the blues, and the result was an album of potent blues guitar playing. (Check out the title cut and "Chicago Smokeshop.") Critics, musicians, and fans were in awe of this masterpiece, and it was clear that Roy Buchanan was home at last. Tragically, his problems with alcohol and substance abuse eventually landed him in a jail cell in Fairfax, Virginia, where he hanged himself on August 14, 1988. His musical legacy, however, is as lofty now as it was over 20 years ago when he was appropriately dubbed "The Best Unknown Guitarist in the World."

Roy Buchanan [on Polydor except where noted], *Roy Buchanan* (1972), *Second Album* (1973), *That's What I Am Here For* (1974), *In the Beginning* (1974), *Rescue Me* (1975), *Live Stock* (1975•), *A Street Called Straight* (Atlantic, 1976), *Loading Zone* (Atlantic, 1977), *You're Not Alone* (Atlantic, 1978), *My Babe* (Waterhouse, 1980), *When a Guitar Plays the Blues* (Alligator, 1985), *Dancing on the Edge* (Alligator, 1986), *Hot Wires* (Alligator, 1987), *Sweet Dreams: An Anthology* (1992).

Recordings featuring Roy Buchanan: **Dale Hawkins,** *Dale Hawkins* (Chess, 1976). **Various Artists,** *The Alligator Records 20th Anniversary Collection* (Alligator, 1991).

Rory Gallagher

Born: *March 2, 1948, in Ballyshannon, County Donegal, Ireland*
Died: *June 14, 1995, in London*
Main Guitar: *Fender Stratocaster*

In the history of rock guitar there are many examples of great British blues-rock guitarists. But there aren't many well-known *Irish* blues-rockers. In the late sixties and seventies, a young blues maven from Ballyshannon named Rory Gallagher rose to the forefront of the blues scene in the U.K., and he has been there ever since.

Gallagher first made waves during the mid sixties with a loud blues trio called Taste. Taste's sound was distinctly heavy blues-rock, and their formation predates Cream's by one year. In 1969 the band signed with Polydor in the U.K. (Atco in America) and released their first album, entitled simply *Taste*. On this album Gallagher revealed his advanced guitar playing in material that was inspired by both American blues and the then-new sounds of heavy metal. On the track "Blister on the Moon" the guitarist executes stereo power chords and bluesy bent notes on his trademark axe, a thoroughly beat-up 1959 Fender Stratocaster. "Sugar

Mama" continues in this same heavy blues vein with more of Gallagher's fast pentatonic runs, feedback tones, and high-register bends.

When Taste broke up in 1971, Gallagher went solo and immediately began attracting a large following in Europe and the U.S. with his accomplished blues guitar work. Forming a band that operated under his name, Gallagher began a nonstop touring schedule so hectic that it virtually destroyed some of his band members. Popular albums from this period, like *Deuce* (1971), *Blueprint* (1973), and *Irish Tour '74* (1974), all serve to confirm his position as one of the foremost blues-rockers of the early 1970s. He refused to sweeten up his music for radio or pop chart appeal, and relied heavily on Elmore James-inspired techniques for his bluesy passion. On *Blueprint* his guitar takes over songs like "Walking on Hot Coals" and "Race the Breeze" with a fine slide showcase. "Unmilitary Two-Step" shows yet another side of Gallagher's playing: his acoustic fingerstyle skills. The guitarist's popularity in the U.S. eventually waned during the eighties, though he will always be one of Europe's most respected blues-rockers.

Taste, *Taste* (Atco, 1969), *On the Boards* (Atco, 1970), *Live Taste* (Polydor, 1971•), *Live at the Isle of Wight* (Polydor, 1972•). **Rory Gallagher** [on Chrysalis except where noted], *Rory Gallagher* (Polydor, 1971), *Deuce* (1971), *Live in Europe* (1972•), *Blueprint* (1973), *Tattoo* (1973), *Irish Tour '74* (1974•), *Against the Grain* (1975), *Calling Card* (1976), *Photo-Finish* (1978), *Top Priority* (1979), *Stage Struck* (1980•), *Jinx* (1982), *Fresh Evidence* (IRS, 1991).

Recordings featuring Rory Gallagher: **Muddy Waters** [on Chess], *The London Muddy Waters Sessions* (1972), *London Revisited* (n/a). **Jerry Lee Lewis**, *The Sessions* (Mercury, 1973). **Albert King**, *Albert Live* (Utopia, 1977•). **Gary Brooker**, *Echoes in the Night* (Polygram, 1985). **Box of Frogs**, *Strange Land* (Epic, 1986).

Dave Edmunds

Born: *April 15, 1944, in Cardiff, Wales*
Main Guitar: *'58 Gibson ES-335*

One modern ambassador of the rockabilly sound is Dave Edmunds, the British guitar star, solo artist, and leader of such popular U.K. acts as Love Sculpture and Rockpile. Like Chris Spedding, Jimmy Page, and other outstanding British guitarists, Edmunds was drawn to the electrifying sounds of rockabilly and its great guitar players during the early years of rock 'n' roll. Though not all of his musical adventures have been in the rockabilly genre, the solid foundation of southern guitar playing he acquired from listening to rockabilly greats like Scotty Moore, Cliff Gallup, and James Burton underlies his guitar sound.

Edmunds formed Love Sculpture in 1967, at the height of the U.K. blues-rock boom, and the band released its first album, *Blues Helping*, in 1968. Edmunds' rockabilly guitar playing belied his proficiency at Clapton-styled blues guitar, especially on the title track, Freddie King's "The Stumble," and on "I Believe to My

Soul." On these cuts Edmunds used fast and distorted pentatonic runs and string bends on his trademark Gibson ES-335 dotneck hollowbody.

Love Sculpture's single version of Khachaturian's "Sabre Dance" (from their second record, *Forms and Feelings*) finally got the band noticed in Britain, primarily due to Edmunds' Middle Eastern-flavored solos. This raucous but untraditional version of "Sabre Dance" was a Dave Edmunds guitar tour de force and quickly found its place on top of the British singles charts in 1968. However, with bands like Keith Emerson's the Nice and the Moody Blues gathering a large reputation for carving up the classics during the late sixties, critics swiftly mislabeled Edmunds' group as a progressive rock band—a tag that was far distant from the act's rockabilly and blues roots. Love Sculpture made one brief U.S. tour, then split up.

In 1970 Edmunds began making solo recordings at Rockfield Studios in Cardiff, Wales. These sessions eventually yielded the single "I Hear You Knocking," a bluesy cover of the original Smiley Lewis number. It became a career maker for Edmunds, and it sold several million copies in America and England. Highlighting the tune were the guitarist's shimmering slide breaks and rhythm playing, which again showed his prowess at blues-flavored guitar work. Two years after "Knocking," Edmunds released his first solo album, entitled *Rockpile*, on which he played virtually every instrument. While recording it, he improved his production techniques to such an extent that, by the mid seventies, he was regarded as something of a studio wizard.

Nineteen seventy-five saw the release of Edmunds' *Subtle as a Flying Mallet*. At the same time, he seriously embraced production work, overseeing records for Foghat, Del Shannon, Brinsley Schwartz, and the Flamin' Groovies. By the time of *Get It* (1977), a new period of Edmunds' career ignited when he teamed up with ex-Brinsley Schwartz bassist/vocalist Nick Lowe. Out of this partnership, the two formed the *group* Rockpile (with the addition of drummer Terry Williams and second guitarist Billy Bremner). Grabbing onto the coattails of the New Wave movement, Rockpile churned out a straight-ahead brand of "roots" rock that combined rockabilly economy and drive with pop vocal idioms from the 1960s.

The result was a rock style known as "power pop," and Edmunds and Rockpile were its prime progenitors in the U.K. On the next two Lowe-backed Edmunds records, *Tracks Wax on 4* (1978) and *Repeat When Necessary* (1979), and Rockpile's only album venture, *Seconds of Pleasure* (1980), the men made a name for themselves as the power pop band of the New Wave era. Key tracks of the Edmunds/Lowe power pop style were Edmunds' solo hit "Girl Talk," Lowe's "So It Goes" and "Cruel to Be Kind," and Rockpile's guitar-dominated hit "Heart" (from *Seconds of Pleasure*), with its effervescent acoustic strumming and melodic rockabilly solo. But shortly after the release of *Pleasure*, contractual problems set in and Rockpile was forced to split up.

Nevertheless, Edmunds continued making his rockabilly-flavored pop on solo records like *Twangin'* (1981) and *D.E. 7th* (1982). Paralleling his solo work at the time were his production credits, which took a large leap forward after his work on the first Stray Cats album and, later, the much-touted Everly Brothers reunion record. In 1983 Edmunds appeared in Paul McCartney's film *Give My Regards to Broad Street*, and in 1985 participated in a much-heralded rockabilly guitar summit with Carl Perkins, Eric Clapton, and George Harrison for a video release. From his energetic stints with Love Sculpture and Rockpile to his skillful production and stylish brand of rockabilly revivalism, Dave Edmunds has established himself as one of the most prestigious elder statesmen of British guitar.

Dave Edmunds [on Swan Song except where noted] *Subtle as a Flying Mallet* (RCA, 1975), *Get It* (1977), *Tracks on Wax* (1978), *Repeat When Necessary* (1979), *Twangin'* (1981), *The Best of Dave Edmunds* (1981), *D.E. 7th* (Columbia, 1982), *Information* (Columbia, 1983), *Riff Raff* (Columbia, 1984), *I Hear You Rockin'* (Columbia, 1986•), *Closer to the Flame* (Capitol, 1990), *The Dave Edmunds Anthology* [1968–90] (Rhino, 1993). **Rockpile,** *Rockpile* (NAM, 1972), *Seconds of Pleasure* (Columbia, 1980). **Love Sculpture,** *Blues Helping* (c. 1967), *Forms and Feelings* (c. 1968), *Classic Tracks, '68–'72* (One-Up, 1974), *Singles, A's and B's* (Harvest, 1980).

Recordings featuring Dave Edmunds: **Mason Ruffner,** *Gypsy Blood* (CBS Associated, 1987). **Nick Lowe,** *Party of One* (Reprise, 1990).

CHAPTER THIRTEEN

Glam Rock
Dresses and Distortion

A musical antidote was in order. As the 1960s waned, adolescents and young adults realized that the pleasing after-effects of the "Summer of Love" were far from permanent. The war in Vietnam wasn't going away, politicians and social leaders were themselves being killed, and the Beatles were on the verge of calling an end to the biggest musical juggernaut of the twentieth century. Life in general was just too serious.

There was no use making matters worse with serious music. Yet one significant downside of guitar-driven rock music in the late sixties and early seventies was how seriously most guitarists took themselves. Obsessed with their own technical abilities, they began to fall prey to the kinds of conceits that often marred jazz: little regard for the audience, a certain preciousness and egotism on the part of musicians, a profound dislike of criticism (constructive or otherwise), and a belief that the music being made was the one key ingredient to widespread political and ideological change. Rock concerts, in particular, became manifestations of this belief, while simultaneously taking on all the aspects of an endurance contest: how long could the guitarists jam, and how long would the audience put up with it? Not much longer, as it would turn out. The whole psychedelic ethic of "peace, love, and harmony" and "let's change the world" created a violent backlash, based largely on the ideology, "Hey, what about *me*?" Welcome to the 1970s—the "Me" decade.

It was this climate that gave birth to the sheer audacity, lunacy, and outrageousness of glamour rock, or glitter rock, which has always been known simply as glam rock, or just *glam*. It's difficult to define the essence of glam rock and its guitar players in a simple statement—there were so many things that gave fuel to the movement. For instance, the extended jams of blues-rock and hard rock, the complexity of art rock, and the self-importance of folk rockers struck many people as downright boring. There were obvious standouts within those genres: the aggressive and destructive stage antics of Jimi Hendrix and Pete Townshend, the theatrical flair of Frank Zappa and Genesis lead singer Peter Gabriel, the cock-rock attitude of Keith Richards and Jimmy Page. But these men were the exception to the rule. In contrast, Eric Clapton, Jeff Beck, Tony Iommi, and most of their brethren were quite content to put on a show which may have dazzled the ears, but left the eyes wanting much more. And with the world becoming an increasingly serious place, audiences wanted desperately to be entertained. They wanted big, bombastic, brilliant, bedazzling, and blinding. In short, they wanted *theater*.

Glam rock gave it to them. "You want to see rock stars?" the glam bands asked rhetorically. "We'll be your rock stars, and we'll be larger than life. We'll dress the part, act the part, and live the part. Tired of watching guys noodle around on their Strats for hours at a time? Fine. We'll give you a show with so much eye candy that you'll be talking about it for weeks. Tired of blues diatribes about cheating women, bad jobs, and workin' for the man? Fine. We'll give you songs about fast women, faster cars, fame and fortune, late-night parties and all-day decadence. We'll give you escape."

That was the idea behind glam, but the motivation behind its individual musicians went far deeper. Since the mid 1960s, guitar playing had become an art and a means to stardom, which meant that a lot more people, especially teenagers, wanted to give it a try. Unfortunately, the standards for entry were extremely high. Hendrix and Clapton, in particular, had set new levels of expectation for rock guitarists, levels that were not within the sights of most aspiring guitarists—then or now. Plus, everyone knew how long it had taken Clapton and Hendrix to get good—hours of practice a day, years of road work, and nightly gigging. In the eyes of aspiring guitarists, that took too long. There had to be a better way. The question, then, was how to be in a band and make a living as a rock guitarist without having to top Hendrix or Clapton?

The answer was simple: Dresses.

Dresses, or any other extreme fashion statement, could hide a myriad of failings, including a lack of musical sophistication or expertise. If people were drawn to a band by its bizarre clothing or questionable sexual orientation or shocking lyrics, they were less likely to notice the often amateurish and stolen riffs. No audience was going to compare a guitarist in eyeliner and glitter to Eric Clapton, but that same audience might still shell out money for the glam guy's records and come to see his shows. (Years later, numerous punk guitarists would use this same tactic to disguise their lack of guitar skills. The difference was that punks replaced the dresses with rage and anger, and hid behind that.)

Glam rockers took their wardrobe cue from the well-dressed mods of the British Invasion, London's Carnaby Street fops, or pure psychedelic tripsters (who often wore form-fitting Victorian-style trousers and billowing blouses), their stage cues and lyrics from Shakespeare and horror films, and their guitar cues from their acclaimed contemporaries. Unlike the Claptons, Becks, and Pages of the late 1960s and early 1970s, however, the glam rockers did not draw directly from the wellspring of the blues, but rather built on the sounds of their time. Few people, for instance, remember that Alice Cooper's first album came out the same year as the first Led Zeppelin album–it sounds as if it must have come years later. Glam guitarists did not create new styles of playing the guitar, because for the most part they were closely following the lead of those that were breaking new ground.

This is not to say that glam didn't produce good guitarists. It did. Cooper's original guitarists, along with Marc Bolan of T. Rex, Mick Ralphs of Mott the Hoople, and Mick Ronson (with David Bowie), were all skilled musicians in their own right, although it is interesting to note that none of them–with the exception of Bolan–were successful solo artists or existed outside of established bands. These guitarists were also surprisingly skilled songwriters, which wasn't necessarily true of the rest of the genre, nor was it true of many other guitarists of the time.

Long-term, glam rock–as performed by its best musicians–established one fact of life for rock and roll: It was possible to play good guitar and look good while doing it. This was a lesson that would not be lost on the metal bands of the 1980s.

T. Rex

Marc Bolan

Born: *Mark Feld, on July 30, 1947, in London*
Died: *September 16, 1977, in London*
Main Guitar: *Gibson Les Paul*

Marc Bolan was the quintessential glam rock guitarist. He was not the best of them, but he was the only guitarist of the genre to make a name for himself as an individual performer without the aid of a band or a riveting frontman–he didn't need one. Bolan was a self-contained glam package.

After spending much of his teen years as a male model, Bolan started playing London area clubs, singing and accompanying himself on acoustic guitar. His songs and playing were typical of the coffeehouse scene at the time (David Bowie being another prime example): simple, chord-based songs with vague lyrics about sex, science fiction, and mind expansion. In keeping with this "Summer of Love" theme, Bolan released several discs under his own name and with local group John's Children (considered the first glam group by some) before founding the overtly hippie-esque Tyrannosaurus Rex with partner Steve Took. The band's first album, *My People Were Fair and Had Sky in Their Hair but Now They're Content to Wear Stars on Their Brows*,

was as full of flower power philosophy as one could get (as well as the influence of J.R.R. Tolkien's fantasy epic *The Lord of the Rings*, from which the title of the album was derived). While being a little on the light side, it did bring attention to the increasingly showy Bolan, which caused Took to leave. Replacing him with Mickie Finn, Tyrannosaurus Rex released *Beard of Stars* and charted with a light acoustic rock single, "Ride a White Swan," in 1970.

Ever alert to changing trends, Bolan added an electric guitar to his repertoire, hired a bass player and a drummer, and shortened the name of the band to T. Rex to reflect a change in direction. It worked better than anyone could have imagined. Bolan proved to be a nimble-fingered guitarist who was willing to experiment with distortion–a far cry from his coffeehouse playing. The band released an album entitled simply *T. Rex* and followed it up with the amazing *Electric Warrior* (1971). This album made Bolan both a glam superstar and a guitar hero in one fell swoop. With tracks like "Jeepster," "Mambo Sun," "Rip-Off," and the monstrous international hit "Bang a Gong (Get It On)," Bolan showed that he could pull licks from incredibly diverse sources, ranging from Chuck Berry on to Keith Richards and Jimmy Page. In the process, he layered on the fuzztone and effects ped-

Marc Bolan

als and used his picking technique to create stuttering and hiccuping effects. His electric repertoire didn't deviate too far from straight-ahead rock (and his acoustic repertoire never strayed too far from acoustic singalongs), but his ability to mix it up both sonically and rhythmically kept his playing interesting.

Following up *Electric Warrior* with *The Slider* (1972), the band gained an international following, although the record was not substantially different from its predecessor. Still, songs like "Chariot Choogle" and "Buick Mackane" saw Bolan keeping up with the times and delving into the territory of heavy metal riffs, à la Zeppelin and Black Sabbath. However, it never appeared that he was ripping those bands off, because he always played his own brand of heaviness at full-tilt boogie shuffle speed, never slowing down long enough to play dirges. This was glam, after all, and the party had to play through every track.

Tanx, the band's 1973 offering, covered even more of the same ground, but glam was beginning to lose its glitter; a year or two later, the movement was all but dead. Despite his keen eye, Bolan's own immense stardom appeared to have blinded him to the passing of the fad. His party-boy image faded as his weight bloated up to comic proportions (like Elvis), and T. Rex's recorded material showed none of the imagination or adventurousness of its earlier work. By the time Bolan realized he had missed the boat, it was already 1976, and his career as glam's poster boy was already over. He broke up the band, did some solo work, and toured with the punk band the Damned in an attempt to make up for lost time (the latter was an effort to show that he still knew how to catch the rising tide of a new trend). Sadly, it was all too late. In 1977 Bolan was killed in a bizarre car crash; his girlfriend smashed the car they were in directly into a tree. (The girlfriend, Grace Jones, would later write the hit "Tainted Love.") He was 30 years old.

Many give Bolan credit for only being in the right place at the right time. This is true in part, although it slights his achievements as a guitarist. His unique playing style and use of effects with simple riffs were far removed from his contemporaries. Bolan was more willing to toy with blues rock, which separated his style from the straightforward playing of Clapton or Beck, and his employment of effects was normally associated with more experimental guitarists like Hendrix and Page. Ultimately, he used the trappings of glam to become one of the first commercially successful guitar heroes—someone who didn't have to wait until he was dead or his career was long gone to be appreciated for his work.

Tyrannosaurus Rex, The Wizard (Decca, 1966), *My People Were Fair and Had Sky in Their Hair but Now They're Content to Wear Stars on Their Brows* (Regal Zone, 1968), *Prophets, Seers & Sages* (Regal Zone, 1968), *The Angels of the Ages* (Blue Thumb, 1969), *Unicorn* (Blue Thumb, 1969), *Beard of Stars* (Regal Zone, 1970). **T. Rex,** *T. Rex* (Cube, 1970), *Electric Warrior* (Reprise, 1971), *The Slider* (Reprise, 1972), *Tanx* (Combat, 1973), *Beginning of Doves* [Bolan solo, recorded c. 1967] (Track, 1974), *Zinc Alloy & the Hidden Riders of Tomorrow* (Combat, 1974), *Zip Gun* (Combat, 1975), *Futuristic Dragon* (Combat, 1976), *Dandy in the Underworld* (Combat, 1977), *Children of Rarn Suite* (Marc on Wax, 1982), *T. Rex Collection* (Combat, 1991), *BBC Radio 1 Live* (ROIR, 1993•).

David Bowie

David Bowie

Born: *David Jones, on January 8, 1947, in London*

Mick Ronson

Born: *May 26, 1947, in Kingston-upon-Hull, Humberside, England*
Died: *April 29, 1993, in London*
Main Guitar: *Gibson Les Paul*

Carlos Alomar

Born: *May 7, 1951, in Ponce, Puerto Rico*
Main Guitar: *Custom Alembic Maverick*

Earl Slick

Born: *October 1, 1951, in New York City*
Main Guitar: *Gibson Les Paul*

Adrian Belew

Born: *1951, in Covington, Kentucky*
Main Guitar: *Fender Stratocaster*

Reeves Gabrels

Born: *June 4, 1956, in Staten Island, New York*
Main Guitars: *Steinberger models*

Ziggy and Ronno. David Bowie was just another London lad singing and playing clubs in the late 1960s when he met up with Mick Ronson in 1969. Ronson—nicknamed Ronnie, or Ronno—had played with a number of London bands, including the Cresters and the Rats, but these had lacked the spark needed to generate commercial success. Bowie, too, was missing a critical element in his repertoire, although he had already demonstrated unique writing skills and a flair for the theatrical. His guitar playing, mostly acoustic, simply didn't provide adequate support for his singing and songwriting. On the other hand, Ronson's exotically distorted and overdriven electric style appeared to be custom-made for Bowie's music, providing a darkness and tension that helped elevate Bowie from the mundane to the masterful. This was evident in their first collaboration, *The Man Who Sold the World* (1971), a haunting LP that showcased both Bowie's songwriting and Ronson's sneering guitar on cuts like "Width of a Circle" and "Superman."

The response to the album pushed Bowie and Ronson to explore even more uncharted territory. After the so-so release *Hunky Dory*, the two reached their collaborative zenith with *The Rise and Fall of Ziggy Stardust and the Spiders from Mars* (1972). Establishing the fictional, vaguely interplanetary, and polysexual character Ziggy Stardust, with his band the Spiders from Mars, Bowie and Ronson launched a full-scale assault on rock convention. They employed hard-driving guitar rhythms and buzzsaw

Mick Ronson

lead lines, but cloaked them in sexually provocative lyrics and tales of life in a quasi-science fictional world. While initially shocking to listeners of the 1970s due to their explicit lyrics, tunes like "Suffragette City" and "Hang on to Yourself" would never have gotten a second listen if it weren't for Ronson's stellar licks and intelligent arranging. The intro guitar to "Suffragette City" that appeared as "Lady Stardust" was still fading out was not only one of the most brilliant examples of musical pacing in all of rock, but in addition, the riff's punch was on a par with the raw aggression of classics like Zeppelin's "Whole Lotta Love" and Mountain's "Mississippi Queen."

Likewise, their stage show emphasized a wholesale renunciation of the live jam session. Instead, the show was scripted out, choreographed, and rehearsed from beginning to end. Costume changes, simulated sex (normally involving Bowie kneeling down in front of Ronson, with his face buried just under Ronson's Les Paul), additional stage performers and cast members, and fully designed sets were everything that Cream, Traffic, and Free were not. Had Ronson not been able to back it all up with his superb playing, it is doubtful that it ever would have worked. But it did work, phenomenally, and Bowie was on his way to becoming one of the most important recording acts of the 1970s.

After *Ziggy*, Bowie and Ronson released *Aladdin Sane*, ostensibly an opus about shattered love and life on the road and in the limelight. Ronson delved into almost perverse sonic realms with the experimental rhythm wailings on "Cracked Actor" and the plaintive, screeching solo on "Time." The only thing that kept this album from establishing Ronson as a guitar hero in his own right was his perceived role as Bowie's sideman.

Pin Ups, the successor to *Aladdin*, was something of a letdown: after the progressiveness of its forerunners, it featured only cover versions of other artists' songs. Ronson, looking for something more, took the opportunity to try his hand at a solo career. He released two solo albums, *Slaughter on Tenth Avenue* and *Play Don't Worry*. The records were well received, but not huge commercial successes, and Ronson decided that he worked better when he wasn't commanding all the attention.

He later teamed up with Ian Hunter, the former frontman for Mott the Hoople. The collaboration was a natural—both men having worked with Bowie—but it never produced the expected results. The two recorded and toured together, their live shows consisting of new material generously sprinkled throughout with the older material that had made them both famous. Ronson later did session work in the late 1980s, and was also in demand for the excellent arranging and producing skills he had developed with Bowie. The guitarist developed liver cancer in 1991, which surprisingly did not slow him down much. Despite his sickness, he played the Freddie Mercury Aids Benefit/Tribute at Wembley Stadium in 1992, and he reunited with both Hunter and Bowie on an album that was released posthumously, *Heaven and Hull* (the title referring to his birthplace). Ronson died in 1993.

Post-Glam. After Bowie and Ronson parted ways, the rock icon began changing guitarists as often as he changed personas. On his first post-Ronson album, *Diamond Dogs*, Bowie chose to play all the guitar parts himself. He handled the task quite well, demonstrating capable chops on the repeated riff to "Rebel, Rebel" and the snaky intro to the title cut. After *Diamond Dogs*, Bowie's projects over the next two decades served as a revolving door for a parade of notable guitarists. First up was Puerto Rican guitarist Carlos Alomar, who joined the singer's band in 1974 (at age 22) and appeared on *Young Americans* (1975) and *Station to Station* (1976). (Alomar had previously played on numerous R&B albums, as well as with the Main Ingredient, a U.S. soul band that scored a hit with "Everybody Plays the Fool.") Since that time, he has appeared on and acted as the *de facto* musical director for just about every Bowie tour and record.

Joining Alomar on most of the mid-seventies albums was Earl Slick, a noted New York session guitarist and gun-for-hire. Slick's golden moment with Bowie was on the great *Station to Station* track "Stay," as compelling a marriage of funk rhythm guitar (Alomar) and hard rock solos (Slick) as has ever been committed to vinyl. Slick later had brief success with the Stray Cats sequel Phantom, Rocker & Slick before disappearing from the rock scene altogether. As for Alomar, in his down-time from Bowie projects, he cut a guitar synth album with a Photon MIDI Converter entitled *Dream Generator* (1988), worked with Mick Jagger, the Pretenders, Yoko Ono, and Paul McCartney, and is currently producing a variety of rising Latin-rock bands.

Adrian Belew (♦) added his howling Strat-abused solos to various cuts on *Lodger* (1979)—notably the single "D.J." And in 1980 King Crimson's enigmatic Robert Fripp (♦) signed on, in time for *Scary Monsters*. Also on that disc was the early guitar synthesist Chuck Hammer, who added strange tones to the radio cut "Ashes to Ashes," though he's barely been heard from since, aside from a solo album called, cleverly enough, *Guitarchitecture* (1982).

A most unusual and promising guitar collaboration followed several years later when Bowie hired a then-unknown Stevie Ray Vaughan (♦) for *Let's Dance* (1983). Vaughan's gutsy blues brought a roughness and earthiness to Bowie's work, especially on cuts like "Cat People (Putting out Fire)" and "China Girl." Like most Bowie collaborations, this one was short-lived, rumor having it that Vaughan quit the band when Bowie offered to pay him only union scale at the U.S. Festival, an event that allegedly netted Bowie himself millions of dollars.

Peter Frampton (♦) temporarily revived his own career as Bowie's guitarist for *Never Let Me Down* (1987) and the accompanying "Glass Spider" tour.

In 1987 Bowie formed Tin Machine, with Reeves Gabrels on guitar, and Tony and Hunt Sales (comedian Soupy Sales' kids) on bass and drums. Tin Machine was not designed to be another Bowie project, but a full-fledged band. The group could not escape the specter of Bowie's past, however, and comparisons were inevitable and not always favorable. Bowie claims that Tin Machine is a long-term project, and throughout the 1990s he has employed Gabrels on his personal projects outside of the band, including *Black Tie, White Noise* (1993). Gabrels is known for his radical sonic experimentation, using everything from vibrators to wind-up toys to wrench unusual sounds from his guitar. He has become a notable session player in his own right.

David Bowie [on Rykodisc/RCA except where noted], *Out of Sight* (Prestige, 1965), *Feelin' Good* (Prestige, 1965), *David Bowie 1966* (Atlantic, 1966), *Love You till Tuesday* (Deram, 1967), *Space Oddity* (Mercury, 1969), *The World of David Bowie* (Decca, 1970), *The Man who Sold the World* (1971), *Hunky Dory* (1972), *The Rise and Fall of Ziggy Stardust and the Spiders From Mars* (1972), *Aladdin Sane* (1973), *Pin Ups* (1973), *Diamond Dogs* (1974), *David Live* (1974•), *Young Americans* (1975), *Station to Station* (1976), *Changesonebowie* (1976), *Heroes* (1977), *Low* (1977), *Lodger* (1979), *Scary Monsters (And Super Creeps)* (1980), *Changes* (1981), *Changestwobowie* (1981), *Another Face* (Decca, 1981), *Let's Dance* (EMI, 1983), *Second Face* (Decca, 1983), *Fame & Fashion* (RCA, 1984), *Tonight* (EMI, 1984), *Never Let Me Down* (EMI, 1987), *Sound + Vision* (1989), *Black Tie, White Noise* (1993), *Outside* (1995). **Tin Machine,** *Tin Machine* (EMI, 1989), *Tin Machine II* (EMI, 1991), *Oy Vey, Baby!* (EMI, 1993•)

Mick Ronson. *Slaughter on Tenth Avenue* (RCA, 1974), *Play Don't Worry* (RCA, 1975), *Heaven & Hull* (Epic, 1994).

Reeves Gabrels, *Modern Farmer* [Gabrels' band] (Victory, 1993), *The Sacred Squall of Now* (Upstart, 1995). **Reeves Gabrels & Dave Tronzo,** *Night in Amnesia* (Upstart, 1995).

Alice Cooper

Glen Buxton

B o r n : *November 11, 1947, in Akron, Ohio*
M a i n   G u i t a r : *Gibson SG Custom*

Michael Bruce

B o r n : *March 16, 1948, in Phoenix*
M a i n   G u i t a r : *Gibson SG Deluxe*

The members of the band that would eventually be called Alice Cooper learned to play their instruments after track meets and during high school recess in Phoenix, Arizona. Known at various times during the mid 1960s as the Earwigs, the Nazz, and the Spiders, the band performed for school sports events and at local grade schools. Glen Buxton was the primary guitarist, learning licks off records and teaching them to the others, but it was Michael Bruce who managed to come up with original guitar hooks that would stick in people's minds.

Deciding to become professional rockers and seek their fame outside of the Phoenix desert (immortalized nearly a decade later in the song "Alma Mater"), the band headed to Detroit and Los Angeles, where they became known collectively as Alice Cooper. The name was chosen for the shock value of having five wildly thrashing males leaping around on a stage in dresses and chrome pants, when the audience was likely to be expecting a blonde folk singer.

Their surreal stage show captured the eyes and ears of Frank Zappa, who signed them to his Bizarre/Straight Record label in 1969. That same year, Alice Cooper released their first record, *Pretties for You*, to near universal disdain. Overall, the recording was lackluster, but the guitar work especially was haphazard and interesting only in spots, as neither Buxton nor Bruce had really progressed beyond the three-chord stage. The album did have big production numbers, like "Fields of Regret," "Living," and "Swing Low, Sweet Cheerio," each of which demonstrated that Alice Cooper had more on its mind than simple rock songs. The follow-up, *Easy Action*, also failed to catch on with the record-buying public. That record, though, showed that Cooper and company were finding inspiration and riffs in places outside of rock and roll—namely, in movie soundtracks and Broadway themes.

Love It To Death (1971) crystallized all of Cooper's disparate influences and produced the single "I'm Eighteen," a gift-wrapped, cut-to-fit anthem for the teen population. With simple chord progressions, arpeggiated notes, and fuzzy guitar, the song was Alice Cooper's gateway to fame. The rest of the album was no slouch, either, as Buxton and Bruce came into their own on cuts such as "Caught in a Dream" and "Long Way to Go." The duo slipped easily into hard rock riffs with simple solos and short fills, yet they created theatrical arrangements that transcended the all-too-common clichés that were part and parcel of early seventies rock. The bass playing of Dennis Dunaway was also a primary factor in shaping the sound of the band, as he often took on leadlike parts in the manner of John Entwistle of The Who.

With "I'm Eighteen" firmly entrenched as an AM radio staple, Alice Cooper went to great lengths to become a concert draw. The cheap dresses and makeup gave way to elaborate stage setups that utilized baby dolls, guillotines, gallows, a boa constrictor, fake blood, white satin suits, and dozens of other props. The band wanted to give audiences theater in the gothic tradition of Vincent Price, not Ethel Merman. The stage act was realized in Cooper's two finest albums, *Killer* (1971) and *School's Out* (1972). Both records stand out for the fine playing of Buxton and Bruce, who ably copped riffs from James Bond and *West Side Story* without dropping their guitar swagger for a moment. "Under My Wheels," from *Killer*, demonstrates the band at its aggressive best, playing the two guitars off of each other using one of the simplest rock progressions. In their hands, the progression was transformed into a classic. The popularity of yet another teen anthem, "School's Out," had as much to do with its lyrics as with its catchy two-chord riff, repeated over and over.

In the wake of *School's Out*, the band became one of the biggest record sellers and concert draws of the early 1970s. Nonetheless, cracks in the band's growing popularity were beginning to show. Frontman Alice Cooper (born Vincent Furnier) became the sole spokesperson for the band, which seemed to relegate the others to the position of sidemen. The timing was interesting, given that Michael Bruce was responsible for penning most of the band's hits. Glen Buxton, unfortunately, had fallen prey to severe substance abuse, which made it difficult for him to show up at either recording sessions or concerts. Session player Dick Wagner had actually been brought in earlier to pick up the slack on *School's Out*, but the situation deteriorated further during the recording of *Billion Dollar Babies*, Cooper's 1973 opus. Wagner's session twin, Steve Hunter, was hired to play on *Babies*, while yet another guitarist, Mick Mashbir, was plugged in off-stage during concerts to cover for Buxton.

Cooper's management was reluctant to toss Glen out of the band during the height of its popularity—such things weren't done in high-profile glam bands circa 1973. Plus, the partying lifestyle was part of the attitude. Unfortunately, it was driving the rest of the band members nuts. Friction heightened over Cooper's role as spokesman and Buxton's lack of contribution to records and concerts. Despite the huge success of *Babies*, which was another album of appealing riff-driven Bruce songs like "No More Mister Nice Guy" and the title track, the Cooper band was tearing apart from the inside out. It recorded its final album, *Muscle of Love*, in 1973. The album was awash with session personnel, including Wagner and Mashbir, not to mention guest vocalists Donovan and Liza Minnelli. Cooper wanted out of the mess in order to be his own man (so to speak), and he decided to leave the others to their own fate.

Alice hooked up with Lou Reed's former touring band, based upon Hunter and Wagner, and embarked on a solo career that began with *Welcome to My Nightmare* and worked its way down from there. Hunter and Wagner provided solid support for Cooper on the albums that followed, but neither of them could contribute songs or an attitude to the solo Alice. Constantly looking for new possibilities to revive his flagging fortunes and plummeting popularity during the 1980s, Cooper tried an endless series of no-name sessionmen, the most famous being Arnold Schwarzenegger look-alike Kane Roberts and future pop pretty boy Kip Winger. Alice regained some of his credibility in 1989 and into the early 1990s with the release of *Trash* and *Hey Stoopid*, which featured guest performances by notable guitarists such as Slash, Joe Satriani, Joe Perry, Steve Lukather, and Richie Sambora, among others. However, *Last Temptation* (1994) had not a hint of guitar genius to it.

The remaining members of the original Cooper band decided to continue recording under the name Billion Dollar Babies. They did not, however, invite Glen Buxton to join them. Instead they hired a guitarist named Mike Marconi to round out their lineup. The band recorded one album, *Battle Axe*, which was largely driven by Bruce's songwriting and vocals. But it was dead on arrival without the strength of the Cooper name. The band broke up, with each of the members going his separate way. Glen Buxton returned to Phoenix, where he gigged in local clubs, and put together a band called Virgin in the early 1980s. Michael Bruce also returned to Phoenix, recording an EP called *Rock Rolls On*. Those endeavors are where the glamour ended for Alice Cooper's original dynamic duo.

The years have been kind to the recorded legacy of Bruce and Buxton. Few bands before or since can boast of such interesting interplay between two guitarists, especially in breaking traditional rocks clichés. They were notable for taking the simple and making it interesting. In their time, they were a formidable team.

Alice Cooper Band [on Warner Bros. except where noted], *Pretties for You* (Bizarre, 1969), *Easy Action* (Bizarre, 1970), *Love It to Death* (1971), *Killer* (1971), *School's Out* (1972), *Billion Dollar Babies* (1973), *Muscle of Love* (1973), *Greatest Hits* (1974). **Alice Cooper** [on Warner Bros. except where noted], *Welcome to My Nightmare* (1975), *Alice Cooper Goes to Hell* (1976), *Alice Cooper Show* (1977•), *Lace & Whiskey* (1977), *From the Inside* (1978), *Flush the Fashion* (1980), *Special Forces* (1981), *Collection* (1982), *Dada* (1982), *Zipper Catches Skin* (1982), *Constrictor* (MCA, 1986), *Raise Your Fist and Yell* (MCA, 1987), *Prince of Darkness* (MCA, 1989), *Trash* (Epic, 1989), *Hey Stoopid* (Epic, 1991), *Last Temptation* (Sony, 1994). **Billion Dollar Babies**, *Battle Axe* (Polydor, 1977).

Mott the Hoople

Mick Ralphs

B o r n : *March 31, 1948, in Hereford, England*
M a i n   G u i t a r : *Fender Stratocaster*

Ariel Bender

B o r n : *Luther Grosvenor, on December 23, 1949, in Worcester, England*
M a i n   G u i t a r : *Gibson Les Paul Junior*

Mick Ralphs was playing in a band called Silence in 1969 when he hired a new singer named Ian Hunter. The group changed its name to Mott the Hoople (after a novel by Willard Manus) and released two interesting but largely ignored records before calling it quits in 1971.

David Bowie, however, had been a fan of Mott, and offered to produce them if they were willing to reunite. The band agreed, and the result was the 1972 glam rock album *All the Young Dudes*. The title track, written by Bowie, hinted at glam's latent homosexual leanings and gave Hunter and Ralphs immediate credibility as Bowie protégés. The album did not rest on the laurels of the title song alone, as was evident on tracks like "Ready for Love" (a Ralphs tune, which he lamely reworked when he joined Bad Company), "One of the Boys," and "Sucker." The record established Ralphs as a good, solid player with a penchant for interesting riffs. His solos, while never extravagant and rarely memorable, were workmanlike and utilitarian, serving to support the band's lyrics and image rather than compete with them.

Using *Dudes* as a jumping-off point and milking the genre to the hilt, Mott became Britain's favorite glam rock outfit. Hunter was never photographed without his Hollywood-style sunglasses, the band always wore thigh-high platform boots, and stage sets included huge marionettes that dangled from the rafters. But *Dudes* was the band's high point, despite the success of the follow-up, *Rock and Roll Queen*—another album that played up the tongue-in-cheek sexuality of glam. In the meantime, Ralphs tired of the outrageous clothing and the nightly fear of falling off his platform heels, and left Mott to team up with ex-Free vocalist Paul Rodgers in Bad Company (♪). He was immediately replaced by Ariel Bender, a guitarist many knew as Luther Grosvenor, formerly of Spooky Tooth. Grosvenor left Tooth in 1972 to record a little-known solo album and then changed his name to Ariel Bender before signing up with Mott in 1973.

After cutting *The Hoople* that year, Bender departed for obscurity, and Mick Ronson came aboard to help the band out on its live dates. The tour had ill effects on Hunter, who was ultimately hospitalized for fatigue. He decided not to return to Mott, as did Ronson, and the remaining members hired singer Nigel Benjamin and guitarist Ray Major as replacements in 1975. Calling themselves simply Mott, and doing away with some of the glam trappings, the band eked out two more records before hanging up their platform boots forever (although several members recorded together under the name British Lions). Ronson and Hunter went on to make several decent records together, while Mick Ralphs is still in Bad Company.

Mott the Hoople [on Columbia except where noted], *Mott the Hoople* (Atlantic, 1970), *Mad Shadows* (Island, 1970), *Wildlife* (Island, 1971), *Brain Capers* (Island, 1971), *All the Young Dudes* (1972), *Rock and Roll Queen* (Atlantic, 1972), *Mott* (1973), *Hoople* (1974), *Live* (1974•), *Drive On* (1975), *Greatest Hits* (1976), *Shouting & Pointing* (1976), *Shades of Ian Hunter—The Ballad of Ian Hunter and Mott the Hoople* (1980), *The Ballad of Mott* (Columbia/Legacy, 1993).

Kiss

Ace Frehley

Born: *Paul Frehley, on April 27, 1951, in New York City*
Main Guitar: *Gibson Les Paul*

Paul Stanley

Born: *Stanley Eisen, on January 20, 1952, in New York City*
Main Guitars: *Ibanez Paul Stanley model, Gibson Flying V*

Bruce Kulick

Born: *December 12, 1953, in Brooklyn, New York*
Main Guitars: *ESP solidbodies*

Kiss began as a four-piece in New York City. Bass player and former grade school teacher Gene Simmons (born Chaim Whitz) and guitarist Paul Stanley had covered Beatles tunes in Wicked Lester, but wanted to form a glam band, using clown and kabuki makeup as their original contribution to the genre. After answering an advertisement in a New York paper, Paul Frehley joined the band as lead guitarist.

From the outset, the band was never taken seriously. Their riffs were admittedly stolen from the best sources ("Firehouse" from Zeppelin's "Misty Mountain Hop," for instance), their songs never ventured far from a four-chord format, and what they lacked in technical ability, they made up for in volume and stage presence. Frehley was hardly a lead guitar dynamo; the majority of his solos relied on bending single notes over and over. Stanley

KISS: Ace Frehley, Paul Stanley, Gene Simmons, Eric Carr

was a faceless rhythm guitar player—no better or no worse than thousands of others. All that was beside the point: Kiss put on the best rock shows in the world. To make their show even more spectacular, they would line up dozens of empty speaker cabinets onstage to make it seem like Kiss had biggest guitar amplification system on planet Earth. Amazingly, the audience bought it.

The first three Kiss studio albums were relatively tepid affairs (Simmons oftentimes likening the sound to "dinosaur farts"), but the aptly titled *Kiss Alive* double disc served up all the fury, frenzy, and fire (literally) of a Kiss concert. Upon the release of the record, the band found its overnight success and whetted the public's appetite for a studio album that would deliver the same high-volume rock goods. Since most of the world had never listened to any of the band's studio records, Kiss had to come up with something that would not be snickered at.

Fortunately, the band succeeded. By all accounts, then and now, *Destroyer* was an exceptional rock album; not from the standpoint of technical guitar playing, but from the marriage of big guitar songs with studio technology. Under the guidance of producer Bob Ezrin (Alice Cooper, Pink Floyd), the band came up with a well-arranged, deftly orchestrated set. Utilizing harmony guitars on "Detroit Rock City" and "Shout It out Loud," thundering power chords on "Do You Love Me," and eerie riffing on "God of Thunder," Ezrin got the more mileage than most people expected out of Paul Stanley and Ace Frehley. The solos were well-choreographed (especially "Detroit Rock City"), but never felt forced or stilted. The success of the record was due as much to the guitarists' ability to make pomp rock sound raw and reckless as to Ezrin's technical direction.

After *Destroyer*, and its breakthrough *piano* single "Beth," Kiss embarked on a long and arduous journey that continues to this day. *Rock and Roll Over* and *Love Gun* followed, as did a simultaneous release of solo albums, which despite "shipping platinum," reportedly didn't sell too well. Considered nothing more than a public relations ploy, they contained little memorable music, with the exception of Frehley's; he had shown that he was capable of both writing and playing his own material, gaining airplay with "New York Groove." But the band began to suffer from its own glam excesses—especially Frehley. Sinking deeper into drug abuse, he became reckless (wrecking cars seemed to be an ongoing pastime) and alienated himself from the other members of the band, especially Simmons and Stanley, who were notorious control freaks.

Frehley was forced from the band in 1982 after a series of poorly conceived and received albums, notably *The Elder* and *Creatures of the Night*. He was replaced by Vinnie Vincent, a Frehley look-alike who was technically a better player than Ace. Upon hiring Vincent, Kiss removed its makeup and shored up its career with *Lick It Up*, a surprising return to its early simplicity. Though a skilled player, Vincent was apparently even more difficult to manage than Frehley, and he was tossed out by Simmons and Stanley. Contemporary metal player Mark St. John was hired in 1984 for *Animalize*, but he was soon diagnosed as having

Reiter's Syndrome and was unable to continue playing with the band. Kiss finally settled on New Yorker Bruce Kulick, formerly of the band Blackjack, who was probably the most well-rounded guitarist to ever join the band's ranks. While he had to play much of Frehley's material over the years, he was instrumental in the band's return to prominence in the late 1980s and early 1990s as a hard rock band par excellence. With Kulick the band recorded *Revenge* (1992), which pushed them back to a popularity rivaling their *Destroyer* days. Interestingly, Vinnie Vincent also received co-writing credit on that album.

Frehley continued on after Kiss with a checkered solo career, releasing albums under his own name and with a loose outfit he called Frehley's Comet. Surprisingly, he emerged as one of the biggest influences on the guitarists of early nineties metal, notably Dimebag Darrell of Pantera and Scott Ian of Anthrax. In hindsight, this may have more to do with his stage antics and simple power chords than any technical proficiency. Still, as a guitarist, he is appreciated—even worshipped—more in retrospect than he ever was during his tenure with Kiss.

In one of the boldest and most unexpected reunions ever, Kiss performed a 1995 MTV "Unplugged" session with Frehley and original drummer Peter Criss as invited guests. The following year, Kulick was sent on sabbatical as the original band—back in makeup—undertook one of the biggest tours in rock history. With Frehley on board (and cleaned up), Kiss' popularity was revived to a degree no one had believed possible.

Kiss [on Casablanca/Mercury except where noted], *Kiss* (1974), *Hotter than Hell* (1974), *Dressed to Kill* (1975), *Alive!* (1975), *Destroyer* (1975), *Rock & Roll Over* (1976), *Originals* (1976), *Love Gun* (1977), *Alive 2* (1977), *Double Platinum* (*Greatest Hits*) (1978), *Dynasty* (1979), *Unmasked* (1979), *Best of the Solo Albums* (1981), *Music from the Elder* (1981), *Creatures of the Night* (1982), *Killers* (Polydor, 1982), *Lick It Up* (Mercury, 1983), *Animalize* (Mercury, 1984), *Asylum* (Mercury, 1985), *Crazy Nights* (Mercury, 1987), *Smashes, Thrashes & Hits* (Mercury, 1988), *Hot in the Shade* (Mercury, 1989), *Revenge* (Mercury, 1992), *Alive III* (Mercury, 1993), *Unplugged* (Mercury, 1996•), *You Wanted the Best, You Got the Best!* (Mercury, 1996•). **Ace Frehley,** *Ace Frehley* (Casablanca, 1978), *Frehley's Comet* (Megaforce, 1987), *Second Sighting* (Megaforce, 1988), *Frehley's Comet Live + 1* (Megaforce, 1988), *Trouble Walkin'* (Megaforce, 1989). **Vinnie Vincent Invasion,** *Vinnie Vincent Invasion* (Chrysalis, 1986), *All Systems Go* (Chrysalis, 1988).

Dick Wagner and Steve Hunter

For two guys that many guitarists have never heard of, Dick Wagner and Steve Hunter spent plenty of time supporting some of the most visible frontmen in the business. The two served as producer Bob Ezrin's "guitar ringers" on many albums, especially those with Alice Cooper and Lou Reed. (It is claimed that he actually used the duo for much of Aerosmith's *Get Your Wings* as well.)

Although Wagner had been a member of a noted early metal act called the Frost in the late sixties, the two guitarists really rose to prominence for their work on Lou Reed's 1973 album *Berlin*.

It was during the subsequent concert tour with Reed, showcased on *Rock and Roll Animal* (1974), that the duo came into their own. The intro to that album, an extended Hunter instrumental leading into Reed's "Sweet Jane" (which had become a glam anthem after Mott the Hoople's cover of it), gave both Wagner and Hunter ample room to show off their individual soloing skills. Easy and restrained, the piece built up slowly to a classic guitar duel, which became explosively loud and raucous just as Reed hit the stage. That cut alone proved the value of employing these two together.

Both guitarists guested on the last two Alice Cooper Band albums, ostensibly to fill in for Glen Buxton. When that band broke up in 1975, Cooper and Ezrin brought in Wagner and Hunter full-time for Cooper's solo debut, *Welcome to My Nightmare*, and for his new touring band. Together and separately, both men have since toured with and recorded for a number of acts, including Peter Gabriel and Hall & Oates. Hunter, in particular, released a solo album, *The Deacon*, in 1989, and played on David Lee Roth's *A Little Ain't Enough* (1991) and *Your Filthy Little Mouth* (1994).

But perhaps Hunter and Wagner's greatest performance was their uncredited stint on Aerosmith's *Get Your Wings*, where they were brought in to add lead-guitar muscle where Joe Perry wasn't cutting it. Both players wail in the classic "Train Kept A-Rollin'," while Wagner also appears on three other cuts, including the popular "Same Old Song and Dance." While this news doesn't do much for Perry's stock, it certainly adds credence to the idea that Steve Hunter and Dick Wagner were among the best hard rockers of the middle seventies.

The Frost [on Vanguard], *Frost Music* (1969), *Rock and Roll Music* (1969), *Through the Eyes of Love* (1970), *Early Frost* (1978). **Dick Wagner,** *Richard Wagner* (Atlantic, 1978).

Recordings featuring Dick Wagner: **Ursa Major,** *Ursa Major* (RCA, 1972). **Alice Cooper** [on Warner Bros.], *School's Out* (1971), *Billion Dollar Babies* (1973), *Muscle of Love* (1974), *Greatest Hits* (1974), *Welcome to My Nightmare* (1975), *Alice Cooper Goes to Hell* (1976), *Lace & Whiskey* (1977), *Alice Cooper Show* (1977•), *From the Inside* (1978), *Zipper Catches Skin* (1982). **Lou Reed** [on RCA], *Berlin* (1973), *Rock and Roll Animal* (1974•), *Lou Reed Live* (1975•). **Elliott Murphy,** *Aquashow* (Polydor, 1973). **Peter Gabriel,** *Peter Gabriel* (Atco,1977). **Tim Curry** [on A&M], *Read My Lips* (1978), *Fearless* (1979). **Hall & Oates,** *Along the Red Ledge* (RCA, 1978). **Burton Cummings,** *Dream of a Child* (Portrait, 1978), *Collection* (Rhino, 1994). **Mark Farner,** *Mark Farner* (Atlantic, 1978). **Lee Aaron,** *Call of the Wild* (Ten, 1986). **Ruth Copeland,** *Take Me to Baltimore* (RCA, n/a).

Steve Hunter, *Swept Away* (Atco, 1977), *The Deacon* (IRS, 1988).

Recordings featuring Steve Hunter: **Alice Cooper** [on Warner Bros.], *Billion Dollar Babies* (1973), *Welcome to My Nightmare* (1975), *Alice Cooper Goes to Hell* (1976), *Lace & Whiskey* (1977), *Alice Cooper Show* (1977•). **Lou Reed** [on RCA], *Berlin* (1973), *Rock and Roll Animal* (1974•), *Lou Reed Live* (1975•). **Crowbar,** *Crowbar* (Epic, 1973). **Doctor John,** *Hollywood Be Thy Name* (UA, 1975). **Jim & Ginger,** *Ain't It Good to Have It All* (ABC, 1975). **Peter Gabriel,** *Peter Gabriel* (Atco,1977). **Bad Boy,** *The Band that Made Milwaukee Famous* (UA, 1977). **Richard Wagner,** *Richard Wagner* (Atlantic, 1978). **Yvonne Elliman,** *Night Flight* (RSO, 1978). **Rob Grill,** *Uprooted* (Mercury, 1979). **Indra Lesmana,** *No Standing* (MCA, 1984). **Flo & Eddie,** *Best of Flo and Eddie* (Rhino, 1987). **Gary Stewart,** *Brand New* (Hightone, 1988). **Leslie West,** *Dodgin' the Dirt* (BBI,1994). **Karla DeVito,** *Wake 'em up in Tokyo* (A&M, n/a). **Angelo,** *Midnight Prowl* (Fantasy, n/a). **Various Artists,** *Guitar Speak* (IRS, 1988). **David Lee Roth** [on Warner Bros.], *A Little Ain't Enough* (1991), *Your Filthy Little Mouth* (1994).

CHAPTER FOURTEEN

Hard Rock and Heavy Metal II
Into the Arena

Talk about the sincerest form of flattery.

When Led Zeppelin, Black Sabbath, and Deep Purple wrote the heavy metal textbook from 1969 through 1974, thousands of metal-wannabe bands suddenly appeared, all trying to copy the masters. And guitarists weren't alone in being entranced by this harder rock; record companies saw the large sums of money that Zeppelin was generating for Atlantic Records and wanted a piece of the action, too. As a result, acts were signed at a record pace and metal blossomed in the early seventies, creating an endless stream of bands trying to emulate the sound of *Led Zeppelin II* or *Machine Head*. Of course, very few succeeded.

On the guitar front, the main metal influences were just four players—Jimi Hendrix, Eric Clapton, Jeff Beck, and Jimmy Page. If you couldn't cop a Clapton lick or a Page stage move, then you weren't a hip six-stringer. (During this period, the combination of a Les Paul and a Marshall stack became the absolute standard, too, thanks to Page.) In all, one might very well sum up the 1973–78 epoch of rock guitar by noting that innovators were out—and emulators were in. Still, for all the bland copyists, a few fine players emerged from the miasma, as well as legions of good "meat 'n' potatoes" rockers—guitarists who weren't terribly original, but could still crank it up and wail like there was no tomorrow.

Aerosmith

Joe Perry

Born: *September 10, 1950, in Boston*
Main Guitar: *Gibson Les Paul*

Brad Whitford

Born: *February 23, 1952*
Main Guitar: *Gibson Les Paul*

Ask mid-seventies hard rock fans who the #1 band of the day was and chances are that the answer will be Aerosmith. Additionally, the group is just as popular in the 1990s as it was back then, which is a strong testament to their enduring appeal. The classic Aerosmith sound blended the best elements of the Yardbirds, the Rolling Stones, the Jeff Beck Group, and Led Zeppelin into a huge blues-based sound that has rocked metal fans on record and in concert for well over 20 years. The most visible member of their lineup has always been frontman and vocalist Steven Tyler, but he has traditionally been flanked by guitarists Joe Perry and Brad Whitford. The duo are as clever and efficient a guitar team as one is likely to find in the hard rock genre.

Aerosmith came together in Sunapee, New Hampshire, during 1970, with a lineup of Tyler, Perry, bassist Tom Hamilton, drummer Joey Kramer, and rhythm guitarist Ray Tabano. By the following summer, Tabano was out and Brad Whitford (imported from another local group, called Justin Tyme) was in. Aerosmith—the name was a bastardization of Sinclair Lewis's novel *Arrowsmith*—shifted its base south to Boston and developed a substantial cult following in the area. In 1972 the band was discovered by Columbia Records president Clive Davis and signed to that label. Nineteen seventy-three saw the release of their first album, titled simply *Aerosmith*, which relied heavily on a swamp rock and blues groove that seemed too confining for the band. The record did, however, feature the band's first single, "Dream On." A local radio favorite, "Dream On" would not become the band's signature tune until

Joe Perry

it was re-released to national radio nearly three years later. In the meantime, Aerosmith released a strong followup, *Get Your Wings* (1974). Ironically, several guitar parts long thought to have been played by Perry were actually cut by session guitarists Steve Hunter and Dick Wagner (♦), including the radio staples "Train Kept A-Rollin' " and "Same Old Song and Dance." Still, neither album made much headway on the charts, in spite of the band's constant roadwork.

Their third album, *Toys in the Attic* (1975) paid off big for Aerosmith, smashing into the upper reaches of the charts with the single "Walk This Way." Other tunes, notably the riff-heavy "Sweet Emotion" and the overdriven title song, drew attention to Aerosmith's full-throttle brand of American rock, earning them regular comparisons with the Rolling Stones. In 1976 the band duplicated the success of *Toys* with *Rocks*. Playing the bad boy rocker image to the hilt, the band increased the volume on *Rocks*, notably in songs like "Sick as a Dog" and "Rats in the Cellar," which ably demonstrated the ability of Perry and Whitford to handle both blues rock and metal. *Rocks* went platinum, as did *Draw the Line* (1977). To top things off, "Dream On" was re-released as a single and bolted to the top of the charts in 1976, providing the band with yet another in a series of megahits. But *Draw the Line* marked a turning point for the band, which seemed to have settled into something of a slump. Most fans didn't understand the Hirschfeld artwork on the album's cover, and they didn't find much drive behind the songs (with the exception of the title track and "Kings and Queens"). The even drabber *Night in the Ruts* followed in 1979.

But while Aerosmith were the rulers of heavy rock 'n' roll from 1975 to 1978–challenged only by Kiss and the continuing enigma that was Led Zeppelin, this did nothing to prevent Perry and Whitford from leaving the group (drugs and personal friction had resulted in onstage fights between members). Perry formed the Joe Perry Project, and Whitford teamed up with ex-Ted Nugent vocalist Derek St. Holmes for the Whitford-St. Holmes Band. Tyler replaced the two with unknowns Jimmy Crespo and Rick Dufay, but it was apparent that these two could not provide the same spark that Perry and Whitford brought to the band. The disappointing *Rock in a Hard Place* was the result, and although this version of the band toured, it was evident that most fans had left with Perry and Whitford.

Since neither Perry nor Whitford found success with their respective bands, they agreed to rejoin Tyler and company for the well-received but commercially unsuccessful *Done with Mirrors* (1985). Bringing in producer Bruce Fairbairn and a group of outside songwriters in a last-ditch attempt to save itself, the band reignited and re-established itself with *Permanent Vacation* (1987), a platinum disc that contained the hits "Dude (Looks Like a Lady)"–containing a berserk Perry solo with a rockabilly tinge–and the power ballad "Angel." Returning to the formulaic approach it had developed nearly two decades earlier (this time without drugs), the band proved even more successful with *Pump* (1990) and *Get a Grip* (1993), reaching heights that sur-

passed their *Draw the Line* days. As of this writing, Aerosmith has almost supplanted Madonna as MTV's pet artist, proof of their ability to attract new fans with more of the same guitar-based power rock that teenagers raved about a full generation ago.

Much of Aerosmith's popularity can be attributed to the gut-bucket riffing of Perry and Whitford. The intricate rhythm work—and Perry's whiplash solo—in "Walk this Way" shows a particularly funky side of the Aerosmith guitar sound, and this is often considered their signature track. Brad Whitford (whose guitar work is often overshadowed by Perry's flashy approach) reveals his own soloing prowess in the blues-metal break of "Round and Round" and the melodic leads to "You See Me Crying" (both from *Toys in the Attic*). Many have complained that Perry and Whitford are just the best players in a simple and hackneyed genre, but this ignores the fact that their songwriting and guitar tradeoffs are among the best in the history of hard rock.

Aerosmith [on Columbia except where noted], *Aerosmith* (1973), *Get Your Wings* (1974), *Toys in the Attic* (1975), *Rocks* (1976), *Draw the Line* (1977), *Live! Bootleg* (1978●), *A Night in the Ruts* (1979), *Greatest Hits* (1980), *Done with Mirrors* (Geffen, 1985), *Aerosmith Classics* (1986●), *Permanent Vacation* (Geffen, 1987), *Classics Live II* (1987), *Pump* (Geffen, 1989), *Pandora's Box* (1991●), *Get a Grip* (1993), *Big Ones* (1994). **Joe Perry Project** [on Columbia], *Let the Music Do the Talking* (1980), *I've Got the Rock 'n' Rolls Again* (1981), *Once a Rocker, Always a Rocker* (1983). **Whitford-St. Holmes Band**, *Whitford-St. Holmes Band* (CBS, 1981).

Recordings featuring Aerosmith: **Various Artists**, *California Jam 2* (Columbia, 1978●). **Various Artists**, *Sgt. Pepper's Lonely Hearts Club Band* (RSO, 1978).

Queen

Brian May

Born: *July 19, 1947, in Hampton, Middlesex, England*
Main Guitar: *"Big Red" (homemade solidbody)*

Brian May was not the archetypal rock guitarist of the seventies. While most players of that decade were batting out pentatonic solos using Les Pauls and cranked Marshall amps, May refined his sound with the use of a Vox AC30 amp and an Echoplex to coax a warm fuzztone from his homemade solidbody guitar (built with his father). And instead of just soloing with plagiarized Clapton and Hendrix licks, Queen's guitarman took these influences and began molding them into his own melodic breaks in two- and three-part harmony. By the end of the decade—when Queen was riding high on a long line of hit singles and albums—May's guitar voice had become an instantly recognizable part of the Queen sound, as identifiable as the voice of flamboyant frontman Freddie Mercury.

After graduating from Imperial College at London University with a degree in physics, May formed Smile with drummer Roger Taylor in the early seventies. When their singer departed, vocalist Freddie Mercury filled the void, and the three were soon joined by bassist John Deacon. In 1972 the four changed their name to Queen. The following year the band signed a contract with EMI Records and released their first album, *Queen*. The unmistakable Queen sound was a slick amalgam of Led Zeppelin's metal crunch with the smooth glitter/glam rock of David Bowie, Mott the Hoople, and the then-fledgling Roxy Music. Queen also put strong emphasis on theatrics with Freddie Mercury's quasi-operatic vocals and onstage antics. Right from the beginning, Queen stood out from the regular rock 'n' roll crowd.

The band's second LP, *Queen II* (1974), contained a hit in the U.K. called "Seven Seas of Rhye," but it wasn't until *Sheer Heart Attack* (also 1974) that Queen scored on both sides of the Atlantic, due to the single "Killer Queen." In addition to Mercury's lush vocal work, Brian May stepped forth on "Killer Queen" with a solo that fused tasty single-note passages with his patented harmony lines and tape echo effects. *Sheer Heart Attack* contained a wealth of outstanding hard rock guitar tracks, among them "Brighton Rock" (a masterpiece of Echoplex techniques), "Now I'm Here," "Tenement Funster," and the high-speed rocker "Stone Cold Crazy." It was an excellent introductory sampler to Brian May's ferocious playing.

In 1975 Queen was elevated to world-class status upon the release of *A Night at the Opera* and the hugely successful single "Bohemian Rhapsody." With a slow, introspective beginning and gradual climb to a raging metal jam and back again, "Bohemian Rhapsody" was akin to Led Zeppelin's "Stairway to Heaven." But while Zeppelin meshed folk influences with heavy metal, Queen opted for the light grandeur of the operetta as part of its hard rock. For sheer cleverness alone, not to mention May's riveting electric work, "Bohemian Rhapsody" rightfully became one of the top singles of 1975 and established Queen in the elite of seventies rock bands. May contributed great playing to the remainder of the disc, notably on his own epic, "Prophet's Song," and the poundingly hard rockers "Sweet Lady," "Death on Two Legs," and "I'm in Love with My Car."

Nineteen seventy-six brought the release of both another hit album and a hit single—*A Day at the Races* and "Somebody to Love." In late 1977 Queen's sixth album, *News of the World*, immediately shot to the top of the bestseller lists side by side with the single "We Will Rock You/We Are

the Champions." The segue between the two-part single featured a dazzling hailstorm of distorted power chords and lead licks from May. Another song from *News*, "It's Late," was notable for May's use of two-handed tapping and hammer-ons in the solo—a year before the rock world was introduced to the master of the two-handed technique, Eddie Van Halen.

In the eighties Queen's music shifted more towards synth-pop as part of Mercury's interest in quasi-Broadway and disco posturing. Despite the strength of songs like "Need Your Love Tonight" and "Hammer to Fall," as well as an interesting collaboration with David Bowie on "Under Pressure" (1981), Queen lost many U.S. fans throughout the decade. In 1983 May released a three-song EP called *Star Fleet Project*, which included Van Halen on guitar. The band partially redeemed itself in 1991 with the impressive rocker *Innuendo*, but Freddie Mercury died of AIDS in November of that year, ending the band's career.

In 1993, a decade after his Starfleet side project, May released *Back to the Light*, a strong effort showcasing his polished chops and the distinct voice that had been part of those lush Queen harmonies for years. He later toured solo as the opening act for Guns N' Roses and has plans for future projects with various artists. Still, it is with Queen that May's legend resides. In addition to his impeccable chops, the guitarist's tall, lithe figure and billowing long hair fully embodied the guitar hero image (as created by Jimmy Page), enamoring him to hordes of worshipping fans around the world. Despite this guitar hero gloss—and the difficulty that many rock critics had in taking Queen seriously—Brian May emerged as a guitarist of the first order, capable of executing both spacious melodic passages and bursts of high-energy metal excitement.

Queen [on Elektra except where noted], *Queen* (1973), *Queen II* (1974), *Sheer Heart Attack* (1974), *A Night at the Opera* (1975), *A Day at the Races* (1976), *News of the World* (1977), *Jazz* (1978), *Queen Live Killers* (1979•), *The Game* (1980), *Flash Gordon* [soundtrack] (1980), *Greatest Hits* (1981), *Hot Space* (1982), *The Works* (Capitol, 1984), *A Kind of Magic* (Capitol, 1986), *The Miracle* (Capitol, 1989), *At the Beeb* (BBC, 1989), *Innuendo* (Hollywood, 1991), *Greatest Hits* (1992), *Made in Heaven* (1995•). **Brian May & Friends,** *Star Fleet Project* (Capitol, 1983). **Brian May,** *Back to the Light* (Hollywood, 1993).

Recordings featuring Brian May: **Lonnie Donegan,** *Puttin' on the Style* (UA, 1978). **Various Artists,** *Concerts for the People of Kampuchea* (Atlantic, 1981•).

Brian May

Bad Company

Mick Ralphs

Born: *March 31, 1948, in Hereford, England*
Main Guitar: *Fender Stratocaster*

In 1974 Bad Company became the first band signed to Led Zeppelin's selective Swan Song label. Led by ex-Free vocalist Paul Rodgers and ex-Mott the Hoople guitarist Mick Ralphs, Bad Company belted out hard rock tunes that were firmly rooted in blues emotion and metal energy. The core of Bad Company's sound was the raunchy power chording and slow, bluesy soloing of Ralphs.

Before spurring Bad Company on to hard rock fame with his metallic guitar work, Ralphs had been a founding member of Mott the Hoople (◀), the British glam rock band led by vocalist Ian Hunter. After several years in the glitter limelight, Ralphs decided to quit Hoople at the peak of its success in 1973. Questing for a "back to basics" rock 'n' roll outfit, he hooked up with Paul Rodgers, who at the time was appearing with a band called Peace. The Ralphs/Rodgers combination clicked, and, after adding drummer Simon Kirke (also from Free) and ex-King Crimson bassist Boz Burrell, Bad Company was formed in late 1973.

By the end of their first year together, it was obvious that Bad Company was hot property. Fans adored Rodgers' powerful vocals and Ralphs' economic solos and power chords. When their debut album was released in 1974, the band topped the album charts and racked up a pair of radio-friendly singles, "Can't Get Enough" and "Movin' On." The album went gold, and on their first tour of America, Bad Company moved from support group to headliner within just a few weeks. The band's second record, *Straight Shooter*, followed its predecessor right up the album charts and produced another Top 10 single, "Feel Like Makin' Love." The Bad Company onslaught continued in 1976 with *Run with the Pack*, which again placed them on the singles charts, this time with "Youngblood." In 1977 the band's popularity sagged a bit with the album *Burnin' Sky*, but bounced back in 1979 with *Desolation Angels* and yet another hit single, "Rock and Roll Fantasy". Ironically, this song's brittle guitar synthesizer solo was played by Paul Rodgers.

Desolation Angels proved to be Bad Company's last hurrah; they released the disappointing *Rough Diamonds* in 1982 and split up that summer. After Bad Company's demise, Mick Ralphs played rhythm guitar on Pink Floyd guitarist David Gilmour's 1984 solo tour, while Rodgers went off to join Jimmy Page in the ill-fated Firm. But it is not always possible to keep a successful hard rock band down, and in 1986 Ralphs and Bad Company were back with a new album (*Fame and Fortune*) and a new singer (Brian Howe), still cranking out the same guitar-based power rock that brought them fame over a decade earlier. Bad Company hit a new high with the aggressive *Holy Water* in 1990, after which they seemed to coast on two sets of past glories. Alas,

in 1995 Ralphs and company released yet another album, *Company of Strangers*, with yet another singer.

Prime Mick Ralphs guitar playing was on early Bad Company recordings such as "Can't Get Enough," "Bad Company," and "Shooting Star," which has a particularly soulful, yet heavily distorted, lead. "Feel Like Makin' Love" epitomized Bad Company's method of juxtaposing light acoustic and heavy electric guitar textures (similar to and probably inspired by Led Zeppelin's approach). On that track, Ralphs mixes a country-styled verse topped with acoustic rhythm strumming and then distorted electric chords in the hook, finishing it off with a fluent metal solo in the rideout. Ultimately, there has never been anything fancy or flashy about his playing—it's been simple, workmanlike, almost clichéd stuff, but extremely effective nevertheless.

Bad Company [on Swan Song except where noted], *Bad Company* (1974), *Straight Shooter* (1975), *Run with the Pack* (1976), *Burning Sky* (1977), *Desolation Angels* (1979), *Rough Diamonds* (1982), *10 From 6* (1985), *Fame and Fortune* (Atlantic, 1986), *Dangerous Age* (Atco, 1988), *Holy Water* (Atco, 1990), *Here Comes Trouble* (Atco, 1992), *How about That* (Atlantic, 1992), *This Could Be the One* (Atlantic, 1992), *Best of Bad Company...Live!* (1993●), *Company of Strangers* (EastWest, 1995).

Recordings featuring Mick Ralphs: **Jim Capaldi,** *Some Come Running* (Island, 1989).

Boston

Tom Scholz

Born: *March 10, 1947, in Toledo, Ohio*
Main Guitar: *Gibson Les Paul goldtop*

Barry Goudreau

Born: *November 29, 1951*
Main Guitar: *Gibson SG*

Besides being a banner year for Peter Frampton, Fleetwood Mac, Paul McCartney, and Stevie Wonder, 1976 also saw the huge success of Boston, whose first album became one of the top smashes of the year. It was the all-time best-selling record by a debut artist up until that time, and is one of the 10 best-selling albums of all time, period. This is all the more amazing given that the band relied on an absurdly simple combination of Zeppelin-flavored metal pyrotechnics and southern California-inspired rock vocal harmonies.

Led by Tom Scholz—the band's lead guitarist, keyboardist, songwriter, producer, engineer, and overall mastermind—Boston became an overnight sensation with the hit single "More Than a Feeling," which propelled the band into the big leagues of seventies rock 'n' roll. Originally a keyboardist, Scholz only began to play the guitar when he was about 20 years old, and even then he took a tentative approach to the instrument. He played in local bands in the city of Boston like the Revolting Tones Revue,

Middle Earth, and Mother's Milk—usually as a keyboard player—with future members of Boston, including Barry Goudreau, who would become Boston's co-lead guitarist.

After completing a Master's Degree in Mechanical Engineering at MIT, Scholz joined the Polaroid corporation in its R&D department. At the same time, he built a home studio and recorded demos for what eventually became the first Boston album. The demos, pristine even by professional studio standards, did not feature an entire band, but an amalgamation of people Scholz knew, including vocalist and rhythm guitarist Brad Delp, bassist Fran Sheehan, drummer Sib Hashian, and Goudreau. After making the rounds and receiving dozens of rejections, the tape fell into the hands of Epic Records, which approached Scholz in 1975 with a recording contract. Scholz scrambled to assemble a full-fledged band, which he named Boston, and put out the demos virtually unchanged as the group's first offering. Within a few weeks of its release in the summer of 1976, the album went gold and screamed towards platinum. Scholz's knack for a catchy chord progression and singer Brad Delp's piercing lead vocals and harmonies were the band's most obvious attributes, but the distorted twin guitars of Scholz and Goudreau created the simultaneously recognizable and inimitable "Boston sound."

The first Boston album demonstrated that, when it came to recording guitars, Scholz's technical expertise in the recording studio was unparalleled. He captured his own playing and that of Goudreau with such clarity, power, and heavy metal crunch that the tracks from the first Boston record remain some of the best-sounding guitar parts ever recorded. In addition to the straight-ahead combination of Les Paul guitar and Marshall amp, he also used various preamps, equalizers, echo units, and some custom-made power attenuators, many of which he made himself. Though neither Scholz nor Goudreau was a technically or stylistically brilliant guitarist, their combined sound was indisputably awesome, overcoming their musical limitations by the sheer force of technology, studio know-how, and a keen feel for ultra-hot riffs. This patented guitar formula was used on every song on the debut set: "More Than a Feeling," "Rock & Roll Band," "Smokin'," and all the rest. Besides this sound, another characteristic of Scholz's and Goudreau's guitar work was their thick harmony solos that appeared in each song. Scholz's solo from "More Than a Feeling" reeked of this approach as he opened with thick doubled phrases (achieved with a Scholz doubling device) before he dubbed in several guitar lines to complete a harmonious guitar choir. "Long Time" provided a forum for Goudreau to step out with some fiery leads and one section of distorted riffs that sounded like a chainsaw toppling a giant oak.

After releasing the album, Boston bolstered its reputation in 1976 and 1977 with aggressive touring across the country, quickly moving from support to headline status (even topping the bill at Madison Square Garden). After a lengthy layoff, the band returned in the fall of 1978 with its second album, *Don't Look Back*. While this album didn't ignite the airwaves like its prede-cessor, it did have the title single (featuring characteristic layers of guitar harmonies, plus Goudreau's hot slide work and rideout solo) and a ballad called "The Man I'll Never Be," containing a long, dramatic solo by Scholz.

Scholz was unhappy with *Don't Look Back*, claiming it was released by Epic before he was finished with it, and he began immediately to plan for its followup. While waiting for the next record to get underway, Goudreau recorded a solo album, which featured Delp and Hashian. This annoyed Scholz, who felt that Goudreau was capitalizing on the bandleader's success. Scholz fired Goudreau, leading to a court battle that eventually involved anyone even remotely connected with Boston. Scholz would ultimately take credit for playing almost all of the instruments on the first record himself, with minimal input from Goudreau (despite the fact that the latter takes the solo on "Long Time," arguably the band's most famous guitar break).

Scholz's inability to produce an album on time—he obsessed over individual waveforms produced by each instrument—prompted legal battles with the record company, which forced an eight-year gap between albums. Switching from Epic to MCA (a move that prompted of one of the nastiest legal battles in record industry history), Boston, with only Scholz and Delp remaining from the original lineup, pushed their way back to the #1 slot on the pop charts in 1986 with the mediocre *Third Stage* and its guitar-powered singles "Amanda" and "Cool the Engines" (now featuring former Sammy Hagar guitarist Gary Pihl in place of the departed Goudreau, who had formed the short-lived Orion the Hunter). After yet another eight-year absence, Scholz finally delivered the extremely flaccid *Walk On* in 1994, which suffered from the absence of frontman Brad Delp, who had joined forces with Barry Goudreau to form RTZ (Return to Zero). Scholz tried to duplicate his previous success by hiring three vocalists that he mixed together in an attempt to emulate Delp, but to no avail. The album was an embarrassment.

Nevertheless, Scholz's later bland work with Boston should not overshadow his work on the first album or his work as something of the guitar world's equivalent of Thomas Edison. During the first half of the eighties, Scholz successfully launched Scholz R&D, a Boston-based electronics company that created several innovative pieces of equipment for guitarists, including the Power Soak amplifier attenuator (for getting high-volume tones at low volumes) and the now-legendary Rockman mini-amp, a Walkman-styled component that became a staple in both top recording studios and young players' bedrooms. Scholz sold the company in 1995 in order to spend more time working on Boston.

Boston, *Boston* (Columbia, 1976), *Don't Look Back* (Columbia, 1978), *Third Stage* (MCA, 1986), *Walk On* (MCA, 1994). **Barry Goudreau,** *Barry Goudreau* (Portrait, 1980). **Orion the Hunter,** *Orion the Hunter* (Portrait, 1984). **RTZ,** *Return to Zero* (Giant, 1992).

Ted Nugent

Born: *December 13, 1948, in Detroit*
Main Guitar: *Gibson Byrdland*

A common sight on American concert stages in the mid seventies was Ted Nugent, "the Motor City Madman," bare-chested and clad in a loincloth, leading his band in a high-volume tribute to the glory of hard rock 'n' roll. From 1975 to the end of the decade, Nugent was one of rock's leading guitar heroes, racking up platinum albums and penning such inane but remarkably catchy metal anthems as "Stranglehold," "Cat Scratch Fever," and "Wango Tango." Though he capitalized on the same Clapton, Beck, and Page heavy guitar clichés that many of his peers did, Nugent hot-rodded them with fast picking, artificial tremolo bar effects, and enough distortion to power every electric guitar in America. All this, along with the axeman's love for the Gibson Byrdland—a hollowbody electric more often associated with country and jazz than rock—made it obvious that Ted Nugent was a breed apart from other 1970s rock guitarists.

After taking up the guitar as a child, Ted Nugent played with his first professional band, the Lourdes, in his mid teens. Nugent had to leave the band when his family moved to Chicago, but quickly formed a new band called the Amboy Dukes. In 1968 the Amboy Dukes scored a hit single with the psychedelic metal song "Journey to the Center of Your Mind," which introduced the young Nugent's savage guitar talents to America by way of a tough fuzztone solo. "Journey to the Center of Your Mind" was the Dukes' high point, though, and while they continued to record and tour (mostly in the South and Midwest), they never achieved any kind of major commercial success. A name change to Ted Nugent & the Amboy Dukes generated more interest in Ted, who proved to be a self-promoter of the first order. He also turned out impressive work, notably a fast, furious pentatonic solo on his cover of Chuck Berry's "Maybellene," from the *Tooth, Fang & Claw* album.

After years as a locally renowned, but nationally unknown, guitar commodity, Nugent broke through in 1975 with a solo record on Epic. This self-titled album, which featured past members of the Amboy Dukes, quickly broke into the Top 30 on the album charts. Ted soon found himself playing to coliseum-sized crowds across the U.S. His followup, *Free-For-All*

Ted Nugent

(1976), did even better, with the title cut presenting the Nuge at his braggadocio best. With the platinum release *Cat Scratch Fever* in 1977, Ted Nugent had finally arrived. *Cat Scratch Fever* caught Nugent in all of his best poses: the cock-rock innuendo and riffs of the title song, the savage beauty of the instrumental "Homebound," and the pedal-to-the-metal power chording of "Death by Misadventure." In addition to his recorded output, Nugent's concert performances stunned audiences everywhere with incendiary guitar solos, onstage acrobatics, and infamous pre-song raps that combined equal amounts of humor and profanity, driving his mostly teenage fans into frothing squeals of delight. He loved using feedback to incite his audiences and would launch into impromptu solos between songs.

In 1978 Nugent released the best-selling *Double Live Gonzo* album, which captured the six-string madman in his perfect forum—the live concert stage. Among the best guitar tracks on the album are "Stranglehold," a brutish mid-tempo rocker with a deep power chord groove and solo of matched-pitch bends, fast pentatonic runs, and his novel whammy effects (he achieved this by pushing up and down on the unobstructed section of strings that runs from the bridge to the tailpiece of his Gibson Byrdland). Also included are such Nugent standards as "Wang Dang Sweet Poontang," his FM hit "Cat Scratch Fever," and "Hibernation," a Lonnie Mack-inspired instrumental in which Nugent executes a series of surprisingly clean and melodic solos.

His star faded quite a bit in the 1980s as he turned out album after album of recycled hard rock. His onstage persona gave way to a high-visibility role as a national hunting activist, especially for the rights of bow hunters (he is an expert bow hunter and founded his own bow-hunting magazine). It seemed for a while that Terrible Ted would be the ultimate 1970s rock casualty. He was saved from the cutout bin when he teamed with Tommy Shaw (ex-Styx) and Jack Blades (ex-Night Ranger) to form Damn Yankees, a short-lived but successful power pop group custom-made for the 1990s. This resurrected interest in Ted as a solo artist has prompted numerous guitarists to come out of the woodwork and cite Nugent (belatedly) as an influence.

Amboy Dukes [on Mainstream], *Amboy Dukes* (1967), *Journey to the Center of the Mind* (1968), *Migration* (1969). **Ted Nugent & the Amboy Dukes** [on Polydor except where noted], *Marriage on the Rocks/Rock Bottom* (1970), *Survival of the Fittest/Live* (1971•), *Call of the Wild* (Discreet, 1973), *Tooth, Fang, and Claw* (Discreet, 1974). **Ted Nugent** [on Epic except where noted], *Ted Nugent* (1975), *Free-For-All* (1976), *Cat Scratch Fever* (1977), *Double Live Gonzo* (1978•), *Weekend Warriors* (1978), *State of Shock* (1979), *Scream Dream* (1980), *Intensities in Ten Cities* (1981•), *Great Gonzos!—The Best of*

Ted Nugent (1981), *Nugent* (Atlantic, 1982), *Penetrator* (Atlantic, 1984), *Little Miss Dangerous* (Atlantic, 1986), *If You Can't Lick' em, Lick 'em* (Atlantic, 1987), *Spirit of the Wild* (Atlantic, 1995). **Damn Yankees** [on Warner Bros.], *Damn Yankees* (1990), *Don't Tread* (1992).

Recordings featuring Ted Nugent: **Various Artists,** *California Jam 2* (Columbia, 1978•). **Various Artists,** *Volunteer Jam VI* (Epic, 1980•).

Joe Walsh

B o r n : *November 20, 1947, in Wichita, Kansas*
M a i n G u i t a r : *Gibson Les Paul Standard*

As lead guitarist for the early-seventies power trio the James Gang, Joe Walsh was well known for his loud guitar solos, rhythm workouts, and slide guitar breaks. Early in his career he was hailed as one of America's answers to the formidable British metal guitarists of the day (e.g., Clapton, Beck, and Page), and gained credibility when Pete Townshend proclaimed him one of his favorite guitarists. From then on, Joe Walsh walked among the elite of in the world of rock guitarists.

Walsh joined the James Gang in 1969 after bumming around Kent State University and the Cleveland rock 'n' roll scene for a few years. With the help of Bill Szymczyk (later producer of the Eagles and Rick Derringer), the James Gang signed with ABC Records in 1969 and cut *Yer Album* that same year. Walsh and the band also hooked up with the Who for a wildly successful tour. In 1970 they cut their second album, *The James Gang Rides Again*, which broke into the Top 20 on the album charts.

With its Led Zeppelin-like metal edge and Walsh's sparkling guitar playing, *The James Gang Rides Again* was an immediate high point in the band's recording career. Guitar hot spots on the album included "The Bomber" and "Funk #49," the latter showing Walsh's picking skills in raw, R&B-styled chord riffs and funky lead licks. From the Gang's next studio outing, *Thirds* (1971), came "Walk Away," perhaps Walsh's best recorded guitar blitz with the band. Setting the pace with a thudding rhythm, Walsh cut loose with power chords and lead lines in the song before venturing into his melodic overdubbed solo. For the finale, the guitarist pulled out all the stops in a brilliant sonic tribute to Jimi Hendrix, complete with uncontrolled feedback, distortion, and an awesome display of multi-octave tremolo dives.

A mediocre live album was issued in mid 1971, and Walsh left the James Gang that November. The following year he formed a new group called Barnstorm and released an album of the same name, though it didn't receive much attention. On his next record, *The Smoker You Drink, The Player You Get* (1973), the members of Barnstorm were relegated to being Walsh's backup band, and the guitarist continued on essentially as a solo act. *The Smoker You Drink* contained Walsh's signature song, "Rocky Mountain Way," a tune that established him as a top-draw rock performer. Bristling with riffing guitar parts and lazy slide figures, "Rocky Mountain Way" became an instant FM hit, especially due to Walsh's clever use of the Talk Box, a popular device for pro-

ducing voice-like sounds that was also being used by artists such as Jeff Beck, Rick Derringer, and Peter Frampton.

Walsh followed up that album with another solid solo effort, *So What*, which contained the killer guitar track "Turn to Stone." In 1976 Walsh accepted an invitation to join the Eagles (♦), just in time to play on their massive-selling *Hotel California*. At the time, critics denounced the partnership, scoffing that Walsh's role as a hard rocker with a tongue-in-cheek attitude could never mesh with the laid-back pop and sentimental lyrics in most Eagles songs. Surprisingly, he proved the pundits wrong, giving the band some of it finest moments. His scintillating solos were heard on such rock classics as "Life in the Fast Lane" and the title track of the album. This partnership lasted until the early eighties, when the Eagles disbanded. During Walsh's tenure with the band, he had a solo hit with the light-humored "Life's Been Good," from his 1978 set *But Seriously, Folks...*, featuring a variety of guitar textures, from acoustic to electric power rhythm to his infamously wicked slide work.

After the Eagles, he released several mediocre solo albums, and his penchant for bizarre humor earned him the moniker "Clown Prince of the Guitar." He had several high points on records, including the soundtrack to *Warriors*, featuring the single "In the City," and an almost brilliant instrumental called "Theme from Boat Weirdos," from *But Seriously, Folks...*. He seemed destined to rehash "Rocky Mountain Way" forever until the Eagles reunion in 1994, which showed that age had not dimmed his clever playing in the least.

James Gang [on ABC except where noted], *Yer Album* (Bluesway, 1969), *The James Gang Rides Again* (1970), *Thirds* (1971), *James Gang Live in Concert* (1971•), *The Best of the James Gang featuring Joe Walsh* (1973). **Barnstorm,** *Barnstorm* (Dunhill, 1972). **Joe Walsh,** *The Smoker You Drink, The Player You Get* (Dunhill, 1973), *So What* (Dunhill, 1974), *You Can't Argue with a Sick Mind* (ABC, 1976•), *But Seriously, Folks...* (Asylum, 1978), *The Best of Joe Walsh* (ABC, 1978), *There Goes the Neighborhood* (Asylum, 1981), *You Bought It, You Name It* (Warner Bros., 1983), *The Confessor* (Warner Bros., 1985), *Got Any Gum?* (Warner Bros., 1987), *Ordinary Average Guy* (Pyramid, 1991), *Songs for a Dying Planet* (Epic, 1992), *Jump the Blues Away* (Verve, n/a), *Look What I Did! The Joe Walsh Anthology* (MCA, 1995). **The Eagles** [on Asylum], *Hotel California* (1976), *The Long Run* (1979), *Eagles Live* (1980•), *Eagles Greatest Hits, Vol. 2* (1982), *Hell Freezes Over* (Geffen, 1994•).

Recordings featuring Joe Walsh: **B.B. King** [on ABC], *Indianola, Mississippi Seeds* (1970), *L.A. Midnight* (1972), *Best of B.B. King* (1973). **Rick Derringer,** *All American Boy* (Blue Sky, 1973). **REO Speedwagon,** *Ridin' the Storm Out* (Epic, 1973). **Dan Fogelberg** [on Epic], *Souvenirs* (1974), *Netherlands* (1977). **Keith Moon,** *Two Sides of Keith Moon* (Track, 1975). **Bill Wyman,** *Stone Alone* (Rolling Stone, 1976). **Rod Stewart,** *A Night on the Town* (Warner Bros., 1976). **Jay Ferguson** [on Asylum except where noted], *All Alone in the End Zone* (1976), *Thunder Island* (1978), *Real Life Ain't this Way* (1979), *Term & Conditions* (Capitol, 1981), *White Noise* (1982). **Emerson, Lake & Palmer,** *Works Vol. 1* (Atlantic, 1977). **Randy Newman,** *Little Criminals* (Warner Bros., 1977). **Graham Nash,** *Earth & Sky* (Capitol, 1980). **Warren Zevon,** *Bad Luck Streak in Dancing School* (Asylum, 1980). **John Entwistle,** *Too Late the Hero* (Atco, 1981). **Don Henley,** *I Can't Stand Still* (Asylum, 1982). **Steve Winwood,** *Back in the High Life* (Island, 1986). **Richard Marx,** *Richard Marx* (EMI-Manhattan, 1987). **Ringo Starr,** *Ringo Starr & His All Starr Band* (Rykodisc, 1990•).

Blue Öyster Cult

Buck Dharma

Born: *Donald Roeser, on November 12, 1947*
Main Guitars: *'61 Gibson SG Custom, Steinberger GM-7*

Once known on the Long Island bar scene as Soft White Underbelly, Blue Öyster Cult rose throughout the seventies to become one of the most original metal bands of the decade. Besides their thunderous power chords and often black-humored lyrics, BOC was noted for their guitar power, supplied primarily by lead guitarist Buck Dharma. The group's eponymous, riff-laden first album was in stores by 1972, and critical acclaim followed for their next two sets, *Tyranny and Mutation* (1973) and *Secret Treaties* (1974). But it wasn't until the live double set *On Your Feet or on Your Knees* in 1975 that the band scored a decisive hit and gained a full national audience.

A flashy soloist in the tradition of Alvin Lee, Buck Dharma added much excitement to many of the Cult's best early works, like "Cities on Flames," "Buck's Boogie," and the group's cover of the Steppenwolf classic "Born to Be Wild," with fleet-fingered pentatonic solos and Tyrannosaurian riffs. In 1976 BOC scored a major hit single with "(Don't Fear) The Reaper," which featured Dharma's vocals and a dramatic, flamenco-flavored lead on electric. The band's golden era followed throughout the late seventies with a string of FM hits and tours that steadily gained them a hard-core following. Among the best of their guitar-dominated tracks of this era were the tongue-in-cheek "Godzilla" (from *Spectres* [1977]), "Burnin' for You," and the absolutely spine-chilling "Joan Crawford" (both from *Fire of Unknown Origin* [1981]). BOC was also a popular concert attraction during this time, and a major highlight of each show was the moment when the other four members of the band would strap on electric guitars and join Dharma at the front of the stage for a crowd-thrilling five-guitar showdown. The band is still recording and touring today, with original members Buck Dharma, vocalist Eric Bloom, and keyboardist/rhythm guitarist Allen Lanier.

Blue Öyster Cult [on Columbia except where noted], *Blue Öyster Cult* (1972), *Tyranny and Mutation* (1973), *Secret Treaties* (1974), *On Your Feet or on Your Knees* (1975•), *Agents of Fortune* (1976), *Spectres* (1977), *Some Enchanted Evening* (1978•), *Mirrors* (1979), *Cultosaurus Erectus* (1980), *Fire of Unknown Origin* (1981), *Extraterrestrial/Live* (1982•), *The Revolution by Night* (1983), *Club Ninja* (1986), *Imaginos* (1988), *Cult Classic Cult* (Caroline, 1994), *Workshop of the Telescopes* (1995•). **Buck Dharma,** *Flat Out* (Columbia, 1982).

Recordings featuring Buck Dharma: **Various Artists,** *Guitar's Practicing Musicians, Vol. I* (Guitar Recordings, 1989•), *Guitar's Practicing Musicians, Vol. III* (Guitar Recordings, 1993•).

Peter Frampton and Humble Pie

Peter Frampton

Born: *April 22, 1950, in Beckenham, Kent, England*
Main Guitar: *Late-fifties Gibson Les Paul Custom*

Steve Marriott

Born: *January 30, 1947*
Died: *April 20, 1991*
Main Guitar: *Gibson SG*

Dave "Clem" Clemson

Born: *September 5, 1949*
Main Guitar: *Gibson Les Paul*

In 1976 the rock world far and away belonged to a slight, golden-haired performer from Britain named Peter Frampton. Until that year, Frampton had been a talented but minor rocker, recording several hard rock albums with Humble Pie at the beginning of the decade and continuing on with his own moderately successful solo career through mid decade. With the release of *Frampton Comes Alive* in March 1976, however, the guitarist became a household name overnight as his album pushed its way to the top of the pop album charts. By the end of the year, *Frampton Comes Alive* had sold approximately 10 million copies (more than any album up until that time), and it established Peter Frampton as America's favorite rock star.

Peter Frampton started playing the guitar at age seven. By the time he was 16, he was a member of a professional pop band called the Herd. In 1967 the band had a hit single in the U.K. with "From the Underground"; they had two more in 1968: "Paradise Lost" and "I Don't Want Our Loving to Die." Few people remember these hits, but they put Frampton in the public spotlight. He was even dubbed "The Face of 1968" by one British pop magazine.

Frustrated at his lack of financial reward in light of all his publicity, Frampton quit the Herd in 1968 to form a group with Steve Marriott, then singer with the Small Faces ("Itchycoo Park"). Frampton and Marriott christened their new outfit Humble Pie and, with the aid of bassist Greg Ridley and drummer Jerry Shirley, cut two albums as a folk-rock unit, inspired largely by recordings from the Band. They then changed gears and set out to rock England and America with a blues-tinged hard rock sound. After releasing several albums to a less-than-zealous public, Pie finally broke big in America with *Rock On* in 1971, following it up later that year with *Performance—Rockin' the Fillmore*, an intense (an intensely successful) live disc. This album showed off Frampton's guitar talents to their fullest as he surged through cut after cut with his impressively melodic, but aggressive, solos. His singular guitar style was heard clearly on rockers like "Hallelujah (I Love Her So)" and the power chording crowd-pleaser "I Don't Need No Doctor."

Following Frampton's exit, the Pie hired Clem Clemson in the lead guitar slot and, in 1972, hit their peak with the album *Smokin'*. Adding R&B vocals to their straight-ahead metal formula, Humble Pie cut the groove-oriented "30 Days in the Hole," which helped propel *Smokin'* to gold-selling status. The half-live, half-studio disc *Eat It!* (1973) continued in this vein, containing "Up Our Sleeve," an uproarious rocker beefed up with Clemson's fat Les Paul solos and Marriott's crushing power riffs pushing the song to hard rock glory. But that was the band's zenith, and they broke up in 1975. Marriott assembled a new version of the band in 1980–81 with little success. A decade later, Frampton and Marriott got together with the hopes of putting the band back together, but the latter suddenly lost his life in a house fire, irrevocably ending the saga of Humble Pie. In hindsight, it was one of the key early metal bands.

As for Frampton's post-Pie career, he briefly pursued studio work, playing with such performers as George Harrison, Harry Nilsson, and Tim Hardin. Finally, he made the move to go solo, and in the fall of 1972 he put out his first solo disc, *Wind of Change*. For the next four years he toured the U.S. almost constantly, taking breaks only to record solo albums, including *Frampton's Camel* (1973; the name of his short-lived band), *Somethin's Happening* (1974), and *Frampton* (1975), arguably his finest studio record ever. Due to this extensive touring and recording, Frampton built up an avid following in America—certainly enough of a following to fuel the concert recordings for his fifth solo outing, a double live album. *Frampton Comes Alive* was released in 1976, and the guitarist suddenly became the most popular musician in the world.

Why was *Frampton Comes Alive* such a huge success? It was simply one of those rare moments where everything came together perfectly: singing, songwriting, band support, audience participation, and, particularly, guitar playing. Through tracks like "Somethin's Happening," "Doobie Wah," the single "Show Me the Way," and his churning cover of the Rolling Stones' "Jumpin' Jack Flash," Frampton played superbly, draping each lick from his Gibson Les Paul Custom with a strong melodic flair and layers of overdrive, phasing, and Leslie speaker effects. "Show Me the Way" and the finale, "Do You Feel Like We Do," also introduced thousands of guitar players to the Talk Box (though Jeff Beck had used it the previous year on his *Blow by Blow*).

After 1976, a.k.a. The Year of Peter Frampton, the guitarist's career crashed as quickly as it had taken off. In 1977 he toured America, selling out the biggest arenas, but his hasty followup LP, *I'm in You*, was a pale pop replica of its predecessor and only yielded the sappy title cut as a moderately successful single. The following year, Frampton appeared in the critically savaged film musical of the Beatles' *Sgt. Pepper's Lonely Hearts Club Band* alongside the Bee Gees; predictably, the movie bombed. To make things worse, he was involved in a car accident in the Bahamas, resulting in a broken arm. By then, however—as a direct result of media hype, overexposure, and poor career decisions—Peter Frampton's popularity had taken a severe dive.

For the next several years, Frampton continued to make albums, but few of them found their ways into the hands of record buyers. He did studio work and toured as a sideman, most notably for David Bowie on the Glass Spider Tour of 1988. Still, he made a few fine discs of his own, like *Premonition* (1986; the single "Lying" contains a hip octave-divided guitar solo) and *Peter Frampton* (1993). Unfortunately, for all his guitar prowess and smart songwriting skills, Frampton may always be known as a relic of the 1970s—the shooting star whose fame fizzled as quickly as it had ignited. This is a sad fate and an unfair eulogy for such a fine player.

Humble Pie, *As Safe as Yesterday* (Immediate, 1969), *Town and Country* (Immediate, 1969), *Humble Pie* (A&M, 1970), *Rock On* (A&M, 1971), *Performance—Rockin' the Fillmore* (A&M, 1971•). **Peter Frampton** [on A&M except where noted], *Wind of Change* (1972), *Frampton's Camel* (1973), *Somethin's Happening* (1974), *Frampton* (1975), *Frampton Comes Alive* (1976•), *I'm in You* (1977), *Where I Should Be* (1979), *Breaking All the Rules* (1981), *The Art of Control* (1982), *Premonition* (Atlantic, 1986), *When All the Pieces Fit* (Atlantic, 1989), *Shine On—A Collection* (1992), *Peter Frampton* (Relativity, 1993), *Frampton Comes Alive II* (IRS, 1995•).

Recordings featuring Peter Frampton: **George Harrison,** *All Things Must Pass* (Apple, 1970). **Doris Troy,** *Doris Troy* (Apple, 1970). **John Entwistle,** *Whistle Rhymes* (MCA, 1972). **Tim Hardin,** *Painted Head* (Columbia, 1972). **Harry Nilsson,** *Son of Schmilsson* (RCA, 1972). **Jerry Lee Lewis,** *The Session* (Mercury, 1973). **Ringo Starr,** *Ringo's Rotogravure* (Atlantic, 1976). **Steve Morse Band,** *Stand Up* (Elektra, 1985). **David Bowie,** *Never Let Me Down* (EMI America, 1987).

Montrose

Ronnie Montrose

B o r n : *November 29, 1947, in Denver*
M a i n   G u i t a r : *Gibson Les Paul*

Aminor kingpin of seventies hard rock, Ronnie Montrose first gained recognition as the lead guitarist in Van Morrison's group. He played on the much-heralded Morrison releases *Tupelo Honey* (1971) and *St. Dominic's Preview* (1972), then played briefly with Boz Scaggs before joining the Edgar Winter Group in 1972. With the Winter band, he appeared on the 1972 album *They Only Come out at Night*, which yielded two hit singles, "Frankenstein" and "Free Ride." The latter tune features some exceptional lead and rhythm work from the guitarist, as well as some input from longtime Winter sideman Rick Derringer (♦). Montrose proved to be a crowd-pleasing live entertainer, too, often trading complex call-and-response vocal and guitar riffs with Winter during his extended solos.

In 1973 Montrose left Winter and formed the band Montrose, a quartet with blatant Led Zeppelin influences. Montrose had minor success with proto-metal tunes, but was perhaps most famous for featuring future Van Halen vocalist Sammy

Hagar. The band's strong debut album was highlighted by the guitarist's ripping lead parts to cuts such as the group's high-volume remake of Elvis Presley's "Good Rocking Tonight" and "Bad Motor Scooter" (which featured one of the first guitar imitations of a motorcycle's shifting gears; this dive bombing technique would later be ripped off by dozens of 1980s metal bands, notably Mötley Crüe). Hagar left Montrose in 1974, and without his cocky, Robert Plant-molded image to front the group, the band quickly deteriorated. After Montrose finally disbanded, having given birth to the future careers of Hagar and Night Ranger, Ronnie formed Gamma, which used synthesizers and guitars to create a sort of high-tech heavy metal. As interesting as it was on paper, the band failed to generate any long-term commercial support.

Montrose's 1978 instrumental solo set *Open Fire* stood out for its variety of material, especially for his hip arrangement of "Town without Pity" for orchestra and cranked-up electric guitar. Since that time, Ronnie Montrose has maintained an eclectic solo career, yet he has never quite managed to find his niche, ranging from hard rock to jazzy fusion and everything in between. A perfect example of what he is capable of at his best is "Blood Alley 152" from the first *Guitar Speak* compilation. It speaks volumes of what Montrose can achieve when he focuses himself.

Montrose [on Warner Bros. except where noted], *Montrose* (1973), *Paper Money* (1974), *Warner Brothers Present Montrose!* (1975), *Jump on It* (1976), *Mean* (Enigma, 1987). **Ronnie Montrose,** *Open Fire* (Warner Bros., 1978), *Territory* (Passport Jazz, 1986), *The Speed of Sound* (Enigma, 1988), *The Diva Station* (1990), *Mutatis Mutandis* (IRS, 1991). **Gamma** [on Elektra], *Gamma I* (1979), *Gamma II* (1980), *Gamma III* (1982).

Recordings featuring Ronnie Montrose: **Herbie Hancock,** *Mwandishi* (Warner Bros., 1970). **Van Morrison** [on Warner Bros.], *Tupelo Honey* (1971), *St. Dominic's Preview* (1972). **Edgar Winter Group,** *They Only Come out at Night* (Epic, 1972). **Kathi McDonald,** *Insane Asylum* (Capitol, 1974). **Gary Wright,** *Dream Weaver* (Warner Bros., 1975). **Tony Williams,** *Joy of Flying* (Columbia, 1979). **Dan Hartman,** *Images* (Blue Sky, n/a). **Various Artists,** *Guitar Speak* (IRS, 1988).

Foghat

"Lonesome" Dave Peverett

B o r n : *1950, in England*
M a i n   G u i t a r : *Gibson Les Paul Junior*

Rod Price

M a i n   G u i t a r : *Gibson Les Paul*

Founded in 1971 as a wholesale spin-off of Savoy Brown (♦), Foghat was originally a British blues/boogie band in the mold of Ten Years After. The band's frontman was "Lonesome" Dave Peverett, a capable rock shouter who also served as the band's second guitarist. However, the bulk of the lead and slide playing was handled by Rod Price, whose fiery blues-based solos torched

such Foghat hits as "Fool for the City," "Rock and Roll Outlaw," "I Just Want to Make Love to You," and the perennial concert favorite "Slow Ride." The band frequently covered Chicago blues classics (Willie Dixon was a primary source of material), giving the songs a British twist and seventies-rock campiness that they would never have received in the era of relative purists like John Mayall and Cream.

Foghat was equally capable of delivering breakneck rock and blues boogie, making them a concert favorite. Their albums, notably *Fool for the City* and *Night Shift*, edged them into the hard rock and FM radio limelight, but it was *Foghat Live* (1977) that captured the band at its full-bore best. This live set, however, proved to be the band's high point. After the respectable *Stone Blue* of 1978—the title track was a modest FM hit and contained more killer slide work from Price—Foghat quietly slipped into rock 'n' roll oblivion on the rails of increasingly tepid material. Obscurity prevailed for most of the 1980s, although the quartet occasionally reunited with different lineups for club gigs. A reunion with the original members has also been rumored for some time. Whatever their ultimate fate, Price and company still have the comfort of knowing that they delivered British rock with an edge and offered some of the finest and most aggressive slide playing heard on either side of the Atlantic.

Foghat [on Bearsville], *Foghat* (1972), *Rock and Roll* (1973), *Energized* (1974), *Rock and Roll Outlaws* (1974), *Fool for the City* (1975), *Night Shift* (1976), *Foghat Live* (1977•), *Stone Blue* (1978), *Boogie Motel* (1979), *Tight Shoes* (1980), *Girls to Chat & Boys to Bounce* (1981), *In the Mood for Something Rude* (1982), *Zig-Zag Walk* (1983), *Best of Foghat, Vols. 1–2* (Rhino, 1990, 1992).

Status Quo

Francis Rossi

B o r n : *April 29, 1949, in Peckham, London*
M a i n   G u i t a r : *Fender Telecaster*

Rick Parfitt

B o r n : *October 12, 1948, in South London*
M a i n   G u i t a r : *Fender Telecaster*

Great Britain's prototypical blues/boogie band, Status Quo rose to towering heights in the English hard rock scene during the seventies, while retaining almost total anonymity in America. Led by guitarists Francis Rossi and Rick Parfitt, Status Quo scored a psychedelic pop single in 1968 with "Pictures of Matchstick Men" before steering their sound in a bluesier direction during the 1970s. Mid-decade releases such as *Piledriver*, *Hello* (both 1973), and *On the Level* (1975) earned the band a huge following, but also the scorn of rock critics, who almost unanimously loathed the group. While neither Rossi nor Parfitt was an extraordinary rock stylist, their dueling Fender Telecaster solos and relentless blues-rock riffing placed them among the most widely heard British pickers of the decade. Status Quo's success continued until the early eighties, when public interest in the band's hard rock boogies began to die down and then dried up altogether.

Status Quo [on A&M/Vertigo except where noted], *Ma Kelly's Greasy Spoon* (Pye, 1970), *Dog of Two Heads* (Pye, 1971), *Piledriver* (1973), *Quo* (1974), *On the Level* (1975), *Blue for You* (1976), *Status Quo Live* (1977•), *Rockin' all over the World* (1977), *If You Can't Stand the Heat* (1978), *Whatever You Want* (1979), *Twelve Gold Bars* (1980), *Never Too Late* (1981), *Collection* (Pickwick, 1985), *In the Army Now* (1986), *Complaining* (1988), *Rock til You Drop* (1991).

Frank Marino and Mahogany Rush

Born: *August 22, 1954, in Del Rio, Texas*
Main Guitar: *'61 Gibson Les Paul/SG*

Like blues-rocker Robin Trower, Canadian-bred Frank Marino established his niche during the seventies as an ardent disciple of Jimi Hendrix. But where Trower leaned more towards Hendrix's spacey, soulful side, Marino laid claim to the guitar legend's hard rocking persona. He employed speedy blues-scale runs and violent tremolo bars effects on the recordings he made with his power trio Mahogany Rush (not to be confused with Rush, Canada's other and far better power trio). Few pentatonic-based guitarists of the early to mid seventies were as technically advanced as Marino, who revealed an exceptional nimbleness in his lead work and often jazz- or blues-tinged compositions.

Marino actually claimed to have been visited by Hendrix while he was in a coma, and mentioned this as gospel truth to anyone who would listen. While few people bought this line, Marino's uncanny ability to mimic Hendrix hinted at something more than mere guitar infatuation. His brand of post-Hendrix hard rock and clean soloing facilities ultimately helped him stand out from the crowd of Hendrix and Clapton imitators. This is evident on *Frank Marino & Mahogany Rush Live* (1978), one of his best efforts. Marino tackled "Johnny B. Goode" with his characteristic high-volume flair and also contributed a remarkably solid cover of Hendrix's "Purple Haze." However, "I'm a King Bee, Baby" showed him in a completely different light, mixing slick blues and jazz licks into his solo. Though his career, like Trower's, was hindered by the frequent comparisons with Hendrix (which he himself fostered), Marino's guitar music was a perfect example of Jimi Hendrix's ongoing influence upon young rock guitarists.

Mahogany Rush [on 20th Century except where noted], *Child of the Novelty* (1974), *Maxoom* (1975), *Strange Universe* (1975), *Mahogany Rush IV* (Columbia, 1976). **Frank Marino & Mahogany Rush** [on Columbia], *World Anthem* (1977), *Frank Marino & Mahogany Rush Live* (1978•), *Tales of the Unexpected* (1979), *What's Next* (1980). **Frank Marino**, *Juggernaut* (1982).

Recordings featuring Frank Marino: **Various Artists**, *California Jam 2* (Columbia, 1978). **Various Artists**, *Guitar Speak II* (IRS, 1990).

Bachman-Turner Overdrive

Randy Bachman

Born: *September 27, 1943, in Winnipeg, Manitoba*
Main Guitars: *Fender Stratocaster, custom Strat-style*

Blair Thornton

Born: *July 23, 1950, in Vancouver, British Columbia*
Main Guitar: *Gibson SG*

As the guitarist for Canadian rockers the Guess Who, Randy Bachman was responsible for the blunt rhythms and simple chording of such radio staples as "American Woman" and "No Sugar Tonight." When he left in 1970, he took those same rhythms and simple chords with him and ultimately found incredible success on his own.

After exiting the Guess Who, Bachman released a solo record, *Axe*, and then joined another Canadian group, Brave Belt. Neither of these endeavors proved overly popular, but Bachman used the experience to round out his rock sound with some country and jazz stylings (rumors from the time had Keith Emerson asking him to join the nascent ELP). When he formed Bachman-Turner Overdrive with brothers Robbie and Tim, along with bassist and vocalist Fred Turner, he combined all these styles and beefed them up with heavily distorted guitars and slick lead playing. This resulting sound made his brand of "blue collar rock" a natural for FM radio in the 1970s.

The band released two albums in 1973, both of which were marvels of guitar songwriting simplicity with a slick technical sheen. After BTO charted with the single "Let It Ride" in 1973, Tim Bachman left the band and was replaced by Blair Thornton, who traded off lead playing duties with Randy. A string of hits followed, most of them fairly formulaic, but always notable: "Takin' Care of Business," "You Ain't Seen Nothing Yet" (both from 1974), and "Roll on Down the Highway" (1975). With "Takin' Care of Business," Bachman single-handedly did more for three chords than anybody since Chuck Berry. On the other hand, "Free Wheelin'," from *Not Fragile*, and "Lookin' out for #1," from *Head On*, showed another side of the Bachman/Thornton guitar team in a series of solos that were notable for their melodicism, clean tone, and jazz-inflected phrasing. It was actually this versatility and all-around rock guitar flair that helped propel Bachman-Turner Overdrive's innocuous three-chord singles to the top of the charts, making the songs more interesting than their pedestrian roots.

But this formula could only sustain just so much repetition, and BTO dropped from the public's hit list quickly after 1976. Randy Bachman attended to his Mormonism, giving up the rock 'n' roll lifestyle of excess for one of religion. He continued to perform, and—speaking of excess—BTO added Leslie West (♦ Mountain) to its touring lineup during the 1980s, billing itself as the "Half-Ton Tour." If there was any other time in rock history that guitarists used their collective body weight as an incentive to lure ticket buyers, we can't think of it. Bachman attempted a comeback in the 1990s, but it was clear that his best work was behind him.

Examples of Randy Bachman's technical expertise and melodic phrasing abound, but many of them are hidden in the nether reaches of his pop work. Due to this fact of his musical life, Bachman has always been a seriously underrated guitarist, something that happens to many players who become staples of radio playlists. However, thanks to "Classic Rock" radio formats, vintage BTO can be heard on the airwaves almost daily, although whether that is good or bad news remains a debatable point.

Guess Who [on RCA], *Wheatfield Soul* (1969), *Canned Wheat* (1969), *American Woman* (1970), *Best of the Guess Who* (1971). **Randy Bachman**, *Axe* (RCA, 1970), *Any Road* (Guitar Recordings, 1994). **Brave Belt** [on Reprise], *Brave Belt* (1971), *Brave Belt II* (1972). **Bachman-Turner Overdrive** [on Mercury except where noted], *Bachman-Turner Overdrive* (1973), *Bachman-Turner Overdrive II* (1973), *Not Fragile* (1974), *Four Wheel Drive* (1975), *Head On* (1976), *Best of B.T.O. (So Far)* (1976), *Freeways* (1977), *Bachman-Turner Overdrive* (Compleat, 1984), *Live! Live! Live!* (Curb, 1986●). **Ironhorse**, *Ironhorse* (Scotti Bros., 1979).

Heart

Nancy Wilson

B o r n : *March 16, 1954, in San Francisco*
Main Guitars: *Ovation acoustic, Dean solidbody*

Howard Leese

B o r n : *June 13, 1951, in Los Angeles*
Main Guitars: *Hamer and Paul Reed Smith solidbodies*

Roger Fisher

B o r n : *February 14, 1950, in Seattle*
Main Guitar: *Fender Stratocaster*

Heart's original guitar threesome of Nancy Wilson, Roger Fisher, and Howard Leese gained six-string recognition in 1976 with their impressive album *Dreamboat Annie*, though the band's allure was based in large part on the appeal of the winsome Wilson sisters. Ann and Nancy Wilson were raised in a musical family and began gigging around Seattle and Vancouver as teenagers. Teaming up with Fisher and Leese, Nancy initially played acoustic guitar while the two men handled electric lead and rhythm chores (Leese also played keyboards). The three guitarists cranked out Zeppelinesque rockers like "Crazy on You" (featuring a beautiful acoustic intro by Nancy that blended flamenco and classical styles) and "Magic Man," which blended metallish electric guitar textures with an acoustic guitar underpinning, helping create the instrumental basis for a long string of hit records for the group.

A good example of their instrumental interplay can be heard on the overly dramatic hit "Magic Man," where the guitar breakdown finds Leese executing the backward-recorded intro lead, Wilson adding robust acoustic underneath, and Fisher topping it all off with a rough hammer-on solo. The group's second album, *Little Queen*, repeated the formula of the first record, but instrumentally was a track-by-track carbon copy of Led Zeppelin's fourth album, from the opening "Black Dog" bombast of "Barracuda" right down to the "Battle of Evermore" mandolins on "Sylvan Song."

Fisher eventually left the band, and since then, Nancy Wilson and Howard Leese have ably handled all the guitar parts, sharing duties on electric and acoustic, lead and rhythm. After a major slump in the early 1980s, Heart struck back hard in 1985 with an album titled simply *Heart*, which displayed more of the duo's hard-edged guitar playing (along with slinky videos and conspicuous cleavage). It struck paydirt again in 1986 with *Bad Animals*, but the renewal stopped there. Bereft of new ideas, the band again dwindled in popularity, though their cult following remained steadfast. In 1993 they launched an "acoustic" tour of the States, playing mostly mid-size theaters, and worked with ex-Zeppelin bassist John Paul Jones on their 1995 acoustic live album.

Heart [on Epic except where noted], *Dreamboat Annie* (Mushroom, 1976), *Little Queen* (Portrait, 1977), *Magazine* (Mushroom, 1978), *Dog & Butterfly* (Portrait, 1978), *Bebe Le Strange* (1980), *Greatest Hits/Live* (1980●), *Private Audition* (1982), *Passionworks* (1983), *Heart* (Capitol, 1985), *Bad Animals* (Capitol, 1987), *Brigade* (Capitol, 1990), *Rock the House—Live!* (Capitol, 1991), *Desire Walks On* (Capitol, 1993).

Recordings featuring Heart: **Various Artists,** *California Jam 2* (Columbia, 1978●). **Various Artists,** *Singles* [soundtrack] (Epic, 1992).

Nancy Wilson

CHAPTER FIFTEEN

Unplugged Singer-Songwriters

A notable development in late-sixties rock was the rise of singer-songwriters. This singer-songwriter school was inherently folk-oriented and wove influences from Bob Dylan, the Byrds, the Beatles, and country music into a soft blend of likable acoustic folk-pop. The mecca for these folkish performers was laid-back Los Angeles (hence its common nickname "L.A. rock"), home of such influential singer-songwriters as Gram Parsons, Jackson Browne, and the Eagles' Glenn Frey and Don Henley. This breed of musician also turned up elsewhere in the world, notably in the British Isles, where groups like Fairport Convention, Fotheringay, Pentangle, Richard and Linda Thompson, Steeleye Span, and Renaissance transformed Celtic ballads and jigs into yet another folk-rock sub-genre.

As was true of several other rock styles, the guitar was an integral part of the singer-songwriter's music, but not necessarily the predominant element. Acts like Poco, Maria Muldaur, and Linda Ronstadt all had good guitar players in their bands, and occasionally a top singer-songwriter was a fine guitarist in his or her own right, as was the case with Joni Mitchell and Neil Young. Though most of the singer-songwriters were roundly ignored by harder rock guitar players (with the highly vocal exception of Jimmy Page), their music was really a hotbed for diverse guitar styles, traversing the spectrum from soft acoustic fingerpicking to well-voiced chordal parts to a surprising number of high-volume rock 'n' roll solos.

Neil Young

Born: *November 12, 1945 in Toronto*
Main Guitars: *Gibson Les Paul, Gretsch 6120*

After bailing out of Crosby, Stills, Nash & Young (◗), Neil Young pursued a brilliant solo career that—while varied and sometimes even disappointing—has never ceased to be interesting and worth watching.

Before joining CSNY, Young had limited post-Buffalo Springfield success with his self-titled debut, an album featuring the fuzztoned rave-up of "The Loner." With the 1969 release *Everybody Knows This Is Nowhere* (featuring a band called Crazy Horse, with Danny Whitten and, later, Frank Sampedro on guitar), Young established himself as a gritty guitar rocker on the haunting "Down by the River" and the pre-punkish "Cinnamon Girl" and displayed his quirky rhythm style on "Cowgirl in the Sand." This latter track is especially noteworthy for its one-note solo, to which Young gives surprising character via wild bends and heavy pick hits. His solo career was put on hold during his stint with CSNY, and then revived with the release of *After the Gold Rush* (1970), with its epic "Southern Man."

Young's career took a decidedly more acoustic and folkie direction with *Harvest* (1972), his cynical version of the laid-back L.A. rock sound. His picking on "The Needle and the Damage Done" and his power chording on "Words" are standouts on the

Neil Young

album. A slew of records followed, notably the hard rocker *Zuma* (1975; with one of Young's best guitar solos on "Cortez the Killer") and the underrated *American Stars 'n' Bars* (1977), which contained Young's guitar opus "Like a Hurricane." He also reunited with Stephen Stills briefly during this period in the Stills-Young Band.

The release of *Rust Never Sleeps* in 1979 pulled Young out of a middle-of-the-road slump. It reunited him with Crazy Horse and displayed him in his two best lights: one side of the record was acoustic and lilting, the other was nervous, primal, and loud. From "Powderfinger" to "Welfare Mothers" to "Hey, Hey, My, My (Into the Black)," Young hammered out a noisy, simple series of chords that were all but obscured by distortion. It was a glorious sound.

Young put Crazy Horse out to pasture yet again, and trying his hand at experimentation, he ventured into techno-rock in 1982 with the universally panned but again underrated *Trans* (featuring Nils Lofgren [◗] on guitar), then into rockabilly with *Everybody's Rockin'* (1983), and even country with *Old Ways* (1985). (Over the years, Young had relied on Crazy Horse only sporadically, and the band deplored this lack of recognition in its 1981 release without Neil, the aptly titled *Left for Dead.*) Continued departures from his bread-and-butter work, including an ill-advised reunion of CSNY (resulting in the critically slammed *American Dream*), did not fare well until a respectable all-blues release in 1988, *This Note's for You*, which took pointed, frequently hysterical jabs at the MTV generation. Seeming to have gotten all these demons out of his system, Young returned to the plaid shirt, scruffy blues jeans, and hyperactive Les Paul solos that had been signatures of his earliest work, and issued a succession of albums that returned him to the forefront of rock 'n' roll.

Starting in 1989 with *Freedom*, on through *Ragged Glory*, *Arc-Weld*, and *Sleeps with Angels* (1994), Young pulled out all the stops, returning to a creative height he hadn't climbed in more than a decade. (Further confounding his followers, he temporarily returned to the acoustic days of *Harvest* by releasing the somewhat bland *Harvest Moon* in 1992; nevertheless, it was a huge seller.) His primitive playing re-awakened a spontaneity in rock that had been missing during the sheen and gloss of the heavy metal 1980s. At the same time, a whole generation of young players embraced the same ethic (and wardrobe) that Young had always lived by—namely, play what you feel, and technique be damned. The up-and-comers, as part of the early 1990s grunge movement, embraced Young as their "godfather." Kurt Cobain of Nirvana—who quoted "Hey, Hey, My, My" in his suicide note—and Mike McCready of Pearl Jam were quick to point out Young's influence in their music. Indeed, many have cited the second side of *Rust* (tracks 6–9) as the first recorded instance of grunge, a term and a style that wouldn't be part of the everyday lexicon for another 12 years. Young brought things full circle by teaming up with Pearl Jam (◗) to record *Mirror Ball* in 1995.

A retrospective of Young's work has been planned since the mid 1980s, but he is apparently against the idea, since he feels that the quality of CDs is inferior to that of vinyl LPs. For Young, the unexpected is always expected. Finally, Young is almost as influential a guitarist as he is a songwriter. He has displayed a complete disregard for well-studied technique, and it has worked to his benefit more than for any other guitarist in rock 'n' roll. From his pristine acoustic playing to his ragged soloing, few players have crossed the line so often and so well.

Neil Young [on Reprise except where noted], *Neil Young* (1968), *Everybody Knows This Is Nowhere* (1969), *After the Gold Rush* (1970), *Harvest* (1972), *Journey though the Past* (Warner Bros., 1972), *Time Fades Away* (1973), *On the Beach* (1974), *Tonight's the Night* (1975), *Zuma* (1975), *American Stars 'n' Bars* (1977), *Decade* (1977), *Comes a Time* (1978), *Rust Never Sleeps* (1979), *Live Rust* (1979•), *Hawks & Doves* (1980), *Re-ac-tor* (1981), *Trans* (Geffen, 1982), *Everybody's Rockin'* (Geffen, 1983), *Old Ways* (Geffen, 1985), *Landing on Water* (Geffen, 1986), *Life* (Geffen, 1987), *This Note's for You* (1988), *Freedom* (1989), *Ragged Glory* (1990), *Arc-Weld* (1991•), *Weld* (1991•), *Harvest Moon* (1992), *Lucky Thirteen* (1993), *Unplugged* (1993•), *Sleeps with Angels* (1994), *Mirror Ball* [with Pearl Jam] (1995), *Broken Arrow* (1996). **Stills-Young Band,** *Long May You Run* (Reprise, 1976). [◗ Crosby, Stills, Nash & Young]

Recordings featuring Neil Young: **Various Artists,** *Woodstock* (Cotillion, 1970•). **The Band,** *The Last Waltz* (Warner Bros., 1978•).

James Taylor

B o r n : *March 12, 1948, in Boston*
Main Guitars : *Gibson and custom Whitebook acoustics*

Among the top purveyors of the folk-pop genre was James Taylor, the gifted singer and songwriter of such memorable soft rock songs as "Fire and Rain," "Country Road," and "How Sweet It Is." In addition to his sensitive songs and likable vocals, one of Taylor's musical trademarks has been the gentle ring of his acoustic steel-string guitar, on which he often displays his considerable skill at fingerstyle playing. Accompanying Taylor on many of his classic seventies recordings was Danny "Kootch" Kortchmar (born in New York in 1946), whose expressive lead and rhythm guitar work has also graced recordings by Carole King, Jackson Browne, and Don Henley. Together, Taylor and Kortchmar made up one of the most engaging guitar teams of the seventies singer-songwriter school.

Taylor came from a musical family and took up the guitar around the age of 12. Drawing influences from Bob Dylan, the Beatles, and various folk musicians, he forged his own identity in coffeehouse performances around New England and the folk haven of Greenwich Village. During the mid sixties Taylor appeared with Kortchmar, whom he had known since his early teens, in a folk duo called James and Kootch. Eventually, they put together an electric band called the Flying Machine, which gained a considerable following in New York towards the end of the decade.

The Flying Machine eventually disbanded, and Taylor moved to London to pursue his singing career. With fortune on his side, he was signed to the Beatles' Apple Records, and in 1969 his first album was released. The record barely dented the American charts, but it was enough to get him signed to Warner Brothers. When released in 1970, Taylor's second album, *Sweet Baby James*, became one of the biggest discs of that year and scored a smash single with "Fire and Rain" (a song about the love he had found in a mental institution). Within a short time, James Taylor became a major rock act, and his albums invariably went gold within weeks of release. Among his classic folk-based ballads of the 1970s were a version of Carole King's "You've Got a Friend," "Walking Man," "How Sweet It Is," and also a cover of Jimmy Jones' "Handy Man" in 1977.

On *Sweet Baby James*, Taylor added Danny Kortchmar to his band, marking the beginning of a long and fruitful six-string partnership. The guitar peaks from that seminal album were on "Oh Baby, Don't You Loose Your Lip on Me," a dual-acoustic blues romp with Taylor providing the tight rhythm support for Kortchmar's steely blues runs; "Suite for 20G," with it jazzy electric breaks and funked-out strumming; and Taylor's beautiful chordal arrangement of Stephen Foster's traditional "Oh Susannah" for voice and solo guitar. Another of their great recorded moments together was on the live version of "Steamroller," from Taylor's 1976 greatest hits package. Starting on a foundation of acoustic chord flourishes from Taylor, "Steamroller" built up to Kortchmar's bluesy electric breaks of limber string bends, strong wrist vibrato, and a barrage of refined blues licks. See, some folkies *can* rock out.

Since the seventies, Taylor has traded in on his fame, producing an occasionally interesting guitar record, but seemingly more content to cover old ground and play to his rapidly graying audience. He has managed to break his own boundaries occasionally, notably with the Latin-flavored "Mexico" and the gritty guitar bump-and-grind of "Only Telling a Lie." His career took a small rebound in 1991 with the gold-selling disc *New Moon Shine*, featuring the catchy track "Copperline," something that sounded like it came right off one of his wonderful early albums.

James Taylor [on Warner Bros. except where noted], *James Taylor* (Apple, 1969), *Sweet Baby James* (1970), *James Taylor and the*

Original Flying Machine—1967 (Euphoria, 1971), *Mud Slide Slim and the Blue Horizon* (1971), *One Man Dog* (1972), *Walking Man* (1974), *Gorilla* (1975), *In the Pocket* (1976), *Greatest Hits* (1976), *J.T.* (Columbia, 1977), *Flag* (Columbia, 1979), *Dad Loves His Work* (Columbia, 1981), *Never Die Young* (Columbia, 1988), *New Moon Shine* (Columbia, 1991), *Live* (1993•).

Eagles

Glenn Frey
Born: *November 6, 1948, in Detroit*
Main Guitar: *Rickenbacker 230GF Glenn Frey model*

Bernie Leadon
Born: *July 19, 1947, in Minneapolis*
Main Guitars: *Martin D-35 and D-28*

Don Felder
Born: *September 21, 1947, in Gainesville, Florida*
Main Guitars: *Gibson Les Paul and EDS-1275 doubleneck*

Joe Walsh
Born: *November 20, 1947, in Wichita, Kansas*
Main Guitar: *Gibson Les Paul*

The undisputed kings of L.A. rock, the Eagles ranked among the most popular and profitable bands of the 1970s. Beginning with "Take It Easy" in 1972, the Eagles racked up a succession of Top 10 singles and best-selling albums throughout the decade that has been rivaled by only a handful of other rock

The Eagles: Timothy B. Schmit, Glenn Frey, Don Felder, Joe Walsh

groups. The essential Eagles sound was a smooth country-rock blend that drew its influences from the Byrds, the Flying Burrito Brothers, and Poco, not to mention the inventive country hybrids of the late Gram Parsons. While the Eagles were known primarily for their catchy, country-styled hits and thick vocal harmonies, their music also featured fine guitar picking from guitarists Bernie Leadon, Glenn Frey, Don Felder, and Joe Walsh.

The original Eagles—Leadon, Frey, drummer and vocalist Don Henley, and bassist Randy Meisner—were members of Linda Ronstadt's backup band. In October 1971 they decided to go off on their own. Frey had previously been in a folk duo with singer John David Souther called Longbranch Pennywhistle, and had worked with Bob Seger. Leadon's credentials included work with bluegrass banjo player Doug Dillard in the Dillard and Clark Expedition and time spent with the Flying Burrito Brothers. When the Eagles formed in 1971, they were signed to the Asylum label, which already had a reputation for producing folky L.A. rock with acts like Jackson Browne and Joni Mitchell. (Asylum was also the brainchild of the man who managed many of these bands, David Geffen.)

The Eagles' first hit, "Take It Easy," displayed the band's guitar talent with Frey's steady acoustic strumming and Leadon's multi-string lead on electric guitar (in addition to fine banjo accompaniment). Leadon's restrained, melodic lead work was also evident on the Eagles' 1975 single "Lyin' Eyes" (from *One of These Nights*). In January 1974 Don Felder was added to the line-up to augment Leadon's lead guitar playing. "One of These Nights," the Eagles' big 1975 single, was one of the best examples of Felder's lead work, showcasing a solo composed of blues-based licks and sustained string bends using an unusually meaty distortion tone.

Bernie Leadon left the group at the end of 1975 (he ultimately turned up in a country band, Run C&W) and was replaced by ex-James Gang guitarist Joe Walsh (♦), who was enjoying the rewards of a successful solo career. While many observers scoffed at the apparent absurdity of mixing Walsh's hard rock bent with the Eagles' mellow style, the combination paid off in spades. With Felder, Frey, and Walsh on guitar, the Eagles issued their most axe-oriented and, indeed, most popular album: *Hotel California* (1976). The title track, one of the top hits of that year, showed off the dual lead guitar playing of Felder and Walsh in unbridled call-and-response solos and harmony guitar lines during the fade-out. Other choice guitar songs on *Hotel California* include the Walsh composition "Life in the Fast Lane," a rocker with funk rhythm grooves and a Walsh slide solo, and "Victim of Love," an unusually heavy Eagles song with a plodding power-chord progression and another fine slide solo from Walsh.

A three-year hiatus followed *Hotel California*, ending in 1979 with the release of another studio album, *The Long Run*. It yielded several more singles for the band ("Heartache Tonight," "The Long Run"), but the band had seemingly run its course, and internal frictions were running high. After a 1980 live album and several well-received solo albums by both Henley and Frey, the Eagles broke up in 1982.

Despite the Eagles' eventual progression into slick AOR rock, their early material (from 1972 to 1976) is highly representative of the L.A. country-rock sound and is among the best music of that genre. Most recently, the band reunited for an MTV "Unplugged" concert and released the album *Hell Freezes Over* (featuring a beautiful Spanish guitar interlude by Walsh and Felder on "Hotel California"). The *Hotel California* lineup was back in force for the reunion release, which also prompted a tour that would set records for rock concert ticket prices (averaging $125 a seat). It was apparent that the band had little of modern merit to offer, relying on the strength of its past successes. For a band that played cleanly and honestly during its heyday, Frey and Henley and company might well go down in history as opportunists after the popular and critical slamming they took when hell froze over.

Eagles [on Asylum], *The Eagles* (1972), *Desperado* (1973), *On the Border* (1974), *One of These Nights* (1975), *Their Greatest Hits/1971–1975* (1976), *Hotel California* (1976), *The Long Run* (1979), *Eagles Live* (1980●), *Eagles Greatest Hits, Volume 2* (1982), *Hell Freezes Over* (Geffen, 1994●). **Glenn Frey**, *No Fun Aloud* (Asylum, 1982), *The Allnighter* (MCA, 1984), *Soul Searchin'* (MCA, 1988), *Solo Collection* (MCA, 1995). **Don Felder**, *Airborne* (Elektra, 1983). [♦ Joe Walsh]

Recordings featuring Bernie Leadon: **The Dillard & Clark Expedition,** *Fantastic Expedition* (A&M, c. 1968). **Flying Burrito Brothers,** *The Last of the Red Hot Burritos* (A&M, 1972). **Gram Parsons,** *Grievous Angel* (Reprise, 1974). **Emmylou Harris** [on Reprise], *Pieces of the Sky* (1975), *Elite Hotel* (1976). **Run C&W,** *Into the Twangy-first Century* (MCA, 1993).

Richard Thompson

B o r n : *April 3, 1949, in London*
M a i n G u i t a r s : *Fender Stratocaster, Lowden acoustics*

On the far side of the globe from the L.A. scene came Richard Thompson, a brilliant vocalist, songsmith, and guitar player that some consider "one of the great buried treasures of British rock," as some critics have called him. To many, Thompson was noteworthy for his stellar singing and songwriting in the late sixties, when he was the leader of England's Celtic-rock supergroup Fairport Convention. Others have praised the dramatic recordings he made with wife Linda Thompson, yielding several classic albums between 1974 and 1982. Still others have singled out Thompson's solo career, which has revealed his stunning talent on guitar, as well as his rich, melancholy vocals and compositions.

Thompson's career goes back to his days with Fairport Convention, which he played with from 1967 until he quit in January 1971. Formed as the English version of Jefferson Airplane, Fairport Convention created a novel sound that blended Celtic ballads, traditional folk songs, and up-tempo jigs with the aggressive sound of electric rock 'n' roll. With co-members Sandy Denny, Ian Mathews, Simon Nicol, and Dave Mattacks (all noted figures of British folk-rock), Thompson released several fine albums that typified electric folk-rock in Great Britain, especially on records like *Fairport Convention* (1968; which contains an exceptional Thompson solo on "Mr. Lacey"), *Unhalfbricking* (1969), and *Full House* (1970).

After Thompson broke with the band in early 1971, he recorded a pair of albums with various friends under the names of The Bunch and Morris On. He cut his first solo album in 1972, entitled *Henry the Human Fly*. Backing him on the effort was vocalist Linda Peters, who also accompanied him on the subsequent tour. Eventually, the two married and continued on, personally and professionally, as Richard and Linda Thompson. The Thompsons' first album together, *I Want to See the Bright Lights Tonight* (1974), was instantly hailed as a rock classic and marked the beginning of several excellent recordings by the duo: *Pour Down Like Silver* (1975), *Sunnyvista* (1979), and their masterpiece, *Shoot out the Lights* (1982).

Throughout these records, Richard Thompson's guitar playing is nothing short of superlative, ranging from the country-styled string bends and chordal licks of "Man in Need" (from *Shoot out the Lights*), to the brutal lead break on "Shoot out the Lights" (with its slap echo effects à la Duane Eddy), to the edge-of-the-pick harmonics, gritty blues runs, and pedal steel-like string bends in "Borrowed Time." Richard Thompson also maintained a strong solo career well into the 1990s (prompted by the Thompsons' divorce in 1982), releasing such praised works as *Guitar, Vocal* (1976), the all-instrumental *Strict Tempo!* (1981), *Hand of Kindness* (1983), *Across a Crowded Room* (1985; which has stunning Stratocaster solos on nearly every track), and *Mirror Blue* (1994). Without fail, Thompson's albums elicit four- and five-star reviews from rock critics, and his career has certainly benefited as a result of their praise. He's also run into the notorious "looking-glass ceiling" of the music business, which prevents normal-looking people from achieving the mass success and adulation that's reserved for prettier and far less talented performers. Fortunately, Thompson's extremely loyal fans know better.

Richard Thompson

Fairport Convention [on Polydor except where noted], *Fairport Convention* (1968), *What We Did on Our Holidays* (1969), *Unhalfbricking* (1969), *Liege and Lief* (A&M, 1969), *Full House* (A&M, 1970), *The History of Fairport Convention* (Island, 1972), *Gladys' Leap* (Varrick, 1985), *Expletive Delighted* (Varrick, 1986), *Moat of the Ledge* (n/a, 1986), *House Full—Fairport Convention Live in L.A.* (Hannibal, 1986•), *Heyday* (Hannibal, 1987). **Richard Thompson**, *Henry the Human Fly* (Island, 1972), *Guitar, Vocal* (Island, 1976•), *Strict Tempo!* (Elixir, 1981), *Hand of Kindness* (Hannibal, 1983), *Small Town Romance* (Hannibal, 1984), *Across a Crowded Room* (Polydor, 1985), *Daring Adventures* (Polydor, 1986), *Amnesia* (Capitol, 1988), *Rumor and Sigh* (Capitol, 1991), *Mirror Blue* (Capitol, 1994), *you, me, us?* (Capitol, 1996). **Richard & Linda Thompson** [on Island except where noted], *I Want to See the Bright Lights Tonight* (1974), *Hokey Pokey* (1974), *Pour Down Like Silver* (1975), *First Light* (Chrysalis, 1978), *Sunnyvista* (Chrysalis, 1979), *Shoot out the Lights* (Hannibal, 1982). **French-Frith-Kaiser-Thompson,** *Live, Love, Larf & Loaf* (Rhino, 1987), *Invisible Means* (Denon, 1990).

Recordings featuring Richard Thompson: **Nick Drake** [on Hannibal], *Five Leaves Left* (1969), *Bryter Layer* (1970). **The Bunch,** *Rock On* (Island, 1972). **Morris On,** *Morris On* (Island, 1972). **Sandy Denny** [on Island], *Like an Old Fashioned Waltz* (1973), *Rendezvous* (1977). **Ashley Hutchings,** *An Hour with Ashley Hutchings and Cecil Sharp* (n/a, c. 1984). **The Golden Palominos,** *Visions of Excess* (Celluloid, 1985). **Bonnie Raitt,** *Luck of the Draw* (Capitol, 1991). **Suzanne Vega,** *99.9° F* (A&M, 1992).

Al Stewart

Born: *September 5, 1945, in Glasgow, Scotland*
Main Guitars: *Gibson and Ovation acoustics*

Stewart grew up in the same town as Robert Fripp and Greg Lake, and the three took guitar lessons from the same music teacher. While Fripp and Lake found their fame and fortune in the progressive rock genre, Stewart took a less obvious route.

After playing lead guitar in a small band called Tony Blackburn & the Sabres, he headed for the same London coffeehouses that provided forums for legendary acoustic guitarists like Bert Jansch and John Renbourn. Stewart developed a style steeped in their brand of Celtic and British folk, yet imbued it with rock and pop sensibilities and a bit of the psychedelic. He was also a witty and insightful songwriter, which helped him to rise above the coffeehouse crowd.

Signing a deal with CBS, he recorded four critically acclaimed records that sold well in the U.K., but nowhere else. On these albums, notably *Love Chronicles* and *Orange*, he was backed by some of Britain's best session players, including Jimmy Page and keyboardist Rick Wakeman. His primary sideman, though, was Tim Renwick, an accomplished nylon-string and electric player who in recent years has toured with Pink Floyd. The two collaborated on a fifth album, *Past, Present, and Future* (1974), which finally brought Stewart attention outside of his homeland. The record included brilliant guitar work on cuts like "Nostradamus" (in open tuning) and "Roads to Moscow" (featuring an Eastern European flavored guitar intro and lead break).

Stewart used *Past, Present, and Future* as a vehicle for exploring his interest in historical events, which was also evident on his next record, *Modern Times* (1975). Utilizing more electric guitar and multitracked acoustics, the album veered from the rockabilly twang of "Apple Cider Reconstitution" to the brooding mayhem of the title cut, which featured a screaming solo from Renwick. This album helped expand Stewart's cult following in the U.S., thus paving the way for his biggest commercial success, *Year of the Cat* (1976). Filled with Middle Eastern melodies, Spanish-influenced rhythm guitar, and still more electric solo work from Renwick, *Cat* made Stewart's career.

Following the release of *Time Passages* in 1978, legal problems with his record company prevented Stewart from maintaining a consistent presence in the public eye. His output rarely varied from its usual high quality, with *24 Carrots* (1980) proving to be an exceptional outing. With new guitar sideman Peter White (who had guested on many of Stewart's earlier albums) and a pickup band called Shot in the Dark, Stewart flirted successfully with hard rock on *24 Carrots*, especially on "Paint by Numbers" and "Mondo Sinistro." Since then, he and White have been nearly inseparable, releasing albums and touring together. (White has a cult following in Britain for his own solo material.) This pairing recorded live acoustic versions of Stewart classics for the guitar duet album *Rhymes in Rooms* (1993).

Al Stewart, *Bedsitter Images* (CBS, 1967), *Love Chronicles* (CBS, 1969), *Zero She Flies* (CBS, 1970), *Orange* (CBS, 1972), *Past, Present, and Future* (Janus, 1974), *Modern Times* (Janus, 1975), *Year of the Cat* (Arista, 1976), *Time Passages* (Arista, 1978), *Early Years* (Arista, 1978), *24 Carrots* (Arista, 1980), *Indian Summer Live* (Arista, 1981•), *Take Off: The Best of Al Stewart* (RCA, 1981), *Last Days of the Century* (Enigma, 1988), *Best of Al Stewart* (Arista, 1988), *Russians & Americans* (RCA, 1984), *Rhymes in Rooms* (Mesa, 1992•), *Famous Last Words* (Mesa, 1993).

Loggins & Messina

Jim Messina

B o r n : *December 5, 1947, in Maywood, California*
M a i n   G u i t a r : *Fender Telecaster*

A talented lead guitarist of the singer-songwriter movement was Jim Messina, one half of the popular singing duo Loggins & Messina. Messina, who was Buffalo Springfield's bassist on their last album and a co-founder of Poco, was hired to produce Kenny Loggins' debut album. He ended up teaming with Loggins, who played rhythm guitar, and the two embarked on a short, but commercially successful, partnership.

Messina embellished many of the duo's songs with country-styled lead breaks on his Fender Telecaster. Among his best pieces were the twangy, pulled-string fills to "Angry Eyes," the Chuck Berry-styled licks in "Your Mama Don't Dance" (both from *Loggins & Messina* [1972]), and his beautiful, flowing

chord solo on "Vahevala" (from the duo's 1972 debut set, *Sittin' In*). Although Loggins went on to find far greater fame on his own, Jim Messina should be given his due as a fine and very underrated player.

Buffalo Springfield, *Last Time Around* (Atco, 1969). **Loggins & Messina** [on Columbia], *Sittin' In* (1972), *Loggins & Messina* (1972), *Full Sail* (1973), *On Stage* (1974•), *Mother Lode* (1974), *So Fine* (1975), *Native Sons* (1976), *Best of Friends* (1976). **Jim Messina,** *Oasis* (Columbia, 1979), *Messina* (Warner Bros., 1981). **Poco,** *Pickin' up the Pieces* (Epic, 1969), *Legacy* (RCA, 1989).

Joni Mitchell

B o r n : *November 7, 1943, in McLeod, Alberta*
M a i n   G u i t a r s : *Martin and Gibson acoustics*

In addition to captivating rock audiences with her meticulously crafted songs, personal lyrics, and engaging soprano voice, Joni Mitchell also proved herself to be a superb rhythm guitarist during her intense heyday in the seventies. Her interesting acoustic work—often accented with spacious chord voicings, open tunings, and accomplished fingerstyle and strumming techniques—turned up on tracks like "Tin Angel" (from *Clouds* [1969]), "People's Parties" (from her 1974 classic *Court and Spark*), and "God Must Be a Boogie Man" (from *Mingus*, her 1979 tribute to the late jazz legend Charles Mingus).

While Joni Mitchell will ultimately be most famous for her songs and singing, she was certainly one singer-songwriter who could hold her own on the guitar. Her songwriting and playing inspired groups as diverse as Crosby, Stills, Nash & Young and Led Zeppelin.

Joni Mitchell [on Asylum except where noted], *Joni Mitchell* (Reprise, 1968), *Clouds* (Reprise, 1969), *Ladies of the Canyon* (Reprise, 1970), *Blue* (Reprise, 1971), *For the Roses* (1972), *Court and Spark* (1974), *Miles of Aisles* (1974•), *The Hissing of Summer Lawns* (1975), *Hejira* (1976), *Don Juan's Reckless Daughter* (1978), *Mingus* (1979), *Shadows and Light* (1980•), *Wild Things Run Fast* (Geffen, 1982), *Dog Eat Dog* (Geffen, 1985), *Chalk Mark in a Rain Storm* (Geffen, 1988), *Night Ride Home* (Geffen, 1991), *Turbulent Indigo* (Warner Bros., 1994).

CHAPTER SIXTEEN

Jazz-Rock Fusion
The Virtuoso Arrives

In 1967 a strange breed of rock 'n' roll made its presence felt. This sound was a heady mixture of rock and jazz, with offshoots into R&B, Indian classical music, and blues. For lack of better terms, it was labeled "jazz-rock," or, somewhat less appropriately, "fusion." At the outset, this jazz-rock was dominated by ersatz rock/big bands like the Electric Flag, Chicago, and Blood, Sweat & Tears, which used brass sections, R&B vocals, and a fair share of fuzzed-out guitar solos to spice up their pop hits. But much of jazz-rock's real identity came from jazzmen (especially those from Miles Davis' post-bebop camp), who were intrigued by the electronic sounds created by rockers like Jimi Hendrix and Sly Stone. Miles' own 1969 masterwork *In a Silent Way* features such straight-ahead jazz stalwarts as keyboardists Herbie Hancock, Joe Zawinul, and Chick Corea, saxman Wayne Shorter, drummer Tony Williams, and guitarist John McLaughlin playing long bop-styled solos. But instead of the steady swing of a jazz rhythm section behind these soloists, static rock progressions fill the background. Miles followed that record with an even more important jazz-rock album, *Bitches Brew* (1970), which actually broke into the upper tiers of the pop charts. With *Brew* establishing that there was a market for such music, the fusion rush was on, and jazz and rock musicians alike converted to this exciting new music.

In the world of fusion, the instrumentalist was king. Obviously, guitar players were immediate beneficiaries of jazz-rock's instrumental bias. Hendrix, Clapton, and Bloomfield had already proven the validity of the rock guitar soloist. Many of the newer jazz-rock guitar players took the notion one step further by creating groups that were completely dominated by guitar. Among them were Larry Coryell (with Chico Hamilton, the Free Spirits, and Gary Burton), Jerry Hahn, and John Abercrombie (with Dreams), all of whom had been combining blues and rock 'n' roll licks with their standard jazz guitar repertoire since the mid sixties.

But it was John McLaughlin who wrote the definitive book of jazz-rock guitar with his high-volume playing and fast fretboard work. During the 1970s McLaughlin's wizardry was showcased in Miles Davis' band, the Tony Williams Lifetime, and his own Mahavishnu Orchestra. After he helped open the fusion floodgates in the early seventies, a steady stream of technically brilliant jazz-rock pickers followed him, including Bill Connors of Return to Forever, Tommy Bolin, George Benson, Al Di Meola (who succeeded Connors in RTF and went on to a popular solo career), and crossover sensations such as Jeff Beck and Pat Metheny. Many of these players were among the first to use guitar synthesizers, and they were responsible for much of the atonal and sonic experimentation that redefined what was considered "musical" in the seventies and eighties.

More important, fusion reacquainted rock with its jazz roots, which are often overlooked in favor of the rustic appeal of blues and country. But make no mistake about it: a number of crucial early rock 'n' roll records were mere derivations of 1940s swing music (notably by Bill Haley), and as such, jazz should be considered as powerful an influence on rock as the aforementioned blues and country genres. And just as the folk and blues booms of the 1960s had created a new generation of musical folklorists and fans, jazz-rock fostered its own re-awareness of jazz music among rock audiences. Furthermore, after weathering the anti-bop sentiments of the mid sixties through early seventies, straight jazz made a comeback later in the decade, perhaps aided by the great fusion explosion.

John McLaughlin

John McLaughlin

B o r n: *January 4, 1942, near Doncaster, England*
M a i n G u i t a r s: *Gibson Les Paul, Gibson and Rex Bogue doublenecks, Ovation and Wechter steel-string and classical acoustics, Synclavier guitar synthesizer*

Few modern guitarists can claim to be the best of their particular genre. For jazz-rock guitarists, though, John McLaughlin is indisputably at the top of the list. He may not have been the first fusion guitarist, but McLaughlin's legendary guitar playing set new standards for rock and jazz guitarists all over the world. Even while rock guitar's technical virtuosos were emerging in art-rock groups during the first few years of the 1970s, they had little on McLaughlin, who is renowned for his incredibly fast fretboard runs, alien jazz harmonies, and amazingly clean technique.

Despite McLaughlin's rise to six-string fame in the early 1970s, he had actually been a part of the British music scene for the better part of a decade. In 1963 the 21-year-old McLaughlin joined the R&B- and jazz-oriented Graham Bond Organization, a band that also featured future Cream stars Jack Bruce and Ginger Baker. During the rest of the sixties, he worked as a session guitarist and played with such popular U.K. performers as keyboardist Brian Auger and teen idol Georgie Fame. Like many other British musicians during that time, McLaughlin was drawn to the mysticism of Eastern religion and Indian music, both of which would have a significant impact on his musical future.

Around 1969 a tape of McLaughlin's guitar playing fell into the hands of Miles Davis' drummer, Tony Williams, who immediately invited McLaughlin to New York to join his new group, the Tony Williams Lifetime. Within a few days of his arrival in the United States, the guitarist found himself jamming with Williams' group and recording in the studio with Miles, who was impressed with the young Englishman's talent. The results of McLaughlin's sessions with Miles were important albums for both rock and jazz: *In a Silent Way* (1969) and *Bitches Brew* (1970). A consequence of the release of these two albums was that jazz-rock exploded, fueled by Miles' mixture of extended jazz improvisations, solid rock grooves, and quasi-African rhythms, and the heavy post-bop guitar breaks of McLaughlin.

At the same time, McLaughlin recorded a solo album called *Extrapolation* with baritone sax player John Surman. More important, he began recording with the Tony Williams Lifetime, a band some connoisseurs consider the greatest fusion band of all time. With drummer Williams, organist Larry Young, and, later, Cream bassist Jack Bruce, McLaughlin reached new heights of instrumental brilliance as a member of Lifetime, both on stage and on record. Together they recorded the hair-raising albums *Emergency!* (1969) and *Turn It Over* (1970). McLaughlin's work with Lifetime coincided with other important solo records, *Devotion* and *My Goals Beyond,* but eventually he left Lifetime to form his own band. Signing up drummer Billy Cobham, bassist Rick Laird, violinist Jerry Goodman, and keyboardist Jan Hammer—each man considered among the world's best on his

instrument—John McLaughlin formed the Mahavishnu Orchestra.

Their first album, *Inner Mounting Flame*, was a hit with rock audiences, and McLaughlin was quickly elevated to guitar hero status. The album's opening track, "Meeting of the Spirits," is a McLaughlin tour de force, containing an endless assault of swift scalar flashes, distorted string-bends, and melodic phrases that combine bebop style with furious rock 'n' roll. "The Noonward Race" carries on this high-intensity guitar playing in the crunchy guitar and drum intro. McLaughlin also highlights his softer acoustic side in "A Lotus on Irish Streams."

The band's follow-up, *Birds of Fire* (1973), was another crossover smash, earning the Mahavishnu Orchestra the #15 spot on U.S. album charts. With Jan Hammer's innovative Moog synthesizer solos and the rest of the group's brilliant ensemble work, *Birds of Fire* became a landmark fusion album, and its title track is still quite possibly the quintessential jazz-rock anthem. Using exotic arpeggiated chords on an electric 12-string (played on a Gibson doubleneck), McLaughlin launches into "Birds of Fire" with a violent, nonlinear melody, followed by a veritable frenzy of notes. The resulting music is nothing short of revolutionary—more so when one considers what other guitarists of the same era were playing. Simply stated, McLaughlin was well ahead of his time.

As is the case with many great bands, however, pressures and personality clashes within the Mahavishnu Orchestra overcame the music, and the band broke up in 1973. Later that year McLaughlin completed an energetic duo recording with Carlos Santana (♪), *Love, Devotion, Surrender,* a record with philosophical overtones that was commercially quite successful. In 1974 a new Mahavishnu Orchestra was formed, but it was noticeably inferior to the original. Yet another lineup change followed, and by the funk-oriented 1976 album *Inner Worlds* (containing the powerful guitar cut "Way of the Pilgrim"), McLaughlin seemed to be rehashing the very music he helped invent. Wisely, he chose to unplug his electric guitar and formed Shakti, a stunning acoustic fusion band that employed several Indian musicians, including violin master L. Shankar. After three incredible albums with Shakti—a band whose creative output and virtuosity may even have eclipsed the original Mahavishnu—McLaughlin briefly went back to his electric for *Electric Guitarist* (1978). He followed that up with *Electric Dreams* (1979), recorded with his short-lived One Truth Band.

Abandoning the electric guitar again, McLaughlin formed an acoustic guitar trio in the early 1980s with Al Di Meola and flamenco master Paco de Lucia (McLaughlin had had an earlier acoustic trio that featured de Lucia and jazz-rocker Larry Coryell). The trio played sold-out shows wherever they went, and their first album, *Friday Night in San Francisco,* was a surprise big-seller. Moving back into a fusion mode, McLaughlin reformed the Mahavishnu Orchestra in 1983 as the slimmed-down Mahavishnu. With this new Mahavishnu, the guitarist sought to again expand the boundaries of jazz-rock guitar playing, with the sonic assistance of a Synclavier digital guitar synthesizer. A fine album simply called *Mahavishnu* was released in 1984 and followed in 1986 by the less intriguing *Adventures in Radioland*. Leaving Mahavishnu behind at the end of the 1980s, he put together a series of smaller acoustic and electric combos, each an apparent effort to re-explore his jazz roots. He also wrote and recorded the Spanish-flavored *"Mediterranean" Concerto* for nylon-string guitar and symphony orchestra.

With his unique guitar voice, mind-boggling technique, and constant musical evolution, John McLaughlin has become something of a living legend. He has been called the most influential guitarist since Jimi Hendrix and is clearly one of the most significant stylists to arrive since Hendrix's death in 1970. He has been as unpredictable as he has been eclectic, equally at home on electric, acoustic, or synthesizer guitars. Many other guitarists find a musical niche for themselves and stick with it (oftentimes to their own detriment), but McLaughlin adopts various styles, reinvents them, and promptly discards them to look for new musical frontiers. Whether for his brilliant technique, engaging compositions, or vast musical diversity, John McLaughlin has embodied fine musicianship and remains the ultimate fusion virtuoso.

Tony Williams Lifetime [on Polydor], *Emergency!* (1969), *Turn It Over* (1970). **Mahavishnu Orchestra** [on Columbia], *Inner Mounting Flame* (1971), *Birds of Fire* (1973), *Between Nothingness and Eternity* (1973•), *Apocalypse* (1974), *Visions of the Emerald Beyond* (1975), *Inner Worlds* (1976). **Shakti** [on Columbia], *Shakti with John McLaughlin* (1976•), *A Handful of Beauty* (1977), *Natural Elements* (1978). **John McLaughlin** [on Warner Bros. except where noted], *Extrapolation* (Polydor, 1969), *Devotion* (Douglas, 1971), *My Goals Beyond* (Douglas, 1971), *Electric Guitarist* (Columbia, 1978), *Best of John McLaughlin* (Columbia, 1980), *Belo Horizonte* (1981), *Music Spoken Here* (1982), *"Mediterranean" Concerto* (Columbia, 1990), *Live at the Royal Albert Hall* (JMT, 1990•), *Que Alegria* (1992), *Free Spirits* [with Joey DeFrancesco] (n/a, 1994), *The Promise* (Columbia, 1996). **Carlos Santana and John McLaughlin**, *Love, Devotion, Surrender* (Columbia, 1973). **John McLaughlin & the One Truth Band**, *Electric Dreams* (Columbia, 1979). **John McLaughlin, Al Di Meola & Paco de Lucia** [on Columbia], *Friday Night in San Francisco* (1981•), *Passion, Grace, and Fire* (1983). **Mahavishnu**, *Mahavishnu* (Warner Bros., 1984), *Adventures in Radioland* (Relativity, 1986).

Recordings featuring John McLaughlin: **John Surman**, *Where Fortune Smiles* (Pye, rec. 1967). **Miles Davis** [on Columbia], *In a Silent Way* (1969), *Bitches Brew* (1970), *A Tribute to Jack Johnson* (1971), *Live-Evil* (1971•), *Big Fun* (1974), *Get up with It* (1975), *You're under Arrest* (1985). **Wayne Shorter**, *Super Nova* (Blue Note, 1969). **Graham Bond**, *Solid Bond* (Warner Bros., 1970). **Carla Bley**, *Escalator over the Hill* (Jazz Composers Orchestra, 1970). **Jack Bruce**, *Things We Like* (Atco, 1971). **James Taylor**, *One Man Dog* (Warner Bros., 1972). **Various Artists**, *Mar y Sol* (Atco, 1972•). **Larry Coryell**, *Spaces* (Vanguard, 1974). **Stanley Clarke** [on Nemporer], *Journey to Love* (1975), *School Days* (1976), *Live 1976–77* (Epic, 1991•). **Various Artists**, *Havana Jam* (Columbia, 1979•). **Various Artists**, *Fuse One* (CTI, 1981). **Miroslav Vitous**, *Mountain in the Clouds* (Atlantic, 1973). **Bill Evans**, *The Alternative Man* (Blue Note, 1985). **Various Artists**, *In from the Storm* [Hendrix tribute] (RCA, 1995).

Al Di Meola

Born: *July 22, 1954, in Jersey City, New Jersey*
Main Guitars: *Gibson Les Paul, ES-175, and custom Al Di Meola model, Ovation acoustics, Paul Reed Smith solidbody*

Shortly after fusion guitarist Bill Connors left Return to Forever in the summer of 1974, leader Chick Corea replaced him with Al Di Meola, a 19-year-old student from Berklee College of Music in Boston. Within two days of joining the band, Di Meola was playing on stage at Carnegie Hall, and the following night he was in Atlanta playing before 40,000 screaming rock fans. Di Meola's first recording with the group, *Where Have I Known You Before*, appeared several months later. By the end of 1975, he had nabbed top honors as "Best New Talent" in *Guitar Player* magazine's Readers Poll.

Certainly, this was an auspicious and lightning-quick introduction to the big leagues of music, but Di Meola showed himself to be capable of handling the task. Few guitarists have ever experienced such a meteoric rise to the top, and fewer still have gone on to make such a reputation for themselves as Di Meola has in the world of jazz-rock.

Di Meola learned hard rock licks off of his record player as a teenager. He got in the habit of damping the strings with the palm of his picking hand so that it would mute the sound and not annoy his parents. Al later made a name for himself at Berklee, where he was honing his jazz technique, when Chick Corea summoned him. The recognition he received with Return to Forever was immediate, although that spotlight was shared with a stellar lineup that included Corea, bassist Stanley Clarke, and drummer Lenny White. Di Meola reached his zenith with the band on *Romantic Warrior*, a jazzy album that veers into the bombast of hard rock, spurred on by intelligently placed power chords and searing lead lines. In 1976, after recording three albums with Return to Forever, he left to embark upon a solo career. By that time he was regularly topping guitar polls everywhere and was considered one

Al Di Meola

of the world's premier fusion guitarists. Al was also only 22 years old.

On his own, Di Meola began to create instrumental albums of—as he once called it—progressive Latin rock. Instead of the eclectic fusion of Return to Forever, this unique style combined the rhythms and moods of Spain, North Africa, Italy, and South America with jazz harmony and even heavy metal textures. His first album, *Land of the Midnight Sun* (1976), bears traces of the Return to Forever sound, but *Elegant Gypsy* (1977), possibly his finest album, demonstrates that Di Meola had indeed created his own distinctive style of jazz-rock. Opening the album is a soaring rocker called "Flight over Rio," a cut that features the guitarist's high-speed solos locked in a vicious sonic duel with Jan Hammer's Moog synthesizer breaks. Although the whole album is a guitar lover's dream, one track that broke the fusion mold yet still captivated guitarists was "Mediterranean Sundance," a duet between Di Meola and flamenco virtuoso Paco de Lucia. Most rock guitarists were awe-struck by the high-speed modal runs and Latin tinged melodies played by the two guitarists on their stereo-panned instruments. This song is historically important for introducing many rock guitar players to the beautiful sounds of Spanish flamenco guitar music and its demanding technique.

Di Meola followed up *Elegant Gypsy* with two more fine studio discs, *Casino* (1978) and the eclectic *Splendido Hotel* (1980). Later in 1980 he took a turn away from his electric musings to join Paco de Lucia and John McLaughlin for a triple acoustic guitar tour. Playing to sold-out houses nearly every night, the tour was a huge success and resulted in a 1981 live recording entitled *Friday Night in San Francisco*. After the tour and a follow-up studio set with de Lucia and McLaughlin, Di Meola briefly returned to his electric work before making a radical stylistic change in 1983. First he made *Scenario*, an album of soft instrumentals that utilizes a Roland guitar synthesizer and a Fairlight digital sampling synthesizer. Then in 1985, *Cielo e Terra* was released, with Di Meola playing only acoustic guitar and the Synclavier digital guitar synthesizer. Soon after, he issued *Soaring through a Dream*, which features Di Meola playing the Synclavier guitar in the context of a band. Music critics, who had for years lambasted the guitarist for his speedy fusion forays and technically precise music, praised his more subdued new work.

Di Meola continues to opt for a less radical style and recording approach in the 1990s, resulting in a mix of the more pastoral sounds of his eighties recordings with the heavier textures of his best-known work of the late seventies. His records also confirm the strong influence of South American composers like Astor Piazolla. He is recording and performing, moving back and forth from larger ensembles (such as his World Sinfonia) and venues to intimate acoustic music and small clubs.

As a ground-breaking guitarist, what set Di Meola apart from most fusion guitar players of the seventies was his pronounced speed and dexterity on the instrument. While playing fast had been the rule for jazz-rock guitar since its inception, Di Meola refined his speedy picking into a controlled on-the-beat tech-

nique that beguiled guitar fans with blinding eighth-, sixteenth-, and thirty-second-note runs up and down the fingerboard. Aside from his renowned speed-picking technique and Latin-styled heavy rock, Di Meola also popularized the "mutola" technique for rock guitarists. This is essentially a method of muting the strings with the palm of the picking hand to produce a percussive, popping sound from the strings, which Di Meola employs as an integral part of his playing (country and jazz great Hank Garland previously used the technique in "Just for Tonight," a song from his 1962 album *The Unforgettable Guitar of Hank Garland*).

It is important to note that Di Meola's guitar work during the seventies clearly prophesied the following decade's obsession with speed and technique, mostly among heavy metal players. He undoubtedly influenced some high-speed guitar mavens such as Yngwie Malmsteen, Tony MacAlpine, and Vinnie Moore. While the guitarist has faced a lot of criticism for his occasionally excessive technique over the years, there can be no doubt that Al Di Meola's brazen playing has added an oft-needed spark to the jazz-rock genre. He is truly a monster guitarist.

Return to Forever, *Where Have I Known You Before* (Polydor, 1974), *No Mystery* (Polydor, 1975), *Romantic Warrior* (Columbia, 1976). **Al Di Meola** [on Columbia except where noted], *Land of the Midnight Sun* (1976), *Elegant Gypsy* (1977), *Casino* (1978), *Splendido Hotel* (1980), *Electric Rendezvous* (1982), *Tour de Force* (1982), *Scenario* (1983), *Cielo e Terra* (Manhattan, 1985), *Soaring through a Dream* (Manhattan, 1985), *Tirami Su* (1987), *Kiss My Axe* (Tomato, 1991), *Orange and Blue* (Mesa, 1994). **Al Di Meola & World Sinfonia,** *World Sinfonia* (Tomato, 1991), *Heart of the Immigrants* (Mesa, 1993). **John McLaughlin, Al Di Meola & Paco de Lucia** [on Columbia], *Friday Night in San Francisco* (1981), *Passion, Grace, and Fire* (1983). **Stanley Clarke, Al Di Meola & Jean-Luc Ponty,** *Rite of Strings* (IRS, 1995).

Recordings featuring Al Di Meola: **Stomu Yamashta,** *Go* (Island, 1976), *Go Too* (Arista, 1977). **Chick Corea,** *Touchstone* (Warner Bros., 1982). **Paul Simon,** *Hearts and Bones* (Warner Bros., 1983). **John McLaughlin,** *The Promise* (Columbia, 1996).

Larry Coryell

Born: *April 2, 1943, in Galveston, Texas*
Main Guitars: *Gibson Super 400, Hagstrom Swede*

Before the public arrival of John McLaughlin in 1969, Larry Coryell was far and away the reigning master of jazz-rock guitar. During his stint with the Gary Burton Quartet from 1967 to 1968, Coryell was widely praised for his then-radical combination of rock and jazz guitar. By the time of his first solo album release in 1968, he was a full-fledged fusion guitar star. He unabashedly coupled pentatonic scales and blues licks with jazz technique and harmony, whipping out everything from flowing melody lines to distorted thirty-second-note runs in his solos. On one level, the strides Larry Coryell was making with jazz and rock in 1968 were very similar to what Eric Clapton was doing with blues and rock at the same time. As a result, Coryell became the most important fusion guitarist of the pre-McLaughlin era.

Coryell started out playing the guitar in his teens near Seattle, Washington, where he was raised. After playing the Pacific Northwest region in rock, jazz, and, occasionally, country bands, Coryell migrated to New York in the mid sixties. There he formed the Free Spirits, one of jazz-rock's very first bands. Soon after, Coryell hooked up with drummer Chico Hamilton's jazz group (replacing his mentor, guitarist Gabor Szabo) and recorded *The Dealer* with them in 1966. "Larry of Arabia" from that album shows Coryell's developing fusion style during an extended solo of bluesy runs, intricate linear phrases, and even repetitive string-pushing licks à la Chuck Berry. What is most important about this early recording, however, is that it's a rare example of pre-Hendrix fusion guitar. The album was recorded a year before Hendrix's momentous debut at Monterey, which heralded the beginning of Jimi's influence on all modern music, especially on jazz-rock guitarists. After Hendrix began his sonic explorations, the sound of fusion guitar changed dramatically, notably with the introduction of fuzztone and feedback as sonic elements.

After departing Hamilton's band, Coryell moved on to vibraphonist Gary Burton's quartet. This band made waves in jazz circles for including the aggressive rock-styled guitar player in their fold, and were thus considered on the vanguard of the new jazz offshoot. Several classic albums were released by this group, including *Duster* and *Lofty Fake Anagram*. "Some Dirge" (from Burton's 1967 *A Genuine Tong Funeral* set) hints at Coryell's move towards a heavier rock approach to jazz guitar as he plays a solo dotted with fast, rock-flavored scale runs, high string-bends, and wrist vibrato tones, all of which are more intrinsic to rock guitar than jazz guitar styling.

Coryell eventually broke the field of jazz-rock guitar wide open with his first solo albums, released in 1968 and 1969. With the first three Coryell recordings, the era of jazz-rock guitar had its formal beginnings. On tracks like "Sex" and "Jam with Albert," Coryell openly acknowledges Jimi Hendrix's influence in a series of inspired rock solos, laden with heavy fuzz, wah-wah, and phase shifter effects. During the first half of the seventies, Coryell continued his jazz-rock explorations in his band Eleventh House, but then turned his attention to acoustic and bebop guitar. In the decades since, he is rarely ever heard playing high-volume fusion. Nevertheless, he remains a vital component of the early fusion sound and is one of its true founding fathers.

Free Spirits, *Out of Sight and Mind* (ABC, 1966). **Chico Hamilton,** *The Dealer* (Impulse, 1966). **Gary Burton Quartet** [on RCA], *A Genuine Tong Funeral* (1967), *Duster* (1967), *Lofty Fake Anagram* (1968), *In Concert* (1968•). **Larry Coryell** [on Vanguard except where noted], *Larry Coryell* (1969), *Lady Coryell* (1969), *Coryell* (1970), *Barefoot Boy* (Flying Dutchman, 1971), *Spaces* [with John McLaughlin] (1974), *At Village Gate* (1975•), *Restful Mind* (1975), *The Essential Larry Coryell* (1975), *Planet End* (1976), *Back Together Again* [with Alphonse Mouzon] (Atlantic, 1977),

Return (1980), *Standing Ovation* (Arista, 1980), *Equipoise* (Muse, 1986), *A Quiet Day in Spring* (Steeplechase, 1988), *Just Like Being Born* (Flying Fish, 1989). **Eleventh House,** *Introducing the Eleventh House* (Vanguard, 1974), *Level One* (Arista, 1975), *Aspects* (Arista, 1976), *Eleventh House at Montreaux* (Vanguard, 1978•). **Larry Coryell & Steve Khan,** *Two for the Road* (Arista, 1976•). **Larry Coryell & Philip Catherine,** *Twin House* (Atlantic, 1977), *Splendid* (Elektra, 1978). **Larry Coryell & Emily Remler,** *Together* (Concord Jazz, 1986).

Recordings featuring Larry Coryell: **Herbie Mann,** *Memphis Underground* (Atlantic, 1969). **Fifth Dimension,** *Earthbound* (ABC, 1975). **Various Artists,** *Fuse One* (CTI, 1981). **Paco de Lucia,** *Castro Marin* (Philips, 1981).

The "Spectrum" Sessions

Tommy Bolin

B o r n : *August 1, 1951, in Sioux City, Iowa*
M a i n   G u i t a r : *Fender Stratocaster*

While many remember Tommy Bolin as the rocker who replaced Joe Walsh in the James Gang and Ritchie Blackmore in Deep Purple, he has also earned a rightful place in rock guitar lore as one of the best fusion players of the early seventies. This is due to his performance on a single album: Billy Cobham's *Spectrum*. This 1973 release was a near-crossover success and contains stunning instrumental improvisation from a lineup that—in addition to Bolin—included Mahavishnu Orchestra alumni Cobham on drums and Jan Hammer on piano and synthesizer.

Originally Tommy Bolin made his name as a whiz kid in Colorado, playing with Albert King and the bands Energy and Zephyr. With Zephyr, he recorded an album in 1969 for the Probe label. Freely mixing hard rock, blues, and jazz elements around a Janis Joplin-styled singer named Cindy Givens, the Zephyr recording provides a revealing look into Bolin's precocious talents (the album is now a much-sought-after collector's item).

Joining Cobham in 1973 for the *Spectrum* sessions, Bolin juiced up several of the extended instrumentals with solos on his Fender Stratocaster. Although almost every track has some of Bolin's bristling electric work, the standouts are "Quadrant 4," "Taurian Matador," and "Stratus," all of which show his facility in mixing pentatonics, distortion, tremolo bar effects, and high-

Tommy Bolin

speed picking. The cut "Red Baron" displays a softer side of Bolin's lead playing; in fact, the funky blues lines, string pops, and slide overdubs with a clean/slap echo tone sound like a blueprint for Jeff Beck's landmark jazz-rock set *Blow by Blow*. The similarities are striking, and perhaps not a little coincidental, given that Bolin would later open for Beck during a tour of the U.S.

Shortly after *Spectrum* was released, Joe Walsh recommended Bolin as his replacement in the James Gang. This period of his career was less than memorable, resulting in his participation on two James Gang records from 1973 and 1974 (*Bang* and *Miami*). The guitarist returned to dabbling in fusion on material from his eclectic 1975 solo album *Teaser*, notably "Homeward Bound" and "Marching Powder." He was recruited by Deep Purple to replace Ritchie Blackmore that same year, in time for what turned out to be a rather lame 1975 set, *Come Taste the Band*. Purple broke up after a world tour, but Bolin was fully immersed in his solo career with the release of *Private Eyes* in 1976. However, he had already become addicted to heroin, a factor that affected his live playing and that many claimed to be a major cause of Deep Purple's dissolution. His skill and personal notoriety were pushing him to guitar hero heights when he died on December 4, 1976, from a drug overdose. Ironically, it was after a gig, opening for Jeff Beck.

Bolin's work on *Spectrum* remains among the best early fusion guitar, and his almost metalish solos brought a heavy rock excitement to the fusion genre—again, well before Beck's similar achievement. With a diverse résumé that included gigs with Albert King, Billy Cobham, the James Gang, and Deep Purple, it is left to the imagination to wonder what musical summits Tommy Bolin and his occasionally inspired guitar playing might have conquered next.

Zephyr, *Zephyr* (Probe/ABC, 1969), *Going Back to Colorado* (Warner Bros., 1971). **James Gang** [on Atco], *Bang* (1973), *Miami* (1974). **Deep Purple,** *Come Taste the Band* (Warner Bros., 1975), *In Concert* (King Biscuit, 1995•). **Tommy Bolin,** *Teaser* (Nemperor, 1975), *Private Eyes* (Columbia, 1976), *The Ultimate…* (Geffen, 1990), *From the Archives* (Rhino, 1996).

Recordings featuring Tommy Bolin: **Billy Cobham,** *Spectrum* (Atlantic, 1973). **Alphonse Mouzon,** *Mind Transplant* (Blue Note, 1974).

Return to Forever

Bill Connors

B o r n : *September 24, 1949, in Los Angeles*
M a i n G u i t a r : *Gibson Les Paul*

One of the Mahavishnu Orchestra's main competitors in the early seventies jazz-rock arena was Return to Forever, a crack outfit led by keyboard virtuoso Chick Corea. The first incarnation of Return to Forever was guitar-less, but in 1973 Corea added axeman Bill Connors to his group (which also boasted esteemed jazz-rock bassist Stanley Clarke and drummer Lenny

White). Connors' guitar work brought a distinct rock dimension to Return to Forever that had not been present on their earlier Latin-flavored jazz albums. The rock touch quickly increased their visibility in the mainstream rock community as well as their overall popularity. Connors' one album with Return to Forever, *Hymn of the Seventh Galaxy*, provided a commanding forum for his solo and ensemble playing with the band. Like Tommy Bolin and Jeff Beck, Connors was clearly a rock-oriented player, and he freely lights up the solos in "Hymn of the Seventh Galaxy," "Captain Señor Mouse," and "Theme to the Mothership" with high-volume distortion and feedback, bent strings, and wrist-vibrato effects. The obvious influence of Eric Clapton is intertwined with a thorough jazz training and also strong inspiration from jazz guitar greats like Wes Montgomery and Jim Hall.

Sensing that jazz-rock was becoming more commercial and moving away from basic jazz ideals, Connors quit Return to Forever in mid 1974. By the following year, he had given up the electric guitar altogether in order to devote himself to the nylon-string acoustic guitar. He recorded several albums of classical and acoustic jazz music during the rest of the decade. In the early eighties, Connors again picked up the electric guitar for a stint with jazz saxophonist Jan Garbarek's quintet. In 1985 he released an electric solo album called *Step It*, featuring a high-energy trio format. He followed that with more electric sets (*Double Up*, *Assembler*) that bore a strong resemblance to the progressive rock style of contemporary Allan Holdsworth.

Return to Forever, *Hymn of the Seventh Galaxy* (Polydor, 1973). **Bill Connors** [on Pathfinder except where noted], *Theme to the Guardian* (ECM, 1974), *Of Mist and Melting* (ECM, 1977), *Swimming with a Hole in My Body* (ECM, 1979), *Step It* (1985), *Double Up* (1986), *Assembler* (1987).

Recordings featuring Bill Connors: **Stanley Clarke,** *Stanley Clarke* (Columbia, 1974).

Post-Fusion: Stern, Scofield, and Henderson

Mike Stern
B o r n : *January 10, 1954, in Boston*
M a i n G u i t a r s : *Fender Telecaster and Stratocaster, Yamaha SA2200*

John Scofield
B o r n : *December 26, 1951, in Dayton, Ohio*
M a i n G u i t a r : *Ibanez Artist*

Scott Henderson
B o r n : *1955, in Florida*
M a i n G u i t a r s : *Ibanez S Series, Fender Stratocaster*

When Miles Davis made his highly publicized comeback in 1981, he introduced a new guitar wizard to the fusion world: Mike Stern. Jazz critics attacked him for his high-volume solos and decidedly rock 'n' roll looks (i.e., long hair and a Stratocaster), but Stern quickly set the record straight with his inspiring leads and ethereal rhythm work for Miles circa 1981–1983. "Fat Time," from Miles' 1981 album *The Man with the Horn*, showcases Stern in a riveting lead break composed of fast repeated licks, overbent string pushes, and bop phrases (the song was Miles' dubious tribute to a then-overweight Stern). In contrast, "Jean Pierre" (from the 1982 live set *We Want Miles*) is full of edge-of-the-pick harmonics and quick, horn-like lines. In 1986 the guitarist spearheaded the rising post-fusion scene with his stunning solo album *Upside Downside*, which has more sublime examples of his bop and metal-based guitar excellence. Since then, Stern has regularly released powerful studio albums, cementing his place at the forefront of modern fusion guitar.

Another leader of the eighties post-fusion movement was John Scofield, a guitarist who also established himself by working as a sideman for Miles Davis. While playing with Davis from 1983 to 1985, Scofield launched a respected solo career. After the 1986 release of his acclaimed effort *Still Warm*, Scofield followed up with another well-received album in 1987, entitled *Blue Matter*. Such pieces as "Blue Matter," "Heaven Hill," and a bop-metal barn burner called "The Nag" display Scofield's exquisite guitarmanship via his use of bluesy bends, complex bop phrasing, Metheny-like processed chordings, and distorted rock lead work. In addition to his many solo releases, Scofield also collaborated with Pat Metheny on the critically lauded 1994 duet album *I Can See Your House from Here*.

Like Mike Stern and John Scofield, Scott Henderson gained attention for his six-string exploits in the post-fusion arena. After teaching at the Guitar Institute of Technology (GIT) for a number of years and playing guitar with violinist Jean-Luc Ponty and bassist Jeff Berlin in Vox Humana (appearing on the group's debut, *Champion*), Henderson landed a job backing Chick Corea on his techno-funk recording *The Chick Corea Elektric Band*. In addition to touring with the Corea group, he also appeared on a lively in-concert disc set called *Players*, with ace instrumentalists Berlin, keyboardist T Lavitz, and drummer Steve Smith. Releasing a solo disc in 1986 entitled *Spears*, Henderson went on to form the electronically driven band Tribal Tech.

Deriving influences from a wide assortment of guitar players, including Allan Holdsworth, Jeff Beck, Pat Metheny, Ritchie Blackmore of Deep Purple, and John Scofield, Henderson's wicked Stratocaster parts fuel tunes like "Big Fun" and "Caribbean" (from *Spears*), combining a hard rock tone and attack with a consummate knowledge of bop and fusion soloing. Henderson and Tribal Tech continued on with *Dr. Hee* (1987), *Nomad* (1989), and *Face First* (1993). In between, he managed to break out of the post-fusion mold by recording *Dog Party* in 1994, an album of high-velocity blues tunes that incorporates his jazz-rock style to excellent effect.

Miles Davis [on Columbia], *The Man with the Horn* (1981), *We Want Miles* (1982•), *Star People* (1983). **Mike Stern** [on Atlantic Jazz except where noted], *Neesh* (Trio, c. 1982), *Upside Downside* (1986), *Time in Place* (1988), *Jigsaw* (1989), *Odds or Evens* (1991), *Standards* (1992), *Is What It Is* (1994), *Between the Lines* (1996).

Recordings featuring Mike Stern: **Vital Information**, *Global Beat* (Columbia, 1986). **Harvie Swartz** [on Gramavision], *Smart Moves* (1986), *Urban Earth* (1986). **Bob Berg**, *Short Stories* (n/a, 1987), *Cycles* (Denon, 1988), *In the Shadows* (Denon, 1991).

John Scofield [on Gramavision except where noted], *Shinola* (Enja, 1982), *Electric Outlet* (1984), *Still Warm* (1985), *Blue Matter* (1987), *Loud Jazz* (1988), *Flat Out* (1989), *Meant to Be* (Blue Note, 1991), *Time on My Hands* (Blue Note, 1990), *Grace under Pressure* (Blue Note, 1992), *What We Do* (Blue Note, 1993), *Best Of...* (Rykodisc, 1994), *Groovelation* (Blue Note, 1995). **Miles Davis**, *Star People* (1983), *Decoy* (Columbia, 1984). **John Scofield & Pat Metheny**, *I Can See Your House from Here* (Gramavision, 1994).

Recordings featuring John Scofield: **Bennie Wallace**, *Twilight Time* (Blue Note, 1985).

Tribal Tech, *Dr. Hee* (Passport Jazz, 1987), *Nomad* (1989), *Tribal Tech* (Relativity, 1991), *Illicit* (Bluemoon, 1992), *Face First* (Bluemoon, 1993), *Primal Tracks* (Bluemoon, 1994), *Reality Check* (Bluemoon, 1995). **Scott Henderson**, *Spears* (Passport Jazz, 1986), *Dog Party* (Mesa, 1994).

Recordings featuring Scott Henderson: **Jeff Berlin & Vox Humana**, *Champion* (Passport Jazz, 1985). **Jean-Luc Ponty**, *Fables* (Atlantic, 1986). **Chick Corea**, *The Chick Corea Elektric Band* (GRP, 1986). **Players**, *Players* (Passport Jazz, 1987).

Pat Metheny

B o r n : *August 12, 1954, in Lee's Summit, Missouri*
M a i n   G u i t a r s : *Gibson ES-175, Roland and Synclavier guitar synthesizers*

Few jazz guitar players ever attain anything even resembling star status, but Pat Metheny certainly is among those rare few. Metheny ranks as one of the most commercially successful jazz guitarists of all time, the primary competition to that claim being guitarist George Benson, who largely achieved fame as a pop and R&B singer. Though Metheny's guitar style is rooted deeply in jazz tradition (especially that of Wes Montgomery and Jim Hall), he has still effortlessly crossed over to instrumental pop on a number of recordings with his Pat Metheny Group and, as a result, gained a sizable audience of mainstream fans.

American Garage (1979) is particularly rock-oriented (notably the title track), while much of his material from *Offramp* (1982) and *First Circle* (1984) shows the guitarist experimenting with international flavors. These recordings also highlight the different sonic textures that Metheny discovered on the Synclavier guitar synthesizer. Despite his wanderings outside the jazz world—especially evident on the weirdly experimental *Zero Tolerance for Silence*—Metheny has always been able to preserve his integrity among jazz fans by regularly issuing recordings with jazz masters like drummer Jack DeJohnette, Charlie Haden, and

Pat Metheny

saxophone/violin legend Ornette Coleman. As with many of fusion's best players, musical evolution has been central to Metheny's career as a contemporary jazz sensation, and his popularity shows little sign of abating.

Gary Burton, *Passengers* (ECM, 1975). **Pat Metheny** [on ECM except where noted], *Bright Size Life* (1976), *Watercolors* (1977), *New Chautauqua* (1979), *80/81* (1980), *Under Fire* [soundtrack] (1983), *Rejoicing* (1984), *Zero Tolerance for Silence* (Geffen, 1994). **Pat Metheny Group** [on ECM except where noted], *Pat Metheny Group* (1978), *American Garage* (1979), *Offramp* (1982), *Travels* (1983•), *First Circle* (1984), *The Falcon and the Snowman* [soundtrack] (EMI America, 1984), *Still Life: Talking* (Geffen, 1987), *Works* (1988), *Works II* (1989), *Letter from Home* (Geffen, 1989), *The Road to You* (Geffen, 1993•), *We Live Here* (Geffen, 1995). **Pat Metheny & Lyle Mays,** *As Falls Wichita, So Falls Wichita Falls* (ECM, 1981). **Pat Metheny & Ornette Coleman,** *Song X* (Geffen, 1986). **Pat Metheny, Roy Haynes, Dave Holland,** *Question and Answer* (Geffen, 1990). **John Scofield & Pat Metheny,** *I Can See Your House from Here* (Gramavision, 1994).

Recordings featuring Pat Metheny: **Joni Mitchell,** *Shadows and Light* (Asylum, 1980•). **Pedro Aznar,** *Contemplacion* (n/a, 1986).

Great Sidemen of the Seventies

In addition to the stars of jazz-rock guitar, there have been countless sidemen and low-profile band members who have become fusion notables in their own right. Chicago's guitarist, the late Terry Kath, was one of the genre's most electrifying but least recognized players. He made his mark at the outset of Chicago's career with an experimental piece called "Free Form Guitar," on *Chicago Transit Authority*. Consisting of Stratocaster feedback, it was years ahead of its time and certainly not what one would expect to find in a horn-driven band. Kath cemented his reputation as a powerful, if relatively unknown, soloist on the cut "25 or

6 to 4," from *Chicago II*. This 1970 pop hit has a memorable descending power-chord hook and a ferocious guitar solo that combines Hendrix-like energy with fast-picked scalar runs—a rarity of the time—and an intense volley of wah-wah pedal effects. It still ranks as one of the greatest solos ever to make it onto Top 40 radio. Kath displays his fine playing on many other Chicago cuts, flaunting his nimble right-hand picking and horizontal modal runs on jazz-tinged hits like "(I've Been) Searching So Long" and "I'm a Man." Though Kath died in 1978 as the result of an accidental gunshot wound, his tenure as Chicago's guitarist marked the band's critical and commercial high point.

Another underpraised sideman is Ray Gomez, who played with Roy Buchanan, Narada Michael Walden, and other rock, pop, and jazz acts, though he is best known as the guitar foil for superbassist Stanley Clarke during the late seventies. Like Jeff Beck, Gomez mixed slick jazz phrasing, and blues and rock licks, along with heavy distortion and the distinctive tone of his Fender Stratocaster. Among his best guitar spots with Stanley Clarke are the extended solos to "School Days" (on Clarke's 1976 album of the same name) and the climactic blues guitar/piccolo bass duel between himself and Clarke on "Quiet Afternoon," from the 1979 set *I Wanna Play for You*. Also extremely noteworthy is "West Side Boogie," an incendiary instrumental from Gomez's 1980 solo album *Volume*, which was later covered by nineties fusioneer Shawn Lane. Other seventies sidemen worth noting are Daryl Stuermer (◗ Genesis), Joaquín Leviano and Jamie Glaser with Jean-Luc Ponty, Icarus Johnson with Stanley Clarke, and studioman Carlos Rios, whose brilliant modal solos lit up Gino Vannelli's 1978 pop-fusion opus, *Brother to Brother*.

Chicago [on Columbia], *Chicago Transit Authority* (1968), *Chicago II* (1970), *Chicago III* (1971), *Chicago at Carnegie Hall* (1971•), *Chicago V* (1972), *Chicago VI* (1973), *Chicago VII* (1974), *Chicago VIII* (1975), *Chicago IX—Chicago's Greatest Hits* (1975), *Chicago X* (1976), *Chicago XI* (1977).

Ray Gomez, *Volume* (Columbia, 1980).

Recordings featuring Ray Gomez: **Stanley Clarke** [on Nemporer except where noted], *School Days* (1976), *Modern Man* (1978), *I Wanna Play for You* (1979•), *Hideaway* (Columbia, 1986), *Stanley Clarke Live 1976–77* (Epic, 1991•). **Narada Michael Walden** [on Atlantic], *Garden of Love Light* (1976), *Awakening* (1979). **Roy Buchanan,** *You're Not Alone* (Atlantic, 1978). **Stacy Lattisaw & Johnny Gill,** *Perfect Combination* (Cotillion, 1984). **Vital Information,** *Global Beat* (Columbia, 1986).

CHAPTER SEVENTEEN

Southern Rock
A Rebel Yell

Call it yin and yang. As disco was driving millions of Americans in the mid 1970s to boogie down, its musical antithesis—a tough, no-frills genre called "southern rock"—was at the zenith of its popularity. The music of southern rock was a back-to-basics formula, sort of a crossbreeding of Carl Perkins' rockabilly boogie and Led Zeppelin's British metal crunch, coupled with a complete disdain of the commercial slickness or glittery excess of mainstream seventies rock. Like its British forebears, it found its best outlet on stage, generating excitement from the virtuosity or aggression of its guitarists, many of whom were inspired soloists. It is not surprising, then, that the best recorded documents by all of southern rock's major artists during this period were live albums.

Much of southern rock's activity was nurtured in two geographic locales: Macon, Georgia, home of Capricorn Records, and Jacksonville, Florida, a somewhat metropolitan enclave that spawned Lynyrd Skynyrd, Molly Hatchet, and .38 Special. Capricorn signed many bands, but its first and most important group was the Allman Brothers Band. The Allmans virtually created the southern rock genre with their ominous twin-guitar, twin-drum attack, and songs that featured raw R&B vocals along with lengthy, jazz-flavored instrumental improvisations.

This latter characteristic provided significant inspiration to talented up-and-coming guitar players in the South during the early 1970s. By mid decade, a hot guitarist—preferably one well-versed in blues, rock, country, and jazz—was a must for any southern rock band, though the consensus seemed to be that two lead guitarists were better than one, and three were better still. Soon, countless bands had rallied under the southern rock flag, and the best guitar players were found in stylistically inventive groups like Skynyrd, the Marshall Tucker Band, the Outlaws, and others. Significantly, the entire southern rock movement was guitar-driven, creating a school of players who were determined only to plug in and rock out. Keyboardists and horn players were hard to find in the genre, which was a joy, given the instrumental excesses of disco, which was predominantly anti-guitar. Thus, guitarists came out of the woodwork in droves to form southern rock bands, which—for a while—provided the only six-string refuge from the mid-seventies dominance of disco.

Allman Brothers Band

Duane Allman

Born: *Howard Duane Allman, on November 20, 1946, in Nashville*
Died: *October 29, 1971*
Main Guitar: *Gibson Les Paul Standard*

Dickey Betts

Born: *Richard Betts, on December 12, 1943, in West Palm Beach, Florida*
Main Guitar: *Gibson Les Paul Standard*

While Hendrix, Clapton, Beck, and Page attracted the lion's share of the guitar hero spotlight in the late sixties and early seventies, another player quietly made a name for himself based on the strength of his incredible playing. Duane Allman, co-leader of the Allman Brothers Band and one of the top rock and R&B session guitarists of his day, was known in guitar circles and among fans for his charismatic blues- and jazz-oriented solos, sturdy rhythm support, and, most of all, his standard-setting bottleneck playing. Allman's short but explosive career with the Allman Brothers Band influenced many of the aspiring rock players who would eventually spur the popular southern rock movement of the 1970s.

Allman Brothers Band: Gregg Allman, Duane Allman, Berry Oakley

Born in Tennessee, Duane Allman moved to Daytona Beach, Florida, with his family in 1957. His younger brother, Gregg, took up the guitar in the early sixties, and Duane, who was fascinated by the instrument, had Gregg teach him how to play. Duane eventually became more proficient on the guitar than Gregg, who decided to find his niche playing keyboards. The brothers began playing locally in a group call the House Rockers, which backed a black vocal group, the Untils. In 1965 the brothers Allman formed a band called the Allman Joys, began touring the southern club circuit, and recorded a single ("Spoonful") for the Dial label. In 1967 Duane and Gregg Allman dissolved the Allman Joys and assembled a new act that eventually became known as Hour Glass. Ultimately, Hour Glass was lured to Los Angeles, where they signed with the Liberty label and opened area nightclub shows for the Doors, among others. Two albums of glossed-up psychedelic rock were recorded for Liberty, but the band broke up in 1968 after achieving little commercial success. Gregg returned to L.A. to work off the rest of the Liberty contract, while the elder Allman brother remained in the South, jamming with various groups, several of which included future members of the Allman Brothers Band.

In late 1968 Duane was asked to play on recording sessions for R&B singer Wilson Pickett at Fame Recording Studio in Muscle Shoals, Alabama. The session was a stunning success, in part due to Allman's suggestion that Pickett cover the Beatles' "Hey Jude"; it became a big hit for Pickett in 1969. Allman was then asked to join the Muscle Shoals Rhythm Section as staff lead guitarist, an offer that he readily accepted. During the next year, Allman played on such noted R&B releases as Aretha Franklin's *Soul '69*—which contains his spectacular, lopsided slide intro on her cover of the Band's "The Weight"—and *This Girl's in Love with You*. He also appeared on King Curtis' *Instant Groove* and Boz Scaggs' debut album, *Boz Scaggs*, which spotlights Allman's tortured extended solo in "Loan Me a Dime." Clearly, Duane possessed an innate and uncanny musical versatility that allowed him to fit into this vast range of styles and artists.

In March 1969 Duane Allman's contract was sold to Phil Walden, who was putting together a new label called Capricorn Records. Walden wanted Allman to find a band, so the guitarslinger headed down to Jacksonville, Florida, where he jammed with various members of local groups like 31st of February (with whom Allman had previously recorded) and the Second Coming. Out of this jam came the framework for the Allman Brothers Band, with Allman, co-lead guitarist-singer-songwriter Dickey Betts, bassist Berry Oakley, and dual drummers Jai Johnny Johanson and Butch Trucks. Sensing that this formation was going to be something special, Allman contacted his brother Gregg in L.A. and told him to come back and join the band as organist and lead vocalist. On March 26, 1969, the Allman Brothers Band was officially born.

The group moved to Macon, Georgia (the new headquarters for Capricorn), and recorded their first album. Blending rock, jazz, country, blues, R&B, and a handful of other influences, the Allman Brothers Band forged a new take on rock 'n' roll with their self-titled debut. The record emphasizes the musicians' instrumental prowess, especially Allman's and Betts' fine lead guitar work, as much as the songs themselves. Although the album didn't crack the top of the charts, the band set out on a long U.S. tour that allowed them to simultaneously hone their onstage chops and incite thousands of fans with their offshoot of bluesy rock 'n' roll.

Nearly a year later, the Allmans released *Idlewild South*, which cemented the group's driving southern sound and increased their popularity. Highlighting the album are tracks like "Revival," an upbeat tune that shows off the trademark twin-guitar harmonies of Allman and Betts, "Don't Keep Me Wonderin'," and "In Memory of Elizabeth Reed," Betts' classic instrumental. Duane Allman also continued doing studio work during this time, playing on albums by Ronnie Hawkins, Laura Nyro, and Eric Clapton's cohorts Delaney & Bonnie.

In the fall of 1970 Duane Allman was asked to participate in another recording venture, which turned out to be one of the milestones of his career: Derek and the Dominos' *Layla and Other Assorted Love Songs*. Though recording sessions had already begun for this Clapton project, Allman fit into the band seamlessly, putting his fat, Les Paul-powered slide and single-note guitar solos alongside Clapton's Strat breaks in blues cuts like "Key to the Highway" and "Have You Ever Loved a Woman." "Why Does Love Have to Be So Sad" is a major guitar hot-spot, but the album's defining moment is "Layla." Besides showcasing Clapton's thundering guitar work, "Layla" captures the two guitar giants' potent harmony guitar parts and Allman's wrenching, if occasionally out-of-tune, slide solos. The bottleneck master closes the piece with some startlingly real imitation bird calls created using his slide.

On March 12 and 13, 1971, the Allman Brothers Band was back in action, taking over New York's Fillmore East for a weekend of concerts. These shows were taped and released that summer as the two-record set *At Fillmore East*. This was the Allman Brothers Band at their finest, with Allman and Betts turning in stellar guitar performances on "Stormy Monday," "Hot 'lanta," and the epic side-long jam "Whipping Post," featuring a relentless barrage of hot bluesy solos. The album's opener, "Statesboro Blues," is another Duane Allman bottleneck tour de force. Betts shines on "You Don't Love Me" in an extended solo that climaxes with a display of amazingly fast picking using a basic blues scale (actually, if Duane hadn't been at the peak of his popularity at the time, this solo would probably have made Betts more famous). *At Fillmore East* ranked as one of the best live recordings of the decade, and over time it has come to be regarded as an essential album for every guitar fan.

That fall the group started work on their fourth album, completing tracks like "Stand Back," "Blue Sky," and "Little Martha," a lovely acoustic duet that is Duane Allman's only original composition with the band. Midway through the sessions, in October 1971, the band went on vacation. Duane was killed during the hiatus from a motorcycle accident. (It was a little over a year after Jimi Hendrix had died.) The Allman Brothers Band had lost their 24-year-old guiding light and strongest musician, but decided to keep on playing together despite the loss. They released *Eat a Peach* in the spring of 1972, an album that contains Duane Allman's last three tracks with the band, plus a few Fillmore East leftovers, including "Mountain Jam." It brilliantly documents the artistic precision of the Allman/Betts guitar team, which later influenced a whole generation of southern players.

Instead of getting another guitar player to fill the void, the band added a second keyboardist to the lineup. Tragically, they also had to add a new bassist, to replace Berry Oakley, who died a year after Duane Allman in a strangely similar motorcycle accident. In 1973 the group released *Brothers and Sisters*, which gave it a huge hit with "Ramblin' Man." Although guitarist Les Dudek appears on the track playing harmony, "Ramblin' Man" contains Dickey Betts' greatest solo, which mixes a melodic sensibility and proficiency with the blues into one magnificent improvisation. Another Betts high spot is "Jessica," an upbeat instrumental that has a typically tasteful and engaging break.

This, however, was to be the commercial peak of the post-Duane Allman lineup of the Allman Brothers Band. In 1975 they released an uninspired record called *Win, Lose, or Draw*, and amid drug scandals, personality clashes, and general apathy, the band folded the next year. After a three-year hiatus, they regrouped in 1979 and issued a relatively popular reunion album called *Enlightened Rogues*, but the music didn't match the fire of *Brothers and Sisters*, much less the earlier Duane Allman days. This version of the band, which included guitarist Dan Toler as Betts' new sparring partner, enjoyed a brief renewal of creative energy, but in 1981 they called it quits yet again.

Apparently, however, a good band can't be kept down. The interest in classic rock during the late 1980s and early 1990s spawned the release of several vintage Allman recordings, including the multi-disc boxed set *Dreams*, *Live at Ludlow Garage 1970*, and the entire Fillmore East shows with Duane Allman, now called *The Fillmore Concerts*. Furthermore, former Dickey Betts Band guitarist Warren Haynes joined the latest incarnation of the Allman Brothers, and their popularity once again skyrocketed, especially on the live circuit (◗ Roots Rock II).

Allman Joys, *Early Allman* (Dial, 1973). **Hour Glass** [on Liberty], *The Hour Glass* (1967), *Power of Love* (1968). **Allman Brothers Band (1969–81)** [on Capricorn], *The Allman Brothers Band* (1969), *Idlewild South* (1970), *At Fillmore East* (1971•), *Eat a Peach* (1972•), *Beginnings* (1973), *Brothers and Sisters* (1973), *Win, Lose, or Draw* (1975), *Wipe the Windows—Check the Oil—Dollar Gas* (1976•), *Enlightened Rogues* (1979), *Reach for the Sky* (Arista, 1980), *Brothers of the Road* (Arista, 1981), *Best of the Allman Brothers Band* (Polydor, 1981), *Dreams* (Polydor, 1989•), *Live at Ludlow Garage 1970* (Polygram, 1990•). **Duane Allman** [on Capricorn], *Duane Allman, An Anthology* (1972), *Duane Allman, An Anthology, Vol. 2* (1974). **Dickey Betts**, *Highway Call* (Capricorn, 1974). **Dickey Betts & Great Southern**, *Dickey Betts and Great Southern* (Arista, 1977), *Atlanta's Burning Down* (Arista, 1978). **The Dickey Betts Band**, *Pattern Disruptive* (Epic, 1988).

Albums featuring Duane Allman: **Wilson Pickett,** *Hey Jude* (Atlantic, 1968). **Aretha Franklin** [on Atlantic], *Soul '69* (1969), *This Girl's in Love with You* (1970), *Spirit in the Dark* (1970). **King Curtis,** *Instant Groove* (Atco, 1969). **Boz Scaggs,** *Boz Scaggs* (Atlantic, 1969). **Clarence Carter,** *The Dynamic Clarence Carter* (Atlantic, 1969). **Arthur Conley,** *More Sweet Soul* (Atco, 1969). **John Hammond,** *Southern Fried* (Atlantic, 1969). **Otis Rush,** *Mourning in the Morning* (Cotillion, 1969). **Barry Goldberg** [on Buddah], *Two Jews Blues* (c. 1969•), *Blasts from the Past* (1971). **The Duck and the Bear,** "Goin' up the Country" [single] (Atlantic, 1969). **Johnny Jenkins,** *Ton-Ton Macoute* (Atco, 1970). **Ronnie Hawkins** [on Cotillion], *Ronnie Hawkins* (1970), *The Hawk* (1971). **Laura Nyro,** *Christmas and the Beads of Sweat* (Columbia, 1970). **Lulu,** *New Routes* (Atco, 1970). **Delaney & Bonnie** [on Atco except where noted], *To Delaney from Bonnie* (1970), *Motel Shot* (1971), *D&B Together* (Columbia, 1972). **Derek & the Dominos,** *Layla and Other Assorted Love Songs* (Atco, 1970). **Various Artists,** *The First Great Rock Festivals of the Seventies* (Columbia, 1971•). **Herbie Mann,** *Push Push* (Embryo, 1971). **Sam Samudio,** *Sam—Hard and Heavy* (Atlantic, 1971). **Cowboy,** *5'll Getcha Ten* (Capricorn, 1971).

Recordings featuring Dickey Betts: **Various Artists,** *Mar y Sol* (Atco, 1973•). **Various Artists,** *Volunteer Jam* (Capricorn, 1976•). **Various Artists,** *Hotels, Motels, and Roadshows* (Capricorn, 1978•). **Don Johnson,** *Heartbeat* (Epic, 1986).

Lynyrd Skynyrd

Gary Rossington
Born: *December 4, 1951, in Jacksonville, Florida*
Main Guitar: *'59 Gibson Les Paul Custom*

Ed King
Born: *September 14, 1949, in Los Angeles*
Main Guitar: *Fender Stratocaster*

Allen Collins
Born: *1952, in Florida*
Died: *January 23, 1990*
Main Guitar: *Gibson Explorer*

Steve Gaines
Born: *1949, in Florida*
Died: *October 20, 1977*
Main Guitar: *Fender Stratocaster*

After the Allman Brothers Band's eventual decline in the mid seventies, the southern rock flag was carried highest and proudest by Lynyrd Skynyrd, a septet out of Jacksonville, Florida, that built its reputation on an unprecedented three lead guitar players. Instead of the Allman Brothers' R&B-flavored numbers and instrumentals of jazz and blues derivation, Lynyrd Skynyrd played guitar-heavy rock that paid homage to the raw purity of blues and country, as well as British heavy rockers like Led Zeppelin, the Jeff Beck Group, and Free. Leading the band was frontman and vocalist Ronnie Van Zant, a barefooted belter with a knack for lyrics full of crisp southern imagery, which initially paved the way for Skynyrd's widespread popularity with fans and critics alike.

Lynyrd Skynyrd was formed in the early seventies with Van Zant, a trio of hot guitarists—Allen Collins, Gary Rossington, and Ed King—plus a keyboardist, and a powerful rhythm section. Several of the band members had gone to high school together, and the name was chosen as a parody of their gym teacher. After jumping on the southern bar circuit, the band was discovered by Al Kooper, who helped get them signed to the MCA label. Lynyrd Skynyrd's first album, *Pronounced Leh-nerd Skin-nerd* (1973), cracked the Top 30 and produced their anthem "Freebird" (a tribute to Duane Allman), which is filled with extended guitar solos and intricate guitar interplay. Rarely had a band shown such complete guitar prowess on a debut album.

Skynyrd landed the opening spot on the Who's "Quadrophenia" tour in 1973, often receiving standing ovations for their rousing stage work and the inevitable show stopper, "Freebird." In 1974 the band captured the commercial market with the hit single "Sweet Home Alabama," a funky rocker with poignant lyrics and several fine Strat solos by Ed King. With this breakthrough, the band's following increased steadily through the release of their next two albums, *Nuthin' Fancy* (1975) and *Gimme Back My Bullets* (1976), which was recorded with only two guitarists, since King had quit the band as a result of exhaustion and drug use (King had also been on the road longer than the others: he was the guitarist for Strawberry Alarm Clock, whose "Incense and Peppermints" hit big in 1967).

A few months later, Lynyrd Skynyrd broke into the national spotlight with a live recording, *One More from the Road*. Like the Allman Brothers' *At Fillmore East* set, this record shows the band in their best playing environment—the concert stage. Recorded at Atlanta's Fox Theater, the album presents all the group's best songs with an extra kick of live adrenaline and guitar energy from Collins, Rossington, and new guitarist Steve Gaines. Scorching guitar solos and heavy rhythm grooves abound, especially on tracks like "Mr. Saturday Night Special," "Gimme Three Steps," and the swinging "T for Texas." As one might expect, the peak of this live extravaganza is the finale, an epic 11-minute-plus version of "Freebird." Starting with melancholy slide work by Rossington, "Freebird" elevates in tension until it explodes into an all-out guitar melee featuring frenzied solos from Collins and Gaines. Right up until the final power chord, the six-string intensity generated by these guitarists is spectacular, and it still stands as one of the finest record-

ed moments of southern rock guitar.

Firmly entrenched in the forefront of southern rock, Lynyrd Skynyrd moved on in triumph, succeeding the million-selling *One More from the Road* with another fine album, *Street Survivors* (1977). FM radio stations regularly played selected cuts from the album, including guitar-based numbers like "What's Your Name," "I Know a Little" (with a wickedly fast intro lick by Gaines), and their grim anti-drug anthem "That Smell," which ends with all three guitarists trading solos like hot potatoes.

On October 20, 1977, just three days after the album's release, tragedy struck Lynyrd Skynyrd. On a post-concert airplane flight to Baton Rouge, Louisiana, their aircraft suffered engine failure and crashed into a swamp near McComb, Mississippi. Ronnie Van Zant and Steve Gaines, along with back-up singer Cassie Gaines and several members of the crew, were killed in the accident, while the surviving members of the band were severely injured. With the loss of their leader, Van Zant, the remaining members had no other choice but to put an end to Lynyrd Skynyrd, much to the heartbreak of millions of Skynyrd fans nationwide (the album cover for *Street Survivors* was also changed, as the original had featured a photograph of Van Zant and Gaines where they appeared to be on fire).

In 1980 several of the Lynyrd Skynyrd musicians returned to active playing in the Rossington-Collins Band, which was led by the band's guitar duo. But after a pair of moderate-selling albums, they realized that the era of the southern rocker was indeed past and quietly broke up.

With the notable exception of the Allman Brothers Band (and possibly the Outlaws), Lynyrd Skynyrd is considered the best southern rock band ever to emerge from below the Mason-Dixon line. In addition to their gritty songs about life and hardships in the South, they had Ronnie Van Zant's powerful vocals and a trio of accomplished lead guitarists who stoked up the band's music with their blues, country, and metal-inspired guitar work. Very few Lynyrd Skynyrd tracks were without a solo spot, and the bulk of them were of a genuinely high quality, exhibiting a wealth of technique, aggression, and, most of all, emotion.

Interestingly, from the ranks of Lynyrd Skynyrd's guitar players, no one single player emerged as a guitar star in his own right, as Duane Allman did in the Allman Brothers Band. This keys into the fact that Lynyrd Skynyrd's music was tightly arranged, not jam-oriented like the Allmans, and this tight ensemble feel was readily apparent on all their recordings. Despite the deep loss felt by the rock community after their 1977 air disaster, the music of Lynyrd Skynyrd (and their guitar players) was still alive and a stirring part of the southern rock tradition. In 1987 the group's survivors—

Lynyrd Skynyrd: Allen Collins, Ronnie Van Zant, Gary Rossington

including original guitarists Gary Rossington and Ed King (Collins was crippled in a car accident and died in 1990)—toured America in a tribute to the tenth anniversary of the crash. Despite tragedies that would have sealed the fate of most bands, Skynyrd is still recording and performing today.

Lynyrd Skynyrd [on MCA except where noted], *Pronounced Leh-nerd Skin-nerd* (1974), *Second Helping* (1974), *Nuthin' Fancy* (1975), *Gimme Back My Bullets* (1976), *One More from the Road* (1976●), *Street Survivors* (1977), *Skynyrd's First…and Last* (1978), *Gold & Platinum* (1979), *Best of the Rest* (1982), *Legend* (1987●), *Southern by the Grace of God* (1988●), *Skynyrd's Innyrds* (1989), *Lynyrd Skynyrd 1991* (Atlantic, 1991), *Lynyrd Skynyrd* [boxed set] (1991), *The Last Rebel* (Atlantic, 1993), *Endangered Species* (Capricorn, 1994). **Rossington-Collins Band** [on MCA], *Anytime, Anyplace, Anywhere* (1980), *This Is the Way* (1981). **Allen Collins Band,** *Here, There & Back* (MCA, 1983). **Rossington** [on Atlantic], *Return to the Scene of the Crime* (1986), *No Exit* (1988). **Steve Gaines,** *One in the Sun* (MCA, 1988).

The Outlaws

Hughie Thomasson

B o r n : *August 13, 1952, in Buchanan, Virginia*
M a i n G u i t a r : *'74 Fender Stratocaster*

Billy Jones

B o r n : *November 20, 1949*
D i e d : *1995, in Florida*
M a i n G u i t a r : *Gibson Les Paul Custom*

One of the three main forces in seventies southern rock was "the Florida Guitar Army," better known as the Outlaws. This Tampa-based outfit had a triple-guitar front line that rivaled, and at times even surpassed, Lynyrd Skynyrd's for pure rock 'n' roll energy and hundred-notes-per-second guitar excitement. Led by pickers Hughie Thomasson and Billy Jones, the Outlaws were decidedly axe-oriented (and even more so after 1977, when rhythm guitarist Henry Paul was replaced with yet another lead player, Freddie Salem). Not content to just grind out solo after solo, the band also showcased close-harmony vocals and catchy rock tunes, including the FM staples "Green Grass and High Tides," "There Goes Another Love Song," and "Hurry Sundown."

In the early seventies, the Outlaws rocked through the Tampa bar scene until they landed a recording contract with Arista records in 1975. The band hit gold with their first album, *The Outlaws*, propelled by the guitar onslaught in the single "Green Grass and High Tides," a 10-minute epic full of Thomasson's and Jones' raw, Claptonesque solos. Just as "Freebird" became Lynyrd Skynyrd's guitar anthem, so did "Green Grass and High Tides" become the Outlaws' theme song and traditional concert show-stopper. In addition to releasing a strong debut, the band secured opening spots on tours by the Who and the Rolling Stones, which greatly increased their fol-

lowing of guitar-hungry fans.

Following their heralded debut came such albums as *Lady in Waiting* (1976), *Hurry Sundown* (1977), and, probably their finest work, the double live set *Bring It Back Alive* (1978), which presents lead guitar-drenched versions of "Lover Boy," "Prisoner," and, of course, "Green Grass and High Tides." Thomasson's blazing Strat solos are ubiquitous on the disc, but it may be Jones who steals the show with his scintillating Les Paul solos. Blending a rich, fat tone with blazingly fast pentatonics and a good ear for melody, Jones shows his ultra-soulful side on "Freeborn Man," while his first break in "Stick Around for Some Rock and Roll" is nothing short of thermonuclear.

After a pair of lukewarm studio albums, the Outlaws were again in the guitar spotlight in 1981 with a near-hit cover of "Ghost Riders in the Sky," which had been cleverly extended to include a flaming volley of guitar solos between Thomasson, Jones, and Salem. Jones left the band soon after (eventually returning to college and getting a degree in mathematics), and as rock tastes shifted towards power pop, the Outlaws' fan-base dried up, as it did for many southern acts.

Unlike Lynyrd Skynyrd, the Outlaws' lyrics contained few hardcore glimpses into the heart of southern culture and, musically, they did not even attempt to duplicate the complex instrumental exploits of the Allman Brothers. Instead, the Outlaws played simple, straight-to-the-heart rock 'n' roll with few embellishments, but with a meaningful commitment to the genre. What they lacked in depth, they more than made up for in fire-breathing guitar solos and an instinctual feel for good, foot-stompin' rock 'n' roll. Their "Guitar Army" label was surely no misnomer.

The Outlaws [on Arista except where noted], *The Outlaws* (1975), *Lady in Waiting* (1976), *Hurry Sundown* (1977), *Bring It Back Alive* (1978●), *Playin' to Win* (1978), *In the Eye of the Storm* (1979), *Ghost Riders* (1980), *Los Hombres Malo* (1982), *Greatest Hits of the Outlaws/High Tides Forever* (1982●), *On the Run* (Raw Power, 1986), *Soldiers of Fortune* (Pasha, 1986), *Hittin' the Road—Live!* (BBI, 1993●), *Diablo Canyon* (BBI, 1994). **Henry Paul Band** [on Atlantic], *Grey Ghost* (1979), *Feel the Heat* (1980), *Anytime* (1981). **Freddie Salem & the Wildcats,** *Freddie Salem & the Wildcats* (CBS, 1982).

Marshall Tucker Band

Toy Caldwell

B o r n : *1948, in Spartanburg, South Carolina*
D i e d : *February 25, 1993*
M a i n G u i t a r : *Gibson Les Paul Standard*

As lead guitarist for the Marshall Tucker Band, Toy Caldwell was among the most distinctive soloists of the entire southern rock school. Eschewing the traditional plectrum or "pick" approach, Caldwell developed an interesting picking style using his thumb to create fast, melodic lines on his Gibson Les Paul. Jazz players are familiar with the legendary Wes Montgomery's proficient use of his thumb for picking, but few rock guitarists have successfully used it.

Caldwell's earliest guitar education came from his father, a semi-professional country guitarist who also never used a pick. After he started playing, Caldwell soaked up influences from country pickers like Chet Atkins and Hank Garland (who was also a renowned jazz player), bluesman B.B. King, and the Beatles. During the late sixties, Caldwell served in Vietnam, and upon his return, he joined a band started by his bass-playing brother, Tommy, which evolved into the Marshall Tucker Band. Eventually Marshall Tucker was signed to the Capricorn label (home of the Allman Brothers), and they released their first album, *Marshall Tucker Band*, in the summer of 1973.

Cruising along on the collective strengths of the band (which included rhythm guitarist George McCorkle), the Marshall Tucker Band's debut set was a commercial success, mostly on the strength of the Toy Caldwell composition "Can't You See." For the next few years, the band rode high on the wave of popularity that southern rock enjoyed during the mid seventies, scoring a long string of best-selling albums, including *A New Life*, *Searchin' for a Rainbow*, and the platinum *Carolina Dreams*.

Throughout all the early Marshall Tucker albums, Caldwell's solos are uniformly dazzling, blending fast jazzy phrases with a plethora of country-styled licks. Among the best are "Can't You See," "Heard It in a Love Song," and "Running Like the Wind." Perhaps the apex of Caldwell's recorded guitar work is on the 1974 *Where We All Belong* set, notably during "24 Hours at a Time," a nearly 14-minute-long piece in which he conjures up a solo that makes effective use of variations in volume and tone, quivering wrist vibrato, and swift lines via left-hand hammer-ons. This is a must-hear track for fans of southern rock, as is Texas swing-inspired "Ramblin' on My Mind" from the same disc.

While Caldwell and the Marshall Tucker Band were an integral part of the southern rock sound, they retained their own musical personality by playing more to the country side of the movement. Most Marshall Tucker songs could have been country hits in their own right, mixing just the right amounts of rock, pop, jazz, and blues into their hybrid sound. In this same way, Toy Caldwell chose a more individualistic country- and jazz-styled sound in his guitar playing than most of his southern rock peers, most of whom assimilated hard rock values from Eric Clapton and Jeff Beck. Besides his influences, Toy Caldwell's creative thumb-picking technique and a soloing style that meshed speed and melody contributed strongly to his special southern rock sound. The guitarist left the Marshall Tucker Band (which had foundered since Tommy's death in a car accident in 1980) in 1985, but died of natural causes in 1993 just as he was getting a solo career off the ground.

Marshall Tucker Band [on Capricorn except where noted], *Marshall Tucker Band* (1973), *A New Life* (1974), *Where We All Belong* (1974•), *Searchin' for a Rainbow* (1975), *Long Hard Ride* (1976), *Carolina Dreams* (1977), *Together Forever* (1978), *Greatest Hits* (1978), *Running Like the Wind* (Warner Bros., 1979), *Tenth* (Warner Bros., 1980), *Dedicated* (Warner Bros., 1981), *Tuckerized* (Warner Bros., 1982), *Greetings from South Carolina* (Warner Bros., 1983), *Just Us* (Warner Bros., 1983). **Toy Caldwell,** *Toy Caldwell* (Cabin Fever, 1992).

Recordings featuring Toy Caldwell: **Charlie Daniels Band,** *Nightrider* (Kama Sutra, 1975). **Various Artists,** *Volunteer Jam* (Capricorn, 1976•). **Various Artists,** *Hotels, Motels, and Roadshows* (Capricorn, 1978•).

Charlie Daniels Band

Charlie Daniels

B o r n : *October 28, 1938, in Wilmington, North Carolina*
M a i n G u i t a r : *Gibson Les Paul Standard*

Tom Crain

B o r n : *c. 1950*
M a i n G u i t a r : *Gibson Les Paul Standard*

As certified "rebels," the Charlie Daniels Band were among the leaders of the southern rock movement. They mined the Top 40 with a string of hit albums, including *Saddle Tramp* in 1976 and *Million Mile Reflections* in 1979, and a best-selling 1979 hit single called "The Devil Went Down to Georgia." The Daniels band features their bulky namesake on lead guitar, as well as picker Tom Crain, both of whom contributed uptempo Allman/Betts-styled guitar harmonies and bluesy solos to many of the CDB's hit recordings. Their guitar playing was often overshadowed by the use of a fiddle on the band's more popular offerings.

Although their recorded output peaked in the early 1980s, the band continues to perform. Daniels also sponsors the annual "Volunteer Jam" concert in Nashville, which features many of the region's top rock and country performers.

Charlie Daniels Band [on Epic except where noted], *Honey in the Rock* (Kama Sutra, 1973), *Fire on the Mountain* (Kama Sutra, 1974), *Nightrider* (Kama Sutra, 1975), *Saddle Tramp* (1976), *High Lonesome* (1976), *Midnight Wind* (1977), *Million Mile Reflections* (1979), *Full Moon* (1980), *Windows* (1982), *A Decade of Hits* (1983), *Homesick Heroes* (1988), *Simple Man* (1989), *Renegade* (1991).

Recordings featuring Charlie Daniels: **Various Artists,** *Volunteer Jam* (Capricorn, 1976•), *Volunteer Jam VI* (Epic, 1980•), *Volunteer Jam VII* (Epic, 1981•).

Molly Hatchet

Dave Hlubek

Born: *1951, in Jacksonville, Florida*
Main Guitars: *Custom Hamer solidbodies, custom "Flying P"*

Duane Roland

Born: *December 3, 1952, in Jeffersonville, Indiana*
Main Guitars: *Gibson Les Paul and reverse Firebird*

Steve Holland

Born: *1954, in Dothan, Alabama*
Main Guitar: *Fender Stratocaster*

A late entry into the southern rock field was Molly Hatchet, a sextet that came as close to pure heavy metal as any top southern group ever got. Fronted by three lead guitarists who resembled British metalers more than rock 'n' roll cowboys, Hatchet created a handful of aggressive albums with distinctly macho names like *Take No Prisoners, No Guts...No Glory*, and their most popular recording, *Flirtin' with Disaster* (1979), gathering a large following of male metal fans in the process. *Flirtin's* high-energy title cut was a sizable FM hit that let their capable lead guitarists, Dave Hlubek and Duane Roland, have a field day with recycled Clapton, Page, and Allman licks. Molly Hatchet's only other distinction from other southern rock bands was that they played louder and used more distortion on their guitars. But as southern rock hit its nadir in the 1980s, so too did the band's popularity. It was not able to make a true metal crossover, and its fortunes waned quickly after *Flirtin' with Disaster*.

Molly Hatchet [on Epic], *Molly Hatchet* (1978), *Flirtin' with Disaster* (1979), *Beatin' the Odds* (1980), *Take No Prisoners* (1981), *No Guts...No Glory* (1983), *The Deed Is Done* (1984), *Double Trouble Live* (1985•).

.38 Special

Jeff Carlisi

Born: *July 15, 1952, in Yonkers, New York*
Main Guitar: *Custom Explorer-style*

Don Barnes

Born: *December 3, 1954, in Jacksonville, Florida*
Main Guitar: *Gibson Les Paul Junior*

Donnie Van Zant

Born: *c. 1950, in Jacksonville, Florida*

W ith the arrival of the 1980s and the trend towards more electronic rock bands, many stalwarts of southern rock were left without an audience and lost much of the widespread popularity they had enjoyed throughout the seventies. Only one band really managed to survive into the eighties as a name-brand commercial success: .38 Special.

The band, which was formed by Donnie Van Zant, the younger brother of Lynyrd Skynyrd's Ronnie Van Zant, played standard-fare, barroom southern rock that was not unique enough to find its way out of the din of hundreds of other similar-sounding bands. Early on, however, .38 Special probably realized that the southern rock sound couldn't go on forever, and by their third album (*Wild-Eyed Southern Boys*, in 1981), they got haircuts and began moving their music in a mainstream direction, largely influenced by the techno-pop music of the Cars. This redirection soon paid off when they scored a hit with "Hold on Loosely."

The band's lead guitarists, Jeff Carlisi and Don Barnes, adapted their blues- and hard-rock-based styles into a more melodic format and added brief but exciting solos in their string of eighties hits, including "Teacher, Teacher" and "Somebody Like You." .38 Special's hit "Caught up in You" remains the band's guitar peak on record, and it was Carlisi who added the tasteful blues licks, octave runs, and high-register repeated riffs to the song's rideout. It still ranks as one of the most memorable FM leads of 1982, a year notable for its lack of good guitar parts on commercial radio.

.38 Special [on A&M except where noted], *.38 Special* (1977), *Rockin' into the Night* (1979), *Wild-Eyed Southern Boys* (1981), *Special Forces* (1982), *Tour de Force* (1983), *Strength in Numbers* (1986), *Flashback* (1987•), *Rock & Roll Strategy* (1988), *Bone against Steel* (Charisma, 1991).

CHAPTER EIGHTEEN

Eclectic Electrics

Strange Brew

Consisting of components from diverse sources or styles.

That's the dictionary definition of the word *eclectic*. In rock 'n' roll, there are several important guitarists who chose not to confine themselves to one particular style or genre of guitar playing, but rather found their niche in assimilating different styles. Since many of these players cross musical boundaries seemingly at whim and draw influences from a myriad of global musical styles, they are referred to as the eclectic guitarists of rock.

Names of eclectic guitarists are not as easily arrived at as are those in the heavy metal or even the glam rock genres. However, they are among the world's best and most esteemed players: Carlos Santana, Ry Cooder, Jeff Baxter, David Lindley, and Lowell George. These and a handful of other guitarists have mixed rock with everything from jazz to country to blues to R&B to reggae to Latin rhythms. To a certain extent, every guitarist who utilizes two or more different musical styles is eclectic, but these exceptionally versatile rock guitarists embody the eclectic guitar label because, in essence, their styles are *all* styles.

Santana

Carlos Santana

Born: *July 20, 1947, in Autlan, Mexico*
Main Guitars: *Gibson SG, Yamaha SG2000, custom Paul Reed Smith*

Towards the end of the psychedelic era, another style of rock 'n' roll emerged from San Francisco. It synthesized musical elements from the Afro-Cuban tradition, American blues and jazz, and straight-ahead rock 'n' roll. The sound was soon dubbed "Latin rock," and its main proponent was an aggressive, percussion-laden sextet called Santana, so named for its lead guitarist, Carlos Santana. The son of a mariachi musician, Santana started out playing the violin but soon dropped it in favor of the guitar. One of his earliest professional guitar experiences was as a young teenager when he earned a living playing in strip joints around Tijuana. Eventually, Santana discovered American blues guitarists like B.B. King, Jimmy Reed, and Otis Rush and began voraciously learning blues-style guitar. In 1962 he moved to San Francisco and, after a few years, formed the Santana Blues Band.

The Santana Blues Band's unique musical twist came when they added congas and timbales to their R&B sound and began playing this fiery Latin rock in local clubs. The band's popularity soared, and by the end of 1968, the still-unsigned band was headlining at the famed Fillmore Auditorium. At Woodstock the rest of the world finally saw what Carlos Santana and his band could really do (the Blues Band suffix was dropped prior to Woodstock). "Soul Sacrifice," a song with pulsating rhythms, drum solo, and Santana's blues-based guitar solos, earned the band a standing ovation and a prominent spot in the film documentary of Woodstock. In late 1969 the first Santana album, *Santana*, was released, earning critical praise and, rare at the time, platinum status. Santana, the band and the guitarist, had clearly arrived.

After the incredible success Santana had with both their appearance at Woodstock and their first album, the band followed up with *Abraxas*, an album that yielded two hit singles, "Oye Como Va" and a cover of Fleetwood Mac's "Black Magic Woman." This 1970 album (named after a deity in Herman Hesse's 1919 novel *Demian*) is a brilliant example of the band's conga-fired rock 'n' roll and Santana's fiery guitar work. Another side that Carlos reveals here is his talent for sensitive ballad playing, which he demonstrates on the beautiful "Samba Pa Ti." Playing off a

Carlos Santana

Imaj7–IIm7 chord progression, he plays melodic solos that reveal his jazz influence, and fuzz- and echo-tinged blues licks.

Santana recorded and toured steadily throughout the seventies, releasing an eclectic array of albums ranging from the hard-rocking *Santana III*, with teenager Neal Schon (♦) joining the group on second lead guitar, to the acclaimed fusion outing *Caravanserai* in 1972. Carlos also participated in an explosive jazz-rock union with Mahavishnu John McLaughlin (♦) on *Love, Devotion, Surrender*. The album explores both guitarists' very public pursuit of their spiritual selves.

After a period of straying from their Latin-rock roots in the mid seventies, the group returned with a vengeance to the percussion-driven rock that made them famous. A series of albums later in the decade culminated with the superb half-live, half-studio album *Moonflower* in 1977. In addition to the band's blistering Latin-rock, the album also includes the spiritualistic jazz-pop of "Transcendence," "Dance Sister Dance," and a blazing fusion workout called "Zulu." On a remake of the Zombies' 1965 hit "She's Not There," Santana's guitar solo is doused with heavy distortion, echo, and wah-wah effects, and in the song's second break, his guitar is so beefed up with effects and volume that it seems on the verge of exploding. The band's updated live version of "Soul Sacrifice" makes the song's predecessors look pale in comparison, including the Woodstock version. Carlos' finest guitar moment on *Moonflower* is his signature tune, the lilting Latin ballad "Europa" (first done on *Amigos* in 1976). Like Clapton's "Layla" or Hendrix's "Voodoo Child (Slight Return)," "Europa" is Santana's personal blues. Using a tonal palette of light distortion, wah-wah, and Leslie speaker effects, Santana fuses rapid scalar runs, wah-wah bursts, and a wide range of fretboard dynamics to create one of his most soulful leads ever.

Outside of his work with the group, Carlos Santana has had a noted solo career, occasionally playing solo concerts and also cutting several nonrock albums. These include *The Swing of Delight*, with modern jazz masters Herbie Hancock, Wayne Shorter, Ron Carter, and Tony Williams, and the blues-oriented *Havana Moon*, with guest Jimmie Vaughan. In 1995, Santana hit the road for a U.S. tour, sharing the bill with fellow guitar legend Jeff Beck.

Santana [on Columbia], *Santana* (1969), *Abraxas* (1970), *Santana III* (1971), *Caravanserai* (1972), *Welcome* (1973), *Greatest Hits* (1974), *Lotus* (1975•), *Borboletta* (1976), *Festival* (1976), *Amigos* (1976), *Moonflower* (1977•), *Inner Secrets* (1978), *Marathon* (1979), *Zebop!* (1981), *Shango* (1982), *Beyond Appearances* (1985), *Freedom* (1987), *Viva Santana* (1988•), *Spirits Dancing in the Flesh* (1990), *Milagro* (Polydor, 1992), *Sacred Fire: Live in South America* (Polydor, 1993•), *Best Of* [boxed set] (1995). **Carlos Santana** [on Columbia], *Oneness/Silver Dreams—Golden Reality* (1979), *Swing of Delight* (1980), *Havana Moon* (1983), *Blues for Salvador* (1987). **Carlos Santana & Buddy Miles,** *Carlos Santana & Buddy Miles! Live!* (Columbia, 1972•). **Carlos Santana & John McLaughlin,** *Love, Devotion, Surrender* (Columbia, 1973). **Carlos Santana & Alice Coltrane,** *Illuminations* (Columbia, 1974).

Recordings featuring Carlos Santana: **Mike Bloomfield & Al Kooper,** *The Live Adventures of Mike Bloomfield & Al Kooper* (Columbia, 1969•).

Various Artists, *Woodstock* (Cotillion, 1970•). **Narada Michael Walden** [on Atlantic], *Garden of Love Light* (1976), *Awakening* (1979). **Giants,** *Giants* (MCA, 1978). **Various Artists,** *California Jam 2* (Columbia, 1978•). **Boz Scaggs,** *Middle Man* (Columbia, 1980). **Aretha Franklin,** *Who's Zoomin' Who* (Arista, 1985). **Clyde Criner,** *Behind the Sun* (RCA/Novus, 1988). **John Lee Hooker,** *The Healer* (Chameleon, 1989), *Mr. Lucky* (Pointblank, 1991).

Little Feat

Lowell George

B o r n : *April 13, 1945, in Hollywood, California*
D i e d : *June 29, 1979*
M a i n G u i t a r : *Fender Stratocaster*

Paul Barrere

B o r n : *July 3, 1948, in Burbank, California*
M a i n G u i t a r : *Gibson ES-335*

Next to Duane Allman, George Harrison, and Ry Cooder, Lowell George stands out as one of rock's premier slide guitarists. During his tenure with Little Feat from 1969 to 1979 and in countless session recordings, George's hellacious bottleneck solos gave rock fans some of the most tasteful guitar work of the period, ranging from blues and folk to New Orleans R&B and rock. His style also incorporated musical elements from Latin, Celtic, Asian, and a variety of other global sources. Besides being a master slideman, he excelled in singing, songwriting, and production, all of which he contributed to albums by artists as diverse as John Sebastian, the Meters, Carly Simon, Chico Hamilton, Robert Palmer, the Grateful Dead, and, of course, Little Feat.

After playing in such early bands as the Factory, the Standells, and the Seeds, Lowell George hooked up with Frank Zappa's Mothers of Invention in the late sixties. He appeared with the Mothers briefly on albums like *Cruising with Ruben & the Jets* (1968) and *Weasels Ripped My Flesh* (1970) before finally deciding to concentrate his musical energies completely on his own band, Little Feat. Little Feat's first album, *Little Feat*, came out in 1971. Although it was favorably received by critics, it fell short in the sales department. Their 1972 follow-up set, *Sailin' Shoes*, received the same treatment, and it was clear that the band would be headed for cult status rather than recognition as a headlining rock act.

For the third Little Feat album, Paul Barrere was brought in on second lead guitar, as was a new bass player and percussionist. With Barrere's phase-shifted rhythm work and single-note leads, George was free to concentrate on his slide playing, which was evident on Little Feat's superb 1973 effort *Dixie Chicken*. Over the top of the title cut's funky groove, the guitarist accents his own vocals with tart slide fills and solo licks. Other fine slide moments on *Dixie Chicken* are on the bouncy rocker "Two Trains" and "Roll 'um Easy," a lilting ballad accentuated by

George's acoustic slide. Despite the overall quality of *Dixie Chicken*, it too achieved little success, and the members of Little Feat broke up to pursue other musical projects.

During this period George immersed himself in session work (as did other Little Feat members), but the following year, the band was back together to give it one more try. The result of this reunion was *Feats Don't Fail Me Now*, which finally cracked the pop album charts and established Little Feat as one of the most original bands of the mid seventies, with its broad blues, funk, and jazz-infused rock. Among Lowell George's slide forays on *Feats Don't Fail Me Now* are cuts like "Rock and Roll Doctor," "Oh Atlanta," and especially "Cold Cold Cold/Triple Face Boogie," where the slide master finishes up his bottleneck break with a piercing slide run over the pickups of his trademark Fender Stratocaster.

Little Feat followed up *Feats Don't Fail Me Now* with an album curiously called *The Last Record Album* (1975), to which George only contributed three songs. The guitarist had even less input on *Time Loves a Hero*, in 1977. Hepatitis and other health problems were cited for the decline of Lowell George's participation in Little Feat. After a live 1978 album and sessions toward a new studio record, the group disbanded again in April 1979. Around this same time, George put out his first solo LP, *Thanks, I'll Eat It Here*, which broke no new ground but provided the basis for a successful solo concert tour across the country. Unfortunately, Lowell George was never able to finish the 1979 tour: on the morning after a particularly good show at the Lissner Auditorium in Washington, D.C., in June of that year, George suffered a heart attack and died. Later, his death was partially attributed to a serious drug problem.

Even though this eclectic slide guitarist's life was cut short, he left a vast legacy of great rock guitar playing in recordings with Little Feat and the many other acts he worked with in the studio. Unlike Duane Allman's high-volume slide style, Lowell George's bottleneck work was more economical and supportive, although he could burst through the song at any given moment with energetic slide licks. And unlike Allman, whose slide solos were predominantly blues-oriented, George's leads used a wider palette of musical colors, assimilating folk and ethnic music from around the country and around the world into his guitar playing. Even though his death cut short the potential for more slide innovation, Lowell George still took rock slide playing to heights that have rarely been scaled since.

Little Feat re-formed successfully in the late eighties with Barrere and newcomer Fred Tackett on guitars.

Little Feat [on Warner Bros. except where noted], *Little Feat* (1971), *Sailin' Shoes* (1972), *Dixie Chicken* (1973), *Feats Don't Fail Me Now* (1974), *The Last Record Album* (1975), *Time Loves a Hero* (1977), *Waiting for Columbus* (1978●), *Down on the Farm* (1979), *Hoy Hoy!* (1981), *Let It Roll* (1988), *Representing the Mambo* (1990), *Shake Me Up* (Morgan Creek, 1991), *Ain't Had Enough Fun* (Zoo, 1995). **Lowell George,** *Thanks, I'll Eat It Here* (Warner Bros., 1979).

Recordings featuring Lowell George: **Frank Zappa & the Mothers of Invention,** *Cruising with Ruben & the Jets* (Verve, 1968), *Weasels Ripped My Flesh* (Bizarre, 1970). **John Cale,** *Paris 1919* (Warner Bros., 1973). **Bonnie Raitt** [on Warner Bros.], *Takin' My Time* (1973), *Streetlights* (1974). **Chico Hamilton,** *The Master* (Enterprise, 1973). **Robert Palmer** [on Island], *Sneakin' Sally through the Alley* (1974), *Pressure Drop* (1975).

Jeff "Skunk" Baxter

Born: *December 13, 1948, in Washington, D.C.*
Main Guitars: *Fender Telecaster, homemade Strat-style, Roland guitar synthesizer*

Jeff "Skunk" Baxter was—and is—one of rock's most accomplished soloists, a guitarist who reached the pinnacle of his visibility in the 1970s. Baxter is best known for his hot six-string work with Steely Dan in the early years of the decade and then with the Doobie Brothers, with whom he appeared from 1974 until their Grammy-sweeping pop album of 1979 *Minute by Minute*. (According to Baxter, the appellation "Skunk" was earned during a rather anti-social period of his youth; he also likes the way it sounds.) Aside from his work with these bands, Baxter has been heavily involved in studio work over the years, playing and recording with acts as strangely diverse as Donna Summer, Glen Campbell, Nazareth, Barbra Streisand, and Dolly Parton.

After playing with the psychedelic rock outfit Ultimate Spinach (with whom he recorded an album in 1968) and doing studio work, Baxter was asked to join Steely Dan in 1972. Instead of being a touring band, however, Steely Dan was essentially a studio group put together by songwriters Donald Fagen and Walter Becker. Sharing guitar duties in the band with the Skunk were bebopper Denny Dias and sessionman Elliott Randall (● Session Players), who provided occasional backup. All three guitarists appeared on the Dan's debut record, *Can't Buy a Thrill*, which includes the hit single "Do It Again" (featuring a wild electric sitar solo by Dias). The year 1973 saw the release of Steely Dan's second set, *Countdown to Ecstasy*, which didn't match the success of their first album, although it's full of great Baxter solos, especially "The Boston Rag" and "Bodhisattva." The latter tune has Baxter following Dias' hot bop break with a twangy second solo and a speedy flamenco-styled run for the finale. But Baxter's best moment on the album—possibly of his entire career—is the combined solo on "My Old School." Using a homemade Strat, the guitarist plays a series of leads throughout the song that reveal his mastery of rock attitude, deep funk, blues soul, country twang, and tasty jazz styles. The song contains four solo spots, but the final lead is a tour de force as Baxter throws in multi-string riffs, scalar and octave runs, power chords, and descending chromatic licks in what amounts to one of the most riveting solos of the decade.

After appearing with Steely Dan on the 1974 release *Pretzel Logic* (which contains a fiery Baxter break on "Night by Night"), the ace soloist left to join the Doobie Brothers, who had already broken into the big leagues of rock with a string of hit singles including "Long Train Runnin' "and "Black Water." He had guested on a few of the Doobies' earlier albums, but joined full-time on *Stampede* (1975), to which he contributed the solo on "Take Me in Your Arms." He also served as the replacement for original guitarist Tom Johnston, who had left the band due to health and drug problems. A successful greatest hits package was issued in 1976, followed in 1977 by *Livin' on the Fault Line.* This album shows the Doobies leaning toward a slicker L.A. pop sound, influenced by new member Michael McDonald's cool vocals and songwriting; still, Baxter burns over the funk-based vamp in "Wheel of Fortune." In late 1978 the Doobie Brothers released their most popular album, *Minute by Minute,* which topped the album charts until well into the next year. Dominated by McDonald's lush pop, the disc confirmed the Doobies' new direction toward less guitar-oriented music. This led to Baxter's departure from the band in the middle of 1979. Nevertheless, he was able to squeeze in some good solos on the disc, especially on the single "Dependin' on You" and "How Do the Fools Survive?"

After exiting the Doobies, Jeff Baxter steeped himself in studio work, especially in the area of production and commercial jingle sessions, primarily in Chicago. He became one of the first guitarists to get heavily involved with guitar synthesizers. Baxter played one of the earliest, if not actually the first, guitar synth solo on a hit record, on Donna Summer's "Bad Girls" of 1979. While many wonder why Baxter has never pursued a solo career, the guitarist himself has stated that his goal as a musician was not to be the star, but instead to be the "ultimate sideman." By the end of the seventies, there was little doubt he was.

Ultimate Spinach, *The Ultimate Spinach* (MGM, 1968). **Steely Dan** [on MCA], *Can't Buy a Thrill* (1972), *Countdown to Ecstasy* (1973), *Pretzel Logic* (1974), *Citizen Steely Dan* [boxed set] (1993). **Doobie Brothers** [on Warner Bros.], *The Captain and Me* (1973), *What Were Once Vices Are Now Habits* (1974), *Stampede* (1975), *Takin' It to the Streets* (1976), *Best of the Doobie Brothers* (1976), *Livin' on the Fault Line* (1977), *Minute by Minute* (1978), *Best of the Doobies, Vol. II* (1981).

Recordings featuring Jeff Baxter: **Buzzy Linhart,** *Buzzy* (c. 1971). **Carly Simon** [on Elektra], *Carly Simon* (1971), *Boys in the Trees* (1978). **Paul Bliss Band,** *Dinner with Raoul* (Columbia, 1978). **Dolly Parton,** *Heartbreaker* (RCA, 1978). **Donna Summer,** *Bad Girls* (Casablanca, 1979). **Barbra Streisand,** *Wet* (Columbia, 1979). **Various Artists,** *FM* [soundtrack] (MCA, 1978). **Nazareth,** *Malice in Wonderland* (A&M, 1980). **Livingston Taylor,** *Man's Best Friend* (Epic, c. 1980). **Various Artists,** *Roxanne* [soundtrack] (1987). **Various Artists,** *Guitar's Practicing Musicians* (Guitar Recordings, 1989).

Albert Lee

B o r n : *December 21, 1943, in Hereford, England*
M a i n G u i t a r s : *Fender Telecaster, Ernie Ball/Music Man Albert Lee model*

Just as some ill-informed folks have made the statement that white musicians can't truly play the blues, one might also think that it would be impossible to find a chicken pickin' country virtuoso from England. In the sixties Eric Clapton and Mike

Bloomfield quickly proved that white musicians could indeed play the blues, and as for a British country guitar wizard, no one needed to look much further than Albert Lee. Although most people associate him solely with country music, his versatility on the guitar has allowed him to play with musicians in a wide variety of contemporary styles, from rockabilly to country to hard-driving rock 'n' roll. During the sixties Lee backed up pop and R&B vocalist Chris Farlowe for a number of years and was a founding member of the British progressive country-rock band Heads, Hands & Feet (with whom he recorded three albums between 1970 and 1973). In the following decade, the guitarist moved into the sideman role, appearing at various times with the Crickets, Jerry Lee Lewis, and Don Everly.

Lee eventually went into session work, showing up on albums by skiffle originator Lonnie Donegan, country singer Rosanne Cash, Jon Lord (of Deep Purple fame), singer-songwriter Jackson Browne, Joe Cocker, and many others. Lee also played on the legendary album *Green Bullfrog* (1971), which is an all-star rock jam, with guitarists Ritchie Blackmore and British session ace Big Jim Sullivan. Several years later, Lee's reputation as a top guitar picker skyrocketed after his appearance on Emmylou Harris' *Luxury Liner* in 1977. There he proved his worth on tracks like "Luxury Liner" and Chuck Berry's "C'est la Vie."

In 1979 Lee joined Eric Clapton's band and appeared with the blues-rock guitar legend on *Just One Night* (1979), *Another Ticket* (1981), and *Money and Cigarettes* (1983). Lee also released his first solo record in 1979, *Hiding,* which contains the uproarious country-stomper "Country Boy," a masterwork of chicken pickin' and cascading echo effects that seemingly allow him to double the speed of his already fast chops. His all-instrumental 1986 disc *Speechless* includes more examples of the guitarist's feverish country work ("T-Bird to Vegas," "Bullish Boogie," and "Cannonball"), as well as his flair for ballad soloing ("Romany Rye"). Albert followed it up in 1987 with another hot guitar showcase, *Gagged but Not Bound.* He continues to astound all with his killer country chops to this day.

Chris Farlowe, *Chris Farlowe & the Thunderbirds* (Charly, c. 1982). **Head, Hands & Feet,** *Head, Hands & Feet* (Capitol, 1971), *Tracks* (Capitol, 1972), *Old Soldiers Never Die* (Atco, 1973). **Emmylou Harris** [on Warner Bros.], *Luxury Liner* (1977), *Quarter Moon in a Ten Cent Town* (1978), *Blue Kentucky Girl* (1979), *Roses in the Snow* (1980), *Light of the Stable* (1980), *Evangeline* (1981). **Albert Lee,** *Hiding* (A&M, 1979), *Albert Lee* (Polydor, 1982), *Speechless* (MCA, 1986), *Gagged but Not Bound* (MCA, 1987). **Eric Clapton,** *Just One Night* (RSO, 1980•), *Another Ticket* (RSO, 1981), *Money and Cigarettes* (Duck, 1983).

Recordings featuring Albert Lee: **Joe Cocker** [on A&M], *With a Little Help from My Friends* (1969), *Stingray* (1976). **Jackson Browne** [on Asylum], *Saturate before Using* (1972), *The Pretender* (1976). **Jerry Lee Lewis,** *The Session* (Mercury, 1973). **Eddie Harris,** *E.H. in the U.K.* (Atlantic, 1974). **Don Everly,** *Sunsets Towers* (Ode, 1974). **Lonnie Donegan,** *Puttin' on the Style* (UA, 1978). **Nicolette Larson,** *Nicolette* (Warner Bros., 1978). **Rodney Crowell** [on Warner Bros.], *Ain't Livin' Long Like This* (1978), *But What Will the Neighbors Think* (1980), *Rodney Crowell* (1981). **Dave Edmunds,** *Repeat When Necessary* (Swan Song, 1979). **Ricky Skaggs,** *Sweet Temptation* (Sugar Hill, 1979), *Don't Cheat in Our Hometown*

(Sugarhill/Epic, c. 1980). **Marc Benno,** *Lost in Austin* (A&M, 1979). **Various Artists,** *Legend of Jesse James* (A&M, 1980). **Everly Brothers,** *The Everly Brothers Reunion Concert* (Passport, 1984•). **Steve Morse Band,** *The Introduction* (Musician, 1984), *Stand Up* (Elektra, 1985). **Dolly Parton, Linda Ronstadt, Emmylou Harris,** *Trio* (Warner Bros., 1987). **Asleep at the Wheel,** *The Wheel Keeps on Rollin'* (Capitol, 1995).

Dire Straits

Mark Knopfler

B o r n : *August 12, 1950, in Glasgow, Scotland*
M a i n G u i t a r s : *Fender Stratocaster, Pensa-Suhr Strat-style*

In the technique-obsessed 1980s, Mark Knopfler became the proverbial breath of fresh air among rock pickers, known largely for his clean toned fingerstyle guitar breaks with Dire Straits. In addition to stirring up the pop world with his fine guitarmanship, the multi-faceted Knopfler was also the group's singer, songwriter, co-producer, and frontman. Under his musical direction, Dire Straits became one of the world's most popular rock 'n' roll bands during the 1980s.

Knopfler and Dire Straits first came to the public's attention in 1978 with the release of their self-titled debut album and its single "Sultans of Swing." Avoiding the high-volume roar of punk rock and the sixties revivalism of New Wave, "Sultans of Swing" presents a no-frills rock 'n' roll song with good lyrics, a catchy hook, and Knopfler's crisp, country- and blues-inspired leads (coupled with his brother David's tight rhythm work). The entire album features Mark's clean Stratocaster work, notably on songs like "Down to the Water Line" and "In the Gallery." The finely crafted solos on Dire Straits' debut, with Knopfler's chordal string bends, melodic pentatonic lines, and quickly picked repetitive licks, caught the ears of many guitar fans and guitarists. By the end of 1978, the guitar world was picking up on the unique "Knopfler sound."

In 1979 Dire Straits issued *Communique*, which didn't make the same splash on the U.S. charts, but still provided a solid follow-up to the first album. Knopfler found himself in demand as a guest guitarist for other rock artists' releases, and within the next few years, he distinguished himself on LPs by

Steely Dan, Van Morrison, Phil Lynott of Thin Lizzy, country great Chet Atkins, and Bob Dylan, one of his major influences.

By *Making Movies* in 1980, Dire Straits had undergone a personnel change due to the departure of David Knopfler, who was replaced by a pair of keyboardists. Despite the change, *Making Movies* proved to be another commercial smash around the globe, and it gained substantial radio air play in the U.S. for the likable pop number "Skateaway."

Dire Straits' upward climb continued with such critically well-received albums as *Love over Gold* (1982), the EP *Twisting by the Pool* (1983), and *Dire Straits Live—Alchemy* (1984). The live set provides guitar fans with a perfect forum to hear Knopfler stretch out on guitar, especially in extended concert versions of "Expresso Love" and "Telegraph Road." Nineteen eighty-five was Dire Straits' biggest year ever, as they cracked the top of the American pop charts with the album *Brothers in Arms*. Leading off with the tongue-in-cheek rocker "Money for Nothing" (with its Billy Gibbons-styled raunch guitar intro), *Brothers* yielded several hit videos and singles, including "Walk of Life" and "So Far Away."

Since the mid 1980s, Dire Straits' future as a band has been questionable, relying solely on Knopfler's whim. He has spent quality time with many other musicians, yet has never formally abandoned his original bread and butter. He is in great demand as a soundtrack composer for films and is still a desirable session artist. This is especially interesting in the 1990s, given that, for two decades, Knopfler has been one of the leaders of roots-oriented rock guitar, cutting a deep swath through the thousands of heavy metal pickers and poseurs with his distortion-free fingerstyle guitar solos. His playing has always borne something of a resemblance to British folk-rocker Richard Thompson's unique style, but Knopfler has distinguished himself with the percussiveness of his fingerstyle breaks and the overall pop flavor of his music. With strong influences from blues, country, and early rock 'n' roll guitar players and his penchant for a clean tone, Mark Knopfler has created a comfortable nook for himself in the vast world of modern rock guitar.

Dire Straits [on Warner Bros.], *Dire Straits* (1978), *Communique* (1979), *Making Movies* (1980), *Love over Gold* (1982), *Dire Straits Live—Alchemy* (1984•), *Brothers in Arms* (1985), *Money for Nothing* (1988), *On Every Street* (1991). **Mark Knopfler,** *Local Hero* [soundtrack] (1983), *Cal* [soundtrack] (1984), *Comfort and Joy* [soundtrack] (1984), *The Princess Bride* [soundtrack] (Warner Bros., 1987), *Screenplaying* (Warner Bros., 1993), *Golden Heart* (Warner Bros., 1996). **Notting Hillbillies,** *Missing and Presumed Having a Good Time* (Warner Bros., 1990). **Chet Atkins & Mark Knopfler,** *Neck and Neck* (Columbia, 1991).

Recordings featuring Mark Knopfler: **Bob Dylan** [on Columbia],

Mark Knopfler

Slow Train Coming (1979), *Infidels* (1983), *Biograph* (1985•). **Phil Lynott** [on Warner Bros.], *Solo in Soho* (1980), *The Philip Lynott Album* (1982). **Steely Dan,** *Gaucho* (MCA, 1980). **Van Morrison,** *Beautiful Vision* (Warner Bros., 1982). **Tina Turner,** *Break Every Rule* (Capitol, 1986). **Various Artists,** *The Color of Money* [soundtrack] (MCA, 1987). **Willy DeVille,** *Uptown Lowlife* (1988).

Ry Cooder

Born: *March 15, 1947, in Santa Monica, California*
Main Guitars: *Fender Stratocaster, Martin 000-18*

It seems that whenever the eclectic guitar is mentioned, Ry Cooder's name is certain to follow. The California native's guitar playing transcends musical boundaries every other bar, effortlessly mixing folk, early jazz, R&B, rock, country, gospel, Hawaiian, and *norteño* (also called "Tex-Mex," a musical style from the southern Texas region near Mexico) song styles into his particularly colorful music. Primarily a rhythm and bottleneck player, Cooder accompanies his easygoing vocals with a diverse assortment of guitar textures, from funky electric chordings and smooth melody lines to open-tuned acoustic strumming and spicy slide fills.

Cooder was deeply immersed in the vibrant folk and blues revivals of the mid sixties. In 1965 he formed a folk, blues, and rock-influenced band, the Rising Sons, with folk legend Taj Mahal. Later Cooder teamed up with rock eccentric Captain Beefheart for his classic *Safe as Milk* recording in 1967. By this time the guitarist had established a reputation as a bottleneck master, and he soon took on session work in L.A. In 1969 Cooder began working with the Rolling Stones, reputedly having a great deal to do with the creation of their massive hit "Honky Tonk Women." He also appeared with the Stones on *Sticky Fingers* in 1971, adding slide to the haunting "Sister Morphine."

Nineteen seventy saw the beginning of Cooder's solo career with the release of his self-titled debut album. While the record garnered positive reviews all around for its atmospheric songs and guitar work, it hardly scratched the charts. The solo albums kept coming, though: *Into the Purple Valley* (1971), *Boomer's Story* (1972), and the gospel-tinged *Paradise and Lunch* (1974). By the mid seventies, Cooder began adding Tex-Mex, gospel, and Hawaiian music into his recordings, and it shows on the songs "Stand by Me" and "Yellow Roses," from his acclaimed 1976 release *Chicken Skin Music*. Especially notable are "Always Lift Him Up" and the chunky finger-plucked rhythm work and acoustic slide fills of "Smack Dab in the Middle."

Besides his solo records, Cooder appeared on many other artists' recordings throughout the decade, including those by Little Feat, Randy Newman, Maria Muldaur, and Arlo Guthrie. In 1977 Cooder put out a live record, *Show Time*, and followed it up in 1979 with the R&B- and early rock-flavored *Bop till You Drop*, which holds the distinction of being the first rock album to be recorded digitally.

In the eighties Ry Cooder's many talents led him to a whole

Ry Cooder

new field of musical endeavor: movie soundtracks. He wrote the scores to *The Long Riders*; *Alamo Bay*; *Paris, Texas*; *Streets of Fire*; and the quasi-tribute to blues guitar legend Robert Johnson, *Crossroads*. This movie featured Cooder's playing under that of actor Ralph Macchio and also featured the considerable six-string talents of Steve Vai. In addition to all of his film and session work, Cooder was also a member of the laid-back but short-lived supergroup Little Village, with John Hiatt, Nick Lowe, and Jim Keltner.

Ry Cooder, [on Warner Bros. except where noted], *Ry Cooder* (Reprise, 1970), *Into the Purple Valley* (Reprise, 1971), *Boomer's Story* (Reprise, 1972), *Paradise and Lunch* (Reprise, 1974), *Chicken Skin Music* (1976), *Show Time* (1977•), *Jazz* (1978), *Bop till You Drop* (1979), *Borderline* (1980), *The Long Riders* [soundtrack] (1980), *Southern Comfort* [soundtrack] (1981), *The Border* [soundtrack] (1982), *The Slide Area* (1982), *Alamo Bay* [soundtrack] (Slash, c. 1984), *Crossroads* [soundtrack] (1986), *Get Rhythm* (Warner Bros., 1987). **Little Village,** *Little Village* (Reprise, 1992).

Recordings featuring Ry Cooder: **Captain Beefheart,** *Safe as Milk* (Kama Sutra, 1967). **Rolling Stones,** *Let It Bleed* (London, 1969), *Sticky Fingers* (Rolling Stones, 1971), *Jamming with Edward* (Rolling Stones, c. 1972). **Randy Newman,** *12 Songs* (Reprise, 1969). **Various Artists,** *Performance* (Warner Bros., 1970). **Little Feat,** *Little Feat* (Warner Bros., 1970). **Maria Muldaur,** *Maria Muldaur* (Reprise, 1973). **Arlo Guthrie** [on Reprise], *Running down the Road* (1969), *Last of the Brooklyn Cowboys* (1973). **Various Artists,** *No Nukes/The Muse Concerts* (Asylum, 1979•). **Eric Clapton,** *Money and Cigarettes* (RSO, 1983). **Steve Douglas,** *King Cobra* (Fantasy, 1984). **Dolly Parton, Linda Ronstadt, Emmylou Harris,** *Trio* (Warner Bros., 1987). **Duane Eddy,** *Duane Eddy* (Capitol, 1987). **John Hiatt,** *Bring the Family* (A&M, 1987).

David Lindley

Born: *March 21, 1944, in San Marino, California*
Main Guitars: *Sears Silvertone, various lap steels and cheapo electrics*

An L.A.-based guitar player who shares Ry Cooder's wide taste for many different international styles of music is David Lindley. Like Cooder, Lindley did extensive work as a sideman and session player, backing rock 'n' rollers from Rod Stewart to Linda Ronstadt to Crosby & Nash. His best-known gig was backing up singer and activist Jackson Browne, with whom he played lap steel and fiddle. Besides providing support to these acts, Lindley had a solo venture in 1981, *El Rayo-X*, an album that features his instrumental prowess and encompassed reggae, R&B, rock, and several ethnic styles (ska, calypso, African popular). In his prime, Lindley was considered a veritable guitar wizard to many artists on the L.A. folk rock scene.

Starting on ukulele at age 14, Lindley picked up guitar and fiddle and eventually became proficient on a variety of string instruments, including lap steel, banjo, mandolin, bouzouki, oud, and more. By the mid sixties, he was an up-and-coming member of the L.A. folk-rock movement and in 1966 formed Kaleidoscope, an electric folk band that also experimented with Middle Eastern and other ethnic music. After recording several albums with them, Lindley joined up with Jackson Browne in 1971 and also played for a while with British rocker Terry Reid. It was his stint with Browne, which lasted until 1980, that cemented his reputation as a legendary sideman. He appeared on the Jackson Browne albums *For Everyman* (1973), *Late for the Sky* (1974), and *The Pretender* (1976), but his guitar skills really caught everyone's attention after his stellar playing on Browne's hit 1977 album *Running on Empty*. Lindley established his trademark guitar sound on the popular title cut and also on "The Load Out/Stay" with throaty, tuneful lap steel solos that often resemble thickly distorted bottleneck leads.

In addition to his guitar talents, Lindley has gained a reputation as a serious guitar collector. But instead of hoarding expensive old Gibsons and Fenders, he zeroes in on cheap guitars from the fifties and sixties, including oddball gems like the Sears Silvertone (often his main electric axe), Teisco, and Goya Rangemaster guitars. With his vast musical influences, his standing as rock's foremost lap-steel soloist, and a humorous sense of the strange and out-of-the-ordinary, David Lindley is one rock guitar player who appears to have been predestined for the title of eclectic guitarist.

Kaleidoscope [on Epic], *Side Trips* (1967), *A Beacon from Mars* (1968), *Incredible Kaleidoscope* (1969), *Bernice* (1970). **Jackson Browne** [on Asylum], *For Everyman* (1973), *Late for the Sky* (1974), *The Pretender* (1976), *Running on Empty* (1977•), *Hold Out* (1980). **David Lindley** [on Asylum except where noted], *El Rayo-X* (1981), *Win this Record* (1982), *Mr. Dave* (WEA, 1985), *Very Greasy* (1988), *World out of Time* (Shanachie, 1992).

Recordings featuring David Lindley: **Graham Nash** [on Atlantic], *Songs for Beginners* (1971), *Wild Tales* (1974). **America,** *America* (Warner Bros., 1972). **Maria Muldaur** [on Reprise], *Maria Muldaur* (1973), *Waitress in a Donut Shop* (1974). **Terry Reid,** *River* (Atlantic, 1973), *Seed of Memory* (ABC, 1976). **Ian Matthews,** *Some Days You Eat the Bear…* (Elektra, 1974). **Linda Ronstadt,** *Heart Like a Wheel* (Capitol, 1974), *Prisoner in Disguise* (Asylum, 1975). **Rod Stewart,** *Atlantic Crossing* (Warner Bros., 1975). **Crosby & Nash** [on Atlantic], *Wind on the Water* (1975), *Whistling down the Wire* (1976), *Live* (1977•). **James Taylor,** *In the Pocket* (Warner Bros., 1976). **Warren Zevon** [on Asylum], *Warren Zevon* (1976), *Bad Luck Streak in Dancing School* (1980). **Lonnie Mack,** *Lonnie Mack and Pismo* (Capitol, 1977). **Karla Bonoff,** *Restless Nights* (Columbia, 1979). **Ry Cooder** [on Warner Bros.], *Jazz* (1978), *Bop till You Drop* (1979), *The Long Riders* (1980). **Jesse Colin Young,** *American Dreams* (Elektra, 1978). **Eddie Money,** *Life Is for the Taking* (Columbia, 1979). **Various Artists,** *No Nukes/The Muse Concerts* (Asylum, 1979•). **Joe Walsh,** *There Goes the Neighborhood* (Asylum, 1981). **Dolly Parton, Linda Ronstadt, Emmylou Harris,** *Trio* (Warner Bros., 1987). **David Crosby,** *Oh Yes I Can* (A&M, 1989). **Various Artists,** *The Indian Runner* [soundtrack] (Capitol, 1990).

Amos Garrett

Born: *c. 1947, in Toronto*
Main Guitar: *Epiphone Sheraton*

As a sideman Amos Garrett's credits include stints with Ian and Sylvia's Great Speckled Bird, Paul Butterfield's Better Days, Bonnie Raitt, Todd Rundgren, and others. However, his best-known piece of guitar work is the knock-out solo on Maria Muldaur's big hit "Midnight at the Oasis" (from her 1973 debut, *Maria Muldaur*). Here, Garrett displays his fingerstyle electric work in a lovely break that combines melodic lines, single-note passages, and the double- and triple-string chord slides and multiple bends that have earmarked his incredible style. While his single-note lines are not unlike Jerry Garcia's, his multi-string chord bends reveal a complex base of influences that extends into rockabilly, jazz, country (especially pedal steel effects), and the blues. So while much of Amos Garrett's other guitar playing reached only a limited number of guitarists' ears, his solo on "Midnight at the Oasis" is still one of the most enchanting guitar leads ever to grace a Top 40 pop hit.

Paul Butterfield's Better Days [on Bearsville], *Better Days* (1973), *It All Comes Back* (1973). **Geoff Muldaur & Amos Garrett,** *Geoff Muldaur & Amos Garrett* (Flying Fish, c. 1978). **Amos Garrett,** *Go Cat, Go* (Flying Fish, 1980), *Amosbehavin'* (Blueprint, 1982).

Recordings featuring Amos Garrett: **Geoff & Maria Muldaur** [on Reprise], *Pottery Pie* (c. 1970), *Sweet Potatoes* (c. 1971). **Todd Rundgren,** *Something/Anything* (Bearsville, 1972). **Maria Muldaur** [on Reprise], *Maria Muldaur* (1973), *Waitress in a Donut Shop* (1974). **Geoff Muldaur,** *Geoff Muldaur Is Having a Wonderful Time* (Reprise, 1975). **Elvin Bishop,** *Hog Heaven* (Capricorn, c. 1979).

Nils Lofgren

Born: *1952, in Chicago*
Main Guitars: *Fender Stratocaster, Hamer and Dean solidbodies*

Nils Lofgren's career encapsulates the huge ups and downs that most rock 'n' rollers go through in their lifetimes. As a teenager Lofgren was tapped by Neil Young to play on his 1970 opus *After the Gold Rush*, as well as for Young's backup band Crazy Horse on their acclaimed 1971 set *Crazy Horse*. Later that year the Hendrix-inspired guitarist formed his own band, Grin (based in Washington, D.C.), and recorded another well-received album, *1+1*. Although fortune seemed to be smiling on Lofgren, Grin began a bumpy ride to rock oblivion, touring and recording feverishly for the next few years with little success.

Later, Lofgren was asked by Neil Young to play on his *Tonight's the Night* album and tour, which turned out to be another boost for the guitarist. After the tour Lofgren gave Grin another go, but by the end of 1974 the group was in pieces. He then moved into a solo career, releasing the critically praised album *Nils Lofgren* in 1975, which contains the Keith Richards tribute "Keith, Don't Go."

Lofgren's solo career picked up with *Cry Tough* in 1976, which broke into the Top 40 album charts. Yet, once again, his solo career did not take off as predicted. A major break for his career seemed to arrive in 1984 when the guitar spot opened up in Bruce Springsteen's E Street Band, after the departure of Steve Van Zant (a.k.a. "Little Steven"). As he did during his 1973 tour stint with Neil Young, Lofgren put his own musical projects on hold to go after this more lucrative gig. He accompanied Springsteen on the huge 1984–85 "Born in the U.S.A." tour, which crisscrossed America and Europe. Recordings from the tour were eventually issued as part of Springsteen's imposing multi-record live set *Live/1975–85*. On the recording Lofgren's formidable lead and rhythm guitar playing were finally heard by a mainstream rock audience, his near-psychedelic guitar solos being particularly highlighted on the single "War." Later, Lofgren was heard on the Boss's 1987 hit "Tunnel of Love," from the studio album of the same name.

After Springsteen dissolved the band and set out alone, Lofgren went back to the obscurity of his solo career. Despite his talent and his ability to play in almost any live situation, he was unable to break out of the role of the invisible sideman. His eclecticism (how many other guitarists could go from Neil Young's electronic *Trans* to Bruce Springsteen's *Tunnel of Love*?) served to keep him busy, but may have also kept him from stepping out on his own. Most recently, Lofgren has been back at work with Springsteen in the re-formed E Street Band.

Nils Lofgren [on A&M except where noted], *Nils Lofgren* (Rykodisc, 1975), *Cry Tough* (1976), *I Came to Dance* (1977), *Night after Night* (1977), *Nils* (1979), *Night Fades Away* (Backstreet/MCA, 1981), *Wonderland* (MCA, 1983), *Flip* (Columbia, 1985), *Nils Lofgren—The Best* (1985), *Code of the Road* (CBS, 1986), *Silver Lining* (Rykodisc, 1991), *Crooked Line* (Rykodisc, 1992), *Damaged Goods* (Transatlantic, 1995). **Grin** [on Spindizzy], *Grin* (1971), *1+1* (1972), *All Out* (1973). **Neil Young,** *After the Gold Rush* (Reprise, 1970), *Tonight's the Night* (Reprise, 1975), *Trans* (Geffen, 1983). **Bruce Springsteen** [on Columbia], *Tunnel of Love* (1987), *Live/1975 85* (1988), *Greatest Hits* (1995).

Recordings featuring Nils Lofgren: **Crazy Horse,** *Crazy Horse* (Reprise, 1970). **Stephen Stills,** *Stephen Stills 2* (Atlantic, 1971). **Ringo Starr,** *Ringo Starr & His All-Star Band* (Rykodisc, 1990).

Landmark Rock Guitar Albums through the Years

1954–55

Although the Sun sessions didn't actually give birth to rock 'n' roll, they marked a huge turning point. Moore's taut rockabilly solos also combined technical prowess with the strong aggressive feel that eventually became a hallmark of countless rock players.

Elvis Presley
The Sun Sessions (RCA [released in 1976])
Main Guitarists: Scotty Moore, Elvis Presley

1956

Danny Cedrone's solo in "Rock around the Clock," with its fast, staccato-picked runs, bluesy bends, and sliding lick at the end, kicked off the youth revolution in what may be the most famous song in rock history.

Bill Haley & His Comets
Rock around the Clock (Decca)
Main Guitarists: Danny Cedrone, Fran Beecher

1958

In the late fifties and early sixties, Berry recorded dozens of rock 'n' roll classics, all of which featured his signature double-stop guitar licks. Songwriter, lyricist, and showman, he is above all one of the most influential rock 'n' roll guitar players ever.

Chuck Berry
One Dozen Berrys (Chess)
Main Guitarist: Chuck Berry

1959

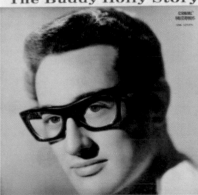

He looked like a nerdy honor-society student, but Buddy Holly blazed through catchy, up-tempo rockers with hip rhythmic guitar riffs and lead fills. To boot, he was rock's first avatar of the Fender Stratocaster, perhaps *the* most popular electric guitar.

Buddy Holly
The Buddy Holly Story (Coral)
Main Guitarist: Buddy Holly

1960

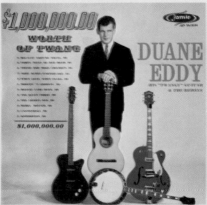

Although many superb rock players came before him, Duane Eddy was really the first real guitar star in rock 'n' roll. His twangy bass-string runs, laden with reverb, defined both a sound and an era, inspiring everyone from the oncoming surf rockers to John Entwistle of the Who.

Duane Eddy
$1,000,000.00 Worth of Twang (Jamie)
Main Guitarist: Duane Eddy

1960

Possibly the most successful instrumental rock act of all time, the Ventures both wrote and covered infectious pop tunes that were so easy to play that anyone with a modicum of musical skill could play them in their own garage band.

The Ventures
Walk, Don't Run (Dolton)
Main Guitarists: Nokie Edwards, Bob Bogle, Don Wilson

1962

Rock wild man Bo Diddley was a sonic innovator of his day, employing distortion, feedback, echo, and tremolo *long* before Beck or Hendrix. He also invented his signature "Bo Diddley" rhythm, which became a pop staple.

Bo Diddley
Have Guitar, Will Travel (Chess)
Main Guitarist: Bo Diddley

1963

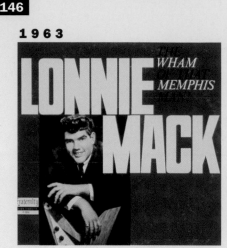

In one short year, this obscure axeman cut guitar-stoked singles like "Memphis" and "Wham!" and then promptly fell off the map. Stevie Ray Vaughan claimed Mack as a major influence and produced his 1985 comeback album.

Lonnie Mack
The Wham of That Memphis Man! (Fraternity)
Main Guitarist: Lonnie Mack

1965

The Beatles finally dropped their Fab Four facade and tackled more complicated material, also employing a wider palette of guitar textures, from 12-string electric to slide to fuzz bass. A major stepping stone on the road to psychedelia and *Sgt. Pepper.*

The Beatles
Rubber Soul (Capitol)
Main Guitarists: George Harrison, John Lennon, Paul McCartney

1965

Dylanesque folk meets electrified Beatles pop on this definitive sixties album. Jim (later Roger) McGuinn created a 12-string sound so distinctive that its influence remains intact over 30 years later. For proof, just turn on the radio.

The Byrds
Mr. Tambourine Man (Columbia)
Main Guitarists: Jim (Roger) McGuinn, David Crosby

1966

Bloomfield's use of twisted modal phrases in a rock context broke new ground, creating his own global blues and further anticipating the psychedelic taste for long, exotic instrumental jams.

The Butterfield Blues Band
East-West (Elektra)
Main Guitarists: Mike Bloomfield, Elvin Bishop

1967

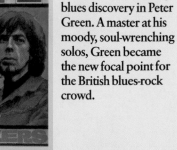

Despite the loss of Eric Clapton to Cream, John Mayall made another startling blues discovery in Peter Green. A master at his moody, soul-wrenching solos, Green became the new focal point for the British blues-rock crowd.

John Mayall and the Bluesbreakers
A Hard Road (London)
Main Guitarist: Peter Green

1967

On this one album, Hendrix rewrote the rock guitar book, defined psychedelia, and prophesied the coming of hard rock. Mixing funk, blues, and proto-heavy rock, he became an instant titan in the six-string universe. Rock's greatest ever?

The Jimi Hendrix Experience
Are You Experienced? (MCA)
Main Guitarist: Jimi Hendrix

1967

It's hard to find one album that captures the Summer of Love, but *Grateful Dead* comes close. Like other San Francisco bands, the Dead freely blended blues, folk, bluegrass, garage punk, and pop, creating a whimsical, down-to-earth style of American guitar rock.

The Grateful Dead
Grateful Dead (Warner Bros.)
Main Guitarists: Jerry Garcia, Bob Weir

1967

British blues-rock embraced American psychedelia on this widely influential disc. Clapton took his fat "woman tone" to the top of the charts with the hit "Sunshine of Your Love" and gave aspiring rock players a whole new model to follow.

Cream
Disraeli Gears (Atco)
Main Guitarist: Eric Clapton

1968

The first complete work to document Beck's post-Yardbirds progress. With the advent of louder amps, Beck assumed a tone steeped in distortion, giving his wild pentatonic licks and power chords new authority and helping define the coming of heavy metal.

Jeff Beck
Truth (Epic)
Main Guitarist: Jeff Beck

1970

Carlos Santana's Latin roots and taste for heavy percussion gave his songs an energy unrivaled by any other psychedelic group. His solos drew from urban blues and British blues-rock, but over the jazz-flavored backdrop of "Samba Pa Ti," his guitar created a brand-new texture.

Santana
Abraxas (Columbia)
Main Guitarist: Carlos Santana

1971

Cooper's shock rock antics were the band's claim to fame, but *Killer* proved that glam guitarists could rock as ferociously and intuitively as any of their less-mascara'd peers. That Buxton and Bruce's playing has stood the test of time is a testament to their ability.

Alice Cooper
Killer (Warner Bros.)
Main Guitarists: Glen Buxton, Michael Bruce

1 9 7 2

While the rest of the rock world was getting primed for glam rock, art rock, and country rock, the Stones stripped their music to the bone and captured their most personal, hard-hitting collection of songs, with the blazing guitars of Richards and Taylor leading the way.

The Rolling Stones
Exile on Main St. (Rolling Stones)
Main Guitarists: Keith Richards, Mick Taylor

1 9 7 3

From his skewed bop phrasing in "Siberian Khatru" to the soaring steel work in "And You & I" to his famous classical piece "Mood for a Day," Howe showed himself on this triple concert LP to be the most skillful all-around player of the seventies.

Yes
Yessongs (Atlantic)
Main Guitarist: Steve Howe

1 9 7 3

With *Birds of Fire,* McLaughlin and Mahavishnu codified the fusion sound and rode it up the pop charts to #15. Within its grooves, the music was still terrifyingly radical: McLaughlin's complex instrumentals and violent, high-speed solos were eons ahead of their time.

Mahavishnu Orchestra
Birds of Fire (Columbia)
Main Guitarist: John McLaughlin

1 9 7 4

Brian May stacked and multitracked harmonies as no one before. In the context of Queen's glossy glam-pop and metal, the results were out of this world. His extended, echo-saturated solo in "Brighton Rock" alone entitles him to the utmost respect.

Queen
Sheer Heart Attack (Elektra)
Main Guitarist: Brian May

1 9 7 6

Page bared the darkness of his soul to create, if not the most popular Zep album, then certainly the heaviest. The pinnacle was "Achilles Last Stand," a 10-minute epic that employed exotic modal climaxes over a driving John Bonham groove.

Led Zeppelin
Presence (Swan Song)
Main Guitarist: Jimmy Page

1 9 7 6

Many have written off Frampton for being too pretty and writing too many radio-friendly hooks, but from the Talk Box musings in the smash "Show Me the Way" to the hard rock riffing on "Do You Feel Like We Do," he proved he knew how to wail on guitar.

Peter Frampton
Frampton Comes Alive! (A&M)
Main Guitarist: Peter Frampton

1977

Di Meola set the guitar world on fire with his Latin-informed fusion, replete with the fastest, most precise guitar work anywhere. Eddie Van Halen was soon considered the best guitarist in rock; Di Meola was widely regarded as the best *in the world.*

Al Di Meola
Elegant Gypsy (Columbia)
Main Guitarist: Al Di Meola

1977

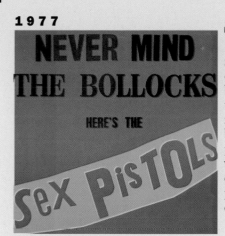

The Sex Pistols had been maligned as inept amateurs, but this disc captured a tight band that could blast through a three-minute rocker like nobody's business. Steve Jones pumped away furiously with giant power chords and ripping, post-Chuck Berry double stops.

Sex Pistols
Never Mind the Bollocks...Here's the Sex Pistols
  (Warner Bros.)
Main Guitarist: Steve Jones

1978

Gorham and Robertson wove their signature harmony guitar lines throughout the album, including the hit "The Boys Are Back in Town," as well as providing incendiary, but remarkably melodic, solos. The band has inspired everyone from Metallica to Corrosion of Conformity.

Thin Lizzy
Live and Dangerous (Warner Bros.)
Main Guitarists: Scott Gorham, Brian Robertson

1978

Throughout this double live package, Thomasson and Jones whipped up a firestorm of red-hot breaks, with Salem throwing in the occasional spot solo to urge them on. Not the most famous southern rock album, but one of the most exciting.

The Outlaws
Bring It Back Alive (Arista)
Main Guitarists: Hughie Thomasson, Billy Jones, Freddie Salem

1979

After the release of this album, just about every rock player on the planet rushed out to buy a chorus pedal like Summers'. His sound was so enchanting one almost forgot all the cool rhythm parts he came up with, including the brilliantly arpeggiated "Message in a Bottle."

The Police
Reggatta de Blanc (A&M)
Main Guitarist: Andy Summers

1979

Young left folk rock for power rock on this half-electric, half-acoustic disc. Brooding dirges like "Powderfinger" and the title cut found him blasting away with angular bends and flying shards of distortion. Too slow for punk, it waited 13 years for a name: grunge.

Neil Young & Crazy Horse
Rust Never Sleeps (Reprise)
Main Guitarist: Neil Young

1979

Schenker burned on this live set, recorded just before he left the group. Few axemen of the decade could rival his clean, fast picking and melodic modal phrases, which helped inspire, for better or worse, the Bach 'n' roll and shred schools of the eighties.

UFO
Strangers in the Night (Chrysalis)
Main Guitarist: Michael Schenker

1980

On this album Morse's eclectic taste and dazzling technique spanned hard rock flash ("Road Expense"), country corn ("Pride o' the Farm"), arty pastiche ("Hereafter"), and pure classical ("Old World"). Here he defined the eclectic virtuoso for the rest of the decade.

Dixie Dregs
Dregs of the Earth (Arista)
Main Guitarist: Steve Morse

1981

By this time, Eddie Van Halen was already the world's most famous rock guitarist. His tapping and tremolo, along with a devilishly fast melange of legato and speed picking, had completely shifted the course of metal guitar away from the blues, in a more modal direction.

Van Halen
Fair Warning (Warner Bros.)
Main Guitarist: Eddie Van Halen

1981

Rhoads mixed Eddie Van Halen's tapping with Michael Schenker's classicism, creating a dark new metal sound. His influence was huge, not only for stoking up the arena-rock furnace, but also for prophesying the Bach 'n' roll phenomenon.

Ozzy Osbourne
Diary of a Madman (Jet)
Main Guitarist: Randy Rhoads

1982

Following their breakthrough in 1980, Rush grew to arena-sized popularity, exposing Lifeson's eclectic, high-tech guitar work to the suburban masses. Here he matched searing solos with textured arpeggios, all doused in heavy distortion, echo, and chorus effects.

Rush
Signals (Mercury)
Main Guitarist: Alex Lifeson

1983

Holdsworth had blown everyone's mind with his uncanny legato technique and avant-bop leads during his stints with U.K., Jean-Luc Ponty, and Bruford. On this, his first major-label release, he revealed his rhythm mastery in tandem with more of those legendary solos.

Allan Holdsworth
Road Games (Warner Bros.)
Main Guitarist: Allan Holdsworth

1983

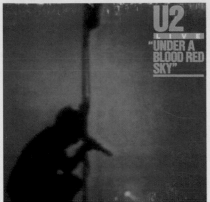

This album captured U2's entire career to that point, with songs such as "Electric Co." and "11 O'Clock Tick Tock" gaining new life because of The Edge's playing maturity. Through his use of calculated digital delay and droning strings, he created a distinctly original sound.

U2
Under a Blood Red Sky (Island)
Main Guitarist: The Edge

1984

With bristling chops and fiery phrasing, SRV did not so much reinvent the blues as add a renewed passion. A master of fills, intros, outros, and turnarounds, he created jagged rhythms and piercing riffs that were equal parts grinding blues and showy rock.

Stevie Ray Vaughan and Double Trouble
Couldn't Stand the Weather (Epic)
Main Guitarist: Stevie Ray Vaughan

1985

This youthful Swede created a blistering neoclassical form of metal, garnished with alternate- and sweep-picking techniques. Due to his inability to move beyond one style, Yngwie's career eventually soured, but for a brief spell, he was the most thrilling guitarist alive.

Yngwie J. Malmsteen's Rising Force
Rising Force (Polydor)
Main Guitarist: Yngwie Malmsteen

1987

Lethal doses of speed, technique, and melody resulted in one of the most popular instrumental guitar albums ever. Satriani's leads, often with deft wah-wah, sounded like vocal lines, and his modal excursions gave guitarists something to chew on for the rest of the decade.

Joe Satriani
Surfing with the Alien (Relativity)
Main Guitarist: Joe Satriani

1988

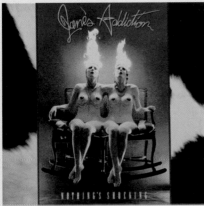

Jane's Addiction was the perfect chronological synthesis between metal and alternative. Navarro slashed and soothed his way over the top of traditional rock guitar conventions, establishing himself as one of the most accomplished players in alternative music.

Jane's Addiction
Nothing's Shocking (Warner Bros.)
Main Guitarist: Dave Navarro

1990

This album set a new standard for rock guitar, not only in speed and technique, but also in experimental playing. "For the Love of God" and "Blue Power" displayed Vai's twisted, brilliant songwriting, while "Two Sisters" showed just how far an imaginative player could go.

Steve Vai
Passion and Warfare (Relativity)
Main Guitarist: Steve Vai

1990

Cliffs of Dover," Johnson's signature track, kicks off with a triumphant flurry of staccato runs and a classically tinged melody. On this album, Johnson blended psychedelia, jazz, and fusion of into a fluid and melodic style that sizzled without becoming overbearing.

Eric Johnson
Ah Via Musicom (Capitol)
Main Guitarist: Eric Johnson

1991

Cobain almost single-handedly deposed the eighties shredder as guitar hero. He was a merely competent player, yet his songwriting skill and jagged tone on cuts like "Lithium" and "Smells Like Teen Spirit" stripped the guitar down to its essence.

Nirvana
Nevermind (Geffen)
Main Guitarist: Kurt Cobain

1992

Eschewing melodicism and technique for simple, brutal riffing, Jourgensen and his studio accomplices helped launch industrial rock. From the opening of "N.W.O." to the skull-crushing main riff of "Just One Fix," Ministry wasn't about guitar *style*, it was about guitar *sound*.

Ministry
Psalm 69 (Sire)
Main Guitarist: Al Jourgensen

1992

Many might claim that the title was an apt description of Darrell's technique: a sledgehammer mix of bruising tone and blinding speed with little regard for subtlety. Yet Darrell took thrash into the realm of technical expertise and inspired a legion of angry young followers.

Pantera
Vulgar Display of Power (Atco)
Main Guitarist: Dimebag Darrell

1993

Jorgenson ignited two-handed runs and tough rock riffs; Ray jumped from country to swing to blues; Donahue spun gossamer chords from surreal bends. But beyond their individual mastery, the Hellecasters proved that guitarmanship still mattered in the punk-fed nineties.

The Hellecasters
The Return of the Hellecasters (Pacific Arts)
Main Guitarists: John Jorgenson, Will Ray, Jerry Donahue

1994

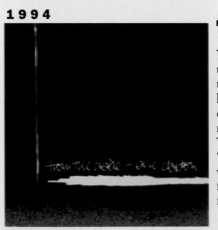

Thirty years after recording with the Yardbirds, Clapton returned to his roots with this all-blues disc, which hit #1 on the album charts and earned FM radio airplay for "I'm Tore Down" and "Motherless Child." It was a victory not only for Clapton, but also for the blues.

Eric Clapton
From the Cradle (Reprise)
Main Guitarist: Eric Clapton

CHAPTER NINETEEN

Punk and New Wave

Apocalypse '77

It wasn't a response; it was a reaction.

In the mid seventies, mainstream rock fans were grooving to light rock from Peter Frampton, Fleetwood Mac, the Eagles, and Stevie Wonder, while others were dancing to the slick sounds of disco and funk. Sick of this harmless and neutered music, the musicians of the underground club scenes in New York and London turned their disdain outward, writing and playing songs that were anti-mainstream. Since the mainstream had become soft, soulless, and soporific, the underground played loud, violently, and incisively. Over time, bands propagating this sound started getting recognition for their noncommercial and seemingly tuneless rock 'n' roll. Various members of these new groups sported short, spiked hair, outrageous makeup, shredded clothing, and metal-studded leather jackets. Soon newscasts (especially in the U.K.) began portraying these brash young rockers as part of a violent youth cult—due primarily to their anti-establishment dress and manner, frequent use of profanity, and generally raucous and occasionally violent club shows. By the end of 1976, this new rock subgenre was menacingly dubbed "punk rock." The punk revolution was on.

When the musical leaders of the movement, the Sex Pistols, made headlines for cursing on a BBC TV show in December 1976, the punk genre caught fire in England. With the ensuing scandal, the Pistols were banned in the U.K., and adolescents the world over immediately found a cause to call their own. In striking similarity to the days when rock began, the parental generation saw this new sound as a threat to the wholesomeness of their children, while the children themselves found it an exciting escape from boredom, both musically and socially. By the summer of 1977—punk's biggest year—bands like the Clash, the Damned, and the Stranglers were pushing their way up the British pop charts.

In America, where the more intellectual and less fashion-oriented punk underground had been thriving for several years, attention was turned to arty New York acts, especially the Ramones, Talking Heads, Richard Hell and the Voidoids (with hot guitarists Ivan Julian and future Lou Reed sideman Robert Quine), Tom Verlaine's Television, Patti Smith (featuring dual guitarists Lenny Kaye and Ivan Kral), and, later, pop-punk crossover Blondie. Los Angeles offered up a spate of retro-punk acts, such as X with rockabilly guitar raver Billy Zoom, and the Blasters with Dave and Phil Alvin on guitars. Seemingly overnight, rock 'n' roll was jammed full of promising young punk bands and primitive guitar adventurers.

Actually, the roots of punk could be traced back to a variety of key American acts, like the hip sixties garage band the Standells ("Dirty Water"), Detroit's MC5 (noted for the great live 1969 album *Kick out the Jams*), and perhaps most important, Iggy Pop and the Stooges, who produced the defining proto-punk platter, *Raw Power*, in 1973. (Iggy was eventually dubbed the "godfather of

The Sex Pistols: Sid Vicious, Johnny Rotten, Steve Jones

punk" by the Sex Pistols, much as Neil Young was tagged the "godfather of grunge" by nineties rockers.) Another vital punk archetype was the Velvet Underground, with Lou Reed on guitar. Reed's solos, an essential element in the Velvet's haunting music, were expressionistic splatter paintings of sound. He sliced through much of the band's material with stark, angular phrases, distorted sounds, and roundly unnerving string bends. This radical, almost antimusic approach to rock guitar rubbed off on a lot of up-and-coming punk pickers, many of whom tried, like Reed, to be the loudest, most primitive, most abrasive guitar players possible.

Ironically, punk and its tamer spin-off, New Wave, were really a return to the simpler roots of rock 'n' roll. Instrumentation in the typical punk band consisted of just guitar, bass, and drums, often played crudely but with plenty of honest emotion and rock aggression. Keyboards and horns were almost universally *verboten* in punk. While jazz-rock was gaining notoriety for its technically advanced musicians during this same period, punk rock offered a new variation on the rock musician. The punk player seemed to be purely concerned with conveying a feeling and venting youthful frustration, while purposely avoiding any fine instrumental proficiency. Thus, the guitar players of punk and New Wave brought to light a revamped version of the guitar-hero—this one using mostly power chords, resurrected Chuck Berry double stops, and new takes on the sonic textures of feedback, overdrive, and, later on, chorus effects.

Sex Pistols

Steve Jones

Born: *May 3, 1955, in England*
Main Guitar: *Gibson Les Paul Custom*

Consider the moniker "Sex Pistols." The phallic name of this band brings to mind images of punk rock at its lewdest, crudest, and, indeed, very best. The Sex Pistols were without question the greatest group of the punk genre, not only because they spearheaded the guitar-dominated revolution while making outstanding music together, but also because the band brought about real change in the semi-stagnant world of late-seventies rock. The centerpiece of the Pistols was Johnny Rotten, an abrasive shouter who constantly spouted his anti-everything viewpoints over the Pistols' locomotive-paced punk beat. But behind the publicity-grabbing frontman (and the band's crafty manager, Malcolm McLaren), a serious power trio was at work: drummer Paul Cook, bassist Sid Vicious, and a punk guitar powerhouse named Steve Jones, whose combination of Chuck Berry-style double-stop licks and metalish power-chord progressions became the virtual standard for punk guitar. Together, this foursome created some of the most important rock of the 1970s and pointed the way to a new direction in music.

Throughout Pistols classics like "God Save the Queen" and

"Holidays in the Sun" (from their only official album, *Never Mind the Bollocks, Here's the Sex Pistols*, in 1978), Jones plays nonstop power chords and mutated double stops. In "Anarchy in the U.K.," he momentarily eschews the double stops, opting instead for some engaging multi-string licks during his solo and a siren's howl of feedback for the finale. On the Sex Pistols' first, last, and only tour of the United States, in early 1978, critics praised Jones' stunning guitar work and attributed much of the band's sound to his stellar playing.

The future of the Sex Pistols was cut short soon after that tour. By its end Johnny Rotten had split from the group in yet another headline-grabbing ploy, and the remaining three members vainly tried to continue touring on their own. But after just a few gigs, they too called it quits, thus ending the short, exhilarating saga of the Sex Pistols. Fortunately, *Bollocks* remains as a testament to the Sex Pistols legacy (which has since been supported by several posthumous releases), a legacy that has clearly been a huge influence on subsequent rock bands and genres. Indeed, the simplicity and ferocity of the Pistols has been adapted and embraced by bands as diverse as heavy rockers Guns N' Roses and grunge ground-breakers Nirvana.

In 1996, the Sex Pistols reunited for the *Filthy Lucre* tour, admitting they were doing it only to cash in on the resurgence of punk. Steve Jones also teamed up with members of Guns N' Roses and Duran Duran that same year to form the Neurotic Outsiders.

Sex Pistols [on Virgin except where noted], *Never Mind the Bollocks, Here's the Sex Pistols* (Warner Bros./Virgin, 1977), *The Great Rock 'n' Roll Swindle* (1978), *Some Product* (1979), *Carry on Sex Pistols* (1979), *Flogging a Dead Horse* (1980), *Filthy Lucre Live* (1996•). **Chequered Past,** *Chequered Past* (EMI America, 1984). **Steve Jones** [on MCA], *Mercy* (1987), *Fire and Gasoline* (1989). **Neurotic Outsiders,** *Neurotic Outsiders* (Maverick, 1996).

Recordings featuring Steve Jones: **Iggy Pop,** *Blah, Blah, Blah* (A&M, 1986), *Instinct* (A&M, 1988). **Andy Taylor,** *Thunder* (MCA, 1987).

The Clash

Mick Jones

Born: *1956, in Brixton, London*
Main Guitars: *Gibson Les Paul and Melody Maker*

Joe Strummer

Born: *John Mellors, on August 21, 1951, in Ankara, Turkey*
Main Guitar: *Gibson Les Paul Junior*

When the Sex Pistols broke up at the beginning of 1978, the rallying cry of the punk rebellion was taken up by the Clash, who were deemed the last great hope of punk rock. Fortunately for punk fans around the world, the Clash delivered *big-time*. During the late seventies, the Clash took their form of punk—which was more political and intellectual than the Sex

Pistols'—and gained widespread success with it, even in the United States, where punk had a lot harder time being commercially accepted. Though they were a four-piece group like the Pistols, the Clash's instrumental arsenal included a two-guitar barrage: the rhythm guitar power chords of singer Joe Strummer and the surprisingly melodic leads of Mick Jones. Together with bassist Paul Simonon and a variety of drummers, they took punk rock rebellion from the streets of London to the top of the American record charts.

After witnessing the Sex Pistols in concert and sensing the birth of a new rock style in late 1975 and 1976, Strummer, Jones, and Simonon abandoned their previous rock and R&B bands (London SS, the 101'ers, Heartdrops) to form their own punk band, the Clash. By the beginning of 1977, the Clash had signed a contract with CBS and began issuing a series of singles that voiced their firm commitment to both important socio-political issues and the guitar-dominated sound of punk. On early Clash singles like "White Riot" and "I'm So Bored with the U.S.A." (included on their debut 1977 set, *The Clash*), the guitar work is distinctly primal but full of punk fervor, especially with Strummer's power chording and Jones' frantic double-stop riffs.

By the second record, *Give 'em Enough Rope* (1978), a new Clash guitar ideal began to emerge side by side with a more crafted pop sound. With Strummer holding down the solid chord parts, Jones started highlighting the vocals with simple but highly effective counter-melodies that breathed new life into the standard power-chord/double-stop vocabulary of most punk guitarists. On songs like "Safe European Home" and the British hit single "Tommy Gun," Jones uses these brief linear phrases in conjunction with octave and power-chord effects to give the music an added harmonic punch. On the track "Stay Free," he steps out as a talented lead player in a break of well-crafted melodic passages that gave new depth to the term punk guitarist.

Throughout the rest of the decade and the first few years of the 1980s, the Clash built up their worldwide following with a series of critically praised albums (*London Calling* in 1979, *Sandinista* in 1980) that contain ele-

Johnny Ramone

ments of reggae, dub, and other ethnic influences from outside of punk. In 1982 the Clash became one of the few punk groups ever to achieve platinum status in the U.S., due to their smash dance single "Rock the Casbah," from the album *Combat Rock*. They also toured the country that year as an opening act on the Who's 1982 "Farewell Tour."

After the success of the early 1980s, the band fractured because of personality problems. Jones formed his own outfit called Big Audio Dynamite, while Strummer continued on for a while with an expanded Clash lineup. Unfortunately, neither band lived up to the punk sound of the original Clash. Nonetheless, after the demise of the Sex Pistols, the Clash were widely recognized as the leaders of the punk movement, and they provided late-seventies rock 'n' roll with some of its strongest new music. As for guitarists Mick Jones and Joe Strummer, they began as rather standard punk players circa 1976–77, but developed into a fascinating guitar team, especially by way of Jones' inventive lead guitar parts. Together, the Clash guitarists created some of the most impressive guitar playing of the entire punk and New Wave era.

The Clash [on Epic except where noted], *The Clash* (1977), *Give 'em Enough Rope* (1978), *London Calling* (1979), *Sandinista* (1980), *Combat Rock* (1982), *Cut the Crap* [without Jones] (1985), *The Story of the Clash, Volume 1* (1988), *The Clash on Broadway* (Legacy/Sony, 1991), *Super Black Market Clash* (1994). **Big Audio Dynamite** [on Columbia], *Big Audio Dynamite* (1985), *No. 10 Upping St.* (1986), *Tighten Up Vol. '88* (1988), *Megatop Phoenix* (1989), *The Globe* (1991), *Higher Power* (1994).

The Ramones

Johnny Ramone

B o r n : *John Cummings, on October 8, 1948, in Long Island, New York*
M a i n   G u i t a r : *Mosrite Ventures model*

Of all the American punk acts, the Ramones probably stick in most people's minds as the top band. They matched the English punks in rough-boy garb and sound, but added a distinctly wry sense of humor to their songs ("I Want to Be Sedated," "Go Mental," and "Now I Wanna Sniff Some Glue"). Johnny

Ramone's guitar excursions are fairly uniform: all basically using eighth-note barre-chord riffs and brief double-stop leads. Using this formula on almost all of the band's releases, Johnny has powered such Ramones LPs as *Leave Home* (1977), *Rocket to Russia* (1977), and *Road to Ruin* (1978), all of which are important releases from the early American punk scene.

Interestingly, the band's biggest contribution to guitar is that they weren't very good in a technical sense. Most of their songs were repetitive and utilized the exact same progressions. However, the sheer volume and intensity of their playing inspired countless teenagers to pick up the guitar and rediscover its emotive value (something that was hard to do after listening to disco). The Ramones were also so simplistic that any novice guitarist could play their songs within minutes, which provided immediate gratification and the impetus to learn more about the instrument. Many early nineties hardcore and grunge bands, and even heavy metal players, have cited the reckless "I don't care what it sounds like as long as it's in your face" abandon of Johnny Ramone as inspiration for their own approach to guitar.

The Ramones officially broke up in the summer of 1996, but as the Sex Pistols proved, one never knows.

The Ramones [on Sire except where noted], *Ramones* (1976), *Leave Home* (1977), *Rocket to Russia* (1977), *Road to Ruin* (1978), *It's Alive* (1979•), *End of the Century* (1980), *Pleasant Dreams* (1981), *Subterranean Jungle* (1983), *Too Tough to Die* (1984), *Animal Boy* (1986), *Halfway to Sanity* (1987), *The Ramones Loco Live—Spain 1991* (1991•), *All the Stuff & More, Vol. 1* (Warner Bros., 1990), *All the Stuff & More, Vol. 2* (Warner Bros., 1991), *Acid Eaters* (RadioActive/MCA, 1994), *Greatest Hits Live* (RadioActive, 1996•).

Recordings featuring the Ramones: **Various Artists,** *Rock 'n' Roll High School* (Sire, 1979).

Pretenders

Chrissie Hynde

B o r n : *September 7, 1951, in Akron, Ohio*
M a i n G u i t a r : *Fender Telecaster*

James Honeyman-Scott

B o r n : *November 4, 1956, in Hereford, England*
D i e d : *June 16, 1982, in London*
M a i n G u i t a r s : *Gibson Les Paul, Zemaitis solidbody*

Robbie McIntosh

B o r n : *c. 1955, in England*
M a i n G u i t a r : *Gibson ES-335*

In England the Pretenders burst to prominence in 1979 as a hip New Wave act with the singles "Stop Your Sobbing" and "Kid." Soon they took a foothold in the U.S. as well with the #14 single "Brass in Pocket." The heart of the Pretenders' early sound was American-born Chrissy Hynde's seductive vocals and the careful twin guitar playing of Hynde and lead guitarist James Honeyman-Scott. Rather than the fuzz-addled guitar antics of many punk bands, the tandem sounds of Hynde and Honeyman-Scott gently urge on Pretenders songs like "Talk of the Town" and "Message of Love" with clean, slightly chorus-enhanced rhythm playing and simple but poignant lead lines.

This is not to say the Pretenders didn't rock. Songs like "Bad Boys Get Spanked," "The Adultress," and "Mystery Achievement" roar at hard-rock speed, while the solo on "Day after Day" blisters and snakes with psychedelic frenzy. At the 1979 Concerts for the People of Kampuchea in London (later a live album), the band tore up the stage with such hard-driving rockers as "The Wait" and "Precious," which were pumped up by Hynde's loud power chording and Honeyman-Scott's double-stop-injected solos.

Tragedy struck the band in 1982 when James Honeyman-Scott died of a drug overdose. The following year bassist Pete Farndon met a similar fate, leaving just Hynde and drummer Martin Chambers. Hynde regrouped the Pretenders with the addition of ace axeman Robbie McIntosh (who later moved on to join Paul McCartney's band) for *Learning to Crawl* in 1984, but the absence of Honeyman-Scott's refreshing New Wave riffs and six-string interplay with Hynde was obviously missed. After a decade of moribund releases featuring a revolving door of musicians, Hynde & Co. scored a comeback single in 1994 with the choice rocker "Night in My Veins."

Honeyman-Scott's influence on New Wave cannot be overstated. His inventiveness and unique style defined the crossover from punk's three-chord aggressive simplicity to New Wave's experimental pop. And while Hynde was—and is—a capable guitarist, it was Honeyman-Scott who really played the riffs that made the Pretenders such an alluring band.

Pretenders [on Sire], *Pretenders* (1979), *Extended Play* [EP] (1981), *Pretenders II* (1981), *Learning to Crawl* (1984), *Get Close* (1986). *The Singles* (1987), *packed!* (1990), *The Last of the Independents* (1994).

Recordings featuring the Pretenders: **Various Artists,** *Concerts for the People of Kampuchea* (Atlantic, 1981•).

Television

Tom Verlaine

B o r n : *Tom Miller, on December 13, 1949, in Mount Morris, New Jersey*
M a i n G u i t a r : *Fender Jazzmaster*

On the American shores of the punk and New Wave invasion was Tom Verlaine, an inventive guitar player whose guitar work with Television was noticeably different from the styles of most British punk pickers. Whereas the Sex Pistols' Steve Jones cranked out his raw Chuck Berry double stops, and Mick Jones of the Clash emphasized melody over muscle, Verlaine and co-guitarist Richard Lloyd broke new sonic ground with harsh scalar runs, off-rhythm chordings, warbly bends, and other effects.

Television came together in the mid seventies out of another New York-based band of Verlaine's called Neon Boys, which also included future punk sensation Richard Hell on bass. They eventually changed their name to Television and were signed to the Elektra label in 1976. The following year saw the release of their debut album, *Marquee Moon*, which has since been lauded by some rock critics as one of the greatest recordings of the American punk movement. Here, the more-celebrated and influential Verlaine unveils his soloing talents in the angular breaks of "Friction" and the title cut. On stage Verlaine also led the band through long solo sections not unlike the extended leads of the psychedelic era, a style that he was frequently associated with.

In 1978 Television issued *Adventure*, which didn't garner the same all-out critical praise as its predecessor, but still has plenty of ear-catching Verlaine solos. Two tracks that stand out for their guitar work are "Foxhole" and "The Fire," the latter a dirge-like piece with Verlaine's stark melody lines, hammer-on licks, and wrist vibrato effects piercing through the song's rideout. In the middle of 1978, Television broke up, and Tom Verlaine commenced on a solo career that resulted in several well-received albums, including *Dreamtime* in 1981. Richard Lloyd also put out a number of acclaimed solo discs after the band's demise. Television finally regrouped with a self-titled reunion set in 1992, though that may have been their last gasp.

In retrospect, many fans and critics regard Television as a highly influential band, while more revisionist-minded folks consider them a bit overrated. In any case, both Verlaine and Lloyd have earned prominent status in the annals of punk and New Wave guitar.

Television, *Marquee Moon* (Elektra, 1977), *Adventure* (Elektra, 1978), *Television* (Capitol, 1992). **Tom Verlaine** [on Warner Bros. except where noted], *Tom Verlaine* (Elektra, 1979), *Dreamtime* (1981), *Words from the Front* (1982), *Cover* (1984), *Flash Light* (IRS, 1987), *The Wonder* (Fontana, 1990), *Warm & Cool* (Rykodisc, 1992). **Richard Lloyd,** *The Blow Up* (ROIR, 1978•), *Alchemy* (Elektra, 1979), *Real Time* (Celluloid, c. 1986•), *Field of Fire* (Moving Target/Celluloid, 1987).

Recordings featuring Tom Verlaine: **Various Artists,** *Guitar Speak III* (IRS, 1991).

CHAPTER TWENTY

Session Players

The Quiet Monsters

Session guitarists have played an important role in rock from the start. When a recording artist or band didn't have its own guitar player (or perhaps the band's guitarist wasn't quite good enough to put on tape), the record producer would simply contract an outside session, or "studio," guitarist to do the gig. By and large, these guitarists are extremely accomplished players who can read music and chord charts well and provide spice to a given recording with colorful improvisation and versatility. A successful session player has to be a virtual guitar chameleon, able to fit in with any style from rock to pop to jazz to country and everything in between.

Studio guitarists have played with the biggest names in rock, though they themselves have not necessarily been rock 'n' roll pickers. Aside from rockabilly pioneers Scotty Moore and James Burton, a veritable army of great country pickers played sessions with Elvis Presley, including legend Chet Atkins, who played rhythm on "Heartbreak Hotel," Hank Garland, Harold Bradley, Grady Martin, and Reggie Young. Jazz players also played early rock dates, in part because of their ability to read music on demand. Bebop specialist Howard Roberts, for example, backed Duane Eddy, the Beach Boys, the Monkees, and Sonny & Cher. Other fine jazz players who sat in on rock gigs were Barney Kessel and the aforementioned Hank Garland.

Of course, it is impossible to discuss studio guitar playing in general without mentioning L.A. studio czar and jazz stylist Tommy Tedesco. Tedesco has played on literally thousands of recordings, including rock dates with Jan & Dean, Kenny Loggins, and even Frank Zappa on his 1968 disc *Lumpy Gravy*. Many claim that Tedesco is the most recorded guitarist in history, and his electric guitar work can be heard on countless TV show themes and movie soundtracks from the sixties, seventies, and eighties. Other legendary session guitarists include Vic Flick (the guitarist who played the "James Bond" theme) and "Big" Jim Sullivan.

Even a number of rock's biggest guitar figures were session guitarists at some point in their careers—James Burton, Jimmy Page, Duane Allman, and Ritchie Blackmore of Deep Purple, for example. Their later success outside of the studio often brought embarrassment to the people that they had recorded with—fame bringing with it a certain amount of historical scrutiny. No one cared, for instance, that Jimmy Page played on Kinks records and Who records when he was a "lowly" guitar for hire. However, when he gained renown as the guitarist for Led Zeppelin, interest in his early work prompted thousands of fans to seek out recordings that he had played on. This meant exposing Page's role on popular recordings and admissions or denials by the offended guitarist.

Page was the exception to the rule; most session players during the sixties toiled in relative, if not lucrative, obscurity. However, during the mid seventies, a rare phenomenon occurred in the studios of Los Angeles and New York: individual studio guitarists were singled out for their performance on recordings by other artists. This was primarily due to their guitar mastery, coupled with a unique

Larry Carlton

sound or tonal quality. These studio players became more than unknown backup musicians; they became semi-stars in their own right. While New York City had its share of noted players (like Steve Kahn, Elliott Randall, Joe Beck, John Tropea, and Eric Gale), it was L.A. that produced the major studio guitar heroes. Wielding a melodic brand of pop-fusion, pickers like Larry Carlton, Lee Ritenour, and Steve Lukather helped to usher in a new L.A. pop sound with their slick, jazz-tinged solos and aggressive rock riffing. By the end of the decade, the appearance of one of these guitarists on a recording was often enough to get guitar fans to buy the album, no matter who the artist was. When Carlton, Ritenour, and Lukather each moved on to solo careers, their spots were dutifully filled by a new generation of monster rock players, including Michael Landau, Carl Verheyen, Dann Huff, and several other talented axemen.

Larry Carlton

B o r n : *March 2, 1948, in Torrance, California*
Main Guitars: *Gibson ES-335, Valley Arts Strat-style*

Larry Carlton is widely considered the dean of the L.A.-based school of pop-fusion guitar. From the late sixties until 1977, Carlton's supple jazz-pop lines were featured on over 4,000 recording sessions for records, movies, television shows, and commercials. Among the many pop and rock notables he recorded with over the years are such artists as Barbra Streisand, Sammy Davis Jr., Joni Mitchell, Ray Charles, Steely Dan, and Glen Campbell. In addition to all of his studio work, Carlton was an integral part of the funk-jazz outfit the Crusaders, and in the late seventies and eighties was a successful solo act. With records like *Larry Carlton* and *Strikes Twice*, the guitar virtuoso established himself as the master of "L.A. fusion," due to the eminently melodic and tasty solos he coaxed from his hallmark guitar, a Gibson ES-335.

Carlton delved into the guitar at the ripe old age of six and absorbed guitar influences from country/rockabilly pickers Joe Maphis and Larry Collins, jazzmen Joe Pass, Wes Montgomery, and Johnny Smith, blues legend B.B. King, and, as a late inspiration, rockers Eric Clapton and Jeff Beck. Carlton first started doing studio work in 1969, gradually building a strong reputation until he was playing as many as 500 sessions a year. He joined the Crusaders in 1972 and stayed with them for four years, playing on discs including *The 2nd Crusade* (1973), *Scratch* (1974), and *Chain Reaction* (1975). During this stint, he developed his volume pedal technique, which allowed him to produce volume swells for solos and rhythm work. This is now a standard effect for electric players of all styles (blues-rocker Roy Buchanan came up with a similar approach around the same time, though he used his guitar's volume knob instead of a pedal). Perhaps Carlton's most famous use of this effect with the Crusaders was on an instrumental cover of Carole King's "So Far Away," recorded for *Crusaders 1* and the live album *Scratch*. Carlton's solo on the live

version was a blend of volume pedal effects and tasteful, jazz-tinged single-note runs that prompted recording artists and session leaders to ask specifically for the "Carlton sound."

Carlton appeared on Joni Mitchell's *Court and Spark* (1974), which is considered the finest album of her career. But his most impressive studio work may well have been with Steely Dan, particularly on *The Royal Scam* (1976). The centerpiece of this classic pop recording is "Kid Charlemagne," on which Carlton takes two breathtaking solos. The first is composed of twisting single-note phrases, bends, and vibrant melody lines (as well as then-novel two-handed tapped notes), while in the fadeout, he plays a joyous off-the-cuff break. His guitar work on "Kid Charlemagne," "Don't Take Me Alive," and the rest of *The Royal Scam* is nothing short of spectacular, and stands as a landmark in the realm of L.A. pop-fusion. Carlton also contributed to Steely Dan's *Gaucho* in 1980, as well as Dan vocalist Donald Fagen's superb jazz-pop solo album of 1982, *The Nightfly*.

After nearly a decade on top of the L.A. studio scene, Carlton went solo in 1977. The following year, his self-titled first album was released to accolades from the guitar community. Included were some of Carlton's best known instrumentals, such as "Room 335" (the name of Carlton's home studio), "Nite Crawler," and "Don't Give It Up," all featuring his patented jazz, rock, pop, and blues-inflected solos. Guitar fans soaked it up, and his next album, *Strikes Twice*, was even more popular. From the infectious pop groove of "Mulberry Street" to the metalish tones of "In My Blood," on to his melodic work in the ballad "For Love Alone," Carlton confirmed his place as one of the tastiest rock pickers of the day.

In the eighties, Carlton continued with several more solo efforts, including *Sleepwalk* (1982) and the bluesy *Friends* (1983). Unfortunately, album sales trailed off when the "L.A. sound" lost some of its audience, and Carlton was dropped by his record label after *Friends*. After a three-year hiatus, he returned to the recording world in 1986 with an all-acoustic effort entitled *Alone/But Never Alone*, showing yet another facet of his guitar versatility. In 1988 the guitarist was critically injured when he was shot by would-be burglars at his home. After a lengthy recovery period, "Mr. 335" returned to performing and recording in the 1990s.

If there is anything to find fault with in Carlton's stellar career, it is his affiliation with the Los Angeles "happy jazz" scene, where every song has a major tonality, a sunny backbeat, and never includes anything resembling a dissonant note. This may have led to some credibility problems for Carlton among straight-ahead jazzers and more straightforward rockers, but for fans of commercial jazz-pop, Larry Carlton remains an absolute legend.

The Crusaders [on Blue Thumb], *Crusaders 1* (1972), *The 2nd Crusade* (1973), *Unsung Heroes* (1974), *Scratch* (1974•), *Chain Reaction* (1975), *Those Southern Knights* (1976), *The Best of the Crusaders* (1976). **Larry Carlton** [on Warner Bros. except where noted], *Singing/Playing* (Blue Thumb, 1973), *Larry Carlton* (1978), *Mr. 335 Live in Japan* [Japanese Import] (1979•), *Strikes Twice* (1980), *Sleepwalk* (1982), *Friends* (1983), *Eight Times Up*

[Japanese import] (n/a•), *Alone/But Never Alone* (MCA, 1986), *Last Night* (MCA, 1987•), *Discovery* (MCA, 1987), *On Solid Ground* (MCA, 1989), *Collection* (GRP, 1990), *Kid Gloves* (GRP, 1992), *Renegade Gentleman* (GRP, 1993). **Lee Ritenour & Larry Carlton,** *Larry & Lee* (GRP, 1995).

Recordings featuring Larry Carlton: **Four Tops,** *Keeper of the Castle* (Dunhill, 1972). **Neil Diamond,** *Jonathan Livingston Seagull* (Columbia, 1973). **Gladys Knight & the Pips,** *Neither One of Us* (Soul, 1973). **Art Garfunkel,** *Angel Clare* (Columbia, 1973). **Billy Joel,** *Piano Man* (Columbia, 1973). **Tom Scott & the L.A. Express,** *Tom Scott & the L.A. Express* (Ode, 1974). **Bobby "Blue" Bland,** *Dreamer* (Dunhill, 1974). **Joni Mitchell** [on Asylum], *Court and Spark* (1974), *The Hissing of Summer Lawns* (1975), *Hejira* (1976). **Joan Baez,** *Diamonds and Rust* (A&M, 1975). **Steely Dan** [on ABC except where noted], *Katy Lied* (1975), *The Royal Scam* (1976), *Aja* (1977), *Gaucho* (MCA, 1980). **Minnie Ripperton,** *Adventures in Paradise* (Epic, 1975). **Hoyt Axton,** *Fearless* (A&M, 1976). **Glen Campbell,** *Bloodline* (Capitol, 1976). **Barbra Streisand** [on Columbia], *Streisand Superman* (1977), *Songbird* (1978). **Various Artists,** *The Wiz* [soundtrack] (MCA, 1978). **Christopher Cross,** *Christopher Cross* (Warner Bros., 1980). **Donald Fagen,** *The Nightfly* (Warner Bros., 1982). **Various Artists,** *Casino Lights* (Warner Bros., 1982•). **Eye to Eye** [on Warner Bros.], *Eye to Eye* (1982), *Shakespeare Stole My Baby* (1983). **Various Artists,** *Against All Odds* [soundtrack] (Atlantic, 1984). **Chet Atkins,** *Stay Tuned* (Columbia, 1985). **Booker T. Jones,** *The Runaway* (n/a, 1989).

Lee Ritenour

B o r n : *January 1, 1952, in Hollywood, California*
M a i n   G u i t a r : *Gibson ES-335*

Hot on Larry Carlton's heels as one of the great studiomen-turned-guitar-heroes in the seventies was Lee Ritenour. Like Carlton, Ritenour started as a full-time studio guitarist in Los Angeles, booking hundreds of sessions every year with some of the biggest names in contemporary music, including Barbra Streisand, Pink Floyd (*The Wall*), Steely Dan, Frank Sinatra, Tony Bennett, and Aretha Franklin. In 1976 Ritenour embarked on a solo recording career while maintaining a high profile as a studio musician. As acclaim poured in for his own albums, he emerged as one of the top jazz-rock guitar stars of the L.A. fusion scene.

Like most skilled studio players, Ritenour started his guitar schooling very young and immersed himself in heavy music studies for most of his childhood. His appetite for musical knowledge was immense, so much so that he reputedly exhausted several teachers before he turned 10 and was gigging regularly by his early teens. Ritenour attended the University of Southern California, where he began studying classical guitar with the eminent Christopher Parkening. He also had occasional lessons with jazz guitar greats Joe Pass and Howard Roberts. Upon graduating, the young guitarist hit the road with bandleader Sergio Mendes for a tour of Japan. During his stint with Mendes, Ritenour was exposed to a huge amount of Latin music, which greatly affected his playing in future years. By the mid seventies, he had broken into the Los Angeles studio scene. His excellent reading and technical skills, along with substantial creativity, placed him among the best session guitarists in town. Soon he was appearing on popular singles by the top acts in rock, funk, and pop, and was doing guitar work for commercials and hit movies like *Saturday Night Fever* and *Grease.*

Not content to play solely on other people's albums, Ritenour recorded his debut solo LP, *First Course,* in 1976. The following year, the guitarist issued three more albums: two direct-to-disc sets for Japanese release, *Gentle Thoughts* and *Sugarloaf Express,* and a stateside disc, *Captain Fingers. Captain Fingers* was popular among U.S. guitar fans and helped establish Ritenour as an L.A. fusion powerhouse. Working with a Gibson ES-335 (and occasionally a 360 Systems polyphonic guitar synthesizer), Ritenour served up his precision jazz-rock on cuts like "Margarita" and a cover of Stevie Wonder's "Isn't She Lovely," which he touched up with melodic leads and some funky slide work in the fadeout jam.

For the next several years, Ritenour continued on his solo voyage with albums like *The Captain's Journey* (1978), *Lee Ritenour and Friendship* (1978), and *Feel the Night* (1979), which featured the guitarist's fluid fusion breaks in the title cut. By the end of the decade, his stature as an L.A. fusionist of note had been recognized in nearly all of the top music polls, as well as by jazz-rock fans around the world. Moving into the eighties, Ritenour released several commercially oriented albums, including *Rit* (1981), the techno-rock flavored *Banded Together* (1984), and even a Latin jazz-styled album of nylon-string guitar music, *Rio* (1982).

After achieving status as a top studio guitarist and guitar hero of L.A. pop-fusion, Ritenour set his sights on another musical horizon—the guitar synthesizer. He was the first guitarist in the U.S. to acquire a SynthAxe (a MIDI synthesizer controller), and he used it to a great extent on his tours and solo recordings, including *Earth Run* in 1986. But the SynthAxe fell into disfavor among its progenitors for a myriad of reasons, and Ritenour returned to the comfort of straightforward electrics for his recordings in the 1990s.

Ritenour is certainly among the best known of all studio guitarists, and the diversity of his work—from Pink Floyd to Frank Sinatra—stands as testimony to that. Like Larry Carlton, however, Ritenour has been guilty of making his records overly slick and commercial, as was the nature of L.A. studio guitarists. But the guitar whiz balanced out the R&B dreck of his quartet Foreplay (which scored a 1993 hit with "Between the Sheets") with a hip homage to jazz great Wes Montgomery on his solo disc *Wes Bound.* Amazingly, these two disparate discs were recorded in the same year, showing Ritenour at his very best and at his very not-so-best. Like all the greatest studio guitarists, Ritenour is nothing if not versatile.

Lee Ritenour [on Elektra except where noted], *First Course* (Epic, 1976), *Captain Fingers* (Epic, 1977), *Gentle Thoughts* (JVC, 1977), *Sugarloaf Express* (JVC, 1977), *The Captain's Journey* (1978), *Lee Ritenour and Friendship* (JVC, 1978), *Feel the Night* (1979), *Rit* (1981), *Rio* (Musician, 1982), *Rit/2* (1982), *Banded Together* (1984), *Earth Run* (GRP, 1986), *Portrait* (GRP, 1987), *Festival* (GRP, 1989), *Stolen Moments* (GRP, 1990), *Collection* (GRP, 1991), *Wes Bound* (GRP, 1993). **Lee Ritenour & Larry Carlton,** *Larry & Lee* (GRP, 1995). **Dave Grusin & Lee Ritenour,** *Harlequin* (1985).

Recordings featuring Lee Ritenour: **Carly Simon,** *Playing Possum* (Elektra, 1975). **Art Garfunkel,** *Breakaway* (Columbia, 1975). **Aretha Franklin** [on Atlantic], *You* (1975), *Sweet Passion* (1977). **Helen Reddy,** *No Way to Treat a Lady* (Capitol, 1975). **Pratt & McClain,** *Happy Days* (Reprise, 1976). **Patrice Rushen,** *Before the Dawn* (Prestige, 1976). **Barbra Streisand/Kris Kristofferson,** *A Star Is Born* [soundtrack] (Columbia, 1976). **Norman Connors,** *You Are My Starship* (Buddah, 1976), *Romantic Journey* (Buddah, 1977), *This Is Your Life* (Arista, 1978). **Earl Klugh** [on Blue Note], *Earl Klugh* (1976), *Finger Paintings* (1977). **Stanley Turrentine,** *Everybody Come on Out* (Fantasy, 1976). **George Duke,** *I Love the Blues, She Heard My Cry* (MPS/BASF, 1976). **Paul Anka,** *The Painter* (UA, 1976). **Seals & Crofts,** *Get Closer* (Warner Bros., 1976). **Ray Charles & Cleo Laine,** *Porgy & Bess* (RCA, 1976). **Brothers Johnson** [on A&M], *Look out for #1* (1976), *Right on Time* (1977). **Barbra Streisand,** *Streisand Superman* (Columbia, 1977). **Various Artists,** *Saturday Night Fever* [soundtrack] (RSO, 1977). **Diana Ross,** *Baby It's Me* (Motown, 1977). **Steely Dan,** *Aja* (ABC, 1977). **Natalie Cole,** *Thankful* (Capitol, 1977). **Leo Sayer,** *Thunder in My Heart* (Warner Bros., 1977). **Gato Barbieri,** *Ruby, Ruby* (A&M, 1977). **Noel Pointer,** *Phantazia* (Blue Note, 1977). **John Handy,** *Carnival* (Impulse, 1977). **Quincy Jones,** *Roots* (A&M, 1977). **Letta Mbulu,** *There's Music in the Air* (A&M, 1977). **John Denver,** *I Want to Live* (RCA, 1977). **Kenny Loggins,** *Celebrate Me Home* (Columbia, 1977). **Various Artists,** *Grease* [soundtrack] (RSO, 1978). **Dave Grusin,** *Dave Grusin & the N.Y.–L.A. Dream Band* (GRP, 1982•). **Frank Sinatra,** *L.A. Is My Lady* (Qwest, 1984).

Steve Lukather

Born: *October 21, 1957, in Los Angeles*
Main Guitars: *Gibson Les Paul Standard, various Strat-style solidbodies, Ernie Ball/Music Man "Luke"*

When Larry Carlton and Lee Ritenour began to concentrate more on their solo careers and less on studio work in the late seventies, a guitar void was left in the L.A. studio scene. It was soon filled by a 19-year-old Californian named Steve Lukather. Lukather had proven himself a versatile guitarist in 1977 when he took over for perennial sideman Les Dudek in Boz Scaggs' band. Scaggs was enjoying immense commercial success, and Lukather's association with him gained him enough exposure and respect that he was instantly in demand for numerous studio dates. Thanks to his incredible chops, Lukather—or "Luke," as he's casually known—

Steve Lukather

quickly became a top L.A. session picker, ultimately doing hundreds of sessions with everyone from Barbra Streisand to Earth, Wind & Fire to Paul McCartney.

In addition to breaking into the lucrative studio scene, the young guitarist's career simultaneously took off in another direction when he became a member of Toto in 1978. Toto was made up of successful session players (keyboardists David Paich and Steve Porcaro, and drummer Jeff Porcaro), and this combination of studio player know-how and high-caliber musicianship paid off when their first album became an instant hit. The first single, a catchy pop-metal number called "Hold the Line," caught on with radio audiences and became a hit, due in part to Lukather's heavy power chording and high-energy solo. When the disc eventually went platinum and Lukather could command triple-scale pay for his studio work, it was clear that one of this axeman's other talents was being in the right place at the right time.

In 1979 Toto issued *Hydra* and reached the charts with Lukather singing the sugary ballad "99." On the studio side, Luke continued to build up his reputation as "the rock 'n' roll studio guitarist," but it wasn't until 1980 that he began to fully unleash his rock guitar mania on other artists' albums. One of the first records to reveal his heavy guitar work was Boz Scaggs' *Middle Man* (1980), which featured its share of killer, high-volume solos and dead-on riffs in the title song, as well as "Breakdown Dead Ahead" and "You Got Some Imagination." Another of Lukather's studio coups in 1980 is on Earth, Wind & Fire's *Faces* LP, where he peels off some of his most tuneful solos on "Back on the Road" and the ballad "You Went Away." With a combination of catchy melodicism and heavy metal drama, Lukather showed that he was a new breed of studio guitarman.

Back with Toto in 1981, Lukather appeared on the band's third album, *Turn Back*, which garnered only disappointing sales and typically scathing reviews from rock critics. But the band bounced back the following year with their most popular record ever, *Toto IV*. Powering the album was a trio of hit singles, "Rosanna," "I Won't Hold You Back," and "Africa," the first two containing searing Luke solos (actually, the track "Lovers in the Night" was the real barnburner here). To boot, Toto picked up eight Grammy awards in 1983 for *Toto IV*, making it one of the biggest albums of the year and an effective snub to all of the critics who had panned the band for so long.

In tandem with Toto's rise to the top, Lukather's studio reputation allowed him to play even more hard rock-styled guitar in pop sessions—a real rarity. He played on records by artists as diverse as the Tubes, Michael Jackson, and Lionel Richie. In 1981 the guitarist's songwriting and lead guitar skills helped the Tubes break into Top 40 radio with "Talk to Ya Later" (from *The Completion Backward Principle*), and two years later his guitar playing on "She's a Beauty" (from *Outside Inside*) propelled them to the top of the charts. In 1982 the guitarist played all of the rhythm guitar and bass parts on Michael Jackson's mega-hit "Beat It" (with Eddie Van Halen taking the famous solo), and he appeared the next year on Lionel Richie's hit single "Running with the Night," taking up a generous amount of tape to cut loose with two frenzied guitar breaks.

One of the peaks of Lukather's recording career came not from a studio gig or from Toto, but from a live club recording with the Greg Mathieson Project. Their 1982 instrumental album *Baked Potato Super Live!* was released in Japan only, but clearly contains some of Lukather's most spectacular guitar work. Here the roots of Luke's style are clearly evident as he blends Jimi Hendrix's metal-infused guitar licks with the tasty jazz and blues-based guitar sounds of Larry Carlton. Lukather's stellar playing on this album is most in evidence on "First Time Around," which features furious melody lines and a solo of distorted metal licks and fast scalar runs. The ballad "I'm Home" also displays his musical dynamics as he effortlessly moves from breezy melody parts to exciting hard rock riffs and blazing solos. It is still a big seller at import record stores.

The 1990s have seen Lukather keeping busy by performing and recording with his band Los Lobotomys (Toto went on indefinite hiatus in the early nineties). He has kept up his studio and session work, and remains one of the most formidable and well-respected players ever to emerge from the L.A. session scene.

Toto [on Columbia], *Toto* (1978), *Hydra* (1979), *Turn Back* (1981), *Toto IV* (1982), *Isolation* (1984), *Dune* [soundtrack] (1984), *Fahrenheit* (1986), *The Seventh One* (1988), *Past to Present 1977–1990* (1990), *Kingdom of Desire* (Relativity, 1992), *Tambu* (1995). **Steve Lukather,** *Lukather* (Fish Kitten, 1991). **Los Lobotomys,** *Candyman* (Viceroy, 1994).

Recordings featuring Steve Lukather: **Terence Boylan,** *Terence Boylan* (Asylum, 1977). **Boz Scaggs,** *Down Two Then Left* (1977), *Middle Man* (Columbia, 1980), *Other Roads* (1988). **Diana Ross,** *Baby It's Me* (Motown, 1977). **Alice Cooper,** *From the Inside* (Warner Bros., 1978). **Deniece Williams,** *That's What Friends Are For* (Columbia, 1978). *Olivia Newton-John* [on MCA], *Totally Hot* (1978), *Greatest Hits, Vol. 2* (1982). **Barbra Streisand** [on Columbia], *Songbird* (1978), *Wet* (1979). **Leo Sayer,** *Leo Sayer* (Warner Bros., 1978). **Hall & Oates,** *Along the Red Ledge* (RCA, 1978). **Valerie Carter,** *Wild Child* (Columbia, 1978). **Manhattan Transfer** [on Atlantic], *Extensions* (1979), *Mecca for Moderns* (1981). **Gary Wright,** *Headin' Home* (Warner Bros., 1979). **England Dan and John Ford Coley,** *Dr. Heckle and Mr. Jive* (Big Tree, 1979). **Elton John** [on MCA], *Victim of Love* (1979), *21 at 33* (1980). **Lee Ritenour,** *Feel the Night* (Elektra, 1979). **Earth, Wind & Fire** [on ARC], *I Am* (1979), *Faces* (1980). **Randy Crawford** [on Warner Bros.], *Secret Combination* (1980), *Windsong* (1981). **Peter Allen,** *Bi-Coastal* (A&M, 1980). **Graham Nash,** *Earth & Sky* (Capitol, 1980). **Donna Summer** [on Casablanca], *The Wanderer* (1980), *Donna Summer* (1982). **Bill Champlin,** *Runaway* (Elektra, 1981). **Peter Frampton,** *Breaking All the Rules* (A&M, 1981). **Quincy Jones,** *The Dude* (A&M, 1981).

Ricki Lee Jones, *Pirates* (Warner Bros., 1981). **Greg Lake,** *Greg Lake* (Chrysalis, 1981). **Peter Cetera,** *Peter Cetera* (Full Moon, 1981). **Patti Austin,** *Every Home Should Have One* (Qwest, 1981). **George Benson,** *The George Benson Collection* (Warner Bros., 1981). **Carole Bayer Sager,** *Sometimes Late at Night* (Boardwalk, 1981). **The Tubes** [on Capitol], *The Completion Backward Principle* (1981), *Outside Inside* (1983). **Greg Mathieson Project,** *Baked Potato Super Live!* (CBS/Sony, 1982•). **Warren Zevon,** *The Envoy* (Asylum, 1982). **Joni Mitchell,** *Wild Things Run Fast* (Geffen, 1982). **Michael McDonald,** *If That's What It Takes* (Warner Bros., 1982). **Laura Branigan,** *Branigan* (Atlantic, 1982). **Kenny Loggins,** *High Adventure* (Columbia, 1982). **Chicago,** *Chicago 16* (Full Moon, 1982). **Michael Jackson,** *Thriller* (Columbia, 1982). **Don Henley,** *I Can't Stand Still* (Asylum, 1982). **Ernie Watts,** *Chariots of Fire* (Qwest, 1982). **America,** *View from the Ground* (Capitol, 1982). **Christopher Cross,** *Another Page* (Warner Bros., 1983). **Lionel Richie** [on Motown], *Can't Slow Down* (1983), *Dancing on the Ceiling* (1986). **Fee Waybill,** *Read My Lips* (Capitol, 1984). **Stephen Crane,** *Kicks* (MCA, 1984). **Various Artists,** *The Official Music of the XXIIIrd Olympiad Los Angeles 1984* (Columbia, 1984). **Paul McCartney,** *Give My Regards to Broad Street* (Columbia, 1984). **Chet Atkins,** *Stay Tuned* (Columbia, 1985). **Eric Clapton,** *Behind the Sun* (Warner Bros., 1985). **Neil Larsen,** *Through Any Window* (n/a, 1988). **Booker T. Jones,** *The Runaway* (n/a, 1989). **Various Artists,** *Guitar's Practicing Musicians Vol. 2* (Guitar Recordings, 1991). **Various Artists,** *In from the Storm* [Hendrix tribute] (RCA, 1995).

Other Studio Stars

One of the most important recording locations of the sixties and seventies was in the area of Muscle Shoals, Alabama, where the ultra-funky Muscle Shoals Rhythm Section powered up hits for Otis Redding, Aretha Franklin, Wilson Pickett, Traffic, Rod Stewart, Bob Seger, and countless others. The mainstay of the studio band at Muscle Shoals Sound Studios (there were other top studios in the area) was rhythm guitarist Jimmy Johnson, who joined in 1962. Within a few years, he had backed up such soul classics as Percy Sledge's "When a Man Loves a Woman," Aretha Franklin's "I Never Loved a Man," and Wilson Pickett's "Mustang Sally." A succession of lead guitarists played with the Muscle Shoals outfit—the most famous among them being Duane Allman. Others included Terry Thompson, Eddie Hinton, and Pete Carr, whose most famous solos can be heard on Rod Stewart's "Tonight's the Night" and Bob Seger's "Main Street." Carr and Allman were also together as members of the pre-Allman Brothers group Hourglass.

Up in New York, studio man Elliott Randall played on thousands of sessions and is still probably best known for his spectacular solos on Steely Dan's first hit, "Reelin' in the Years." (1972). Combining sumptuous melodic phrases with rock attitude and ample fuzztone, Randall's breaks in "Reelin' in the Years" presented one of the earliest pop lead guitar parts that actually fused both heavy rock dynamics and jazz intellect. In addition, it is also one of the hottest guitar solos ever to turn up on AM radio. The guitarist has also worked with the Doobie Brothers, Joan Baez, Carly Simon, and David Sanborn, among many others, and currently lives and plays in London.

On the opposite coast, Jay Graydon remains one of the great

guitar wizards from the L.A. studios. Like most studio players, he earned his reputation by way of his extraordinary guitar versatility and by playing hundreds of sessions every year. As his stature increased, so did the visibility of his recorded guitar parts (this was evident in his much-lauded solo on Steely Dan's 1977 hit single "Peg"). After conquering the role of studio guitarist, Graydon moved on to become a producer-player, eventually working on albums by the Manhattan Transfer and Al Jarreau. On the Transfer's 1979 hit "Twilight Zone," he recorded one of his most famous breaks, a harmonized solo of fast bop phrases, blues runs, and dizzying chromatic fantasies. This multitracked recording method also became something of a Graydon guitar hallmark.

Known more as a great sideman (and then as a solo artist) than as a 9-to-5 session player, Robben Ford was one of the most exciting pop-fusion guitarists to emerge in the 1970s. During the early part of that decade, Ford worked in various blues outfits with harpist Charlie Musselwhite, singer Jimmy Witherspoon, and his own Charles Ford Blues Band (named after his father). In 1974 he played on George Harrison's only U.S. tour, after which he joined saxman Tom Scott's L.A. Express (replacing Larry Carlton). With the L.A. Express, he played on two exquisite albums by Joni Mitchell— *Miles of Aisles* (1974) and *The Hissing of Summer Lawns* (1975), besides cutting an album with the band itself.

Ford's work with Harrison and the L.A. Express gained him a great deal of exposure, and he then won studio gigs with Barbra Streisand, Kenny Loggins, and many others. Within a few years, Ford—like Larry Carlton and Lee Ritenour before him—caught the solo bug, recording a solo album in 1979, *The Inside Story*, using a Gibson ES-335 just as they did. A mixed bag of jazz, rock, blues, and funk, the disc is full of Ford's characteristically inspired guitar work. "Magic Sam," in particular, is marked by chunky chording and a solo of bent blues licks, melodic runs, and a jazzman's use of chord tensions. "Tee Time for Eric," on the other hand, is a clean funk blowout, with Ford laying down a constant rhythm groove to take flight in a flowing single-note solo—his specialty.

In the 1980s Ford continued on as a blues-picker-turned-studioman-turned-fusion-guitar-hero in a stint with the Yellowjackets, a band of fellow session maestros. After the group's first album, however, Ford took a less active role in the band. One of his highlights with the Yellowjackets was captured on a live album from the 1982 Montreux Jazz Festival, *Casino Lights*. On the track "Monmouth County Fight Song," Ford rips through a brilliant blues-based solo, composed of mature modal lines, distorted pentatonic licks, and some extremely tasteful modulating phrases. A few years later, Ford's guitar magic was heard in jazz legend Miles Davis' fusion band. Then, in 1988, Ford released a solo blues album entitled *Talk to Your Daughter*, which was critically well received. In the 1990s he led his own blues band, the Blue Line, using his own Fender Robben Ford Model solidbody guitar.

Recordings featuring Jay Graydon: **Steely Dan**, *Aja* (ABC, 1977). **Manhattan Transfer** [on Atlantic], *Extensions* (1979), *Mecca for Moderns* (1981). **Al Jarreau**, *High Crime* (Warner Bros., 1984).

The Charles Ford Band, *The Charles Ford Band* (Arhoolie, 1972). **Robben Ford,** *The Inside Story* (Elektra, 1979), *Talk to Your Daughter* (Warner Bros., 1988). **Robben Ford & the Blue Line,** *Robben Ford & the Blue Line* (Stretch, 1992), *Handful of Blues* (Blue Thumb, 1995).

Recordings featuring Robben Ford: **Jimmy Witherspoon,** *Spoonful* (L.A. International, c. 1973), *Live at the Mint* (Private, 1996•). **George Harrison,** *Dark Horse* (Apple, 1974). **Joni Mitchell** [on Asylum], *Miles of Aisles* (1974•), *The Hissing of Summer Lawns* (1975). **Tom Scott & the L.A. Express,** *Tom Cat* (Ode, 1975). **L.A. Express,** *L.A. Express* (Caribou, 1976). **Barbra Streisand/Kris Kristofferson,** *A Star Is Born* (Columbia, 1976). **Kenny Loggins,** *Celebrate Me Home* (Columbia, 1977). **Yellowjackets** [on Warner Bros.], *Yellowjackets* (1981), *Mirage a Trois* (1983). **Various Artists,** *Casino Lights* (Warner Bros., 1982•). **Brandon Fields,** *The Other Side of the Story* (Nova, 1986).

CHAPTER TWENTY-ONE

Hard Rock and Heavy Metal III
New Heroes for a New Age

A change was in the wind. Rock guitar by the mid 1970s had largely become a stagnant pool of bland imitators of Clapton, Beck, Page, and Hendrix. Innovation was a rare commodity, yet endless hordes of white suburban teenagers still lapped up the often uninspired licks of the period's mainstream hard rock guitarists.

Towards the end of the decade, a group of disparate players began pushing the envelope of hard rock and heavy metal guitar, adding a refined technique and eclectic influences—especially classical music—to their repertoire. In Clapton and Page's day, the pentatonic blues scale or, at most, the funky Dorian mode were the basis for solos. The new players supplemented these scales with the more flavorful minor Aeolian or dominant Mixolydian modes. New techniques such as legato hammer-ons and pull-offs added a fresh melodic flair, while the aged and fading tremolo unit was retooled and revived as a must-have hardware component. Tools and tricks aside, the new guitar heroes were simply faster, slicker, and more musically knowledgeable then their predecessors. Whether it was a metal icon like Eddie Van Halen or a Euro-radical like Uli Roth of Scorpions, the new generation of hard rocking guitarists was steadily twisting the standardized rock solo into a brave new language. While this era is generally considered a minor one in heavy metal history, in reality it was something of a golden age for the guitar.

Eddie Van Halen

Born: *January 26, 1955, in Nijmegen, Holland*
Main Guitars: *Homemade Strat-style solidbody, Ernie Ball/Music Man Van Halen Model, Peavey Wolfgang*

Like an electric shock reviving a heart attack victim, Eddie Van Halen single-handedly grabbed the dying art of seventies rock guitar and zapped new life into it. While most rock guitarists relied on pentatonic blues scales for their solos and a Jimmy Page-inspired Gibson Les Paul Standard with Marshall stacks for gear, Van Halen strapped on a homemade Stratocaster (composed of pieces from various manufacturers) and soloed with hammer-on runs, deep tremolo bar dives, and a brilliant two-hand tapping technique.

His tapping method involved the fretboard hand executing a repeated but highly movable hammer-on motif, while the picking hand tapped another note higher up on fingerboard. After he unveiled this technique in 1978 on the classical-sounding finale from his monumental solo "Eruption" (from *Van Halen*), rock guitarists around the globe appropriated tapping for their own use. Soon thereafter, Eddie Van Halen was touted by fans, critics, and other guitarists as the newest and most significant guitar hero of the day.

Early Years. Born in Holland, Edward Van Halen immigrated with his family to California in 1967. Van Halen already played classical piano, but upon arrival in the U.S., the young musician was immediately taken with the music created by John Mayall's Bluesbreakers and Eric Clapton's Cream. Inspired by these exciting rock 'n' roll sounds, Van Halen took up drums, while his brother Alex learned guitar. But he found that he wasn't particularly proficient on the drums, and switched roles with Alex, who—for his part—had shown no particular proficiency for guitar playing.

Eddie later played in

Eddie Van Halen

local rock groups like the Broken Combs, Trojan Rubber Co., the Space Brothers, and Mammoth before the two brothers formed Van Halen around 1973, with singer David Lee Roth and bassist Michael Anthony. Over the next few years, Van Halen worked their way up the southern California rock ladder, gaining a large following by gigging constantly in and around Los Angeles, especially at clubs like The Whiskey and Gazarri's. By the mid seventies, the band had graduated to opening gigs for major rock acts playing in the L.A. area, like Santana, UFO, and guitarist Nils Lofgren. Kiss bassist Gene Simmons heard Van Halen and was impressed enough to finance the band's first demo tape. Their brief collaboration with Simmons failed to result in a record deal, but the band continued to play local showcases and sent the tape out as a promo piece. In the spring of 1977, Van Halen signed with Warner Brothers and entered the studio with producer Ted Templeman (of Doobie Brothers fame) and engineer Donn Landee. Within a few days, Van Halen had recorded over 30 songs for their first album. Released early in 1978, *Van Halen* still stands as one of the great hard rock albums of all time, and arguably, the group's finest effort.

Recordings. Before the record's actual release, radio listeners were bombarded with Van Halen's thundering cover of the Kinks' 1964 classic "You Really Got Me" (ironically, one of the progenitors of heavy metal) and their own composition "Runnin' with the Devil." Both cuts featured Eddie running amok with uncanny ad lib solos and power riffs. When the album was released, Van Halen's "Eruption" brought guitar fans to their knees as Eddie performed high-speed hammer-ons, tremolo bar leaps, and the legendary two-hand tapping finale. With a high level of melodic drama, technical virtuosity, and all-out metal crunch, "Eruption" became the most influential unaccompanied rock solo since Jimmy Page's "Heartbreaker" lead of 1969. The entire debut album was consistently brilliant, featuring both fleet-fingered virtuosity and sonic experimentation throughout. The definitive example was "Ain't Talkin' 'bout Love," which showcased Van Halen's flanged and phased guitar and his ability to make simple chord progressions musically interesting. No one in the history of guitar got more exciting mileage out of a two-chord song (Am and G) than Van Halen did on this cut. With the immediate and sudden success of its first record, the band hit the road as the opening act for Black Sabbath.

After release of *Van Halen II* (1979), the group moved to headliner status and embarked on a world concert tour. The second Van Halen disc featured the band's first bona fide hit in "Dance the Night Away," a cut which made them more accessible to a wider (more pop-oriented) rock audience. They did not ease up on their drive or volume, however, as the album featured metal guitar masterworks such as "Somebody Get Me a Doctor," "Bottoms Up," and "Light Up the Sky." As a pseudo-sequel to "Eruption," Eddie recorded a solo acoustic guitar track for *Van Halen II* entitled "Spanish Fly," which he performed on an Ovation nylon-string. Even though he used many of the same techniques that were employed on his original electric extrava-

ganza, Van Halen's application of these techniques to the acoustic guitar was simply ear-boggling. It was yet another great unaccompanied solo by the young guitar wizard.

By the arrival of *Women and Children First* (1980), Eddie Van Halen was topping guitar polls everywhere and had clearly become the most influential rock guitar player since the days of Clapton, Page, and Hendrix. To emulate Eddie, young guitarists everywhere scrambled to learn his two-handed tapping style and purchased Strat-style electrics with whammy bars and humbucking pickups in the bridge position (one of Van Halen's biggest influences, Allan Holdsworth, used this same guitar setup in the band U.K.). *Women and Children First* featured another radio hit, the song "And the Cradle Will Rock," which, ironically, utilized a distorted electric piano made to sound like a guitar, and a hammer-on solo heavily inspired by Holdsworth.

Cranking out another new studio album the following year (making it four in four years), Van Halen brought forth *Fair Warning* in 1981. *Fair Warning* signaled a different direction for the band by featuring the increased use of overdubbing and the layering of multiple guitar parts. This was especially notable since earlier group efforts had practically been recorded live in the studio. The intro of the lead-off song, "Mean Streets," displayed another new "trick" from Eddie Van Halen: slapping the fretboard of the guitar with his hands to get a percussive, harmonic-filled sound. Nineteen eighty-two saw the release of *Diver Down*, which was yet another hit for the band. However, many fans claimed that it was not one of VH's best efforts, primarily because of its short length and overabundance of cover material. Among the bright spots are "Cathedral," which contains a sterling example of Albert Lee-style cascade echo effects, and the acoustic intro to "Little Guitars," in which Van Halen plays two parts at once, via a combination of hammer-ons and fast picking.

Outside of the band and *Diver Down*, Eddie Van Halen appeared on a song that exposed his guitar playing to nearly every household in America, and perhaps the world. The cut was Michael Jackson's "Beat It," the #1 single from the all-time best-selling album, *Thriller*. After session master and Toto guitarist Steve Lukather (♦) laid down a hot power chord and bass groove, Van Halen played a brilliant solo that incorporated all of his patented techniques: hammer-on climbs, harmonics, tremolo bar drops, and, of course, his trademark two-hand taps. After the landmark success of "Beat It," there were very few people who could claim that they had never heard Van Halen's guitar playing.

A two-year Van Halen sabbatical followed *Diver Down* as the band geared up for their next musical move. That move came at the onset of 1984 with the album *1984* and its single "Jump." A major departure for the band, "Jump" featured Eddie Van Halen playing synthesizer in lieu of his usual power guitar riffs, although he contributed a scorching axe break to the song's midsection. While keyboard textures had been used on earlier Van Halen tracks, the bold use of the guitarist's Oberheim OB-Xa synthesizer on "Jump" signaled the beginning of a lucrative new era for Van Halen: both the album and the single raced to the top of the record sales charts. Other songs off of *1984*, including "I'll Wait," "Hot for Teacher," and "Panama," received considerable radio and MTV airplay, and all seemed bright for Van Halen. After a successful tour, yet another long layoff period followed, during which David Lee Roth cut a solo EP that spawned several singles and popular videos of the songs "California Girls" and "I'm Just a Gigolo." Before long, rumors were ripe that Roth was ready to make a movie. After several months of music industry speculation, the band made an announcement that Roth had left Van Halen due to friction with his bandmates. The ensuing predicament as to who could replace a showman as flamboyant as Roth even caused Warner Brothers to recommend that Eddie and the boys carry on using a different name for their band. Eddie refused—it was *his* name, after all—and he put the issue to rest at the beginning of 1986: ex-Montrose vocalist and solo artist Sammy Hagar would be Van Halen's new vocalist.

Van Halen released the album *5150* in the spring of 1986. As if to quell any doubts that Hagar would be able to fill Roth's shoes, the record became one of the biggest selling albums of the year. Named after Van Halen's home studio and the police code for "psycho on the loose," *5150* featured even more keyboards than its predecessor, along with Alex Van Halen's triggered-drum work and Eddie's increasingly pop-oriented compositions. The disc *5150* went to #1 on the record charts—the first Van Halen album to do so—and racked up hits with "Why Can't This Be Love," "Dreams," and "Love Walks In." A hugely successful tour followed, with Sammy Hagar handling guitar chores on those songs that required Eddie on keyboards. With its increasingly slick commercial sound, and favorable reviews for *5150* from the mainstream press, Van Halen went from being a top heavy metal outfit to one of the most popular groups in eighties rock 'n' roll.

Mainstream popularity also brought with it mainstream scrutiny. Eddie's marriage to actress Valerie Bertinelli, their attempts to have a child, and his highly publicized bouts with alcoholism all became fodder for the tabloid press. Outside of Eric Clapton, no other guitarist had ever attracted so much public prying into his personal life. This did not deter his musical pursuits, however, and 1988 found the band leading the huge "Monsters of Rock" tour around the country (with Scorpions, Dokken, Metallica, and Kingdom Come). That same year, Van Halen also released the rather limp studio set *OU812*, a somewhat lyrically overwrought and musically safe excursion that never strayed far from mainstream pop. Perhaps sensing a bit of its own malaise, in 1991 the band released the pounding *For Unlawful Carnal Knowledge*, and followed that up with a live set, *Right Here, Right Now*, in 1993. *Balance* was released in 1995, reaching double platinum status within four months, making Van Halen the only guitarist in history to have all of his studio records go multi-platinum.

In mid 1996, Van Halen shocked fans and the rock press when it announced that Sammy Hagar had left the band. According to Eddie, Hagar had been less than enthusiastic about Van Halen projects ranging from the *Twister* soundtrack to a

greatest hits package to a new studio album. A public battle followed: Hagar claimed he was fired, Eddie maintained that Hagar had quit. During this same period, Roth re-emerged and offered to contribute to the greatest hits record. He was brought back into the band to add two new songs to the *Best of, Volume 1* album, but the old animosities resurfaced, and Roth was back on the street soon thereafter. Eddie eventually decided to add an entirely new face to the picture when he announced that Gary Cherone, the lead singer of Extreme, would be joining the band as its full-time vocalist. Tracks for a new studio album were already complete by October 1996.

Style and Technique. Eddie Van Halen's legacy is immense. While Van Halen was certainly not the first rock guitarist to use the two-hand tapping method—Steve Hackett of Genesis, Harvey Mandel, Billy Gibbons of ZZ Top, and Larry Carlton each used the technique earlier—he was certainly the one who introduced it to the rest of the guitar world, and he was singularly responsible for making it famous. The same holds true for his tremolo bar work: Jimi Hendrix was a famous practitioner of multi-octave whammy drops, but—due to the technical limitations of Fender Stratocaster tremolo units and Bigsby vibrato bars (that is, for fear of putting the guitar out of tune or breaking a string)—few guitarists after Hendrix used the device so dramatically. With the advent of locking-nut tremolo units like the popular Floyd Rose and Kahler models, not to mention Eddie's own tremolo-spring setup, Van Halen revived the radical use of the whammy bar. His lead prompted almost every player on the planet to buy a guitar with a tremolo unit—a craze that eventually extended to bassists and acoustic guitarists. It was a true hardware revolution.

As for Van Halen's occasional use of legato hammer-ons, there were also earlier proponents of that technique, namely Randy California of Spirit, Bill Nelson of Be Bop Deluxe, and the veritable master of legato, Allan Holdsworth. Still, Van Halen made the technique his own by combining it with super-fast picking and violent, crazed string bends—perhaps an abstraction of the guitarist's early fascination with the bluesy string bending of Eric Clapton. Thus, Van Halen's genius might be found in the way he dug up old techniques and reinvented them as wild new forms.

Like Chuck Berry, Eric Clapton, Jimi Hendrix, Jeff Beck, and Jimmy Page in their own time, Eddie Van Halen exerted so powerful an effect on rock guitarists—especially during the period from 1978 to 1984—that even those players who didn't listen to him directly felt his influence. This happened for the simple reason that his sound and style filtered down through the rock guitar world so relentlessly that eventually it seemed as if every other player was copping his licks and learning his solos. Though there have been many superb guitarists since rock's inception, only exceptional guitarists like Berry, Hendrix, Clapton, and, later, Yngwie Malmsteen sparked this sort of all-pervasive guitar frenzy. Today, Van Halen is considered one of *the* great rock players of all time, and for overall impact, ranks as equal to Hendrix and Clapton.

Van Halen [on Warner Bros.], *Van Halen* (1978), *Van Halen II* (1979), *Women and Children First* (1980), *Fair Warning* (1981), *Diver Down* (1982), *1984* (1984), *5150* (1986), *OU812* (1988), *For Unlawful Carnal Knowledge* (1991), *Right Here, Right Now* (1993•), *Balance* (1995), *Best of, Volume 1* (1996). **Various Artists,** *Twister* [soundtrack] (Warner Bros., 1996).

Recordings featuring Eddie Van Halen: **Nicolette Larson,** *Nicolette* (Warner Bros., 1978). **Michael Jackson,** *Thriller* (Epic, 1982). **Brian May & Friends,** *Star Fleet Project* (Capitol, 1983). **Various Artists,** *The Wild Life* [soundtrack] (MCA, 1984). **Sammy Hagar,** *Sammy Hagar* (Geffen, 1987).

Rush

Alex Lifeson

Born: *Alex Zivojinovic, on August 27, 1953, in Surnie, British Columbia*
Main Guitars: *Gibson Les Paul Standard, ES-355, EDS-1275 doubleneck, and Howard Roberts model, Strat-style solidbodies, Paul Reed Smith solidbody, various steel-string and classical acoustics*

Alex Lifeson has been at the forefront of innovative rock guitar since the late 1970s. His creative, high-energy guitar playing with Rush, the high-tech power trio from Canada, utilizes a distinctive guitar sound comprising incendiary solos, textured rhythm work, and a tasteful use of electronic sound effects.

Recordings. Rush was formed in 1968 by Lifeson, bassist-vocalist Geddy Lee (born Gary Lee Weinrib), and drummer John Rutsey. For several years the trio pounded out hard rock tunes on the Toronto bar circuit, gradually building themselves a strong following north of the border. In 1974 Rush released their eponymous first album, which was a collection of Led Zeppelin-styled heavy rockers. By their second album, *Fly by Night*, Rutsey had been replaced by drummer-lyricist Neil Peart, and Rush began several years of touring across the U.S., opening shows for bands like Aerosmith and Kiss. The 1976 release of *2112*, their hugely popular fourth album, helped to establish Rush as a band with serious talent and a unique twist on hard guitar rock. The album also gained the band a sizable cult following in the U.S. and Canada, an amazing accomplishment for a group that had received very little commercial radio airplay. Lifeson's playing on these first few Rush albums was straight from the British rock school (e.g., Clapton, Beck, and Page) and utilized an abundance of fast left-hand hammer-ons and blues scale clichés. Among the guitar highlights of this era were his solos on "Bastille Day" (from the 1976 live set *All the World's a Stage*), most of the leads from the extensive *2112* suite, the explosive riffing in "Something for Nothing," and the lush chording of "The Twilight Zone."

On *A Farewell to Kings* (1977) and *Hemispheres* (1978), Rush moved from its heavy metal roots into the synthesizer-dominated art rock genre. The band's recordings contained lengthy concept pieces reminiscent of Yes, Genesis, and Pink Floyd, except that Rush performed them with a definite hard rock edge based on Lifeson's overdriven guitar. With *A Farewell to Kings*,

Lifeson started to delve into the sounds of art rock guitarists like Steve Howe and Steve Hackett, developing a more melodic approach to soloing that could be heard in songs like "Xanadu," with its dramatic, Lydian-flavored intro, and "Closer to the Heart." Like Howe and Hackett, Lifeson is a proficient classical guitarist, and he used nylon-string guitar segments to open several Rush pieces, like "A Farewell to Kings" and "The Trees" (from *Hemispheres*). Rush's music during this time was extremely complex, employing difficult tempo changes and a variety of key signatures within individual pieces—something rarely found in hard rock.

In 1980 the band abruptly changed direction again and issued *Permanent Waves*. It had noticeably shorter songs and, in light of the New Wave movement, signaled the band's move towards a less ornate, more electronic sound. This stylistic change quickly paid off, as *Waves* cut into the U.S. Top 10 album charts and established Rush as one of the top progressive bands in rock. A series of critically acclaimed studio albums and successful tours promoted this formula, keeping Rush on the charts and making the band a rock radio mainstay. These records included *Moving Pictures* (1981), which featured some of Lifeson's most scorching riffs on the song "Red Barchetta," *Signals* (1982), *Grace under Pressure* (1984), *Presto* (1989), and *Counterparts* (1993), to name a few.

Style and Technique. Lifeson has also been a proponent of cutting and pasting solos, meaning that he would often record several solos for a song and then take the best parts of each and strip them into one continuous piece. Some of his best electric solos are on tracks such as "La Villa Strangiato," a complex instrumental suite that features a slow solo reminiscent of Peter Green's soulful playing with Fleetwood Mac; "The Spirit of Radio," with its groundbreaking proto-shred solo; and "Limelight," which betrayed Holdsworth's influence on Lifeson with its subtle tremolo bar effects and highly melodic runs.

As he continued to mature as a guitarist, Lifeson also developed an economic approach to soloing in the New Wave-influenced eighties that exuded taste and texture over speed (interestingly, at the same time most of his peers headed for shred city). A good example of this can be heard in "Afterimage" (from *Grace under Pressure*), which Lifeson tracked with guitar textures ranging from big chordal splashes, effects-ridden lead fills, and a solo of multi-string riffs and shimmering chords.

In addition to his brilliant lead work, Lifeson has also proven himself a skilled rhythm guitarist and, like Andy Summers of the Police, has made extensive use of chorus and echo effects in his arpeggiated chord progressions and suspended-fourth chords. He also moves easily from staccato strums to fluid acoustic passages, and seems equally at home with bombast and finesse. For sheer rock guitar versatility and dynamics, Lifeson has few equals.

Rush [on Mercury except where noted], *Rush* (1974), *Fly by Night* (1975), *Caress of Steel* (1975), *2112* (1976), *All the World's a Stage* (1976•), *A Farewell to Kings* (1977), *Hemispheres* (1978), *Permanent Waves* (1980), *Moving*

Pictures (1981), *Exit: Stage Left* (1981•), *Signals* (1982), *Grace under Pressure* (1984), *Power Windows* (1985), *Hold Your Fire* (1987), *A Show of Hands* (1988•), *Presto* (1989), *Roll the Bones* (1991), *Chronicles* (1991•), *Counterparts* (1993), *Test for Echo* (Atlantic, 1996). **Alex Lifeson,** *Victor* (Atlantic, 1995).

Randy Rhoads

Born: *December 6, 1956, in Santa Monica, California* ·
Died: *March 19, 1982, in Leesburg, Florida*
Main Guitars: *Gibson Les Paul Custom, Carl Sandoval custom Flying V, Jackson/Charvel custom V-style*

At the beginning of 1982, Randy Rhoads was the heir apparent to Eddie Van Halen. His hot guitar work for ex-Black Sabbath vocalist Ozzy Osbourne on the albums *Blizzard of Ozz* and *Diary of a Madman* proved that he was an inventive and original metal axeman. With dark, minor-tonality riffs and solos that incorporated two-hand tapping, the hammer-on/pull-off technique, classical influences, and his omnipresent double- and triple-tracking signature, his magnetic playing attracted scores of hero-worshipping fans. He was a rising star in the rock guitar world who won top honors as best new guitarist in guitar polls and was roundly praised for his concert performances and recorded work with Ozzy. Sadly, on March 19, 1982, Rhoads was killed in a freak plane crash during an Ozzy tour. To the heartbreak of his countless fans, the promise of Randy Rhoads' great talent was never fulfilled, though he remains one of the most popular guitarists of the 1980s.

Before landing the Ozzy gig in 1979, Rhoads had been one of the top guitarists on the Los Angeles rock scene. For several years, he and his band Quiet Riot (later a briefly popular act on their own) had ruled the southern California metal circuit, along with rival band Van Halen. Although Quiet Riot had toured internationally and was on the verge of a record deal, Rhoads kept his options open. As luck would have it, Ozzy Osbourne began auditioning musicians for a new band in L.A. after tiring of Black Sabbath (◆), the band he had fronted for close to a decade. Legend has it that Ozzy's L.A. search proved fruitless and that he was about to leave California when someone recommended he listen to a local guitar teacher named Randy Rhoads. Amidst towers of Marshall stacks, Rhoads strolled into the audition with a little practice amp, started tuning his axe, and played some soft fretboard harmonics. After listening to the constant high-volume drone of countless metal aspirants and clones, Ozzy offered Rhoads the gig on the spot.

Rhoads relocated to England and recorded the first Ozzy solo album, *Blizzard of Ozz*. Upon its release in 1980, the disc stormed up the charts, and Rhoads was immediately thrust into the guitar spotlight. Establishing his monstrous sound and lightning-quick chops with the opening track, "I Don't Know," Rhoads then injected his multitracked guitar work into many of the record's rockers, like "Crazy Train," "Mr. Crowley," and "Suicide Solution." In contrast, he served up classical-styled fingerpicking for the gentle acoustic guitar ballad "Dee." Perhaps most astounding to listeners and guitar fans was his ability to repeat his solos perfectly, note for note and take after take, in order to create multiple, and identical, layers of individual sections. This was so far removed from the idea of one-take or live solos that it appeared positively alien to many hard rockers.

After a short tour of Europe to support *Blizzard of Ozz*, Ozzy and company went right back into the studio to record a second album, *Diary of a Madman* (1981). Now fully settled into his role with Ozzy's band, Rhoads let loose with his most inspired guitar work, filling up song after song on *Diary* with wildly inventive guitar parts. On such Ozzy classics as "Over the Mountain," "Diary of a Madman," and, especially, the guitar favorite "Flying High Again," Rhoads used harmonics, tremolo effects, fast-picked modal runs, muted phrases, tapping, hammer-ons, multitracking, and classical arpeggios for his showcase solos. Clearly, this was a player with a *very* strong creative vision.

But within a few months of launching the subsequent tour, Rhoads was dead. Amazingly, what he did achieve on the two albums and several tours with Ozzy Osbourne (as well as two earlier Japanese LPs with Quiet Riot) was still being discussed and analyzed more than a decade after his death. Some called his guitar techniques mere "tricks" (such as

Ozzy Osbourne, Randy Rhoads

hammer-ons, tapping, classical-styled riffs, and tremolo effects), but thousands more absorbed and assimilated these sizzling techniques into their own playing, thereby effecting a change in the sound of rock guitar. Rhoads' talent was reaffirmed with the posthumous release of a live album called *Tribute* in 1987, which proved that his chops were no studio fluke. Another fascinating posthumous disc was *The Randy Rhoads Years*, a retrospective of his early Quiet Riot recordings, which showed how astoundingly advanced the guitarist was even in the late seventies (though Quiet Riot itself was a rather conventional metal band).

Although Rhoads was in many ways trapped into rehashing Van Halen techniques by virtue of the era in which he played (as he regularly admitted in interviews), his guitar parts were prophetic in their use of classical ideas, effectively predating–and clearly influencing–the coming shred revolution. Not since Ritchie Blackmore of Deep Purple had a top metal player been so aware of the possibilities of using baroque motifs in heavy rock 'n' roll. Rhoads' playing also had parallels with that of Jimmy Page. Like Page, Rhoads had a real talent for using the recording studio as an instrument in and of itself. This was evident in his many complex guitar overdubs and effects treatments. Another similarity between the two was their overpowering guitar hero appeal, i.e., the visual mystique of the handsome, even pretty, player whose thin figure was countered by the mighty blast of his guitar and amp stacks. It's an indelible image that has been copied countless times, but rarely do guitar players manage to merge it into a complete guitar hero aura. Randy Rhoads, however, truly was one of those players.

Quiet Riot [on CBS Sony], *Quiet Riot I* (1977), *Quiet Riot II* (1978), *The Randy Rhoads Years* (Rhino, 1993•). **Ozzy Osbourne** [on Jet], *Blizzard of Ozz* (1980), *Diary of a Madman* (1981), *Mr. Crowley* [EP] (1981•). **Ozzy Osbourne & Randy Rhoads**, *Tribute* (CBS, 1987•).

Thin Lizzy

Scott Gorham

B o r n : *March 17, 1951, in Los Angeles*
M a i n G u i t a r : *Gibson Les Paul*

Gary Moore

B o r n : *April 4, 1952, in Belfast, Northern Ireland*
M a i n G u i t a r : *Gibson Les Paul*

Brian Robertson

B o r n : *February 12, 1956, in Glasgow, Scotland*
M a i n G u i t a r : *Gibson Les Paul*

Eric Bell

B o r n : *March 9, 1947, in Belfast, Northern Ireland*
M a i n G u i t a r : *Fender Stratocaster*

Snowy White

B o r n : *March 3, 1948, in Barnstaple, North Devon, England*
M a i n G u i t a r : *Gibson Les Paul*

John Sykes

B o r n : *July 27, 1959, in Blackpool, England*
M a i n G u i t a r : *Gibson Les Paul*

The highly influential hard rock quartet Thin Lizzy achieved little more than cult celebrity status in America during the seventies and early eighties, but was considered a superstar group in England during that time. The band's classic seventies guitar line-up of Scott Gorham and Brian Robertson created extraordinary tandem guitar work and helped make Thin Lizzy one of the most powerful live bands of the decade. Gary Moore—who played with the band at three different points during the decade—was another integral part of the band's history, adding his state-of-the-art chops to the band's already incendiary sound. Other fine players like Eric Bell, Snowy White, and John Sykes rounded out the compelling Thin Lizzy guitar saga.

Scott Gorham

Recordings. Before their mid-decade glory days, Thin Lizzy was a trio featuring bassist-singer-frontman Phil Lynott, drummer Brian Downey, and guitarist Eric Bell. Formed in 1970, early Lizzy was closer to psychedelic blues-rock than heavy metal. The Hendrix-inspired Bell tore through tracks like "The Rocker" with a deft use of wah-wah, phasing, and distortion effects, and soloed in "Black Boys on the Corner" with fiery blues licks. He left the band in 1974 (later playing with a number of blues acts), to be temporarily replaced by blues-rock master Gary Moore. Moore appeared on only a smattering of recordings at this time, including the full-throttle rocker "Little Darling." He left after a few months to play fusion with drummer Jon Hiseman in Colosseum II. Two obscure German players named John Caan and Andy Gee held the Lizzy guitar reins for a brief period, and then Gorham and Robertson signed on for what would be Lizzy's golden age.

The two first appeared with Thin Lizzy for the relatively weak *Nightlife* (1974), but achieved full strength in 1976 with

Jailbreak (although the recording itself was a typical mid-seventies production, with a lamentable lack of bottom end). The single "The Boys Are Back in Town" brought the album into the U.S. Top 20 and helped Gorham and Robertson gain recognition for their outstanding harmony guitar lines on the song. Other guitar strong points of the disc were the heavy metal riffing of "Jailbreak," "Emerald," and Warriors," as well as the screaming blues-metal breaks on "Cowboy Song"—with Gorham taking the first solo and Robertson burning through the second. The follow-up album was the Robertson-dominated *Johnny the Fox*, issued in late 1976 to solid acclaim. With strong thematic cuts like "Johnny," the record had almost as much potential as *Jailbreak*, but without the sales to back it up.

During 1976 Thin Lizzy toured America as opening act for Queen. This tour became semi-legendary for the guitar battles that took place every night between Thin Lizzy's Gorham and Robertson, and Queen's Brian May; at some gigs, Thin Lizzy blew the headliners off the stage. For some reason, though, the band never caught on in the United States. To make matters more difficult, the group was operating as a trio by the release of the remarkably solid *Bad Reputation* in 1977. Due to friction between Lynott and Robertson, the guitarist departed prior to the recording of the album, leaving Gorham alone to fill both roles. Gorham absolutely shone on the record, although Robertson was eventually brought back to cut great solos to the rockers "Opium Trail" and "Killer without a Cause."

Nineteen seventy-eight brought the release of Thin Lizzy's finest recorded moment: the stunning *Live and Dangerous* set, which caught the band in prime form during several Gorham-Robertson shows. While the record was a testament to how well these musicians worked together, Robertson was ousted from the band again and went off to join Motorhead. He was soon replaced by Gary Moore for the fine 1979 follow-up, *Black Rose*. Another stellar period ensued, with Moore adding blistering breaks to "Toughest Street in Town" (notable for its insane pre-shred solo), "Get out of Here," and the Celtic-inspired title epic, which featured Moore trading hot solos with himself via over-dubbing. Gorham kept up the heat with muscular solos on "Waiting for an Alibi" and the second break to "Got to Give It Up"—one of his best ever. However, further infighting during the subsequent U.S. tour led to the departure of Moore and the end of a very promising Lizzy lineup.

To fill in during the search for a permanent replacement, players like Midge Ure (later of Ultravox) and Dave Flett of Manfred Mann's Earth Band sat in for a few months of touring. Subsequent albums featured Gorham pairing off with co-guitarists Snowy White (a longtime Pink Floyd sideman) and John Sykes (later of Whitesnake), but they were not nearly as impressive as the band's earlier work. Lynott pulled the plug on Lizzy in 1983, although their final disc, *Thunder and Lightning*, had shown a spark of their former glory. It also displayed Sykes' explosive lead work, which was certainly one of the earliest pure shred exhibitions on record.

Style. Few would dispute that the Gorham-Robertson period was the band's strongest era. Credit for this rested largely with singer Phil Lynott, who was in top songwriting and vocal form, and with the interplay between Gorham and Robertson. These two made up the most coherent British guitar team since Andy Powell and Ted Turner of Wishbone Ash. Defining Thin Lizzy's guitar sounds were the duo's highly contrasting lead styles, as evidenced by Robertson's wah-wah inflected metal breaks and Gorham's more melodic and soulful approach. With this combined guitar and songwriting prowess, Thin Lizzy's late-seventies albums regularly broke into the British Top 5, while the acclaimed *Live and Dangerous* stayed on the charts for over a full year.

Despite their individual abilities, few of Lizzy's guitarists were able to strike out on their own. Robertson's stint with Motorhead was relatively uneventful, while Gorham went on to do work sporadically with Supertramp, Asia, and then his own band, 21 Guns. Snowy White returned to relative obscurity. John Sykes achieved some fame (and presumably fortune) as David Coverdale's guitar foil during the heyday of Whitesnake. He then formed his own band, Blue Murder, with bassist Tony Franklin and drummer Carmine Appice, and then proceeded to drop off the map. Currently, rumors abound that a Thin Lizzy reunion is imminent, under the creative auspices of Gorham.

Solo Moore. Only Gary Moore made a substantial name for himself outside of the confines of Thin Lizzy. After his sudden exit from the band in 1979, he began a solo career with *Back on the Streets*, a part-rock, part-fusion affair that saw chart success via the ballad hit "Parisienne Walkways." (The original version featured Lynott on vocals; after Moore left Lizzy, these were erased and replaced with the guitarist's own singing.) Moore briefly tried working in a band format again with G-Force, and also played sideman for Greg Lake of ELP. Eventually he went back to solo work, cutting the Deep Purple-flavored albums *Corridors of Power* (1983) and *Victims of the Future* (1984). In 1985 he reconciled with Phil Lynott and recorded a new single, "Out in the Fields," which scored big in England. It was a brilliant piece of high-tech metal that featured Moore's new interest—the guitar synthesizer—as well as his patented flash guitar breaks. Sadly, Lynott died in early 1986 after years of drug and alcohol abuse.

Moore's next solo effort, *Run for Cover*, included everything from bombastic metal cuts to airplay-oriented pop tunes, and was roundly praised by rock critics. While U.S. fans failed to pick up on it, it was a success for Moore abroad. In 1987 Moore put out his fifth American solo album, *Wild Frontier*, a powerful tribute album to Lynott that featured some of Moore's most poignant songwriting and guitar work to date. Among the tracks were a metal remake of the Easybeats' 1967 hit "Friday on My Mind" and several Celtic-flavored rockers with members of the Irish traditional group the Chieftains as featured guests. Unfortunately, the guitarist's next effort, *After the War*, strayed from this elegant Celtic-rock formula and returned to bland, straight metal.

In 1990 Moore made the smartest leap of his career, cutting

a full blues-rock album called *Still Got the Blues*. The record was largely based on the British blues he grew up listening to, notably John Mayall's Bluesbreakers, Fleetwood Mac, and Cream. To boot, his main guitar for the project was Peter Green's original 1959 Les Paul, which he had purchased from the Fleetwood Mac guitarist some 20 years earlier. The album was a major success, and Moore's career was rejuvenated. His fiery, metal-influenced blues solos also won the guitarist a new range of fans, and the similarly well-received albums *After Hours* and *Blues Alive* followed in the same vein. He then teamed up with Cream alumni Jack Bruce and Ginger Baker in the *de facto* supergroup BBM, which many wrote off as recycled Cream despite Moore's brilliant playing. Nonetheless, once Moore found his blues-rock niche, he cemented his reputation as one of Great Britain's finest rock soloists.

Thin Lizzy [on Mercury except where noted], *Thin Lizzy* (Decca, 1971), *Shades of a Blue Orphanage* (Decca, 1972), *Vagabonds of the Western World* (Decca, 1973), *Nightlife* (1974), *Fighting* (1975), *Jailbreak* (1976), *Johnny the Fox* (1976), *Remembering, Part One* (Decca, 1976), *Bad Reputation* (1977), *Live and Dangerous* (Warner Bros., 1978•), *Rocker: 1971–1974* (London, 1978), *Black Rose/A Rock Legend* (Warner Bros., 1979), *The Continuing Saga of the Ageing Orphans* (Decca, 1979), *Chinatown* (Warner Bros., 1980), *Renegade* (Warner Bros., 1981), *Thunder and Lightning* (Warner Bros., 1983), *Life—Live* (Warner Bros., 1984•), *Lizzy Lives* (Grand Slamm, 1989), *Dedication* (1991). **Phil Lynott** [on Warner Bros.], *Solo in Soho* (1980), *The Philip Lynott Album* (1982). **Wild Horses**, *Wild Horses* (EMI, 1980), *Stand Your Ground* (EMI, 1981). **21 Guns**, *Salute* (RCA, 1992).

Recordings featuring Eric Bell: **The Dreams**, *The Best of the Dreams* (Dolphin, 1969). **Noel Redding Band**, *Clonakilty Cowboys* (RCA, 1976), *Blowin'* (RCA, 1976). **Brush Shiels**, *Brush Shiels* (Hawk, 1977). **Mainsqueeze**, *Live* (Expulsion, 1983•). **Bo Diddley**, *Hey, Bo Diddley Live* (Conifer, 1986•). **Smiley Bolger**, *Ode to a Black Man* (Stagelight, 1989).

Recordings featuring Scott Gorham: **Pat Travers**, *Putting It Straight* (Polydor, 1977). **Supertramp**, *Brother, Where You Bound* (A&M, 1985). **Phenomena II**, *Dream Runner* (Arista, 1987). **Heads Up**, *The Long Shot* (Polydor, 1989). **Asia**, *Then and Now* (Geffen, 1990). **Air Pavilion**, *Kaizoku* (Polydor, 1990). **Phenomena III**, *Inner Vision* (Parachute, 1993).

Recordings featuring Brian Robertson: **Pat Travers**, *Making Magic* (Polydor, 1977). **Steve Ellis**, *The Last Angry Man* (Ariola, 1978). **Peter French**, *Ducks in Flight* (Polydor, 1978). **Roy Sundholm**, *Chinese Method* (Ensign, 1979). **Eric Burdon**, *Darkness Darkness* (Polydor, 1980). **Motorhead**, *Another Perfect Day* (Bronze, 1983), *The Birthday Party* (GWR, 1990), *Welcome to the Bear Trap* (Castle, 1990).

Recordings featuring Snowy White: **Peter Green**, *In the Skies* (PVK, 1979). **Roger Waters & Various Artists**, *The Wall—Live in Berlin* (Mercury, 1990•). **Blues Agency**, *Change My Life* (c. 1990).

Recordings featuring John Sykes: ▶ Whitesnake.

Skid Row, *Skid* (1970), *34 Hours* (1971). **Gary Moore Band**, *Grinding Stone* (CBS, 1973). **Thin Lizzy** [on Warner Bros. except where noted], *Nightlife* (Mercury, 1974), *Remembering, Part One* (Decca, 1976), *Black Rose* (1979), *The Continuing Saga of the Ageing Orphans* (Decca, 1979), *Life—Live* (1984•). **Colosseum II**, *Strange New Flesh* (Bronze, 1975), *Electric Savage* (MCA, 1977), *War Dance* (MCA, 1977). **G-Force**, *G-Force* (Jet, 1980). **Gary Moore**, *Back on the Streets* (Jet, 1978), *Corridors of Power* (Mirage, 1983), *Rockin' Every Night—Live in Japan* [Japanese import] (Virgin, 1983•),

Dirty Fingers (Jet, 1984), *Live* (Jet, 1984•), *Victims of the Future* (Mirage, 1984), *White Knuckles* (Raw Power, 1985), *Run for Cover* (Mirage, 1985), *Wild Frontier* (Virgin, 1987), *After the War* (Virgin, 1989), *Still Got the Blues* (Charisma, 1990), *After Hours* (Charisma, 1992), *Blues Alive!* (Charisma, 1993•), *Blues for Greeny* (Charisma, 1996). **Gary Moore & Phil Lynott**, *Out in the Fields* [EP] (10 Records, 1985). **BBM**, *Around the Next Dream* (Virgin, 1994).

Recordings featuring Gary Moore: **Rod Argent**, *Moving Home* (MCA, n/a). **Andrew Lloyd Webber**, *Variations* (n/a, 1978). **Gary Boyle**, *Electric Glide* (Gull, n/a). **Robin Lumley & Jack Lancaster**, *Peter and the Wolf* (n/a, c. 1979). **Eddie Howell**, *Gramophone Record* (Warner Bros., n/a). **Cozy Powell**, *Over the Top* (Ariola, 1980), *Tilt* (Polydor, 1981). **Phil Lynott**, *Solo in Soho* (Warner Bros., 1980). **Greg Lake** [on Chrysalis], *Greg Lake* (1981), *Manoeuvres* (1983). **The Beach Boys**, *The Beach Boys* (Caribou, 1985). **Various Artists**, *Ferry Aid* (n/a, 1987). **The Traveling Wilburys**, *Vol. 3* (WB/Wilbury, 1990).

AC/DC

Angus Young

B o r n : *March 31, 1959*
M a i n G u i t a r : *Gibson SG*

Malcolm Young

M a i n G u i t a r : *Gretsch Jet Firebird*

While most of the world's top heavy metal acts originated in America or Europe, Australia laid claim to one of the genre's most popular and loudest bands, AC/DC. Led by two sibling guitarists—Angus Young on lead and Malcolm on rhythm—AC/DC took record charts, radio, and concert arenas by storm in the late seventies with their simple, meat 'n' potatoes brand of hard rock. While most metal outfits were havens for musical excess, the Young brothers modeled the AC/DC sound on overwhelming simplicity: solid power chords, a thunderous beat, and catchy vocal choruses to make the songs radio-worthy. With this talent for economy, AC/DC racked up a handful of hit albums beginning in 1979 with discs such as *Highway to Hell*, *Back in Black*, and *For Those about to Rock, We Salute You*.

Angus and Malcolm Young formed AC/DC in 1974 with singer Bon Scott. The band earned its stripes playing the notoriously difficult bar circuit in Sydney, Australia, and in 1975 AC/DC recorded their first album, *High Voltage*. Directing the production was Angus and Malcolm's older brother George Young and his partner Harry Vanda (once leaders of the sixties pop band the Easybeats, known for their hit "Friday on My Mind"). Crafted with volume and aggression in mind, *High Voltage* and its successor, *TNT*, became big hits in Australia.

In 1976 AC/DC successfully toured the U.K., which helped them to gain an international following. *Let There Be Rock* (1977) put the band on the U.S. and U.K. record charts with their "Down Under" blue-collar hard rock anthems. The final step to superstardom came with the release of *Highway to Hell* in 1979. Produced by Robert John "Mutt" Lange, the disc crackled with the twin guitar muscle of the brothers Young, winning the band a legion of rabid new fans. Scott, however, died of alcohol poisoning while the band was rehearsing for their follow-up recording.

With new singer Brian Johnson, AC/DC forged on and in 1980 released *Back in Black*. This record put the band over the top with the hits "You Shook Me All Night Long," "Hells Bells," and the raging title track. Driven by the Youngs' simple guitar formula, *Back in Black* made its way to the top of record charts all over the world and established AC/DC as a heavy metal supergroup. Onstage, AC/DC became a major concert draw, due in part to Angus' school-boy garb (complete with knickers and cap), peripatetic body movements, and an eyebrow-raising striptease finale.

On a musical level, *Back in Black* introduced the Youngs' guitar work to millions of metal guitar fans worldwide. With Malcolm executing the crisp power chords on his Gretsch semi-solidbody (a very unusual axe for heavy metal), Angus filled up the rest of each song's harmonic midsection with a complement of doubled rhythm work, repeated hammer-on licks, and slow blues-based solos from his trademark Gibson SG. From "You Shook Me All Night Long" to "Hells Bells" to "Shoot to Thrill," the Young brothers used this exact formula on almost every track, choosing consistency over experimentation in their high-volume guitar playing.

Over the next decade, AC/DC duplicated this sound on such albums as *Fly on the Wall, Who Made Who*, and *The Razor's Edge*. During a decade when speed and technique dominated most rock guitarists' styles, the two guitar siblings thrived on clean power chords, economical rhythm arrangements, and aggressive, blues-based solos. In all, Angus and Malcolm Young proved that even the loudest and most crass of heavy metal bands could incorporate tasteful guitar as part of their presentation.

AC/DC [on Atlantic except where noted], *High Voltage* (Atco, 1976), *Let There Be Rock* (Atco, 1977), *Powerage* (1978), *If You Want Blood, You've Got It* (1978•), *Highway to Hell* (1979), *Back in Black* (1980), *Dirty Deeds Done Dirt Cheap* (1981), *For Those about to Rock, We Salute You* (1981), *Flick of the Switch* (1983), *'74 Jailbreak* (1984), *Fly on the Wall* (1985), *Who Made Who* [soundtrack] (1986), *Blow up Your Video* (1988), *The Razor's Edge* (Atco, 1990), *Live* (Atco, 1992•), *Ballbreaker* (East-West, 1995).

Minor Metalers

If any group illustrated the dramatic changes taking place in hard rock guitar from 1978 to 1980, it was the Pat Travers Band. During that span, the quartet had two aggressive lead guitarists: Pat Travers (born in 1954 in Canada), a hot pentatonic-based soloist who represented the blues-rock sound of sixties and seventies metal guitar, and Pat Thrall, a nimble stylist whose fast and melodic fusion lines were emblematic of the new generation of metal guitarists guided by the music of Eddie Van Halen. This version of the Pat Travers Band cut only a very few albums together, but the results keenly showed the metal guitar transition, espe-

cially on the live *Go for What You Know* (1979), which contains the semi-hit "Boom Boom (Out Go the Lights)." Thrall's break is angular and jarring, revealing his fusion training, while Travers stokes the furnace with a meaty blues-metal break. A ballad from the set, "Stevie," starts with Thrall playing an elegant cascade echo part, while Travers jams in the song's rideout with straight rockin' pentatonics. On *Crash and Burn* (1980), the guitar barn-burner "Snortin' Whiskey" features a Travers break full of blues-based bends, while Thrall creates a strange midsection comprising a violent low-register riff with glassy funk rhythms on top. The combining of the two players' solos during this time showed a rare détente between two generations of hard rockers, and, although short-lived, it was extremely exciting.

Another rock stylist who defied categories was Rik Emmett, Triumph's inspired and eclectic guitarist. Although the band's format was essentially pop-metal, Emmett (born July 10, 1953, in Toronto) didn't just restrict himself to the sound of an electric solidbody plugged into a stack of tube amplifiers. He proved himself a talented classical, jazz, blues, country, and acoustic fingerstyle guitarist and, amazingly, still found room for Triumph's standard hard rock fare. "Fantasy Serenade," "Fingertalkin' " (from *Progressions of Power*, 1980), and "A Minor Etude" reveal his varied acoustic skills, while "Suitcase Blues" (from *Just a Game*) and "Take My Heart" display his jazz education with cool bluesy playing. Still, Emmett could rock like anything, as he ably showed in everything from "Lay It on the Line" to the radio hit "I Live for the Weekend" to "Somebody's out There" (from *The Sport of Kings*, 1986), on which he played a full run of power chord rhythms and crunchy solos. As if to prove how atypical he was, Emmett often played his heaviest Triumph riffs on a Framus Jan Akkerman hollowbody. By any guitar standards, *that's* eclectic.

Pat Travers [on Polydor except where noted], *Pat Travers* (1976), *Putting It Straight* (1977), *Hot Shot* (1984), *Blues Tracks* (BBI, 1992). **Pat Travers Band** [on Polydor], *Heat in the Street* (1978), *Go for What You Know* (1979•), *Crash and Burn* (1980), *Radio Active* (1981), *Boom Boom/The Best of Pat Travers* (1985). **Pat Travers' Black Pearl**, *Pat Travers' Black Pearl* (1982). **Hughes/Thrall Band**, *Hughes/Thrall* (Boulevard, 1982).

Recordings featuring Pat Thrall: **Automatic Man** [on Island], *Automatic Man* (1976), *Visitors* (1977). **Stomu Yamashta** [on Island], *Go* (1976), *Go Live from Paris* (1978•). **Alphonso Johnson**, *Spellbound* (Epic, 1978). **Narada Michael Walden**, *Awakening* (Atlantic, 1979). **Esquire**, *Esquire* (Atlantic, 1987). **Sly Dunbar & Robbie Shakespeare**, *Rhythm Killers* (n/a, 1987). **Meat Loaf**, *Bat out of Hell II* (MCA, 1994).

Triumph [on RCA except where noted], *Triumph* (Attic, c. 1977), *Rock & Roll Machine* (1978), *Just a Game* (1978), *Progressions of Power* (1980), *Allied Forces* (1981), *Never Surrender* (1983), *Thunder Seven* (MCA, 1984), *Stages* (MCA, 1985•), *The Sport of Kings* (MCA, 1986), *Surveillance* (MCA, 1987). **Rik Emmett**, *Absolutely* (Charisma, 1991).

Recordings featuring Rik Emmett: **Diane Heatherton**, *Heatherton Rocks* (Epic, n/a). **Justin Page**, *Justin Page* (Capitol/EMI, n/a).

CHAPTER TWENTY-TWO

Pop Experimenters
Beyond Top 40

Music fans got hungry for melodies again.

This was one of the cheerier side effects of the 1970s punk/New Wave revolution. Not content with the pummeling riffs that had fueled rock for years—thanks to Led Zeppelin, Black Sabbath, and Blue Öyster Cult—audiences at the end of the decade decided that the word "pop" wasn't dirty anymore. Suddenly, it was acceptable to coat rock 'n' roll with a sprinkling of melodic ear-candy. Elvis Costello was considered pop and he was cool; the Knack was pop and they were considered cool; Styx was pop and, amazingly, even *they* were cool. In keeping with renewed public fascination for the Beatles (as evidenced in the cheesy Broadway play *Beatlemania*), audiences yearned for talented songwriters with an ear for melody, arrangements, and a catchy lyric or two.

As heavy metal hit its commercial (though not artistic) low point, lots of guitar players hopped on the melodic bandwagon. They helped to hash out a new subgenre, which was termed "power pop," a musical style that had rock roots reaching as far back as the Beatles' "I Wanna Hold Your Hand" and even earlier to Buddy Holly's "Peggy Sue." The rise of power pop eventually gave birth to its own spinoff, a slightly harder-sounding variation known as pop-metal. Coupling loud and distorted guitars with mainstream pop vocals and melodies, pop-metal yielded such American favorites as Journey, Foreigner, Toto, REO Speedwagon, and Styx. No matter how slick, insipid, or commercial these bands were, their songs generally had a nice, breezy melody, which was enough to assure them of heavy radio play, astronomical record sales, and sold-out stadium concerts.

While these bands were generally led by vocalists with angst-ridden falsettos and whitewashed Robert Plant complexes, their guitarists tended to be quite capable—if not completely invisible. REO Speedwagon's Gary Richrath was an inventive rocker who played excellent slide, while Tommy Shaw and James Young provided Styx with pop-metal's only guitar duo, and a compelling one at that. Toto was propelled by session wizard Steve Lukather, and Journey relied heavily on the guitar chops of former Santana guitarist Neal Schon.

Some of the guitarists of power pop and pop-metal managed to make a name for themselves as significant contributors to the guitar lexicon. There were others, however, who just cashed their big royalty checks and left the business after the demise of their respective bands. As was true of all of the musical genres prevalent in the late 1970s and 1980s, finding outstanding musicians and musical value was a matter of digging through the rubbish that filled the record charts and discovering the occasional gems buried deep within.

Adrian Belew

Born: *December 23, 1949, in Covington, Kentucky*
Main Guitars: *Modified Fender Stratocaster and Mustang, Roland guitar synthesizer*

Showered with plaudits including "The World's Premier Electric Guitarist," "Sonic Radical," and "The Future of Rock Guitar," Adrian Belew was a significant force in rock guitar during the 1980s and the darling of guitar critics and fans everywhere. Balancing his guitar tones between the clean, crisp twang of a Fender Stratocaster and the limitless sonic textures that emanated from a Roland guitar synthesizer—with animal noises and industrial burps prominently featured—Belew soared to prominence with Robert Fripp's King Crimson (◆), circa 1981 to 1984. Belew also earned widespread acclaim for his stage and studio work with Frank Zappa, David Bowie, Talking Heads, and then as a solo artist.

Before Belew found his niche as an avant-garde guitar extremist, he slugged it out in club bands and Top 40 acts for many years. In 1977, while playing in a Nashville club with his band Sweetheart, Belew was discovered by Frank Zappa. Zappa got in touch with Belew and invited him to L.A. to audition for his band. Belew passed the audition (on the second try) and was hired for a year-long gig with Zappa's touring band. Aside from guitar duties on stage, Belew also dressed in costumes and did skits for fans on Zappa's 1978 tour (some of which appeared on the *Sheik Yerbouti* album). During one show, Belew met David Bowie while Zappa was taking an extended solo. The two expressed their admiration for each other's music, and there, on the spot, Belew was hired for Bowie's next tour.

Belew played on the 1978 world tour, portions of which eventually appeared as the live album *Stage*. Next, Belew joined Bowie in the studio for the avant-pop *Lodger* set, to which he contributed the feedback- and tremolo-tinged solos on such gems as "Red Sails," "D.J.," and "Boys Keep Swinging." After the Bowie gig ended, Belew set up base in Springfield, Illinois, and formed a band called Ga-Ga. The group played the club circuit and gained a sizable following, but no record deal ever materialized. In 1980 Ga-Ga was asked to open for Robert Fripp's New Wave dance band, the League of Gentlemen, in New York. (Belew had met Fripp while on tour with Bowie.) Once there, Adrian was asked to do some studio work for Talking Heads. His guitar playing appeared on *Remain in Light* (1980); his wrenching solo on "The Great Curve" was one of the recording's strong points. With Ga-Ga not going anywhere, Belew hitched up with Talking Heads for a tour of the U.S., Europe, and Japan, which was chronicled by the Heads' live set *The Name of This Band is Talking Heads*. By 1981 Belew's abrasive guitar parts with Bowie and Talking Heads had earned him his reputation as an inventive soloist, and he began doing session work for the likes of Garland Jeffreys, Robert Palmer, Herbie Hancock, Joe Cocker, and Talking Heads spin-offs like the Tom Tom Club and Jerry Harrison's solo work.

Something beyond studio work opened up for Adrian Belew in 1981. After the demise of the League of Gentlemen, Robert Fripp put together a new band, called Discipline, with ex-Yes drummer Bill Bruford and bass/Stick player Tony Levin. He asked Belew to join the new lineup, and after a few weeks of jamming, Discipline turned into a new King Crimson. The new version of the band was musically based on the interlocking but contrasting guitar styles of Belew and Fripp (both of whom were using Roland GR-300 guitar synthesizers) and the formidable rhythm section of Bruford and Levin. Later in 1981, King Crimson released a record called *Discipline*, which was praised by fans and critics alike. Belew's chiming Strat chordings on "Elephant Talk" and "Matte Kudasai" (also featuring his unusual overhand slide style), as well as the tremolo bar effects on "Frame by Frame" and "Thela Hun Ginjeet," added a dimension of deft unpredictability to this powerful incarnation of Crimson.

King Crimson also performed a series of club dates around the U.S. and abroad that brought fans old and new out in droves. Based on this exposure, Belew quickly became the newest man to watch in rock guitar, and by 1982 all of the major guitar magazines had large write-ups on his unusual guitar style. During the summer of 1982 King Crimson released *Beat*, which displayed more of Belew's strange and beautiful guitar parts on "Waiting Man," "Two Hands," and "Neal and Jack and Me." To cap off an extremely successful year, in 1983 Belew released his solo album *Lone Rhino*. The next year he followed it up with another strong effort, *Twang Bar Master*, several cuts of which were done on a guitar in nonstandard tuning (E–A–D–A–B–E, low to high).

At the beginning of 1984 King Crimson put out *Three of a Perfect Pair*, the last in a trilogy of Crimson discs. It was also the end of this version of the band. With each Crimson member seeking new musical horizons, Belew himself retreated from the spotlight after his high-profile years on the vanguard of rock guitar. In late 1986 he re-emerged with *Desire Caught by the Tail*, an ambitious recording that consisted solely of Belew playing guitar synthesizers, guitar, and percussion. Though not as accessible as his previous efforts, the record was still very well received and marked another step up in Belew's endlessly fascinating career.

He then made a few albums with his band the Bears, while also recording brilliant solo discs like the power-pop jewel *Here* (1994). Later that year he again joined Robert Fripp in a new version of King Crimson, this time with the lineup expanded to include another drummer (Pat Mastelotto) and another bass/Stick player (Trey Gunn). The guitarist also signed with Caroline records to produce a series of avant-garde guitar records under the moniker Adrian Belew Presents.

King Crimson [on Warner Bros. except where noted], *Discipline* (1981), *Beat* (1982), *Three of a Perfect Pair* (1984), *Vrroom!* (Discipline, 1994), *Thrak* (Virgin, 1995), *B'Boom* (Discipline, 1995•). **Adrian Belew,** *Lone Rhino* (Island, 1983), *Twang Bar Master* (Island, 1984), *Desire Caught by the Tail* (Island, 1986), *Mr. Music Head* (Atlantic, 1989), *Young Lions* (Atlantic, 1990), *Inner Revolution* (Atlantic, 1992), *Here* (Caroline, 1994), *The Guitar as Orchestra* (Adrian Belew Presents, 1995). **The Bears** [on Primitive Man], *The Bears* (1987), *Rise and Shine* (1988).

Recordings featuring Adrian Belew: **Frank Zappa,** *Sheik Yerbouti* (Zappa, 1979•). **David Bowie,** *Stage* (RCA, 1978•), *Lodger* (RCA, 1979), *Sound + Vision* (Rykodisc, 1989). **Talking Heads** [on Sire], *Remain in Light* (1980), *The Name of This Band Is Talking Heads* (1982•). **Garland Jeffreys,** *Escape Artist* (Epic, 1981). **The Melons,** *Snake Melon Show* (n/a). **Tom Tom Club,** *Tom Tom Club* (Sire, 1981). **Herbie Hancock,** *Magic Windows* (Columbia, 1981). **David Byrne,** *The Catherine Wheel* (Sire, 1981). **Jerry Harrison,** *The Red and the Black* (Sire, c. 1982). **Robert Palmer,** *Maybe It's Alive* (1982•). **Laurie Anderson,** *Mister Heartbreak* (Warner Bros., 1984). **Paul Simon,** *Graceland* (Warner Bros., 1986). **Various Artists,** *Guitar Speak III* (IRS, 1991). **Nine Inch Nails,** *The Downward Spiral* (Interscope/Nothing, 1994).

Neal Schon

Born: *February 27, 1955, in San Mateo, California*
Main Guitars: *Gibson Les Paul, Schon solidbody*

Neal Schon is one of those rare rock instrumentalists who rose from teen prodigy to successful career player. In the process, he achieved world renown and a plethora of platinum albums by the time he was 25 years old. Schon is most famous for his work with Journey, a San Francisco-based rhythm section that developed into one of the most commercially successful pop bands of the 1980s. The guitarist's other impressive credentials include the fact that at the age of 15 he was asked to join both Santana and Eric Clapton's Derek & the Dominos. Players who are 30, much less 15, aren't often asked to play in the presence of such guitar masters, but for guitar hot-shot Neal Schon, it was just another footnote to his long and impressive rock 'n' roll career.

Schon started playing the piano at age five and took up the guitar at 10. After learning note-for-note solos from classic Cream and Jimi Hendrix albums, Schon played in Bay area nightclubs, where he was discovered by Santana members Gregg Rolie (keyboards) and Michael Shrieve (drums). The three became friends, and Schon eventually jammed with the Santana band. Eric Clapton then heard the young phenomenon at a local rehearsal hall and, after jamming with Neal, offered him a spot in Derek & the Dominos. After sizing up the merits of his alternatives—the Dominos were heavily into drugs at that point—Schon chose to work full-time with Santana. He joined the group just in time to record their popular album *Santana III* (1971). His distorted guitar work can be heard on tracks like "No One to Depend On," "Jungle Strut," and, most notably, "Taboo." In 1972 Schon appeared with Santana on the fusion-oriented *Caravanserai* LP and on the lackluster *Carlos Santana & Buddy Miles! Live!*

He grew dissatisfied working with Santana and left late in 1972 to pursue new musical ventures. In 1973 Schon put together a hot rhythm section under the guidance of San Francisco manager Walter "Herbie" Herbert. With a lineup that included Schon, keyboardist-vocalist Gregg Rolie (from Santana), bassist Ross Valory, ace session drummer Aynsley Dunbar, and rhythm guitarist George Tickner, the quintet dubbed themselves Journey. In 1975 they recorded their self-titled debut, which focused mainly on the band's instrumental talents (especially on guitar-dominated tracks like "Of a Lifetime" and "Kohoutek"). Journey toured incessantly and recorded two more albums (without Tickner) that showed off their fine musicianship, *Look into the Future* (1976) and *Next* (1977), the latter containing Schon's flash guitar breaks on "People."

Despite their solid rock style, Journey's early albums sold poorly. In 1978, vocalist Steve Perry joined the band, allowing Rolie to concentrate more on keyboards, arranging, and backing vocals. This, in tandem with the production skills of Roy Thomas Baker (of Queen fame), resulted in *Infinity*, an album that mixed the band's heavy metal roots with soft pop accents and lush vocal harmonies. The new pop-metal bent was extremely successful, and *Infinity* became Journey's first hit album. Schon's guitar was still out front in the new softer mix, and his hot rock solos cut through hits like "Wheel in the Sky" and "Lights" with everything from tasty blues licks to high string pushes and fast pentatonic runs.

With their foot in the door of success, Journey pushed on with increasingly popular and radio-friendly albums, including *Evolution* (1979), *Departure* (1980), and their biggest hit, *Escape* (1981). *Escape* sold well into the millions and produced three major hit singles: "Don't Stop Believin'," "Who's Crying Now," and the gentle ballad "Open Arms." "Don't Stop Believin' " featured some of Schon's rawest guitar work, especially his fast, muffled fade-ins, chordal crunch riffs, and string bends. Despite Journey's progression towards the lighter side of rock, Neal Schon regularly reminded the group's fans that his guitar playing was hard rock right to the core.

Journey's success story continued throughout the mid eighties with *Frontiers* (1983) and *Raised on Radio* (1986). Schon also delved into some solo projects, like his two fusion-oriented records with synthesist Jan Hammer and his 1984 metal-fest with Hagar-Schon-Aaronson-Shrieve (HSAS), entitled *Through the Fire*. Journey fizzled out by the end of the decade, and Schon pursued a variety of endeavors. He founded his own guitar company, which had only a few years of limited success before it went out of business. Schon teamed up with former members of the Babys and Journey to form Bad English, a short-term band that had some radio success and one platinum album. A quick stop in a one-off band called Hardline occurred in 1992, and then he released another solo album in 1995. The record, called *Beyond the Thunder*, features acoustic playing in an almost New Age vein, and reveals very little of Schon's hard rock leanings (a tack that had proven successful for former Starship guitarist Craig Chaquico). The guitarist was then lured back to play with his former Santana bandmates (minus Carlos) in the band Abraxas, and also joined a Journey reunion.

Santana [on Columbia], *Santana III* (1971), *Caravanserai* (1972). **Journey** [on Columbia], *Journey* (1975), *Look into the Future* (1976), *Next* (1977), *Infinity* (1978), *Evolution* (1979), *In the Beginning* (1979), *Departure* (1980), *Captured* (1980•), *Escape* (1981), *Frontiers* (1983), *Raised on Radio* (1986), *Journey's Greatest Hits* (1989). **Neal Schon & Jan Hammer** [on RCA], *Untold Passion* (1981), *Here to Stay* (1983). **Hagar-Schon-Aaronson-Shrieve,** *Through the Fire* (Geffen, 1984•). **Bad English** [on Epic], *Bad English* (1989), *Backlash* (1991). **Hardline,** *Double Eclipse* (MCA, 1992). **Neal Schon,** *Late Nite* (Columbia, 1989), *Beyond the Thunder* (Higher Octave, 1995).

Recordings featuring Neal Schon: **Carlos Santana & Buddy Miles,** *Carlos Santana & Buddy Miles! Live!* (Columbia, 1972•). **Jeff Berlin & Vox Humana,** *Champion* (Passport Jazz, 1985). **Michael Bolton,** *The Hunger* (Columbia, 1988). **Jimmy Barnes,** *Freight Train* (Geffen, 1988).

The Police

Andy Summers

B o r n : *December 31, 1942, in Blackpool, England*
M a i n   G u i t a r s : *Fender Telecaster, Hamer solidbody, Roland guitar synthesizers*

Without question, Andy Summers was the most the influential rhythm guitarist of the 1980s. His signature sound combined reggae, pop, jazz, and R&B

Andy Summers

rhythms with a slew of electronic effects (the most important being chorus and echo), effectively creating a vast, symphonic sound. Each of the Police's numerous hit songs ("Roxanne," "Don't Stand So Close to Me," and "Every Breath You Take") spotlighted his stylized guitar work, which often came in the form of restrained rhythm passages or skillfully overdubbed guitar parts that formed a miniature guitar orchestra. Like many adventurous rock players in the eighties, Summers explored the guitar synthesizer, and he used this musical tool on several Police projects, as well as on his noteworthy recordings with Robert Fripp.

Though Summers' rise to fame with the Police seemed relatively quick, his role in British rock extended back to the 1960s. With solid grounding in jazz and classical guitar, Summers landed his first professional gig with Zoot Money's Big Roll Band in the mid sixties. Later he got involved with London's burgeoning psychedelic underground movement, first playing with the obscure Dantalion's Chariot, and joining the original Soft Machine in 1968. Summers moved on to Eric Burdon's Animals, with whom he appeared on the album *Love Is* (1968). By then, the Animals were on their last legs, and Summers moved on yet again. After a period of classical guitar study at California State University at Northridge, he returned to England and backed the likes of vocalist Kevin Coyne and ex-Soft Machine bassist Kevin Ayers before the punk revolution hit.

In mid 1977 Summers first came into contact with the Police, an up-and-coming punk act featuring bassist-singer Sting, drummer Stewart Copeland, and a guitarist named Henry Padovani. Summers joined the outfit, and the Police played as a quartet before Padovani quit later that year. A pre-Summers Police single, "Fall Out," had been released with moderate success, but the group didn't really start to take off until the appearance in 1979 of the single "Roxanne." With Summers' staccato reggae strums, a firm beat, and Sting's seductive vocals, "Roxanne" hit it big on British and American airwaves, and marked the Police as a punk/New Wave act to be watched. A successful U.S. club tour followed, and after pulling together $6,000 of their own money, the trio recorded *Outlandos d'Amour* (which A&M released later in 1979). The Police's effervescent pop, reggae, and punk-infused tunes—"Can't Stand Losing You," "So Lonely," and "Born in the 50's"—and gimmicky bleached-blonde image were an instant hit with rock fans around the globe.

Later in 1979, the Police followed up with another smash record, *Reggatta de Blanc*, which contained the popular FM hit "Message in a Bottle." From that point until 1983, the Police were on a platinum roll, releasing *Zenyatta Mondatta* (1980), *Ghost in the Machine* (1981), and the #1 mega-album *Synchronicity* (1983). The group also went on several successful international tours, going beyond the standard rock 'n' roll stops in America, Europe, and Japan to such exotic locales as India, Southeast Asia, and Africa.

Throughout all of their albums and singles, Andy Summers' guitar work is omnipresent. On "Message in a Bottle," "Don't Stand So Close to Me," and "Every Breath You Take," Summers' guitar is as integral to the song as Sting's vocal hook, especially in the way he uses arpeggiated chord patterns and carefully harmonized lines in lieu of basic barre chords and lead licks. His use of tasteful electronic effects can be heard in "Reggatta de Blanc," "Behind My Camel," and "Wrapped around Your Finger." For guitar synthesizer textures, "Don't Stand So Close to Me" and "Secret Journey" are good examples (as are his two duet LPs with Robert Fripp). And as a progenitor of reggae-rock guitar, Summers brilliantly employs clipped chord strumming on songs like "The Bed's Too Big without You," "Man in a Suitcase," and "Spirits in the Material World." Though known primarily as a rhythm expert, Summers also pulls off some accomplished lead work, notably in "Peanuts," "Message in a Bottle," and the tortured atonal break in "Driven to Tears."

Although he opted to pursue a low-key jazz-fusion career after the breakup of the Police in 1983, Andy Summers has left a legacy of dramatically altering the sound of rock guitar, primarily through his sublime rhythm chops and his sonic texturing. Though his recorded catalog is not extensive compared to those of many other musicians of the period, he has left an indelible stamp on the genre that is impossible to ignore.

Zoot Money's Big Roll Band, *All the Happening Zoot Money's Big Roll Band at Klook's Kleek* (Epic, 1966). **The Animals** [on MGM], *Love Is* (1968), *The Greatest Hits of Eric Burdon and the Animals* (1969). **The Police** [on A&M], *Outlandos d'Amour* (1979), *Reggatta de Blanc* (1979), *Zenyatta Mondatta* (1980), *Ghost in the Machine* (1981), *Synchronicity* (1983), *Every Breath You Take: The Singles* (1986). **Robert Fripp & Andy Summers** [on A&M], *I Advance Masked* (1982), *Bewitched* (1984). **Andy Summers** [on Private Music except where noted], *2010* [soundtrack] (A&M, 1984), *Down and out in Beverly Hills* [soundtrack] (MCA, 1986), *Weekend at Bernie's* [soundtrack] (n/a), *XYZ* (MCA, 1987), *Mysterious Barricades* (1988), *The Golden Wire* (1989), *World Gone Mad* (1991), *Synaesthesia* (CMP, 1996). **Andy Summers & John Etheridge,** *Invisible Threads* (Mesa, 1994).

Recordings featuring Andy Summers: **Kevin Coyne** [on Virgin], *Matching Head and Feet* (1975), *Heartburn* (1976), *In Living Black and White* (1977). **Kevin Ayers,** *Yes We Have No Mañanas—So Get Your Mañanas Today* (Harvest, 1976). **Various Artists,** *No Wave* (A&M, 1979). **Various Artists,** *Propaganda* (A&M, c. 1980). **Kevin Lamb,** *Sailin' down the Years* (Arista, n/a). **Eberhard Schoener,** *Video Magic* (Harvest, 1981), *Music from Video Magic and Flashback* (n/a, 1987). **Sting,** *...Nothing Like the Sun* (A&M, 1987).

U2

The Edge

B o r n : *David Howell Evans, on August 8, 1961, in Dublin*
M a i n   G u i t a r s : *Fender Stratocaster, Gibson Explorer*

While many top guitar players of the eighties and early nineties relied on flawless technique, theoretical knowledge, and speedy solos, U2 guitarist The Edge made brilliant use of his *lack* of fine technique. Instead, he created an extraordinary style based on a simplicity of ideas, economy of notes, and passionate feeling. From the first moment of U2's 1980 debut

The Edge

Aid concert and the 1986 Amnesty International tour. The spring of 1987 was all but dominated by U2's next album, *The Joshua Tree*, and the single "With or without You." Aside from his usual guitar theatrics and electronic treatments, The Edge integrates blues and folk influences into his playing on the album, and makes room for stellar acoustic guitar parts. Standout tracks include "Where the Streets Have No Name," "I Still Haven't Found What I'm Looking For," and the unnerving, Hendrix-inspired "Bullet the Blue Sky."

On the strength of their albums and roadwork, U2 became a major rock icon, and The Edge and singer Bono both became celebrities in their own right. However, by the 1990s, the band was in danger of devolving into self-parody, so it completely overhauled its musical approach. Led by The Edge's guitar, U2 pushed beyond their passionate and textured eighties rock sound into uncharted electronic and industrial sounds and grittier rhythms on *Achtung Baby* and *Zooropa*. The former disc shows that The Edge can power-riff and feed back as well as any alternative guitarist, while *Zooropa* (1993) actually relies more on samples and synthesizers than on The Edge's distinctive style. Though it is his early echoed sound that will be his greatest legacy, The Edge must also be cited for his willingness to take chances and experiment with guitar techniques that aren't part of his patented sound. Given the potential longevity of U2, The Edge's role as the definitive "guitar anti-hero" may be a relevant image well into the next millennium.

U2 [on Island], *Boy* (1980), *October* (1981), *War* (1983), *Under a Blood Red Sky* (1983•), *The Unforgettable Fire* (1984), *Wide Awake in America* (1985•), *The Joshua Tree* (1987), *Rattle and Hum* (1988•), *Achtung Baby* (1991), *Zooropa* (1993). **The Edge,** *Captive* [soundtrack] (Virgin, 1987). **Passengers,** *Original Soundtracks 1* (Island, 1995).

Recordings featuring The Edge: Jah Wobble, *Snake Charmer* (Island, c 1983). **Robbie Robertson,** *Robbie Robertson* (Geffen, 1987). **Various Artists,** *Folkways: A Vision Shared* (CBS, 1988).

The Cars

Elliot Easton

B o r n : *December 18, 1953, in Brooklyn, New York*
M a i n G u i t a r s : *Various Dean solidbodies, Fender Telecaster and Stratocaster, Gibson Les Paul and Flying V*

Ric Ocasek

B o r n : *March 23, 1949, in Baltimore, Maryland*
M a i n G u i t a r : *Gibson SG*

During the Cars' platinum-strewn glory days from 1979 to 1985, Elliot Easton proved himself a true rock guitar craftsman, less interested in speed or flash than in turning in short, tuneful leads that were as hook-filled as the songs themselves. Deriving influences from country, blues, and early rock 'n' roll

album, *Boy*, on through the group's successful *Zooropa*, The Edge has applied his unique guitar voice to songs like "I Will Follow" and "Gloria," the breakthrough singles "Sunday Bloody Sunday" and "New Year's Day," and the anthems "Pride (In the Name of Love)" and "I Still Haven't Found What I'm Looking For."

Defining U2's sound from the outset, The Edge uses heavy dabs of cascading echo along with both clean and distorted tones to paint soft, haunting soundscapes that are contrasts of simplicity and depth. For example, the early song "I Will Follow" is graced with the guitarist's quick-strummed open chordings and power riffs tied in with a midsection interlude of spacious chordal harmonics. In much the same way, "Gloria" makes use of chord fragments and ethereal echo effects, but adds emotional minor-key slide solos. The ripping live versions of these and other key tracks pervade the band's 1983 set *Under a Blood Red Sky*, making it among The Edge's finest guitar exhibitions.

In 1984, U2 went to the top worldwide with *The Unforgettable Fire* and its hit "Pride (In the Name of Love)." During the next two years U2 won millions of new fans with their popular live appearances, including shows at the legendary Live pickers—especially his hero George Harrison—southpaw Easton developed an eclectic style that uses everything from rockabilly chicken pickin' ("My Best Friend's Girlfriend") to sustained E-Bow lines ("Since You're Gone") à la Robert Fripp.

After a few semesters at the Berklee College of Music and stints in some Boston-area club bands, Easton joined the Cars in 1977. The band lineup was already in place: vocalist/rhythm guitarist/songsmith Ric Ocasek, bassist/vocalist Ben Orr, keyboardist Greg Hawkes, and drummer David Robinson. After Easton signed on, the Cars gained a considerable local following in the area and were signed to the Elektra label. In mid 1978 their first album, *The Cars*, was released and yielded the popular single "Just What I Needed." The song had just enough economy and melody along with hard rock punch to make it a radio staple—and the definitive prototype of the New Wave movement. The song was propelled in no small part by the burst of string bends and ascending chordal climbs within Easton's solo. The album and its follow-up, *Candy-O* (1979), were extremely successful, the latter disc containing the riff-laden hit single "Let's Go." *Panorama* (1980) features Easton's expansive guitar work on "Touch and Go," an unusual single that alternates between a 5/4 beat and a rockabilly-tinged chorus. For the chorus, Easton provides low Duane Eddy-styled twang lines while taking one of his rare extended breaks. Ever the consistent hitmakers, the Cars issued *Shake It Up* in 1981 (their fourth platinum disc in a row), featuring Easton letting loose another hook-filled solo in the title hit single.

Much of Elliot Easton's notoriety as a rock guitarist came from his reputation as "solo specialist." Though he shared rhythm duties with leader Ric Ocasek (who clearly knew how to write a memorable chord riff), Easton's real forte with the Cars was the lead break, which was almost a song unto itself due to its clear melodicism. His diversely influenced and occasionally imitative guitar breaks are the perfect complement to Ocasek's stark pop songs, offering bursts of electric color in the middle of the Cars' three-chord rock 'n' roll tunes. In 1985, Easton briefly stepped out of the Cars fold to release his first solo effort, *Change No Change*, which includes the Beatlesque single "Shayla" and a brisk guitar-dominated cut called "(Wearing Down) Like a Wheel." Sadly, when New Wave passed, so did the Cars, relegating most of the band—including Easton—to anonymity. Ocasek may get most of the credit, but Easton is easily one of the tastiest guitarists of the 1980s.

The Cars [on Elektra except where noted], *The Cars* (1978), *Candy-O* (1979), *Panorama* (1980), *Shake It Up* (1981), *Heartbeat City* (1984), *Greatest Hits* (1985), *Door to Door* (1987), *Just What I Needed: The Cars Anthology* [boxed set] (Rhino, 1995). **Elliot Easton,** *Change No Change* (Elektra, 1985).

Recordings featuring Elliot Easton: **Boulder,** *Boulder* (Boulder, 1979). **Peter Wolf,** *Lights Out* (EMI America, 1984). **Jules Shear,** *Watch Dog* (EMI, 1984). **Peter Gordon,** *Peter Gordon* (Columbia Masterworks, c. 1985). **Espionage,** *ESP* (Elektra, c. 1985). **Jon Anderson,** *Three Ships* (Elektra, c. 1985). **Various Artists,** *Shots in the Dark* (Donna/Del-Fi, 1996).

Rock Icons: Bruce Springsteen and Prince

Guitar hero status and accolades are rarely given to singer-songwriters. The conventional wisdom is that they aren't "dedicated" guitarists, and that their primary talents lie elsewhere—regardless of their six-string ability. In America, this was especially true of two very good guitarists who rarely were noted for their exceptional playing: Bruce Springsteen and Prince.

On Springsteen's 1978 album *Darkness on the Edge of Town*, the singer-songwriter-guitarist went far beyond his earlier axe exploits, demonstrating to the world that he didn't just use his Fender Esquires and Stratocasters as stage props (though he did do that well). While his previous records had plenty of guitar work (*Born to Run*, for one), none matched the bluesy, fuzztone-riddled breaks he draped across *Darkness*. "Adam Raised a Cain," "Badlands," "Streets of Fire," "Candy's Room," and "Prove It All Night" each contain energetic string-pushing solos that make listeners think twice before labeling Springsteen (born September 23, 1949, in Freehold, New Jersey) just a great singer and songwriter. After his stormy guitar rampages on that album and on subsequent recordings like *The River* (1980), the best-selling *Born in the U.S.A.* (1984), and especially *Live/1975–85* (1986), critics had to concede that Springsteen was an excellent rock 'n' roll guitar player.

Although Springsteen dominated the mainstream of the mid-eighties rock scene with his guitar music, he did have stiff competition from Prince, whose 1984 breakthrough threatened to overwhelm both the Boss and mass popster Michael Jackson. This Minneapolis-bred funk-rocker (born Prince Rogers Nelson, on June 7, 1958) spent several years honing his act prior to the explosive release of the film *Purple Rain* and its immensely successful soundtrack album. Like Springsteen, Prince is an energetic showman and rock personality, yet is also adept at many instruments, most notably the guitar. The #1 hit single "Let's Go Crazy" rages with his aggressive power riffing, octave-divided bass-string lines, and string-bending solo. To cap it off, Prince ends the song with speaker-blowing high bends and pentatonic runs down the neck of his Fender Telecaster, all soaked with wah-wah. The title ballad contains a long, dramatic solo that, in the film, Prince plays on a custom scroll-shaped solidbody. Blending sensual string pushes, fast picked phrases, and a catchy melodic motif, this solo is one of the clear high points of the soundtrack, and is perhaps Prince's best solo—*ever*.

Bruce Springsteen [on Columbia], *Greetings from Asbury Park* (1973), *The Wild, the Innocent, and the E Street Shuffle* (1973), *Born to Run* (1975), *Darkness on the Edge of Town* (1978), *The River* (1980), *Nebraska* (1982), *Born in the U.S.A.* (1984), *Bruce Springsteen & the E Street Band Live/1975–85* (1986•), *Tunnel of Love* (1987), *Chimes of Freedom* (1988), *Human Touch* (1992), *Lucky Town* (1992), *Greatest Hits* (1995).

Recordings featuring Bruce Springsteen: **Various Artists,** *No Nukes/The MUSE Concerts for a Non-Nuclear Future* (Asylum, 1979•). **Various**

Artists, *Folkways: A Vision Shared* (CBS, 1988). **Roy Orbison & Friends,** *A Black and White Night Live* (Virgin, 1989•). **Various Artists,** *Philadelphia* [soundtrack] (Epic, 1993).

Prince [on Paisley Park/Warner Bros.], *For You* (1978), *Prince* (1979), *Dirty Mind* (1980), *Controversy* (1981), *1999* (1982), *Purple Rain* (1984), *Around the World in a Day* (1985), *Parade* (1986), *Sign o' the Times* (1987), *Lovesexy* (1988), *Graffiti Bridge* (1990), *Diamonds and Pearls* (1991), *Love Symbol Album* (1992), *Hits/B-Sides* (1993), *The Gold Experience* (1995).

Melodic Masters

One fascinating player of the late sixties and early seventies was Randy California (born Randolph Woolfe, on February 20, 1951, in Los Angeles). California was the guitarist for Spirit, the cult pop-rock band that ingeniously blended Beatlesque power pop, jazz, folk, heavy metal, and art rock into a singularly appealing sound. Spirit never became a major success, but came close on *Twelve Dreams of Dr. Sardonicus* (1970), a complex pop suite that contained the hit "Nature's Way" and ably demonstrated California's eclectic guitar talent. Throughout the album, his guitar parts varied from folksy acoustic fingerpicking and R&B rhythms to volume swells and echoey slide sections, and on to the fuzz-drenched Strat solos of "Mr. Skin" and "When I Touch You." The latter two pieces carry a strong influence from California's one-time jamming partner Jimi Hendrix. Also of note is his groundbreaking solo to "Street Worm," during which he uses fast scalar legato hammer-ons in a way that was not commonly found in rock circles until Eddie Van Halen and Allan Holdsworth made them a rock staple nearly a decade later.

A noted guitar luminary since his arrival in the 1960s has been Todd Rundgren, formerly leader of the prophetic sixties pop group the Nazz ("Open My Eyes," "Hello It's Me"). Rundgren's 1972 solo hit "I Saw the Light" includes a sparkling multitracked lead break, as does the rocker "Couldn't I Just Tell You" (both on his stellar 1972 solo effort *Something/Anything*). In the middle of the decade, he shifted focus to his occasionally brilliant techno-pop band Utopia. With Utopia, Rundgren welded his metalish Beck- and Clapton-based guitar licks into the group's synthesizer-heavy framework. Rundgren's fiery lead work during this period appears on such songs as "The Icon" and "Freak Parade," from *Utopia* (1974), "Communion with the Sun," from *Ra* (1977), and "Trapped," from *Oops! Wrong Planet* (1977). "Last of the New Wave Riders," from *Adventures in Utopia* (1979), however, contains one of those definitive "guitar orgasms," as Rundgren builds his solo to a frenzy and grabs a singing high note, sustaining it for all its worth over a dramatic riff. Although he was far more famous for his singing and songwriting, Todd Rundgren has proven himself to be an impressive guitar player time and time again.

Even higher up the Top 40 food chain was the popular success of Elton John. Elton's on-and-off lead guitarist during the height of his popularity was a lanky Scot named Davey Johnstone, who added tuneful electric solos to many of the pop singer's hits.

Johnstone's best blues-based leads include the absolutely ferocious "Funeral for a Friend/Love Lies Bleeding," "Saturday Night's Alright for Fighting" (both from *Goodbye Yellow Brick Road*, 1973), and the rocker "Meal Ticket," from the Elton John hit opus *Captain Fantastic and the Brown Dirt Cowboy* (1975). Though he was hardly a household name in the guitar world, Davey Johnstone's quality guitar work with Elton John brought his guitar sound to millions of pop fans and gave AM hit radio a hefty share of first-rate rock guitar playing.

Among the most popular acts of the seventies and early eighties was Fleetwood Mac. In 1975 the band revamped the original blues-rock sound that had been established in their Peter Green days (♦ U.K. Blues Revival) and metamorphosed into a slick commercial act led by singer Stevie Nicks and guitarist Lindsey Buckingham (born on October 3, 1947, in Palo Alto, California). The Mac's self-titled 1975 album sparked several hit singles and entrenched Fleetwood Mac on radio playlists for years to follow. In 1977 the band released *Rumours*, one of the three best-selling records of all time, which contained a good sample of Buckingham's versatile guitar work on nearly every cut. "Gold Dust Woman" revealed some shimmering rhythm textures, but the folk-inspired guitarist stepped out on lead in some surprisingly strong fingerstyle electric solos, particularly on "Don't Stop" and "Go Your Own Way."

A late entry into the 1970s pop-metal arena (à la Styx and Journey) was Foreigner, the British-American outfit led by ex-Spooky Tooth guitarist Mick Jones. Foreigner's radio-ready hard rock made for above-average radio fodder during the last few years of the decade and well into the eighties, and produced a fistful of hits. Jones (not to be confused with the Clash guitarist of the same name) was never a flashy guitarist, and his guitar work was rarely excessive—unlike others in the genre. Instead, he simply made his solo fit the song, and most of the time he was right on target. Jones' best guitar playing is evident in the carefully structured, yet effective, guitar breaks and power riffs on early Foreigner hits like "Feels Like the First Time," "Cold as Ice," and "Double Vision." His finest break is generally regarded to be his bluesy bump-and-grind lead to "Hot Blooded" (on *Double Vision*, 1978), which features low bends, sustained crunch notes, and some exceptionally funky R&B licks from a '61 Gibson Les Paul through a Marshall amp. According to the guitarist, the aged amp actually caught fire while he was recording this *hot* solo.

During the seventies and eighties, Gary Richrath was the lead guitarist for REO Speedwagon. Despite that group's musical decline in its latter years, Richrath's playing on REO's earliest albums established the band as one of the Midwest's hardest rockers. A capable bluesy rocker and a deft manipulator of the wah-wah pedal, Richrath had no trouble screaming through hard rockers like "Being Kind Can Hurt Someone Sometimes" and "Down by the Dam," or mixing it up on "Golden Country" and "Lost in a Dream." Part of the band's original appeal was that Richrath also delved into realms not usually explored by mainstream rock guitarists. A lot of rock and pop guitar players got their first taste of chicken pickin' by listening to his instrumental tour de force "Flying Turkey Trot." Richrath was also an accomplished slide player, learning the craft from Joe Walsh. If for nothing else, though, Richrath should be revered for writing "Riding the Storm Out," the definitive three-chord rock anthem. REO's most popular and commercially successful years were marred by their syrupy radio material, and Richrath had a smaller role in that overly orchestrated environment. He left the group in the early 1990s to record on his own.

With a guitar-driven brand of power pop that predated the Steve Perry-era Journey and Foreigner by several years, the Babys set a standard as one of the best and most influential bands of the genre. Although they were labeled bubblegum and pop (in the worst sense of the word) during their time, the members of the band were some of the most imitated musicians of the day. With vocalist John Waite (later a successful solo artist and member of Bad English), drummer Tony Brock (a future member of Rod Stewart's band), bassist Ricky Phillips (also a member of Bad English, and of the Coverdale-Page band), keyboardist Jonathan Cain (later of Journey and Bad English), and guitarist Wally Stocker, the band had a penchant for catchy but difficult chord combinations and time signatures. Songs like "Midnight Rendezvous," "Give Me Your Love," "Rodeo," and "Postcard" were impressive rockers that offset the radio dreck of "Isn't It Time" and "Every Time I Think of You." With a style rooted in the hard-rock power chording of the second British Invasion, Stocker excelled at brutish guitar tones and riffs that pulled the Babys' material above the rest of the power pop crowd. He rarely strayed from straight-ahead hard rock or acoustic ballads, and kept his playing simple yet excruciatingly raw. Surprisingly, he was the only member of the Babys who did not re-emerge in a more successful band after the group's demise in 1980.

Behind Pat Benatar's string of pop-metal hits in the late seventies and early eighties was the electric sound of her lead guitarist, co-songwriter, and husband, Neil Geraldo. Riding on the heavy metal fringes of the New Wave movement, Benatar catapulted to national stardom with her 1979 album *In the Heat of the Night*, containing the single "Heartbreaker." The song garnered attention for its piercing vocals and tight pop arrangement, and Geraldo received kudos from the guitar community for his distorted power chordings and hammer-on lead work. After that, the guitarist's gritty lead parts were heard on such Pat Benatar singles as "Hit Me with Your Best Shot," "Treat Me Right," "Fire and Ice" (all 1981), and "Shadows in the Night" (1982), which are laden with his legato scale work and squealing guitar tones. By mid decade, Pat Benatar had run her course as the queen of hard rock, but Neil Geraldo's brief tenure in the guitar hero spotlight marked him as one of the first rock players to demonstrate Eddie Van Halen's deep influence upon guitarists of the period.

One talented, but only briefly popular, eighties band was Big Country, from Scotland. They turned heads in 1983 with the single "Big Country," off their album *The Crossing*. Using soft fuzztone, chorus, and E-Bow effects, guitarists Stuart Adamson and

Bruce Watson created a unique bagpipe tone for the song, as well as for several others, including the axe-laden title cut to their 1984 follow-up EP *Wonderland*. Despite the high quality of Big Country's rock (the rhythm section consisted of popular British players Mark Brzezicki on drums and Tony Butler on bass), their later material was dismissed as being too much like that contained on *The Crossing*, and the band swiftly—and perhaps prematurely—disappeared from the eighties rock scene altogether.

When it was announced in the early 1980s that Yes (◗) was reforming with relative newcomer Trevor Rabin standing in for progressive guitar virtuoso Steve Howe, many were skeptical about this dinosaur band's return. But Yes fans couldn't have been more surprised to hear the new Yes album *90125* (1983). The revitalized Yes had a new, contemporary sound, and Rabin (born January 13, 1955, in Johannesburg, South Africa) dazzled listeners with his advanced chops, arranging, and songwriting. Rabin had previously played in a successful South African pop band called Rabbitt and also had a few solo albums to his credit. Upon relocating to Los Angeles (via London), he hooked up with several former Yes-men to form the band Cinema. The overwhelming number of Yes alumni in the project prompted it to be billed as a Yes reunion, and *90125* was released as a new Yes album. Rabin's best-known spot on the recording is the hit single "Owner of a Lonely Heart," where he pumps out the central power chord theme and arpeggiated chordal highlights.

The concert follow-up disc, *9012Live*, earned Rabin even more respect for his acoustic solo "Solley's Beard." Whereas Howe was a fingerstyle master (as heard in "Mood for a Day" and "Clap"), Rabin proved himself a flatpicking monster, on a par with such super-pickers as Al Di Meola and John McLaughlin for speed and technical excellence. *Big Generator* was a solid studio follow-up to *90125*, though subsequent Yes discs *Union* (a 1991 joint album with the Yes splinter band Anderson, Bruford, Wakeman, Howe) and *Talk* (1994) were major disappointments. Regardless of Yes' fortunes, Rabin has been in demand as a studio whiz, both as guitarist and as producer; he did soundtrack work for the movies *Twister*, *Eraser*, and *Glimmer Man*, and has created guitar samples for Apple Computer. In addition, his talents as an artist outside of Yes are ably demonstrated on his various solo records. It remains a testimony to his strength that he was able to win over so many Steve Howe fans and still establish his own place in the pantheon of progressive rock—and power pop—guitar greats.

Spirit [on Epic except where noted], *Spirit* (Ode, 1968), *The Family that Plays Together* (Ode, 1969), *Clear* (Ode, 1969), *Twelve Dreams of Dr. Sardonicus* (1970), *The Best of Spirit* (1973), *Spirit of '76* (Mercury, 1975), *Farther Along* (Mercury, 1976), *Future Games* (Mercury, 1977), *Spirit Live* (Potato/Illegal, 1977◗), *Potatoland* (Rhino/Beggar's Banquet, 1978), *Time Circle* (1991). **Randy California**, *Kaptain Kopter and the Twirlybirds* (Epic, 1973).

Recordings featuring Randy California: **Various Artists**, *Guitar Speak* (IRS, 1989), *Night of the Guitar Live!* (IRS, 1989◗).

Nazz, *Nazz* (SGC, 1968), *Nazz Nazz* (1969), *Nazz III* (1970), *Best of Nazz* (Rhino, 1984). **Todd Rundgren** [on Bearsville except where noted], *Runt* (Ampex, 1970), *Something/Anything* (1972), *A Wizard, a True Star* (1973), *Todd* (1974), *Initiation* (1975), *Faithful* (1976), *Hermit of Mink Hollow* (1978), *Back to the Bars* (1978•), *Healing* (1981), *The Ever Popular Tortured Artist Effect* (1983), *Nearly Human* (Warner Bros., 1989), *Anthology 1968–85* (Rhino/Bearsville, 1989), *2nd Wind* (Warner Bros., 1991). **Utopia** [on Bearsville except where noted], *Todd Rundgren's Utopia* (1974), *Another Live* (1975•), *Ra* (1977), *Oops! Wrong Planet* (1977), *Adventures in Utopia* (1979), *Deface the Music* (1980), *Swing to the Right* (1982), *Utopia* (Network, 1982), *Oblivion* (Passport, 1984), *POV* (Passport, 1985), *Trivia* (Passport, 1986), *Anthology* (Rhino/Bearsville, 1989).

Recordings featuring Todd Rundgren: **Meatloaf,** *Bat out of Hell* (Cleveland International, 1977).

Elton John [on MCA except where noted], *Madman across the Water* (1971), *Honky Chateau* (1972), *Goodbye Yellow Brick Road* (1973), *Caribou* (1974), *Greatest Hits* (1974), *Captain Fantastic and the Brown Dirt Cowboy* (1975), *Rock of the Westies* (1975), *Here and There* (1976•), *Blue Moves* (1976), *Greatest Hits, Vol. II* (1977). **Davey Johnstone,** *Smiling Face* (MCA, 1973). **China,** *China* (n/a, c. 1978).

Fleetwood Mac [on Warner Bros. except where noted], *Fleetwood Mac* (Reprise, 1975), *Rumours* (1977), *Tusk* (1979), *Fleetwood Mac Live* (1980•), *Mirage* (1982), *Tango in the Night* (1987), *Greatest Hits* (1988), *25 Years—The Chain* (1992). **Lindsey Buckingham & Stevie Nicks,** *Buckingham Nicks* (Polydor, 1973). **Lindsey Buckingham,** *Law and Order* (Asylum, 1982), *Go Insane* (Elektra, 1984), *Out of the Cradle* (Reprise, 1992).

Spooky Tooth, *You Broke My Heart So I Busted Your Jaw* (A&M, 1973), *Witness* (Island, 1973), *The Mirror* (Island, 1974). **Foreigner** [on Atlantic except where noted], *Foreigner* (1977), *Double Vision* (1978), *Head Games* (1979), *4* (1981), *Foreigner Records* (1982), *Agent Provocateur* (1984), *Inside Information* (1987), *Unusual Heat* (1991), *Mr. Moonlight* (Rhythm Safari, 1995). **Mick Jones,** *Mick Jones* (Atlantic, 1989).

Recordings featuring Mick Jones: **George Harrison,** *Dark Horse* (Apple, 1974).

Pat Benatar [on Chrysalis], *In the Heat of the Night* (1979), *Crimes of Passion* (1980), *Precious Time* (1981), *Get Nervous* (1982), *Live from Earth* (1983•), *Tropico* (1984), *Seven the Hard Way* (1985), *Wide Awake in Dreamland* (1988), *Best Shots* (1989), *True Love* (1991).

Big Country [on Mercury except where noted], *The Crossing* (1983), *Wonderland* (1984), *Steeltown* (1984), *The Seer* (1986), *Peace in our Time* (Warner Bros./Polygram, 1988).

Rabbitt [on Capricorn], *Boys Will Be Boys* (1976), *A Croak & a Grunt in the Night* (1977). **Trevor Rabin** [on Chrysalis except where noted], *Trevor Rabin* (1978), *Face to Face* (1980), *Wolf* (1980), *Can't Look Away* (Elektra, 1989). **Yes** [on Atco/Atlantic except where noted], *90125* (1983), *9012Live: The Solos* (1985•), *Big Generator* (1987), *Union* (Arista, 1991), *Yes Years* (1991•), *Talk* (Victory, 1994).

Recordings featuring Trevor Rabin: **Manfred Mann's Earth Band,** *Chance* (Warner Bros., 1981). **Noel McCalla,** *Night Time Emotion* (Epic, c. 1980).

CHAPTER TWENTY-THREE

Euro-Metal
A Distant Roar

Heavy metal was dead. At least that's what many music magazines loudly proclaimed as the 1970s whimpered to a close. The idea was reinforced by the late-decade lethargy of such metal dinosaurs as Led Zeppelin, Black Sabbath, and the then-defunct Deep Purple. The rising popularity of punk and New Wave were concrete reinforcements of this proclamation, especially as these bands slagged their rock forefathers in the press.

In Europe, however, metal lived on in working-class bands that rocked nightclubs and small concert halls filled with hardcore metalheads. The term "heavy metal underground" emerged as a moniker for this arcane generation of hard rockers, a group of young people who knew that, in the late seventies, heavy metal was anything but dead. British music magazines picked up this underground metal phenomenon and gave coverage to up-and-coming bands like Judas Priest (who actually had started recording in 1974), Motorhead, Saxon, Angelwitch, Tygers of Pan Tang, Samson, Iron Maiden, and Def Leppard. These bands, and this new movement, were subsequently dubbed "The New Wave of British Heavy Metal."

On the continent, Germany embraced this same genre with a fervor unseen in any other European country. The German metal quintet Scorpions began tearing up the metal scene all over Europe and also made major inroads into the eager and profitable Japanese market, where they recorded a very popular live album in 1978. Michael Schenker, Germany's first internationally known guitar hero

(and brother of Scorpions guitarist Rudolf Schenker), found worldwide acceptance after years of touring and recording with the British metal band UFO, which had pulverized even the jaded America audience with its 1977 album *Lights Out*.

This new wave of European heavy metal sparked a renewed interest in the genre from rock fans around the world, allowing many of the underground bands to achieve huge success in the 1980s. This avalanche of quality Euro-metal, coupled with the arrival of Van Halen and the resurrection of Ozzy Osbourne, prompted a worldwide revival of heavy metal—a revival that contributed to the eventual downfall of disco, southern rock, and punk. For the next decade, heavy metal would be among the world's most popular styles of music.

UFO

Michael Schenker

Born: *January 10, 1955, in Sarstedt, West Germany*
Main Guitar: *Gibson Flying V*

Even though Eddie Van Halen virtually dominated heavy metal guitar in the late seventies and early eighties, there was a significant cult following for a radically different kind of metal guitar hero: Michael Schenker. From 1973 until 1979, Schenker's lead guitar powered the British heavy rock outfit UFO and inspired thousands of young guitarists with his stylistic emphasis on speed, drama, and, perhaps above all, melody. Unlike Van Halen's radical use of hammer-ons and the tremolo bar, German-born Schenker used sheer tech-

Michael Schenker

nique to make his mark on heavy metal guitar, especially with his lightning-fast picking runs. By combining technical expertise and strong emotional drive, he was eventually recognized as one of Europe's greatest metal guitar heroes and one of Eddie Van Halen's *very* few rivals of the time.

Schenker began studying guitar at the age of nine, when he started to learn songs by listening to records in order to teach them to his older brother, Rudolf. After playing in local bands like Enervates, the Cry, and Copernicus, he formed Scorpions with Rudolf around 1970 and recorded the album *Lonesome Crow* (1972). In 1973, Michael left Scorpions to join the British hard rock group UFO, whose guitarist had quit during a German tour (Scorpions had been the opening act). Although the 18-year-old guitarist spoke little English, he fit into UFO perfectly, as demonstrated on his fine first effort with the band, *Phenomenon* (1974). The record contained guitar work that would establish songs like "Doctor, Doctor" and "Rock Bottom" as classics in the UFO repertoire. Schenker's blazing leads on the latter track show how advanced he was relative to his peers—nothing else from 1974 even comes close to it for sheer dynamism and progressiveness. In terms of technique alone, he was at least four or five years ahead of his time in rock circles.

Over the next few years, Schenker and UFO released several well-received albums: *Force It* (1975), *No Heavy Petting* (1976), and the brutally intense *Lights Out* (1977). The band also acquired a reputation as a strong live act, which helped to cement Schenker's own reputation as an astounding guitarist. By 1977, Michael could rightly lay claim to being Europe's foremost guitar hero. Still, the pressures of touring and an overindulgent rock 'n' roll lifestyle began to take their toll on the German superpicker. On the eve of UFO's *Lights Out* tour of America, Schenker simply disappeared. The band toured anyway, with Schenker clone Paul Chapman sitting in for the missing guitarist, but the absence of the real thing brought the band few new fans and disappointed the diehards.

Eventually, the stressed-out axeman came out of hiding and rejoined UFO for the excellent studio disc *Obsession* (1978) and a double live album, *Strangers in the Night* (1979). Among Schenker's fans, there was little doubt that *Strangers in the Night* was the guitarist's finest recording with UFO, and it remains a brilliant testament to his time with the band. From his blindingly fast sixteenth-note runs in "Mother Mary" to the dramatic string-pushing break in the 6/8 rocker "Love to Love" to his magnificent 10-minute lead blitz in "Rock Bottom," Schenker set his trademark Gibson Flying V on fire with his personal formula for "heavy melodic" guitar: swift modal runs, twenty-second-fret string bends, wah-wah effects, and heavy doses of emotion and drama. Within the context of heavy metal guitar, this album is clearly a masterpiece.

Sadly, *Strangers in the Night* marked the end of Schenker's stint with UFO. At the end of 1979, he left the band to rejoin Scorpions temporarily, recording several strong solos on *Lovedrive* and playing occasional gigs with them in Europe. In 1980, he announced the formation of his own Michael Schenker Group (also known as MSG) and that year issued an eponymous debut album. Containing typically high-voltage solos on "Armed and Ready" and "Cry for the Nations," the album revealed him to be in prime form. After a successful tour opening for southern rockers Molly Hatchet, the Schenker band recorded *MSG*, which yielded the near-hit "On and On" and gained the group a sizable amount of FM radio airplay. Schenker continued his solo rampage with *One Night at Budokan* (1982), *Assault Attack* (1983), and *Built to Destroy* (1984).

In 1987, he teamed up with singer Robin McCauley to form a *new* MSG—the McCauley-Schenker Group—and released the commercially oriented *Perfect Timing*. But the album never took off, and after two further records, the band fell apart. Schenker went back into seclusion, taking the time to release an all-acoustic solo album entitled *Thank You* on his own label. A planned tour with Scorpions in 1993 fell through when Michael broke his foot in an accident. But he did reunite with UFO for the album *Walk on Water* and a club tour.

It is important to note that while Michael Schenker's impact on heavy metal guitar has been huge, he's ironically had very little commercial success. Among the many heavy metal guitar players he influenced are Joe Satriani, Jeff Watson of Night Ranger, and Kirk Hammett of Metallica. It's unfortunate that during his heyday Michael Schenker never received the widespread recognition for his guitar work he so obviously deserved. Yet, had he not personally chosen to abandon the 1977 *Lights Out* tour with UFO, things might have been substantially different—for both Schenker and the band. As it turned out, Michael became a famous guitar cult hero, but not an overwhelming guitar star like Van Halen. Regardless of his degree of stardom, it is clear that Michael Schenker created some of the most exciting six-string playing of the 1970s and 1980s, and became a legendary figure in the history of metal guitar.

UFO [on Chrysalis], *Phenomenon* (1974), *Force It* (1975), *No Heavy Petting* (1976), *Lights Out* (1977), *Obsession* (1978), *Strangers in the Night* (1979•), *Essential UFO* (1992•), *BBC Radio One Live in Concert* (Griffin, 1995•), *Walk on Water* (Zero, 1995). **Scorpions,** *Lonesome Crow* (Brain, 1972), *Lovedrive* (Mercury, 1979). **Michael Schenker Group** [on Chrysalis], *Michael Schenker Group* (1980), *MSG* (1981), *One Night at Budokan* (1982•), *Assault Attack* (1983), *Built to Destroy* (1984), *Essential Michael Schenker Group* (1992), *BBC Radio One Live in Concert* (Griffin, 1995•). **MSG** [McCauley-Schenker Group], *Perfect Timing* (Capitol, 1987), *Save Yourself* (EMI, 1989), *MSG* (Impact, 1991). **Michael Schenker,** *Thank You* (n/a, 1992).

Recordings featuring Michael Schenker: **Contraband,** *Contraband* (Impact, 1991).

Scorpions

Rudolf Schenker

Born: *August 31, 1948, in Sarstedt, West Germany*
Main Guitar: *Gibson Flying V*

Ulrich (Uli Jon) Roth

Born: *December 1954, in Dusseldorf, West Germany*
Main Guitar: *Fender Stratocaster*

Matthias Jabs

Born: *October 25, 1957, in Hanover, West Germany*
Main Guitar: *Gibson Explorer*

Michael Schenker

Born: *January 10, 1955, in Sarstedt, West Germany*
Main Guitar: *Gibson Flying V*

From their humble beginnings in what was then West Germany, Scorpions slowly fought their way to the top of the international metal scene, ultimately competing for chart space and concert venues with the likes of Van Halen and Judas Priest. Their brand of Euro-metal was fueled by various guitarists along the way, each of whom was skilled in the art of six-string pyrotechnics. The single, unchanging core of this group was rhythm guitarist Rudolf Schenker, who had sense to surround himself with some of the best lead players Europe had to offer: his brother Michael Schenker, proto-shredmeister Ulrich Roth, and jack-of-all-trades Matthias Jabs. Combined with Klaus Meine's superb rock vocals and a bombastic rhythm section, these guitarists produced—at their very best—irresistible hard rock 'n' roll. At their worst, Scorpions created a vast library of misogynous metal that relied as much on clichés as on bad hairdos.

Scorpions formed circa 1970 with a lineup that included the two Schenkers along with Meine and a rhythm section. With Michael Schenker handling lead duties, the band recorded the album *Lonesome Crow* in 1972 for the local label Brain. The band suffered an immediate setback the following year when Michael left to join UFO. Scorpions briefly broke up,

Scorpions: Matthias Jabs, Rudolf Schenker

but eventually re-formed when Meine and Schenker teamed up with virtuoso guitarist Ulrich Roth and his band Dawn Road. In 1974, Scorpions released an album called *Fly to the Rainbow*, but it wasn't until *In Trance* (1975) that the band found an international audience. Breaking out from the German metal market, *In Trance* hit big on the continent and whetted the appetites of increasingly voracious metal fans in Japan. The following year, the stellar *Virgin Killer* was issued and established the quintet's popularity around the globe.

The record proved to be one of Scorpions' best guitar records ever. The track "Pictured Life" screams out of the blocks with a burst of harmony guitar lines and is carried forward by Rudolf Schenker's abrasive rhythm work and Roth's fast descending trills. Another intense guitar track, "Polar Nights," shows the influence of Jimi Hendrix on Roth's playing. The highlight of the disc is "In Your Park," where Uli Roth demonstrates the art of using arpeggios within a rock solo—truly an exquisite lead. Interestingly, this type of playing didn't enjoy widespread use until the mid 1980s, when Eric Johnson and Yngwie Malmsteen made "arpeggios" the guitar buzzword of the period. Finally, there is "Catch Your Train," an up-tempo rocker that features Roth's extremely fast sixteenth-note and blazing Mixolydian-mode runs. Roth proved himself to be technically well ahead of his peers with this record; perhaps the only other metal guitarist able to play with Roth's level of skill in the mid seventies was Rudolf's brother Michael.

After the success of *Virgin Killer*, Scorpions came back with another heavy effort, *Taken by Force* (1978), and issued their first live album, the much-heralded but poorly recorded *Tokyo Tapes*. However, Uli Roth grew disenchanted with Scorpions' metal formula and left the band to head out on his own (resulting in an obscure solo career centered in Europe, where he ambitiously attempted to blend Hendrix-style metal with classical music). Carrying on, Scorpions auditioned nearly 200 guitarists before choosing a young German metalist named Matthias Jabs, who had previously worked with Lady. Yet, just four months later, Jabs was out. Michael Schenker had quit UFO and Scorpions were eager to have him back, so Jabs was terminated. Michael rejoined the band for some studio sessions, as well as for some live shows around Germany. However, the younger Schenker's personal problems resurfaced, and he started missing gigs. In a repeat of his performance with UFO, Michael eventually walked out and left Scorpions for good.

Scorpions approached Jabs and again asked him to join the band, this time on a more permanent basis. Jabs agreed, and set about the task of filling the lead guitar slot. He appeared with the band during a small tour, and then contributed cuts to Scorpions' 1979 set *Lovedrive*, which also featured tracks recorded by Michael Schenker. *Lovedrive* proved to be Scorpions' U.S. break-through disc, based partly on the success of the title cut and the popularity of "Another Piece of Meat" with the growing number of hard rock and heavy metal radio stations.

The band toured America to deepen their foothold in the States, opening for Ted Nugent, who was at the peak of his popularity. For their next record, *Animal Magnetism* (1980), Jabs—although not nearly the virtuoso that Roth and Michael Schenker were—handled the bulk of the solo work, sharing lead duties with Rudolf Schenker on a few tracks. The album went gold in the U.S. and paved the way for their next release, *Blackout* (1982), which contained Scorpions' first major hit in America, "No One Like You." On the title cut alone, Jabs offers up a complete selection of the most popular guitar tricks of the day, from hammer-ons to fast, Schenkeresque pentatonic runs. On the strength of *Blackout*'s success, coupled with massive amounts of radio rotation, Scorpions headlined U.S. arenas in preparation for their follow-up, *Love at First Sting* (1983). Jabs' lead work is showcased on the record's hit, "Rock You Like a Hurricane," in a furious lead of quick hammer-ons, muted scalar phrases, and edge-of-the-pick harmonics. While impressive, Jabs' playing still resides in the shadow of both Schenker and Roth. Instead of breaking new ground as a guitarist, Jabs seems more content to solidify the overall sound of Scorpions.

Love at First Sting firmly entrenched Scorpions at the forefront of eighties heavy metal, making them one of the top concert draws in the world. More hugely successful albums in the same vein followed, including allowing them to hit platinum with *World Wide Live* (1985), *Savage Amusement* (1988), *Crazy World* (1991), and *Face the Heat* (1993). Unfortunately, by the time the latter disc was released, the band had fallen into a formulaic rehashing of its repertoire. Scorpions even fell into the trap that had ensnared newer and less savvy metal bands—recorded maudlin ballads about world tragedy and lost love.

Fans had already turned away from metal by this time, and Scorpions found themselves losing popularity as part of a worldwide metal backlash. To boot, a planned reunion with Michael Schenker in 1993 never took place. Regardless of where the band ends up commercially, it does have a substantial guitar legacy that it will leave behind, due in no small part to the pioneering work of Uli Roth and the introduction of Michael Schenker.

Scorpions [on RCA except where noted], *Lonesome Crow* (Brain, 1972), *Fly to the Rainbow* (1974), *In Trance* (1975), *Virgin Killer* (1976), *Taken by Force* (1978), *Tokyo Tapes* (1978•), *Lovedrive* (Mercury, 1979), *Best of Scorpions* (1979), *Animal Magnetism* (Mercury, 1980), *Blackout* (Mercury, 1982), *Love at First Sting* (Mercury, 1983), *Best of Scorpions, Vol. 2* (1984), *World Wide Live* (Mercury, 1985•), *Savage Amusement* (Mercury, 1988), *Best of Rockers and Ballads* (Mercury, 1990), *Crazy World* (Mercury, 1991), *Face the Heat* (Mercury, 1993), *Live Bites* (Mercury, 1995•), *Pure Instinct* (Atlantic, 1996). **Uli Roth's Electric Sun** [on Metronome], *Earthquake* (c. 1979), *Fire Wind* (c. 1980). **Uli Jon Roth,** *Beyond the Astral Skies* (EMI, 1985).

Recordings featuring Scorpions: **Various Artists,** *Stairway to Heaven/Highway to Hell* (Mercury, 1990).

Iron Maiden

Dave Murray

B o r n : *December 23, 1956, in London*
M a i n   G u i t a r : *Fender Stratocaster*

Adrian Smith

B o r n : *1956, in London*
M a i n   G u i t a r : *Ibanez Destroyer*

"The New Wave of British Heavy Metal" was in full swing as the 1970s came to a close, and rockers around Europe were head-banging to the sounds of Judas Priest, Motorhead, and many others. Among the others was a band from London's East End with the apt name of Iron Maiden. Formed in 1975 by bassist-songwriter Steve Harris, Iron Maiden employed a metal method largely based on heaven-versus-hell lyrical themes and fine musicianship, especially that of lead guitarist Dave Murray.

Like Black Sabbath 10 years earlier, Maiden and their doom-metal formula clicked with audiences (the name Iron Maiden played off the dichotomy of heavy and light originated by Led Zeppelin, and was the actual name of a torture device used during the Spanish Inquisition). After the release of a 1979 EP called *The Soundhouse Tapes* and an appearance on the compilation record *Metal for Muthas*, the band gained a substantial British following. Dennis Stratton was added on second guitar (after a brief stint by guitarist Tony Parsons), and, by the end of the year, Maiden struck a recording deal with EMI. Such was their "underground" popularity that their self-titled 1980 debut album entered the U.K. Top 5 in its first week. However, Stratton quickly departed the band and was replaced by ex-Urchin guitarist Adrian Smith. Iron Maiden then undertook large tours opening for Judas Priest and Kiss.

With Murray and Smith tearing up recordings and concerts with their polished harmony guitar lines, power chords, and individual solo bursts, Iron Maiden continued on the headbangers' trail with *Killers* (1981), an album that enabled them to tour the U.K., Europe, Canada, the U.S., and Japan. In celebration of the tour's success and the attendant increase in record sales, Maiden issued a mini live record later that year entitled *Maiden Japan* (a pun on Deep Purple's classic live set *Made in Japan*). Even better things were on tap for Maiden in 1982: the addition of new vocalist-songwriter Bruce Dickinson (replacing Paul Di'anno) and the release of what is generally regarded as the band's finest record, *The Number of the Beast*, though the title's satanic reference also stirred up a respectable amount of controversy. Internationally, *The Number of the Beast* sold well into the millions and cracked the Top 40 in America. The record's appeal rested not only on Dickinson's distinctive vocals, but on the tight interplay, solid songs, and brutish twin guitar work of Murray and Smith.

A mammoth world tour followed, with dates opening for Scorpions, Judas Priest, and Rainbow. In 1983 the band offered up *Piece of Mind* and another tour, and in 1984 Iron Maiden recorded *Powerslave*. This disc included such fine Murray and Smith guitar tracks as "Aces High" and "Two Minutes to Midnight," which were highlights of the colossal "World Slavery Tour '84–'85." This particularly opulent Maiden stage show used ancient Egyptian themes and pyramids along with an appearance by the band's 10-foot-tall monster mascot, Eddie. Subsequently, Maiden issued its first full-length live album, *Live after Death*. In 1986, their keyboard-oriented album *Somewhere in Time* effortlessly shot into the U.S. Top 10.

All was not well in the Maiden camp after so much relentless touring. Adrian Smith left the group to form his own act, ASAP, and was replaced by Jannick Gers. Bruce Dickinson then released a solo record. With the metal backlash in full swing, *Fear of the Dark* (1992) was the first Maiden record in a decade not to go gold in the U.S., much less platinum. Dickinson left the band in 1994 after a semi-successful farewell tour.

Iron Maiden [on Capitol except where noted], *The Soundhouse Tapes* [EP, local release] (1979), *Iron Maiden* (Harvest, 1980), *Killers* (Harvest, 1981), *Maiden Japan* (Harvest, 1981•), *The Number of the Beast* (Harvest, 1982), *Piece of Mind* (1983), *Powerslave* (1984), *Live after Death* (1985•), *Somewhere in Time* (1986), *Seventh Son of a Seventh Son* (1988), *The First Ten Years* [British release] (EMI, 1990), *No Prayer for the Dying* (Epic, 1990), *Fear of the Dark* (Epic, 1992), *A Real Live One* (1993•), *A Real Dead One* (1993•), *X Factor* (Castle, 1996). **ASAP,** *Silver and Gold* (Enigma, 1990).

Recordings featuring Iron Maiden: **Various Artists,** *Metal for Muthas* (EMI, 1979). **Various Artists,** *New Wave of British Heavy Metal '79 Revisited* (Metal Blade, 1991).

Judas Priest

Glenn Tipton
B o r n : *October 25, 1948, in Birmingham, England*
M a i n G u i t a r : *Gibson SG*

K.K. (Kenneth) Downing
B o r n : *c. 1952, in Birmingham, England*
M a i n G u i t a r : *Gibson Flying V*

The band that spearheaded "The New Wave of British Heavy Metal" was Judas Priest. Although Priest became one of the most popular international bands of the eighties, the group had actually been recording since the mid seventies. The Judas Priest sound merges the power rock of Deep Purple with the doom-and-gloom themes of Black Sabbath, carving out their own niche with the highly distinctive wailing of vocalist Rob Halford and the high-energy, though hardly innovative, guitar work of guitarist duo Glenn Tipton and K.K. Downing.

Judas Priest began gigging in early seventies around the British Midlands and finally settled into a solid lineup in 1973, with guitarists Tipton and Downing and vocalist Rob Halford fronting the quintet. In 1974, they landed a contract with the independent Gull label, issuing the blues-influenced LP *Rocka Rolla* that same year. After building up a solid following on the road, they released their brilliant second album, *Sad Wings of Destiny* (1976), which features "Victim of Changes," a lengthy tune showcasing the guitarists at their interplaying best. The band then moved to CBS records in 1977 and recorded *Sin after Sin*, a disc that contains a surprisingly solid metal version of Joan Baez's folk ballad "Diamonds and Rust."

Stained Class (1978) topped charts around the world and allowed the band to tour in the U.S. and Japan. Another studio set followed, *Hell Bent for Leather* (1979; U.K. title: *Killing Machine*), which includes the violent guitar-driven "Delivering the Goods" and the title track. Priest closed out the first chapter of their metal career with the hugely successful *Unleashed in the East (Live in Japan)*, which contains new guitar-powered versions of "Sinner," "Ripper," and "Genocide."

The next year, Judas Priest embarked on a new phase of their career, one that was less visceral and more radio-friendly. *British Steel* (1980) featured two popular FM hits, "Living after Midnight" and "Breaking the Law." While Priest didn't sacrifice any drive or volume for the airplay, they did tone down the Satanic innuendoes, added more melody to the vocal lines, and dispensed with the tempo-changing arrangements that had made some of their early work more interesting than the standard Brit-metal fare. With *Screaming for Vengeance* (1982), Priest hit the metal big-time, scoring their first platinum album in America and headlining arenas all over the world. *Defenders of the Faith* (1984) came next and gave Judas Priest another hit. Although neither album was groundbreaking, Tipton and Downing were able to show off their individual styles to better effect on these records. Tipton played the more linear, classically oriented breaks (fast modal phrases, hammer-on arpeggios, thirty-second-note runs), while Downing presented himself as the power blues-rocker, using high-speed pentatonic climbs and a strong wrist vibrato.

Like Scorpions and other successful Euro-metal bands, Judas Priest started to devolve into self-parody in the late 1980s. Priest's practice of replacing its drummers every other year prompted the "dying drummer" gag in the movie *This Is Spinal Tap*; indeed, many have claimed Priest as the inspiration for all of *Spinal Tap*. The band was also involved in a highly publicized and protracted court battle over its alleged use of disguised lyrics and "back-masking," the process of recording vocals in reverse. In Priest's case, a mother claimed her son had committed suicide after hearing the band issue the edict "Do it." The band was found innocent of any wrongdoing.

Subsequent releases sounded like they were manufactured on an assembly line, repeating time-worn hooks and avoiding innovation at all costs (although the guitarists did use a guitar synth on the 1986 tune "Turbo Lover"). In 1992, Halford left the band to form the more thrash-oriented band Fight, leaving Tipton and Downing musically adrift. The group prepared to release a new record in 1996 with the help of a new, and completely unknown, vocalist.

For better or worse, Tipton and Downing were the definitive metal guitar duo. Leather-clad, metal-studded, posed, preened, and cranked to 11, they decimated listeners on record and in concert with a relentless barrage of heavy metal fifth chords and alternating solos. They must be commended for not falling prey to power pop ballads, but they do have to take some grief for not doing more with their abilities. Given their pre-eminence as guitarists in one of the biggest heavy metal bands of the 1980s, it seems that they had the freedom to be more experimental, if not adventurous. Still, they were good at what they did, and there is no denying them their due in that regard.

Judas Priest [on Columbia except where noted], *Rocka Rolla* (Gull, 1974), *Sad Wings of Destiny* (Janus, 1976), *Sin after Sin* (1977), *Stained Class* (1978), *Hell Bent for Leather* (1979), *Unleashed in the East* (1979•), *British Steel* (1980), *Point of Entry* (1981), *Screaming for Vengeance* (1982), *Defenders of the Faith* (1984), *Turbo* (1986), *Priest...Live!* (1987•), *Ram It Down* (1988), *Painkiller* (Columbia, 1990), *Metal Works '73–'93* (1993).

Def Leppard

Steve Clark

Born: *April 23, 1960, in Sheffield, England*
Died: *January 8, 1991*
Main Guitar: *Gibson Les Paul*

Phil Collen

Born: *December 8, 1957, in London*
Main Guitar: *Ibanez Destroyer*

Pete Willis

Born: *February 16, 1960, in Sheffield, England*
Main Guitar: *Hamer Standard*

Vivian Campbell

Born: *in Belfast, Northern Ireland*
Main Guitar: *Charvel Strat-style*

As a band of teenagers, Def Leppard gained a name for itself in Britain in the early 1980s on the strength of two hard-rocking early albums, *On through the Night* (1980) and *High 'n' Dry* (1981). The band toured ceaselessly and also made videos of their songs, which gave them a leg up on the competition when MTV finally arrived.

During the recording of the band's third album, guitarist Pete Willis left the group (sources differ on whether he was fired or resigned), leaving the band with only one guitarist, Steve Clark. After a lengthy search, Phil Collen was recruited from Girl to team up with Clark. Following a nearly two-year delay, the band released *Pyromania*, an album that was in the right place at the right time. It defined commercial metal and would be the definitive metal album of the 1980s: melodic, heavy, loud, played by relatively attractive males with big haircuts and plenty of pout, and most importantly, filled with good guitar work. The album's centerpiece, "Photograph," summed it all up in under five minutes. Built on an impressively catchy riff by Clark, "Photograph" features singer Joe Elliot layering lots of background vocals and harmonies over the simple refrain, while Collen plays a

Phil Collen

tuneful, speed-capped solo. In retrospect, Collen's solo on this song probably constitutes the first shred break ever to appear in a major rock hit.

With the success of *Pyromania*, Def Leppard became one of the biggest concert draws in the world. Unfortunately, various internal problems arose, including a horrible car crash that caused drummer Rick Allen to lose his left arm. As Allen relearned the drums—with the aid of a specially designed electronic kit —the band was forced to wait four years to release its next record. Nevertheless, *Hysteria* (1987) immediately followed *Pyromania* into the realms of multi-platinum sales by way of ample video exposure and hits like "Pour Some Sugar on Me" and "Love Bites." Having reconquered the metal world, Leppard was again at the top of its game.

Unfortunately, guitarist Steve Clark died in January of 1991, due to complications from alcoholism. Def Lep's next album, *Adrenalize*, was recorded with just the four surviving members, although it did include a few tracks recorded before Clark's death. After an extensive search, Clark was replaced by ex-Dio and Whitesnake guitarist Vivian Campbell, who toured with the band and appeared on the album *Retro Active* in 1993. Campbell was fully in evidence on *Slang* (1996), a raw and marked departure from the group's slicker metal offerings.

Def Leppard [on Mercury], *On through the Night* (1980), *High 'n' Dry* (1981), *Pyromania* (1983), *Hysteria* (1987), *Adrenalize* (1992), *Retro Active* (1993•), *Slang* (1996).

Recordings featuring Def Leppard: **Various Artists,** *New Wave of British Heavy Metal '79 Revisited* (Metal Blade, 1991).

CHAPTER TWENTY-FOUR

Instrumental Rock II
Pushing the Limits

Living on the edge. Apart from mainstream rock players, there has always been a cult of players who have been intent on breaking barriers, whether it be regarding speed, sound, or style. They're seemingly not interested in garnering hits—just the respect and admiration that come from being among the most accomplished guitarists on the planet. Thousands of players have diligently pursued this chimera, but few have captured it.

Not surprisingly, the bulk of the music produced by these guitarists is instrumental, designed to showcase the instrument and not a vocalist. The music is oftentimes rigorous and intricate, even oppressively so, but it is a rock sub-genre that makes no excuses for its complexity. The guitarists who play at this level usually do not give in to record company pressures or radio requirements, which is why most instrumental guitar records are found on obscure independent labels. In short, there aren't big bucks at this end of the rock guitar spectrum. But there is something about being recognized by one's peers as being among the best that somehow makes up for the lack of financial reward.

The guitarists that have embodied this ethic are few and far between. People like Jeff Beck, Steve Morse, and Allan Holdsworth—all outlined below—have been major influences on several generations of guitar players, and they made names for themselves as far back as the sixties and seventies. But since that time, there have been few instrumentalists who have had immediate impact on their fellow players. This is surprising given that every year since the dawn of shred, circa 1984, countless players have recorded their own instrumental guitar records. The bulk of them have been horrible, self-indulgent affairs that were more concerned with chops than substance. However, there are players who rise above the maelstrom and make authoritative musical statements. Among the most recent additions to this list are David Torn, Mike Keneally, and Shawn Lane, all of whom can respectfully be called guitarists' guitarists.

Coming from the same school as Robert Fripp, Adrian Belew, and Frank Zappa, Torn and Keneally operate on rock's avant garde fringe, twisting tones and hitting dissonant notes at every opportunity. Think of them as rock's answer to such jazz-noise terrorists as Sonny Sharrock, Bill Frisell, and Terje Rypdal. Torn has released such compelling solo discs as *Cloud about Mercury* (1987), *Door X* (1990), and the largely improvisational *Polytown* (1994), all of which revealed his unusual guitar voice. Mistakenly labeled as an Allan Holdsworth clone early on, Torn

developed his own sound based on an ungodly amount of effects processing gear. In addition, his guitar of choice was anything but mainstream—a custom Klein solidbody—but such departures from the norm are part of what makes David Torn such an intriguing player.

Mike Keneally, on the other hand, is a distinguished graduate of Frank Zappa's touring band who has released several solo albums of erratic guitar behavior, notably *hat* (1993) and *Boil That Dust Speck* (1994). Strange sounds, bizarre time signatures, and flashes of technical brilliance highlight his work, all served up in a churning sonic soup that must be listened to over and over to be digested. He also recorded and toured with Zappa progeny Dweezil and Ahmet as part of their band Z (▶ Shred).

A less radical, but equally impressive, guitar instrumentalist is Shawn Lane, a Memphis virtuoso who promises to be one of the major players of the 1990s. For a time, Lane was an underground legend—players on the caliber of Steve Morse and Eric Johnson spoke of him as one of the best unknown players around—but the guitar community at large could not even find him. After years of this obscurity, Lane released his solo disc *Powers of Ten* in 1992. The record delivered everything that had previously just been rumored. With great taste, melodic sense, and positively stupefying chops, the guitarist burned throughout the album, especially on the tuneful "Get You Back," a cover of Ray Gomez's "West Side Boogie," and the stunning "Gray Pianos Flying," in which he played one of the fastest recorded runs in guitar history. To top it off, the guitarist played every instrument on the album, produced and engineered it, and also proved himself to be a virtuoso pianist on two classically styled tracks, "Powers of Ten: Suite" and "Piano Concerto: Transformation of Themes." A true virtuoso in every sense of the word.

Jeff Beck

Born: *June 24, 1944, in Wallington, Surrey, England*
Main Guitars: *Fender Stratocaster and Telecaster, Gibson Les Paul Standard*

After his Beck, Bogert & Appice fiasco (▶ the Jeff Beck Group), Jeff Beck returned to the forefront of rock guitar in the spring of 1975 with an album called *Blow by Blow*. Instead of the blues-rock clichés he had been serving up since the mid sixties, Beck moved into the realm of jazz-rock with this album, an instrumental tour de force that meshed rock ("Highway Jam"), fusion ("Scatterbrain"), R&B ("She's a Woman"), and funk ("You Know What I Mean") with unerring precision. Produced by George Martin—who was behind the boards for all the Beatles records—*Blow by Blow* went to the top of the album charts and re-established Beck as rock's premier guitar player and a successful harbinger of the new jazz-rock sound.

With the rhythm section of pianist Max Middleton (from the last incarnation of the Jeff Beck Group), bassist Phil Chen, and drummer Richard Bailey, Beck was at peak form on *Blow by Blow*. One of the album's highlights was his rendition of Stevie Wonder's "Cause We've Ended as Lovers," a stormy guitar ballad that Beck dedicated to guitar virtuoso Roy Buchanan. He filled the piece with an enchanting Strat solo that exhibited a dazzling array of tonal colorings and subtle dynamics, making the track one of the guitar masterworks of the seventies. After the release of *Blow by Blow*, Beck embarked on a successful tour of the United States as part of a double fusion bill with John McLaughlin (◗) and the Mahavishnu Orchestra.

The British guitar wizard followed up his 1975 triumph with yet another hit instrumental album, *Wired* (1976). This time, Beck utilized the talents of drummer/composer Narada Michael Walden and synthesizer master Jan Hammer (both expatriates of the Mahavishnu Orchestra). With Hammer's crisp synth work spicing up several cuts, *Wired* had a more electronic feel than *Blow by Blow*, as shown on tracks like "Blue Wind" (a piece that garnered a considerable amount of FM radio airplay) and Beck's rock version of Charles Mingus' "Goodbye Pork Pie Hat." Towards the end of 1976, Beck undertook another large tour (giving Jan Hammer and the boys equal billing), which resulted in the rather ho-hum *Jeff Beck with the Jan Hammer Group Live* (1977). A rehash of the studio tracks from the previous two records, this live record was something of a throwaway— not mediocre enough to diminish Beck's reputation as a top fusion soloist, but not exciting enough to break any new musical ground.

With the exception of a 1978 tour of Japan with bassist Stanley Clarke and drummer Simon Phillips, Beck went into seclusion for the next few years, opting to spend his free time pursuing his other passion—the restoration and collection of cars. He finally re-emerged in 1980 with *There and Back*, another solid jazz-rock outing. Top tracks included such instrumentals as "El Becko," "Star Cycle," "The Golden Road," and "The Final Peace," one of Beck's most elegant guitar ballads.

After this release, Beck again dropped out of sight for a few years, occasionally popping up for all-star gigs like the Secret Policeman's Ball in 1981 or the 1983–84 ARMS tour, with its spectacular cast of British rock stars, including Eric Clapton and Jimmy Page (marking the first time the three guitar heroes had ever performed together). In 1984, Beck also guested on several albums by Mick Jagger, Tina Turner, and Rod Stewart, contributing typically off-the-wall leads on each one. Only a player of Beck's caliber would be allowed to rip relentlessly on commercial rock releases like these, and only Beck could pull it off and make his skewed solos fit into slick AOR grooves.

In the summer of 1985, Jeff Beck released his first solo album in half a decade, *Flash*. Here, he finally moved away from fusion with a strong record that mixed electronic funk rhythms with a smattering of metal guitar solos, dubbed "black metal." His truly ear-piercing take on the heaviness of the genre was played to the hilt on "Ambitious" and the horrifically jagged intro to "Gets Us All in the End." Critics and fans heralded the album as Beck's welcome return to rock 'n' roll, and he also scored some radio and MTV airplay with a wonderful remake of Curtis Mayfield's "People Get Ready," with old bandmate Rod Stewart on vocals.

Another hiatus followed, and in 1989 Beck released a solid instrumental album called *Jeff Beck's Guitar Shop* (with artwork that spoofed his automotive obsessions), featuring drummer Terry Bozzio and keyboardist Tony Hymas. Beck took this band out on the road, sharing the bill in the U.S. with Stevie Ray Vaughan. In 1991 *Beckology* was issued, a three-disc boxed set covering his career. He then released a pair of diverse studio sets: *Frankie's House*, which was the soundtrack to a television film set in the Vietnam era, and *Crazy Legs* (1993), a raucous rockabilly tribute to his idol Cliff Gallup, the original guitarist with Gene Vincent & the Blue Caps (◗). Even longtime Beckophiles were amazed at how closely the guitarist mimicked the subtleties of Gallup's then-radical style. Others simply wondered why.

After nearly 30 years at the forefront of rock guitar, Beck clearly is one rock musician who neither rests on his laurels nor is content to play only in one particular musical style. Despite his many musical forays—into blues-rock, heavy metal, fusion, and contemporary funk—Beck always maintains a firm grip on his rock 'n' roll roots. Though some have

Jeff Beck

tried to categorize Beck and his diverse musical masks, only one label truly fits him: Guitar Icon. His future is always questionable, as he seems not to be concerned with the public clamoring for more of his records and more concert performances. Instead, he reluctantly picks up the mantle of guitar hero only when he breaks away from his favorite passion, working on hot rods.

Jeff Beck [on Epic], *Blow by Blow* (1975), *Wired* (1976), *Jeff Beck with the Jan Hammer Group Live* (1977•), *There and Back* (1980), *Flash* (1985), *The Best of Jeff Beck, 1967–1969* (Fame, 1985), *Beckology* (1991•), *Crazy Legs* (1993). **Jeff Beck, Tony Hymas, Terry Bozzio,** *Guitar Shop* (Epic, 1989). **Jeff Beck & Jed Leiber,** *Frankie's House* [television soundtrack] (Epic, 1992).

Recordings featuring Jeff Beck: **Stanley Clarke,** *Journey to Love* (Nemperor, 1975), *Modern Man* (Nemperor, 1978), *I Want to Play for You* (Nemperor, 1979), *Time Exposure* (Epic, 1984). **Narada Michael Walden,** *Garden of Love Light* (Atlantic, 1976). **Billy Preston,** *Billy Preston* (A&M, c. 1976). **Upp,** *This Way* (Epic, 1976). **Badger,** *White Lady* (Columbia, 1976). **Various Artists,** *The Secret Policeman's Other Ball, The Music* (Island, 1982•). **Tina Turner,** *Private Dancer* (Capitol, 1983). **The Honeydrippers,** *The Honeydrippers, Vol. 1* (Esparanza, 1984). **Vanilla Fudge,** *Mystery* (Atco, 1984). **Various Artists,** *White Boy Blues, Classic Guitars of Clapton, Beck, and Page* (Compleat, 1984). **Box of Frogs,** *Box of Frogs* (Epic, 1984), **Rod Stewart,** *Camouflage* (Warner Bros., 1984). **Mick Jagger** [on Columbia], *She's the Boss* (1985), *Primitive Cool* (1987). **Jon Bon Jovi,** *Blaze of Glory* [soundtrack] (Mercury, 1990). **Buddy Guy,** *Damn Right I've Got the Blues* (Silvertone, 1991).

Steve Morse

Born: *July 28, 1954, in Hamilton, Ohio*
Main Guitars: *Modified Fender Telecaster, Ernie Ball/Music Man Steve Morse model*

Steve Morse stands first and foremost among rock's greatest guitar virtuosos. On one level, he is a master technician, able to execute single-note passages, chordal changes, and solos with such speed and accuracy that guitar aficionados around the world have been left dumbstruck. On another level, he is nearly the ultimate *eclectic* guitarist, as he has proved in his stints with the Dixie Dregs, Kansas (♦), Deep Purple, and his own Steve Morse Band. While eclecticism is nothing new to rock guitar, very few players have been able to fuse so many diverse influences into one valid style, and still be so adept at playing each genre independently. Besides composing and play-

Steve Morse

ing pieces that reflect a multitude of musical sources, Morse can play rock, country, classical, bluegrass, funk, heavy metal, blues, and jazz-fusion guitar with the absolute best players in those fields. Simply put, Steve Morse is a rock guitar marvel.

Background. Raised in Michigan and Georgia, Morse took up the guitar in the early 1960s, inspired by the Beatles, the Rolling Stones, and the Yardbirds. Later, after seeing a concert by classical guitarist Juan Mercadel during high school, Morse realized there was more to guitar than three-chord rock. As a result, he enrolled in the University of Miami's renowned music program, which at the time counted fusion guitarist Pat Metheny, Weather Report bassist Jaco Pastorius, and drummer/producer Narada Michael Walden among its distinguished faculty or visiting musical guests.

During his days at the University of Miami, Morse's bluesy hammer-on guitar style gave way to a more controlled linear method that utilized picking on every note. His knowledge of classical and jazz guitar technique, music theory, and composition also increased dramatically during this period. Morse formed a school rock ensemble with violinist Allen Sloan, drummer Rod Morgenstein, and bassist Andy West (with whom Morse had played in a high school band called the Dixie Grits). Fleshing out the lab band with a keyboardist, the five formed a group that became known as the Dixie Dregs. Using Morse's complex instrumental compositions, the young musicians began formulating a new rock sound, which was profoundly influenced by John McLaughlin's Mahavishnu Orchestra, yet emphasized a heavy rock 'n' roll beat and unbridled hard rock flair.

Recordings. After gigging for a while on the southern bar circuit around Augusta, Georgia, the Dixie Dregs were heard by the right people at Capricorn Records, who promptly signed them in late 1976. The group's first outing, *Freefall*, was released in the spring of 1977 and displayed the band's prodigious talents on guitar-dominated songs like "Freefall," "Moedown," and "Refried Funky Chicken," which boasted some expert wah-wah guitar from Morse. The high point of *Freefall* was an uptempo fusion romp called "Cruise Control" (a longtime Dregs concert favorite), which showed off the group's musical talent in a finale featuring each member trading off solos of two bars, then one bar, then half a bar, and then soloing on an incredible one beat each.

In 1978 the Dixie Dregs went into the studio with producer Ken Scott, who had worked with the Mahavishnu Orchestra, Stanley Clarke, and Jeff Beck. With Scott at the helm, the group recorded *What If*, which contained such Dregs classics as the great rocker "Take It off the Top," "Odyssey," and "Night Meets Light." After the release of the record, the band hit the road, opening for major rock acts like Santana, Styx, and the Doobie Brothers, and playing their own club dates.

Nineteen seventy-nine brought the release of *Night of the Living Dregs*, some of which was recorded at the 1978 Montreux Jazz Festival in Switzerland, where the group brought down the house with a hot version of "The Bash."

The following year, Morse and company shortened their name to just the Dregs and jumped record labels to Arista. There they recorded three fine Morse-produced albums during the early eighties: *Dregs of the Earth* (1980), *Unsung Heroes* (1981), and *Industry Standard* (1982). By this time, the Dregs had acquired a large cult of dedicated followers and received near-universal accolades from critics for their "electric chamber music." Morse himself was regularly recognized as a stellar rock guitarist, winning guitar polls year after year and influencing thousands of young players with his myriad of tones, technique, and uniquely tasteful soloing style. Another source of fascination for Morse fans was his customized electric guitar: a one-of-a-kind Fender Telecaster with a Strat neck and various humbucker, single-coil, and guitar-synth hex pickups—an eclectic guitar for an eclectic guitarist.

However, by 1983 the Dregs reached the bottom of the barrel. Their adherence to mostly instrumental rock had produced no big hits, and the band was suffering from record company pressures, internal tension, and business problems. By the end of the year, the Dregs broke up. Morse took some time off, but soon appeared in various concert settings with a variety of other musicians. First, he went on tour opening for the Trio—the super-acoustic coupling of John McLaughlin, Al Di Meola, and Paco de Lucia—and fans spoke in awe about the nights Morse blew them off the stage. Later, Steve briefly formed an electric trio with bassist Jerry Peek and a drummer, dubbing them Morse Code.

Eventually, Morse Code turned into the Steve Morse Band (a trio with Morse, Peek, and Dregs drummer Rod Morgenstein), and a new album arrived in the summer of 1984, entitled *The Introduction*. The band followed that record with *Stand Up* (1985), a strong second effort that showed the guitarist moving full-speed into the world of guitar synthesizers. *Stand Up* also featured an array of guitar guests, including Eric Johnson, Albert Lee, and Peter Frampton. In 1986, Morse made a surprise career move, venturing away from his all-instrumental format to join Kansas for their comeback album *Power*. Then, during 1987–88, the guitarist temporarily took a break from the music business to work as a commercial airline pilot, while simultaneously working on a second Kansas disc and another solo project.

In 1990, he garnered acclaim for his acoustic-oriented *High Tension Wires*. He followed that record with a revised Steve Morse Band (ultimately featuring bassist Dave LaRue and drummer Van Romaine), which cut several solid, if somewhat predictable, instrumental albums. A Dixie Dregs reunion produced well-received live and studio albums, while Morse kept busy with his own projects, notably the intense *Structural Damage* (1995), and joining up with Deep Purple. Morse replaced the temperamental Ritchie Blackmore (and Blackmore's temporary replacement, Joe Satriani) for an international tour and a new Purple

record. Clearly, Steve Morse's main career priority is to keep moving on.

Style and Technique. One of Morse's greatest attributes as a rock stylist is that he has been able to achieve near-perfect picking and musical diversity without ever losing a basic feel for high-energy rock 'n' roll. His heavier rock playing with the Dregs reflects the fast scalar runs and chordal comping of jazz along with the low-register string bends and fuzzed-out riffing of metal ("Take It off the Top," "Road Expense," "Native Dance," "Cruise Missile"). Then again, spellbinding country guitar tracks like "Gina Lola Breakdown," "The Bash," and "Pride o' the Farm" rank with Nashville's finest picking. There are, of course, other styles that he has mastered and made his own, as evidenced in his funk guitar breaks ("Ice Cakes," "Kat Food") and art-rock anthems, the best of which include "Long Slow Distance," "Hereafter," and "Day 444." Finally, he has created several beautiful and finely crafted classical guitar pieces ("Northern Lights," "Little Kids," "Go for Baroque") that go far beyond the musical boundaries of most rock 'n' roll pickers.

As a sonic groundbreaker, Morse has constantly pushed himself and his instrument to the limit. The proof of this resides in his recordings with the Dregs, the Steve Morse Band, and Kansas, and is obvious in his high-voltage concert performances. Via his sheer command of both electric and acoustic guitar, Morse has inspired a slew of guitarists to rise above the limitations of playing in one style. While he hasn't achieved the mass radio success of such heavy rock guitar superstars as Eddie Van Halen or Neal Schon, Morse's musical focus has always been on contemporary guitar music and its evolution. It is hardly an exaggeration to say Steve Morse is one of the most respected guitarists to have ever picked up the instrument.

Dixie Dregs [on Capricorn except where noted], *Freefall* (1977), *What If* (1978), *Night of the Living Dregs* (1979), *Dregs of the Earth* (Arista, 1980), *Best of the Dixie Dregs* (Grand Slamm, 1987). **The Dregs** [on Arista], *Unsung Heroes* (1981), *Industry Standard* (1982), *Bring 'em Back Alive* (Capricorn, 1992•), *Full Circle* (1994). **Steve Morse Band** [on MCA except where noted], *The Introduction* (Musician, 1984), *Stand Up* (Elektra, 1985), *Southern Steel* (1991), *Coast to Coast* (1992). **Kansas** [on MCA], *Power* (1986), *In the Spirit of Things* (1988). **Steve Morse**, *High Tension Wires* (MCA, 1989), *Structural Damage* (High Street, 1995), *Stressfest* (High Street, 1996). **Deep Purple**, *Purpendicular* (RCA, 1996).

Recordings featuring Steve Morse: **Various Artists**, *Hotels, Motels, and Roadshows* (Capricorn, 1978•). **Steve Walsh**, *Schemer-Dreamer* (Kirshner, 1980), **Art in America**, *Art in America* (Pavillion, 1983). **T Lavitz**, *Storytime* (Passport Jazz, 1986). **Triumph**, *Surveillance* (MCA, 1987). **Lynyrd Skynyrd**, *Southern by the Grace of God* (MCA, 1988•). **Various Artists**, *Guitar's Practicing Musicians* (Guitar Recordings, 1989), *Guitar's Practicing Musicians, Vol. 2* (Guitar Recordings, 1991). **Various Artists**, *Guitar Speak III* (IRS, 1991). **Michael Manring**, *Thonk* (High Street, 1994).

Allan Holdsworth

Born: *August 6, 1948, in Bradford, Yorkshire, England*
Main Guitars: *Modified Fender Stratocaster, Charvel Strat-style, Steinberger, Carvin, and DeLap electrics, Gibson SG*

Since Allan Holdsworth's rise to prominence in the mid 1970s, his instrumental voice has added a whole new sound and technical approach to rock guitar. In lieu of the clipped staccato of most guitarists' picking styles, Holdsworth's technique falls into the area of the legato, blending smooth hammered-on lines and melodic phrasing into a sound not unlike a saxophone or a violin. Also, his innovative use of tremolo bar effects has provided a subtle embellishment to his splendid guitar work with such acts as Soft Machine, the New Tony Williams Lifetime, Gong, Bruford, Jean-Luc Ponty, U.K., and his own solo projects.

Allan Holdsworth

Holdsworth's earliest musical inspiration came from his father, an accomplished pianist, and his large collection of jazz records. Holdsworth didn't actually take up the guitar until he was around 16. After playing locally and in London for a few years, Holdsworth hooked up with ex-Colosseum drummer Jon Hiseman and formed the heavy rock outfit Tempest. This radical rock band lasted only a few months; after one album in 1972, Holdsworth left to join the experimental rock band Soft Machine. He appeared on Soft Machine's *Bundles* (1975), which showed off the guitarist's intricate lead style in "Hazard Profile, Part One" and his fine acoustic guitar talents on "Gone Sailing."

Holdsworth had musical aspirations beyond Soft Machine and left the group in 1975. Fortuitously, he was put in contact with the legendary jazz-rock drummer Tony Williams, who tapped him for the guitar slot in his band, the New Tony Williams Lifetime. Holdsworth appeared on two Lifetime efforts, *Believe It* (1975) and *Million Dollar Legs* (1976), both emphasizing strong funk-fusion grooves and the band members' individual soloing talents. Also during 1976, Holdsworth recorded his first solo set, *Velvet Darkness*, a disc that contained powerful electric work as well as three extraordinary acoustic guitar pieces: "Last

May," "Kinder," and "Floppy Hat." The guitarist brilliantly translated his hammer-on legato to the acoustic guitar—no mean feat, considering that the technique usually relies on the sustain that electric guitars and amps produce. Unfortunately, this album was less than successful in the fusion world, and, worse, the New Tony Williams Lifetime was forced to disband due to bad management.

However, Holdsworth's guitar talents had been noticed, and soon he was recording with several acts as a featured soloist. In 1977 he appeared with Gong on their progressive instrumental album *Expresso* (and on *Expresso II* the following year). Holdsworth also recorded with Jean-Luc Ponty on his crossover-jazz set *Enigmatic Ocean*.

Until 1977, Holdsworth had largely been associated with the fusion world, but that year, he appeared on ex-Yes and King Crimson drummer Bill Bruford's instrumental rock album *Feels Good to Me*. As a result, the guitarist's image and audience began to change. Instead of the free-form jams and experimental numbers that marked Holdsworth's early career, Bruford's music presented instrumental rock in a compact, structured form, not unlike the art-rock music of the early 1970s. Though still burdened by the "spotlight soloist" label, Holdsworth was outstanding in this environment, highlighting the tuneful music with his own flashy, but melodic, leads (best heard on songs like "Feels Good to Me," "Either End of August," and "Adios a la Pasada"). For both Holdsworth and the Bruford band, the record was a stellar achievement.

In 1978, his rock affiliation deepened as he and Bruford formed U.K. with singer/bassist John Wetton and keyboardist/violinist Eddie Jobson. A distinctly progressive rock band with supergroup leanings, U.K. won huge numbers of fans and made its way onto the record charts with its debut album. Holdsworth may have been the biggest beneficiary of U.K.'s success, as guitar fans around the world discovered his fast legato playing and tremolo bar effects in compositions like the popular suite "In the Dead of Night." Among the guitarists enthralled with this fine disc were Alex Lifeson of Rush, Joe Satriani, and Eddie Van Halen, who ultimately cited Holdsworth as one of his favorite guitarists. In retrospect, the debut U.K. album has proven to be one of the most important records in the history of progressive and art rock.

Musically, Holdsworth was again primarily relegated to soloing duties within U.K., while Jobson and Wetton handled most of the songwriting and arranging. Miffed at this underling role, Holdsworth left U.K. and returned to the Bruford band. Still, the rock world had noticed the 30-year-old guitar master's performance on the U.K. disc. By the release of the next Bruford album, *One of a Kind* (1979), the guitar world was primed for great things from Holdsworth. An acknowledged classic in instrumental rock, *One of a Kind* was just what it claimed to be: a once-in-a-lifetime meeting of four great musicians—Holdsworth, Bruford, bassist Jeff Berlin, and keyboardist Dave Stewart. Holdsworth rose to the occasion, giving nearly every track a splash of his soloing skills, including fast modal runs and a variety of colorful tremolo nuances. From "Hell's Bells" to "One of a Kind, Part One" to " Five G" to his own "The Abingdon Chasp," Holdsworth blazed away on the album. His playing mesmerized guitarists on every continent and made him one of the most influential players of the time.

Ironically, Holdsworth's career temporarily plummeted from this musical peak when he left the Bruford camp. Again, his departure was due to his frustration at being pigeonholed as a soloist, a constant state of affairs that overlooked his superb rhythm playing skills. He formed False Alarm, a band that played his brand of instrumental music exclusively. Since the music was hardly commercially oriented, Holdsworth and his band (subsequently called I.O.U.) struggled for the next few years without a recording contract, ultimately recording an album in 1982 with money out of their own pockets. Then, at the urging of Eddie Van Halen, Warner Brothers signed Holdsworth for a mini-album, which resulted in *Road Games* (1983). On this effort, Holdsworth's unique musical vision finally attained reality, with both vocal and instrumental compositions that revealed a myriad of tonal textures, powerful solos, and, at last, his ethereal rhythm playing.

After *Road Games*, Holdsworth's career got back on track when he formed a new group that revolved around himself, bassist Jimmy Johnson, and drummer Chad Wackerman. He took this band on the road and recorded for both the Enigma and Relativity labels, releasing several brilliant albums, including *Metal Fatigue* (1985), *Atavachron* (1986), and *Hard Hat Area* (1994). These records crossed a myriad of musical boundaries and firmly reinforced his reputation as a musical groundbreaker and guitar virtuoso. *Atavachron* also marked Holdsworth's debut with the SynthAxe, a six-string synthesizer controller that hooked up to a synthesizer via MIDI (Musical Instrument Digital Interface). Not surprisingly, the results were stunning.

As a guitarist constantly pushing forward the technical and tonal limitations of his instrument, Allan Holdsworth has been the creator of some of rock's most intriguing modern guitar work. He initially emerged as a vibrant fusion soloist, broadening

the tonal borders of the rock guitar with his work in Bruford and U.K. During the early years of the 1980s, his legato hammer-on and tremolo bar techniques went hand-in-hand with Eddie Van Halen's similar methods (barring the two-handed tap, which was Van Halen's sole domain) to influence an entire generation of rock guitar players. He also pioneered the use of cutting-edge technology as part of a guitarist's arsenal with his groundbreaking synthesizer work. And as of this writing, he may also be the best improvisational soloist in the history of rock music.

Tempest, *Tempest* (Warner Bros., 1973). **The New Tony Williams Lifetime** [on Columbia], *Believe It* (1975), *Million Dollar Legs* (1976). **Allan Holdsworth,** *Velvet Darkness* (CTI, 1976), *I.O.U.* (self-produced, 1982), *Road Games* [EP] (Warner Bros., 1983), *Metal Fatigue* (Enigma, 1985), *Atavachron* (Enigma, 1986), *Sand* (Relativity, 1987), *Secrets* (Intima, 1989), *Wardenclyffe Tower* (Restless, 1992), *Hard Hat Area* (Restless, 1994). **Bruford** [on Polydor], *Feels Good to Me* (1977), *One of a Kind* (1979). **U.K.,** *U.K.* (Polydor, 1978). **Allan Holdsworth & Gordon Beck,** *The Things You See* (JMS, 1980), *With a Heart in My Song* (JMS, 1989). **MVP,** *Truth in Shredding* (Legato, 1991).

Recordings featuring Allan Holdsworth: **Soft Machine** [on EMI], *Bundles* (1975), *Land of Cockayne* (1981). **Gong** [on Virgin except where noted], *Gazeuse* (1977), *Expresso* (1977), *Expresso II* (Arista, 1978). **Jean-Luc Ponty** [on Atlantic], *Enigmatic Ocean* (1977), *Individual Choice* (1983). **Gordon Beck,** *Sunbird* (n/a, 1979). **Nucleus,** *Belladonna* (Vertigo, n/a). **Krokus,** *Change of Address* (Arista, 1986). **Stuart Hamm,** *Radio Free Albemuth* (Relativity, 1988). **Jack Bruce,** *A Question of Time* (Epic, 1989). **Chad Wackerman,** *Forty Reasons* (CMP, 1991). **Gongzilla,** *Suffer* (Lolo, 1995).

Eric Johnson

Born: *August 17, 1954, in Austin, Texas*
Main Guitar: *Fender Stratocaster*

Eric Johnson is one of those superb guitarists who initially became famous for not being famous. Like Roy Buchanan before him, Johnson has had a reputation among other guitarists as a true *player*. Since 1974, Johnson had been receiving rave reviews about his awesome guitar talents from the likes of Johnny Winter, Jeff Baxter, Steve Morse, and Billy Gibbons, but the guitar public at large had heard nothing of his music. He had released an album with his Austin-based fusion band, the Electromagnets, in the mid seventies and had later participated in some sessions for Carole King, Cat Stevens, and Christopher Cross (playing lead on "Minstrel Gigolo," from Cross' popular debut album). Still, the life of a session guitarist was hardly high-profile, and Johnson remained a mystery guitar hero. In 1981 he was asked to join Steve Morse's Dixie Dregs after violinist Allen Sloan left, but Johnson turned the job down. He was then reportedly offered gigs with fusion bass star Stanley Clarke and prog-rockers U.K., but declined them as well.

Fortunately, the guitarist finally decided to make his move in the mid 1980s. First, he appeared on a song from Steve Morse's album *Stand Up*; then, after signing a record deal with Reprise Records, he recorded his debut, *Tones*, in 1986. Bolstered by extensive coverage in the major guitar magazines, *Tones* found an

Eric Johnson

tarist rocked through instrumentals ("Righteous," "Trademark"), catchy vocal tunes ("Desert Rose," "High Landrons," "Nothing Can Keep Me from You"), and such eclectic fare as the country tune "Steve's Boogie" and the acoustic "Song for George." There was even a Wes Montgomery tribute called "East Wes." With his devilish chops, poofed-up hairdo, and eternal grin, Eric Johnson had finally arrived.

Of course, after Johnson arrived, he promptly disappeared again. He did tour with his hero B.B. King in 1994 and appeared on a Chet Atkins television special. He also filmed an extremely popular instructional guitar video, but that was the extent of his offerings until 1996, when he released *Venus Isle*, his first album in six years. Complete with Johnson's trademark perfection, it also featured a significant amount of his keyboard playing

audience eager to get a taste of Johnson's guitar mastery. Interweaving clean-toned rhythm textures with Hendrix-inspired hard rock sections, Johnson powered his way through songs like "Friends," "Emerald Eyes," and "Bristol Shore" with speed-picking lines, pop melodies, and shimmering koto-like harmonics. Although it wasn't the blow-away performance some insiders were expecting, it was still a very impressive debut.

Again the years slipped by, and in 1990 Johnson switched over to Capitol Records, quietly releasing *Ah Via Musicom*. He had recorded the entire album twice, since he was unhappy with the first version—a testimony to his perfectionism and evidence of his disregard for music industry schedules and deadlines. Initially, the album appeared to flop. While the guitar and music magazines sang its praises, it seemed to end up being nothing more than another six-string small event. However, radio station DJs starting playing "Cliffs of Dover," Johnson's signature instrumental from the album. The song had previously been available only as a plastic flexi-disc contained in a 1986 issue of *Guitar Player* magazine. Surprisingly, the once-unknown guitarist had a bona fide radio hit on his hands with "Cliffs of Dover," which pushed *Ah Via Musicom* up the pop charts. The track itself was a guitar marvel. Opening with a trumpeting, call-to-arms lick on his vintage Strat, Johnson launched into a brisk, major-tonality rocker that featured all his best attributes: fast eighth- and sixteenth-note alternate picking, a terrific sense of melody, and undeniable soulfulness. The rest of the album was just as remarkable, as the gui-

and singing. There was more than enough to keep guitar purists happy, though, with rockers like "Camel's Night Out" and a blues tribute entitled "S.R.V." During the time it took to record *Venus Isle*, Johnson developed tinnitus, which has affected many rock guitarists, including Pete Townshend and Jeff Beck. In the fall of 1996, he undertook a tour with Joe Satriani and Steve Vai, which was billed as G3.

Johnson is known as a perfectionist, even in a genre where perfectionism is the norm. His commitment to tone has led to the story—perhaps apocryphal—that he can identify the brand of batteries used in effects boxes because of the variances in tone that they cause. Johnson's chops are similarly awe-inspiring. Although they aren't of the Yngwie Malmsteen mach-speed variety, his fast eighth- and sixteenth-note chops are as quick as a very agile country or bebop player, and then some. He also exhibits a strong Jimi Hendrix influence, particularly within his clean-toned rhythm playing (which occasionally bears a Pat Metheny mark, too). Unlike heavy-handed Hendrix aspirants such as Frank Marino or Robin Trower, Johnson seems to convincingly nail down the guitar legend's prowess for combining rhythm, taste, and, above all, feel. Better still, he takes Hendrix licks and transforms them into something new and intriguing, which is a rarity among rock players. Johnson is notable for being able to stand above the pack, keep his originality, and leave his audience always wanting more.

The Electromagnets, *The Electromagnets* (EGM, 1975). **Eric Johnson,** *Tones* (Reprise, 1986), *Ah Via Musicom* (Capitol, 1990), *Venus Isle* (Capitol, 1996).

Recordings featuring Eric Johnson: **Cat Stevens,** *Back to Earth* (A&M, 1978). **Christopher Cross,** *Christopher Cross* (Warner Bros., 1979). **Carole King,** *Pearls* (Capitol, 1980), *One to One* (Atlantic, 1982). **Steve Morse Band,** *Stand Up* (Elektra, 1985). **Various Artists,** *Guitar Speak* (IRS, 1989). **Stuart Hamm,** *The Urge* (Relativity, 1991).

Joe Satriani

Born: *July 15, 1956, in Westbury, New York*
Main Guitar: *Ibanez JS Series*

Joe Satriani became one of the biggest and most important guitar heroes of the 1980s on the strength of his vast array of fretboard techniques and harmonically adventurous guitar style. The success of his instrumental tunes—so melodic that you could sing along with them—proved that instrumental guitar music could be interesting, exciting, and commercially acceptable. Few guitarists have ever achieved such personal success and acclaim outside of the context of a band.

Satriani grew up on Long Island, New York, where he picked up the guitar around the age of 14. Within a year, he was accomplished to the point of being able to give lessons to other aspiring guitarists. Among his first students was a fellow Long Island resident, Steve Vai. In the late 1970s, Satriani moved to California and settled in the Bay area. There he taught guitar in and around Berkeley, giving lessons to such future notables as Kirk Hammett (Metallica) and Alex Skolnick (Testament). He also spent time playing the club circuit with his own trio, the Squares.

Recordings. In 1984 Satriani released a self-titled EP on his own label, Rubina (named after his wife), but poor distribution limited the record's audience. Undaunted, Satriani used his credit cards to finance his next record, *Not of This Earth*. This strong fusion-based effort eventually brought the guitarist accolades for his extraordinary guitar techniques, which ranged from advanced blues scale work to fast hammer-on legatos to tremolo bar and two-hand tapping tricks to blinding scalar chops. The strongest endorsement came from Steve Vai, who was then riding high on the success of his playing with David Lee Roth. Vai brought Satriani to Relativity Records, which ultimately released *Not of This Earth* in November 1986, more than a year after Joe had finished recording his tracks.

While waiting for Relativity to get *Not of This Earth* into stores, Joe played guitar with San Francisco popster Greg Kihn and began recording new tracks for another album, called *Surfing with the Alien*. Released in October 1987, *Surfing* proved to be one of the best-selling instrumental guitar albums of all time. Fueled by the ferocious title cut and heavy rockers like "Satch Boogie," *Surfing* got immense amounts of radio airplay and catapulted Joe into the realm of guitarist extraordinaire. What separated *Surfing* from its predecessors was that Satriani

cut away the fusion excesses and opted for a more straightforward rock sound. Among the album's best guitar tracks were the title track—laden with solos that incorporated violin-like taps, hammering, and tremolo bar effects—and "Ice Nine," a song notable for its Hendrix-toned Stratocaster melody and crystalline chord strokes. Surprisingly, some of Joe Satriani's most interesting playing on *Surfing with the Alien* was on softer pieces like "Always with You, Always with Me" and "Midnight," a remarkable piece of neoclassical guitar music that used highly original tapping techniques and effects.

After winning most major guitar polls for 1987 and becoming the veritable player of the year, Satriani made headlines by interrupting his own tour (twice) to take over Jeff Beck's seat as guitarist for Mick Jagger's solo tour in 1988. In October 1989, Satriani released *Flying in a Blue Dream*, which further demonstrated his mastery of a variety of styles. In a bold move for an instrumental guitarist, Satriani sang on several of the record's cuts. While purists cried foul, Joe's adventurousness did not seem to cut into his popularity at all. He toured successfully for the next few years, and then released *The Extremist* in 1992, a darker and moodier album, which spawned the hit "Summer Song" (later used by Sony as the soundtrack to a Walkman commercial).

After the release of the double live/studio album *Time Machine* in 1993, Satriani removed himself from the public eye, emerging just long enough to fill Ritchie Blackmore's spot in Deep Purple for an international tour. In 1995 he released *Joe Satriani* (actually the second album to bear that title), which found him exploring blues and jazz in addition to his trademark searing rockers. Throughout 1996 he toured the world to enthusiastic crowds—an anomaly in the "anti-guitar hero era"—and then headlined a series of dates as part of G3, the guitar tour that also featured Eric Johnson and Steve Vai.

Style and Technique. Stylistically, Satriani is an anomaly. He has incredible chops, speed, and technique, yet he is also a compelling songwriter. Very few of his compatriots have written instrumental tunes that stand on their own as songs—and not simply as displays of guitar virtuosity. Satriani writes and plays *singable* instrumentals, an aspect that is enhanced by his deftly effective use of wah-wah pedals. This flair for melodic voicing is particularly evident in "Back to Shalla-Bal" and "The Crush of Love." He has a thorough working knowledge of guitar theory, which he applies meticulously to his writing, and his use of the pitch axis theory, a twentieth century compositional technique, is unrivaled in modern guitar. By any standard, Satriani will rank as one of the most important rock guitarists of the 1980s and 1990s.

Joe Satriani [on Relativity except where noted], *Joe Satriani* [EP] (Rubina, 1984), *Not of this Earth* (1986), *Surfing with the Alien* (1987), *Dreaming #11* (1988●), *Flying in a Blue Dream* (1989), *The Extremist* (1992), *Time Machine* (1993●), *Joe Satriani* (1995).

Recordings featuring Joe Satriani: **Greg Kihn Band,** *Rock & Roll & Love* (EMI, 1985). **Danny Gottlieb,** *Aquamarine* (Atlantic Jazz, 1987). **Stuart Hamm,** *Radio Free Albemuth* (Relativity, 1988). **Alice Cooper,** *Hey Stoopid!* (Epic, 1991).

CHAPTER TWENTY-FIVE

Shred
Built for Speed

Shred. It means to tear up, to splinter. It first gained popularity as an indication of speed on ski slopes, where "shredders" would cut fast and furiously through the snow, often with dangerous and seemingly insane maneuvers. "Shredding" came to denote speed coupled with barely controlled recklessness. The recklessness part was just for show; every shredder knew what he was doing.

The same word came to be used in the guitar community during the mid 1980s as a means of describing a whole new class of speed-driven players. Of course, fast guitar playing was nothing new. Back in the thirties, Django Reinhardt's acoustic swing with the Quintet of the Hot Club of Paris made jaws drop. In the fifties, jazzers like Tal Farlow and Howard Roberts, as well as country-jazz player Hank Garland, regularly tore up their fretboards with lightning-quick runs. And country music had no end of fast pickers, the paramount example being the notorious speedster Jimmy Bryant. In rock 'n' roll, Bill Haley's sideman Danny Cedrone and Gene Vincent's guitarist Cliff Gallup could have been designated as proto-shredders for their high-speed picking. And then there were fast pickers like Dick Dale and Alvin Lee, who also used speed for speed's sake. In one way or another, all of these players contributed to the development of shred.

But if you buy into the theory that most major technical innovations in jazz guitar eventually filter down to rock music (certainly valid in Cedrone's and Lee's cases), then the real roots of modern shredding spring largely from two players: John McLaughlin and Al Di Meola. With their groundbreaking fusion records of the seventies, McLaughlin and Di Meola showed rock players how to play fast, cleanly, and, most important of all, how to do it with a distorted, hard rock guitar tone. Their fat tones on *The Inner Mounting Flame* and *Elegant Gypsy*, respectively, were identical to Eric Clapton's famous "woman tone" from Cream's *Disraeli Gears*. (This was because they used their neck pickup or rolled off the treble knob.) Certainly, fusion players had gotten their share of influences from Clapton and especially Hendrix.

On the rock side, late-seventies pyrotechnicians like Michael Schenker, Uli Roth, and Gary Moore also figured into the oncoming shred attack. By the early eighties, a few metal players had actually begun to use bare-bones attempts at shred on recordings. A few of the best early examples were Alex Lifeson's solo on the Rush hit "Spirit of Radio," John Sykes' work on Thin Lizzy's 1983 platter *Thunder and Lightning*, and Phil Collen's lead on the 1983 Def Leppard smash "Photograph." These are the direct ancestors of shred.

Moreover, the new shredders were all rock players who were striving to move beyond basic pentatonics in their solos, yet they did not subscribe wholly to the popular legato/tremolo approach of Eddie Van Halen. Instead, they were more partial to the classical mindset, as it had been employed by Deep Purple's Ritchie Blackmore, Randy Rhoads, and Van Halen himself in the finale to his "Eruption" solo. Many of them cited Bach and Paganini as their sole sources of inspiration, claiming to have never listened to the pivotal British rock, metal, and fusion guitarists. (Such claims were ludicrous even at the time—if all these teenage boys were buying classical albums, how come Paganini wasn't outselling Cream?)

Like Clapton, Beck, and Bloomfield in the sixties, this school of guitarists was all heading in the same direction, slowly pushing towards a common, but still foggy, goal. Back in 1966, Eric, Jeff, and Mike were stumbling through the mist until they ran smack into a behemoth called Jimi Hendrix. Eighteen years later, fledgling shredders ran into their generation's version of King Kong—the terrifying monster guitarist whom no one could beat. Its name was Yngwie.

Yngwie Malmsteen

Born: *June 30, 1963, in Sweden*
Main Guitar: *Fender Stratocaster*

In 1983–85, Eddie Van Halen's position as rock's #1 guitar hero was seriously challenged and partially usurped by Yngwie Malmsteen, a 20-something Swedish superpicker with both attitude and chops. While most heavy rock guitarists of the day were busy copping Van Halen's two-handed tapping and tremolo bar tricks, Malmsteen's forte was straight power picking; he was able to flash across the fretboard of his modified Fender Stratocasters with staggering agility and alternate-picking precision. In those two short years, the ambitious guitarist cruised through two minor bands—Steeler and Alcatrazz—and then established himself as a solo artist of note with his own group, Rising Force. His blinding chops and classically infused rockers attracted thousands of metal guitar fanatics, and, in a case of déjà vu recalling Clapton's tenure with the Bluesbreakers, the slogan "Yngwie Is

God" became a popular catch phrase. By mid decade, the guitarist was arguably the most popular guitar player in heavy metal, as well as the progenitor of such terms as *Bach 'n' roll*, *neoclassical metal*, and, perhaps most prevalently, *shred*. For better or worse, a new era of rock guitar had dawned.

Yngwie Malmsteen became enamored with the idea of being a guitar hero after seeing Jimi Hendrix on Swedish television the day Hendrix died, September 18, 1970. The seven-year-old immediately took up the guitar, and got his next shot of inspiration on his ninth birthday when he received a copy of Deep Purple's *Fireball*. The record featured the charged guitar work of Ritchie Blackmore, a musician whose sense of bravado and classical panache Malmsteen would eventually incorporate into his own performing. With the combined influences of Hendrix and Blackmore, as well as a deep love for the music of Johann Sebastian Bach and Nicolò Paganini, the young Malmsteen set to work developing a flawless technique for classically influenced metal guitar.

After playing with several local groups, Yngwie formed Rising Force in 1978. Built around Yngwie's guitar acrobatics, Rising Force eventually made a name for itself in Sweden and even did some recording for CBS in the early eighties (the results of which were never released). Yngwie's big personal break came in 1983, when he was featured in *Guitar Player* magazine's "Spotlight" column, a section for talented unknown guitarists. Mike Varney, author of the column and head of his own Shrapnel Records, sensed the Swede's unheralded talent and invited Yngwie to the U.S. to play with Steeler, a small-time metal act that he felt would give him greater exposure to American audiences. He recorded one self-titled album with the quartet, but tensions within the group forced his departure by the end of 1983. In retrospect, it is an almost amusing recording, since it pitted Yngwie's groundbreaking shred solos against the blandest, most generic-sounding metal possible. On the bright side, however, was the guitarist's sizzling solo "Hot on Your Heels," which exhibited his famed shredding as well as a rare piece of Van Halenesque tapping. There was also an acoustic flamenco intro that implied that Yngwie had spent more than a little time listening to Al Di Meola.

Yngwie Malmsteen

As Yngwie had predicted, his appearance with Steeler enhanced his reputation as a speed-picking prodigy, and, after fielding offers from ex-UFO vocalist Phil Mogg and ex-Rainbow/MSG vocalist Graham Bonnet, he went off to form Alcatrazz with Bonnet. During the guitarist's brief and stormy tenure with Alcatrazz, he went from being a hot newcomer on the U.S. metal scene to an international guitar star. Alcatrazz released only one studio album with Yngwie, *No Parole from Rock 'n' Roll*, while a concert album, *Live Sentence*, was released after his exit. Amidst the many rockers on the release, Malmsteen's stunning axe work was shown off in fine style on "General Hospital," "Island in the Sun," and "Kree Nakoorie." But again, Yngwie's volatile temperament grated on his bandmates. Adding to the problem was that he was 10 to 20 years younger than his bandmates and didn't come from the same musical background. So he finally quit Alcatrazz in the middle of 1984 to go solo; he was eventually replaced by Steve Vai (⧫).

While many famous rock guitarists take years to work their way up the ladder of popular acclaim, Yngwie at the age of just 21 was an undisputed metal guitar hero. Signing with Polydor-Japan, he released his first solo record, *Yngwie J. Malmsteen's Rising Force*, at the end of 1984. It contained a relentless barrage of classical-metal instrumentals, each precisely laid out to display his fast modal runs, diminished scale work, high bends, deep tremolo dives, tapping, and clean classical passages. *Marching Out* (1985) found Yngwie taking his music in a slightly more commercial direction by adding vocals to his already strong instrumental repertoire. By 1986, it was clear that the guitarist had set his sights on mainstream commercial success with the release of *Trilogy*, his most tuneful and mass audience-oriented record yet. National tours opening for Emerson, Lake & Powell and other high-profile bands increased public recognition of Yngwie, and *Trilogy* broke into the Top 50 on the U.S. record charts. Malmsteen continued in this vein with the release of *Odyssey* (1988). Like Ritchie Blackmore before him, however,

Yngwie situated himself at the center of a revolving door of band members who came in and out of Rising Force with irritating frequency.

Despite his sudden rise to fame, the guitarist was the target of ample criticism. Malmsteen's prodigious talent was countered by his infamous temper and vanity. These personality quirks, along with weak interview skills, gave rise to almost as many detractors as fans. The media also attacked his chops-ridden music, calling it excessive and over-indulgent, and heated debates rose up between pro-Yngwie and anti-Yngwie factions about his guitarmanship and music.

As time went on, it also became clear that the guitarist wasn't planning to push his musical vision beyond the licks that he had demonstrated on his first few albums. While the rest of the rock guitar world moved into grunge, alternative, and blues-revival modes, Malmsteen continued to play his formulaic neoclassical bombast. Not surprisingly, this intransigence cost the guitarist several record deals, as well as many fans who grew tired of his dizzying shred solos and frequent classical allusions. Sadly, his personal life, including publicized fights with his mother-in-law and extreme weight gain, generated more interest than his playing.

Putting aside all the notoriety, however, Yngwie Malmsteen remains a remarkable guitarist, and he did take heavy metal guitar in a dramatically new direction away from the early-eighties Van Halen school. He wasn't the first rock guitarist to use classical influences or blinding speed, yet his skillful application of classical motifs in a metal context and his command of the electric guitar were nothing short of genius. He was incredibly influential, inspiring thousands of rock players to improve their technique, apply arpeggios and exotic modes to the once pentatonic-based art of lead guitar, and, overall, raise their musical sights. Like Jimmy Bryant and Al Di Meola before him, the Swede had a picking technique that was beyond reproach. Love him or hate him, but Yngwie Malmsteen is unquestionably rock's King of Shred.

Steeler, *Steeler* (Shrapnel, 1983). **Alcatrazz** [on Rocshire], *No Parole from Rock 'n' Roll* (1983), *Live Sentence* (1984•). **Yngwie J. Malmsteen's Rising Force** [on Polydor], *Rising Force* (1984), *Marching Out* (1985), *Trilogy* (1986), *Odyssey* (1988), *Trial by Fire—Live in Leningrad* (1990•), *Eclipse* (1990), *Fire and Ice* (Elektra, 1992). **Yngwie Malmsteen,** *The Seventh Sign* (CMC Int'l, 1994), *Magnum Opus* (Viceroy, 1995).

Recordings featuring Yngwie Malmsteen: **Hear 'n' Aid,** *Stars* (n/a, 1986).

Steve Vai

B o r n : *June 6, 1960, in Carleplace, New York*
M a i n   G u i t a r : *Ibanez JEM*

As a member of Frank Zappa's (♦) multifaceted band early in the 1980s, Steve Vai made a name for himself within Zappa's organization as an ace transcriber and a player of impossible guitar parts. The Long Island native had taken guitar lessons in his early teens from neighbor Joe Satriani and had become enamored of Zappa's eclectically intricate music, learning parts off of albums note for note. While at the Berklee College of Music in Boston, Vai began writing out transcriptions of Zappa's more complex songs. He ultimately sent these transcriptions to Zappa, who was so impressed by their accuracy that he hired young Vai as a "stunt guitarist" for his band. Vai joined Zappa for several albums and tours (a stint memorialized in the Zappa song "Stevie's Spanking").

Zappa albums being sporadic affairs, Vai took to recording his own music. In 1984 he released a homemade solo album, *Flex-able*, which showcased him as a heavy rock guitar player in his own right. His unique style was highlighted on stunning, even groundbreaking instrumentals such as "The Attitude Song" and "Call It Sleep." Riding on the praise for *Flex-able*, he then joined Alcatrazz, the metal group that had recently bid adieu to Yngwie Malmsteen (♦), and played on the band's *Disturbing the Peace* (1985). Next, Vai recorded a magnificent instrumental track called "Blue Powder," which appeared on a flexi-disc in *Guitar Player* magazine. On this one-off cut, he fused soulful, almost bluesy licks (at least for Vai), wild swooping bends and harmonies, and furious speed picking to create a fresh new path for metal guitar. In fact, there were so many tones and textures on "Blue Powder" that it almost defied description. Finally, if these achievements weren't enough, Vai also starred as Jack Butler, Satan's guitar virtuoso, in the film *Crossroads*, which was loosely

Steve Vai

based on the legend of blues guitar master Robert Johnson. By the end of 1985, Steve Vai was fully primed for the big time.

Vai's big break came in 1986, when he was asked to join the backup band for ex-Van Halen vocalist David Lee Roth. Teamed up with super-bassist Billy Sheehan and drummer Gregg Bissonette, Vai found a heavy rock format that allowed him room for his relentlessly clever guitar riffs, solos, and ad libs. The resulting album, *Eat 'em and Smile*, revealed Steve Vai as a state-of-the-art metal stylist, capable of both the commercial and the extreme. What set him apart from most other metal pickers was his radical harmonic vocabulary, which was likely a result of his work with Frank Zappa. Add to that great technique, killer multitrack guitar harmonies, and new variations on Van Halen's old whammy tricks (not to mention his chiseled rock star looks and over-the-top stage presence), and a new guitar god was born.

The first single off *Eat 'em and Smile*, "Yankee Rose," featured an amusing vocal rap between Roth and Vai, who created vocal effects on his Strat-style electrics with a wah-wah pedal, sick bends, and more tremolo madness. Still, the track "Big Trouble" may have been the album's guitar tour de force, a track to which Vai added thick, shimmering chords and spot licks under Roth's vocals. His solo was a master class of unusual tones, fast-picking chops, whammy dives and pulls, harmonic chirps, feedback manipulation, and a final cascade of fretboard tapping that made even the most experienced two-handers drop their jaws. Not surprisingly, at the end of 1986, Steve Vai was soaking up top honors in major guitar polls and soon became hard rock's #1 guitar hero, ending the short reign of Yngwie Malmsteen.

Following this burst of success, Steve Vai's career coasted for a few years. He played on Roth's follow-up, *Skyscraper*, and then joined MTV metal favorites Whitesnake. David Coverdale's pop-metal band was in peak form, coming off the sales of an extremely successful eponymous album in 1985. However, Whitesnake guitarist John Sykes had departed, and replacement Adrian Vandenburg allegedly hurt his hands in a freak accident. Coverdale hired Vai to do the one-off record, but the album was a surprising disappointment (most of the music had been completed by the time Vai arrived). Vai toured with the band, simultaneously helping Ibanez develop his JEM series guitars, including a seven-string model that was quite revolutionary for the time.

Just as the Whitesnake ship was sinking and Steve was getting a reputation as the best gun for hire in the guitar world, he took the time to release a solo record in 1990. Called *Passion and Warfare*, the album exploded up the charts. The highest-charting guitar album since Jeff Beck's *Blow by Blow*, this disc even landed him time on MTV for the video "The Audience Is Listening." Although Vai fans had heard most of the techniques on the album before, it was still an extremely exciting and well-rounded statement, showing new audiences what Vai was capable of. *Passion and Warfare* contained a remix of the earlier "Blue Powder" and the stunningly melodic "For the Love of God." Vai also got players' attention with "Ballerina 12/24," where he fingerpicked arpeggios that were turned into an enchanting soundscape with the assistance of an Eventide H3000 Harmonizer.

Switching directions yet again, Vai formed a band known simply as Vai, which released one record in 1993, *Sex & Religion*. With its glass-gargling vocals (courtesy of one Devin Townshend) and strange metal-meets-grunge-meets-guitar-acrobatics, no one was quite sure what to make of the disc. Too strange to be commercially successful, it was a disappointment for both fans and guitar aficionados. Vai persevered in light of near-universal criticism, but after a small tour, the group disbanded. Steve then took a two-year hiatus before returning to top-notch form with the 1995 hard rock EP *Alien Love Secrets*. Complete with sexy grooves and even light ethereal touches, the EP brought Vai back to the top of the guitar heap on cuts like "Bad Horsie" and "The Boy from Seattle." After a tour opening for Bon Jovi and an aborted collaboration with Ozzy Osbourne (which was broken up by Ozzy's record company, although Vai penned music that ended up on *Ozzmosis*), Vai released the long-awaited *Fire Garden* in late 1996. The lengthy album was a diverse record that included two phases: an instrumental set and a vocal set, with Steve handling himself surprisingly well in the role of vocalist. Like Eric Johnson and Satriani before him (both of whom he toured with as part of G3), Vai received criticism for stepping out of his guitar hero role and stepping in front of a microphone. Yet there was no denying that his guitar playing was still pushing the boundaries of conventional rock guitar.

What has differentiated Steve Vai from most of his metaloid peers is, among other things, his advanced knowledge of music theory and his willingness to take chances on his instrument. While most tremolo-groping rock guitarists of the eighties were content with pressing down their whammy bars à la Van Halen, Vai madly pulled his into the upper registers, discovering uncharted regions of tremolo effects. And, while other guitarists were stuck with either the Van Halen/Holdsworth legato hammer-on style of soloing or the Di Meola/Malmsteen school of staccato speed-picking, Vai moved between the two styles with supple ease, adding his own unique touches along the way. He has firmly established himself as one of modern rock's best players, and, along with Eric Johnson's "Cliffs of Dover" and Stevie Ray Vaughan's "Texas Flood," his "Blue Powder" is certainly one of the finest guitar performances of the 1980s. On the strength of his innovation alone, Steve Vai is worthy of a place in the pantheon of guitarists that includes Hendrix, Clapton, and Van Halen.

Frank Zappa [on Barking Pumpkin], *Tinsel Town Rebellion* (1981), *Shut up 'n' Play Yer Guitar* (1981), *You Are What You Is* (1981), *Ship Arrived Too Late to Save a Drowning Witch* (1982), *The Man from Utopia* (1983), *Them or Us* (1984•), *Thingfish* (1984), *Jazz from Hell* (1986), *You Can't Do that on Stage Anymore Sampler* (1988•), *Frank Zappa: Guitar* (1988), *You Can't Do that on Stage Anymore, Vol. 1* (1988•), *Guitar World According to Frank Zappa* (1988), *You Can't Do that on Stage Anymore, Vol. 3* (1989•), *You Can't Do that on Stage Anymore, Vol. 4–6* (1992•). **Steve Vai,** *Flex-able* (Urantia, 1984), *Flex-able Leftovers* (Urantia, 1984), *Passion and Warfare* (Relativity, 1990), *Alien Love Secrets* [EP] (Relativity, 1995), *Fire Garden* (Epic, 1996). **Alcatrazz,** *Disturbing the Peace* (Capitol, 1985). **David Lee Roth** [on

Warner Bros.], *Eat 'em and Smile* (1986), *Skyscraper* (1988). **Whitesnake,** *Slip of the Tongue* (Geffen, 1989). **Vai,** *Sex & Religion* (Relativity, 1993).

Recordings featuring Steve Vai: **Public Image, Ltd.,** *Album* (Elektra, 1985). **Bob Harris,** *The Great Nostalgia* (Mastahna, 1986). **The Epidemics,** *The Epidemics* (Shankar/Caroline, 1986). **Randy Coven,** *Funk Me Tender* (TPL/Guitar, 1987). **Western Vacation,** *Western Vacation* (Akashic, 1987). **Various Artists,** *Guitar's Practicing Musicians* (Guitar Recordings, 1990). **Various Artists,** *Bill & Ted's Excellent Adventure* [soundtrack] (Interscope, 1991). **Alice Cooper,** *Hey Stoopid!* (Epic, 1991). **Various Artists,** *Zappa's Universe* (Verve, 1993). **Various Artists,** *PCU* [soundtrack] (Fox, 1991).

The Shrapnel School

Even before Yngwie Malmsteen's departure from both Steeler and Shrapnel Records, label boss Mike Varney was looking for the next generation of monster guitarists. With his help, a horde of young neoclassical shredders came bursting out of the woodwork, thus initiating the Shrapnel School of guitar. Some were good; many were simply Yngwie copycats. (Unfortunately, as most shred playing proved time and again, there was perhaps no other time in rock history when its guitar players were so far removed from the music's original blues roots and its inherent emotions.) Regardless of their individual inventiveness, shred guitarists helped to define the metal guitar sound of the eighties, and for that they deserve a footnote in guitar history.

Two of the first players out of the Shrapnel gate were Tony MacAlpine and Vinnie Moore. Like neoclassical forerunner Yngwie, Tony MacAlpine played a baroque/heavy metal mélange that included as much high-speed picking as dramatic classically influenced motifs, much of the latter owing to his conservatory training in classical piano. During his brush with notoriety from 1985 to 1987, the prolific guitarist appeared on four albums for the Shrapnel label. He released two solo discs, *Edge of Insanity* and *Maximum Security* (with guitar guests Jeff Watson and George Lynch), collaborated on *Project: Driver* with MacAlpine-Aldridge-Rock-Sarzo, and, finally, served as a keyboardist on guitarist Vinnie Moore's classical metal debut, *Mind's Eye.*

Combining his talents as a classical pianist with those of a technically oriented lead guitarist, MacAlpine attracted attention for his near-flawless technique, fast scalar picking, tapping tricks, and relentless classical arpeggios. Among his best solos from this period were his shred-happy live solo "Quarter to Midnight," from *Edge of Insanity* (1985), the overdubbed breaks in "Nations on Fire" on *Project: Driver,* and his leads to "The King's Cup," "Autumn Lords," and "Hundreds of Thousands," from *Maximum Security* (1987). MacAlpine has recorded steadily since then, gaining a cult of followers for his slickly polished chops, but turning others away with his rigidly technical and often cold lead style.

Much of this same criticism was also leveled at Vinnie Moore, who was considered the third link in the neoclassical chain after Yngwie Malmsteen and Tony MacAlpine. Like those two, Moore was discovered by talent scout Mike Varney through

his "Spotlight" column and joined the band Vicious Rumors to play on their album *Soldiers of the Night.* Moore gained a substantial following for his clean, high-speed picking with his first solo effort, *Mind's Eye* (1986). Varney signed the young Delaware-bred guitarist to Shrapnel and then employed such noted players as ex-Dixie Dregs bassist Andy West and drummer Tommy Aldridge to back Moore up. Clearly a big Al Di Meola fan, Moore gained immediate recognition for his accomplished baroque-metal breaks, especially on the track "Daydream," while the intro to "Saved by a Miracle" admirably displayed his chops on acoustic guitar, an instrument that tends to separate the men from the boys when it comes to technique. Still, like many of his shred peers, he found his career hindered by a noted lack of songwriting skills and musical evolution. By the end of the 1980s, he was a sideman in Alice Cooper's band and continued to record solo for a limited audience.

Of all the many young Bach 'n' Rollers from the late 1980s, Paul Gilbert of Racer X managed to pull away from the shred masses via an exciting, over-the-top lead style. Gilbert first came to public attention at the ripe old age of 15 in Mike Varney's "Spotlight" column and soon relocated from his native Greensburg, Pennsylvania, to Hollywood, were he attended and later taught at the Musicians' Institute (a.k.a. the well-known shredders' haven GIT). By the end of 1986, he was recording for Varney's Shrapnel label and produced the album *Street Lethal* with his band, Racer X.

Where MacAlpine and Moore's solos were polished to perfection, Gilbert pushed the speed limit, adding a refreshing degree of rock 'n' roll grit and unpredictability to his lines. A good example was his stunning break on "Frenzy," where he traded alternate-picked and tapped solos with himself at uncanny speeds. Musically, however, Racer X was conventional eighties hairdo metal, despite their being the most popular band in Los Angeles. *Second Heat* (1987) featured the addition of Gilbert's guitar protégé, Bruce Bouilett. With Bouilett and bass shredder John Alderete, Paul began to explore fast classical harmonies along with two- and three-way tapping sections, such as in the intense instrumental "Scarified." After folding the band a few years later, Gilbert shifted gears dramatically and formed the pop-metal act Mr. Big. The band scored a big hit in 1991, ironically, with the mellow acoustic ballad "To Be with You." Unlike many other guitarists of the eighties, Gilbert had the foresight to jump off the shred bandwagon before the genre crashed in the nineties.

Other shredders of the Shrapnel saga include such fine players as Michael Lee Firkins, Greg Howe, James Byrd, future Megadeth (♦) guitarist Marty Friedman, Derek Taylor, and Ron Thal, as well as forgettable hairdo metalers like Joey Tafolla and Richie Kotzen. But as popular taste moved away from hi-tech metal, so too did Shrapnel's roster. In the 1990s, Mike Varney opened up the subsidiary label Blues Bureau International and signed vintage favorites like Pat Travers, Rick Derringer, Leslie West, and the Outlaws. While many players still consider

Shrapnel a dirty word for its pivotal role in the oft-criticized shred revolution, the label nevertheless made a sizable dent in rock guitar history and also deserves credit for finding such expert players as Malmsteen, Gilbert, and Firkins. As with anything else, one must take the good with the bad.

Steeler, *Steeler* (1983). **Tony MacAlpine,** *Edge of Insanity* (1985), *Maximum Security* (1987), *Premonition* (1994). **Vinnie Moore,** *Mind's Eye* (1986), *Time Odyssey* (1988). **Racer X,** *Street Lethal* (1986), *Second Heat* (1986). **Cacophony [Marty Friedman & Jason Becker],** *Speed Metal Symphony* (1987), *Go Off!* (1989). **Greg Howe,** *Greg Howe* (1988), *Howe II* (1989), *Uncertain Terms* (1994). **Richie Kotzen,** *Richie Kotzen* (1989), *Fever Dream* (1990). **Michael Lee Firkins,** *Michael Lee Firkins* (1990), *Howling Iguanas* (1994), *Chapter Eleven* (1995). **Derek Taylor,** *Dystrophy* (1994). **Ron Thal,** *The Adventures of Bumblefoot* (1995). **James Byrd,** *Octoglomerate* (1994), *Son of Man* (1995).

Dio [on Warner Bros.], *Holy Diver* (1983), *The Last in Line* (1984), *Sacred Heart* (1985), *Intermission* (1986•). **Riverdogs,** *Riverdogs* (Epic, 1990). **Def Leppard** [on Mercury], *Radio Active* (1993), *Slang* (1996).

Recordings featuring Vivian Campbell: **Various Artists,** *Guitar's Practicing Musicians* (Guitar Recordings, 1989). **Jack Bruce,** *A Question of Time* (Epic, 1989). **Various Artists,** *New Wave of British Heavy Metal '79 Revisited* (Metal Blade, 1991).

Minor Shredheads

There were so many shredders during the peak of the genre that to include full entries for each one would be impossible. Still, from among the hordes (and there *were* hordes), a few notables rose above the fray. A very early member of the shred school, Vivian Campbell, came out of a popular Irish band called Sweet Savage to join ex-Rainbow and Black Sabbath singer Ronnie James Dio in the self-titled Dio. A Gary Moore fan, Campbell smoothly blended chops with commendable soul on such notable Dio cuts as "Rainbow in the Dark," "The Last in Line," and "Rock 'n' Roll Children." Later, the mercurial guitarist toured with Whitesnake, jumped in and out of several no-name bands, and then joined Def Leppard (♭) after the death of guitarist Steve Clark.

Frank Zappa's son Dweezil also joined the shred ranks for a while, cutting a few Van Halen-inspired solos on his dad's albums before striking out on his own with the 1986 disc *Having a Bad Day*. He later formed the band Z with his brother Ahmet and guitar extremist Mike Keneally.

Competing with Mark Varney's Shrapnel label for shred glory (and dollars) was David T. Chastain's Leviathan label, which specialized in producing speed guitar discs. Chastain himself was the label's hottest property, attracting a big cult of guitarists to his blazing Di Meola- and Holdsworth-inspired shred style. And from Japan, Loudness guitarist Akira Takasaki made a brief noise in 1985 as the next big thing, but his penchant for copping Van Halen, Malmsteen, and Lifeson licks note for note soon put his shred ambitions on permanent hold.

Other minor rockers of note include Jennifer Batten, the vicious two-handed tapper who rocked out on Michael Jackson's *Bad* tour and cut a solo album in 1991 called *Above, Below & Beyond* (featuring a wild version of "Flight of the Bumblebee"). There was also England's sole shred champ, Dave Sharman, who released a killer guitar album called *1990* and then promptly fell off the face of the planet.

CHAPTER TWENTY-SIX

Hard Rock and Heavy Metal IV
The MTV Years

It's a case of style over substance. The huge success of southern Californian axe heroes like Eddie Van Halen and Randy Rhoads in the early 1980s gave rise to an entire Los Angeles-based guitar scene. Imitators of Van Halen and Rhoads appeared in locust-like numbers up and down the Sunset Strip, every one of them ready and willing to pass themselves off as clones of the two guitar maestros.

In another time, in a different place, only a handful of these guitarists would have been worth a second listen. But this time they had something going for them that no other generation of rock guitarist ever had—MTV. Music Television created a market for music based in large part on physical appearances, stage moves, and rock songs that reveled in big-breasted bimbos and a frat-boy attitude towards partying. No doubt, commercial shallowness was king.

Unfortunately, large amounts of established rock acts didn't fit this picture; they were either too old, too plain looking, or just not telegenic enough for a youth culture that now expected to see its rock stars up close and personal on TV. In a way, MTV created its own void: it needed good-looking and non-threatening rockers, and they weren't readily available. Since necessity is the mother of invention, MTV—aided by the record companies—went out and got them.

Waiting in the wings, or more literally, on the streets, was southern California's horde of aspiring metallists. With licks learned from Hollywood's famed Guitar Institute of Technology or just right off *Van Halen* or *Diary of a Madman*, the Van Halen-wannabes fit the bill for MTV perfectly. Clad in spandex and leather, they moussed up their hair and applied make-up liberally to their lips and eyes, all the while singing about sex, drugs, and drinking. The irony was thick: rockers dressed up to the point of transvestitism singing macho tunes of female conquest and domination. In all, it was not a pretty picture.

It was, however, a temporarily lucrative picture. "Hair bands" and poseurs, as these musicians were called, got signed in droves to major labels and had their pouting faces and choreographed guitar twirls plastered all over MTV. If ever Andy Warhol's assertion that everyone would get their 15 minutes of fame was true, it was true to an unprecedented degree in the time that MTV embraced heavy metal. Guitarists and vocalists, especially, were the prime beneficiaries of the instant recognizability that MTV afforded, and there many of them. White Lion's Vito Bratta, Quiet Riot's Carlos Cavazo, Warrant's Joey Allen and Erik Turner, Poison's C.C. DeVille, Cinderella's Tom Keifer, the Ratt guitar team of Robben Crosby and Warren DeMartini, L.A. Guns' Tracii Guns, and Great White's Mark Kendall all had their temporary moments in the guitar hero spotlight. Not one of them produced more than an album's worth of consistently high-quality playing, if that. Ratt's DeMartini was perhaps the only guitar standout of the bunch, capable of playing blazing runs over inventive melodies, but that was only relative to his peers: his playing was still extremely derivative of Van Halen. And more of a Jimmy Page stylist, Cinderella's Keifer was proficient at translating raw blues into well-honed pop-metal songs. The rest, however, were formulaic to the point of being cookie-cutter copies of each other

This, of course, didn't prevent them from being wildly successful. The market ate up their records and concerts at a frenzied pace, fueled primarily by the endless and relentless exposure that these bands received on MTV. Such success

Guns N' Roses: Izzy Stradlin, Slash

translated into even more copycatting on the part of the guitar community. Guitarists were judged on their looks more than their chops, and it seemed like Ratt and Poison were only the tip of the iceberg. For awhile, many feared that the poseur parade might never end.

Fortunately, it did end, killed swiftly and mercilessly by grunge. But grunge also killed off the guitar hero, even if that guitar hero was only a disposable MTV poseur. Only a handful of guitarists from this era were inventive enough to rise above the detritus of metal's disintegration, but they were the people that had been head and shoulders above the rest of the guitar pack anyway: Slash, George Lynch, Nuno Bettencourt, Night Ranger's Jeff Watson and Brad Gillis, and Vernon Reid of Living Colour.

For the rest, it was a quick trip back to the day jobs they had left several years earlier in order to pursue rock 'n' roll glory. This much must be admitted, however: MTV and metal may not have had much substance, but it was a fun ride while it lasted. If only for a moment, any guitarist with the right amount of eyeliner and lipstick could be a guitar god. Stardom was never easier—or more temporary.

Guns N' Roses

Slash

Born: *Saul Hudson, on July 23, 1965, in Stoke, England*
Main Guitar: *Gibson Les Paul*

Izzy Stradlin

Born: *Jeffrey Isabelle, in 1962, in Florida*
Main Guitar: *Gibson ES-125*

Gilby Clarke

Main Guitars: *Gibson Les Paul, Fender Telecaster*

No one brought the aggressive swagger of cock rock back to the fore during the 1980s more than Guns N' Roses. Sex, drugs, and rock 'n' roll were everything the band was about, and it paraded its vices to the top of the record industry, dragging lawsuits and tabloid tales with it every step of the way. Led by social misfit W. Axl Rose (born Bill Bailey), the Gunners played hard and they rocked hard. The musical end of this was accomplished largely through the efforts of lead guitarist Slash, whose roots in seventies-styled musical excess served to give GNR the sound that would sell millions of albums.

Slash was born Saul Hudson to an Africa-American mother and a Jewish father, something he would have to defend once GNR became popular. He was weaned on Led Zeppelin, Aerosmith, Jeff Beck, and Ted Nugent, learning basic blues-based riffs and pentatonic scales. He joined a number of hard rock bands during the early 1980s in Los Angeles, at one point hook-

ing up with bassist Michael "Duff" McKagan. Ultimately, their band merged with the existing Guns N' Roses, which had featured Tracii Guns as lead guitarist. (Tracii was the "Guns" in Guns N' Roses; he went on to minor success with his own L.A. Guns and Contraband, the latter featuring Michael Schenker.) Thus, Slash effectively replaced Guns and teamed up with the "Roses" part of the band, vocalist Axl Rose. Already on board with GNR was rhythm guitarist Izzy Stradlin, a Keith Richards fan who had been a friend of Axl's when the two lived in Indiana as youths.

The band slogged it out on the Sunset Strip during the 1980s, living the traditional life embodied in rock 'n' roll horror stories: bad drugs, no money, a whole band living in a one-room apartment, eating rice and noodles, etc. The group did make a name for itself with its extremely aggressive rock 'n' roll, a throwback to early Aerosmith, yet with an even harder, almost punk edge. This, coupled with GNR's reputation for debauchery, elevated them to near-mythical status in southern California even before they were signed.

In 1987, the band was approached by Geffen (Slash's father worked in the art department there), which released the band's debut, *Appetite for Destruction*, later that year. The record immediately became one of the biggest sellers of the decade, powered by riff-heavy metal tunes like "Welcome to the Jungle," and "Sweet Child o' Mine," the latter track featuring a screaming wah-wah solo from Slash. While the music was tight and loud—an update of the formula that Led Zeppelin has used to great effect 15 years earlier—Axl Rose's lyrics and public comments got the band more publicity than the music. His racial slurs and drug references had moralists crawling out of their skins. Many of them berated Slash for not keeping a tight rein on Rose; after all, Slash was part of the ethnic group that Rose slammed. However, Slash seemed not to care—his own public drunkenness, private drug problems, and tabloid romances kept him busy enough.

The band released the EP *G N' R Lies* in 1988, a record that was largely a compilation of some of the band's older tunes. Like its predecessor, it sold millions of copies, keeping GNR on the radio with the immensely popular, but musically bland, ballad "Patience." Escalating drug use in the band, however, seemed to keep GNR on the brink of self-destructing. First to go was drummer Steve Adler, who was replaced by Matt Sorum. Adler was fired for his erratic ways, and sued the band. This did not stop GNR from releasing two albums simultaneously in 1991, *Use Your Illusion I* and *II*. Both albums were platinum upon their release, which was an unprecedented feat (although many decried the greedy nature of the venture: with the high retail prices of individual CDs, couldn't the band have released a cheaper double CD set?). The band headed out on the road, and then fired Izzy Stradlin, replacing him mid-tour with Kill for Thrills guitarist Gilby Clarke, who was also a sometime session player in L.A. Stradlin's departure was as nasty as Adler's, yet he went somewhat more quietly. Later, he recorded his own fairly solid solo record, which was very much in the Keith Richards/X-Pensive Winos vein.

GNR took a recording and touring break after *Illusions*, opting instead to play out their lives in the tabloids. They returned in 1993 to release *The Spaghetti Incident?* an album of cover tunes that included everything from Nazareth to the New York Dolls. Unfortunately, it also contained a song penned by notorious murderer Charles Manson, which again brought the band so much scathing press that the negativity overshadowed the record. Still on a touring hiatus, Clarke was fired for no apparent reason. He had just released a solo album, *Pawnshop Guitars*, which had included all the members of GNR on it. He had even joined Slash in a side project, Slash's Snakepit, when he found out that Axl had canned him.

It became clear that Rose was the personnel director of the band, and that most of the problems and firings could be attributed to him. Yet Slash did nothing to prevent Axl from toying with the band's future. Instead, he bided his time until the next GNR record by releasing *Slash's Snakepit* in 1995, an album that was full of by-now-rote GNR riffs and melodies. The public did not snatch this one up, though, perhaps growing tired of both GNR's general attitude and their overdrive, neither of which seemed appropriate for the alternative climate of the mid 1990s.

Still, Slash may have been one of the last guitar stars of the nineties. He embodied the same cockiness that was part and parcel of the best guitarists of the British Invasion. A clear Michael Schenker fan, he also stuck very close to the pentatonic minor and blues scales, rock's driving musical forces (there was the occasional foray into the Mixolydian mode, but even that wasn't far removed from roots rock). He relied on straightforward rock gear: Les Pauls, Marshalls, an occasional wah-wah. In short, the guy was as stripped down as a guitarist can get when it comes to playing rock 'n' roll. By not attempting to join the athletic ranks of people like Steve Vai or Joe Satriani, Slash nailed a niche—that of pure rocker—and controlled it like nobody since Joe Perry of Aerosmith. Many guitar purists wrote him off as a parody of himself, but in truth, the guy knew how to rock, and he had an amazing knack for memorable riffs, subtle melodies (as in the mega-hit "November Rain"), and well-placed solos. His offstage antics aside, Slash deserves much more credit than his association with Axl Rose will probably earn him.

George Lynch

Guns N' Roses [on Geffen], *Appetite for Destruction* (1987), *G N' R Lies* [EP] (1988), *Use Your Illusion I* (1991), *Use Your Illusion II* (1991), *The Spaghetti Incident?* (1993). **Slash's Snakepit**, *Slash's Snakepit* (Geffen, 1995).

Recordings featuring Slash: **Michael Jackson**, *Dangerous* (Epic, 1992).

Recordings featuring Gilby Clarke: **Kill for Thrills** [on MCA], *Dynamite from Nightmareland* (1990), *Commercial Suicide* (n/a). **Gilby Clarke,**

Pawnshop Guitars (Virgin, 1994). **Candy,** *Whatever Happened to Fun?* (Mercury, 1985).

Recordings featuring Izzy Stradlin: **Izzy Stradlin,** *Izzy Stradlin & the Ju Ju Hounds* (Geffen, 1992).

Dokken

George Lynch

Born: *September 28, 1954, in Spokane, Washington*
Main Guitars: *Charvel Strat-style, ESP George Lynch model*

To many metal guitar aficionados, George Lynch was the foremost stylist of the MTV era. He took the tricks and techniques of the Van Halenites, added unbridled frenzy and a seriously heavy tone, and created a unique sound and style that instantly placed him above his peers and, arguably, even above his own bandmates in Dokken.

Lynch was encouraged to learn the guitar as a boy, and was largely self-taught. His original influences were Jimi Hendrix and Jeff Beck, and he developed a flair for heavy riffs and melodic solos. When his family moved to California, he played in a variety of high school bands before teaming with future Dokken drummer Mick Brown to form the Boyz. This band patrolled the SoCal circuit in the late 1970s alongside the likes of Quiet Riot and Van Halen before hooking up with lead vocalist Don Dokken. The band eventually made its way to Germany (with Juan Croucier on bass, who later left to join Ratt), where they secured an album deal with Carrere Records. While touring incessantly, the band—now known as Dokken—released its first record, *Breaking the Chains*, in 1982. The album showed that Lynch was more than another flash in the rising SoCal mode. His lead lines tended to be both fast and melodic, a rare merger amongst guitarists of the time, excepting Van Halen, Rhoads, and Michael Schenker.

Returning to America, Dokken signed a deal with Elektra and released *Tooth and Nail* in 1984 (with bassist Jeff Pilson). Lynch again proved himself to be a guitarist worth listening to on cuts like "Paris Is Burning" and "Just Got Lucky," where he incorporated two-handed tapping at speeds that made most listeners' heads spin. Aided by MTV airplay, Lynch gained the requisite amount of notoriety for his golden boy/rock star looks and wildly decorated guitars, which featured graphics and shapes ranging from skull-and-crossbones to tiger stripes.

The band hit its stride with *Under Lock and Key*, which produced several chart-toppers, including "It's Not Love" and "In My Dreams." The band also recorded several ballads, which proved to be the precursors of the power ballads that MTV foisted on an unsuspecting public at every turn during the late 1980s. For Dokken, however, ballads worked quite well, as evidenced by tunes such as "Slippin' Away." Lynch was a more than capable acoustic player, yet he lost none of his electric ferocity on the instrument.

With high MTV exposure, sold-out U.S. concerts, and platinum albums, the band was asked to contribute the theme song to the movie *Nightmare on Elm Street 3: Dream Warriors*. Another album followed in 1988, *Back for the Attack*, which featured the definitive Lynch instrumental, "Mr. Scary." Based on a freight-train riff and a lead line that was reminiscent of Robert Plant's vocal in Led Zeppelin's "Immigrant Song," Lynch pulled out every stop in his book, creating one of the truly mesmerizing and jaw-dropping metal guitar showcases of the 1980s.

However, Dokken's success was burdened by increasing personality conflicts within the band, especially between Lynch and Don Dokken. The band's 1988 live album *Beast from the East* (featuring stellar versions of Dokken hits including "Mr. Scary") proved to be their last. Don Dokken declared that he was going solo and taking the band moniker with him. After a nasty legal battle, he was prevented from recording or performing simply as Dokken; he had to use his full name so as to prevent confusion over who—or what—the band comprised. He eventually recorded a solo album with John Norum, the Swedish guitar hotshot who had been with the pop-metal one-hitter Europe.

Lynch took Brown and formed Lynch Mob, which released its debut album in 1990 with vocalist Oni Logan and bassist Anthony Esposito. The album satisfied hardcore Lynch fans—all the licks were there—but something was missing in the songwriting. The 1992 follow-up, titled simply *Lynch Mob*, replaced Logan with Robert Mason, but saw no appreciable increase in the band's popularity despite the heavy radio rotation of the single "Tangled in the Web." In 1993 Lynch took time off from being in bands. He released a solo record, *Sacred Groove*, featuring a variety of session players and vocalists, including Ray Gillen and Glenn Hughes. The album had some brilliant playing, including Latin-flavored acoustic pieces and even sitar, but Elektra Records didn't quite know what to do with it, and sales stalled.

The following year, Lynch was asked to participate in a Dokken reunion, which he rejected. However, both Columbia Records and JVC Japan clamored for a Dokken record—as long as Lynch was included. In late 1994, Lynch relented, adding guitar tracks to a mostly completed Dokken project called *Dysfunctional* (the title being a wry commentary on the band's interpersonal relationships). Released in 1995 by Columbia, the largely mediocre record spawned a single, "Too High to Fly," and put Lynch back out on tour, playing to highly receptive audiences.

Despite Dokken's on again/off again love affair with itself and with its fans—the band was still selling platinum albums when

it first broke up—Lynch himself has rarely offered up anything other than fine displays of guitar pyrotechnics and taste. The less-than-enthusiastic audience response to Lynch Mob may have been partially due to the band's covering some already familiar turf, but *Sacred Groove* effectively proved that Lynch could play in unexpected and unexplored realms when given the chance—or seizing the opportunity. Out of all the post-Van Halen SoCal guitarists, George Lynch was the only one who spawned his own legion of imitators and adherents. His impressive soloing, blistering two-handed style, and killer tone set him apart from most other guitarists of the day, and continue to make him one of the most singularly interesting guitarists to make the transition from the 1980s to the 1990s.

Dokken [on Elektra except where noted], *Breaking the Chains* (Carrere/Elektra, 1982), *Tooth and Claw* (1984), *Under Lock and Key* (1986), *Back for the Attack* (1987), *Beast from the East* (1988•), *Dysfunctional* (Columbia, 1995). **Lynch Mob** [on Elektra], *Wicked Sensation* (1990), *Lynch Mob* (1992). **George Lynch**, *Sacred Groove* (Elektra, 1993).

Recordings featuring George Lynch: **Various Artists,** *Nightmare on Elm Street 3* [soundtrack] (n/a, 1987). **Tony MacAlpine,** *Maximum Security* (Mercury, 1987). **Various Artists,** *Guitar's Practicing Musicians, Vol. 3* (Guitar Recordings, 1994). **Various Artists,** *L.A. Blues Authority* (Shrapnel/BBI, 1992).

Extreme

Nuno Bettencourt

B o r n :   *September 20, 1966, in the Azores*
M a i n   G u i t a r s :   *Washburn NB Signature models*

Born in the Azores, off the coast of Portugal, Bettencourt moved with his family to Massachusetts, where he took up the guitar. Perhaps inspired by the acoustic flash of his birthland, Nuno soon fused the styles of electric players like Eddie Van Halen, Yngwie Malmsteen, and Al Di Meola into a heavy metal style that had enough spark and intelligence to set him apart from the other MTV-generation hacks.

After playing around the Boston area, Nuno joined Extreme, which released its first, eponymous, album on A&M in 1989. An interesting freshman effort, the record was notable more for what it promised than what it actually contained. Showing glimpses of Nuno's awesome chops, it still didn't break too far out of the heavy metal mold. *Extreme II: Pornograffitti* (1990) broke not only the mold, but also broke Extreme into the big leagues. With a bewildering array of song styles—heavy metal, ballads, funk, etc.—the album found fans from a variety of genres. The two soppy hits "More than Words" and "Hole Hearted" became MTV staples, and the former, an acoustic piece in the vein of the Everly Brothers, became the first in a wave of metal-acoustic ballads that would shortly saturate the airwaves.

Barely halfway into his twenties, Nuno was revered for both his acoustic and electric prowess by guitarists around the world.

His ability to play a variety of styles equally well showed the potential for becoming a guitar icon in his own right. But Extreme was hampered by its audience's inability to figure out just exactly what the band was all about, torn between the ideals of heavy metal and pop ballads. Just as frustrating was vocalist Gary Cherone's by-the-numbers style of heavy metal singing.

The band managed to repeat some of the success of *Pornograffitti* in 1992 with *III Sides to Every Story*, an extended recording that picked up on some of the social and political themes that its predecessor had touched on. While it was a strong album, it did not sell as well as expected. The band toured behind it and then released *Waiting for the Punchline* in 1995. Unfortunately, by that time, no one was waiting for Extreme. This dismal album tried to deliver a harder edge, but it ultimately ended up sounding like recycled metal. It dropped off the charts with nary a whisper.

Bettencourt's chops were as strong as ever, especially on the instrumental "Midnight Express." Again, the big problems were trying to define the band's sound and the lack of vocal originality. While Nuno and the band still maintained a hard-core following, it was readily apparent after *Punchline* that Nuno's extensive talents could be put to better use in another environment. As of the 1995, his most enduring legacy is *Pornograffitti*, which, under better circumstances, would be considered his starting point. His command of the instrument shows that he is capable of more.

Extreme [on A&M], *Extreme* (1989), *Extreme II: Pornograffitti* (1990), *III Sides to Every Story* (1992), *Waiting for the Punchline* (1995).

Recordings featuring Nuno Bettencourt: **Various Artists,** *Guitar's Practicing Musicians, Vol. 2* (Guitar Recordings, 1991).

Night Ranger

Jeff Watson

B o r n : *c. 1957, in Sacramento*
M a i n   G u i t a r : *'56 Gibson Les Paul goldtop*

Brad Gillis

B o r n : *c. 1958*
M a i n   G u i t a r : *Modified '62 Fender Stratocaster*

Although Night Ranger has been summarily (and perhaps appropriately) lumped in with the eighties hairdo metalers, they did actually possess one of the most potent guitar teams of the decade: Jeff Watson and Brad Gillis. Gillis had previously played with seventies funk act Rubicon and was the fill-in guitarist in Ozzy Osbourne's band following the death of Randy Rhoads (♪ Arena Rock), playing on the so-so live album *Speak of the Devil.*

Originally formed in 1979, Night Ranger debuted on record with *Dawn Patrol* in 1982. The powerful album was a surprise success, with the hard rock single "Don't Tell Me You Love Me" surging to #40 on the singles chart. The next two albums, *Midnight Madness* and *7 Wishes*, were bona fide hits, earning platinum sales, MTV videos, and sell-out concert crowds.

Bolstered by the sharp pop-metal songwriting of bassist/vocalist Jack Blades and drummer Kelly Keagy, the two guitarists dropped hot solos literally all over these recordings—it's hard to find a track that doesn't have a smokin' solo or two. Watson's two-handed tapping, Schenkeresque pentatonics, and speedy alternate picking à la Di Meola turned up in "Don't Tell Me You Love Me," while his famed eight-fingered tapping approach appears in the radio hit "(You Can Still) Rock in America." Looking back, this was one of those rare instances when a guitarist actually built upon Eddie Van Halen's tapping style, rather than just copping it blatantly.

In contrast to his partner's tapping prowess, Gillis' forte was melody and tremolo bar effects, but like Watson, instead of copying Van Halen's famed whammy dives, he started the trend of pulling the bar up, which later was codified by Steve Vai. A good example is his potent first solo in "Eddie's Comin' out Tonight," a track ignited by thrilling dual harmonics at the end. Gillis also played the band's most famous solo, the elegant whammy-inflected break in the otherwise lightweight ballad "Sister Christian," a #5 hit in 1984. And despite their pigeonholed roles—Gillis being "the melodic guy" and Watson "the speed guy"—each could trade places easily: listen to Gillis burn through the first solo in "Passion Play," while Watson gets tasteful in "Call My Name."

Nevertheless, Night Ranger quickly crapped out after their mid-eighties heyday, with Blades going on to further pop fame in Damn Yankees, featuring guitarists Tommy Shaw of Styx and Ted Nugent (♪). Both Watson and Gillis later cut passable solo albums (Watson's guests included Steve Morse and Allan Holdsworth). Later, Gillis re-formed the band as a power trio and cut one dismal album, though by 1996 the original lineup was back in the studio for a full-scale reunion.

Night Ranger [on MCA except where noted], *Dawn Patrol* (Boardwalk, 1982), *Midnight Madness* (1983), *7 Wishes* (1985), *Big Life* (1987), *Man in Motion* (Camel, 1988), *Greatest Hits* (Camel, 1989), *Live in Japan* (1990•), *Feeding off the Mojo* (Drive, 1995). **Jeff Watson,** *The Lone Ranger* (Shrapnel, 1992). **Brad Gillis,** *Gilrock Ranch* (Guitar, 1993).

Recordings featuring Brad Gillis: **Rubicon,** *Rubicon* (20th Century, 1977). **Ozzy Osbourne,** *Speak of the Devil* (Jet, 1982). **Various Artists,** *Guitar's Practicing Musicians, Vol. 2* (Guitar Recordings, 1991).

Recordings featuring Jeff Watson: **Tony MacAlpine,** *Maximum Security* (Mercury, 1987). **Various Artists,** *Guitar's Practicing Musicians* (Guitar Recordings, 1989). **Steve Morse,** *Southern Steel* (MCA, 1991).

Living Colour

Vernon Reid

Born: *c. 1959, in London*
Main Guitars: *ESP and Hamer Strat-style*

Vernon Reid remains one of the most difficult guitarists of the eighties to define. Brought up on calypso and jazz, he entered the hard-rock arena by the side door, kicking it down with his powerful band Living Colour.

Reid was exposed to music early on, and most of his influences were jazz musicians like Ornette Coleman and John Coltrane. After hearing Cream and Santana, he picked up the guitar. From the jazz world he listened to Wes Montgomery and Charlie Christian, while his rock influences tended to be of the eclectic variety: John McLaughlin and Carlos Santana.

He gigged around the New York club scene during the mid eighties, playing in avant garde and jazz bands such as Defunkt and Decoding Society. He also formed the Black Rock Coalition, an organization of New York bands aimed at creating awareness for African-American rock acts and combating racism in the music industry. He ultimately formed Living Colour with vocalist Corey Glover, and the band became an instant word-of-mouth hit in New York. Welding funk, metal, and fusion into a very workable hard rock style, Reid became famous for his completely unexpected and over-the-top playing. He used jazz chord voicings in a rock format (employing ninths and even thirteenths), but took the then-clichéd whammy bar to its extreme, threatening to rip the bridge off the body with the amount of diving and soaring he did with the bar.

Reid came to the attention of Mick Jagger, who used him on his solo album *Primitive Cool*. Jagger then produced several demos for the band, and their notoriety grew even further. They were signed to Epic, and their debut record, *Vivid*, was released in 1988. The song "Cult of Personality," originally a record considered too raucous for rock radio, was picked up by MTV, which turned it into an overnight hit. The song was Reid at his finest, flailing away at hard rock convention while turning in a wildly distorted and contorted shred solo. Other songs, including "Glamour Boys" and "Open Letter (to a Landlord)" showed that Living Colour was pushing the limits of hard rock.

The release of *Vivid* was heralded as a new direction for heavy metal. With Corey Glover's socio-political lyrics and Reid's masterful metal-fusion

style, it seemed that Living Colour could do no wrong. The fact that the band, composed of all African-Americans, was succeeding in a white-dominated genre made them all the more important. Reid, in particular, was singled out as being the first black guitarist since Hendrix to have a direct effect on the white world of hard rock guitar. His ability to incorporate so many diverse styles so powerfully made everyone—regardless of race—sit up and take notice. Still, his critics scoffed at his solo flurries as mere expositions of aimless speed and harmonic nonsense rather than precise technique and avant-garde jazz harmony. Later on, he eased back on the speed approach and started employing a tastier, more tuneful variation on the two-handed tapping maneuvers of the day.

Living Colour released *Time's Up* in 1991. Although it not launch the direct assault of *Vivid*, it did show that the band was not at a loss for new ideas. Internal problems forced the departure of the band's bassist, Muzz Skillings, who was replaced by Doug Wimbish in time for *Stain* in 1993. With Reid in full swing, the album roared with the same intensity as *Vivid*—perhaps more. But the songwriting in general was not as exciting as Reid's playing, and it seemed the only reason to listen to the band was to hear what Reid was going to do next (a problem shared by Nuno Bettencourt in Extreme). The album received high praise, but it did not sell as well as the band hoped. Disenchanted, the various members went their separate ways, and Living Colour officially broke up in 1995. Nevertheless, Reid's playing with Living Colour, and with artists such as Mick Jagger, Janet Jackson, and Carlos Santana, stands as some of the most aggressive and imaginative of the late 1980s and early 1990s. Reid left a legacy that will be hard to duplicate, and his original approach to metal guitar puts him in the category of the instrument's true stylists.

Living Colour [on Epic], *Vivid* (1988), *Time's Up* (1991), *Stain* (1993). **Vernon Reid**, *Mistaken Identity* (550/Sony, 1996).

Recordings featuring Vernon Reid: **Ronald Shannon Jackson**, *Eye on You* (About Time, 1980), *Street Priest* (Moers, 1981), *Mandance* (Antilles, 1982), *Barbeque Dog* (Antilles, 1983). **Ronald Shannon Jackson & the Decoding Society**, *Decode Yourself* (Island, 1984). **Defunkt**, *Thermonuclear Sweat* (Hannibal, 1984). **Jay Haggard**, *Riverside Dance* (India Navigation, 1985). **Mick Jagger**, *Primitive Cool* (Rolling Stones, 1987). **Public Enemy**, *Yo, Bum Rush the Show* (Def Jam, 1987). **Bill Frisell & Vernon Reid**, *Smash & Scatteration* (Rykodisc, 1989). **Janet Jackson**, *Rhythm Nation 1814* (A&M, 1989). **Carlos Santana**, *Spirits Dancing in the Flesh* (Columbia, 1990). **Garland Jeffreys**, *Don't Call Me Buckwheat* (RCA, 1992). **Jermaine Jackson**, *You Said* (LaFace, 1992). **Gravediggaz**, *Six Feet Deep* (Gee Street, 1994). **Barrington Levy**, *Barrington* (MCA, 1993). **Michael Hill's Blues Mob**, *Bloodlines* (Alligator, 1994).

Vernon Reid

CHAPTER TWENTY-SEVEN

Arena Rock
The Sound of Big Bucks

Instant audience. Instant ticket sales. As bands were rocketed to success by MTV, the number of people who bought their albums and attended their concerts rose commensurably. In the past, bands sold albums by dint of heavy touring schedules and constant roadwork. With MTV, they now gained massive numbers of fans without ever playing a single gig. And when the time came to actually play in concert, the popularity of these bands was such that they were booked right into arenas. While many of them did do the requisite amount of work in clubs and on the local bar circuit, others were propelled quickly to arena status without taking the time to get road-hardened. In many cases, it was like a twisted game of Monopoly: go straight to Park Place, and don't bother to pass Go.

Arenas had always been the province of hard-working, long-time road warriors who had finally made it big—bands like the Rolling Stones, Led Zeppelin, Aerosmith, and Pink Floyd. In the late 1970s and early 1980s, arenas were home to art rockers like Yes, Genesis, and Rush, along with the subsequent wave of more commercial groups like Journey, Kiss, and Foreigner. With MTV creating a ready-made market for brand-new bands, arenas completely eclipsed clubs as part of a tour. In fact, in many places, the club circuit died or went dormant, as MTV bands headed for enormodomes and major festivals (Monsters of Rock, Castle Donnington,

Reading) in every city they played.

Certain bands milked this to the extreme. Mötley Crüe, a band that took Kiss's makeup and added a huge dose of misogyny and chemical abuse, became was one of the major arena acts during the late 1980s. Despite minimal deviation from the standard rock formula, Crüe staged elaborate shows, and their concerts were headbanging affairs, appealing mostly to testosterone-charged males. Guitarist Mick Mars (born on April 4, 1955) was hardly anybody's model of guitar inventiveness, but he pounded out his fifth-chords and simple solos with enough bravado to keep Crüe in the running with other four-chord metal bands. Other bands took the simple metal formula to the arenas with multiple guitarists and radio-friendly songs, notably Tesla and Skid Row. Along with these performances came the required MTV video, showing these bands playing in front of hundreds of thousands of screaming fans.

And one cannot discuss arena rock without mentioning that endlessly reviled entity known as Winger, the pop-metal quartet that scored two platinum albums in 1988–90. But just a few years later, their career hit the skids, and they broke up in obscurity. To add insult to injury, the band soon became tagged as the stereotypical eighties hair band and were the targets of endless lampooning on MTV's "Beavis & Butthead" cartoon. Although frontman Kip Winger did have all the requisites for eighties success and nineties scorn—big hair, good looks, pouty vocals—Winger the band actually boasted stellar musicianship, notably from ex-Dregs drum virtuoso Rod Morgenstein and for-

Whitesnake: Vivian Campbell, Adrian Vandenburg

mer studio guitarist Reb Beach (Chaka Khan, Bee Gees, Twisted Sister). Amidst the trite lyrics and Toto-esque riffs on their first album (as well as a pathetic remake of Hendrix's "Purple Haze"), Beach dropped in a number of hot tapping and shred breaks, notably on "Madalaine," Hungry," and "Seventeen." Even slicker was the #19 hit "Headed for a Heartbreak," which featured a pair sultry breaks that mixed equal parts of Holdsworthian legato, Van Halenesque whammy bar antics, and Lukather-like string bends and melody. While Beach was hardly an original stylist, he could still certainly *play*, as these solos amply prove.

Then there were the Led Zeppelin clones, which somehow filled a stadium-sized need for guitar rock that no one knew existed. Kingdom Come rose to dazzling heights on the strength of an album that was by-the-book Zeppelin (although their guitarist made the outlandishly stupid claim of never having heard Jimmy Page), but deservedly crashed and burned after the novelty wore off. In between, they took their show on the road, playing in front of huge festival crowds the world over, including Van Halen's mammoth Monsters of Rock tour of 1988.

Arenas helped to make bands wealthier and more famous than clubs ever could, which was certainly part of their appeal. But as the 1990s rolled in, fewer and fewer bands could sell out arenas on their own. The spectacle, high gloss, and lack of intimacy inherent in 20,000-seat venues crumbled before the in-your-face aggression of grunge and mosh pits. The value of smaller theaters and clubs, where the guitarist was within touching distance—and not some tiny dot on a stage a quarter of a mile away—shut down the arena tours almost overnight. Bands like Great White, Skid Row, and Tesla went from headlining arenas to barely filling local clubs. The backlash against the arena crowd affected even the biggest names in the business, many of whom joined up with other bands of similar or lesser stature to ensure packed houses.

Still, the arenas were the breeding grounds for several bands that were primed for huge things right from the start, and they did propel a number of good, yet otherwise unknown, guitarists into the spotlight. As the century came to a close, these were the last of the big-time guitarists, regardless of their skill or their ultimate longevity.

Whitesnake

John Sykes
B o r n : *July 27, 1959, in Blackpool, England*
M a i n G u i t a r : *Gibson Les Paul*

Adrian Vandenburg
M a i n G u i t a r : *Gibson Les Paul*

Vivian Campbell
B o r n : *in Belfast, Northern Ireland*
M a i n G u i t a r : *Charvel Strat-style*

Steve Vai
B o r n : *June 6, 1960, in Carleplace, New York*
M a i n G u i t a r : *Ibanez Jem*

Micky Moody
B o r n : *August 30, 1950, in Middlesborough, England*
M a i n G u i t a r : *Gibson Les Paul*

Bernie Marsden
B o r n : *May 7, 1951, in Buckingham, England*
M a i n G u i t a r : *Gibson Les Paul*

Mel Galley
B o r n : *March 8, 1948, in Cannock, Staffordshire, England*
M a i n G u i t a r : *Gibson Les Paul*

David Coverdale was one of a handful of lead vocalists, along with Ozzy Osbourne and Ronnie James Dio, who went through lead guitarists as if they were kids going through candy. Yet Coverdale always managed to find the six-stringer with the right combination of chops, looks, and expertise for the job.

After the demise of the fourth incarnation of Deep Purple in 1976, Coverdale embarked on a solo career. For guitar duties he called on Micky Moody, an old friend Coverdale had known from his pre-Purple days. Moody had been in the Roadrunners with British rock vocalist Paul Rodgers, and was struggling along in a little-known British band called Tramline. He agreed to work with Coverdale on his solo projects, perhaps because Coverdale had a record deal, but didn't see himself as a lead guitarist. Coverdale wanted two guitarists anyway, and contacted Bernie Marsden, who had served brief stints in UFO and Paice, Ashton & Lord.

With Moody and Marsden in tow, Coverdale recorded two records under his own name, *Whitesnake* and *Northwinds*, both of which were bland blues-rock affairs. Touring around Britain, the band he had assembled (which included Neil Murray on bass) was billed variously as the David Coverdale Band and David Coverdale's Whitesnake. Under the latter name they released an EP called *Snakebite* in 1978. And when former Deep Purple keyboardist Jon Lord joined later that year, the band became known simply as Whitesnake.

Regardless of the name, the band's offerings were generally rehashed rock in the vein of Free and even Bad Company. (Coverdale was known as "Coverversion" in the U.K. for his tendency to mimic Paul Rodgers on record.) Moody and Marsden were competent players, but neither was especially exciting or adventurous. Their lone standout performance was the 1980 recording *Ready an' Willing*, an album that marked the appearance of Deep Purple drummer Ian Paice in the lineup. "Fool for Your Loving" and the title cut broke through the basic blues-rock formula to touch on heavy metal, and "Ain't Gonna Cry No More," an acoustic piece featuring Moody on 12-string, raved up to near-metal levels by its conclusion. Whitesnake's overall lack of musical adventurousness did not endear them to the American market, which ignored the band completely, although they were popular in both Japan and Europe.

Musical malaise and the opportunity for solo records by the band's members put Whitesnake on ice in 1982, with Coverdale himself looking to join another band (he was approached by Michael Schenker and Tony Iommi). When Coverdale decided to keep going it alone, he repackaged Whitesnake, this time with Moody and new guitarist Mel Galley, who had been with Trapeze (which had also been home to Glenn Hughes, bassist and vocalist for Deep Purple during Coverdale's tenure). With Cozy Powell now on drums, the band stumbled through *Saints an' Sinners* before undertaking the recording of *Slide It In* in 1983. While the album was being mixed, Coverdale and Moody had a falling out during a tour with Thin Lizzy. Moody left, recommending that Thin Lizzy's (◗) John Sykes replace him. At the end of the tour, Thin Lizzy disbanded, freeing Sykes to accept Coverdale's offer.

Sykes was British, but had grown up in Spain. He could not speak Spanish, however, and he spent his free time playing guitar, listening especially to Eric Clapton, Ritchie Blackmore, and Johnny Winter. Thus, he was steeped in hard rock with an appreciation for the blues. In addition, Sykes was an incredibly fast player, relying on sheer picking and fingering prowess rather than two-handed tapping. When his family moved back to England, he joined Tygers of Pan Tang, a progressive hard rock outfit that had some success in the U.K. From there he joined Thin Lizzy on their last tour before meeting up with Whitesnake.

Slide It In was released in the U.K. in early 1984, but Whitesnake's American record company, Geffen, wanted it remixed before putting it out in the U.S. Sykes redid many—but not all—of Moody's parts before Geffen was happy. The album featured the song "Love Ain't No Stranger" and the Zeppelinesque title track, both of which had a strong heavy metal flavor previously lacking in Whitesnake's playing. Both tunes became popular in America, signifying Whitesnake as an emerging metal powerhouse.

Meanwhile, Galley broke his arm in a freak accident when Sykes fell on Galley's arm as they were goofing off in a parking lot. The arm became infected, damaging some nerves and permanently taking Galley out of the band. Whitesnake carried on as a four-piece and recorded what is considered the definitive commercial metal album of the eighties, *Whitesnake* (also known as "Serpens Albus," or "Whitesnake '87"). The success of the album owed as much to Coverdale's Robert Plantisms as to its overall light/heavy Zeppelin quality. Sykes roared through the album, delivering heavy-edged yet lightning-quick runs throughout most of the tracks. His solos on "Bad Boys" and "Still of the Night" set

new standards in FM rock circles for fretboard speed. Moreover, they weren't based on the neoclassical-style runs of most shredders; Sykes just played rock licks tremendously fast. Despite the upbeat melodicism of the tunes, his tone gave the entire record a heavy, bombastic feel that was almost Sabbath-like in its intensity. Sykes also showed that he could play as gracefully at slower tempos, as on the sudsy ballad "Is This Love?"

Interestingly, the two biggest songs on the record had appeared on previous Whitesnake albums: "Cryin' in the Rain" and the FM hit "Here I Go Again" (which was co-written by Marsden). The album version of the latter track was not heard much by the public; instead, a super-slick take made it to video and radio. Even more ridiculous is that by the time the record was released in the U.S., Sykes wasn't even in the band. The album had actually been recorded in late 1985 and early 1986, and then put on hold while Coverdale underwent surgery for sinus infections. In the intervening year, Sykes had quit Whitesnake over differences stemming from who was going to oversee the mixing of the record. Everyone else had left as well, since they were not being paid for just sitting around.

After recovering from his operation, Coverdale had an album, but no band. With the record tearing up the charts, he had to get one—fast. His first priority was recording a video, so he hired two musicians who were readily available: ex-Dio axeman Vivian Campbell (◗ Shred) and Dutch guitarist Adrian Vandenburg (whose self-titled band had had a minor hit with "Burning Heart"). Vandenburg had known Coverdale for years and had played on the album version of "Here I Go Again" that Geffen had asked for on the American remix of *Slide It In*. He was also considered as a possible Whitesnake guitarist when Sykes was hired. Now he would be playing Sykes' parts on video and on stage. (During the video, Vandenburg aped Jimmy Page's famed violin bowing, eliciting cries of outrage from the guitar community and Page himself.) To make matters more complicated, the hit radio version of "Here I Go Again" featured a solo by American studio guitarist Dann Huff. Go figure.

The band toured the world, becoming one of the biggest acts of the late eighties. All was not joy in Whitesnake, however, as Campbell was fired in 1988 without ever recording with the band; he subsequently went on to an outfit called Riverdogs before settling in with Def Leppard (◗) as the deceased Steve Clark's replacement. When it came time to release the next Whitesnake record, expectations were high that a decent lineup would be able to repeat the success of "Serpens Albus." Strangely, Vandenburg allegedly injured both his hands during what he claimed were strenuous finger exercises. Thus, he was not able to play on the next record. Instead, heavy rock's top guitar gun, Steve Vai (◗), was brought in to play on the entire album, which was called *Slip of the Tongue*. Although Vandenburg wrote much of the album, he didn't play a lick on it. Vai brought his patented histrionics to the project, but even he couldn't salvage a band that had clearly played itself out by 1989. Indeed, his playing may have been too much for Whitesnake; after all, Sykes had defined the

Whitesnake sound by playing basic rock with a keen sense of pop melody and fretboard finesse. And, once again, the album's standout was a retread: "Fool for Your Loving," which had appeared previously on *Ready an' Willing*. This time, though, Americans weren't buying in such great numbers. The record, which sold reasonably well, was still a big disappointment.

Whitesnake was put on hold once again while Coverdale evaluated his career. He teamed with Jimmy Page in the ill-fated Coverdale-Page partnership, which saw Page reduced to playing Whitesnake tunes on tour. Jumping on the reunion bandwagon, Coverdale resurrected Whitesnake with a greatest hits record in 1994 and a subsequent tour that featured Vandenburg and former Ratt guitarist Warren DeMartini.

Whitesnake [on except where noted], *David Coverdale/Whitesnake* (n/a, 1977), *Northwinds* (n/a, 1978), *Snakebite* [EP] (n/a, 1978), *Trouble* (UA, 1978), *Lovehunter* (UA, 1979), *Ready an' Willing* (UA, 1980), *Live…In the Heart of the City* (UA, 1980 •), *Come an' Get It* (Atlantic, 1981), *Saints an' Sinners* (Liberty, 1982), *Slide It In* (Geffen, 1984), *Whitesnake* (Geffen, 1987), *Slip of the Tongue* (Geffen, 1990), *Greatest Hits* (Geffen, 1994).

Ozzy's Axemen

Jake E. Lee

Born: *Jakey Lou Williams, c. 1960, in Virginia*
Main Guitars: *Strat-style solidbody, Gibson SG*

Zakk Wylde

Born: *January 14, 1967, in New Jersey*
Main Guitar: *Gibson Les Paul*

Ozzy Osbourne's solo career had taken off with the release of *Blizzard of Ozz* and *Diary of a Madman*, and he'd effectively freed himself from the constraints of always being known as the ex-vocalist for Black Sabbath. This was due in no small part to the superb skills and writing ability of guitarist Randy Rhoads (♦), who also brought the guitar fanatics into Ozzy's camp. But with Randy's death in a plane crash in March 1982, Ozzy was left without a lead guitarist to help him maintain his post-Sabbath popularity.

Rhoads died while the band was on tour, and Ozzy had to hire a replacement in order to complete the run. Few professional guitarists were available on such short notice, but Ozzy did find one: Bernie Torme, a somewhat reserved six-stringer who had spent time with Ian Gillan's band, Gillan. Torme learned most of the band repertoire in 10 days, and then hit the road with Ozzy. The stress, the publicity, and the insanity surrounding Ozzy was too much for Torme, and he bailed from the tour after only three weeks, never to be heard from again.

During Torme's leg of the tour, Ozzy continued auditioning guitarists in hopes of finding a full-time replacement for Randy. One of the guitarists who fit the bill was Brad Gillis, but Gillis was interested only in a temporary gig, preferably the one that Torme had won. Gillis had just begun recording with his own band, Night Ranger (♦), and felt that the exposure with Ozzy could do him some good. When Torme left, Gillis was brought in, with the knowledge that he would not be Ozzy's full-time axeman. It was a strange agreement for an unknown guitarist to make, but it seemed to work for both Ozzy and Gillis. The tour carried on with Gillis in the guitar slot. Much of the material was Sabbath-oriented, partially out of Ozzy's inability to deal with Rhoads' death. A live album, *Speak of the Devil*, came out of the tour. The 1982 record featured only Sabbath tunes, which Gillis handled adequately if not imaginatively. Critics also slammed Osbourne for the album: it appeared to be a direct slap in the face of his old Black Sabbath cohorts, who were releasing their own live album with Ronnie James Dio on vocals. With the album released, Gillis went back to Night Ranger, and the search for a new guitarist began again.

A casting call in L.A. brought guitarists and wannabes out of the woodwork. Ozzy finally settled on a half-Japanese flash guitarist named Jakey Lou Williams, who went by the name Jake E. Lee. He had been one of the throngs of L.A. guitarists who had been up and down the Sunset Strip plying their wares, and at one time or another he had served duty in Rough Cutt, Ratt, one of Ronnie James Dio's bands, and a slew of other SoCal groups. Lee was an incredibly fast player who had the looks and stage moves down pat. Although nowhere near the diverse stylist that Rhoads was, he did have a knack for writing memorable heavy metal tunes, and he played with more than the requisite amount of flash.

Lee's first album with Osbourne, *Bark at the Moon* (1983), picked up Ozzy's career where *Diary of a Madman* had left off. (Ozzy himself didn't like *Speak of the Devil*, saying it was made merely to fulfill contractual obligations, and it stiffed in the stores.) Though not as neoclassical or exquisite as its predecessors, *Bark at the Moon* had a bit more metal punch, notably on the songs "Rock and Roll Rebel," "Waiting for Darkness," and the title track. The follow-up, *The Ultimate Sin* (1986), was even heavier, and recalled early Sabbath. It also showed Lee hitting his stride with Ozzy after years of touring and working together. But Ozzy, who had been in and out of rehab clinics during the mid eighties, was less than stable. He had been firing band members left and right (or they had left in dismay) ever since 1980. Despite all of the wonderful and warm things they said about each other in the press, Ozzy and Jake just weren't cutting it together. Lee left after the *Ultimate Sin* tour, claiming that he wanted to have more control over his career and to play more a more blues-oriented rock 'n' roll.

While Lee went on to form Badlands (a short-lived band that featured occasional Sabbath vocalist Ray Gillen), Ozzy once again put out the call for a new guitarist. Playing with Ozzy was getting to be the prime guitar gig in the world, a guarantee of immediate fame and a certain degree of professional fortune and success. It was like co-starring in the year's biggest movie. Thus, hundreds of guitarists sent their tapes into Ozzy's camp, just praying that he would call.

The one who received the nod was a 19-year-old from New Jersey, Zakk Wylde. A diehard Sabbath fan, Wylde was well-versed in Ozzy's catalog. He also shared Ozzy's penchant for loud and raucous good times, which Ozzy took to immediately. With Wylde in the lineup, Ozzy recorded *No Rest for the Wicked* in 1988, an album that seemed to go even further back to Ozzy's dark metal roots. While Wylde was capable of plenty of flash, the songs took on a more dirge-like quality than they had had even with Jake E. Lee, calling to mind the style of Tony Iommi. Ozzy continued selling out stadiums around the world, and then released one of the strongest and most popular records of his solo career, *No More Tears*, in 1991, containing the radio hit "Mama, I'm Coming Home."

Ozzy announced after the *No More Tears* tour that he was retiring from touring, and perhaps from recording. This meant that Wylde was out of a job. However, his time with Ozzy had made him a valuable commodity in the musical marketplace, and he signed a record deal with Geffen Records. Even though he was from New Jersey, Wylde had something of a redneck image. He started his own band, Pride and Glory, which played heavy rock with a southern influence in the vein of Lynyrd Skynyrd, the Outlaws, and Blackfoot. Wylde also served as the band's lead singer, something that almost no self-respecting metal guitarist had ever done with any degree of success. But he had a good voice, and that, combined with his metal bent, made Pride and Glory quite palatable as a hard-kicking rock 'n' roll band.

While Zakk was recording Pride and Glory's debut, Ozzy decided to come out of retirement (which surprised almost no one). Ozzy asked Zakk to contribute some tracks to a new record, which he did, but Zakk was committed to his own band. So Ozzy went to the best gun-for-hire available—Steve Vai. The pairing produced several cuts, but Ozzy's record company ultimately rejected them. It was something of an odd match: Vai had a well-known spiritual side, which made his partnership with the Ozzy and his Satanic parodies a bit confusing. Wylde was brought back to complete the project, and even to record over some of Vai's tracks. The album, *Ozzmosis*, was released in 1995. Ozzy later toured with new guitarist Joe Holmes.

Ozzy has always had a penchant for hooking up with outstanding guitarists who are also good songwriters. Almost universally, they have proven to be the right people at the right time (Torme and Gillis excepted), and their association with him has often proven to be the high point of their careers.

Ozzy Osbourne [on Jet/Epic Assoc.], *Blizzard of Ozz* (1980), *Diary of a Madman* (1981), *Speak of the Devil* (1983●), *Bark at the Moon* (1984), *The Ultimate Sin* (1986), *No Rest for the Wicked* (1988), *Just Say Ozzy* [EP] (1990●), *No More Tears* (1991), *Live & Loud* (1993●), *Ozzmosis* (1995). **Badlands** [on Atlantic], *Badlands* (1989), *Voodoo Highway* (1991). **Pride & Glory,** *Pride & Glory* (Geffen, 1994). **Zakk Wylde,** *Book of Shadows* (Geffen, 1996).

Recordings featuring Zakk Wylde: **Various Artists,** *L.A. Blues Authority* (BBI, 1992). **Various Artists,** *Guitar's Practicing Musicians, Vol. 3* (Guitar Recordings, 1994).

Queensrÿche

Chris DeGarmo
Born: *June 14, 1963, in Washington state*
Main Guitar: *ESP Strat-style*

Michael Wilton
Born: *February 23, 1962, in Washington state*
Main Guitar: *ESP Strat-style*

Chris DeGarmo and Michael Wilton both grew up in the Seattle area, learning songs by seventies hard-rock groups. They met as teenagers and in 1981 formed Queensrÿche with the intent of creating a band that was so tight it would never have to play the club circuit to prove itself. Wilton, who had attended the Cornish Music Institute to study classical guitar, came to the band with a heavy fusion/progressive bent, while DeGarmo brought an appreciation of British maestros Jimmy Page and David Gilmour, along with a penchant for artful arrangements.

Their first release, an EP entitled simply *Queensrÿche*, sold nearly 50,000 copies in and around the band's home town, primarily by word of mouth. Taut arrangements, pile-driving heavy metal, vocalist Geoff Tate's quasi-operatic vocals, and an art-rock flair similar to Rush pushed Queensrÿche above the run-of-the-mill metal mongers. The success of the EP sent EMI Records rushing to sign the band, and the company released *The Warning* in 1984 (after reissuing the original EP in 1983). The record did not deliver the overnight success that some had expected, but the band began a rigorous

Queensrÿche: Michael Wilton, Chris DeGarmo

touring schedule during which it opened for arena metal bands such as Dio and Iron Maiden.

The Warning and the subsequent *Rage for Order* (1986) produced several notable tunes, including "Take Hold of the Flame" and "Walk in the Shadows," respectively. Wilton and DeGarmo were careful to play to their individual talents, and rarely stepped on each other's toes when playing, providing an interesting guitar interplay uncommon to metal. The first two records merely hinted at the potential for the band, while their lack of bombast and the absence of a Mötley Crüe-style party attitude failed to put them in the same league as Poison and Cinderella (which ended up being a blessing). Management problems and the glut of glam metallers filling up the enormo-dromes also kept a cap on Queensrÿche, relegating them to minor-league status during the mid eighties and forcing them to play the smaller venues they had hoped to avoid.

Then came *Operation: Mindcrime*. Perhaps the most expertly crafted concept album since the Who's *Tommy*, the 1988 record featured scintillating lyrics and vocals from Tate, along with a dual barrage of riffs and tasty solos from DeGarmo and Wilton. The album was almost flawless from the perspective of guitar: the slower pieces were properly moody and not sappy, while the heavier numbers relied on strong riffs and counter-melodies instead of flash and fretboard pyrotechnics. "Revolution Calling" had the two guitarists playing scorching harmony solos, "I Don't Believe in Love" went from heavy riff groove to slowly arpeggiated verse lines, and "Eyes of a Stranger" brought it all to a heady conclusion with a growling back and forth of power chords and staccato leads. Throughout, DeGarmo and Wilton played with admirable aggression, making the songs and their instruments work together so that the guitar parts never became their own showpieces. Rarely in metal had this integration of guitar and song been accomplished with such precision.

With *Mindcrime* the band built upon its cult following, and over the course of two years the album became a metal classic—thanks in part to Queensrÿche's commitment to touring and delivering highly theatrical and visual shows. Then, with the long-awaited release of *Empire* in 1990, the band's popularity was chiseled in stone. *Empire* became one of the hottest albums of the year, driven by the acceptance of a number of tunes on mainstream radio (and the regular rotation of their videos on MTV). The title track, written by Wilton, had a repeating riff in the best Zeppelin mode, incorporating Rush-like tempo changes and segues. The album's biggest hit, however, was an acoustic piece penned by DeGarmo, "Silent Lucidity." The song reveled in Pink Floyd ethereality, from its soothing vocals and distorted samples to its use of atmospheric string backing and up-front acoustic guitar. A simple open-chorded song, its acoustic starkness was in direct contrast to most of Queensrÿche's heavier material.

The band toured extensively behind *Empire*, releasing an annoyingly edit-crazed video (à la MTV) and disc of the *Mindcrime* segment of the shows. Then they retreated into seclu-

sion for two years before releasing the somewhat disappointing *Promised Land* in 1994. The record was the darkest and moodiest piece the band had ever done, but with less of the metal explosiveness of their earlier efforts. This came as something of a shock to *Mindcrime* purists and those expecting more Floydian flights of fancy on the order of "Silent Lucidity." There were more than the usual number of acoustic-oriented pieces from DeGarmo, as well as the sheer overload of songs like "I Am I" and "Damaged," which featured a backwards intro by Wilton. The band took off on an arena tour of the world in 1995, proving themselves to be one of the last metal bands of the 1980s that could fill arenas on their own merit without resorting to co-billing or festival-style conglomerations.

In retrospect, neither DeGarmo nor Wilton ever capitalized on the basic tricks of the trade that defined guitar heroes, which is perhaps one of the reasons that they were not often singled out for their individual work. As true band members, they never sought the spotlight outside of their roles in creating an overall sound. Nonetheless, they were both adept at all the styles that make up hard rock: power chording, repeated riffs, acoustic picking, and searing solos. They blistered when necessary, but were also masters of keeping it simple (illustrated to great effect by the two-note harmonics and gentle whammy bar on "Jet City Woman," as well as the endlessly sustained single notes on "Waiting for 22"). Their insistence on putting the songs first—and playing guitar parts that contributed to making those songs memorable—placed them in that exclusive category of accomplished guitarists who know what to leave out, and when.

Queensrÿche [on EMI], *Queensrÿche* [EP] (1981), *The Warning* (1984), *Rage for Order* (1986), *Operation: Mindcrime* (1988), *Empire* (1990), *Operation: Livecrime* (1991•), *Promised Land* (1994).

Bon Jovi

Richie Sambora

Born: *July 11, 1959*
Main Guitar: *Fender Stratocaster*

No rock group blended the premise of hard rock, pop sentimentality, and the arena mentality to better advantage than Bon Jovi. Led by the telegenic Jon Bon Jovi (born Jon Bongiovi), the group combined catchy rockers and ballads with the right amount of stage-show antics and coliseum pyrotechnics. The band was also fortunate in that it was anchored in solid musicianship and songwriting, much of it from lead guitarist Richie Sambora. A workmanlike player in the mold of stalwarts like Mick Ralphs, Jethro Tull's Martin Barre, and BTO's Randy Bachman, Sambora was able to switch gears between heavy pop-metal and acoustic ballads without sacrificing anything along the way. For better or worse, he is perhaps the quintessential arena-rock guitar hero.

Prior to joining Bon Jovi, Sambora had played with a number of New Jersey bands in the late seventies and early eighties, and had earned a name for himself as a session player and part-time sideman. One of his bands, Mercy, had actually signed a record deal with Led Zeppelin's Swan Song label. Unfortunately, John Bonham's death and Zeppelin's subsequent breakup brought about the demise of Swan Song, leaving Sambora and company in the dust.

Sambora then went out on the road with a group called Duke Williams & the Extremes. He also did sessions whenever he could, and during a session in Chicago, he was asked by his friend Alec Jon Such to join a band back in New Jersey. Intrigued, Sambora returned and met with Such, who was playing bass for a singer-guitarist named Jon Bon Jovi. Sambora hit it off well with Bon Jovi, and the two began writing songs together. Their first collaborative effort was *Bon Jovi* (1984), an album of light rock tunes that featured the minor hit "Runaway." Undaunted by not breaking into the big time with their debut release, Bon Jovi and Sambora hit the road in what would become a pattern of incessant and ferocious touring. *Fahrenheit 7800*, the band's 1985 follow-up, was less than well received, producing a so-so radio track called "In and Out of Love." But MTV was catching on to the band—especially Jon Bon Jovi's good looks and big hair—and Sambora was keeping up the musical end by writing more consistently catchy riffs.

Nothing in the air—or on the airwaves—prepared anyone for the success of *Slippery When Wet*. Like Whitesnake's eponymous 1987 album (which came the following year), *Slippery When Wet* was the right offering from the right band at the right time. One of the best cuts on the album, "Livin' on a Prayer," contained a *très* cool talk-box riff courtesy of Sambora, while the acoustic "Wanted Dead or Alive," with Sambora playing slick arpeggios on an Ovation 6/12-string doubleneck, became an arena anthem (arguably giving impetus to similar acoustic offerings by Mr. Big and Extreme).

The band went right from the *Slippery* tour back to the record racks with *New Jersey* in 1988, another success, which maintained a similarly high position on the charts for the next year. Sambora and Jon Bon Jovi seemed to be wearing on each other's nerves after so many months on the road, though, and the band took a hiatus as everyone went their separate ways. Sambora went on to attract headlines for his relationship with Cher, and many of his fans felt that he had fallen prey to the Hollywood lifestyle. He played on albums by Cher and Alice Cooper before releasing his own solo disc, *Stranger in This Town*, which actually featured a guest performance by Eric Clapton. Meanwhile, Jon Bon Jovi wrote the soundtrack for *Blaze of Glory*, which found him recording with Jeff Beck. Apparently, the two were trying to make simultaneous bids for credibility, especially in light of the critics' constant wrath.

Time healed all wounds, and Bon Jovi reunited for *Keep the Faith* (1992). The metal scene, and the arena scene, had imploded, and Bon Jovi adapted to the new climate by sporting shorter hair and writing more "poignant" songs. Surprisingly, it worked. However, the lack of full-throttle guitar put the band squarely into the middle-of-the-road category. Nonetheless, in the summer of 1995, the band sold out Wembley Stadium in London two nights in a row. The opening act? Van Halen. Go figure. The release of *These Days* in 1995 (following a hugely successful greatest hits collection in 1994) proved that Bon Jovi, and Richie Sambora, had a worldwide fan base. Most of it, however, was not in the U.S.

Despite his reunion with Bon Jovi in its stripped-down mode, Sambora had not given up his Hollywood ways. He married TV vixen Heather Locklear (formerly wife of Mötley Crüe's Tommy Lee) in a highly publicized ceremony in 1995. In the end, Sambora's romantic liaisons may make him more famous than his guitar playing ever did. Such is the life of an arena rocker.

Bon Jovi [on Mercury], *Bon Jovi* (1984), *Fahrenheit 7800* (1985), *Slippery When Wet* (1986), *New Jersey* (1988), *Keep the Faith* (1992), *Crossroads—Best Of* (1994), *These Days* (1995). **Richie Sambora,** *Stranger in This Town* (Mercury, 1991).

Recordings featuring Richie Sambora: **Cher,** *Cher* (Geffen, 1987). **Alice Cooper,** *Trash* (Epic, 1989).

CHAPTER TWENTY-EIGHT

Roots Rock II

Modern Soul Stirrers

Emotion needed to stage a comeback. The early 1980s was a dark period for blues guitar, especially within the rock community. Many guitarists were learning to play synthesizers as their second instrument and steering their six-string work more toward the technical end of the spectrum. Soul was out; chops were in. On the record charts, synth-pop acts like Devo, Duran Duran, the Human League, the Eurythmics, and Gary Numan hit it big, promoting the sounds of drum machines and synths and performing robotlike live shows.

The mechanization of music provided ammunition for the return of the roots rockers. The enemy was the emotionless drone of quantized drum machines, and a new generation of earthy, blues-inspired guitarists united against it. Out of this movement, only one bona fide guitar superstar emerged—Stevie Ray Vaughan—but lots of other notable six-stringers climbed the charts with ripping, axe-fueled blues-rock or rockabilly. Their likes included the Stray Cats, Robert Cray, the Fabulous Thunderbirds, Mason Ruffner, Jeff Healey, and Eric Gales. Even Eric Clapton's career got a jump-start from this roots revival. On the country side of the movement, a fad dubbed "heartland rock" hit its zenith via such icons as Bruce Springsteen, John Cougar Mellencamp, the ever-eclectic Neil Young, and Tom Petty. (There was even a brief folkie fad, thanks to acoustic divas Suzanne Vega and Tracy Chapman.) Although synthesizers weren't completely purged from rock music until the grunge revolt of 1991, the roots genre kept getting bigger, until blues music was almost mainstream in the mid nineties. As evidence of this phenomenon, Clapton scored huge hits with his blues-based albums *Unplugged* (1992) and *Back to the Cradle* (1994), while the careers of great bluesmen like B.B. King, Otis Rush, and Buddy Guy were brighter than ever.

Stevie Ray Vaughan

Born: *October 3, 1954, in Dallas*
Died: *August 27, 1990, in East Troy, Wisconsin*
Main Guitar: *'59 Fender Stratocaster*

Stevie Ray Vaughan first entered the consciousness of guitar fans by way of his growling blues guitar solos on David Bowie's 1983 "comeback" album *Let's Dance* and its spin-off hit singles "Let's Dance," "Cat People (Putting out Fire)," and "China Girl." Oddly enough, Vaughan's hot Texas-style blues playing and Bowie's kinetic techno-pop blended perfectly together and created one of the most popular recordings of the early 1980s. In addition, it provided both musicians with a much-needed boost to their careers.

Stevie Ray Vaughan

While making the Bowie record, Vaughan was also cutting an album with his own group Double Trouble, under the tutelage of legendary producer John Hammond, the man credited with discovering Charlie Christian, Billie Holiday, Bob Dylan, and Bruce Springsteen, among others. Late in 1983 Vaughan's album *Texas Flood* was released on the Epic label. It received near-unanimous raves from the guitar community, especially for the fiery blues leads on the title cut. His raunchy, string-bending guitar solos, incredible Strat tone, and reverent electric tributes to his main inspiration, Jimi Hendrix, won Stevie Ray Vaughan a legion of fans in both the electric blues and pop communities. Thus, in the course of one year, 1983, and on two recordings, *Let's Dance* and *Texas Flood*, Vaughan emerged as the pre-eminent blues-rock guitar stylist of the day.

Stevie Ray Vaughan's guitar roots went deep into the legendary Texas music scene, which was rich in styles ranging from blues and rock to country and Tex-Mex. Stevie and his older brother Jimmie Vaughan (◊) picked up the guitar early and were smitten with the guitar work of bluesmen such as Howlin' Wolf, Muddy Waters, T-Bone Walker, Albert King and B.B. King. Stevie Ray developed a strong taste for heavy rock guitar as well and immersed himself in the sounds and styles of Lonnie Mack, Eric Clapton, Jeff Beck, and Hendrix. He spent much of the 1970s on the Texas blues and rock circuit, developing his muscular guitar style in a long succession of bar bands like Blackbird, the Nightcrawlers, Cobra, and the Triple Threat Revue.

In 1978 Vaughan formed the trio Double Trouble with drummer Chris "Whipper" Layton and bassist Tommy Shannon (who had previously been with Johnny Winter). During a club show in the early 1980s, the group was seen by Keith Richards and Mick Jagger of the Rolling Stones, and they invited the band to play at a private party in New York. The gig brought them to the attention of record producer Jerry Wexler, and he then managed to get them a spot at the 1982 Montreux Jazz Festival in Switzerland. After a hot set there in front of thousands of mesmerized fans, Vaughan met David Bowie (◊), who asked him to play on the *Let's Dance* sessions.

With the release of the Bowie disc and his own *Texas Flood*, Vaughan's career skyrocketed. He was soon receiving music awards for best new guitarist and best guitar album. He left the Bowie camp (allegedly Bowie was only willing to pay him union scale for an appearance at the huge US Festival) and set out on his own. In 1984 Vaughan followed *Texas Flood* with *Couldn't Stand the Weather*. It contains a remake of Hendrix's "Voodoo Child (Slight Return)," which generated a storm of both positive and negative criticism from Hendrix purists. Other highlights are the title song, "Scuttle Buttin'," and "Stang's Swang," on which the Texas blues-rocker tried his hand at jazz.

Vaughan cranked out another studio disc in 1985, *Soul to Soul*. Continuing in the same blues-rock vein as its predecessors, the record is notable for the addition of keyboards and saxophone to Double Trouble. The track "Look out for Little Sister" gained the band a considerable amount of radio air play, the most

that Vaughan had received since his stint with Bowie. Stevie Ray also became known as a powerhouse showman, entrancing audiences with his outlandish psychedelic outfits and cowboy hats, as well as with such Hendrix-inspired tricks as playing his trademark Fender Stratocaster behind his head or back. The aura of Vaughan's live performances was captured on his album *Live*, which was released in 1986.

After years of wrestling with a drug problem, the guitarist finally cleaned up his act and released one of his best albums, *In Step*, in 1989. The record contains the radio hit "Crossfire," a track full of smokin' blues solos and the guitarist's best singing ever. A year later he cut the relaxed *Family Style* with his brother Jimmie and seemed to be at the height of his popularity. In August 1990, after performing with Eric Clapton, Robert Cray, and his brother Jimmie at a blues-rock concert at Alpine Valley in East Troy, Wisconsin, Stevie was killed when the helicopter he was riding in crashed late at night. The guitar world mourned one of its favorite sons, and in true Hendrix fashion, posthumous Stevie Ray Vaughan releases began appearing the following year.

In the eighties era of speed-picking shredders, Vaughan's blues attack was a welcome relief from most rock guitarists' infatuation with technique and fretboard calisthenics. While there was no doubt that Vaughan was a rock guitarist (as opposed to a predominantly blues-oriented player like his brother Jimmie), his use of blues influences in rock 'n' roll had an overwhelmingly positive effect on the international guitar scene. In his few years in the limelight, the Texas guitarslinger was singled out with several awards (including a Grammy) and commanded a considerable legion of fans all around the world. And, as is typical in the premature passing of rock stars, the guitarist was deified after his death. Many players still talk about him in the hushed tones of reverence usually reserved for Jimi Hendrix. Vaughan's death also sparked a flood of Strat-toting Stevie Ray wannabes, who blandly rehashed the patented Vaughan sound. Still, no matter how hard the imitators tried to prove otherwise, there was only one Stevie Ray Vaughan. He was an American guitar original.

Stevie Ray Vaughan & Double Trouble [on Epic], *Texas Flood* (1983), *Couldn't Stand the Weather* (1984), *Soul to Soul* (1985), *Live* (1986•), *In Step* (1989), *The Sky Is Crying* (1991), *In the Beginning* (1992). **The Vaughan Brothers,** *Family Style* (Epic, 1991).

Recordings featuring Stevie Ray Vaughan: **David Bowie,** *Let's Dance* (EMI America, 1983). **Johnny Copeland,** *Texas Twister* (Rounder, n/a). **Marcia Ball,** *Soulful Dress* (Rounder, n/a). **Various Artists,** *Blues Explosion* (Atlantic, n/a). **Lonnie Mack,** *Strike Like Lightning* (Alligator, 1985). **Bennie Wallace,** *Twilight Time* (Blue Note, 1985). **Don Johnson,** *Heartbeat* (Epic, 1986). **Various Artists,** *Back to the Beach* [soundtrack] (n/a, 1987). **Bill Carter,** *Loaded Dice* (Epic, 1988). **A.C. Reid,** *I'm in the Wrong Business* (n/a, 1988).

Bonnie Raitt

Born: *November 8, 1949, in Burbank, California*
Main Guitar: *'69 Fender Stratocaster*

Once lumped in with the L.A. folkie crowd dominated by Jackson Browne, the Eagles, and Joni Mitchell, singer-guitarist Bonnie Raitt has always been firmly rooted in the blues since she began recording in the 1970s. Coming from a musical family (her father John was a renowned Broadway showman), Bonnie started playing the guitar at age eight. She was exposed to the Mississippi blues of Fred McDowell and Muddy Waters while still a teenager, and she continued searching out blues records while a student at Radcliffe College in Massachusetts. She left school to play the blues bar circuit, eventually making her way to California in the late 1960s. Many of her early recordings and concert appearances were graced by fine slide and acoustic guitar breaks (such as "Finest Lovin' Man" or "Love Me Like a Man"), but it was her gravelly, sultry singing style that gained her initial rave reviews. Her voice is the driving force behind such records as *Streetlights* (1974), which contains her signature ballad "Angel from Montgomery," and *Sweet Forgiveness* (1977), which features a near-hit version of Del Shannon's "Runaway." Raitt's talents were also part of the 1979 "No Nukes" benefit concert at Madison Square Garden in New York, which later became a hit live album. Still, it was her singing—and not her masterful slide work—that established her as a recording act.

As such, she was never mainstream enough to be a major act. So after years of being a second-tier act on the Warner Brothers label (her last album for the label, *Nine Lives*, only reached #115), Raitt switched to Capitol in the late eighties. Focusing on her blues roots and skillful guitar playing, she scored a #1 album with the aptly titled *Nick of Time* in 1989. The record spawned the singles "Have a Heart" and the title cut, which pushed Raitt to the level of arena headliner a mere 18 years after the release of her first album. The cut "Thing Called Love" spotlights Raitt's potent electric slide licks, as does the sultry funk track "Love Letter." With the release of *Nick of Time*, rock 'n' roll had a new bottleneck master to contend with. To top it off, the guitarist swept the 1989 Grammy Awards, walking away with four awards. "Bonniemania" had begun.

Her 1991 album *Luck of the Draw* was another immediate smash. It features the rollicking "Something to Talk About," which is draped with lazy slide figures and Raitt's typically sexy vocals. Even sexier is the funk rocker "Tangled and Dark," a track pumped up by killer bottleneck and some over-the-top erotic lyrical metaphors. A minor hit off of the disc was "Not the Only One," featuring the electric work of British guitar great Richard Thompson (◗). Raitt's *Longing in Their Hearts*, released in 1994, proved that her popularity was not a trendy thing. Having firmly planted herself in the hearts and minds of pop fans and blues aficionados, Raitt has all the makings of a long-term "overnight" success. Her slide playing alone has endeared her to guitarists the world over, many of whom have compared her slide skill to that of Duane Allman. If she were a male guitarist, it's most likely that she would already have been deemed a guitar god. As it is, she may be blues-rock's only guitar goddess.

Bonnie Raitt [on Warner Bros. except where noted], *Bonnie Raitt* (1971), *Give It Up* (1972), *Takin' My Time* (1973), *Streetlights* (1974), *Home Plate* (1975), *Sweet Forgiveness* (1977), *The Glow* (1979), *Green Light* (1982), *Nick of Time* (Capitol, 1989), *The Bonnie Raitt Collection* (1990), *Luck of the Draw* (Capitol, 1991), *Longing in their Hearts* (Capitol, 1994).

Recordings featuring Bonnie Raitt: **John Lee Hooker,** *The Healer* (Chameleon, 1989). **Roy Orbison and Friends,** *A Black and White Night Live* (Virgin, 1989◗). **David Crosby,** *Oh Yes I Can* (A&M, 1989). **Various Artists,** *A Tribute to Stevie Ray Vaughan* (Epic, 1996).

Danny Gatton

Born: *September 4, 1945, in Washington, D.C.*
Died: *October 4, 1994, in Maryland*
Main Guitars: *'53 Fender Telecaster and Danny Gatton Telecaster*

During a troubled but colorful career, Danny Gatton established himself as a true Tele terror, able to mix rock, jazz, country, and blues with uncanny finesse. But no matter how great a player he was, Gatton was never able to find a national audience, and frustrated with the music business and depressed at the death earlier in the year of band member Billy Windsor, he committed suicide in late 1994. His legacy, however, remains formidable.

With a list of influences that ranged from Charlie Christian and Howard Roberts to Les Paul to James Burton, Danny Gatton first gained a national reputation after on-and

Danny Gatton

off-again gigs with the likes of Roger Miller and Bobby Charles, along with the release of two impressive but hard-to-find solo albums, *American Music* (1976) and *Redneck Jazz* (1978). Gatton's reputation as a guitar maestro was spread even more as a result of his session work, live bootlegs, and recordings with rock 'n' roll singer Robert Gordon, with whom he appeared on two discs, *Are You Gonna Be the One?* in 1981(with such stand-out guitar tracks as "Lover Boy" and "Too Fast to Live, Too Young to Die") and Gordon's 1982 compilation set *Too Fast to Live, Too Young to Die*. Still, fame eluded him. Gatton released his third solo record in 1987, *Unfinished Business*, and received an avalanche of publicity. His live performances became legendary too, especially his *shtick* of playing slide with a full bottle of beer and dumping the beer on his guitar. Then, as he was toweling the neck off, he'd start to play hot solos right through the towel. Audiences would inevitably go nuts as a result.

After years as a word-of-mouth legend, the virtuoso signed with a major label, Elektra, and released *88 Elmira Street* in 1991. It is a superb record that contains many examples of the guitarist's wildly eclectic chops, such as the rockin' "Funky Mama" and the rockabilly-fired "Elmira St. Boogie." However, his follow-up record, *Cruisin' Deuces*, didn't even chart, and he lost his record deal within a few months. Subsequent recordings like *Relentless*, with jazz organ virtuoso Joey DeFrancesco, or the all-jazz *New York Stories* won rave reviews, but hardly put Gatton on the map. At the time of his death, Gatton's career seemed to have stalled. It was only the admiration of legions of guitar fans that kept him in business at all.

Stylistically, however, the guitarist was at the peak of his abilities. His fingerstyle chicken-pickin' techniques, pedal steel imitations, slide guitar, fast flatpicking jazz, and bluesy rock playing are all in abundance on his last recordings. Outside of Steve Morse and Steve Howe, Gatton was one of the most well-versed guitarists this side of the 1960s. It may have been this eclecticism that hindered his career, since the music industry has always been infamous for pigeonholing artists into a specific niche and then marketing their music accordingly. It was also somewhat curious that Gatton chose to live in rural Maryland and pursue his solo career from there, when he could have easily maintained a very lucrative studio career in Nashville, New York, or Los Angeles. He claimed to want to maintain a normal life for his family, but being in Maryland kept him out of the spotlight that could have improved his career prospects.

Truly bizarre comparisons can also be made between Gatton and fellow roots virtuoso Roy Buchanan (♪): both were based in Washington, played Telecasters, were extremely versatile roots players, were dubbed "The World's Greatest Unknown Guitarist," and ultimately, both took their own lives. And like Buchanan, Gatton chased his own elusive six string vision to the exclusion of anything else. As for his legacy, Gatton ranks as one of the greatest Tele masters who ever lived, the personification of the guitar term "monster." To those outside the music community, he may actually have been the world's greatest unknown guitarist.

Robert Gordon [on RCA], *Are You Gonna Be the One?* (1981), *Too Fast to Live, Too Young to Die* (1982). **Danny Gatton,** *American Music* (Ripsaw, 1976), *Redneck Jazz* (NRG, 1978), *Unfinished Business* (NRG, 1988), *88 Elmira Street* (Elektra, 1991), *New York Stories* (Blue Note, 1992), *Cruisin' Deuces* (Elektra, 1993). **Tom Principato & Danny Gatton,** *Blazing Telecasters* (K.O. City Studio, 1991). **Danny Gatton & Joey DeFrancesco,** *Relentless* (Big Mo, 1994).

Recordings featuring Danny Gatton: **Bobby Charles,** *Bobby Charles Invades the Wells Fargo Lounge* (n/a), **Big Al Downing,** *Big Al Downing* (Team, c. 1983), **Link Wray,** *Fire and Brimstone* (n/a). **Cindy Bullens,** *Desire Wire* (UA, 1978). **Chris Isaak,** *San Francisco Days* (Reprise, 1993). **Arlen Roth,** *Toolin' Around* (Blue Plate, 1993).

Jimmie Vaughan

Born: *March 20, 1951*
Main Guitar: *Fender Stratocaster*

At the beginning of the 1980s, a new name was being heralded as an up-and-coming figure of blues-rock guitar: Jimmie Vaughan. As guitarist for the Fabulous Thunderbirds, Jimmie Vaughan (older brother of guitar hero Stevie Ray Vaughan) won praise from fans, critics, and great bluesmen for his no-frills blues guitar style and dynamic lead/rhythm technique. Having the only chord-playing instrument in the Thunderbirds, Vaughan combined his single-note lead work with a variety of multi-string and chordal riffs to create his roots rocking sound. He did this in much the same way Buddy Holly did with the Crickets and Keith Richards did with the Rolling Stones.

Unlike younger brother Stevie, Jimmie grew up as more of a blues traditionalist. While Stevie cranked up the amps and dressed outlandishly, Jimmie favored a more laid-back guitar style and conservative approach. The two of them played the local clubs in and around Austin, with Stevie eventually heading to the Coast and Jimmie hooking up with some local bluesmen to form the Fabulous Thunderbirds. The Thunderbirds began recording in 1979, releasing highly praised discs including *What's the Word* and *T-Bird Rhythm*, as well as touring all over the U.S. and England. Despite the fine musical quality of the LPs, record sales were poor, and the music seemed in complete opposition to the synthesized techno-rock of the time.

With ZZ Top's techno-blues blast to the top of the charts in 1983, coupled with Stevie Ray Vaughan's first solo venture that same year, a shift in rock listening brought back a blues-rock revival by mid decade. In 1986 the Fabulous Thunderbirds issued *Tuff Enuff*, which—on the strength of its title cut—shot into the upper regions of the pop album charts and placed the band among the top blues-rock outfits in the country. Another hot cut from the album is "Wrap It Up," which features more of Vaughan's minimalist blues textures and riffs. A few more hits followed, but when their popularity waned in 1990, the T-Birds called it quits (they later re-formed with guitarists Duke Robillard and Kid Bangham). Later that year Vaughan released *Family Style*, a record that featured the brothers Vaughan together at last. Tragically, Stevie was killed in a helicopter crash not long after the recording was finished.

Jimmie Vaughan took a few years off after the death of his brother in 1990, but re-emerged in 1994 with *Strange Pleasure*, an album of barreling roadhouse boogies and cool blues licks.

The Fabulous Thunderbirds [on Chrysalis except where noted], *The Fabulous Thunderbirds* (Takoma, 1979), *What's the Word* (1980), *Butt Rockin'* (1981), *T-Bird Rhythm* (1982), *Tuff Enuff* (CBS Associated, 1986), *Hot Number* (CBS Associated, 1987). **The Vaughan Brothers,** *Family Style* (Epic, 1991). **Jimmie Vaughan,** *Strange Pleasure* (Epic, 1994).

Recordings featuring Jimmie Vaughan: **Asleep at the Wheel,** *Served Live* (Capitol, 1979●). **Lou Ann Barton,** *Old Enough* (Asylum, 1982), *Forbidden Tones* (Spindletop, 1986). **Bill Carter,** *Stompin' Grounds* (SouthCoast, 1985), *Loaded Dice* (Epic, 1988). **Carlos Santana,** *Havana Moon* (Columbia, 1983). **Various Artists,** *An Austin Rhythm and Blues Christmas* (Austin, n/a). **Stevie Ray Vaughan,** *Couldn't Stand the Weather* (Epic, 1984), *Live* (Epic, 1986●). **Various Artists,** *Porky's Revenge* [soundtrack] (Columbia, 1985). **Ron Levy,** *Ron Levy's Wild Kingdom* (Blacktop, 1986). **Various Artists,** *Gung Ho* [soundtrack] (n/a, 1986). **Denny Freeman,** *Blues Cruise* (Amazing, 1986), *Out of the Blue* (Amazing, 1988). **Various Artists,** *Cocktail* [soundtrack] (n/a, 1988). **Various Artists,** *A Tribute to Stevie Ray Vaughan* (Epic, 1996).

Minor Masters

Blues guitarist, vocalist, and songwriter Robert Cray crossed over onto the pop charts in a big way in 1986 and early 1987 with his hit album *Strong Persuader* and its infectious single and video "Smoking Gun." Cray spent part of the 1970s backing blues guitarist Albert Collins before striking out on a solo career in 1978 with *Who's Been Talking*. Later, solo sets like *Bad Influence* in 1983, (which contains the modern blues classics "Phone Booth" and "Bad Influence") and *False Accusations* in 1985 built up the guitarist's popularity and earned him several W.C. Handy awards as blues performer of the year. With *Strong Persuader* and *Smoking Gun*, he finally gained a vast audience for his pop, gospel, and funk-fired blues. He also gained outspoken admiration from such rock stars as Eric Clapton, Phil Collins, and Elvis Costello.

As a guitarist, Cray is no less intriguing, stoking up his infectious altered blues cuts (like *Strong Persuader*'s "Smoking Gun," "Right Next Door (Because of Me)," and "Fantasized") with the blues tones of his vintage Fender Stratocasters. Although not an excessively flashy player, Cray's clean electric textures and string-bending finesse helped make "Smoking Gun" a radio and MTV staple. His live shows opening for Eric Clapton and Huey Lewis were among the best performances of 1987 (he also made an exciting appearance at that year's Grammy awards ceremony). Aided by a strong voice, excellent songwriting skills, and more than ample good looks, Robert Cray's blues guitar mastery gave his career the boost it needed and made his prospects for a long haul in rock and blues seem almost predestined.

Among the most critically lauded new acts of the eighties was Los Lobos. Rising from the clubs of their native East Los Angeles, Los Lobos was a textbook example of the term "eclectic guitar." On their popular recordings, like the 1984 hit *How Will the Wolf Survive?* and *By the Light of the Moon*, in 1986, guitarists and multi-instrumentalists Cesar Rosas and David Hidalgo melded diverse musical influences such as blues, heavy rock, country, polka, swing, R&B, norteño (or Tex-Mex), rockabilly, and traditional Mexican folk music genres into one highly original rock style.

Instrumentally, the two guitarists also intermingled their rock-inspired electric guitar parts (à la Clapton and Hendrix) with the sounds of the bajo sexto, an acoustic bass guitar that is often used in Mexican folk music. In addition to their acclaimed work on Los Lobos albums, the guitar and vocal talents of Rosas and Hidalgo were also tapped for recordings by Paul Simon, the Fabulous Thunderbirds, Ry Cooder, Bob Dylan, and Elvis Costello. In 1987 the band's contributions to the wildly successful film *La Bamba* (the film biography of singer Ritchie Valens) made Los Lobos a household name, largely on the strength of their rollicking cover of the Valens hit single "La Bamba." Further critical acclaim followed the release of their stellar album of traditional Mexican folk music *La Pistola y el Corazon*.

Unquestionably, the leaders of the early 1980s rockabilly revival were the Stray Cats, a roots rock trio not from the South, but, ironically, from Long Island, New York. After conquering England, Europe, and Japan, the Stray Cats topped the U.S. rock scene in 1982 with their best-selling album *Built for Speed* and its hip hit singles "Rock This Town" and "Stray Cat Strut." While synthesizer-filled techno-rock kept a stranglehold on the U.S. pop scene at the time, the Stray Cats' rockabilly frolics were a refreshing change of pace, and the band quickly found thousands of fans, especially among the college set. The core of the Stray Cats sound was the singing, songwriting, and extremely authentic rockabilly picking of Brian Setzer (born on April 10, 1959, in Massapequa, New York), the band's blonde-pompadoured frontman. Every Stray Cats song crackles with Setzer's fifties-influenced stylizations, as he played everything from fingerstyle rhythm parts à la Scotty Moore to sparkling lead lines that brought both James Burton and Cliff Gallup to mind. His axe of choice, of course, was the definitive rockabilly guitar, a Gretsch 6120 Chet Atkins model.

After the Cats first broke up in the mid eighties, Setzer came out with his own solo album in the spring of 1986, entitled *The Knife Feels Like Justice*. Surprising fans and critics alike, *The Knife* showed the ex-Stray Cats guitarman in a new light, playing sixties-styled rock somewhat akin to recordings by John Cougar Mellencamp, Tom Petty, and John Fogerty. His powerful 1988 set *Live Nude Guitars* swung back towards rockabilly (it contains ferocious axe tracks like "Rebelene" and "Rockability"), while a few years later he received rave reviews for his *Brian Setzer Orchestra*, which attempted to mix the post-Sinatra schmaltz of Harry Connick Jr. with the rockabilly twang of Scotty Moore. Amazingly, the blend worked.

One very cool blues-rocker of the 1980s who had a brief but exciting run in the spotlight was Mason Ruffner. A potent Strat soloist from Fort Worth, Texas, Ruffner's second solo album, *Gypsy Blood*, caught the ear of the blues-rock community, which pushed the disc to #80 on the rock charts. Produced by Dave

Edmunds, the album mixes blues progressions with synth-driven grooves, creating a hip sound that ably complements ZZ Top's synth-fueled experiments of the same era. In addition to being a passionate singer and songwriter, Ruffner's soulful solos and rhythms really spark this album to life, notably on the title cut, the swampy "Runnin'," and on the barrelhouse boogie strains of "Baby, I Don't Care Anymore." Yet even with subsequent praise from Edmunds and Jimmy Page, who invited the guitar flash to open for the Firm's 1987 tour, Ruffner's career fizzled out pretty fast. By the nineties he was listed as M.I.A. within rock circles, and at last report, he was playing nightclubs in Texas.

Jeff Healey was another bright light of the late-eighties blues-rock scene. Born on March 25, 1966, this blind guitarist developed an unorthodox over-the-neck fretting technique that nevertheless was as bluesy and soulful as any conventional guitar approach (the technique resembled that used on mountain dulcimers or lap steel guitars). His debut album, *See the Light*, hit platinum via the hit ballad "Angel Eyes," yet the guitarist could also tear it up, as was evident in his remake of the Beatles' "While My Guitar Gently Weeps," from his second album, *Hell to Pay* (George Harrison joined him on the track). Still recording and performing today, Healey's career has cooled somewhat since his 1988–90 heyday, but he still made a notable mark on the initial blues-rock revival movement and won the praise of B.B. King, Gary Moore, and Stevie Ray Vaughan.

The Atlanta-based Black Crowes issued their debut album, *Shake Your Money Maker*, in 1990, and after several months of hard touring, the single "Jealous Again" caught on with radio audiences and became a major hit, as did subsequent singles "Twice As Hard," "Hard to Handle," and "She Talks to Angels." Each cut was graced with singer Chris Robinson's whiskey-toned bray, which was indebted to early Rod Stewart and Otis Redding. Guitarists Jeff Cease and Rich Robinson also relied heavily on early-seventies Brit-rock for their primary inspiration, in particular the Rolling Stones, the Faces, and Humble Pie. Their copping of famous British styles made them an able latter-day Mick Taylor/Keith Richards duo, replete with Cease's updated Chuck Berry licks and uncluttered blues bends and Robinson's open-tuned rhythm work.

Cease was let go from the band in 1991 after a series of tours with Heart and ZZ Top, and he was replaced with the even more retro-minded Marc Ford, formerly of the local L.A. power trio Burning Tree. *Southern Music and Harmony Companion* (1992) continued to mine the vintage British sound and debuted at #1 on the Billboard album charts. Despite the energetic performances on the album (such as on the radio hit "Remedy"), the band's perennial mining of vintage rock material (interpreted by many as blatant rip-offs) soured many fans and critics. *Amorica* (1995) continued in this vein, winning some fans and losing others, though there seemed to be an established cult of Crowe followers around the country. Guitarwise, however, the fresh blast of Brit-rock energy that was unleashed with the first album turned into a maudlin pool of six-string clichés, and as of this writing,

Shake Your Money Maker remains the band's definitive axe recording.

Finally, they said it couldn't be done: no one could replace Duane Allman in the Allman Brothers Band (♦). Although the group had tried on a number of occasions, it wasn't until the Allmans re-formed in 1990 with new guitarist Warren Haynes that they truly found Duane's replacement. Cranking out solos next to founding member Dickey Betts, the addition of Haynes to the lineup proved a master stroke. Right from the start, Haynes lays his fiery slide and single-note leads next to Betts' more lyrical breaks on impressive discs like *Seven Turns* (1990), *Shades of Two Worlds* (1991), and *An Evening with the Allman Brothers: First Set* and *Second Set* (1992, 1995). The fans noticed too. After teetering on the edge of "oldies" classification for several years, the Allman Brothers all of a sudden became hip among the 18-to-22-year-old college crowd. Their live performances became true events that attracted many Grateful Dead followers and long-time jam fans.

Stylistically, Haynes was able to beat the Duane comparisons by playing some classic Allman solos in the spirit of the great guitarist, but he judiciously added his own jazz- and blues-powered inflections. Undeniably, the addition of Warren Haynes to the Allman Brothers lineup improved the band's sagging fortunes. The group continues to record and tour, and Haynes' reputation is such that he was able to sign a record deal with Relativity (home of Joe Satriani and Steve Vai) for his own band Gov't Mule.

Robert Cray, *Who's Been Talking* (Tomato), *Bad Influence* (Hightone, 1983), *False Accusations* (Hightone, 1985), *Strong Persuader* (Hightone/Mercury, 1986), *Don't Be Afraid of the Dark* (Mercury, 1988), *Midnight Stroll* (Mercury, 1990), *I Was Warned* (Mercury, 1992), *Some Rainy Morning* (Mercury, 1995). **Robert Cray, Johnny Copeland & Albert Collins,** *Showdown* (Alligator, 1985).

Recordings featuring Robert Cray: **Chuck Berry,** *Hail! Hail! Rock 'n Roll* [soundtrack] (MCA, 1987•). **Tina Turner,** *Tina Live* (Capitol, 1988•). **John Lee Hooker,** *The Healer* (Chameleon, 1989). **Eric Clapton,** *Journeyman* (Duck/Reprise, 1990).

Stray Cats [on EMI America except where noted], *Stray Cats* (Arista, 1981), *Gonna Ball* (Arista, 1982), *Built for Speed* (1982), *Rant 'n' Rave* (1983), *Rock Therapy* (1986), *Blast Off* (1989). **Brian Setzer,** *The Knife Feels Like Justice* (EMI America, 1986), *Live Nude Guitars* (EMI-Manhattan, 1988), *Brian Setzer Orchestra* (Hollywood, 1994).

Recordings featuring Brian Setzer: **Dave Edmunds,** *Twangin'* (Swan Song, 1981). **Various Artists,** *La Bamba* [soundtrack] (Slash, 1987). **Arlen Roth,** *Toolin' Around* (Blue Plate, 1993).

Mason Ruffner [on CBS/Associated], *Mason Ruffner* (1985), *Gypsy Blood* (1987).

Recordings featuring Mason Ruffner: **Bob Dylan,** *Oh Mercy* (Columbia, 1989).

Los Lobos [on Slash/Warner Bros. except where noted], *...And a Time to Dance* (1983), *How Will the Wolf Survive?* (1984), *By the Light of the Moon* (1986), *La Pistola y el Corazon* (1988), *The Neighborhood* (1990), *Kiko* (1992), *Just Another Band from East L.A.: A Collection* (1993), *Papa's Dream* [with

Lalo Guerrero] (Music for Little People, 1995).

Recordings featuring Los Lobos: **Ry Cooder,** *Alamo Bay* [soundtrack] (Slash, c. 1984). **The Fabulous Thunderbirds,** *Tuff Enuff* (CBS Associated, 1986). **Elvis Costello,** *King of America* (Columbia, 1985). **Paul Simon,** *Graceland* (Warner Bros., 1986). **Roomful of Blues,** *Live at Lupo's Heartbreak Hotel* (Varrick, 1987). **The Long Ryders,** *Two Fisted Tales* (n/a, 1987). **Various Artists,** *La Bamba* [soundtrack] (Slash, 1987). **John Lee Hooker,** *The Healer* (Chameleon, 1989).

Jeff Healey Band [on Arista], *See the Light* (1989), *Hell to Pay* (1990), *Feel This* (1992), *Cover to Cover* (1995).

Recordings featuring Jeff Healey: **Various Artists,** *Road House* [soundtrack] (Arista, 1989).

Black Crowes [on Def American/American], *Shake Your Money Maker* (1990), *Southern Music and Harmony Companion* (1992), *Amorica* (1995), *Three Snakes and One Charm* (1996).

Allman Brothers Band (1990–94), *Seven Turns* (Epic, 1990), *Shades of Two Worlds* (Polygram, 1991), *An Evening with the Allman Brothers Band: First Set* (Epic, 1992•), *Where It All Begins* (Epic, 1994), *An Evening with the Allman Brothers Band: Second Set* (Epic, 1995•). **Warren Haynes,** *Tales of Ordinary Madness* (Megaforce, 1993). **Gov't Mule,** *Gov't Mule* (Relativity, 1995).

CHAPTER TWENTY-NINE

Thrash
The Dark Side of the Force

There was a black hole in rock music. As the heavy metal powerhouses of Led Zeppelin, Black Sabbath, and Deep Purple all fell into various stages of demise and dormancy in the early 1980s, a void was left for the kind of riff-heavy and dirgelike rock that had helped define rock guitar throughout the early 1970s. As synth-pop, R&B, and even country gained footholds on the music charts of the day, it seemed as if heavy metal would be relegated to the cemeteries and netherworlds that had been an essential component of its lyrics.

Of course, metal wasn't really going to die—it went underground. Numerous bands adopted Tony Iommi and Black Sabbath as their patron saints and carried on with drop-D tunings and root-fifth chromatic riffs. But it was now the 1980s, and the new bands had to do something to update the legendary Sabbath sound. A number of choices were readily apparent: add pop to the formula and create the pop metal confection that came to dominate arenas and MTV in the 1980s or else turn down a darker path. Inside of seeking out the pop sunshine, some metalers chose to speed up the metal gloom and make the lyrics grislier, more Satanic, and more disturbing than Sabbath ever had, while also stripping the melody lines out of the chord progressions and solos. Others got lead singers who could barely carry a tune and whose lack of vocal control made them sound like tortured hounds from hell.

Pop metal obviously owed little to its Sabbathian forefathers, but bands in the metal underground were by-the-numbers Sabbath with slight twists on the original theme. Fast Sabbath became speed metal; grisly Sabbath became death metal; punk Sabbath became thrash. Unfortunately, almost all of these genres bought into the vocalist as screamer instead of singer, which lent a musical sameness to their offerings.

Thrash metal grew up on the two coasts of the U.S. via legions of Sabbath imitators who also relied heavily on the influences of AC/DC, Judas Priest, Iron Maiden, Thin Lizzy, and even Motorhead. But the East Coast contingent found itself butting heads with and fusing with the New York/Washington, D.C., hardcore punk scene, giving their heavy metal a certain unrestrained recklessness, and even a social consciousness. On the other hand, the West Coast thrashers pulled ideas from some of the skate punks and rappers of the Los Angeles area. All of them eschewed—at first—any of the subtleties of Sabbath's softer side (pieces like "Fluff" or "Laguna Sunrise"), concentrating only on the traditional pile-driving and headbanging of simpler and more intense riffs. Angry and indignant, thrash was what Black Sabbath would have sounded like if Johnny Rotten had been lead vocalist in place of Ozzy Osbourne or Ronnie James Dio. Gone was any of the polish of 1970s heavy metal production, along with the leather and studs. In their place were primitive production, meaning few effects other than distortion, and jeans and T-shirts. Thrash sounded like Sabbath, but it was more visceral and more confrontational, with almost no trace of the blues roots of early Sabbath. The use of double bass drums and lightning fast bass lines heightened the effect of aural fury that came from thrash bands. Anthrax had the definitive New York sound, while groups like Suicidal Tendencies captured the thrash audiences of California.

Speed metal was different from thrash in that the punk recklessness was replaced with solos that were a bit more on the shred side, and the rhythm guitars emphasized flurrying right hands over flurrying left hands. However, many thrash bands played tunes that crossed over into speed metal, and the distinction between the two metals was often blurred, although there were some speed metal standouts. Chief among them was Testament's Alex Skolnick, a student of Joe Satriani's, who brought technical proficiency and an appreciation of modal playing and legatos to the genre.

Death metal emerged—unbelievably—from Florida, the so-called Sunshine State. Maybe it was a backlash against all the sun and surf, or maybe it was the most extreme form of rebellion that adolescents could shove down the throats of a growing retirement community, but cities from Orlando to Miami vomited up increasing numbers of death metal bands on a monthly basis. Claiming that their allegiance to Satan was real and not just a parody of Black Sabbath, death metal bands like Mercyful Fate, Venom, and Morbid Angel played thrash with a necrophiliac attitude that appealed to a limited but rabid audience. These bands certainly got plenty of coverage in the press, but record sales were usually—how shall we say?—short-lived. Other than lyrics, there wasn't much guitarwise to separate death metal bands from their more popular thrash and speed brethren. Nonetheless, fine axemen such as Chuck Schuldiner of Death and James Murphy of the Obsessed (and later Testament) managed to attract a cult following within their limited domain.

In the late 1980s and early 1990s, all of these metal idioms helped to crack open the mainstream, making the generic term "heavy metal" a catchall once again. Metallica, Anthrax, Megadeth, and Slayer were different bands playing different types of metal, but heavy metal seemed like the best way to classify them all. Every one, however, drew the strength of its sound from Sabbath, and a new generation of hard rockers pushed these groups to the top of the rock charts. Sure, it may have been recycled Sabbath, but it was still a metal they could call their own.

Metallica

James Hetfield

Born: *August 3, 1963, in Los Angeles*
Main Guitar: *ESP Explorer*

Kirk Hammett

Born: *November 18, 1962, in San Francisco*
Main Guitars: *ESP Strat-style and Kirk Hammett model*

The single driving force that made thrash metal palatable and commercial in the late 1980s was Metallica. Taking Sabbath-styled riffs, screaming vocals, and lyrics about the agonies of war and society, Metallica carved out a niche that made it the biggest heavy metal band to enter the 1990s.

The band was formed in 1981 by vocalist and guitarist James Hetfield and drummer Lars Ulrich. Hetfield had begun playing piano as a boy, then switched to guitar, borrowing his brother's Stratocaster to learn rock songs that he listened to. After bouncing bass players and guitarists in and out of the band, Metallica's first somewhat stable lineup was rounded out by bassist Cliff Burton and lead guitarist Dave Mustaine, a player whose rhythm style was very similar to that of Hetfield's. The two formed a tight rhythmic duo that played staccato root-fifth chords over frenetic pedal points, but Mustaine's lead playing was nothing to write home about.

Playing the Bay area club circuit, the band was radically different from anything that San Francisco had ever produced in the way of hard rock. Instead of psychedelic blues jams, Metallica played American heavy metal in the best British tradition. They were fans of the "New Wave of British Heavy Metal" acts, such as

Iron Maiden and Samson, as well. The band also established the "play-as-you-are" tradition in heavy metal: street clothes instead of spandex and leather. This gave them a much closer tie-in to their fans, who were looking for metal they could sink their teeth into.

As the band gathered local accolades and plenty of regional fame, it signed to the independent label Megaforce. Unfortunately, Mustaine, who was highly volatile to begin with, became more difficult to deal with as an increasing fascination with drugs overtook him. As the band was traveling cross-country to record their first album, Hetfield ousted Mustaine, replacing him with Kirk Hammett, another San Francisco guitarist who was then playing lead in a band called Exodus.

Although the four had originally wanted to call their 1983 debut *Metal up Your Ass*, the more eloquently titled *Kill 'em All* was still enough to do the trick, selling over 300,000 copies, no small thanks to the blazing songs written largely by Hetfield and Ulrich. Interestingly, the version of "Hit the Lights" that kicks off the album is less like what we now call "thrash" than an embellishment on the high-speed boogies and metal shuffles of Motorhead and their New Wave of British Heavy Metal (NWOBHM) counterparts; even Kirk Hammett's speedy, Schenker-inspired pentatonic solos seem rather conventional in hindsight (in one interview, Hetfield admitted that the popular "Seek & Destroy" was also a bit of a retread, this time from a Diamondhead song). However, by the second track, "The Four Horsemen" (co-written with Dave Mustaine), the essential sound of thrash comes into focus, mostly from Hetfield's furiously galloping rhythm riff and grim lyrics, as well as from the varying tempos, Hammett's melodic solo, and the overall complexity of the arrangement.

Even more quintessentially thrash are "Whiplash" and "Metal Militia," both of which explode with the kind of frenzied rhythm strums that James Hetfield made an essential skill for all speed metal guitarists to learn and master. Other interesting cuts on *Kill 'em All* are "Blitzkrieg," a song whose central chord progression is, perhaps unconsciously, a reworking of Jan Akkerman's main guitar riff from Focus' 1973 hit instrumental "Hocus Pocus," and also "(Anesthesia) Pulling Teeth," which revealed to many the four-string talents of bassist Cliff Burton, who although not a technical virtuoso, was able to play an extremely expressive solo that relied as much

Kirk Hammett

on sheer confidence and conviction as on the actual notes he produced from his instrument.

The next major milestone in the widening thrashscape was the appearance of Metallica's second album, *Ride the Lightning*. Where *Kill 'em All* showed a band just taking its first speed metal baby steps, *Ride the Lightning* revealed those same musicians up and running like a gang of healthy young thugs. *Lightning* also showed the band cutting away the remaining blues-based touches of the NWOBHM and playing pure thrash, though Metallica purposely threw in a ballad, the gripping "Fade to Black" (with its Thin Lizzy-like guitar harmonies). The album also revealed the maturation of Metallica's songwriting talents, with all members contributing ideas from the group's "riff tapes," which are recordings of various band jam sessions. Later, Hetfield and Ulrich had the task of going through these tapes in search of the strongest riffs and then assembling them into full songs (a not-uncommon method of songwriting, with Van Halen and Rush also among its notable practitioners).

Moreover, *Ride the Lightning* gave a clearer illustration of Metallica's unusual recording style than the first set. Strong advocates of sound-on-sound recording, the band recorded every instrument separately, which isn't unheard of in metal circles. But where many groups give their guitarists the roles of lead guitar and rhythm guitar as rough delineators of who solos and who doesn't, Metallica stuck to these titles rigidly. So in reality, what one hears on a Metallica album is not really a metal quartet playing together but a power trio—Hetfield, Burton (later Newsted), and Ulrich—and a de facto "solo specialist," Kirk Hammett, who *only* does leads. All the other rhythm guitar parts and harmonies (and the odd solo) are Hetfield, though in concert, both players share rhythm duties.

Hammett's reputation as a thrash flash also took a significant leap forward from his work on *Ride the Lightning*. Coming from a background immersed in Jeff Beck, Jimi Hendrix, and particularly UFO's Michael Schenker, the guitarist began taking

James Hetfield

greater chances with his leads at this time, something likely related to the lessons he had started taking the year before from Joe Satriani. Satriani's input helped Hammett break out of the pentatonic box mentality and go beyond the speedy Schenkerisms that he showered upon *Kill 'em All*. And while the influence of the great UFO/MSG picker was still prevalent—witness "Fight with Fire"—the Metallica axeman also began adding classical elements to his speedcore repertoire, as heard in his breaks to the title track and "Creeping Death," where he takes a strong neoclassical solo. Considering that he recorded this lead in the spring of 1984, it's also clear that Kirk Hammett was not only breaking ground with thrash, but also with Bach 'n' roll, since it was at this same time that Yngwie Malmsteen was just gaining initial recognition for his popular baroque metal style.

Yet for all their breakthroughs, Metallica was still considered a minor band, at least relative to the darling pop metal bands of MTV. In 1986 the band showed the public where it really was planning on going over the long term, with the release of *Master of Puppets*, which was the turning point for both Metallica and the new generation of guitar metal. On "Battery," Hetfield introduced nylon-string classical guitars, an apparent oddity that he put to good use in Metallica's repertoire from that point forward. The song then changes gear, diving into anvil-smashing riffs—a transition that would become another Metallica trademark. Hammett adds a wah-wah pedal to his solo, a device that had all but disappeared from the standard metal stomp box arsenal. His tone was vastly improved from previous Metallica efforts, making his Strat- and Flying V-powered speed runs easier to hear and his nervous, Tony Iommi-like vibrato all the more unnerving. From his performance on the record, Kirk Hammett was thereafter regarded as the premier guitarist of thrash, as the abundance of articles about him in rock and guitar magazines proved in the ensuing months. Hetfield also emerged as a tasty soloist, as heard in the first break to "Master of Puppets."

A tour with Ozzy Osbourne in support of *Puppets* almost made Metallica a household name, elevating Kirk Hammett to metal guitar poster boy in the process, but the frenzy was stopped short by the death of bassist Cliff Burton, who died on September 27, 1986, when the band's tour bus was involved in a freak accident in Sweden. Taking time to regroup with former Flotsam and Jetsam bassist Jason Newsted, the band put out an EP of cover material the following year called *Garage Days Revisited*. The EP bought them some time to regain their footing and incorporate Newsted into the band. The efforts paid off, and the release of *...And Justice for All* in 1988 pushed the band nearly to the top of the charts. The record's showcase is the signature tune "One," a multi-section anti-war opus that incorporates all the staccato riffs, acoustic interludes, tempo changes, speedy shred riffs and node-producing vocals that Metallica was now justly famous for. Other key tracks on the album, like "Blackened," layer lots of Hetfield guitars (four of them are piled up for the backwards intro to the song) into the best that thrash had to offer.

Metallica went out on that year's "Monsters of Rock" tour with Van Halen, Scorpions, and Dokken and was also nominated for a Grammy award in hard rock. They played "One" in front of millions of television viewers—many of whom were perhaps appalled at the huge wall of sound beating its way through their tiny TV speakers. This incongruity—the Grammys were normally showcases for weenie rock favorites and bland middle-of-the-road entertainment personalities like Whitney Houston—was only heightened by the band's loss of the hard rock award to veteran, but hardly relevant, art-rockers Jethro Tull. Obviously, this was hardly justice for all, but Metallica got their revenge with the release of their next record, the eponymous *Metallica*, in 1991.

The all-black album, often referred to as *None More Black* (a parody of Spinal Tap's *Smell the Glove*), was not only Metallica's mainstream breakthrough, but it also became the standard-bearer of post-Sabbath metal. With the churning riffs of "Enter Sandman" and the acoustic heaviness of "The Unforgiven" and "Nothing Else Matters," Metallica came up with a heavy metal combination that MTV and the Billboard charts could finally love. Some of the dirges were gone, replaced with a little more refinement on the part of Hetfield's vocals and a little more melody in his riffs (as well as tons of pumped-up bass), but the album was the pinnacle of everything that Metallica had been evolving towards. Hammett backed off from some of the speed merchant madness as well, making the entire record more accessible on every level.

The band took to the road for nearly two years after the record's release, sending the black album deep into multi-platinum status and selling out arenas the world over. It released a monstrous boxed set of the tour, called *Live Shit...Binge and Purge*, which contained all sorts of Metallica goodies and memorabilia. Despite its price tag of nearly $100, the box set sold incredibly well, and the band was well on its way to living a life of luxury—a far cry from their days as working-class heroes of the metal underground. After a two-year break, Metallica began recording a new album in 1995. The band re-emerged with *Load*, a less metalish and more hard-rock album that downplayed the

group's previous headbanging. Sporting a new alterna-look, including fashionable clothes and short haircuts, the band angered a lot of long-time followers, but that didn't stop *Load* from debuting and staying at #1. The record also highlighted an increased contribution from Hammett in the band's sound and compositions (there were actually songs throughout the band's career that had featured only Hetfield, with no playing by Hammett). To further confound critics and fans, the band headlined the formerly alternative-driven rock festival Lollapalooza.

As for Metallica's monstrous guitar legacy, the band is first and foremost James Hetfield's brain child. As the principal songwriter (along with Ulrich), Hetfield defines the band's sound, and plays all of the rhythm parts. In fact, he is certainly one of rock's most important rhythm players and belongs in the same hallowed halls as Keith Richards, Steve Cropper, and Pete Townshend. It is not popular to think of Hammett as his sidekick, but in reality, that has been Hammett's role. He was brought in to add the flash to Metallica's songs *after* Hetfield had crafted them, his role being specifically that of soloist and not lead or main guitarist. This, of course, didn't stop Hammett from becoming a guitar icon among metalheads—his speed metal chops as derived from Schenker, Satriani, and Malmsteen were certainly a cut above anything his peers were doing in the mid eighties, and his place in metal lore is well assured. But if you really want to pinpoint the true guitar genius in Metallica, one need not look much further than Hetfield.

Metallica [on Elektra], *Kill 'em All* (1983), *Ride the Lightning* (1984), *Master of Puppets* (1986), *Garage Days Revisited* [EP] (1987), *...And Justice for All* (1988), *Metallica* (1991), *Live Shit...Binge and Purge* (1993•), *Load* (1996).

Megadeth

Dave Mustaine

Born: *September 13, 1961, in La Mesa, California*
Main Guitar: *Jackson/Charvel V-style*

Marty Friedman

Born: *December 8, 1962, in Washington, D.C.*
Main Guitar: *Jackson/Charvel Strat-style*

Dave Mustaine grew up in southern California and got his first exposure to the guitar from his sister's boyfriend. Soon he was playing in various bands, whipping off Led Zeppelin, Rush, Pat Travers, and Iron Maiden covers. In the early 1980s, he hooked up with James Hetfield, the guitarist and leader of a relatively new band called Metallica. The two shared an appreciation for bone-crunching riffs played at warp speed with right-handed frenzy, and Mustaine signed on as second guitarist, which in Metallica terms, was the equivalent of lead guitarist.

The playing of Mustaine and Hetfield in early Metallica helped define the speed and thrash of the new heavy metal, but

Mustaine was not an easy person to deal with. Always outspoken, intelligent, and opinionated, he began to alienate Hetfield and Lars Ulrich with his increased drug use and belligerence. Just as Metallica was ready to record their debut album, *Kill 'em All*, Mustaine was booted. He had already helped write songs for the record, but he had become more of a hindrance than a help to the band's career.

Stung, Mustaine hooked up with bass player Dave Ellefson, and the two formed Megadeth in 1984. The band was built on the same slash-and-burn rhythm style that Metallica had pioneered, but Mustaine's snarling vocals and politically based vitriol added a nastier and more visceral bent to Megadeth's thrash. In constructing Megadeth, Mustaine also followed the same methodologies established by Hetfield in Metallica: the second guitarist was the soloist or lead guitarist, but the reins of the band stayed in the rhythm guitarist's hand. In Megadeth, that was Mustaine. The first of many lead guitarists to cycle through the band was Chris Poland. He played on the band's 1985 independent release, as well as on its Capitol Records debut, *Peace Sells...But Who's Buying?*, in 1986. Poland was largely overshadowed by Mustaine's primal and heavy-handed rhythms, but he did add some color to the music, the result of some jazz influences. Ultimately, Poland wasn't up to the day-to-day confrontations with Mustaine, so he was ousted from the band. In his place came Jeff Young, a technician trained at the Guitar Institute of Technology (GIT) who added an appreciation for shredding and scalar runs to the thrash of Mustaine & Co. But Young only lasted for one album, *So Far, So Good...So What?* (1988). Even though he contributed some of the most interesting Megadeth guitar solos up to that point, the pressure of dealing with Mustaine caused Young to turn in his resignation.

Mustaine once again held auditions for a new lead guitarist. This time Marty Friedman showed up. Friedman had already established himself as a bona fide guitar shredder with his outfit Cacophony, a Shrapnel Records guitar collaboration with fret-burner Jason Becker. He had also released a solo record on the label, *Dragon Kiss* (1988). Thus, Friedman was one of the "Shrapnel School Shredders" (◗ The Shrapnel School), a tag he was trying to live down, and Megadeth was the perfect forum. Signing on with Mustaine in time for *Rust in Peace*, the band put together one of its most cohesive efforts to date. The cohesion may have had as much to do with Mustaine's publicized decision to give up drugs and to have the band attend weekly therapy sessions. Whatever it was, it worked. Highlighted by "Hangar 18" (which had solos by both Mustaine and Friedman), *Rust in Peace* had plenty of crunching chords, lots of arpeggiated picking, and Friedman's neo-shred soloing oozing over the top of it all. It was blistering and muscular, and it cemented Megadeth's reputation as the biggest non-mainstream purveyor of thrash in the business.

That album was just the precursor to the band's 1992 breakthrough *Countdown to Extinction*. Finally getting through more than one album with the same strong lineup, Mustaine reached the heights of popularity and critical acclaim that his old band mates in Metallica had scaled the year before. Adding more melody and more flash—along with even more scathing lyrics about the grim plight of youth—than on previous albums, Megadeth roared to its zenith on cuts like "Ashes in Your Mouth," an acidic burner with multiple time changes and overlapping guitars and the swelling "Symphony of Destruction." A long stint on the road ensured that the album would rack up multi-platinum sales.

Not resting on its laurels, the group came back with its ultimate tome of disaffected youth, *Youthanasia*, in 1994. Igniting the press and conservative religious groups with its cover of babies on a clothesline (a pun on "hanging our youth out to dry"), *Youthanasia* showed even more thematic variations from Megadeth. The slow-tempo acoustic lines of "À Tout le Monde" gave way to the breakneck riffing of "Train of Consequences" and "Family Tree." The band was looser and perhaps a little more lushly arranged than in the past, causing some fans to cry, "Sell out!" Nonetheless, the record was a more than worthy follow-up to *Countdown*, and it debuted in the top 10 of the Billboard charts, going platinum within weeks of its release.

Megadeth [on Capitol except where noted], *Killing Is My Business…And Business Is Good* (Combat, 1985), *Peace Sells…But Who's Buying?* (1986), *So Far, So Good…So What?* (1988), *Rust in Peace* (1990), *Countdown to Extinction* (1992), *Youthanasia* (1994).

Anthrax

Scott Ian

B o r n : *Scott Ian Rosenfeld, on January 31, 1963, in New York City*
M a i n G u i t a r : *Jackson/Charvel Surfcaster*

Danny Spitz

M a i n G u i t a r : *Jackson/Charvel Strat-style*

Anthrax's brand of thrash was decidedly more adventurous than any of its peers, veering at times from glam to punk to rap to speed metal to blues-based hard rock.

Formed in New York at the height of the early 1980s punk scene, Anthrax went through several guitarists before hitting on the rhythm and lead combination of Scott Ian and Danny Spitz in 1983. Interestingly, the guiding light in the band was drummer Charlie Benante, who came up with the basic song structures before passing them over to Scott Ian. Lead singer Joey Belladonna was a bit over the top as a frontman, but the band made it all work. Perhaps most important, Anthrax did not have quite the same level of self-absorption that both Metallica's James Hetfield and Megadeth's Dave Mustaine had. Thus, they were able to move between genres with relative ease.

Their live reputation as mainstays of the New York-New Jersey club circuit got them signed to Megaforce Records, which released the aptly titled *Fistful of Metal* in 1984. All of Anthrax's early efforts were flat-out thrash attacks, with Ian providing the rumble that immediately identified Anthrax as among the heaviest of the metal bands in the mid 1980s. Songs were usually played using fifth chords, with chugging pedal points providing the overall sonic drive. The band had sported some of the pop metal look in its early day, but intensified their image as they got more and more raves from the thrash community. Never willing to be as subtle or angry as Megadeth and Metallica, the band was not above playing with a sense of humor and even self-deprecation.

A series of albums on Island pushed the band to the second tier of thrash, behind Metallica and Megadeth, but they still didn't have national support. Anthrax decided to cast all of their various images away in exchange for fierceness and grimness as the 1990s dawned (Ian shaved his head, giving the quiet guitarist the appearance of a demonic thrasher). Further enhancing their reputation as a band willing to take chances, they recorded with rap stars Public Enemy on a remake of that band's "Don't Believe the Hype" in 1991. They also did a concert tour with the rappers, taking modern music's most aggressive players and putting them on the same bill.

In 1992 Anthrax tossed Belladonna out of the band, opting for the more aggressive vocals of John Bush, who had been with Armored Saint. The change was widely heralded as a move that would make Anthrax the equal of their more commercially suc-

cessful peers. The new lineup released *Sound of White Noise* on Elektra Records in 1993. Anthrax incorporates the sinister tremolo strains of Angelo Badalamenti (the creator of the spooky "Twin Peaks" soundtrack) on "Black Lodge" and goes for the throat with the overdriven cuts "Potters Field" and "HyProGlo." Yet even though the album is a stellar and consistent effort, it was not the breakthrough the band had hoped for. Still they remained MTV darlings, contributing a lengthy piece to the album *Beavis and Butthead Experience*.

Regardless of their ultimate popularity, Ian and Spitz are two of the most important thrash guitarists, combining rhythm and lead guitar in equal doses for a frenzied speed and thrash metal that at times is even more aggressive and head pounding than Megadeth and Metallica. Perhaps because of their musical diversity (and the absence of a domineering singer-rhythm guitarist), they are not as easy to categorize as Megadeth and Metallica, but that in no way should diminish the sledgehammer ferocity they brought to thrash in its earliest days. Scott Ian's and Danny Spitz's contribution to the genre is arguably as important as that of Hetfield and Mustaine. Ironically, Spitz was fired in late 1994, apparently after losing interest in playing the guitar at all. In early 1996 the band announced that the lead guitar slot would be taken by Paul Crook, a New York shredder who had appeared on *Stomp 442*.

Anthrax [on Island except where noted], *Fistful of Metal* (Megaforce, 1984), *Armed and Dangerous* (1985), *Spreading the Disease* (1986), *Among the Living* (1987), *I'm the Man* [EP] (1987), *State of Euphoria* (1988), *Persistence of Time* (1990), *Attack of the Killer B's* (1991), *Sound of White Noise* (Elektra, 1993), *Live—The Island Years* (1994•), *Stomp 442* (1995).

Slayer

Kerry King

M a i n G u i t a r : *Jackson Kerry King model*

Jeff Hanneman

M a i n G u i t a r : *Jackson V*

From the outset Slayer's goal was to be the meanest, ugliest, and most violent of all the thrash bands. And that meant more than minor chords and tuning down to D or E♭. Leaving politics and the pains of adolescence to Megadeth and Metallica, Slayer staked out the "horror show" turf, putting the rigors of thrash alongside lyrics of rigor mortis. In the process they foreshadowed death metal and grindcore, but played fast enough to make all the thrashers sit up and take notice.

Formed in Los Angeles in 1982, Slayer took their initial cue from Alice Cooper and Kiss, dressing outlandishly and wearing makeup. They also sported Kerry King and Jeff Hanneman as a dual lead guitarist team, much like seventies rock bands did. But the glam metal trappings were a mere front: the band played like

Black Sabbath and sang songs that would have made any Satanist proud.

Hanneman started playing at age 18 and met up with King only a month after picking up the guitar. King had played since he was in the seventh grade, and he was in band by the time he ran into Hanneman. Both guitarists loved seventies metal, especially Judas Priest and Iron Maiden, although they were interested in the diverse guitar styles of players like AC/DC's Angus Young and Yngwie Malmsteen.

Their first album, *Show No Mercy* (1984),was released on the Enigma label and shows way too much of the band's early glam influences. By and large, the band and the album were dismissed as professional parodies—a sort of early-day GWAR, if you will. Switching labels the following year, the band delivered *Hell Awaits*, a psychotic first exploration into the depths of Satanism and physical torture. This time people listened. The musicianship is improved, as is lead singer Tom Araya's voice, making the band sound less like hacks and more like metal fiends. The sludgy riffs, which were pure Sabbath, are offset by some of King's and Hanneman's faster solos, giving Slayer entrée into the speed metal realm.

The success of fellow thrash bands Metallica and Megadeth in getting record deals, along with increased southern California interest in Slayer's stage show, incited a record company bidding war for Slayer. Def Jam, then a rap and hip hop label, came out the winner and offered up *Reign in Blood* in 1986 as the prize. CBS Records, however, wouldn't distribute the record because of lyrical content (isn't it funny how times have changed?), and distribution was taken over by Geffen Records, never a label to miss a chance for free publicity. *Reign in Blood* went on to be Slayer's breakthrough; never again would they be so heavy or so brutal. With echoing guitars, an occasional shred-style arpeggiation, and songs like "Angel of Death," Slayer defined demon-inspired thrash.

Although the band was more a household name for their antics than for their music, they continued to slog away, releasing better-selling albums with each turn, but never quite rising to the heights of Metallica or even Megadeth. Part of this was due to the fact that the band never deviated much from their blood and guts formula, and part of it was that newer death metal and grindcore acts in the early 1990s were doing it with more conviction. In retrospect, Slayer's music doesn't even have quite the gruesome edge as recent death metal bands. But in 1982 no one else was doing the full-fledged cemeteries-and-Satan act, so Slayer can rightly be credited as having invented the style that is popularly known as death metal. Quite possibly, their guitar playing was the heaviest ever played to that point, making it an integral part of the band's hellish aura. The twin guitars of King and Hanneman have not been replicated to such an exact degree by any latter-day adherents of 1990s metal, making Slayer true guitar pioneers in their own right.

Slayer [on Def American/American except where noted], *Show No Mercy* (Enigma, 1984), *Hell Awaits* (Restless, 1985), *Reign in Blood* (1986), *South of Heaven* (1988), *Seasons in the Abyss* (1990), *Decade of Aggression: Live* (1991•), *Divine Intervention* (1994).

CHAPTER THIRTY

Alternative
Guitar on the Edge

What's in a name?

In the mid 1980s, the term "alternative" came to be used to categorize any music that didn't fit nice and neatly into the tidy little domains of hard rock, heavy metal, or mainstream pop. The word was more of a curse than a cure for listeners, as well as for those musicians who played different styles of rock. The problem was that alternative was too loosely defined. The only way to make sense of the word was to ask "alternative to what?" The only concise answer was "alternative to whatever had come before."

Alternative was first known as underground music and then college music. The latter tag was more appropriate to the mid 1980s, because underground music by that time applied almost exclusively to club music from New York, London, Berlin, and L.A. The term "college music" worked better for a number of reasons. The music was a little more mentally demanding and a little more self-revealing than mainstream rock. Calling this college music implied that college listeners were more discerning and perhaps more intellectually attuned to this headier and less blatantly sex-driven style of music (as opposed to 1980s mainstream rock and pop metal, which appealed largely to high-school-aged headbangers). College music was also given its name because it was college radio stations that gave air play to bands like R.E.M., the Replacements, and U2 when mainstream stations ignored them.

As college music made its way out of the confines of college campuses, led by Hüsker Dü and R.E.M., it took on the guise of alternative music. Quickly, alternative became the name for everything that wasn't mainstream. Alternative was grunge before grunge got a name. Alternative was post-punk pop rock, with a shorter and less alliterative name. Most important, alternative was definitely not hard rock. The unusual aspect of this fact was that—like hard rock—alternative was defined first and foremost by the sound of its guitars. Whatever was not mainstream rock guitar was alternative guitar. Pioneered by players as different as Bob Mould and Dave Navarro, alternative guitar forms flirted with the excesses, the experimentation, and the fringe of rock. The sounds ranged from big and jangly to surgically precise to atmospherically psychedelic. As long as it wasn't obvious, it was alternative.

With the success of R.E.M., a host of bands broke out of the alternative niche—barely. Several alternative groups even had enough overdriven guitars in their sound that the bands approached hard rock, but it was usually an anomaly. For instance, guitarist Paul Westerberg and his Replacements were the prototypical college music band. Rough, gruff, with a knowing wink and a "party till we die" attitude à la the Faces, the Mats—as they were lovingly known—could have been an excellent mainstream rock band. But Westerberg's playing (and that of early lead guitarist Bob Stinson, who died in 1994 after years of substance abuse) was too wild, too out-of-control, to fit within the confines of commercial FM rock. Nevertheless, their music was thrilling, reckless rock 'n' roll that was marked by ringing guitar riffs, impassioned vocals, and a freight-train drum beat. "Bastards of Young" (from *Tim* in 1985) is perhaps the ultimate Mats rocker, typically mixing pop melody with primal guitar riffing and a sloppy solo. "I'll Be You," a compelling mid-tempo tune from the big-label *Don't Tell a Soul* in 1989, shows more studio polish, but fortunately Westerberg's raw guitar still shines through, along with the tasty acoustic slide of new lead guitarist Slim Dunlap. But while his alternative peers like R.E.M. and Sonic Youth broke through to larger audiences, the Mats disintegrated in 1990 after *All Shook Down* (actually a Westerberg solo album released under the Replacements name). As of the mid 1990s, Westerberg has seemingly become the Todd Rundgren of the alternative generation: a creative genius whose vast legacy of great songs and recordings is contrasted by his lack of commercial success. He's just another talented songwriter who slipped through the cracks of pop fame.

At the other end of the spectrum was Faith No More. While not a college band in the classic sense, the group's funk, metal, avant-garde, and pseudo-jazz defied categorization. To make it easy on critics and fans, Faith No More was summarily lumped into the alternative category. While the Replacements briefly flirted with the mainstream charts, Faith No More got huge—temporarily—with the 1990 rap-metal rant of "Epic." While this song proved to be a one-off hit, it did accomplish two important things in the alternative universe: it was an early example of white musicians playing rap (although white rockers "borrowing" from black musicians is nothing new), and it was also the first bit of thrash metal guitar to reach commercial FM radio and MTV. Metallica was certainly a huge band at the time, but they didn't have their widespread breakthrough until 1991. Although not credited as such, Jim Martin's midrange power chording on "Epic" may actually have been thrash's true coming-out party.

Like anything else that sticks around long enough, alternative bands made their way into the mainstream, in the 1990s. In fact, the mainstream was alternative in the nineties (or alternative was the mainstream—take your pick). Smashing Pumpkins, led by guitarist and vocalist Billy Corgan with his penchant for root-fifth (no third) chords, broke into the mainstream in 1993 with their album *Siamese Dream*, a record full of densely layered guitar parts and psychedelic tone (reminiscent of the textured guitar work by British bands like My Bloody Valentine, the Cure, Curve, and Catherine Wheel). For all his fey geekiness, Corgan knew how to crank up the heavy tone on his guitars, giving tunes like "Cherub Rock" a buzz-saw edge that was distinctive and immediately identifiable. Even the strangest of alternative bands gained some credibility in the 1990s. Primus, a nerdy funk rock group led by bass virtuoso Les Claypool, got MTV air play and was a major draw at concerts and festivals. Or the Rollins Band, whose music married skull-crushing power chords from Chris Haskett with the vocals and socio-political sermons of Henry Rollins (former leader of the pioneering post-punk act Black Flag). Amazingly, audiences loved it, and the band scored a big video and radio hit in 1994 with "Liar." There was no telling which alternative bands were going to strike the proper chord with audiences.

Long-term success and visibility came only to a few bands from the alternative world. Since alternative was so spread out in terms of its musical diversity, its lyrical content, and the sound of its guitars, it never became a proper self-contained genre. Those alternative bands or artists that made it to the top of the rock pile did so on the quality of their incredibly unique sounds and unique approach to rock music. Of course, those unique sounds didn't last long. The minute an alternative band made it big, the record companies launched a thousand "band *du jour*" copycats. When it came to real originality, the guitarists in the seminal alternative bands were the only ones worth listening to.

Hüsker Dü

Bob Mould

Main Guitar: *Ibanez Flying V*

Bob Mould invented alternative guitar. Period. That should be enough of a description of the man to send guitarists running to the record stores for his back catalog, but things are never so easy. An acknowledged pop guitar genius, Mould never broke through to the mainstream, despite single-handedly shaping the course of college music and influencing the generation of guitar anti-heroes that followed in his footsteps.

Mould's early fame was made in Hüsker Dü, one of the first bands to find major success at the college level while remaining virtually unknown in the mainstream world. Hailing from Minnesota (like fellow college rock ground-breakers, the Replacements), Hüsker Dü played raucous and fast—a lot like any other post-punk pop band. But Hüsker Dü—the name was taken from the name of a popular American board game that originated in Sweden—had one thing that was significantly different from its peers: Bob Mould's guitar playing.

Mould began playing guitar at age 16, inspired by the wailing frenzy of the Ramones. By playing around with barre chords and variations on standard chords, Mould found that he could get the ringing sound of the Ramones while adding his own sparkling twist. The result was as flurried and furious as the Ramones, but with more tonal variations and less punk rock bluntness.

Forming Hüsker Dü in 1979 with drummer Grant Hart and bassist Greg Norton, Mould introduced his style to the rock guitar world—starting in Minneapolis. Instead of writing songs with the big barre chords that were standard fare for all rock 'n' roll, Mould played simple open chords. But he still slashed away at all six strings with a fury, creating a big droning sound that was only hinted at by three-finger acoustic players. While hard rock bands used barre chords to help block off or dampen unnecessary strings, Mould used open chords so that those extra strings would stay open, and he flailed away at all of them like a maniac. The result was a wall of drones and dissonance that was usually heavily overdriven to give it a unique texture—perhaps like the soundtrack created when buzz bombs provided the serenade to the nighttime air raids on London during World War II.

Throughout the early 1980s, Hüsker Dü toured incessantly, playing the Midwest college circuit and then venturing out across the nation. The band appealed to punks, but instead of preaching anarchy, Mould and Hart (the other primary songwriter in the band) looked at the darker side of personal relationships. The band's reputation spread quickly, gaining them a cult following in the U.S. and Europe by 1985. All during this time, Mould was becoming a renowned but unlikely guitar hero—he looked like a corn-fed farm boy with a bad haircut. Nonetheless, people flocked to the band's shows and bought up their early independent record releases like *Zen Arcade* and *Flip Your Wig* in droves. In 1985 Hüsker Dü came up with one of the best guitar anthems of the alternative eighties: "I Apologize" from the album *New Day Rising*. In this track Mould's slash-and-burn power chords dominated the backdrop for three minutes and thirty seconds of totally distorted bliss. There's no solo, but no need for one either: the guitarist's manic riff says it all.

This brought Hüsker Dü to the attention of Warner Brothers, who signed the band in 1986. As the first alternative band with a major label deal (predating R.E.M.'s signing with Warner Brothers by more than a year), Hüsker Dü was poised for the limelight and the mainstream with the release of *Candy Apple Grey* (1986). The album went nowhere, so expectations were higher for the follow-up, *Warehouse: Songs & Stories* (1987). Perhaps one of their best and most accessible albums, *Warehouse* was a double-disc culmination of the band's sound: fast, big, edgy, nervous, and brilliantly noisy.

But that album went nowhere just as fast. Fed up with life on the road, tired of internal friction, and devastated by the suicide of Hüsker Dü's manager that same year, Mould packed it in. Hüsker Dü was simply no more as of January 1988. But ever the workaholic, Mould signed a solo deal with Virgin Records and released *Workbook* in 1989. Working with a new bassist and drummer (a consistent band lineup throughout Mould's career), the album was not as edgy as Hüsker Dü's thrashing wall of sound. Instead Mould used acoustic guitars and a more subdued sonic approach as accompaniment to his dark voice and introspective songs. It did, however, contain the hit single "See a Little Light," which kept Mould in the public eye. His second solo record, *Black Sheets of Rain* (1990), was more of a return to seething guitar form. Cascading guitars provide the dense textures for the title song and "Hanging Tree," while crackling electric licks reinforce the sound of the album's remaining tracks, including "It's Too Late" (which has a three-chord break much like ELO's "Do Ya" from a decade before) and "Stop Your Crying."

Surprisingly, Mould shifted gears and formed a new band called Sugar following the release of *Black Sheets of Rain*. Signed to Ryko, the band (with David Barbe on bass and Malcolm Travis on drums) released its debut, *Copper Blue*, in 1992. The album was everything that guitar fanatics had hoped for from Mould, and Sugar revealed itself to be a razor sharp power trio with the heart of a pop band. Serpentine licks coil around Mould's blitzkrieg rhythms on "A Good Idea," which is also interspersed with perverse bits of guitar squealing. The minor hit "If I Can't Change Your Mind" made it to the airwaves with optimistic acoustic strains and a mainstream pop hook, as did the tougher sound of "Changes." Mould gets downright heavy with "Fortune Teller," a song that foreshadows the release of *Beaster* in 1993. An example of Mould's guitar playing at its most frazzled, this EP features songs that weren't included on *Copper Blue*. The edginess of Mould and the band is highlighted on "JC Auto" and "Titled," which bleed with six-string fury and epilepsy-inducing rhythms, while "Come Around" shows Mould at his acoustic and electric guitar best, injecting droning electric lines over the big repeated chords of a bristling acoustic.

Sugar's *File Under: Easy Listening (FU:EL)* was released in 1994 and features the hit single "Your Favorite Thing." It was a much lighter pop exercise for the band, and the album sold well right out of the chute. However, it doesn't have the overall punch that listeners had come to expect from Mould and Sugar, and lack of support failed to make it the monstrous breakthrough to the big time that everybody had expected for Mould. His admission

of homosexuality during interviews for the album may not have helped, but overall the album just did not have the hooks or the bite that its predecessors had. In 1995 Sugar released *Besides*, a compilation of outtakes and live performances from the record vaults.

Mould, more than any other alternative guitarist, can claim to have personally redirected mainstream rock guitar playing in his image. His influence—obvious or not—was demonstrated by grunge and neo-punk bands, and his unique rhythm style became *de rigueur* for the guitarists that made their way to the mainstream in the 1990s. Mould is also nothing if not prolific, and his legacy is far from finished.

Hüsker Dü, *Land Speed Record* (SST, 1982•), *Metal Circus* (SST, 1983), *Zen Arcade* (SST, 1984), *New Day Rising* (SST, 1985), *Flip Your Wig* (SST, 1985), *Candy Apple Grey* (Warner Bros., 1986), *Warehouse: Songs & Stories* (Warner Bros., 1987), *Everything Falls Apart* (Rhino, 1993), *The Living End* (Warner Bros., 1994•). **Bob Mould** [on Virgin except where noted], *Workbook* (1989), *Black Sheets of Rain* (1990), *Poison Years* (1994), *Bob Mould* (Rykodisc, 1996). **Sugar** [on Ryko], *Copper Blue* (1992), *Beaster* (1993), *File Under: Easy Listening* (1994), *Besides* (1995).

Sonic Youth

Thurston Moore

Born: *1958*
Main Guitars: *Fender Jazzmaster and Jaguar*

Lee Ranaldo

Born: *1959*
Main Guitars: *Fender Jazzmaster and Jaguar*

Thurston Moore and Lee Ranaldo were part of the late 1970s and early 1980s New York underground art rock and noise scene (being distinct, at that time, from the college rock scene). Growing up in the New York tri-state area during the mid 1970s, they played in not-so-traditional New York rock bands such as the Coachmen, the Arcadians, and Flux. The two teamed up and worked together with—and were heavily influenced

Sonic Youth: Lee Ranaldo, Kim Gordon

by—avant-garde guitarist and composer Glenn Branca and his late 1970s experimental guitar symphonies. Learning the basics of Branca's take on performance art and *musique concrète*, they used found objects to play the guitar, including nails, drumsticks, pieces of wire, etc. They left Branca to form Sonic Youth in 1981, with Moore's wife Kim Gordon (bass, vocals) and eventually Steve Shelley (drums).

Forerunners of the modern school of deconstructed guitar playing, Sonic Youth was notorious for ripping strings off their Fender fretboards with screwdrivers and drumsticks to literally tear noise from the guitar. Their live show, coupled with some quirky but catchy songwriting, gained the band a strong following in New York, and they began releasing records on various independent labels.

The band was so avant-garde that they were basically an acquired taste, since many of their songs were pushing the guitar to its sonic (and perhaps tolerable) limit. Long, drawn-out jams that were played over droning strings oftentimes obscured Sonic Youth's ability to structure a coherent and interesting tune. But that was the point. Moore, especially, was interested in breaking down conventions of everyday rock 'n' roll, and he did it by pushing his guitar to the extreme. None of this had much to do with technical fretboard finesse; instead, it had everything to do with seeing how much strangeness could be coaxed from a guitar without actually killing it in the process.

Sonic Youth, like many early 1980s alternative bands, released records on various independent labels almost as fast as they could make them. Outstanding among these many releases were *EVOL* (1986) and *Daydream Nation* (1988), the latter featuring the band's college hit "Teenage Riot," perhaps the first single ever to be written in G–A–B–D–E–G tuning. It wasn't until Sonic Youth inked a deal with Geffen Records that they first gained a large audience outside of New York. Like any alternative band that signed to a major label in the late eighties or early nineties, the band was accused of selling out, but nothing could have been further from the truth. *Goo*, released in 1990, showed that Moore could be both melodic and tonally abrasive on cuts like "Tunic (Song for Karen)" and "Disappearer." Surprisingly, he also knew how to rock with a groove, as evidenced by the album's one hard rock hit, "Kool Thing." For diehard experimentalists, there is plenty of white noise and guitar abuse on the tunes "Mildred Pierce" and "Scooter & Jinx."

The album got the band the opening spot on Neil Young's tour the following year, and then they took time off to record *Dirty*, which was released in 1992. More accessible than any Sonic Youth record to date, *Dirty* covered much of the same ground as *Goo*, but with more hooks and more noise. Even though the band was noisier and more melodic, the album was something of a breakthrough for Sonic Youth's patented dissonance. Songs like "Sugar Kane" (in G–A–B–D–E–G tuning), the riff-laden "Purr," and the melodic feedback of "JC" gave old and new fans huge doses of everything that Sonic Youth was known for. *Experimental Jet Set, Trash and No Star* (1994), however,

failed to live up to the success of the previous records, rehashing much of what the band had offered up on *Goo* and *Dirty*, but without the freshness. Moore and Gordon took time out to have a baby, and Moore also released a solo record in 1995, *Psychic Hearts*.

Obviously, Sonic Youth was radical for their guitar abuse and the insertion of screwdrivers and other pointed tools into the strings. In addition to using these implements, the band changed tunings so frequently on its songs that they had to tour with a dozen guitars apiece for Moore and Ranaldo—each tuned to a different key. The band avoided traditional guitar tunings in order to get a "wall-of-noise" signature sound, evident on *Daydream Nation* and *Goo*. Most were experimental tunings that Moore and Ranaldo came up with themselves; they then created chord structures within those tunings through trial and error. Many of the tunings were so dissonant as to not make any sense at first glance, (such as F♯–F♯–G–G–A–A, low to high) while others involved the simplicity of tuning the guitar to octaves of only two notes (such as G–D–D–D–D–G).

Although they ignored standard modes in search of specific aural feelings, Moore and Ranaldo managed to patch together rhythmic textures and drones that inspired a whole generation of experimental and alternative bands, ranging from texture bands to grunge rock. Lead guitar, per se, was nonexistent in the band's repertoire, but with all of that strange noise coming out of their six strings, no one missed the solos.

Sonic Youth, *Sonic Youth* [EP] (SST 1982), *Confusion Is Sex* (SST 1983), *Kill Your Idols* (Zensor, 1983), *Sonic Death* (SST, 1984), *Bad Moon Rising* (Homestead, 1984), *Starpower* (SST, 1986), *EVOL* (SST, 1986), *Sister* (SST, 1987), *Daydream Nation* (Blast First/Enigma, 1988), *Master Dik* (SST, 1988), *Goo* (DGC, 1990), *Dirty* (DGC, 1992), *Experimental Jet Set, Trash and No Star* (DGC, 1994). **Thurston Moore,** *Psychic Hearts* (Geffen, 1995).

Jane's Addiction

Dave Navarro

Born: *June 7, 1967, in Los Angeles*
Main Guitar: *Fender Stratocaster*

Dave Navarro grew up in Los Angeles during the late 1970s and early 1980s. As a member of the marching band at his Sherman Oaks high school, he met up with drummer Steve Perkins, and the two formed a speed metal band called Disaster when Navarro was 16. He was inspired by European alternative bands such as Love and Rockets and Bauhaus, who favored minimalist guitar playing instead of shredding and big monster chords. He also listened to Led Zeppelin and the Cure, a combination that gave him an appreciation for guitar atmospherics without necessarily having to rely on heavy chord progressions.

Navarro, Perkins, and bassist Eric Avery hooked up with L.A. singer Perry Farrell, an artsy punk with a taste for the bizarre. Forming Jane's Addiction, the band put in heavy club time on the

Sunset Strip, where it gained a name for its avant-garde brand of rock. The band released a record of one of its live shows from the infamous Roxy, which sent major labels scurrying to sign Jane's Addiction. Warner Brothers emerged the victor and released *Nothing's Shocking* in 1988.

The album was touted as a new direction for rock music, even more extreme and compelling than the offerings by alternative bands and grungemeisters. From the opening strains of *Nothing's Shocking*, it's evident that Jane's Addiction was nothing ordinary. The melancholy bass line intro to "Up the Beach" gives way to soaring power-chord drones that fade out and feed back into the mix, followed by a progression of orchestral guitars that tumble down in echoing waves of chromatic lead lines. "Ted, Just Admit It" is a loose yet inventively raw series of guitar doodlings played over voice samples and a light jazz-funk groove. Then the song rips open with blazing chords, string scratchings, and staccato strumming. "Standing in the Shower...Thinking" features Navarro in a funk and phase-shifted frenzy, along with some classic blues-rock style lead lines. Clearly, this is a guitarist who can incorporate diverse influences without missing a trick. "Summertime Rolls" is as atmospheric as anything played by texture guitarists such as the Church's Marty Willson-Piper, and the rest of the album, including the lushly acoustic "Jane Says" and the quasi-pop single "Had a Dad" explore similarly diverse territory. Even the more straightforward songs are filled to capacity with swirling psychedelia, recalling both Jimi Hendrix and Jimmy Page. The one component holding it all together is Perry Farrell's eerie voice and Navarro's overriding sense of instrumental melody.

Despite the sudden rise to fame, the band members were not all that stable in their day-to-day lives. Farrell was reveling in his role as spokesperson for the alternative nation. Drugs were running rampant in the band, and Navarro was hit especially hard. He had flirted with a drug habit since shortly after his mother was killed by her ex-boyfriend when Navarro was only 15. Rumors circulated about Jane's Addiction not even being up to putting out another record, but in 1990 the band released *Ritual de lo Habitual*. Featuring another bit of twisted cover art from Farrell, the album instantly got MTV air play with the single "Been Caught Stealing," a rather simple affair by guitar standards. Other cuts, including "Stop!" and "Classic Girl," capture the experimental zeal of the first record, with Navarro contributing his masterful guitar ambiance to the tracks. But the rest of the record devolves into near narcissism, reaching points of self-indulgence that seemed to be more a part of Farrell's ego than any sort of musical adventurousness.

Although it lacks much of the appeal of the first record, *Ritual de lo Habitual* was considered the band's breakthrough. Farrell, however, was having none of it. Just as the record went gold, he announced that he was taking the band out on its farewell tour, which would be a traveling extravaganza known as Lollapalooza. His decision shocked not only his band mates, but also fans and the record company. True to his word, Farrell broke up Jane's Addiction after organizing Lollapalooza, and the members went off to separate projects. Farrell immediately re-emerged with Porno for Pyros, while Dave Navarro did a fine one-off album under the name Deconstruction. After contemplating leaving the record business, Navarro was asked to join Red Hot Chili Peppers (♪) in 1993. At the time the Peppers were coming off their biggest album to date, and also one of the biggest albums of the previous year, *Blood Sugar Sex Magik*. Interestingly, it was the mainstream breakthrough of Jane's Addiction that allowed bands like the Peppers to get more notice, despite the fact that the Peppers had been slogging it out for far longer than Jane's.

The importance of Jane's Addiction to guitar players is solely that it brought Dave Navarro into the mainstream. A brilliantly inventive guitarist who easily fuses rock with nuances taken from numerous other sources, he also applies effects to the guitar with an unusually intuitive sense. His sonic explorations paved the way for the rebirth of effects pedals and processors in the normally stripped-down setup of post-punks and grunge players. His tasteful innovation make him a guitarist worth searching out, as Red Hot Chili Peppers discovered.

Jane's Addiction, *Jane's Addiction* (Triple X, 1987), *Nothing's Shocking* (Warner Bros., 1988), *Ritual de lo Habitual* (Warner Bros., 1990). **Deconstruction,** *Deconstruction* (1994).

Recordings featuring Dave Navarro: **Alanis Morissette,** *Jagged Little Pill* (Maverick, 1995). **Porno for Pyros,** *Good Gods Urge* (Warner Bros., 1996).

R.E.M.

Peter Buck

Main Guitar: *Rickenbacker*

R.E.M. took the roots of the rootsiest American music—country, folk, lilting ballads, smatterings of R&B—and turned it into the biggest alternative success story of all. They did it with insightful lyrics, angst-ridden and often mumbled vocals, and the simplest guitar playing this side of Neil Young.

Formed in Athens, Georgia, by a group of college friends, R.E.M. played modest-tempo rock with a distinct southern folk bent to it. Although it was the era of American punk, there was little that was punk about R.E.M. Peter Buck's chiming guitars were more reminiscent of the Byrds and Buffalo Springfield than anything resembling 1970s radio or arena rock. Yet there was a modern quality to the music, mostly in the arrangements, that kept the band from being dismissed as a group of folkies.

A self-financed single "Radio Free Europe" made the band local Georgian heroes in 1981 and brought IRS Records to their door. IRS re-released the band's EP *Chronic Town*, which started R.E.M.'s slow climb up the college rock path to international fame. Immediately embraced by a host of college radio stations around the country, R.E.M. became the flag bearers of college music, a band so different and so good that mainstream radio just didn't know what to do with them.

Over the course of several IRS albums, the band's fan base expanded exponentially, growing even into Europe. Each successive record was more accomplished and more finely tuned than the last, but the basic formula never varied. Stipe mumbled the lyrics, Buck played ringing arpeggiated chords punctuated only rarely by lead licks, and drummer Mike Mills and bassist Bill Berry kept the band in time. While much of R.E.M.'s college-level appeal was derived from Stipe's enigmatic lyrics and garbled vocals, the backbone of the group was Buck and his guitar. Rarely overdriven or reliant on riffs (except in the case of atypical straight rock tunes like "Driver 8"), Buck could be counted on to deliver clean, crisp, rarely processed rhythm guitar parts that always had just enough force behind them to rise above the ballady-bluegrassy sound of most folk guitarists. His playing and songwriting jelled perfectly in creating excellent alterna-pop songs that were part rock, part folk, part backwoods, but never quite fully mainstream pop (such attributes call to mind parallels with the Band from the 1960s and 1970s). The addition of mandolin on various tracks also cemented the southern aspect of the band's sound.

The formula was relatively simple, but no one had come up with it before, which put R.E.M. years ahead of the pack. There were bands that had done similar things, yet they had never gotten all the same pieces together at the same time: CSNY had done something like it, but hadn't included the Beatlesque pop sensibilities; Hüsker Dü had done something like it without the nod of respect to Americana; the Band had done something like it without any of the quirky joy. Thus, R.E.M. put their sound on original songs like "Can't Get There from Here," "Gardening at Night," "Fall on Me," and "(Don't Go Back to) Rockville." In some cases Buck and the band could have been dismissed as country players trying to add a rock edge (or vice versa), but their songs were too up-tempo, too individual, and too intelligent to be so easily categorized.

After signing a well-publicized deal with Warner Brothers in 1988, R.E.M. released *Green* (in an all orange package). There are several all-out rock numbers, which the band wasn't known for ("Orange Crush," "Turn You Inside Out"), with the obvious acoustic tracks and quasi-pop songs tucked innocuously in between them. Following up with the huge-selling *Out of Time* in 1991 and *Automatic for the People* in 1992, Buck stays close to the near-acoustic quality of his Rickenbackers for the generally somber numbers that adorn those records ("Losing My Religion," "Nightswimming," "Everybody Hurts").

Buck's biggest departure from the R.E.M. norm—and indeed, the band's biggest stylistic departure—was *Monster* in 1994. The group had been promising a gritty and raw rock album for several years, but had continually opted for the slow and singable qualities found on *Out of Time* and *Automatic for the People*. *Monster* was not a singable album; it was 180 degrees removed from everything R.E.M. had ever done. With rip-roaring

guitars, fuzztones, and effects in full view, Buck lets loose right from the record's first cut "What's the Frequency, Kenneth?" With amp tremolos cutting through the sound (like Johnny Marr and the Smiths on "How Soon Is Now?"), Buck takes a backwards solo that is both spacey and plaintive and altogether perfect for the song. Feedback, echo, and tremolo find their way to other corners of the record (notably on "Crush with Eyeliner" and "I Took Your Name"), while Buck gets downright thrashy on "Let Me In." There are one or two R.E.M. standards ("Strange Currencies"), but overall the band strips itself of its former sound as successfully and completely as U2 had done with *Achtung Baby*.

Buck is a pioneer in bringing roots-based musical forms to the mainstream via the backdoor of alternative, but his playing is not groundbreaking. Notable variations in his playing are few: the herky-jerky opening licks of "Shiny Happy People," the sinister riff of "Driver 8," the neo-punk lines of "I Remember California." This is not to say that Buck repeats himself. Rather, he has staked out a territory that he can wander around in freely, and that territory happens to have jangly open chords and occasional distortion. His solos are more often than not simple lines based on the main melody. Like Neil Young before him, these are things that he does well, perhaps better than anyone else, and his fusion of Americana into an alternative success story has inspired thousands of guitarists and hundreds of bands, many of whom are easily dismissed as R.E.M. clones simply by listening to their guitars. As such, Buck's playing is as important to the success of R.E.M. as Michael Stipe's vocals and lyrics.

R.E.M. [on Warner Bros. except where noted], *Chronic Town* (IRS, 1982), *Murmur* (IRS, 1983), *Reckoning* (IRS, 1984), *Fables of the Reconstruction* (IRS, 1985), *Life's Rich Pageant* (IRS, 1986), *Dead Letter Office* (IRS, 1987), *Document* (IRS, 1987), *Eponymous* (IRS, 1988), *Green* (1988), *Out of Time* (1991), *Automatic for the People* (1992), *Monster* (1995).

Red Hot Chili Peppers

The Red Hot Chili Peppers are every alternative guitarist's dream, but ultimately they are not a guitar band. Instead, they have gone through seven different guitar eras, like a musical Elizabeth Taylor and her six-string husbands, always trying to push the edge of what is considered alternative. Their succession of guitarists has pushed the Chili Peppers to the edge, but the music has always been anchored by the uncanny bass sensibilities of the band's musical director, Flea. For the Chili Peppers, the guitarists themselves haven't meant as much to the band as the kinds of curve-ball attitudes that each one has brought to the table. Each guitarist's kink has added another wrinkle to the already heavily kinked sound of the Peppers.

Formed by bassist Flea (born Michael Balzary), vocalist Anthony Kiedis, and guitarist Hillel Slovak in 1983, the Red Hot Chili Peppers were initially as much about shock value as they were about making music. The band was different from the outset in that they incorporated a heavy funk groove into their brand of rock, and they attracted a small but ardent following. However, living in the post-punk world of alternative music, the Peppers fell prey to heroin (the resurgence of the drug in the late 1980s and early 1990s seemed almost endemic to major players on the alternative scene: Kurt Cobain, Courtney Love, Scott Weiland of Stone Temple Pilots, Kelley Deal of the Breeders), which set in motion a cycle that would continually affect the band's progress in an adverse manner.

Slovak left the band at one point, and his spot was filled by Jack Sherman, who was tossed out when Slovak decided he wanted back in. The Peppers recorded several funk-driven albums with Slovak, including a cover of Sly Stone's "If You Want Me to Stay," which gave the band early credibility with the hip white crowd that was getting into funk in the mid 1980s. The band almost lost it, however, when Slovak died of a heroin overdose in June 1988, just as the Peppers were gaining national attention. He was replaced in August by Duane McKnight, but McKnight proved to be not much more than a guitar temp. He was replaced by the end of that year with John Frusciante, a guitarist whose crazed rhythm work and utterly outside lead playing was allegedly a manifestation of his own personality. He arrived just in time for the recording of *Mother's Milk* (1989), which features the band's dead-on alternative version of Stevie Wonder's "Higher Ground." Frusciante's fractured style is all over the place, and he plays in funk-reggae spasms on tunes like "Knock Me Down." But he and the band found their ultimate groove two years later on *Blood Sugar Sex Magik*. With the exception of his acoustic playing on the MTV and radio hit "Under the Bridge," Frusciante concentrated on skewed electric guitar passages that followed Flea's bass lead into the odd-time realms of hip hop, funk, rap, and metal. Through it all, Frusciante's jagged style of combining, for example, rock rhythms with a rap groove (as on "Give It Away") were quirky enough to keep him in the musical blend along with Flea and Kiedis.

But overall, he did get lost behind the two. During the tour to support *Blood Sugar Sex Magik*, Frusciante threw in the towel, ostensibly succumbing to the rigors of life on the road (he released an almost unlistenable album of experimental guitar music on the American label in late 1994 called *Niandra Lades and Usually Just a T-Shirt*; 11 of the tracks were listed simply as "Untitled"). Arik Marshall, an L.A. guitar fixture who had played with Flea in a pickup band called Trulio Disgracias, was called in to fill the remaining dates on the tour. Marshall didn't last long either, and he was out before the Peppers even began working on their next record. He was replaced in mid 1993 by Jesse Tobias, who was around for even less time than Duane McKnight.

By mid 1994 the band finally settled on Dave Navarro, formerly of Jane's Addiction (♪). Navarro had been through a well-publicized nasty period with drugs, but was straightened out and in the middle of a post-Jane's project called Deconstruction. Navarro's experience with Perry Farrell and the breakup of Jane's Addiction had been so acrimonious that he had contemplated

giving up music altogether. But the offer from the Peppers came at the right time (rumors were that he was also being considered for Guns N' Roses), and he signed up with the band in time to play at the 1994 Woodstock Festival. The Peppers then headed into the studio, where a "Jane Meets the Chilis" ethic prevailed. However, the record was delayed several times over the next year, seemingly because of the newness of the arrangement. The real reason surfaced in mid 1995: Kiedis was trying to re-kick his heroin habit. The band emerged in late 1995 with *One Hot Minute* and shocked fans and detractors with Navarro's aggressively psychedelic buzzsaw playing (and homoerotic videos and *Guitar* magazine cover). The album yielded the hit "Warped," and after a successful 1996 world tour, the band continued to deny rumors that they were breaking up.

Each Pepper guitarist has helped push the band farther along a path of continual change. Despite the limitations of Kiedis' vocals, this progression has made the Peppers always interesting and increasingly adventurous with each subsequent album.

Red Hot Chili Peppers [on EMI except where noted], *Castles* (n/a), *Freaky Styley* (1985), *Uplift Mofo Party Plan* (1987), *Abbey Road* [EP] (1988), *Mother's Milk* (1989), *Blood Sugar Sex Magik* (Warner Bros., 1991), *What Hits!?* (1992), *One Hot Minute* (1995).

CHAPTER THIRTY-ONE

Euro-Pop, Euro-Goth, Euro-Rock
Lord Byron Meets the Stratocaster

Synths couldn't cut it alone. As musical audiences became bored with, and overdosed on, techno-pop's repetitive drone, pop and rock groups gradually brought guitars back into the mix to make things more interesting. Synthesizers just weren't keeping people's interest, and the dynamic range of the electric guitar seemed to be a means of injecting some power and excitement into the genre.

So as techno-pop was broken into fragments, various musical factions in Britain took the shards and carried them off in different directions. One faction came to be known as dream-pop or "shoegazers" (for their habit of looking at the ground while playing the guitars on stage). They were musicians who played trancelike, ethereal music that was composed of numerous guitars playing heavy droning chords wrapped in echo effects and phase shifters. During the mid 1980s, the leading purveyors of dream-pop were My Bloody Valentine, Lush (with female guitarists Miki Berenyi and Emma Anderson), and Curve (led by former Eurythmics sideman Dean Garcia). The acknowledged godparents of the movement were My Bloody Valentine, a British-Irish foursome that ultimately defined textured guitar playing and dream-pop with their 1988 debut LP, *Isn't Anything*. Fueled by the guitar conjurings of leader Kevin Shields and guitarist Belinda Butcher, My Bloody Valentine filled up tape track after tape track with guitars

Johnny Marr

and vocals in various stages of anguish (Shields, in particular, was later cited by a number of musicians as the guitarist who really opened the doors to full-scale post-techno guitar experimentation). Like many of the bands that followed them, even through the mid 1990s, My Bloody Valentine created a sound that intertwined strange guitar feedback and drones with the mesmerizing voice of a female singer.

Another faction took techno-pop towards the trappings of heavy metal, yet they didn't completely embrace the doom and gloom that was so often part of British metal. Instead these musicians embraced a more romantic vision of darkness—a gothic and Victorian attitude of tragic nineteenth-century poetry in the tradition of Byron, Shelley, and Keats. They became known simply and categorically as goth rockers and Euro-goths. In an inspired move, they took the overly synthesized roots of techno-pop, including the drum machines, and added the same influences that had made Led Zeppelin so unique more than a decade before: Middle Eastern scales and instruments, Celtic acoustic music, and even North African rhythms. Two bands that initially fused these styles onto the remains of techno-pop were the Southern Death Cult (later just known as the Cult) and the Sisters of Mercy.

The Sisters of Mercy comprised lead singer Andrew Eldritch and guitarist Wayne Hussey, along with various bass players and a drum machine known as Doktor Avalanche. The band was technically quite sloppy, but their rhythmic attempts at combining dance music and Middle Eastern sounds with heavy guitars made for a most interesting and unique combination. After *First and Last and Always* in 1985, which contained the dance hit "Walk Away," Hussey went off on his own to form the Mission UK. That band took the goth formula even further, but dispensed with the drum machines and pop rhythms. Throughout the late 1980s, the Mission UK released increasingly experimental albums that skirted with psychedelia, heavy metal, acoustic folk, and ethnic percussion—all the things that had made for interesting 1970s rock (not surprisingly, Led Zeppelin's John Paul Jones produced their

1988 release *Children*). The band's 1990 album *Carved in Sand*, featuring guitarist Simon Hinkler and guitar sidemen such as Tin Machine's Reeves Gabrels, was the pinnacle of the Mission's career, if not the pinnacle of the entire goth movement. Acoustic guitars lace many of the tracks, notably "Amelia," while chiming guitars and heavy power chords lend a surreal atmosphere to "Deliverance" and "Into the Blue," the last tune featuring a remarkable display of whammy bar diving and soaring by Gabrels.

Meanwhile, Eldritch and the Sisters of Mercy had carried on with a variety of guitarists until the release of *Vision Thing* (1990), a superb heavy-metal-meets-goth affair that has more drive and melody than any other form of heavy rock offered that year. Monstrous riffs on the title cut and "Dr. Jeep" have all the gloom and doom of early Sabbath, yet with a melodic flair that transcends strict heavy metal. However, the rise of grunge and alternative music spelled the end for goth (which was too conceptually themed and theatrical for new audiences), and both the Sisters and the Mission UK faltered and folded after these releases.

The dream-pop bands themselves never became too successful until the second generation of the style, which produced a more pop-oriented (in the best British sense of the term) crop of bands. In the mid 1990s, these groups—including Oasis, Bush, Elastica—climbed up the charts on the merits of swirling and heavily effected guitars, while bands like Catherine Wheel forged those same textured guitars to a harder rock sound, anticipating the gradual rebirth of hard rock in Britain. This second generation is less spatially disorienting than its predecessors, yet it still finds plenty of use for every guitar effect under the sun, especially those that have their roots in 1970s stomp boxes.

Ultimately, the first wave of post-techno bands had limited success during the mid 1980s. Their run was cut short by grunge in America and alternative and house music in Britain and Europe. Only a handful managed to outlive the vagaries of popular taste, partially due to their international followings, their innovative vocalists, and the distinctive sounds of their guitarists.

The Smiths

Johnny Marr

B o r n : *John Maher, on October 31, 1963, in Manchester, England*
M a i n   G u i t a r s : *Fender Stratocaster, various Gretsch models*

Johnny Marr learned guitar on his own as a teenager, picking up the instrument around the age of 13. He had little interest in joining a band; instead, he wanted to write songs that other people would record, because he never saw himself as an entertainer or performer. Thus, he spent most of his late adolescence writing songs on his guitar to the accompaniment of a drum machine.

When he was introduced by a mutual friend to singer and songwriter Steven Morrissey in 1982, that all changed. While both Morrissey and Marr had originally wanted to stay out of the spotlight and get known simply for their songwriting skills, it became apparent that no one could musically interpret their songs as well as the two of them could. They promptly formed the Smiths and within a year had released their first record, simply entitled *The Smiths*.

For the next four years, the Smiths were the most popular pop band in the U.K., but their peculiar British style never really appealed to a large American audience. The band was equal parts Morrissey's angular vocal stylings and intimate lyrics and Marr's incredible sense of musical harmony. His guitar lines were flawless examples of pop structure, so smooth and concise that Morrissey could sing about his girlfriend being in a coma and still have it work musically as a memorable pop song (which he did on "Girlfriend in a Coma" in 1987).

Marr and Morrissey complemented each other perfectly, allowing the Smiths to explore strange political and personal themes without sounding like sociopaths or idiots. Marr's guitar high point with the band is the atypical "How Soon Is Now?" from *Hatful of Hollow* (1984). Applying heavy amp tremolo to a series of overdubbed guitars, Marr creates a perfectly timed guitar thumping that is offset by the wailing of two individual notes, creating a truly ominous and spooky backdrop for the already moody and spooky Morrissey. The track was revolutionary for the way that Marr manages to construct an entire rhythm line from the tremolo, and nothing like it had ever been heard before, other than as a sound effect.

The Smiths got famous fast, and internal frictions took hold almost from the start. After half a dozen albums in four years, Marr decided that he did not want to spend his entire career with Morrissey and the Smiths. In 1987 he left the band to go out on his own, and media expectations were that he would become Britain's next rock guitar god. Instead, Marr chose to become Britain's ultimate sideman, working with Paul McCartney, The The, the Pretenders, Bryan Ferry, the Cult's Billy Duffy, and Talking Heads. It was Morrissey, who most thought would be lost without Marr, that went on to a successful solo career, proving once again the old rock guitar adage that "every lead guitarist needs a great lead singer in order to survive, but the last thing a lead singer needs is a great lead guitarist."

Marr finally settled down, temporarily, with New Order vocalist Bernard Sumner and the members of the Pet Shop Boys to form Electronic, which released one record in 1991. They did have a notable British hit "Getting Away with It," but that was Marr's last public splash. After Electronic, he emerged from time to time in the music press as part of some hoped-for collaboration, but none of them ever materialized. As it stands, Marr's legacy is as one of the best pop guitarists of the 1980s, and that legacy rests squarely—whether he likes it or not—on the shoulders of his playing with the Smiths.

The Smiths [on Sire], *The Smiths* (1984), *Hatful of Hollow* (1984), *Meat Is Murder* (1985), *The Queen Is Dead* (1986), *Louder than Bombs* (1987), *Strangeways Here We Come* (1987), *Rank* (1988 •). **The The** [on Epic], *Dusk* (1993), *Solitude* (1993).

Recordings featuring Johnny Marr: **Everything but the Girl,** *Everything but the Girl* (Sire, 1984). **Billy Bragg** [on Elektra], *Talking with the Taxman about Poetry* (1986), *Don't Try this at Home* (1991). **Electronic,** *Electronic* (Warner Bros., 1991).

The Cure

Robert Smith

Born: *April 21, 1957, in Crowley, Sussex, England*
Main Guitars: *Fender Jazzmaster, various Gibsons*

No band better fused the detritus of techno-pop with the gloomy leanings of goth rock better than the Cure. Through the 1980s and the 1990s, the band rose slowly through the rank and file to become one of the most successful bands of the early 1990s, relying on the ethereal guitar playing of Robert Smith and the lead bass lines of Simon Gallup.

Smith formed the Cure in 1976 during the early years of Euro-disco and the electronic sounds of such European synth acts as Kraftwerk and Tangerine Dream. His playing was of the standard 1960s pop type, yet he wrote songs of extreme self-despair and existentialism (the band's first hit, "Killing an Arab," was inspired by *The Stranger,* the archetypal existential novel by Albert Camus). The Cure released some material through a European independent label before signing with Fiction, a small label distributed by Polydor. In 1979 the band released *Three Imaginary Boys* and then *Seventeen Seconds* in 1980. With the release of *Faith* in 1981, Smith hit upon the proper gloomy formula for a generation of adolescents that had no faith in anything—self-loathing and the pain of no love. His voice, lyrics, and guitar playing were so anti-punk that the British press picked up on the Cure and its plaintive style as being the best that Britain had to offer. Plus, Smith's regular habit of wearing all black, along with black eyeliner, smudged lipstick, and rat's-nest hair endeared him to the disenfranchised of British society.

With *Pornography* in 1982, Smith demonstrates a penchant for guitar layering, open chords, droning strings, and dense arrangements. His single-mindedness, however, drove the remaining members out of the band (the Cure had always had a reputation as something of a revolving door outfit). Seemingly without any personnel for the Cure, Smith joined British punk band Siouxie and the Banshees as their temporary guitarist in 1983. He also joined the Banshees' side project the Glove, which proved to be a short-lived endeavor. All the while he strengthened his guitar chops, using the Banshees as the means to a harder-edged personal style.

Resurrecting the band in 1984 for *The Top,* Smith added his increasingly dark guitars to the mix, but brought in former Cure sessionman Porl Thompson on guitar for the next record, *The Head on the Door.* The band broke through in America with *Kiss Me, Kiss Me, Kiss Me* in 1987, but it wasn't until *Disintegration* in 1989 that the Cure found their perfect voice. Driven throughout by the melodic lines of bassist Simon Gallup, Smith and Thompson literally weave together a hypnotic tangle of guitars that is as dense and melodic as anything ever put on vinyl. Tracks like "Fascination Street" are wrapped around a jarring bass line, with guitar feedback, lead licks, and repeated riffs floating in and out of the mix. Conversely, "Lullaby" features a simple two-chord pattern sliced through with a jangly lead line and funky bass. Although the approach to guitars is different on each cut, there is no mistaking them as Cure tunes: Smith had become a master at the art of layering different guitar parts together in one inextricable thread.

After a successful tour of the world in 1989 and 1990, the Cure was the most important band in nontraditional rock circles, able to sell out stadiums that had largely been the domain of metal groups. In 1992 the band issued *Wish,* an even denser guitar package—as if that's possible—that features third guitarist Perry Bamonte. Tracks like "Open" and "From the Edge of the Deep Green Sea" are so tightly packed with guitars that it's hard to aurally separate out just how many guitars Smith had crammed into the tracks. Even with all that density, the record is not overproduced, nor does it lose any of its melodic gloominess. "Open," in particular, has a single growling riff floating somewhere near the top of a two-chord progression while screaming licks—not solos—swell in from the outside corners of the mix before feeding back into droning noise that washes out when the next set of licks flange in from the opposite side of the mix. With so many guitars in the mix, "Open" threatens to create sensory overload in unsuspecting listeners.

In terms of their six-stringing, the Cure was never a lead guitar band. Any outstanding guitar parts tended to be repeated riffs or occasional licks that seemed planned as part of the overall song. Jangly acoustic guitars jelled with heavy electrics and wah-wah riffs, but they were always song components and not individual showcases. Smith and Thompson are both quite capable guitarists, yet they always play with personal restraint. Their self-indulgence comes not with the way they play, but how many parts they play, and how many effects they apply to those parts.

Thompson left the band after the *Wish* tour (captured on the LP *Show* in 1993) and ended up joining with Jimmy Page and Robert Plant as second guitarist for their Page/Plant reunion album and tour. For *Wild Mood Swings* (1996), former roadie Perry Bamonte took over the reins from Thompson, which gave a simpler, yet less appealingly moody, guitar texture to the band's music.

The Cure [on Fiction/Elektra], *Three Imaginary Boys* (1979), *Boys Don't Cry* (1980), *Seventeen Seconds* (1980), *Faith* (1981), *Pornography* (1982), *The Top* (1984), *The Head on the Beach* (1985), *Standing on a Beach* (1986), *Kiss Me, Kiss Me, Kiss Me* (1987), *Disintegration* (1989), *Mixed Up* (1990), *Wish* (1992), *Show* (1993•), *Paris* (1993•), *Wild Mood Swings* (1996).

The Cult

Billy Duffy

Born: *May 12, 1961, in Manchester, England*
Main Guitar: *Gretsch White Falcon*

Billy Duffy grew up listening to Bill Nelson of Be Bop Deluxe, Steve Jones of the Sex Pistols, and Thin Lizzy's Brian Robertson and Scott Gorham. From these disparate influences, he created a heavy style that incorporated the brashness of punk with the bombast of melodic heavy metal and the polish of 1970s progressive rock.

Duffy played with Theatre of Hate in 1982, but exited in 1983 to team up with vocalist Ian Astbury in the Southern Death Cult, which shortened its name to Death Cult with Duffy's arrival. Astbury was steeped in the early goth movement and had added Native American imagery to his take on the genre, while Duffy's love was with hard rock and punk. Finally shortening their name to just the Cult, they released their first record, *Dreamtime*, in 1984. Their first taste of success came in 1985 with the album *Love* and its single "She Sells Sanctuary." The song was a goth milestone, combining heavy guitar with pulsating, even danceable rhythms. But the album is a chaotic affair, leaning at times towards moody dance music and other times towards post-punk abrasiveness.

Pursuing a heavy touring schedule, the band went into the studio to record their next album, but failed to find a cohesive mix of Astbury's and Duffy's input. They hired producer Rick Rubin, who turned the material into a solid hard rock entity that was released as *Electric* in 1987. From their cover of Steppenwolf's "Born to Be Wild" to the near-metallic power of "Wildflower" and "Love Removal Machine," the Cult cranks up the volume and doesn't stop. Duffy leads every song with power chords and thick riffs that bring together the best rhythm styles of the Rolling Stones and Led Zeppelin with the unpolished recklessness of punk. His fills are pure hard rock in the tradition of Richards, Iommi, and Page, while his solos have a searing quality that finds its roots in heavily amplified blues-rock. There hadn't been rock like this in the U.K. since the late seventies.

Electric proved to be immensely popular, and the band set out on a world tour, with a then-unproven Guns N' Roses as their opening act. The time spent on the road solidified the band's hard rock sound, and they discarded the final remains of its goth days. In 1989 the Cult released *Sonic Temple*, their biggest and most aggressive album ever. The cover photo alone, with Duffy wearing a low-slung Les Paul and an upraised arm ready to strike, hints at the album's contents. Unleashing an even more violent barrage of guitars than that found on *Electric*, *Sonic Temple* proved that the Cult was the only British rock band playing hard and heavy rock as if they meant it. From the finger-ripping opening strains of "Sun King" to the phased licks of "Fire Woman" on to light acoustic picking and electric harmony leads of "Edie (Ciao Baby)," the band covers the entire hard rock map in a way that few had done since the demise of Led Zeppelin. Duffy was elevated to near guitar-god status, and the only thing keeping him from being a guitar deity was the reluctance of the British press to admit that such guitar bombast was valid in the late 1980s. In America, however, Duffy and the Cult were selling thousands of albums and selling out coliseums. One more monster album would put them into the big leagues forever.

Unfortunately, that album never came. *Ceremony*, the 1991 follow-up to *Sonic Temple*, fell right into the trap laid for big rock acts by grunge. People didn't want British guitar bombast, they wanted the post-punk Seattle sound. This proved untimely for the Cult. The album is musically sound, featuring much of the same diversity as *Sonic Temple*, but lyrically Astbury retreats to the Native American fetish of his Southern Death Cult days—a move that put off many fans in the politically correct 1990s. Songs such as the title cut and "If" are fleshed out with sensuous grooves and multitracked guitars that show Duffy in fine form. Despite its many high points, the album is not of the same quality as *Sonic Temple* from beginning to end. To make matters worse, *Ceremony* was just the wrong album at the wrong time. One year earlier and it would have stormed the charts, one year later and it never would have been released.

The band retreated to lick its wounds and to sort out a variety of personal problems and frictions caused by nearly a decade on the road. They returned with the eponymous 1994 LP, *The Cult*, which featured more acoustic playing but considerably less of the malevolent beauty of *Sonic Temple*. It seemed as if the band had some of their fire plucked out during the metal backlash of the early 1990s. The group broke up when Astbury left to form the Holy Barbarians in late 1995, although there were rumors that Duffy would continue on without him. Regardless, Duffy is still the last hard rock guitar star to come out of Britain during the 1980s and 1990s. Few dare to play as flamboyantly and as venomously as he does, and

Billy Duffy

his in-your-face style may be the last one Britain sees until the twenty-first century.

The Cult [on Sire], *Dreamtime* (1984), *Love* (1985), *Electric* (1987), *Sonic Temple* (1989), *Ceremony* (1991), *The Cult* (1994).

The Church

Marty Willson-Piper
M a i n   G u i t a r : *Rickenbacker electric 12-string*

Peter Koppes
M a i n   G u i t a r : *Fender Stratocaster*

Although their origins in Australia kept the band from being a direct part of the Euro-pop or Euro-goth movements, the Church created their own guitar-oriented psychedelic and dreamy style that dovetailed perfectly with musical trends in both the U.K. and America during the late 1980s and early 1990s.

The band was formed in 1981 with Steve Kilbey on bass and vocals, Marty Willson-Piper on lead guitar, Peter Koppes on rhythm guitar, and Richard Ploog on drums. They released their first album in Australia shortly after this lineup was in place. Initially the Church was a fairly straightforward pop rock group, but with each successive album, they experimented with more guitar textures and nuances. Willson-Piper's increased use of a Rickenbacker 12-string added jangly cascades of sound to the records, evoking at times the more adventurous outings of the Byrds. Koppes' playing was more straightforward, holding down the rhythm patterns and generally providing unadulterated rock licks. Both of them were enamored of effects boxes, which got put to better and more extensive use as their careers progressed.

It was on *Heyday* in 1985 that the Church found their own unique musical voice, writing and playing tightly wound pop songs that are bathed in guitar psychedelia and Steve Kilbey's detached vocals. The opening track, "Myrrh," is a prime example, using arpeggiated notes strewn over quickly strummed chords and a pulsing bass line that are all offset by chiming harmonics, volume swells, and amp-tremolo segues. Other tunes, including "Tantalized" and "Night of Light," are more obvious rockers that the band bends slightly out of shape with echo effects and over-processed power-chord droning.

The Church had their first American hit with *Starfish* (1988). It contains "Under the Milky Way," which became a radio and MTV staple. The song incorporates all the elements that the band had as a standard part of its arsenal: Willson-Piper's open-chord strumming of suspended and major seventh chords on the 12-string, Koppes' complementary six-string rhythm chording, and the generous use and abuse of guitar sounds like feedback and drones slashing into the song at all the right points. This formula is put to even better use on "Hotel Womb," which builds on a simple riff that turns into a shimmering open-chord progression

that in turn fragments into several separate and surreal guitar sections. On "Blood Money" and "Reptile," the band layers these same textures over tighter and more agitated rock riffs, elevating their power pop to hard rock levels. Often the only thing that keeps the Church from being a hard rock band is their ability to take the rougher edges off the guitars with sweeping effects and the use of open chords instead of barre chords.

Having defined themselves once and for all with *Starfish*, the band followed up with *Gold Afternoon Fix* (1990) and *Priest = Aura* (1992), both of which produced the requisite singles. But neither effort was as warmly received as *Starfish*, and the band's popularity waned in the U.S. All of the band members have been pursuing side projects, and between them they released nearly two dozen solo or collaborative albums outside of the Church during the 1980s and 1990s, including stints with Jack Frost, All about Eve, Tom Verlaine, and Hex. Citing personal and professional differences, Richard Ploog left the band before *Priest = Aura*, and then Peter Koppes left after the record's release, ostensibly to seek his own muse. By 1994 the band consisted of just Kilbey and Willson-Piper, who released *Sometime Anywhere* that same year as a duo. In mid 1996 the Church released *Magician among the Spirits*, which featured guest performances by Koppes, even though the band had become essentially a Kilbey and Willson-Piper partnership.

With a fairly extensive catalog of recorded work, the Church's guitar playing styles are well-documented. Willson-Piper is a master of utilizing open chords to maximize the droning effects of open strings. He gets more mileage out of three-finger chord structures on a Rickenbacker electric 12-string than many guitarists do with five-finger barre chords on a Strat, utilizing techniques as simple as accenting the bass notes while plucking or strumming the root or repeating a haunting arpeggio over and over. Koppes was the perfect foil: he fills in the wide open guitar spaces with a more traditional approach to electric playing.

Guitar pairings that allow each guitarist to play completely different parts and still mesh with each other do not come along frequently, and it is doubtful that anyone will be able to duplicate the Church's brand of textured and psychedelic guitar rock for some time to come.

The Church [on Arista except where noted], *Of Skins and Heart* (1981), *The Blurred Crusade* (1982), *Seance* (1983), *Remote Luxury* (1984), *Heyday* (1985), *Starfish* (1988), *Gold Afternoon Fix* (1990), *Priest = Aura* (1992), *Sometime Anywhere* (1994), *Magician among the Spirits* (White/Deep Karma, 1996).

CHAPTER THIRTY-TWO

Grunge
Death of the Guitar Hero

The pendulum swung back hard at the beginning of the nineties. Drawing from the well of heavy metal, punk, and seventies pop rock, grunge became the *de facto* sound of rock 'n' roll in the early nineties. Led by a flannel-shirted and army-booted group of musicians from Seattle, grunge reflected the anger, angst, and aimlessness of the post-baby boom generation. It also brought about, with the release of a single song, the death of the rock guitar hero. Indeed, grunge is as much about guitar anti-heroes as anything else.

The whole decade of eighties metal and its various incarnations (pop, glam, thrash, heavy, etc.) produced a musical backlash of unprecedented proportions. While bands like Mötley Crüe and Whitesnake pouted and preened their way through videos that rejoiced in the rock-star-as-millionaire pose, thousands of aspiring guitarists in the late eighties consciously rejected that ideal. As part of the poorly named, demographically challenged Generation X, young rockers knew instinctively that the rich rock star ethic was nonsense. This new generation of adolescents was told that they would never have the things their parents had—the first time in the history of America that this would be so—and they weren't buying into the glamour and greed of the obviously spoiled and sated metal rock stars. Instead, they drew their inspiration from three of the most misunderstood and maligned forms of electric

music—metal, punk, and seventies pop—and fused them all together.

First and foremost, these up-and-coming guitarists embraced the raw and primitive playing style of punk, emphasizing energy and lack of finesse over technique and precision. They culled their playing styles from the Sex Pistols, the Dead Boys, and even Neil Young (many people feel that side two of Young's *Rust Never Sleeps* was the first set of true grunge songs). Also figuring in the mix were essential eighties post-punks like the Replacements, Hüsker Dü, Black Flag, and the highly influential Melvins (featuring guitarist King Buzzo), out of Aberdeen, Washington.

Then the grunge riffers went back to the roots of heavy metal, giving their punk playing style a more ominous and distorted sound. As such, the sound of grunge guitar is heavier and more layered than punk, resembling at times the thick bludgeoning guitars of Black Sabbath, Uriah Heep, Slade, and other groups from the heyday of early metal. By combining metal with punk's recklessness, the result was a free-form slag of melodic sound popularly known—for lack of a better term—as grunge.

The third element was just as important, though. Finding twisted solace in the lightweight cheeriness and mindless pop of Cheap Trick, the Knack, Abba, and even various mop-top outfits of the sixties, grunge bands extracted the melodic hooks, vocal lines, and simple guitar solos from these groups and grafted them onto their punk/metal sound. The result was everything that most metal was not: catchy, spontaneous, rhythmic, raw, angst-ridden, and even—gasp—

Kurt Cobain

singable. The best grunge songs could be TV commercials for a dispossessed generation.

The earliest proponents of grunge were from the rainy musical hinterland of Seattle, which had produced Jimi Hendrix, Heart, and Queensrÿche—but little else. Some claim it was the rain, some claim it was the slump in the logging industry, some claim it was just the lack of opportunity, but Seattle had plenty of angry teens, and plenty of them played guitar. A local record label, Sub Pop, captured the angst of these bands in the late eighties, putting out records by Seattle bands that gradually attracted national attention to the then-unnamed rock 'n' roll hybrid.

The chief purveyors of the sound were Nirvana and Green River, the latter band being the spawning ground for future grungemeisters Mother Love Bone and Mudhoney. Mother Love Bone, in turn, served as the nucleus of Pearl Jam, perhaps the most commercially successful of the grunge bands and the one rock group that brought grunge squarely into the mainstream. The Sub Pop label fostered grunge right up until its commercial breakthrough, which came with the major-label release of Nirvana's *Nevermind* in 1991. The first single off the album, "Smells Like Teen Spirit," changed the course of guitar playing, and commercial record releases, for the rest of the decade.

From that point forward, the dam burst open. Record companies descended on Seattle, signing everything that moved—and lots of things that didn't. Anything that wasn't metal or blues or techno was grunge (or the more absurd "alternative"), even if it wasn't from Seattle. Good hard rock bands like Stone Temple Pilots, from San Diego, were considered grunge simply because there was no way else for the media to pigeonhole them. The playing style and attitude of STP's guitarist Dean DeLeo actually owes more to the existence of Jimmy Page and Joe Perry than anything resembling the anti-rock star ethic of grunge (to boot, he's a big Allan Holdsworth fan, which is about as far away from grunge as one can get). STP's releases have been multi-platinum sellers that cross several genres, yet the band has had to fight the grunge tag and comparisons to groups like Pearl Jam. Dinosaur Jr.'s J. Mascis, considered a near-guitar god of grunge for such stripped-down masterpieces as *Green Mind* (1991) and *Where You Been* (1993), has been summarily lumped in with the grungers, despite the fact that he plays crisp solos—regularly—and has a distinctive guitar sound. His laid-back punk-meets-folk style has little to do with grunge, but this meant nothing to a world bent on grungifying everyone.

This attempt to classify bands in the nineties, and the failure to do it with any consistency, ensured that almost any loud guitar band with an album out between 1991 and 1995 got tagged as a grunge band. Yet, like any rock genre, especially those driven by loud guitars, grunge experienced a backlash. Industrial, retro, glam, and mid-nineties Euro-pop (as purveyed by Catherine Wheel, Bush, Oasis, and their ilk) drew popular attention away from grunge. The anti-celebrity attitude of most grunge artists (epitomized by Kurt Cobain's suicide and Eddie Vedder's public pursuit of privacy) also fueled fan disdain and led audiences to less oppressive, more upbeat music.

The transition away from grunge has been an easy one for guitarists to make. Grunge is hardly a demanding musical style, and glam and Euro-pop are just as easy to play on the guitar—in most cases grunge is just lots of loud, distorted, power-chord strumming, often in dropped-D tuning. Most of the difference is simply in the approach to tone: retro, glam, and the others use choruses, flangers, and echo units in place of fuzzed-out distortion. As grunge has begun sailing into the sunset, more and more styles have risen up in its wake. There has been more punk: Offspring, Green Day, and Korn, for example. There is also more rootsy, retro, and refined "alternative" rock: Soul Asylum, Spin Doctors, Live. There've been more reunions: Page & Plant, Dokken, Mountain, the Beatles. Never has the diversity of the electric guitar been more evident than in the various styles that have emerged to take the place of the place of grunge since the mid nineties. For a time, it's been anything goes. To be a guitarist in the mid nineties—any kind of guitarist—has meant an unlimited array of opportunities. It just hasn't meant being a guitar god. Anonymity, unfortunately, is the price of unrestrained musical diversity.

Nirvana

Kurt Cobain

Born: *February 20, 1967, in Seattle*
Died: *April 8, 1994, in Seattle*
Main Guitar: *Fender Jaguar, Mustang, and Jag-Stang*

Despite his personal demons, Kurt Cobain proved to the world that a guitarist didn't have to be particularly fast, gifted, technically adept, or even in tune to be considered a guitar hero (or, more accurately, guitar *anti*-hero). What mattered—and has always mattered in the creation of popular music—was the ability to convey emotion and passion within the limited confines of six strings. This was something that Cobain did better than most of the musicians of his generation.

Cobain's simple chord progressions and pop melodies, played with reckless abandon at full volume, became the signature style of grunge guitar, although Cobain admitted to a lack of interest in the guitar as an instrument to be mastered. Nirvana's "Smells Like Teen Spirit" (a subtle reworking of the same structure that ran through Boston's "More than a Feeling") became the hallmark of grunge guitar: elementary chord structure, overdriven and distorted sound, and minimal solos.

Suffering through a broken family life on the outskirts of Seattle, the left-handed Cobain played guitar as a matter of course—it gave him something to do. He was influenced by numerous "indie" punk bands, including the Vaselines, the Pixies, and the Raincoats, but also by the melodic pop bands of the seventies. He put this formula to use in his band Nirvana, the resulting music being something he described as "the nineties version of Cheap Trick or the Knack."

Playing the dreary club circuit between Olympia and Seattle, Nirvana would wear dresses, smash equipment, berate the audiences—anything to get a rise, a response from their crowds. Cobain and the band were simply loud thrashers at first, but as he became a more confident singer and songwriter, the guitar playing followed. His style rarely deviated from simple chords, and his solos were of the Neil Young variety—herky-jerky, quick, and with traces of the vocal line in them.

Their stage reputation, and a repertoire of increasingly catchy songs, got them signed to Sub Pop, which released their first album, *Bleach*, in 1989. Though it was an independent release, *Bleach* took off, making its way to the offices of Geffen records, which quickly signed the band. Geffen was on a signing binge, and Nirvana was expected to be one of the label's "baby bands," meaning that the label might nurture the band over several albums in hopes of seeing Nirvana break into the big time (major Geffen acts at the time were Aerosmith, Guns N' Roses, and Whitesnake). Nirvana's first album for Geffen, *Nevermind*, broke all the industry barriers, going to #1, becoming the surprise hit of 1991–92, and changing the face of rock music for the rest of the decade. Cobain's fuzzed, full-throttle guitar on songs like "Lithium" and "Breed" showed that he had gained control over his instrument, reining in some of the reckless—and oftentimes tuneless—cacophony of his punk inclinations. Instead, on *Nevermind* he created tight arrangements and cut-to-the-quick guitar lines. The solo on "Smells Like Teen Spirit" was quintessential Cobain: it was a direct reading of the vocal line, simple and chromatic, yet smeared with layers of dirty effects. To boot, the infectious chorus featured slamming power chords and a sick series of bends to top it off. It was grunge incarnate.

Still, the band was ill-prepared for its success, and as *Nevermind* became the definitive album for a generation of angry adolescents, Cobain retreated from the limelight. While planning the follow-up to *Nevermind*, Nirvana released *Incesticide*, an album of outtakes and B sides from various stages of the band's career. Rumors of internal problems swelled up around the band, the most notable of which was Cobain's use of heroin (ostensibly to offset the pain of a stomach malady). He also became a news item—the last thing he wanted—by keeping romantic company with Courtney Love, the outspoken lead singer of the band Hole.

In 1993, Nirvana unveiled *In Utero*. The album lived up to expectations created by *Nevermind* and caused a media frenzy with its anatomically correct cover art. (Many record chains and department stores would not carry it.) While every bit as hard as *Nevermind*, *In Utero*—which debuted at #1—also offered a much softer and even relaxed Cobain, especially on tunes like "Penny Royal Tea" and the hit "All Apologies." The lyrical content was still as vitriolic as ever, but Cobain had found a less over-the-top way of conveying his anger musically.

It seemed as if Cobain and Nirvana had come to grips with

their popularity as they embarked on a tour in support of *In Utero*. Cobain married Courtney Love, had a child, and appeared to be settling into his role as reluctant spokesman for a generation. But his heroin problem had gotten worse, and he was hospitalized while on tour in Italy in early 1994. Then, in April 1994, Cobain was found dead in his Seattle home. He had committed suicide with a shotgun blast to his head; he had been dead three days before his body was discovered.

It was a tragic end to an extremely short but influential career. Later in 1994, when Geffen released *Unplugged in New York*, a recording of Nirvana's performance on the MTV show "Unplugged," it too soared to the top of the charts. The semi-acoustic record showed that Cobain was not entirely comfortable with anything but an electric guitar; perhaps there wasn't enough angry punch in an acoustic. He even added an unusual fuzz-acoustic on their compelling remake of David Bowie's "The Man Who Sold the World."

Although Cobain will be remembered more as a cultural icon than as any type of guitar hero, his playing—from the seething force of his hardest rock songs to the lightness of his never-precious ballads—was the standard by which a nation of grunge guitarists would be judged. That's not a bad legacy for a lefty guitarist from Seattle who didn't think he played all that well.

Nirvana [on Geffen except where noted], *Bleach* (Sub Pop, 1989), *Nevermind* (1991), *Incesticide* (1992), *In Utero* (1993), *Unplugged in New York* (1994).

Pearl Jam

Stone Gossard
B o r n : *July 20, 1966*
M a i n   G u i t a r : *Gibson Les Paul*

Mike McCready
B o r n : *April 5, 1965, in Seattle*
M a i n   G u i t a r : *Fender Stratocaster*

Pearl Jam guitarists Mike McCready and Stone Gossard often sound more like a seventies retro band than any of their grunge compatriots. Although Gossard's compositions feature new patterns, the two guitarists also sometimes utilize chord progressions that would not have been out of place on albums from the heyday of hard rock in the seventies or even the psychedelia of the late sixties. They make the old riffs new again, which—as the Rolling Stones and U2 proved before them—is the mark of any great rock 'n' roll band.

Gossard played with bassist Jeff Ament in the seminal Seattle indie punk band Green River. When that band folded, Gossard and Ament formed Mother Love Bone, a Seattle band that was more glam than grunge. This was due to lead singer Andrew Wood, who was something of a Robert Plant-meets-David Lee

Roth frontman, complete with the retro clothes and big rock star swagger. Mother Love Bone was on the verge of its first major label release when Wood died of a heroin overdose. Shattered, the remaining band members went their separate ways.

Gossard and Ament hooked up with Mike McCready, a Hendrix-loving guitarist steeped in the bluesy rock of the sixties and early seventies. They put together a band, without a lead singer, and recorded a number of demos. Through a series of happy accidents, they came into contact with Eddie Vedder, who moved to Seattle from San Diego to sing with the band. He added vocals to the demos, and the result was a new band, Pearl Jam, and a complete album, *Ten*. Pearl Jam was signed by Epic Records, which released *Ten* to an underwhelming response in 1991. Its (then) unidentifiable sound was hard for radio stations and the media to finger; they couldn't tell if it was hard rock, retro rock, proto-punk, or anything else. When Nirvana's *Nevermind* took the music world by storm, only then could people point to Pearl Jam and say, "Oh, they're a *grunge* band. We like that." With the grunge tag firmly affixed, *Ten* started making its way up the charts, eventually going multi-platinum. The band's reputation as a hard-working live band and the memorable hooks from *Ten* placed Pearl Jam at the forefront of grunge, successfully putting them eye-to-eye with Nirvana in the minds and wallets of the record-buying public. (This led Kurt Cobain to disparage Pearl Jam; he felt that they were too slick and commercial-sounding to be considered a grunge band.)

Ten was a diverse offering that showed how well Gossard and McCready worked together. Gossard was the primary songwriter, and also a big believer in riffs. McCready was more the laid-back soloist and utility man who had been weaned on the blues-inspired music of guitarists like Jimi Hendrix, Jimmy Page, and Jeff Beck. Thus, they never got in each other's way. The first single from the album, "Alive," featured a deceptively light rock guitar sound coupled with a punchy riff and lead lines. Throughout *Ten*, the two guitarists were able to link this light/heavy atmosphere in a way that was not—surprisingly—anything like Led Zeppelin or other practitioners of light/heaviness.

Stone Gossard

On *Ten*, slower cuts like "Black" were made to sound more ragged by applying a thick buzz-saw tone to the guitars. On the other hand, "Why Go" and "Once" blazed in true heavy rock fury, with both guitarists pumping away at overlapping rhythm lines.

Like Nirvana, Pearl Jam became reluctant heroes for a generation. Gossard and McCready remained suitably invisible, though, eschewing any attempts to make them guitar stars. The band's follow-up, *Vs.* (1993), showed both guitarists more highly charged, but perhaps not as focused. The songs did not stand out as individually as those on *Ten* had, although there was no dearth of powerful and even maniacal guitar material. The lead riff on "Rearview Mirror" (surprisingly, written by Vedder), along with the nasty guitar growlings of "Rats" and "Leash," showed that Pearl Jam as a band was taking a heavier approach to their sound; Vedder was also bashing away on rhythm guitar at various points on the album. Yet there were still enough blues-rock and seventies references to make sure the band kept its unique sound, notably on "Glorified G" and even the near-folk of "Daughter." It was apparent that Gossard had relinquished some of the songwriting tasks as the band drew on the influences of all its members.

During a suitably long hiatus (by grunge standards), the band shut itself off from the world, leaving tabloids to speculate about Eddie Vedder's mental condition or the fate of the various members of the band (drummer Dave Abbruzzese was actually fired). With absolutely no fanfare, the band released *Vitalogy* in 1994. Though immensely successful, it was a confusing record that rambled all over the musical map. Nothing stuck out as being of the caliber of the early songs, although "Not for You" was a top draw from the set. Other tracks included sonic weirdness à la the Beatles' "Revolution #9." (Interestingly, the band did not release the Hendrix-inspired "Yellow Ledbetter"—which was a takeoff on "Little Wing"—or their stellar acoustic cover of Victoria Williams' "Crazy Mary," both of which had become radio hits before the release of *Vitalogy*.)

While preparing to tour—and fighting with Ticketmaster about it—McCready and Gossard went off to work on some side projects. McCready joined with Layne Staley of Alice in Chains to record as Mad Season, which released a record in 1995. Gossard dabbled in a number of things; he had already recorded with a group called Brad the previous year. Then, a massive Pearl Jam tour of the U.S. during the summer of 1995 sold out in minutes. There was also their participation as the backing band on Neil Young's album *Mirror Ball*. Clearly, the band's outside interests were not interfering with the public's voracious appetite for all things Pearl Jam.

At the band's peak, it could do no wrong. Many critics have cited vocalist Eddie Vedder as the band's only unique component, wrongly dismissing the instrumental aspect of Pearl Jam as a seventies cover band in nineties clothes. This claim, unfortunately, has detracted from Stone Gossard's and bassist Jeff Ament's innovative song structures, which make Pearl Jam much more interesting and unique than if they were in fact merely the grunge version of the Black Crowes. McCready plays with the requisite amount of sixties and seventies chops, while Gossard remains grunge's best riffmeister, drawing from punk and heavy metal sources. The two are quite competent, although their most obvious strength is Gossard's songwriting abilities. Their decision to remain somewhat invisible amidst the publicity that surrounds the band ensures that, as part of Pearl Jam, neither will be regularly singled out for individual accomplishment.

Pearl Jam [on Epic], *Ten* (1991), *Vs.* (1993), *Vitalogy* (1994), *No Code* (1996).

Recordings featuring Pearl Jam: **Neil Young,** *Mirror Ball* (Reprise, 1995).

eclipsed when grunge broke out nationwide. Thayil grew up in Chicago, teaching himself how to play guitar just so that he could write songs (his mother, a music teacher, was unaware of her son's interest). He eventually moved to Seattle, ostensibly because it was far from the Midwest. Hooking up with various players in the area, he finally teamed with rhythm guitarist and vocalist Chris Cornell to form Soundgarden (named after a public sculpture in Seattle). In this partnership, Thayil concentrated on riffing and spartan solos, while Cornell worked on chording.

After releasing several indie records in the late eighties, Soundgarden signed to A&M, which promptly released *Louder than Love*. Although Thayil cites bands like Kiss, the New York Dolls, the Stooges, and even early Chicago as influences, it's evident from this record that the band drew pretty extensively from the Black Sabbath well. Not only are Thayil's dirge-like riffs right out of the Tony Iommi playbook, but lead singer Chris Cornell's vocals bear an uncanny resemblance to "Sweet Leaf"-era Ozzy Osbourne.

Perhaps unwittingly, Soundgarden strengthened the Sab connection even further when it did a note-for-note cover of Sabbath's "Into the Void"—right down to the reverb'd outro—as a bonus track on *Badmotorfinger* (1991). On that album, Thayil's Sabbath comps are even more in evidence, as his dropped-D tuning reinforces the Iommi comparisons. The break that occurs dead smack in the middle of the MTV hit "Rusty Cage" is vintage Sabbath, right down to the abrupt time changes. Yet "Rusty Cage" is also a perfect example of how Thayil has found new paths on

Soundgarden

Kim Thayil

B o r n : *September 4, 1960, in Seattle*
M a i n   G u i t a r : *Guild S-100*

Chris Cornell

B o r n : *July 20, 1964, in Seattle*
M a i n   G u i t a r : *Gretsch Silver Jet*

Despite their Seattle origins, Soundgarden is more of a heavy metal band than a grunge outfit. Admittedly, it interweaves the lyrical anger of grunge into its music, but the band owes more to Black Sabbath than to any other single source.

Kim Thayil and company had a big following in Seattle as a local metal band, a fact that was all but

Soundgarden: Kim Thayil, Chris Cornell

an otherwise obvious heavy metal route. The opening riff is a tense fusion of psychedelic riff repetitiveness with a near-metal edge, which creates an almost dizzyingly hypnotic mood that is as far from heavy metal as it is from grunge.

Badmotorfinger was a minor success, but Soundgarden remained in the shadow of grunge—Seattle's best-kept secret. Part of the problem was the inability of the music press to classify the monstrous guitar sound of the band. It was too aggressive and hard to be grunge as defined by the likes of Nirvana, but too flexible and melodic to be considered heavy metal. *Superunknown*, released in 1994, changed all that. In fact, the release of *Superunknown* was touted by the press as being the epitome of anti-grunge, making the album the media-designated leader of the grunge backlash.

The title track is the best example of the mature Soundgarden (meaning that it relies very little on obvious past influences). It has a catchy repeated pull-off riff and ferocious wah-wah playing, both of which make it less Sab-like than its predecessors. "Spoonman," the first single off the album, still hearkens back to the seventies—yet it has a distinctly nineties edge, using the sliding chord progression that defined songs like "Cinnamon Girl" and "American Woman." With *Superunknown*, Thayil got to a point in his playing where he could effortlessly meld the styles of his forebears and not make them sound like they were just tossed into some musical blender.

The success of the record made Soundgarden one of the most successful bands of 1994. Its touring schedule and heavy MTV rotation (notably of the churning single "Black Hole Sun," featuring cool Leslie rhythm parts) kept *Superunknown* at the top of the charts for nearly a year, and in that time four of its tracks became radio hits. Still, Thayil is something of a guitar anomaly in the mid nineties: not a bluesman, not a metal monger, and not even a grungemeister. Instead, he manages to synthesize all those styles in a unique way, a fact of life which has kept him—and Soundgarden—afloat after the demise of grunge.

Soundgarden [on A&M except where noted], *Ultramega OK* (SST, 1989), *Louder than Love* (1990), *Badmotorfinger* (1991), *Superunknown* (1994), *Down on the Upside* (1996).

Alice in Chains

Jerry Cantrell

Born: *March 18, 1966*
Main Guitar: *G&L Rampage*

During the grunge era, Jerry Cantrell and company were perhaps the most melodic and musically experimental of all the Seattle bands, rising above the grunge tag with both acoustic and heavy numbers that defied any obvious categorization. In the process, Jerry Cantrell became one of the most accomplished and respected players of the early nineties, something aided by

his guitar-heroesque appearance. Yes, even grunge guitar fans are not above the lure of basic sex appeal.

Cantrell picked up the guitar at 17, at the same time as he was serving as the president of his high school choir. His first instrument, a Fender Mustang copy, had only two strings. The absence of the other four strings didn't phase him, though; he was still able to learn heavy riffs by AC/DC, Ozzy Osbourne, and Van Halen, and got a good working knowledge of fret and string relationships. His mother eventually bought him four more strings when it was evident he wasn't going to give the instrument up.

In the mid eighties, he formed Alice in Chains with three other Seattle-area musicians, notably vocalist Layne Staley. The band played the club circuit, performing intricately heavy songs that flew in the face of the minimalism that was leading to grunge. Cantrell's playing had a certain bottom-heavy crunch similar in tone and feel to that of Tony Iommi (and shared by fellow Seattle non-grunger Kim Thayil), but his riffs and chord progressions reflected a more melodic seventies rock style. He even counted Elton John and Lindsey Buckingham-era Fleetwood Mac as being among his primary songwriting influences, but also subscribed to the light-but-heavy philosophy of vintage bands like Iron Butterfly and Led Zeppelin. This eclectic approach to the Seattle sound, coupled with Staley's tortured vocals and societal angst, separated Alice in Chains from almost every one of their Northwest peers.

The band's 1990 debut, *Facelift*, featured the hard-rock radio single "Man in a Box," an extraordinarily dark chorded piece that found Cantrell mining the deepest, densest of the guitar while employing the infamous eighties talk box. The rest of the album was full of similar foreboding dirges that traded the gothic doom of the seventies for the personal despair of the nineties. As if to prove that he was not another metal mutant, Cantrell changed gears on the band's next record, a 1992 EP called *Sap*, which was a collection of five acoustic songs. Cantrell's acoustic playing was not of the ballad sort; rather, he played lushly arranged tunes that had the melodicism of the best nonelectric offerings from Jethro Tull and Pink Floyd. His sense of harmony belied the band's predominantly metal sounding grunge, providing the band with a layered sound that was utterly foreign to Seattle's shores. This aspect of the band's sound may have had more to do with Cantrell's choir experience than any amount of time spent copping licks from old AC/DC records.

The band went out on tour with Van Halen (Cantrell and Eddie Van Halen became notorious friends during this stint) and then released *Dirt*, a record that went on to sell millions of copies. Employing single-step chromatic riffs on the songs "Junkhead" and "Rooster," Alice in Chains gave obvious nods to songs like Sabbath's "Sweet Leaf" and Zeppelin's "Dazed and Confused." On the completely opposite side of the scale, the single "Would" was an ethereal exercise in psychedelia and sparse playing. Cantrell was all over the map, but it all sounded like Alice in Chains.

After the band headlined at Lollapalooza, word leaked out

that singer Staley had a serious heroin problem (something that became *de rigueur* for many groups associated with grunge). The band punted several high-profile gigs due to Staley's inability to perform, including the 1994 Woodstock Festival. While figuring out what to do with Staley, Alice in Chains released another EP, *Jar of Flies*. Cantrell's playing was even more diverse than it had been on any of the previous albums, blending acoustic strumming with metal riffing and meshing it all with phase shifters, echo, and distortion. As potentially unpalatable as this might have sounded, the result was brilliant, earning Cantrell even more kudos from the community, and defining him as one of the few truly interesting guitarists of the grunge movement.

Staley's continued struggle with drugs kept Alice in Chains from recording. He was ultimately able to pull things together to the point that, in late 1995, the band released the well-received *Alice in Chains*. The group also made a rare concert appearance on MTV's "Unplugged" during 1996, which resulted in a live album, and then opened for Kiss on several dates of its huge reunion tour. There were, however, continued concerns about Staley's health. Regardless of whether or not the singer cleans up his act for good, it's certain that Cantrell will not only land on his feet, but will do well wherever he does land. His compositional style ensures that he will be one of the most watched—and listened to—guitarists at the end of the century.

Alice in Chains [on Columbia], *Facelift* (1990), *Sap* [EP] (1992), *Dirt* (1992), *Jar of Flies* [EP] (1994), *Alice in Chains* (1995), *Unplugged* (1996•).

Recordings featuring Jerry Cantrell: **Twisted Willie,** *Twisted Willie* (1996). **Various Artists,** *The Cable Guy* [soundtrack] (Columbia, 1996).

CHAPTER THIRTY-THREE

Industrial and Grindcore

Noise as Art

Metal was starting to mutate. Towards the end of the eighties and into the nineties, the original "heavy" metal spawned thrash metal, speed metal, death metal, pop metal, art metal, funk metal, and a thousand variations in between. They were all propelled by unique guitar styles that emphasized the appropriate tonal colorings (usually dark and minor-flavored) or speed (usually fast) as necessary. Through all of this, perhaps the most excruciating styles to which heavy metal gave birth were industrial, grindcore, and that beast known as death metal.

Industrial was actually born in the techno-world of the late seventies. Throbbing Gristle, a band whose name alone would launch a thousand industrial groups, began recording and performing as a heavy "performance" band. Their music consisted of tape loops patched together randomly, guitars distorted beyond reason, and heavily effected vocals, while their club gigs had many of the elements of a live sex show. There was, however, no rhythm to the music, which made it quite unpopular in mainstream circles. A band of Throbbing Gristle's contemporaries, called Cabaret Voltaire, took some of the more palatable ideas from Gristle and set them to the pulsating rhythm tracks that were part and parcel of the British dance club scene. Though neither Throbbing Gristle nor Cabaret Voltaire achieved huge success with their experimentation, they did lay the foundation for the essential elements of industrial: taped or sampled sounds and noise, heavy drum (or drum machine) beats played at blood-curdling volume with mind-numbing repetition, and distorted vocals dealing with songs of pain and torture—in the literal sense of the term.

Industrial remained an underground attraction throughout the eighties, even as more bands attempted to make it musically more structured. Groups like Einsturzende Neubauten and KMFDM from Germany, along with Foetus, Nitzer Ebb, and Killing Joke from the U.K., slowly added discernible guitar parts to their mix, with varied results. It wasn't until 1988, when a band called Ministry released *The Land of Rape and Honey*, that industrial found its niche. Ministry, led by Al Jourgensen, essentially fused heavy metal guitars and chord patterns with the noisy machine-like rhythms and samples of industrial music. From there, a natural course of events brought guitars into the dominant role in industrial, relegating the drums and the noise to supporting parts. Bands like Ministry and Nine Inch Nails, which made industrial a commercially successful musical form, led industrial into the nineties with guitars blazing and computers blinking away.

Interestingly, the use of industrial sounds behind heavy guitars was not new in the mid eighties. Pink Floyd had put tape loops of machines and various pulsing mechanical equipment behind David Gilmour's ringing strummed C and E minor chords on "Welcome to the Machine," from *Wish You Were Here*, in 1975. Pop-rocksters Loverboy had dabbled in industrial sounds by simulating pile drivers in the intro to the 1982 hit "Standing in the Strike Zone," and even Foreigner took repeated anvil-like sounds and used them as the basis for the rhythm to "Stranger in My Own House," from *Agent Provocateur* (1984). These were experiments, but they did prove to be precursors of guitar-based industrial music. In the nineties, guitar bands like Pitchshifter, Stabbing Westward, Machines of Loving Grace, and even former pop-metalers Shotgun Messiah meshed their heavy guitar songs with tape machines, samples, and even vintage tone-generating synthesizers to further the cause of modern industrial music.

While industrial took guitar experimentation to new and tortured heights by adding elements of noise to the music, another movement sought to do the same thing by speeding the guitars up to near hyperspeed. They created rhythmic sledgehammers not with drum machines and tape loops, but with speedily riffed guitars. Grindcore began in the late eighties, when a number of British thrash metal bands decided, somewhat oxymoronically, that even thrash was still not aggressive enough for their tastes. Grind was a Brit term for thrash, so there was a natural connection there—a blend of thrash and hardcore. But grindcore was thrash on amphetamines, mixed in with Darth Vaderesque vocals, industrial noise, and lyrics pulled from a coroner's handbook. Grindcore had none of the truly blatant quasi-religious or demonic overtones of death metal, but it was similar in form and content. More than being a vehicle for personal philosophy, however, grindcore was about physically and mentally abusing listeners with guitar sounds to the point of disorientation and even pain.

As grindcore caught on in America during the early nineties, many metal guitar aficionados argued that grindcore was just a British version of thrash or death metal. This was a misinformed oversimplification. Starting with Napalm Death, the band credited with giving a defined shape to grindcore, a whole generation of British grindcore guitarists pushed thrash-style playing as fast as it could go. Napalm Death in turn begat Godflesh and Carcass, and from there, the incestuousness of the grindcore scene was as blatant as its lyrics were grisly. The names of the bands alone provided an indication of the mindset of this generation of metal purveyors: Morbid Angel, Nocturnus, Entombed, Terrorizer, Carnage, Cadaver, Lawnmower Deth, Hellbastard, Painkiller, Naked City, and on and on.

Outside of Godflesh and Carcass, there was not much musically to separate the guitar styles of the grindcore assemblage from their forefathers in the thrash and death camps—except for speed. This was not to say that grindcore guitarists didn't bring anything new to the modern guitar table. Just as James Hetfield, Dave Mustaine, Scott Ian, and Kirk Hammett overran the increasingly bland conventions of early-eighties heavy metal—as hashed out by Mötley Crüe and Ratt—grindcore guitarists were pushing their instruments to even further limits. The boundaries this time around, though, were physical: just how fast could a human being flail away at the strings of a guitar and still make sounds that might be considered musical?

In many cases, the question was rhetorical, because it didn't matter. Napalm Death was famous for recording 30-second blasts of guitar fury that were almost unrecognizable as anything that resembled songs. On the other hand, Napalm Death alumni Justin Broadrick (Godflesh) and Bill Steer (Carcass) were among the most accomplished guitarists of the genre, able to manipulate their instruments with the agility of scalpel-wielding surgeons. While Broadrick favored inventive dissonance and distorted experimentation, Steer was a card-carrying member of the fast-is-best grindcore guitar club. Most grindcore bands avoided solos in favor of noises usually only heard during battlefield massacres, yet Steer had no compunction about speeding his way through post-Yngwie neoclassical solos, admirably shredding over the rhythmic carnage dished out by his bandmates. Steer's lead break on "Buried Dreams," from Carcass' 1994 disc *Heartwork*, was pure eighties shred. His chops, and the harmony lead tradeoffs he did with second guitarist Michael Amott, were right from the neo-flash handbook, making him the only outstanding soloist of the grindcore pack. The fact that he made shred guitar playing work within the molten intensity of grindcore was all the more to his musical credit.

Unfortunately, to get a handle on most grindcore, one had to put up with a slew of glass-gargling vocalists that made AC/DC's Bon Scott and Henry Rollins sound like opera stars. It was part of the style, but it tended to obscure the meatiness and velocity of the underlying riffs. In addition, grindcore as a musical pur-

suit was also something of an endurance contest. Not only were the guitars required to be fast and often razor sharp, but the bass and drums were similarly jet-propelled. The average grindcore tune would give even the most dedicated shredder second thoughts about what speedy chops were all about. Thus, in some respects, grindcore was worth exploring just to hear what really constituted "fast" relative to both rhythm and lead playing. Alas, many guitarists shunned grindcore because of the lyrical and vocal travesties it involved. The closest thing they could get to experiencing the speed and intensity of the genre was to play their vinyl Metallica and Black Sabbath discs at 45 or 78 rpm.

Both industrial and grindcore were acquired tastes, but they were the musical styles that prompted the most radical guitar experimentation in the nineties. Guitarists who dismissed them as noise missed the point of using the guitar as a lethal weapon.

Ministry

Al Jourgensen
Main Guitars: *Miscellaneous Ibanez solidbodies*

Mike Scaccia
Main Guitars: *Miscellaneous Ibanez solidbodies*

Al Jourgensen gave up guitar playing when he discovered his first synthesizer. He decided to be part of the new techno-music revolution of the eighties that was being led by Human League and Thomas Dolby, and there was no place for guitars in techno. Forming a duo called Ministry, Jourgensen recorded an album called *Cold Life*, which was released as an EP in 1983. It featured no guitars and was nothing more than a rehash of British techno; in fact, it was boring. For the next several years,

Ministry: Al Jourgensen *(center)*

Jourgensen put out bland synth-pop on the Wax Trax label before realizing he was making a big mistake.

Jourgensen was not a techno-dweeb. He was an angry and rowdy young man who had tried to fit himself into the mold of the then-popular musical styles that revolved around synthesizers and drum machines. After four years, he switched to industrial. Many of the same elements were there—the computerized gear, the production, the remixing, etc.—but electric guitars were there, too, and bands like KMFDM were showing that it could be done well. He jumped into industrial and switched record labels in the process. But he was reluctant to make the transition from techno-pop to industrial while incorporating guitars all at the same time. He released a strictly industrial album in 1986, *Twitch*, and then—feeling more confident—he picked up the electric guitar for *The Land of Rape and Honey* (1988). With this record, he stuck to simple metal chords in the vein of popular metal contemporaries like Mötley Crüe. The album was an underground favorite, since it was still an industrial record spiced with thick guitars.

It wasn't until *Psalm 69* (1992) that Jourgensen nailed everything. The album was guitar-driven, but it had big production, lots of eerie biblical voices, samples of world leaders' speeches, and plenty of other industrial hallmarks. But it was the guitars that made *Psalm 69* such a definitive industrial work. Huge masses of guitars, riffing incessantly over tunes such as "N.W.O." and "Just One Fix," bombarded listeners. Like early industrial, there was a heavy beat, but this was the monstrous blast of digitized kick drums, not the tinny electro-beeps of cheap drum machines. Jourgensen and partner Paul Barker layered miles of guitars on top of each other, creating a weighty guitar army that marched on relentlessly. Some of the songs had an obvious Sabbath inspiration, while others, like "Jesus Built My Hot Rod," seemed to be a compendium of styles that even included rockabilly.

Jourgensen was nothing if not shrewd. Not only did he have the good sense to bail out of the techno scene, but once he decided to rock hard, he also decided to look the part. Biker gear, long hair and beard, sunglasses, and boots all contributed to his new image as the outlaw of industrial. And the success of *Psalm 69* supported this claim. That success also took the band out on tour, where it made a name for itself on the Lollapalooza tour (which also helped Nine Inch Nails gain a following). Jourgensen and Barker hired guitarist Mike Scaccia, who had been with death metal band Rigor Mortis, to help beef up their stage sound. At times, other guitarists were invited onstage, providing a three- or four-guitar lineup that bludgeoned audiences with cranked amps and skull-shattering riffs. Headbanging was now in the hands of the guitarists, and not the crowd.

Ministry—onstage or in the studio—has always been Jourgensen accompanied by an ever-shifting aggregation of friends and associates playing with the band whenever they were in town or near a local recording studio. It got to the point where there were so many of these people peripherally involved in Ministry that Jourgensen started grouping them into side projects; Ministry couldn't handle them all. Thus, Revolting Cocks,

Pailhead, 1000 Homo DJs, and Lard all became satellites in the Jourgensen/Ministry orbit. Their numbers included members of Nine Inch Nails, Fugazi, and Cabaret Voltaire, among others.

Ministry went on hiatus during 1994 and early 1995 to record a new album and to give Jourgensen time to set up a studio in Austin. That didn't stop him from releasing a variety of one-offs with his side projects, all of which got deeper into the guitar-based industrial music that he helped pioneer. If any single person can be credited with making the electric guitar a successful instrument in the industrial arena, it's Al Jourgensen. Others did it before, and NIN has made more money doing it, but none have done it as well as Ministry.

Ministry [on Sire except where noted], *Twitch* (1986), *The Land of Rape and Honey* (1988), *A Mind Is a Terrible Thing to Taste* (1989), *In Case You Didn't Feel Like Showing Up* (1990•), *Psalm 69: The Way to Succeed and the Way to Suck Eggs* (1992), *Filth Pig* (Warner Bros., 1996).

Nine Inch Nails

Trent Reznor

Born: *May 17, 1965, in Mercer, Pennsylvania*
Main Guitar: *Gibson Les Paul*

Trent Reznor is the one-man band known as Nine Inch Nails. His inventive use of guitars revolutionized the way the instrument is used in digital recording, and NIN is the band that made guitar-driven industrial music a commercial gold mine. As if that weren't enough, the guitars on NIN albums are possibly among the most bizarre sounding ever laid down on computer disk and tape.

Reznor grew up in Ohio and Pennsylvania, bounced from relative to relative. Along the way, he learned piano and bit of guitar, but also became infatuated with computers. He played in several no-name bands in Cleveland before deciding that he could best express his musical ideas by himself. Taking advantage of the Macintosh computer and the variety of music software packages available for it, especially sequencers, Reznor pieced together bits of sound and music to create songs, adding his vocals and some guitar to provide a melodic consistency. This experimentation resulted in *Pretty Hate Machine* (1989), a record that went nowhere when it was released by indie label TVT. While Reznor's tunes had all the elements of industrial music, they were more disarming in that they featured traditional pop-style structures. Thus, it took a while for listeners to decipher what they were hearing, but over the next two years, NIN and *Pretty Hate Machine* climbed their way to mass acceptance.

Asked to participate on the 1991 Lollapalooza tour, Reznor hurriedly assembled a band and proceeded to amaze and impress with his destructive stage shows. Just as NIN began making money and a gaining a national reputation, Reznor and TVT entered a legal battle over the future of NIN. To satisfy his obligations, Reznor released *Broken* in 1992, a stunning EP soaked in some of the most horrific guitar sounds ever put to disc. With *Broken*, Reznor ventured into what he called "male hard rock," trying to capture (or deflect) the rage and disgust he felt during his record company difficulties. From the first moment of the EP, it's clear that the guitar had become Reznor's sound device of choice. The opening cut, "Wish," delivers—at a machine-gun pace—guitars so distorted and overdriven that they're almost unrecognizable. His industrial rage transforms simple guitar parts into chainsaws and mutant machines, bent and beaten by his technological massaging and shattered-glass approach to layering.

But it is "Last" that is NIN's guitar *tour de force*. Not only does it evoke some of the best of heavy metal with its incessant riffs—à la Black Sabbath and Judas Priest—but Reznor also twists the sounds of the guitars into something uniquely his own. On the second verse in particular, he pushes NIN's emerging signature guitar sounds to the breaking point (they sound like they'll shatter under the weight of all the distortion) and then deftly drops in two beats of a different guitar sound. These new guitars, gated and slightly pitch-bent, create a total contrast with the rest of the track. It's one of the coolest guitar sounds to reach the ears of record listeners in the nineties.

The rest of *Broken*—and its evil remixed twin, *Fixed*—follows in the same vein, pushing guitars way up into the mix and delivering the strongest slice of true industrial angst that NIN would ever produce. (Reznor considers himself a pop artist and not an industrial musician.) With *The Downward Spiral* (1994), however, Reznor transcended industrial and heavy metal to become a bona fide mainstream star. The record was an immediate success, and NIN headlined shows around the world. Although *The Downward Spiral* backed off the angry guitar overdrive of *Broken* by a notch, Reznor went in other directions with the guitar. Notably, he brought in Adrian Belew to help out on a number of tracks. Given Belew's own experimental guitar work, particularly the array of elephant sounds and otherworldly guitar voices that he created on his own records and with King Crimson, he was a unique choice to complement Reznor's noise fury. Perhaps no other contemporary guitarist of any renown would have fit the bill as well; no one else (save perhaps Allan Holdsworth) took an extreme enough sonic approach to the guitar. Belew's most obvious contribution to the album is the closing riff to the opening song, "Mr. Self Destruct." Replete with Adrianesque slides and squeals, the guitars are actually looped back in a repeating pattern for nearly 45 seconds throughout the song's closing. This is a perfect example of the kinds of guitar manipulations that run through Reznor's albums—the passage is so mutated and bizarre that it is virtually unrecognizable as a guitar part in the linear and traditional sense of the term.

Elsewhere on *The Downward Spiral*, Reznor even manages to drop in some acoustic guitar work on "The Becoming," a nice touch that evokes the tasteful seventies styles of acoustic guitarists such as CSNY and Al Stewart. He inserts this acoustic simplicity into the sampled screams and pulsing synth beats found in most NIN songs, and with his sense of compositional craft, weaves them together naturally.

The Downward Spiral and its successful tour (wherein NIN reproduced its guitar sounds by means of additional guitarists) brought Reznor a great deal of notoriety. He was asked to do the soundtrack for the highly controversial film *Natural Born Killers*, he started his own record label (Nothing Records), and he got involved in producing and assisting other artists with their projects. One of these involved fellow industrialist Al Jourgensen and his side band 1000 Homo DJs.

In all, Reznor will always be noted primarily for his skills as a songwriter and a frontman, but his guitar playing should not be overlooked, due to its sheer experimental nature and the radical approach he took to recording guitars.

Nine Inch Nails, *Pretty Hate Machine* (TVT, 1990), *Broken* [EP] (TVT, 1992), *Fixed* [EP] (TVT, 1992), *The Downward Spiral* (Interscope, 1994), *Further Down the Spiral* (Interscope, 1995).

Godflesh

Justin Broadrick

M a i n   G u i t a r : *Fender Stratocaster*

The most adventurous of the grindcore guitarists, Justin Broadrick first picked up the guitar at age 10. His stepfather, an ardent fan of Jimi Hendrix and Pink Floyd who kept a Stratocaster around the house, taught Justin the basics of the instrument. Broadrick progressed to playing simple British punk tunes, especially those of the Stranglers, before moving into the heavier realms of Black Sabbath and industrial forefathers Killing Joke. He joined the lineup of what was arguably the first grindcore band, Napalm Death, at the age of 16. With that band long enough to record its debut LP, *Scum*, which was notable for its 30-second-long tracks of guitar violence, Broadrick soon left due to boredom. Eager to explore other avenues, he teamed up with the little-known Head of David—as their drummer. He left HOD soon thereafter, complaining that the band was going in a pop-metal direction similar to Whitesnake or Bon Jovi.

In 1988 he formed Godflesh. Immediately heralded as the future of all things metal, Godflesh attracted attention for the originality of its sound: industrial angst welded to metal hammering. The setup was as simple as Broadrick's single-minded drive—one guitar, one bass, one drum machine, occasional vocals. But Broadrick (and collaborator G.C. Green) took the grindcore style and slowed it way down, using the Sabbath philosophy of dirge-like throbbing and detuned strings to evoke the pain of life. The band's debut, a primitive affair called *Streetcleaner*, was released in 1989 on Earache Records, the mother ship of early grindcore bands. The record was followed by *Slavestate*, *Cold World*, and, in 1992, *Pure*. The latter album featured a variety of strange time shifts and the band's starkest and deepest guitar tones, especially on "Wasn't Born to Follow" and "Monotremata." Along the way, Broadrick and company, which grew to include an additional guitarist and an occasional drummer, flirted with doom-laden techno-style dance rhythms, samples, MIDI, and even more intense walls of sound, never once forsaking the apocalyptic power of the guitar. Godflesh also attracted the attention of eighties guitar icon Joe Satriani and Metallica's Kirk Hammett, both of whom touted Broadrick's playing.

The 1994 EP *Merciless* was the epitome of Broadrick's attempt to create music that could actually melt speakers. In particular, the swelling riffs of "Flowers"—coupled with catchy but cranium-piercing harmonics played in alternating time signatures—seemed to grow louder and louder with each second. The track "Blind" featured a guitar sludge that combined riffing, droning chords, feedback, and guitar samples into an oddly melodic and hypnotic track. Broadrick tuned his Stratocaster and the accompanying bass down a step and a half to maximize the bottom end of the sound, while playing with a metal pick to elicit higher-pitched squeals from the strings. Many of the rhythm instruments on *Merciless* were actually guitar samples deftly arranged to simulate drums. Godflesh released a full-length record, *Selfless*, at the end of 1994, and then headed out on a world tour.

Broadrick, like many of his industrial and grindcore contemporaries (Jourgensen, Reznor), is also a master in the studio. His reputation for getting the most out of digital recording systems has prompted bands as diverse as speed-metal merchants Pantera and nineties alternative-popsters the Lemonheads to ask him for remixes of their tunes.

Broadrick's merit as a guitarist stems not from a unique playing style, but from his ability to see beyond the limits of the guitar. For someone who rarely puts vocals on his records, he conveys some devastating emotions. In a perverse way, Godflesh utilizes one of the most direct forms of guitar playing to emerge since the perfection of acoustic ballads. With ballads or even guitar etudes, the lyrical quality of the acoustic guitar conveys emotions without words. With most rock music, on the other hand, words are necessary to define the precise feeling behind the music; rock guitar tunes could be about almost anything: sex, drugs, power, love, violence, or a host of other topics—all of which are defined by the lyrics. With Godflesh, there's no need for words—the listener knows the doom and despair are there just by experiencing the pulsing rhythm and horrific tonality of the guitars. The guitars in Godflesh are nothing if not raw, naked emotion.

Godflesh [on Earache/Columbia], *Streetcleaner* (1989), *Slavestate* (1990), *Cold World* [EP] (1991), *Pure* (1992), *Merciless* [EP] (1994), *Selfless* (1994), *Songs of Love and Hate* (1996).

CHAPTER THIRTY-FOUR

Hard Rock and Heavy Metal V

Rage 'n' Roll at the End of the Century

The nineties are a curious time for guitarists. Grunge destroyed the guitar hero, and only people like Steve Vai and Joe Satriani have kept their eighties hero status intact, although just barely. Others before them, like Jimmy Page and Eddie Van Halen, have maintained their roles as guitar icons, but they've been doing that for decades. No one new is rising up to claim the mantle.

Various six-stringers have been on the verge of "making it" when they disappeared overnight. Or, in even more bizarre occurrences, guitarists have risen out of nowhere to become overnight sensations, but their glory has hung by a thread as thin as their next *Billboard* chart position. Blame a short-sighted record industry, a schizophrenic MTV, and a fickle buying public.

A number of hard rock guitarists have stood ready to pick up at the crossroads where thrash, death, pop, glam, and every other metal intersected. An unknown band called Candlebox took more than a year to climb to the top of the charts in 1994. When Candlebox arrived, their previously unknown guitarist, Peter Klett, was suddenly filling up the pages of the guitar magazines. Conversely, John Christ took a long and dirge-laden route to stardom with his Satanic-cartoon band, Danzig. Propelled by the blessings of the ever-influential Beavis & Butthead (a statement we make, sadly, in all seriousness), Danzig was ready to be the next big-time arena act with its 1994 release *Danzig 4*. For whatever reason—overhype, oversaturation, overkill—the album died on arrival, and Christ's rise to stardom, along with that of Dio clone Glenn Danzig, was stopped short. Going even further, Ty Tabor of King's X was touted as being the one guitarist who was going to set the standard for tasteful guitar playing in progressive metal circles. That was in the late eighties; as of the mid nineties, he still wears that tag. Prong's guitarist, Tommy Victor, went from being a soundman at CBGB's in New York in the late eighties to being hailed as the next great guitar thrashmeister of the nineties—all on the strength of one MTV video and a powerful 1994 album entitled *Cleansing*. Other players who've stepped briefly into the guitar-god spotlight, only to be bumped out a few weeks later by the next in line, include Page Hamilton of Helmet, J. Yuenger of White Zombie, and Tom Morello of the politically charged Rage against the Machine. Will these players become our future axe icons, or are they just one-offs in the endless parade of guitar poster boys? Who knows?

In short, the nineties just aren't designed for longevity. Corporations are breaking up and going bankrupt; so are bands. Corporations are also looking for short-term returns; record companies are no exception. It takes a great deal to stand out from the crowd in the nineties for any length of time, and only two guitarists have been able to do it for more than 15 minutes—total. The interesting thing is that Dimebag Darrell and John Petrucci are in two of the most dissimilar bands to make the charts in the nineties (they've shared the same record label, though). Maybe that's why the two of them have come to be the only hard rock guitar heroes for the anti-hero age.

Dimebag Darrell

Pantera

Dimebag Darrell

Born: *Darrell Abbott, on August 20, 1966, in Dallas*
Main Guitars: *Dean ML, Washburn Dimebag Darrell model*

Pantera led the second generation of thrash and speed metalers out of the closet with guitarist Dimebag Darrell's blitzkrieg chops and frontman Phil Anselmo's misogynistic and usually brutish lyrics. In the process, they became the most successful thrash-mongers to emerge in the wake of Metallica's and Megadeth's commercialization in the early nineties.

Encouraged by his father, Darrell learned guitar as a child while growing up outside of Dallas, copping Ace Frehley licks and Randy Rhoads runs off of albums. From Kiss, he got a sense of the outrageous; from Rhoads and guitarists like Eddie Van Halen and Michael Schenker, he got speed and a flair for flashy techniques. He also developed a penchant for Texas bluesman Bugs Henderson and other bluesy players. An admitted soloing fanatic, the teenage Darrell entered local battles of the bands and guitar competitions just to blast the pants and fingers off all challengers. In this way he won gear that allowed him and his brother Vinnie to form Pantera with a bass player known only as Rex. In the mid eighties the band played basic rock and roll—Kiss and Aerosmith covers *ad infinitum*—until it hooked up with vocalist Anselmo. Deciding to make their music as brutal as possible, the band opted for a thrash metal direction, abandoning all pretense of mainstream rock as it headed into the nineties.

The band's first release was *Cowboys from Hell* (1990), an album of hardcore thrash tunes that won the band an immediate following amongst metal radio listeners. The prime cut was "Cemetery Gates," a track that careened all over the spectrum with Darrell's leads and heavily distorted chords. Using a simple chromatic chord progression, the band set the tone for its music: basic underlying musical themes played at frenetic speeds that were only broken up by Darrell's solos. The rhythm section of Rex and Vinnie managed to keep things interesting while Darrell stepped outside of the main riffs to solo, avoiding overdubs as often as he could (à la Van Halen).

A heavy touring ethic whipped the band's early fans into a frenzy, which sent Pantera's second release, *Vulgar Display of Power*, scurrying up the charts in 1992. Even more mind-boggling than its predecessor, *Vulgar Display* set new metal standards for its combination of merciless tone, speed, and chops. Opening with "Mouth for War," a cut that showcased Darrell's finger-blurring runs and bent harmonic notes, Pantera established a take-no-prisoners attitude on every track. Another killer track was "Rise," which featured fast single-note picking that brought to mind the modal mastery of Scorpions' Uli Roth.

In short order, Darrell became the darling of young metal fans who were already tiring of Metallica's and Megadeth's flirtations with acoustic songs and mainstream success. To them, Darrell, in all his primitive and down-home glory, was the real thing. No pretenses, no effects (save for a DigiTech Whammy Pedal), Darrell was just a regular guy who could play tasty, blazing solos over Pantera's brain-crushing riffage. A guitar hero for the nineties was in the making, and this was not lost on the guitar magazines and the product manufacturers, who picked up on Darrell's four-letter vocabulary and rough-shod attitude like kids diving for Halloween candy. Ironically, Pantera toured as the opening act for Skid Row, whose career was already faltering. To be charitable, it could be said that a significant proportion of fans showed up each night to catch Pantera's blistering set (and participate in mosh pit acrobatics).

The buzz from *Vulgar Display of Power* barely prepared the world for *Far beyond Driven* (1994). Anticipation for the album was so high it debuted at #1 in *Billboard*. Yet the record was so over-the-top that even diehard fans had to say "enough." *Far beyond Driven* was, at its core, a continuous onslaught of intense speed riffing and double bass drumming, fueled to psychotic levels by Anselmo's Neanderthal tirades. The album delivered what everyone had wanted—but it delivered too much of it. With the exception of a note-for-note cover of Black Sabbath's "Planet Caravan," Pantera didn't let its listeners come up for a moment's air. Darrell showed no restraint, only an attempt to play more notes faster and with more aggression than he ever had before.

While the album did well, it didn't have the staying power that the band's minions had hoped for. Instead, Pantera was in danger of becoming a parody of itself—even after a mere three albums. The "Cowboys from Hell" image had worn a little thin, and the band hadn't done anything to shore it up (Darrell had even changed his public moniker from "Diamond" back to the stoner-oriented "Dimebag"). In addition, *Far beyond Driven* hadn't broken any new ground, and Anselmo's limitations as a vocalist and especially as a lyricist were more evident than ever.

The standouts on the album were Darrell and Vinnie, whose collective playing still made thrash fans bang their heads that much harder. Darrell's chops alone ensure that he will be held in high regard by metal fans of all stripes, no matter what fate might befall Pantera in the future.

Pantera [on East/West], *Cowboys from Hell* (1990), *Vulgar Display of Power* (1992), *Far beyond Driven* (1994), *The Great Southern Trendkill* (1996).

Dream Theater

John Petrucci

Main Guitars: *Ibanez custom RG and John Petrucci model*

If shredding and technical proficiency were all but dead by the mid nineties, no one told Dream Theater's John Petrucci, who has become the only beacon of hope in a quickly dwindling flash guitar community.

Petrucci played guitar in high school, learning licks and attending clinics by Steve Morse, one of his primary influences. He went on to attend the Berklee College of Music in Boston, where he met other musicians that would become the core of Dream Theater. A fan of Al Di Meola, Yngwie Malmsteen, Steve Howe, and Alex Lifeson, Petrucci also listened to harder bands like Iron Maiden and Metallica. Dream Theater was thus born as a hard progressive rock band in the early nineties.

Combining Rush-like bombast with a not-quite-classical shred mentality, Dream Theater carved a niche for themselves as an art-rock band with few peers, aside from Queensrÿche and King's X, neither of whom matched their high-caliber musicianship. The group's first release went largely unnoticed, but its 1992 follow-up, *Images and Words*, opened the eyes and ears of mainstream fans and diehard shredders alike. Featuring ultra-slick new vocalist James LaBrie, the main attraction was the neo-Rush sound of the album's single, "Pull Me Under," which displayed Petrucci's knack for intense solos that combine melody, fretboard wizardry, and astounding speed.

The record's art-rock feel filled a void that no one knew existed, and sales of *Images and Words* well surpassed the 200,000 mark. Unfortunately, the next Dream Theater release, *Awake* (1994), was an exercise in self-indulgence. With nothing nearly as accessible as "Pull Me Under," the album stalled on the charts. The fact that most of the songs were over six minutes, and as long as 11 minutes, kept the band off the airwaves and out of regular MTV rotation, though the album did sizable international business, especially in Japan. While *Awake* didn't offer any signs of stylistic development from the band, Petrucci's chops were as slick and surgically precise as ever. Undaunted, the band released an EP in mid 1995 that featured a single epic, the 20-minute-plus "A Change of Seasons." The band may have been preaching to the converted, however, and signs were that it was already in the "Tales from Topographic Oceans" stage of its career.

Dream Theater [on East/West except where noted], *When Dream and Day Unite* (Mechanic, 1989), *Images and Words* (1992), *Live at the Marquee* (Atco, 1993•), *Awake* (1994), *A Change of Seasons* [EP] (Elektra, 1995•).

CHAPTER THIRTY-FIVE

The Future of Rock Guitar?

Riding the Cycle

Where will rock guitar go in the coming decades? Moreover, will there even be such a thing as rock guitar down the road? The answer is yes—at least for the foreseeable future. Of course, this is usually the part of a book where the author says that it is impossible to see where music will go in the future. Nevertheless, while we don't have a crystal ball, tarot cards, or tea leaves, it actually is possible to anticipate the various paths rock guitar might take. All one has to do to see the future of guitar is to view its past, which is what this book has been all about.

The key to this concept is simply understanding the basic cycles of art (which in itself is probably a microcosm of understanding human nature, but that's a story for another day). If you look at the history of art, at least as it has existed over the last 600 to 800 years, a cyclical pattern emerges. This pattern is prevalent in all art forms, whether it be painting, architecture, literature, or thrash metal. For example, in the Middle Ages, lofty Gothic cathedrals and flat Byzantine religious paintings attempted to convey a sense of otherworldliness and subtle beauty through refined proportions and calculated effects. At the end of the fifteenth century, however, the Renaissance ushered in a new artistic movement that was bent on depicting life in as naturalistic, three-dimensional, and "earthy" a way as possible. In the following centuries, art swung back and forth: the stylized baroque era, the whimsical rococo, the restrained classical style, the emotional romantic period. This cycle—or pendulum, if you prefer—continues its undulation today.

How does this pertain to rock guitar? As the pages of this book have revealed, rock guitar has its own cycle that—just like fine art—shifts between polar opposites: earthiness vs. gaudiness, riffs vs. melodies, and three-chord anthems vs. technical chops. Rock guitarists, just like any other artists, are torn between two opposing forces: emotion on the one hand, technique on the other.

Back in the 1950s, when rock began, the music was raw and gritty. There were certainly concessions to show biz and stage presence, but the overall vibe of the times was simply to rock out and have a good time. This was embodied by early rock guitar masters Scotty Moore, Chuck Berry, and Bo Diddley. By the early sixties, however, rock lost much of its rough edge, and the music

of the surf bands and British invasion acts was a bit neater and cleaner than the rock acts of the fifties. Melody took precedence over fiery drum beats and wild guitar solos, which went along with the clean-cut look and matching suits of the Beatles, the Shadows, and the Beach Boys. A few years later, psychedelia brought unvarnished emotion back to the forefront with long, bluesy solos and folkie acoustic strumming to complement the "back to nature" spirit of the times.

And so rock guitar rolled on, shifting back and forth through various divine vs. secular eras. Early seventies heavy metal and glam rock gave way to punk and New Wave. Synth-pop and neo-classical metal dominated the eighties, only to be put out to pasture in the nineties by grunge, alternative, and industrial/grindcore.

So, what next? Chances are, the music cycle will swing back to keyboards and melodies by the end of the century, which usually brings technically advanced guitar work along with it. (Another axiom to remember here: whenever keyboards are popular—be it Steinways, Farfisas, Hammonds, Moogs, or Roland synths—fiery and flashy guitar chops aren't far behind. When keyboards disappear, you get lots of punky guitar riffs but very few solos or guitar heroics. Kurt Cobain demonstrated this better than anyone.)

Let's say the cycle does come back around. The obvious question then is: What stylistic mountains are there yet to conquer? Certainly, the speed barrier has been permanently broken, thanks to McLaughlin, Di Meola, Malmsteen, and a host of other hot pickers. Technical wizards like Holdsworth and Van Halen have delved into the athletic and scalar aspect of the instrument, seemingly doing everything to a guitar that can be done with two hands. Of course, that's what they said about Hendrix, and he showed up a decade before Van Halen. It is always easy to fall into the "everything that can be done has been done" trap, but without our crystal ball, we can't really see which boundaries will be the next to fall.

As for the electric guitar, it has remained relatively unchanged in its half century on the planet. This occasionally makes it seem as if we've learned all we will ever need to know about the essence of the instrument. But the guitar synthesizer—once touted as "the next big thing"—has yet to take to off and conquer the guitar universe. Until synths get their own Eddie Van Halen to bring that sound and technology over to the masses, it will remain an obscure rock tool. In fact, at this point in time, the plain old acoustic guitar is more popular than ever, reaffirming the notion that the guitar is a simple, Everyman instrument. Though there are those in the six-string community who strive to bring high tech to guitarists, most players are generally reluctant to indulge in the benefits of the digital age (notably MIDI). Instead, they are happy just to strum a few chords on the front porch or plug in and jam with their bands. No muss, no fuss—just easy playing. The most adventurous guitarists seem to have little interest in changing the shape and sound of their guitars; instead, they want to see what they can do with the equipment at hand. Literally.

The immediate future for guitar gods is more in doubt, however. The disposable culture of MTV and rapid radio rotations provides little in the way of long-term exposure necessary for guitar icons to develop their followings and their techniques over years and years—and in some cases, over decades. Modern culture just doesn't have that long an attention span. Even today, the major musical icons—not just guitarists—are those who are holdovers from the sixties and seventies. It often seems as if the newest generation of musicians isn't given the time to develop stylistically and artistically. Instead, if a record falls short of expectations, the musician finds him- or herself out on the street, usually owing the record company plenty of cash to make up for advances and promotional money. Looking around these days, one can't find a newer player who presides over a substantial body of work, such as that created by Jimmy Page, Eric Clapton, Keith Richards, or even Van Halen.

With the increasing focus on home entertainment as an alternative to a night out, people may not spend their evenings out watching bands or crawling through clubs where new talent is honing its chops. Rather, with the onset of music via the Internet, artists may be available in much the same way as pay-per-view cable movies. If you missed them this month, however, you might never hear them again—unless you're surfing around the bargain-basement bin. Thus, guitarists will have to leap increasingly higher cultural hurdles over the next few years, and only the most inventive will survive. And of those, only a handful will rule. Of course, there are those who might say that these hurdles are always there in every generation, and that history is just repeating itself.

No matter what the medium, the guitar will continue on as the essential rock instrument, be it electric, acoustic, or synthesized. Although keyboard fads and digital flings come and go, the guitar remains the tool that defines rock 'n' roll, and that has not changed in nearly 50 years. Until someone comes up with another polyphonic instrument that can convey a similar sense of aggression, power, and thrust, the six-string will remain rock's greatest artifact. In the end, the guitar *is* rock 'n' roll.

Index

Photo Credits

The publisher and authors wish to thank the following for the use of photographs that appear in this book:

Debra Boulanger: 264 (Newquist). Bob Cavallo: cover (Beck), 90, 109, 137, 190. Ross Halfin: cover (Hammett). Tracy Hart: 216. Stephen C. LaVere: 8, Robert Johnson Studio Portrait. Hooks Bros., Memphis, 1935. © 1989 Delta Haze Corporation. All Rights Reserved. Used by Permission. Jean-Pierre Leloir: 48. Kevin Nash: 264 (Prown). Charles Peterson: 242. Joseph Sia: cover (Hendrix). Jim Steinfeldt: cover (Van Halen). Kevin Westenberg: 5.

MICHAEL OCHS ARCHIVES/Venice, CA

16, 19, 23, 26, 27, 29, 31, 37, 39, 81, 97, 120, 130, 133, 153, 205. Waring Abbott: 118. Tom Copi: 46. David Corio: 155. Richard Creamer: 101. Joe Hughes: 208, 250. Larry Hulst: cover (Page), 59, 72. John Beecher: cover (Berry), 12, 14. Richard McCaffrey: 116. Don Paulsen: 54. Peter Sherman: cover (Vaughan). Jon Sievert: 79, 106, 122, 124, 182, 184, 191, 193, 198. Neil Zlozower: 203.

RETNA LTD.

Jay Blakesberg: 246. Larry Busacca: 213, 240. Monica Dee: 232. John Halpern: 218. Lance Mercer: 245. Tony Mottram: 254. Don Powers: 199. Michael Putland: cover (Clapton), 33, 68, 82. Jennifer Rose: 209. Luciano Viti: 158. David Wainwright: 169. Chris Walter: 63, 161, 168.

LGI PHOTO AGENCY

David Anderson: 75. John Bellissimo: 142. Ralph Fitzgerald: 129. M. Gerber: 71. Lynn Goldsmith: 164, 175. Melissa Hill: 115. Steve Jennings: 187, 224, 225. Richard Pasley: 104. Raj Rama: 141. Mark Solomon: 177.

STAR FILE

126. Bob Gruen: 43. Chuck Pulin: 96. Eugene Shaw: 195, 237.

About the Authors

A guitarist for over 20 years, Pete Prown is editor-in-chief of America's premier guitar gear magazine, *Guitar Shop*. He has been a regular contributor to *Guitar* magazine (formerly *Guitar for the Practicing Musician*) since 1987, as well as writing for *Guitar Player*, *Car Stereo Review*, *Relix*, and *Music Alive*. Other projects include writing the liner notes to such compact disc retrospectives as *Essential UFO* and *Essential Michael Schenker* (EMI/Chrysalis Records) and recording the CD/guitar-instructional book *Modal Riffs for Guitar* (Cherry Lane). He lives with his wife and three children in Rose Valley, Pennsylvania.

HP Newquist is the editor-in-chief of *Guitar* magazine, one of the best-selling guitar magazines in the world. He has written several books, including *Music & Technology* (Billboard Books), *The Brain Makers* (Macmillan), and *Virtual Reality* (Scholastic), and his writing has appeared in hundreds of magazines. He plugged in his first guitar at age 15, and still believes that few things in life compare to playing a single power A chord with the volume set to "10." He lives with his wife and daughters in Manhattan.